THE ENCYCLOPEDIA OF THE PHARAOHS

Volume I

THE ENCYCLOPEDIA OF THE PHARAOHS

Volume I

Predynastic to the Twentieth Dynasty

(3300 – 1069 BC)

DARRELL D. BAKER

Typography by Norman Jacobson

STACEY
INTERNATIONAL

The Encyclopedia of the Pharaohs
Volume I

© Darrell D. Baker 2008

Stacey International
128 Kensington Church Street
London W8 4BH
Tel: +44 (0)20 7221 7166 Fax: +44 (0)20 7792 9288
E-mail: info@stacey-international.co.uk
www.stacey-international.co.uk

ISBN: 978-1-905299-37-9

The LaserHieroglyphics™ font that appears in this work is available from

Linguist's Software Inc., P O Box 580, Edmonds, WA 98020-0580, USA

Tel: +1 (425) 775-1130

Printed in the UAE by Oriental Press

CIP Data: A catalogue record for this book is available from the British Library

All rights reserved. No part of this publication may be reproduced,
stored in a retrieval system, or transmitted in any form or by any means,
electronic, mechanical, photocopying, recording, or otherwise, without the prior
permission of the copyright owners

Contents

Map – Key Sites in Ancient Egypt	vii
Foreword	viii
Author's Preface	ix
Chronology of Ancient Egypt	xi
Dynastic King List	xiii
The Encyclopedia	1
Appendix: Apocryphal Kings of the Fourteenth Dynasty	507
The Royal Titulary	511
Glossary	513
Abbreviations	521
Bibliography	525
Index: Alphabetical King List	573

Dedication

This book is dedicated to the staff of the Interlibrary Loan department of the University of California, Irvine. This group knows no boundaries when it comes to locating an article, journal, microfilm or book on any subject in any language – at least that's the way it appears to me. This encyclopedia could not have been written without the hard work and caring attitude of Suzy Jung, Pam Lazarr, Gerry Lopez, Dianna Sahhar, Pat Staump, Michele Upton, Linda Michelle Weinberger and the rest of the crew.

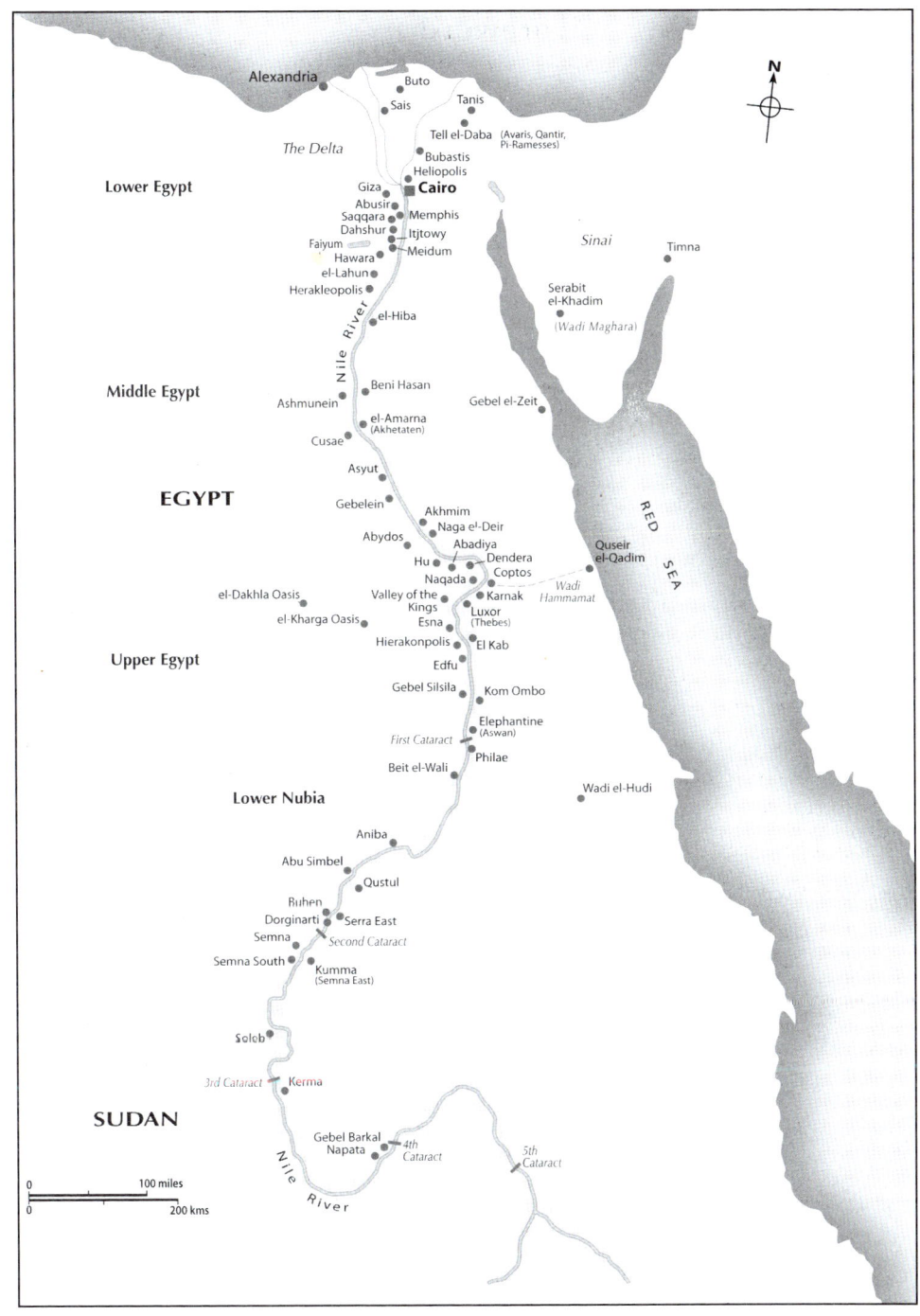

The map shows the key sites in Ancient Egypt referred to in the Encyclopedia

Foreword

Clearly Cecil B. DeMille ought to be thanked not only for producing some of the most magnificent films to have graced the silver screen, but also for inciting and inspiring Darrell Baker's interest in ancient Egypt which has resulted in this book. Although there are several books on Egyptian pharaohs, few are as easy to use, as comprehensive, or as honest – the ignorance of Egyptologists concerning the most basic information about many of Egypt's rulers is considerable. Of course, this very absence of knowledge also underlines the possibility of endless exciting discoveries regarding the kings of Egypt by future Egyptologists, and provides a great deal of scope for creativity in the interim.

Darrell's book brings together the basic facts concerning Egypt's pharaohs from a diverse number of sources. Each entry provides illustrated (and spelt) variations on each king's different names, the length of their reign, the burial place, the survival of the body, and their consorts; records their appearance in king lists; and provides details about their reigns. The references for each entry are superb, and the index is enormously useful as it provides the (many) different variations in spelling for each name. Norman Jacobson should also be thanked for forcing Darrell to persevere with this project and for producing a beautiful book that is a pleasure to use. May he and Darrell continue to collaborate, both in text and image.

Salima Ikram
Professor of Egyptology,
American University in Cairo

Aidan Dodson
Department of Archaeology
and Anthropology,
University of Bristol

2008

Author's Preface

When I was ten years old, I saw Cecil B. DeMille's *The Ten Commandments* for the first time. Utterly enthralled, I tried to learn everything I could about Egypt's mysterious past and the shadowy figures who had been her earliest rulers. I soon moved from my *Columbia Viking Desk Encyclopedia* to the works of Leonard Cottrell and James Henry Breasted. Eventually, I began looking for a book that would provide me with thumbnail sketches of the lives of each of Egypt's pharaohs – but by the time I was 12 years old, I concluded that the book I sought did not exist, and that it would be up to me to write it. I began to organize the meagre information I was able to glean onto index cards, and soon amassed 1,400 cards covering the reigns of about two dozen kings. Lacking the magical assistance of personal computers (this was, after all, 1958) the weight of the project deterred me, and I set it aside. However, I kept the cards, vowing to eventually complete the book.

The project lay dormant for the next 36 years, and might never have been resurrected had I not met Norman Jacobson. At the time we began collaborating on this book, Norm knew virtually nothing about Egypt, although he found it fascinating; I knew even less about computers, and viewed them as the overpriced toys of a generation of immature man-children. Even though my attitude has softened somewhat, it is undoubtedly true that Norman has learned a great deal more about Egyptology than I have learned about computers. To Norm, this is my book and he is a technical assistant – but to me, he is a partner in an enterprise that could not have been possible without his extraordinary ability, perseverance, and dedication.

Special thanks are also owed to the following, without whom this book would not have been possible: John Adams, Aidan Dodson, Salima Ikram, Donald B Redford, Susan Redford, Caroline Rider, Donald P Ryan, Barbara Shorf, Ian Stevens, Jonathan Van Lepp, Charles Watkinson and Bruce Warner.

As grateful as I am to all of the friends and colleagues mentioned above, I owe the most to my wife, Tina. She has been my helpmate

Encyclopedia of the Pharaohs

and support through the many long years of research and writing that it has taken to produce this book. She has travelled endless miles, trudged through countless museums and ruins, and staggered under the weight of the masses of research material that had to be collated, alphabetized, indexed, filed, cross referenced, and photocopied. She has corrected my English grammar and my countless run-on sentences. She has set aside a great deal of her own life in order to help see me through this project. She is the *m3ʿt* and *mr* in my life.

The *Encyclopedia of the Pharaohs* does not pretend to be any more than its title suggests. Its sole purpose is to present straightforward facts about the kings of Ancient Egypt as synthesized from a vast array of credible sources. In keeping with the encyclopedia format, the book uses no footnotes, bibliographic references are given with each entry, and the complete list of reference provides a reading list in excess of 700 titles. Because the book is aimed at a wide audience, my bibliography includes sources available at any good public library as well as obscure and often out-of-print works, of interest only to the most serious scholars.

Finally, this volume of the encyclopedia covers the rulers of Egypt from the late Predynastic era (ca.3300 BC) to the close of Dynasty XX (1069 BC). I am bringing down the curtain a thousand years before what most historians consider the end of the Pharaonic Civilization, the death of Cleopatra VII in 30 BC. The stretches of Egyptian history, following the close of Dynasty XX are periods of jumbled records, ephemeral rulers and foreign domination which placed many invaders on Egypt's throne. The rulers of this complex period, while of great historical interest to many Egyptologists, are best treated as a group distinct from royal predecessors.

I hope that the book will prove valuable to the full spectrum of students of Egyptian history, from the serious professional scholar to the equally serious occasional 12 year old.

Darrell Baker
Portland, Oregon

Chronology of Ancient Egypt

Predynastic Period	**5500-3150 BC**
Badarian Period	5500-4000
Naqada I Period	4000-3500
Naqada II Period	3500-3300
Early Naqada III Period—Dynasty "00"	3300-3200
Late Naqada III Period—Dynasty "0"	3200-3150
Archaic Period	**3150-2686 BC**
Dynasty I	3150-2890
Dynasty II	2890-2686
Old Kingdom	**2686-2125 BC**
Dynasty III	2686-2613
Dynasty IV	2613-2494
Dynasty V	2494-2345
Dynasty VI	2345-2181
Dynasty VII/VIII[1]	2181-2125
First Intermediate Period	**2160-2055 BC**
Dynasty IX/X[1]	2160-2025
Dynasty XI (Thebes only)	2125-2055
Middle Kingdom	**2055-1795 BC**
Dynasty XI (All of Egypt)	2055-1985
Dynasty XII	1985-1795

---

[1]The Manetho List (see "Manetho" in Glossary) separates kings into Dynasties VII and VIII and Dynasties IX and X. However, there is no apparent reason for these divisions, as the second dynasty in each case seems to be merely an extension of the first with no dynastic break.

Second Intermediate Period   **1795-1550 BC**

Dynasty XIII/XIV[2]   1795-1650
Dynasty XV   1650-1550
Dynasty XVI and XVII   1650-1550

New Kingdom   **1550-1069 BC**

Dynasty XVIII   1550-1295
Dynasty XIX   1295-1186
Dynasty XX   1186-1069

Third Intermediate Period   **1069-664 BC**

Dynasty XXI   1069-943
Dynasty XXII   943-720
Dynasty XXIII   835-720
Dynasty XXIV   732-718
Dynasty XXV   753-656

Late Period   **664-332 BC**

Dynasty XXVI   664-525
Dynasty XXVII   525-404
Dynasty XXVIII   404-399
Dynasty XXIX   399-380
Dynasty XXX   380-343
Dynasty XXXI   343-332

Dynasty of Macedon   **332-310 BC**

Dynasty of Ptolemy   **310-30 BC**

Roman Period   **30 BC-395 AD**

References:

Murnane 1983 Appendix: Capsule King List and History of Ancient Egypt
Shaw and Nicholson 1995 Chronology

---

[2]Dynasty XIV was a series of ephemeral kings whose territory was confined to the eastern Delta, and was contemporaneous with Dynasty XIII, which ruled from Memphis and Itjtowy in the Faiyum.

Dynastic King List

Predynastic Period   <u>5500-3150 BC</u>
Early/Late Naqada III Periods   <u>3300-3150 BC</u>
Dynasties 00/0

King List
(none)

Unplaced Kings

A(?)
Crocodile
De
Double Falcon
Hat-Hor
Iry-Hor
Ka
Ny-Hor
Pe-Hor
Scorpion I
Scorpion II
  (immediately
  precedes
  Narmer)
Sma
Zeser

Unplaced Kings
Palermo Stone
…a
Khayu
Mekh
Neheb
…pu
Seka
Tiu
Tjesh
Wadjin

Archaic Period	**3150-2686 BC**
Dynasty I	**3150-2890 BC**

King List	*Unplaced Kings*
Narmer	(none)
Aha	
Djer	
Djet	
Den	
Merneith	
Anedjib	
Semerkhet	
Qa'a	

Dynasty I or II

King List	*Unplaced Kings*
(none)	Ba
	Seneferka

Dynasty II	**2890-2686 BC**

King List	*Unplaced Kings*
Hotepsekhemwy	Neferkare
Nebre	Neferkaseker
Ninetjer	Nubnefer
Weneg	Sekhemib/Peribsen
[...]	Sened
Khasekhemwy	

Old Kingdom	**2686-2125 BC**
Dynasty III	**2686-2613 BC**

King List	*Unplaced Kings*
Djoser	Qahedjet
Sekhemkhet	Sanakht
[...]	Sedjes
Khaba	
Huni	

Dynasty III or IV

King List	*Unplaced Kings*
(none)	Sharu

Dynasty IV	**2613-2494 BC**

King List	*Unplaced Kings*
Seneferu	Bikka
Khufu	
Djedefre	
Khafre	
Menkaure	
Shepseskaf	

Dynasty V 2494-2345 BC

King List
Userkaf
Sahure
Neferirkare (I)
Neferefre
Shepseskare
Niuserre
Menkauhor
Djedkare
Unas

Unplaced Kings
(none)

Dynasty VI 2345-2181 BC

King List
Teti
Userkare
Pepi I
Merenre I
Pepi II
Merenre II

Unplaced Kings
(none)

Dynasty VII/VIII 2181-2125 BC

King List
Netjerkare Siptah
Menkare
Neferkare
Neferkare Neby
Djedkare Shemai
Neferkare Khendu
Merenhor
Neferkamin
Nikare
Neferkare Tereru
Neferkahor
Neferkare Pepi-Sonb
Neferkamin Anu
Qakare Ibi
Neterkaure
Neferkauhor
Neferirkare (II)

Unplaced Kings
Hotep
Imhotep (possibly Dynasty IX/X)
Isu
Iytjenu
Khui
(Wadjkare?)

First Intermediate Period   2160-2055 BC
Dynasty IX/X   2160-2025 BC

King List   *Unplaced Kings*
Khety I
Neferkare
Khety II
Senen…
Khety III
Khety IV
Shed…y
H…
Khety V
Merykare

Imhotep (possibly Dynasty VII/VIII)
Ity
Mery…[hathor?]
Se…re Khety

Dynasty XI (Thebes only)   2125-2055 BC

King List   *Unplaced Kings*
Intef   (none)
Montuhotep I
Intef I
Intef II
Intef III

Middle Kingdom   2055-1795 BC
Dynasty XI (All of Egypt)   2055-1985

King List   *Unplaced Kings*
Montuhotep II   (none)
Montuhotep III
Montuhotep IV

Dynasty XII   1985-1795 BC

King List   *Unplaced Kings*
Amenemhet I   (none)
Senwosret I
Amenemhet II
Senwosret II
Senwosret III
Amenemhet III
Amenemhet IV
Sobekneferu

Second Intermediate Period   1795-1550 BC

King List
(none)

Unplaced Kings
Aaqen
Abiya
...hebre
Hotepkare
...hotep[re?]
Khaenptah
Kha...re
Merytowy
Montuwoser
Pepi
Sekhemkare
...sekhem[re?]
Sekhemrekhutowy
Sewadj...re
Sharek
Sobek
Sobekhotep
...webenre (b)
...webenre (c)
Woserkhau
Woser...re (I)
Woser...re (II)

Dynasty XIII   1795-1650 BC

King List
Sobekhotep I
Sonbef
Nerikare
Amenemhet V
Qemau
Hornedjheritef
Efni
Amenemhet VI
Nebnennu
Sehotepibre
Sewadjkare I
Nedjemibre
Sobekhotep II
Ranisonb
Hor
Khabau
Djedkheperu
Sebkay
Amenemhet VII
Wegaf
Khendjer

Unplaced Kings
Ini II
Khuiqer
Neferhotep II
Pantjeny
Sekhaenre
Senaaib
Senebmiu
Wepwawetemsaf

Dynasty XIII (continued)

King List

Imyremeshau
Intef IV
Seth (I)
Sobekhotep III
Neferhotep I
Sihathor
Sobekhotep IV
Sobekhotep V
Sobekhotep VI
Iaib
Aya
Ini I
Sewadjtu
Ined
...hori
Sobekhotep VII
[...]
Mer...re
Merkheperre
Merkare
[...]
Montuhotep V
... mosre
Ibi
...hor
Se...kare
Sankhptahi
...re
Se...enre

Dynasty XIV   1795-1650 BC

King List   *Unplaced Kings*
Yakbim   Khamure
Ya'ammu   Nuya
Qareh   Sheneh
'Ammu   Shenshek
Sheshi   Wazad
Nehsy   Ya-k-'-r-b(?)
Khakherure   Ya'qub-Har
Nebfawre
Sehebre
Merdjefare
Sewadjkare II
Nebdjefare
Webenre
[...]

Dynasty XIV (continued)
King List

...djefare
...webenre (a)
Awibre (II)
Heribre
Nebsenre
[...]
...re
Sekheperenre
Djedkherure
Seankhibre
Nefertum...re
Sekhem...re
Kakemetre
Neferibre
I...re
Khakare
Akare
Hapu... (II)
'Anati
Bebnum
[...]
...re
[...]
...[re]
...[re]
Senefer...re
Men...re
Djed...re
[...]
Inek(?)
'A...
'Ap...

Dynasty XV   1650-1550 BC
King List   *Unplaced Kings*
Semqen   (none)
'Aper-'Anati
Sakir-Har
Khyan
Apepi
Khamudi

Dynasty XVI   1650-1550 BC

King List   *Unplaced Kings*
[...]   Dedumose I
Djehuty   Dedumose II
Sobekhotep VIII   Montuemsaf
Neferhotep III   Montuhotep VI
Montuhotepi   Senwosret IV
Nebiryraw I
Nebiryraw II
Semenre
Bebiankh
Sekhemre-shedwaset

Dynasty XVII   1650-1550 BC

King List   *Unplaced Kings*
Rehotep   Nebmaatre
Sobekemsaf I
Intef V
Intef VI
Intef VII
Sobekemsaf II
Senakhtenre
Seqenenre
Kamose

<u>**New Kingdom**</u>   <u>1550-1069 BC</u>

Dynasty XVIII   1550-1295 BC

King List   *Unplaced Kings*
Ahmose   (none)
Amenhotep I
Thutmose I
Thutmose II
Hatshepsut
Thutmose III
Amenhotep II
Thutmose IV
Amenhotep III
Akhenaten
Smenkhkare
Neferneferuaten
Tutankhamen
Ay
Horemheb

Dynasty XIX   1295-1186 BC

King List   *Unplaced Kings*
Ramesses I   (none)
Sety I
Ramesses II
Merenptah
Amenmesse
Sety II
Siptah
Tawosret

Dynasty XX   1186-1069 BC

King List   *Unplaced Kings*
Setnakht   (none)
Ramesses III
Ramesses IV
Ramesses V
Ramesses VI
Ramesses VII
Ramesses VIII
Ramesses IX
Ramesses X
Ramesses XI

The Encyclopedia

Dynasty 00

Length of Reign:	Unknown
Tomb:	Unknown
Mummy:	Unknown

Consorts:	Unknown	**Variant Names:**	None
Manetho:	Not given		
King Lists:	None		

Two rock drawings in the limestone cliffs behind Armant, near Thebes, provide the only documentation for the existence of this king. These two graffiti, both representing a very early form of serekh, can be dated to a time prior to Dynasty I in that period sometimes referred to as Dynasty 00.

In both cases, the carvings are roughly done. A Horus falcon stands atop a serekh which contains what is probably the hieroglyph for "p." The sign below the "p" is unclear; it may be nothing more than a crudely drawn bottom section to the serekh. In any event, the falcon over the "p" sign is reminiscent of another possible early ruler, Pe-Hor, from Qustul in Lower Nubia.

References:
T. Wilkinson 1995 pp. 205-210
Winkler 1938 pp. 10, 31, pl.
 XI.2 & 3

Dynasty 00

Length of Reign:	Unknown
Tomb:	Tarkhan, Tomb 412(?)
Mummy:	Unknown

Consorts:	Unknown	**Variant Names:**	None
Manetho:	Not given		
King Lists:	None		

Although proposed as the name of an early ruler, these signs, written in ink on a jar found by Petrie in Tomb 412 at Tarkhan, more likely belong to a nobleman. The name is not in a serekh, nor does the bird appear to represent a Horus falcon.

References:
Petrie 1913 p. 9, pl. XXXI. 71   T. Wilkinson 1999 p. 54
von der Way 1993 pp. 100-101

Dynasty 00

Length of Reign:	Unknown
Tomb:	Unknown
Mummy:	Unknown

Consorts:	Unknown	**Variant Names:**	None
Manetho:	Not given		
King Lists:	None		

This possible ruler, whose name remains untranslated, is attested to by a serekh on a pottery jar from the eastern Delta (provenance unknown) and from two serekhs on pottery from Tura. The name is made up of what appear to be three *hd* ("mace") signs, with a falcon above in the Delta example and no falcons on the Tura examples. Further differences in the Tura serekhs include the hd signs extending to the bottom of the serekh, replacing the vertical lines which are normally used to represent the palace facade. Also, three circles are added beneath the serekhs. As with many other serekhs from this period, it is possible that they merely represent royal property. However, the falcon above the name on the Delta jar would seem to indicate that the serekhs do contain a royal name.

References:

Fischer 1963a pp. 44-46,
  figs. 1, 3.a and c, pl. VI. a, c
Junker 1912 p. 46, fig. 57.1-2
van den Brink 1996 p. 146,
  figs. 2 III.17-19, pl. 30.a

von der Way 1993 pp. 99, 101
T. Wilkinson 1999 pp. 55-56

...a   Predynastic

...a
...a

Length of Reign:	Unknown
Tomb:	Unknown
Mummy:	Unknown

Consorts:	Unknown	**Variant Names:**	None
Manetho:	Not given		
King Lists:	P		

  ...a is one of a group of nine kings known only from the Palermo Stone. Each name is followed by a representation of a squatting king wearing the crown of Lower Egypt. Whether these names are to be taken as historic personages or mythic "ancestors" is not known.

References:

Clagett 1989 pp. 66, 97-98
Edwards 1971 pp. 3-4
Gardiner 1961 pl. III

O'Mara 1979 p. 5
T. Wilkinson 2000 pp. 62, 85-86, 88

'A...

'A... Dynasty XIV

Horus Name:
Unknown   **Nomen:** Unknown

Prenomen:

i...
'a...

Two Ladies: Unknown

Golden Falcon: Unknown

Length of Reign:	Unknown
Tomb:	Unknown
Mummy:	Unknown

Consorts:	Unknown	**Variant Names:**	I... Ineb(?)
Manetho:	Not given		
King Lists:	T: (G 9.15; R 10.14; vB 8.23)		

Perhaps the fiftieth king of Dynasty XIV, 'A... is one of a group of kings known only from the Turin Canon. The papyrus' fragmentary state allows for varying interpretations as to the positioning of some of the kings of this dynasty. However, 'A...'s place seems secure. Both Gardiner and Ryholt see a possible *nb* (⌣) sign following the determinative. Ryholt does not acknowledge the *nb* sign in any of the several Dynasty XIV king lists in his book, whereas Gardiner reads the name as "Ineb?"

References:

Gardiner 1959 pl. III, Col. IX #15
Gardiner 1961 p. 442 9.15
Ryholt 1997a pp. 95 Col. 10.14, 98 #50, 380 File 14/50, 409 #50

von Beckerath 1999 pp. 110 #24, 111 #24

A(?)		Dynasty 0

Length of Reign:	Unknown
Tomb:	Unknown
Mummy:	Unknown

Consorts:	Unknown	**Variant Names:**	None
Manetho:	Not given		
King Lists:	None		

This king is known from a graffito cut into a sandstone outcropping some 10 to 12 km. southwest of Umm el-Dabadib at the Kharga Oasis in the western desert. The serekh was discovered by the North Kharga Oasis Survey under the direction of Dr. Salima Ikram. The hitherto unattested royal name seems to show evidence of royal activity in the farther reaches of the western desert as early as the Protodynastic Period.

References:
Ikram 2004
Ikram and Rossi 2004 pp. 211-215

Aaqen   SIP

Horus Name: Unknown   **Nomen:**

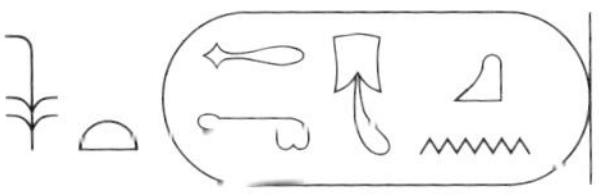

ꜥꜣ-kn
Aaqen

Prenomen: Unknown

Two Ladies: Unknown

Golden Falcon: Unknown

Abiya

Length of Reign:	Unknown
Tomb:	Unknown
Mummy:	Unknown

Consorts:	Unknown	**Variant Names:**	Aqen
Manetho:	Not given		
King Lists:	None		

This king is known only from a priest's ancestor-list from Memphis and is most likely fictitious. Von Beckerath would place this king in Dynasty XIII.

References:

Borchardt 1935 pp. 96-112, pl. 2 and 2a
Ryholt 1997a p. 402 File N/9

von Beckerath 1999 pp. 104 #n, 105 #n

Abiya   SIP

Horus Name: Unknown   **Nomen:**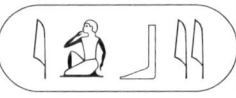

'a-b-ya
Abiya

Prenomen: Unknown

Two Ladies: Unknown

Golden Falcon: Unknown

Length of Reign:	Unknown
Tomb:	Unknown
Mummy:	Unknown

Consorts:	Unknown	**Variant Names:**	Abai
Manetho:	Not given		
King Lists:	None		

This name is known only from a priest's ancestor-list from Memphis and is most likely fictitious. Von Beckerath places this "king" in Dynasty XIII.

References:

Borchardt 1935 pp. 96-112, pl. 2 and 2a
Ryholt 1997a p. 402 File N/8

von Beckerath 1999 pp. 104 #m, 105 #m

Aha   Dynasty I

Horus Name

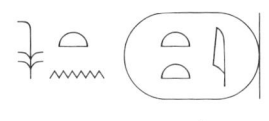

ꜥḥꜣ
Aha

Nomen: *tti*
Teti

Two Ladies: *nbty tt*

Golden Falcon: Unknown

Length of Reign:	Unknown
Tomb:	Abydos, Umm el Qa'ab, B 10/15/19
Mummy:	Unknown

Consorts:	Bernerib Khenthap(?)	**King Lists:**	Ab: (1); P
Manetho:	Athothis (A, E)	**Variant Names:**	Hor-Aha

The second king of Dynasty I, Aha was the son of Queen Neithhotep and probably king Narmer. His Horus name, Aha, means "the fighter." He was no doubt aptly named, as it is likely that Egypt had not fully adjusted to its newly united condition and that pockets of hostility remained. It also seems that Aha was concerned with possible problems from the south, as an ebony label found at Abydos appears to record an expedition against the Nubians. It is unknown whether this was a full-fledged effort at conquest or a means toward establishing a secure southern boundary at the First Cataract, but the latter is the more likely.

A damaged serekh found at En-Besor in Israel was once thought to belong to Aha, but in fact belongs to the pharaoh Den.

The Palermo Stone holds a record of the final two years of Aha's reign, and Cairo Fragment number five would appear to give accounts of three years earlier in the reign. The information given thereon is useless in an historic sense, but gives us an idea of the sort of religious celebrations being held during this period. For instance, in the five years attributed to Aha, two and possibly three record what is called "The Festival of the Birth of Anubis." What is also interesting is the reference to "six months and seven days," which undoubtedly refers to the last partial year the king ruled.

As for the length of Aha's reign, the Egyptian sources give us only the five years surviving on the Palermo Stone. Manetho gives 57 years according to Africanus, while according to Eusebius, Aha reigned 27 years.

Manetho tells us that Aha built the palace at Memphis, and was also said to have been a skilled physician who wrote books on anatomy.

From an ebony label discovered at Abydos, we know that Aha founded or at least endowed a temple of Neith at Sais, in the Delta. This may have been in order to help salve the wounds of the recently subjugated northerners or it may have been in honor of the king's mother, Neithhotep, who appears to have been from the Delta.

A large mudbrick mastaba with a palace-facade design discovered near Naqada in Upper Egypt was once thought to have belonged to Aha, but it seems more likely to have been built by him for Neithhotep.

There has been much controversy concerning Aha's burial site: was he buried in the B 10/15/19 complex at Abydos, or in Tomb Number 3357 at Saqqara? The battle of Abydos vs. Saqqara as the place of royal burials has raged since the discovery of a large Dynasty I and II cemetery at Saqqara. The latest research tends to point toward Abydos as being the Royal Cemetery, while the northern tombs would seem to be the graves of wealthy nobles. Furthermore, the Abydos tomb is connected with a triple row of graves of servants who were undoubtedly killed so that they might serve their king in his next life. There are no such subsidiary graves around the Saqqara tomb.

It should be noted that some scholars favor a theory which would identify Aha as the king Menes of legend; however, see NARMER.

References:

Clagett 1989 pp. 67-68
Dodson and Hilton 2004 pp. 44-45, 46, 48
Emery 1939
Emery 1949 vol. I pp. 5-6, 7, 71-81, pl. 14-20
Emery 1958 vol. III pp. 37-72, pl. 21-84
Gardiner 1961 p. 430
Gophna 1987 pp. 23-40
O'Connor 1989 pp. 54, 58-60
Petrie 1900, 1901a, 1902b
Schulman 1983 pp. 249-251
Troy 1986 pp. 94, 152 # 1.5
Uphill 1984
Verbrugghe and Wickersham 1996 pp. 111, 187
von Beckerath 1999 pp. 38 #1, 39 #1
Waddell 1940 pp. 29 ff.
T. Wilkinson 1999 pp. 3, 63 fig. 3.1 #1, 68, 70-71, 125, 153, 159, 161, 178 fig. 5.3 #3, 179, 180, 202, 203, 221, 222, 223, 224, 233, 234, 266, 281, 291, 292, 297301-302, 317, 318 fig. 8.9 #3, 320, 337,
T. Wilkinson 2000 pp. 90-91, 238-240, 256

Ahmose   Dynasty XVIII

Horus Name:

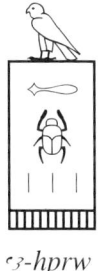

ꜥꜣ-ḫprw

Nomen: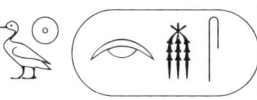

iꜥḥ-ms
Ahmose

Prenomen:

nb-pḥti-rꜥ
Nebpehtire

Two Ladies:

nbty twt-mswt

Golden Falcon: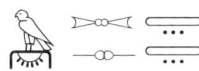

bik-nbw ṯs-tꜣwy

Length of Reign:	25 years
Tomb:	Unknown; probably at Dira Abu'n-Naga
Mummy:	Royal Cache at Deir el-Bahri Now at Cairo Museum: JE26210; CG61056

Consorts:	Ahmose-Nebta Ahmose- Nefertiri Satkamose(?)	**King Lists:** **Variant Names:**	Ab: (66); S. (47) Ahmes Ahmosi
Manetho:	Amos (A) Amoses (E) Amosis (E)		

    The first king of Dynasty XVIII, Ahmose was the son of the Dynasty XVII king Seqenenre Taa and Queen Ahhotep, and the brother of king Kamose. He would have been about ten years old at his accession to the throne if the latest examinations of his mummy are to be believed; according to recent research, he died at about the age of 35. An inscription found in the Tura quarries gives a regnal year of 22. Manetho, according to Josephus, gave Ahmose a reign of 25 years and 4 months. A reign of 25 years, plus or minus a few months seems certain.

The young king certainly inherited a touchy situation. Lower Egypt from the Delta south to the area around Memphis was under the control of the Hyksos and their Egyptian vassals, and Egypt's southern border, at the First Cataract, was probably under the threat of invasion from the Nubians.

Queen Ahhotep, the king's mother, undoubtedly guided her son's early years on the throne. It has even been suggested that she served as coregent for a time. Whatever might lie behind her prominence, she was later remembered for having been crucial to the struggle for Theban control of all Egypt.

It would appear that Ahmose did not begin a campaign against the Hyksos until around his tenth or eleventh year on the throne. There is reason to believe that the Hyksos' power was already waning when Ahmose began his northern advance. In any event, by regnal year 15 at the latest, the Hyksos capital, Avaris, in the eastern Delta, was taken. Sharuhen in southern Palestine, seemingly the last Hyksos bastion, was put under a siege that would last three years. (It should be noted that some Egyptologists think Ahmose began operations against the Hyksos within a year or two of his accession, and that some scholars think that the siege of Sharuhen lasted six years.)

After the fall of Sharuhen, Ahmose was able to turn his attention toward the south. The prince of Kush had been in league with the Hyksos kings since at least the reign of Kamose. Now that Ahmose had freed Egypt, he moved to re-establish the southern territory lost after the fall of the Middle Kingdom. The initial success of the first campaign into Nubia was followed by two "mopping up" actions.

Exactly how far into Nubia Ahmose was able to march is unsure. Certainly he was able to reclaim territory at least as far as the Second Cataract, where he reopened the fortress of Buhen, which had been sacked during the Second Intermediate Period. Buhen became the administrative center of Kush under a bureaucrat Ahmose appointed. The position became known as the "Viceroy of Kush" in the time of Ahmose's successor, Amenhotep I, and was to remain a powerful position for centuries.

Some time after the expeditions to Nubia, an insurrection in middle Egypt, fomented by former Hyksos allies and supporters, necessitated some military action.

Year 22 saw Ahmose return to Syria-Palestine, campaigning in the area of Djahy and perhaps marching as far north as the Euphrates river.

Once Egypt had been reunited, a stable government became imperative. The Theban royal house had been responsible for the southern portion of Egypt only; now it was necessary for it to govern the entire country. What was more, with the defeat of the Hyksos and the prince of Kush, it was also necessary to maintain and defend extended boundaries. Ahmose saw to it that Egypt and Kush were governed along the lines of the bureaucratic system used so successfully during the latter portion of Dynasty XII. As far as Egypt's boundaries were concerned, these were to be defended by a fairly new innovation: a standing, professional army.

At the beginning of his reign, Ahmose married a lady of the royal family, Ahmose-Nefertiri. This woman was either his niece (the daughter of king Kamose), or Ahmose's full sister. The royal couple had several children, including the future Amenhotep I and his wife, Meryetamen.

There is not much left of the temples and other buildings constructed during this reign; it is thought that the majority were built of mud brick and have either weathered away or were pulled down and the brick reused. At Karnak, Ahmose built an addition to the Temple of Amen-Re. The floor, ceiling and supporting columns of the structure were made of cedar wood. At Abydos, the King constructed mud brick cenotaphs for himself and his grandmother, Tetisheri.

Ahmose's tomb has yet to be discovered, but was undoubtedly located at Dira Abu'n-Naga in the Theban Necropolis. The king's mummy was discovered in the Royal Cache at Deir el-Bahri. The body, which measured 1.635 m. tall, was that of a man of about forty years old who suffered from arthritis of the back and knees.

References:
Aldred 1998 pp. 149-150
Breasted 1906 vol. II pp. 3-16
Dodson and Hilton 2004 pp. 21, 114, 122, 123, 124-126, 126-127, 128-129, 130, 131, 139
Forbes 1998a pp. 614-615
Grajetzki 2005 p. 50
Grimal 1992 pp. 199-200
Ikram and Dodson 1997 p. 24
Ikram and Dodson 1998 pp. 321-322
T. James 1965 pp. 7-22
Lehner 1997 pp. 190-191
Lichtheim 1976 pp. 12-13
Partridge 1994 pp. 45-47
D. Redford 1992 pp. 127-130, 138-139
Ryholt 1997a p. 280, table 81
G. Smith 1912 pp. 15-18
Tyldesley 2006 pp. 88-90
Verbrugghe and Wickersham 1996 pp. 140, 198
von Beckerath 1999 pp. 132 #1, 133 #1
Waddell 1940 pp. 109, 111, 115, 117

Akare Dynasty XIV

Horus Name: Unknown

Nomen: Unknown

Prenomen:

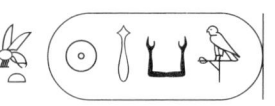

ˁ₃-k₃-r ˁ
Akare

Two Ladies: Unknown

Golden Falcon: Unknown

Length of Reign:	Unknown
Tomb:	Unknown
Mummy:	Unknown

Consorts:	Unknown	**Variant Names:**	Aakare Ankhkare ...ka[re?]
Manetho:	Not given		
King Lists:	T: (G 8.25; R 9.25; vB 8.25)		

Perhaps the thirty-first king of Dynasty XIV, Akare is one of a group of kings known only from the Turin Canon. The papyrus' fragmentary state allows for varying interpretations as to the positioning of some of the kings of this dynasty. However, Akare's place seems secure. The exact transliteration of the name is debated, with Gardiner and Ryholt reading the name as "Akare" while von Beckerath sees the hieroglyph (ˁ₃) as (ˁnḫ) and reads it as "Ankhkare."

A recent study of the Turin Canon indicates that Gardiner's column IX #27 joins with his VIII #25. This eliminates IX #27 ...kare (...k₃[rˁ]) as a possible prenomen.

References:

Gardiner 1959 pl. III, Col. VIII #25
Gardiner 1961 p. 441 #8.5 as "Aakare"
Ryholt 1997a pp. 24, 95 Col. 9 #25, 98 #31, 380 File 14/31, 409 table 95 #31

von Beckerath 1999 pp. 110 #26, 111 #26

Akhenaten   Dynasty XVIII

Horus Name:

Nomen: *imn-ḥtp*
Amenhotep

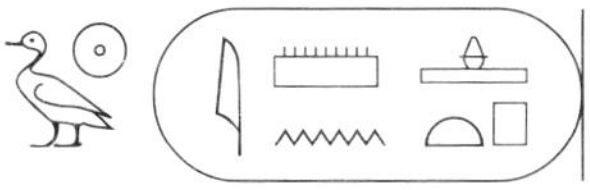

Prenomen: *nfr-ḫprw-rꜥ wꜥ-n-rꜥ*
Neferkheperure-waenre

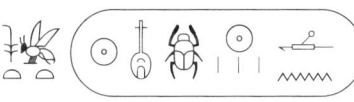

kꜣ nḫt kꜣi-šwti

Two Ladies: *nbty nsyt-m-iptswt*

Golden Falcon: Unknown

Horus Name:

Nomen: *ꜣḫ-n-itn*
Akhenaten

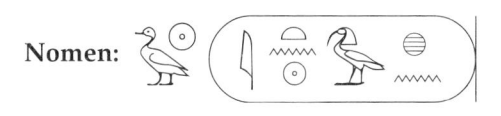

Prenomen: *nfr-ḫprw-rꜥ wꜥ-n-rꜥ*
Neferkheperure-waenre

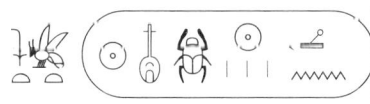

kꜣ nḫt mry-itn

Two Ladies: *nbty wsr-nsyt-m-ꜣḫtitn*

Golden Falcon: Unknown

Akhenaten

Length of Reign:	17 years		
Tomb:	Amarna: TA26		
Mummy:	Unknown		
Consorts:	Kiya Nefertiti	**Variant Names:**	Aakhu-en-aten Akhenkheres Akhenkherses Aten-khu-en Ikhnaton Khu-en-aten
Manetho:	Achencheres (J) Acherres (A, E) Akherres (A, E)		
King Lists:	None		

    The tenth pharaoh of Dynasty XVIII, Akhenaten is without a doubt the most controversial ruler in Egyptian history. He has been called "the first individual in history," "the first monotheist," a "Philosopher-King," and "Egypt's most intriguing king." He has also been referred to as a "false prophet," and a ruler who was "autocratic and unsympathetic," who "destroyed his people's myths." Within a few years of his death, his name was proscribed and if necessity forced a reference to him, he was called "the criminal," or "the enemy." He has been likened unto Moses, not to mention Oedipus. He has been analyzed by Freud, and if coffee table books are discounted, he is arguably the most written-about person in scholarly and popular Egyptological literature.

    Akhenaten was a son of Amenhotep III and Queen Tiye, and at birth was named Amenhotep, after his father. He seems not to have been first in line for the throne, as that honor originally went to his older brother, Thutmose, who died at an early age. When he ascended the throne, he was called Amenhotep IV; he changed his name to Akhenaten, probably in regnal year five.

    Egyptologists have debated for more than a century the question of whether there was a coregency between Amenhotep III and Akhenaten, and there is still no consensus on the issue. Theories range from 12 years (Aldred and Johnson) to either a brief coregency (fewer than three years) or to no coregency at all (Redford). The uncertainty stems from the lack of any direct evidence and the presence of some indirect evidence. The absence of any double-dated monuments is striking, especially given the large number of documents and other attestations about both reigns. On the other hand, recent scholars have noted cultural similarities in the latter part of Amenhotep III's reign and Akhenaten's early regnal years. In particular, the profound changes in religious and artistic styles that mark the reign of the son seem to have begun during the last decade of the father's reign. This evidence, while not conclusive, tends to support a coregency of some sort, but perhaps only for a few years.

In any case, the religious "revolution" of Akhenaten's reign was rooted in changes that took place near the end of Amenhotep III's tenure as pharaoh, although these changes had begun during the reign of Akhenaten's grandfather, Thutmose IV.

Among the changes in Egyptian culture that marked the reign of Akhenaten, the most profound was the rise of a monotheistic solar religion, which began shortly after he ascended the throne. Amenhotep IV was presumably crowned at Thebes, in the temple of Amen at Karnak. The high priest of Amen would have officiated, thus assuring the god's blessing upon the new pharaoh. Scarabs issued soon after the coronation refer to Amenhotep IV as chosen by Amen to rule. The priests, not to mention Amen himself, must have been somewhat taken aback when Amenhotep began construction throughout Egypt of temples, not to Amen, but to Aten, the largest being one that directly abutted the site of Amen's temple at Karnak.

Aten ("sun disk") was viewed as the physical manifestation of Re beginning in the Middle Kingdom. Gradually, he achieved the status of a separate god. However, it was not until the reign of Amenhotep III that Aten began to assume prominence over other gods. Akhenaten, building upon the foundation laid by his father, elevated Aten to a status unprecedented in the history of Egyptian religion. By regnal year five, he had changed his name from Amenhotep ("Amen is Satisfied") to Akhenaten ("Illuminated Manifestation of Aten") and moved his capital from Thebes to the new city of Akhetaten (now el-Amarna).

Having begun his reign by building the temple to Aten, Akhenaten later shut down temples throughout Egypt, with special attention to those temples dedicated to Amen. These changes meant that the traditional religion of the ruling elite no longer enjoyed official state support. The once-powerful priesthood, stripped of revenue, no longer had a significant voice in Egyptian religious, political, and economic life. Throughout Egypt, Akhenaten had the names of other gods (especially Amen) erased from monuments and other public edifices. Aten was, in effect, the only god, and Akhenaten and his family bore a uniquely personal relationship to this deity. Although there was a priesthood of Aten, "Akhenaten alone was said to have true knowledge of the god." In fact, it seems possible that Atenism in its purest form was in actuality a very personal communion between the god and his manifestation on earth, Akhenaten. Converts to the new religion (and there were many among the courtiers and nobility) could expect to bask in the reflected radiance of Aten as it trickled down from Akhenaten and his immediate family. Needless to say, Atenism had nothing to offer the common people. Indeed the temple closures robbed many of employment, not to mention spiritual comfort. Worse yet, Akhenaten's "religious revolution" was devastating to the Egyptian psyche. The concept of "maat" (order, consistency, truth) had provided the foundation for culture, politics, and religion throughout recorded Egyptian history. By dismantling the principal cultural institutions of his people, Akhenaten deprived them of the comfort and stability provided by centuries of tradition.

Changes in the artistic styles of the era paralleled the dramatic religious changes. For more than 2,000 years, depictions of Egyptian royalty followed strict conventions; a carving of Dynasty I pharaoh Den striking his enemy on the head with a mace looks much like one of Dynasty XVIII's Thutmose III. Beginning with the building of the Temple of Aten at Karnak from regnal years one through five, portrayals of Akhenaten and his family reflected an entirely new, caricature-like style. Faces were elongated, bodies became relatively androgynous, buttocks and lips were exaggerated. Freed from the strict protocols of the past, Egyptian artists temporarily embraced a more naturalistic style when portraying animals and other (non-royal) people. A particularly graphic illustration of the changes can be seen in the tomb of the nobleman Ramose, where a series of representations of the pharaoh were begun following the traditional canon but were completed in the newer style.

The Aten temple at Karnak appears to have been built in conjunction with the new pharaoh's celebration of a Sed Festival. This celebration, ideally observed after 30 years of rule to rejuvenate a failing monarch, was held in regnal years three or four. A likely reason for the premature festival might be, as Dodson suggests, that Amenhotep IV held the celebration to "mark a fundamental change of direction for the reign." Certainly a change was imminent. Within a year Amenhotep had become Akhenaten, and within another year Thebes was abandoned for Akhetaten.

Akhetaten (Horizon of the Aten) was a city of mud brick and sandstone built on the east side of the Nile about 200 km. north of Thebes. The site, a crescent of land hemmed in on three sides by cliffs and the river on the fourth, had never been dedicated to any god; virgin soil for the new religion. The city at its height ran for some 7 km. from north to south and included residential suburbs, two Aten temples immediately adjacent to the king's house (one of modest proportion, one large enough to contain 750 altars), two palaces, various administrative offices, and a village for the workmen. Estimates of the city's population range from 20,000 to 50,000. The city limits and immediate environs were marked with a roughly circular series of 14 boundary stelae, located on both sides of the Nile. Each of the stelae depicted Akhenaten and his family worshipping the Aten.

Akhenaten's family at the time of the move to Akhetaten consisted of his wife, Queen Nefertiti, and two daughters, Meryetaten and Meketaten. Although Nefertiti's parentage is unknown, there is speculation that her father may have been General Ay, an influential courtier who later became the fourteenth pharaoh of Dynasty XVIII. In or about regnal year seven a third daughter, Ankhsenpaaten, was born. Over the next few years three other daughters followed. Kiya, a secondary wife of the king, may have given birth to several of Akhenaten's children, including possibly

Smenkhkare and Tutankhaten (later Tutankhamen). Akhenaten's mother, the dowager Queen Tiye, may have resided at Akhetaten, at least on a part-time basis. With Tiye was a princess named Beketaten who was perhaps the last child of Amenhotep III.

Akhenaten was not very attentive to his realm's political relationships, allowing some treaties and alliances to fall into disarray. Nubia required little effort, and was handled much as it had been by his predecessors. Gold, so much needed for building projects and commerce, was extracted from the Nubian mines. Local populations were still enslaved and sent off to Egypt and her allies in Syria-Palestine. At some point, probably around regnal year 12, the king ordered the suppression of a small-time revolt, which netted under 150 Nubian captives and 361 head of cattle. The number of tribesmen killed in the fighting is not recorded, but we do know that some of the captives were impaled alive. As Amenhotep IV, the pharaoh built a town-enclosure and temple to Amen, Mut, and Khonsu, as well as a temple to the Aten at Sesebi. A temple to Aten was also built at Kawa, at the Third Cataract. At the temples built by Amenhotep III at Soleb and Sedeinga, Amenhotep IV is shown worshipping both himself and his father (who was equated with the sun god Re at both sites).

The political situation in Syria-Palestine was much more complicated than that of Nubia. Egypt held sway over a score or so petty kingdoms in the region that maintained some independence although they paid annual tribute to the pharaoh. The Egyptians maintained garrisons throughout the region, and in return for their tribute these principalities frequently called upon the Egyptians for support in their endless squabbling. There were, historically, two other major players in the region, the Hittites to the north and the Mitannians to the northeast. After three generations of calm relations with the Egyptians, the region was destabilized during Akhenaten's reign, first by Hittites who invaded Mitannian-held territory in northern Syria and then by a dynastic struggle among the Mitannians. This allowed the Hittites to attack and destroy the Mitannian capital and take much of the territory that had been given to Egypt by treaty during the reign of Thutmose IV, 60 years before. All of this and much more is discussed in the Amarna Letters (see Glossary). By the end of Akhenaten's reign, Egypt's control of the region was all but nonexistent.

In addition to likely serving as coregent to his father, Amenhotep III, for an indeterminate period of time, recent scholarship strongly suggests that Akhenaten also shared the throne with two other individuals: Ankhkeperure Smenkhkare, his possible son, and Nefertiti, his wife and chief queen (under the name Ankhkhpereure Neferneferuaten). Because of the three possible coregencies, it would not be unreasonable to postulate that Akhenaten never ruled independently.

It is most likely that Akhenaten, before abandoning Thebes for Akhetaten, had ordered construction of his tomb begun. An unfinished tomb in the Valley of the Kings (WV25) has been suggested as the site. The pharaoh was actually interred in his tomb in the Royal Wadi at Amarna. When cleared by the Antiquity Service in 1891-1892, fragments of funerary furniture, broken ushabtis, and such items made it clear that several burials had taken place in the tomb. Certainly Akhenaten, the princess Meketaten, and probably Nefertiti were buried there. Also, fragments of a sarcophagus found in the tomb have recently been confirmed as belonging to Queen Tiye; the queen mother may have been laid to rest near her son.

The mummy of Akhenaten has never been discovered, or at least not recognized as such. On more than one occasion it has been suggested that the skeleton found in KV55 (a royal cache discovered in the Valley of the Kings) is that of Akhenaten, rather than Smenkhkare, as is the usual identification. Another theory has put forth the possibility that the mummy from the Deir el-Bahri cache, usually identified as Amenhotep III, is actually Akhenaten. Estimates for age at death for the skeleton are between 23 and 35 years; a recent estimate of age for the mummy is about fifty years. Either one might be Akhenaten.

References:

Aldred 1988
Do. Arnold 1996
Bryan 2000 pp. 274-290
N. Davies 1903-08
Dodson 1995 pp. 96-108
Dodson forthcoming pp. 1-13
Dodson and Hilton 2004 pp. 13, 24, 142-143, 144-145, 146-147, 148, 149-150, 154-157
Eaton-Krauss 2001 pp. 48-51
Freed et al. 1999
Giles 1997
Gohary 1992
Grajetzki 2005 pp. 59-61, 61-62
Hall 1913 pp. 195-197 #s 1945-1969, 276-278 #s 2676-2688
Hornung 1999
Ikram and Dodson 1998 pp. 315, 318
W.R. Johnson 1996 pp. 65-82
Kemp 1989 pp. 261-317
Loeben 1994 pp. 104-109
Martin 1974
Martin 1989a
Montserrat 2000
Moran 1992
Murnane 1977 pp. 123-169, 169-179, 231-234

Newberry 1906 pp. 104 #IV, 167-168 #s 13, 19-25, 26, 28, pl. I #IV, XXXI
Peet et al. 1961
Perepelkin 1978
Petrie 1894
Petrie 1978 pl. XXXVI #s 18.10.1-55
D. Redford 1967 pp. 88-169, 170-182
D. Redford 1984
Reeves 1988 pp. 91-101
Reeves 1990b pp. 40-41, 42-49, 58-59 note 157
Reeves 2001
Reeves and Wilkinson 1996 pp. 10, 116-121
Samson 1978
Samson 1982 pp. 61-67
Thomas 1994 pp. 72-81
Tyldesley 1998
Tyldesley 2006 pp. 125-134
van Dijk 2000 pp. 274-286
Velikovsky 1960
Watterson 1999
R. Wilkinson 2000 pp. 25, 51, 60, 78, 82, 140-141, 164-165, 232
R. Wilkinson 2003 pp. 36-39, 58, 206, 209, 236-241

Amenemhet I — Dynasty XII

Nomen: 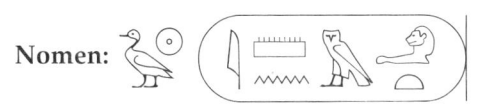 *imn-m-ḫ3t*
Amenemhet

Early Names:

Horus Name: *sḥtp-ib-rʿ*

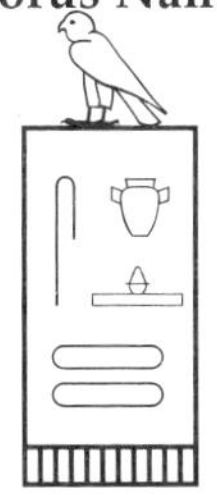

Prenomen:  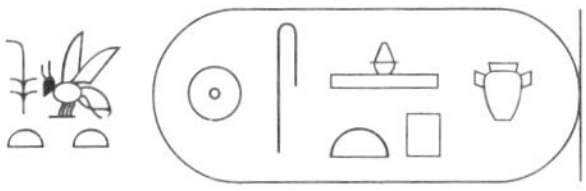 *sḥtp-ib-rʿ*
Sehotepibre

Two Ladies: 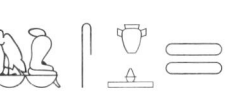 *nbty sḥtp-ib-rʿ*

Golden Falcon:  *bik-nbw sm3*

Later Names:

Horus Name: *wḥm-mswt*

Prenomen: 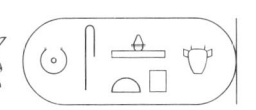 *sḥtp-ib-rʿ*
Sehotepibre

Two Ladies: 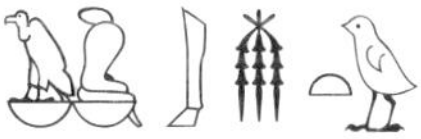 *nbty wḥm-mswt*

Golden Falcon: 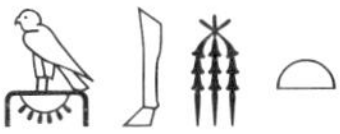 *bik-nbw wḥm-mswt*

Amenemhet I

Length of Reign:	30 years
Tomb:	Pyramid at Lisht: "The Places of the Appearance of Amenemhet"
Mummy:	Unknown

Consorts:	Neferitatjenen	**Variant Names:**	Ammenemes Amunemhat
Manetho:	Ammanemes (A) Ammenemes (A, E)		
King Lists:	Ab: (59); S: (39); T: (G 5.20)		

The first pharaoh of Dynasty XII, Amenemhet I appears to have been the son of commoners, the God's Father Senwosret and a lady named Neferet (I), who is given the title King's Mother. All we know about Amenemhet's father comes from the title God's Father, which at this point of Egyptian history apparently was used to denote the non-royal father of a pharaoh. The King's Mother, Nefret, is known from an offering table found at Lisht, and from a literary work, the Prophecy of Neferty, where she is described as a "woman of Ta-Seti" (the first nome of Upper Egypt, whose capital was at Elephantine).

Amenemhet I was probably the vizier and general of the same name who is mentioned on four inscriptions found in the Wadi Hammamat dating to the second regnal year of Montuhotep IV. The inscriptions were set up to commemorate the visit by 10,000 soldiers, laborers and stone-cutters under the command of Amenemhet who were there to cut the stone for Montuhotep's sarcophagus. These inscriptions also record two unusual happenings. First, a gazelle gave birth on the very stone picked for the sarcophagus lid, and, second, after a storm and flash flood, a well some ten cubits square was discovered in that desolate region, a well that had previously gone completely unnoticed: "No eye had seen it..." not "soldiers of old, and kings who had lived aforetime." Both events were looked upon as somewhat miraculous and so undoubtedly added to Amenemhet's prestige. It has been suggested that the two "miracles" happening during Amenemhet's command of the expedition might have been viewed as a sign that the gods especially favored him.

The Turin Canon ignores Amenemhet's predecessor, Montuhotep IV (as do all of the king lists), and records instead a kingless period of seven years. Montuhotep's highest known regnal date is his second year, which leaves five years during which Egypt was most probably embroiled in civil strife, some of which was undoubtedly violent. At the end of this period, Amenemhet I sat on the throne of the Two Lands. It should be noted that a fragment of stone bowl found at Lisht bears the Horus name of Amenemhet on one side and the nomen and partial Horus name of Montuhotep on the other, leading some Egyptologists to posit a coregency between the two. While this isn't impossible, it seems highly unlikely.

Amenemhet's claim to the throne was bolstered by the Prophecies of Neferty, which contained a story predicting his ascension to the throne to save and revitalize a crisis-torn Egypt. Throughout ancient Egyptian history, such "prophetic" political narratives were written to justify a variety of actions taken by pharaohs.

Attestations for Amenemhet I at Thebes are few: an offering table from the temple of Ptah bearing his Horus name, two statue fragments from Karnak (only one of which bears the king's name), and possibly the beginnings of a funerary complex. Attestations from the rest of Egypt include a red granite offering table from Memphis, a red granite doorway and seated statue of the king from Khatana-Qantir, and the remains of a temple from Ezbet Rushdi. Attestations are also to be found at Tanis (a red granite statue usurped by Merenptah of Dynasty XIX), and at Bubastis, where are found the remains of a temple. Remains of a seated statue attributed to this king come from Heliopolis. From the Faiyum area comes the bottom part of a dual statue of Amenemhet and Bastet. Architectural elements come from Abydos, Dendera and Coptos. A great many remains from Amenemhet come from Armant, mostly stone blocks bearing wall reliefs, inscriptions, ceiling decorations, and the like; one of these blocks gives a date of Amenemhet's first regnal year. There are also the remains of two seated statues and an inscribed pillar. From Tod comes the lower part of a dual statue of the king with the goddess Sekhmet.

Outside the borders of Egypt, Amenemhet I appears to be the earliest pharaoh on record to have explored the turquoise mines at Serabit el-Khadim in Sinai. An inscription found at Ayn Soukhna, the coastal jumping-off point for expeditions to and from Sinai, tells us that Amenemhet explored the area in his Seventh Year. He was also much interested in Nubia. At Abu Handal, some 150 km. south of the Egyptian border at Aswan, we find rock inscriptions dating to Amenemhet's rule which make it very clear that Egyptian interest in Nubia was intense and would be pursued to the bloody end. One inscription, dated to the king's year 29, ends "we came to vanquish Wawat," while another inscription tells us that "the Nubians of the entire remaining part of Wawat were slaughtered...I sailed victoriously upstream, slaughtering the Nubian on his river bank(s)...I sailed downstream...I put fires to their houses." Exactly how much of Nubia was controlled by Egypt during Amenemhet's rule is uncertain, but it appears as though the planned subjugation of Nubia began under this king.

At some point during Amenemhet's reign, civil strife seems to have again become an issue. The stele of Nesu-Montu, an overseer of troops, tells us how he overthrew enemies of the pharaoh and led "the battle for the two lands." Perhaps it was just such internal unrest that prompted Amenemhet to declare his son Senwosret as

Amenemhet I

coregent in the former's year 20. While not numerous, there are a fair number of double-dated attestations for the coregency, and in some cases where dates were not given, the cartouches of both kings are juxtaposed in such a way as to signify the sharing of the throne. It may be at this point of his reign that Amenemhet moved the capital from Thebes to a new town called Amenemhet Itjtowy, ("Amenemhet, seizer of the Two Lands"). The town has not yet been discovered, but undoubtedly was very near Lisht, where Amenemhet's pyramid was built. The town was at what the ancients considered the exact border between Upper and Lower Egypt.

An unfinished funerary complex at Thebes which might have rivaled Nebhepetre Montuhotep's temple at Deir el-Bahri, had it been completed, was probably intended as Amenemhet's final resting place. The site was abandoned when Amenemhet moved the court from Thebes to Itjtowy, and a new tomb site was chosen at Lisht, not far from the new capital. The new tomb was a pyramid with a base of 86 x 86 m. and a height of 55 m. Built of poor quality stone, blocks pilfered from other monuments (those of Khufu, Khafre, Unas and one of the Pepis), sand and mudbrick, the pyramid is today a jumbled pile some 20 m. tall. The entrance to the tomb, in the middle of the north side, is at ground level, with a slightly sloped passageway that leads to a small square room; a vertical shaft in its floor then leads downward to the burial chamber. Over the pyramid's entrance stood the north chapel, now long gone. The complex included a mortuary temple (called "Amenemhet is High and Beautiful"), two mastabas and a series of tomb shafts for the burials of consorts, princesses and perhaps loyal courtiers.

"Regnal year 30...The god ascended to his horizon, the King of Upper and Lower Egypt, Sehotepibre, flew up to heaven...," so The Story of Sinuhe describes the passing of Amenemhet I. The author of The Instruction of King Amenemhet for His Son Senwosret is a bit more graphic: "It was after supper, night had come. I was taking an hour of rest....As my heart began to follow sleep, weapons for my protection were turned against me...." Thus died Amenemhet I. We don't know why assassins, evidently members of his body-guard, struck the pharaoh down. Perhaps it was a plot to install a rival on the throne. If so, the culprits were swiftly crushed by Senwosret, who also seems to have hurriedly completed his father's pyramid and its complex.

Manetho gives a reign of 16 years for Amenemhet, his Ammenemes, which is certainly too low. The Turin Canon records a reign of 2[9], while the stele of an official named Intef is dated to year 30 of Amenemhet I and year 10 of Senwosret I.

References:

Berman 1986 pp. 5-7, 10-14, 14-18, 19-23, 36-42, 55-90, 107-110, 173-213
Breasted 1906 vol. I pp. 211-216
Callender 2000 pp. 156, 158-160
Couyat and Montet 1912 pp. 79-81, 97-98, 100-102, 79-81, pl. XXIX #s113, XXXVI and XXXVII

Dodson 2003 pp. 84, 85-86, 129
Dodson and Hilton 2004 pp. 19, 90, 92-93, 96-98
Gardiner 1959 pl. II, Col. V.20
Gardiner 1961 p. 439
Gardiner and Peet 1952 pl. XIX #63, XXI #71, XXII #70, XCI, XCII
Gardiner and Peet 1955 pp. 36, 38-39, 84
Goedicke 1971
Grajetzki 2005 p. 30
Grajetzki 2006 pp. 26, 28-35
Habachi 1954 pp. 448-458
Hayes 1953 pp. 167-168 and fig. 102
Lehner 1997 pp. 38, 168-169, 226
Lichtheim 1975 pp. 135-139, 139-145, 222-235
Murnane 1977 p. 2-5, 8, 228
Peden 2001 pp. 21-22, 35, 36, 68
Tidyman 1995 pp. 103-110
Tyldesley 2006 p. 70
Valbelle and Bonnet 1996 pp. 7-8, 83, 127-129
Verbrugghe and Wickersham 1996 pp. 138, 195-196
Verner 1997 pp. 155, 383-384, 396-399, 400, 404, 465
von Beckerath 1999 pp. 82 #1, 83 #1
Waddell 1940 pp. 63, 65, 67, 69, 71
Winlock 1947 pp. 56-57
Zaba 1974 pp. 31-35 #4, 54-56 #27, 99-109 #73, 174 #168

Amenemhet II Dynasty XII

Horus Name:

ḥkn-m-mꜣʿt

Nomen:

imn-im-ḥꜣt
Amenemhet

Prenomen:

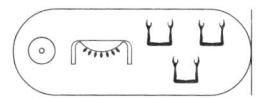

nbw-kꜣw-rʿ
Nubkaure

Two Ladies:

nbty ḥkn-m-mꜣʿt

Golden Falcon:

bik-nbw mꜣʿ-ḥrw

Length of Reign:	35 years
Tomb:	Pyramid at Dahshur: "The Ba of Amenemhet"
Mummy:	Unknown

Amenemhet II

Consorts:	Kaneferu Keminub(?) Senet(?)	King Lists:	Ab: (61); S: (41); T: (G 5.22)
Manetho:	Ammenemes (A, E)	Variant Names:	Ammenemes Amunemhat

The son of Senwosret I and Queen Never (III), Amenemhet II was the third pharaoh of Dynasty XII. The first mention we have of him comes from the tomb of the nomarch of Beni Hasan, also named Amenemhet. We are told that the nomarch led an expedition to Kush during the reign of Senwosret I, that he was accompanied by the "oldest son of the king, of his body, Ameny," and that the expedition was so successful that "the king's son praised god for me." Some time after this Nubian adventure, Amenemhet seems to have become coregent with his father. The partnership lasted between three and four years, until the death of Senwosret in his regnal year 45.

Attestations for Amenemhet II are not numerous in Egypt: a pair of colossal sphinxes, one found at Tanis, but originally from Memphis or Heliopolis; inscribed offering tables from Nebesha and Khatana in the Delta; and part of a series of royal annals preserved on two stone blocks from the temple of Ptah at Mit Rahina (Memphis). From the temple of Thoth at Hermopolis come the jambs of a limestone gateway which show the pharaoh making an offering to that god. At Tod, two metal boxes bearing the king's name and containing a small treasure of silver and lapis lazuli objects were discovered in the temple of Montu. Also known is an assortment of scarab-seals, cylinder-seals and plaques. Amenemhet's name is to be found on more than two dozen private stelae in various parts of Egypt. A graffito from the alabaster quarry at Hatnub commemorates an expedition there in year 20.

Outside Egypt, Amenemhet II is attested in Sinai, at the turquoise mines at Serabit el-Khadim, where a series of stelae and graffiti record at least three expeditions sent in years 2, 11 and 24. Royal annals tell of an Egyptian force sent to "hack up the land" somewhere in Sinai, and they also tell of the capture of two unnamed towns and the taking of over 1,500 prisoners on the Lebanese coast. However, peaceful relations were carried on with Byblos and Tunip. At Ras Shamra (ancient Ugarit), in Syria, a statuette of a princess dates to Amenemhet II, as does a fragment of statue bearing the name of his vizier, Senwosretankh. At Megiddo, the fragments of four statuettes of Thothhotep, the nomarch of Hermopolis, were discovered. From Qatna comes a sphinx inscribed with the name of Ita, a daughter of Amenemhet II.

Some time after year 11, at least one expedition was sent to the amethyst mines at Wadi el-Hudi in Lower Nubia.

Two stelae from Wadi Gasus on the Red Sea coast document an expedition to Punt in Amenemhet's twenty-eighth year.

Amenemhet II

Amenemhet II chose not to be buried near his father and grandfather at Lisht, but instead to build his pyramid and funeral complex at Dahshur, about 12 km. to the north. Today the monument is nothing more than a mound of mud bricks referred to locally as the "White Pyramid" in reference to the white limestone blocks that once made up its core, and because of the millions of shards of white limestone found with the brick. Except for limited and hurried excavations done by deMorgan in 1894-95, the complex has not been explored, and so we are unsure of the pyramid's base and height, although the base is estimated to have been about 50 x 50 m. The entrance to the structure was in the middle of the north side, hidden by a small chapel. A passage led downward, past two granite portcullises, to the burial chamber, which contained a quartzite sarcophagus sunk into the floor. From the burial chamber, a shaft drops down and a passage doubles back beneath the entrance corridor for a short way; at its end is a hole in the floor which was evidently intended to hold the king's canopic chest.

Outside the pyramid lie the few remains of the mortuary temple. Just beyond that are two pylon-like ruins that may be all that is left of the gateway into the complex, although they may be the remains of tombs. On the opposite side of the pyramid, deMorgan discovered six tombs, that of a prince Amenemhetankh, those of princesses Ita, Khnemet, Itaweret and Sithathormerit, and that of a queen named Keminub. The royal offspring are almost certainly the children of Amenemhet, but Queen Keminub should evidently be placed in Dynasty XIII. The valley temple has never been discovered.

Manetho gives his Amenemmes (II) a reign of 38 years and says that the king was killed by his own eunuchs. This is obviously a confusion between Amenemhet II and his grandfather Amenemhet I, who evidently was killed by his bodyguard. The highest date known for Amenemhet II is a year 35.

References:

Anthes 1928 p. 78, Gr. 50, pl. 8, inscrift XIII, 32, Gr. 50
Bourriau 2000 p. 187
Callender 2000 pp. 163-164
Dodson 2003 pp. 88-89, 132
Dodson and Hilton 2004 pp. 90, 92-94, 96-97
Fay 1996
Gardiner 1959 pl. II, Col. V.22
Gardiner 1961 p. 439
Gardiner and Peet 1952 pl. XIX #s 75, 78, XX #74, XXI #s 71,72, 76, XXI A #73, XXII #s 76, 79
Gardiner and Peet 1955 pp. 34, 36, 48, note f, pp. 77-78 #s 47-49, 86-89 #s 71-79
Grajetzki 2005 pp. 31, 38
Grajetzki 2006 pp. 28, 36, 43, 45-48, 108, 109, 114, 125, 126, 136, 146, 162, 169, 172, 174, 189
Hall 1913 pp. 10-11 #s 102-108, 265 #s 2608, 2609
Jidejian 1968 p. 25
Lehner 1997 pp. 101, 171, 174, 184, 226
Malek 1992 p. 16
Murnane 1977 pp. 5-6
Newberry 1906 pp. 111 #s 1-4, 116 #11, pl. s VI #s 1-4, VIII #11
Peden 2001 pp. 27, 32, 35
Petrie 1889 #s 219-221
Petrie 1978 p. 19, pl. XIII, 12.3 #s 1-17
Sadek 1980 pp. 40-41 #18
Tufnell 1984 p. 362 #s 3031-3032, pl. LII #s 31-32
Tyldesley 2006 p. 72
Verbrugghe and Wickersham 1996 pp. 138, 196
Verner 1997 pp. 187, 385, 406-408, 465

Amenemhet III

von Beckerath 1999 pp. 84 #3, 85 #3
Waddell 1940 p. 67, 71

Wilson 1941 pp. 225-236

Amenemhet III   Dynasty XII

Horus Name:

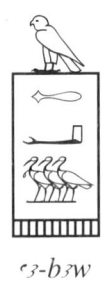

ꜥꜣ-bꜣw

Nomen:

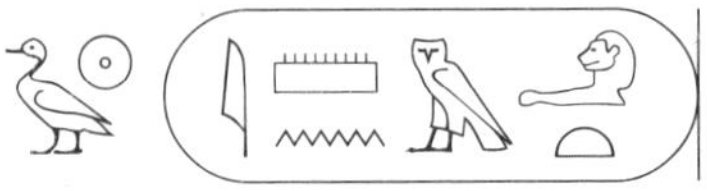

imn-m-ḥꜣt
Amenemhet

Prenomen:

ni-mꜣꜥt-rꜥ
Nimaatre

Two Ladies:

nbty iṯi-iwꜥt-tꜣwy

Golden Falcon:

bik-nbw wꜣḥ-ꜥnḫ

Length of Reign:	46 years
Tomb:	Pyramid at Dahshur: "Amenemhet Lives" Pyramid at Hawara
Mummy:	Unknown

Consorts:	Aat Hotepti(?) Khenmetnefer- hedjet	**King Lists:**	Ab: (64); S: (44); T: (G 5.25)
Manetho:	Lachares (A) Lamares (A, E) Lamaris (E) Lampares (E)	**Variant Names:**	Ammenemes Amunemhet Maot-en-ra Nymaatra

The sixth pharaoh of Dynasty XII, Amenemhet III was almost certainly the son of his predecessor, Senwosret III. Amenemhet's mother is not known. It has been suggested that at some point in the reign of Senwosret III Amenemhet was elevated to the throne as a coregent, and recent research points in that direction. The juxtaposition of names, a few double-dated articles, as well as new evidence for an additional twenty years of reign for Senwosret III, all point to a long father-son association. A coregency of twenty years is what is indicated, so that Amenemhet's regnal year one corresponds to Senwosret's year 20.

Although attestations for Amenemhet III in Egypt are relatively common, they consist mostly of small items: the base of a statue from Tell el-Yahudiya, a palace at Bubastis which attests to a Sed festival for the king, additions to a wall built by Senwosret II at El Kab, a statue and portions of a gateway at Memphis, papyri from Kahun, inscriptions recording two expeditions to Wadi Hammamat, his name added to a lintel of Dynasty XI pharaoh Intef III at Elephantine, etc. There is a marked lack of monumental architecture. This is partially due to the ravages of time, but also to the fact that a great deal of Amenemhet's resources were spent on the development of the Faiyum area and on the construction of two pyramids.

Outside of Egypt, Amenemhet paid a great deal of attention to the turquoise mines in Sinai, sending at least twenty-five expeditions to Wadi Maghara and Serabit el-Khadim. The first of these expeditions was in regnal year two, and the last in year 45. A shrine to Hathor at Serabit el-Khadim was begun by Amenemhet III, but completed by his successor, Amenemhet IV. A tomb in the royal necropolis at Byblos has yielded an obsidian vase set in gold and bearing the prenomen of Amenemhet III.

Nubia received constant attention during the reign of Amenemhet III: inspection tours by officials and enlargements of some of the forts at the Second Cataract. No military actions have been confirmed, but there seems to have been some sort of a rebellion, evidently in regnal year nine.

Amenemhet III's original intent was to be interred at Dahshur, where a pyramid was built but never occupied by the king. The pyramid, which was evidently begun in the king's first regnal year (we have a builder's graffito that is dated to year two), measured 105 x 105 m. to the side and rose 75 m. high. The pyramid, like his father's, was constructed entirely of mud brick, built in a series of "steps," and sheathed in a limestone casing that was 5 m. thick. Today, the casings are gone, having been pulled down and carried away in antiquity for use elsewhere, and the pyramid is a great heap known as the Black Pyramid, due to the color of the remaining brick core. Amazingly enough, the pyramid's capstone, inscribed with the nomen and prenomen of the king, was discovered pretty much intact. It seems likely that the capstone was never set in place, and was perhaps kept in the temple at the funerary complex. The burial chamber was reached by an entrance at foundation level, near the southeast corner of the pyramid. After descending stairs, a series of corridors, stairways and rooms finally led to the actual burial chamber of the king. It had never been occupied.

A separate entrance to the pyramid, located on the west side, led to burial chambers for two of Amenemhet's queens, Aat and an unknown woman. Aat's skeleton suggests that she was in her mid-thirties at time of death, while the unnamed queen was in her mid-twenties. A few items were overlooked by the tomb robbers: Aat's burial chamber yielded pieces of jewelry, duck-shaped alabaster containers, the canopic chest and one canopic jar, and a few other items. The chamber of the unnamed queen contained, among other things, several duck-shaped alabaster containers, stone mace-heads, and some jewelry. A passageway connected the queens' "suite" to that of the king. The pyramid was surrounded by two sets of walls, and a mortuary temple and chapel were built on the east side. A causeway led to a valley temple. Based on severe internal and external damage, Reeves believes that the pyramid was completed by regnal year 15, probably hastily. The structure's foundation was unable to support its immense weight; walls collapsed and parts of the structure sank. Shoring up with brick and timber helped, but the pyramid had to be abandoned. However, it was obviously considered sturdy enough to use for the burial of the two queens. Amenemhet deserted Dahshur and began a new pyramid complex at Hawara in the Faiyum.

The new pyramid measured 105 x 105 m. and stood 58 m. tall. Although the base was the same as that of the pyramid at Dahshur, the height was 17 m. less, which alleviated stress; Dahshur had been an expensive lesson. Construction seems to have begun in or about regnal year 15. As with the pyramids of his father and grandfather, Amenemhet III's tomb was constructed of mud brick and cased with limestone. Like those of his predecessors, the casing is long gone and the pyramid is a heap of mud brick, albeit the best preserved of the lot. The burial chamber, carved into a huge block of either sandstone or quartzite, contained the king's sarcophagus and canopic chest, as well as a sarcophagus and canopic chest that seems to have belonged to the king's daughter, Neferuptah. This princess has the distinction of being the first woman in Egyptian history to have had her name enclosed in a cartouche. However, sarcophagus aside, Neferuptah appears to have been buried in her own pyramid some two kilometers away at Hawara-South. The interior of the pyramid was explored for the first and last time by Petrie in 1889, and much of it, including the burial chamber, was found to be flooded. Since that time the entire substructure has filled with water and is completely inaccessible

Amenemhet III's funerary complex at Hawara encompassed an area of at least 60,000 square m. Used as a quarry since Roman times, the site is today little more than a vast area of limestone chips, but it is described by classical writers as a labyrinth, a great warren of temples and courts. Herodotus describes the area as a building having 12 covered courts and surrounded by a wall. The building, a two storied affair, supposedly contained 3,000 rooms that were connected by "baffling and intricate passages from room to room and from court to court." Petrie was able to draw plans for part of the area, and it appears to have contained a vast number of columned halls, chapels and rooms once decorated with statuary and relief work.

Manetho gives his Lamares a reign of only eight years. The Turin Canon gives Amenemhet III 40+ years. The highest date from a contemporary source is Kahun Papyrus XIV, which gives a year 46. It is known from a lintel found at Bubastis that Amenemhet III celebrated a Sed Festival in his regnal year 30. Sometime in year 43 or 44 Amenemhet III installed Amenemhet IV as coregent. It is assumed that they were father and son, although the younger Amenemhet's mother, Hotepti, does not bear the title "King's Wife" and nowhere is Amenemhet IV's paternity given.

References:

D. Arnold 1987
Bell 1975 p. 229 note 11
Cron and Johnson 1995b pp. 48-50, 58-66
Dodson 2000/2001 pp. 40-47
Dodson 2003 pp. 94-97, 134
Dodson and Hilton 2004 pp. 28, 90, 91, 92-93, 95, 96-99, 110-111
Farag and Iskander 1971
G. Fraser 1900 pp. 5-6 #s 35-39, pl. II #s 35-39
Gardiner 1959 pl. II, Col. V.25
Gardiner 1961 p. 439
Gardiner and Peet 1952 pl. X-XIV, XVI-XVIII, XXII-XL, XLIV, XLVII, LIII-LIV, LXXXIII, LXXXV
Gardiner and Peet 1955 pp. 15, 16, 24, 28, 30, 33, 34, 35, 36, 37, 39, 49, 66-70 #s23-31, 73 #41(?), 76 #46, 78-80 #s 83-117, 129-130 #124, 133-134 #s 131-132, 141-142 #s 142-143, 144, 205-208 #s 405-406, 409
Goyon 1957 pp. 91-92 #70, pl. XX
Grajetzki 2005 p. 34
Grajetzki 2006 pp. 51, 52, 55, 57, 58 61, 70, 85, 101, 102, 107, 109, pl. II-III
Hall 1913 pp. pp. 14-16 #s 141-154, 267-270 #s 2622-2638

Herodotus 1954 pp. 188-189
Ikram and Dodson 1998 pp. 31, 83, 84, 93, 116, 167, 203, 252 illustration 347 #s B-C, 253, 279, 315, 318
Jidejian 1968 p. 25
Lehner 1997 pp. 19, 34, 35, 101, 176
Leprohon 1980
Murnane 1977 pp. 9-13, 13-20, 20-23, 228-229, 229
Newberry 1906 pp. 46, fig. 22, 88, fig. 93, 111-113 #s 1, 10-15, 119-121 #s 25-29, 36, 37 pl. VI #s 1, 10-15, IX #s 25-29, 36, 37
Peden 2001 pp. 41-42
Petrie 1912 pp. 28-35, pl. XXIII-XXIX
Petrie 1978 pl. XIII-XIV 12.6 #s 1-28
Ryholt 1997a pp. 159 note 580, 214, table 47
Tufnell 1984 p. 364 #s 3072-3092, pl. LIII #s 3072-3092
Tyldesley 2006 p. 73-74
Uphill 2000
Verbrugghe and Wickersham 1996 pp. 138, 196
Verner 1997 pp. 177, 187, 232, 388, 419, 421-431, 433, 465
von Beckerath 1999 pp. 86 #6, 87 #6
Waddell 1940 p. 69, 71, 73
Wegner 1996 pp. 249-279

Amenemhet IV — Dynasty XII

Horus Name: ḫpr-ḫprw

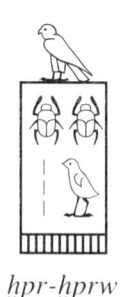

Nomen: imn-m-ḥ3t
Amenemhet

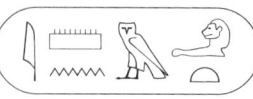

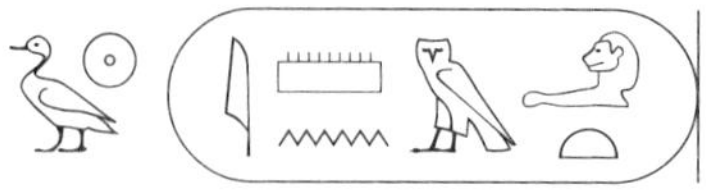

Prenomen: m3ˁ-ḫrw-rˁ
Maakherure

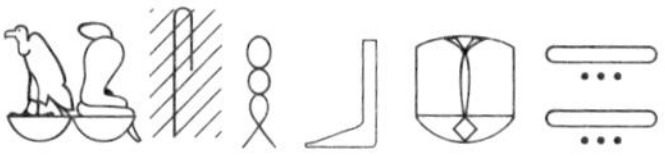

Two Ladies: nbty [s]ḥ3b-t3wy

Golden Falcon: bik-nbw sḫm-nṯrw

Length of Reign:	13 years
Tomb:	Unknown
Mummy:	Unknown
Consorts:	Sobekneferu(?)
Manetho:	Ammenemes (A) (E)
King Lists:	Ab: (65); S: (45); T: (G 6.1)
Variant Names:	Ammenemes, Amunemhat

The seventh pharaoh of Dynasty XII, Amenemhet IV's relationship to his immediate predecessor Amenemhet III is unknown; the fact that Amenemhet IV refers to the elder king as "father" several times isn't proof of an actual blood relationship, since the term is sometimes used as an honorific, sometimes can refer to a grandfather, and sometimes is used to refer to a predecessor. Amenemhet IV's mother was the King's Mother Hetepi, whose figure and titles are shown on a wall in the temple of the goddess

Renenutet at Medinet Maadi in the Faiyum. Since this one carving is the only reference we have to her, it is impossible to rule her out as having been a wife or perhaps a concubine of Amenemhet III.

Whatever the actual relationship between Amenemhets III and IV, it appears that the older Amenemhet chose to name the younger as coregent, not an uncommon practice during Dynasty XII. The length of the coregency is uncertain; some scholars favor as little as one year, others two, and some as many as seven. The majority favor two years and, if they are correct, the coregency would probably have begun in Amenemhet III's forty-third year.

It has been suggested that the senior Amenemhet's daughter, Sobekneferu, might have been married to Amenemhet IV. Whether or not she was his sister, the marriage would have added security to his hold on the throne, but this is no proof of such an arrangement.

Very few attestations for Amenemhet IV are to be found in Egypt, and those that are known are almost always in conjunction with Amenemhet III. A pedestal from Karnak carries both kings' names. The temple of Renenutet at Medinet Maadi mentioned above was probably built by both Amenemhets III and IV, although it is possible that the latter simply finished it after the former's death. Several funerary stelae of officials bear both names. Amenemhet's name has been found alone at the Wadi Shatt el-Rigal, where there is a graffito bearing his prenomen and dated to his third year. Sphinxes inscribed with his name have been found at Abukir, in the Delta. Several scarabs, a cylinder-seal, and an inscribed plaque are also known.

Scholars assume that a pyramid for Amenemhet IV would have been built, or at least begun, but to date no tomb or funerary monument has been found. This king's name has been found in the mortuary temple of Amenemhet III's pyramid at Dahshur, and some scholars have considered whether Amenemhet IV might have been interred in the former king's tomb. It has also been suggested that one of two anonymous pyramids at Mazghuna may have belonged to this king.

Unlike in Egypt, Amenemhet IV's name is well attested at Sinai, where he sent four expeditions to the turquoise mines at Serabit el-Khadim. Amenemhet IV's last expedition to that region was in year nine of this reign; the mines would not be visited again until the time of Ahmose in Dynasty XVIII, a period of some 200 years. Amenemhet IV is responsible for at least the completion of a shrine at the temple of Hathor.

From Nubia, at the Second Cataract, we have records for the heights of the Nile's flooding for years five, six and seven of Amenemhet IV's reign. There is also a stele from the amethyst mines at Wadi el-Hudi, dated to year two of his reign. From Byblos on the Lebanese coast comes an obsidian chest decorated with gold and bearing Amenemhet's prenomen. Tomb II at the royal necropolis of Byblos has yielded a stone vase with Amenemhet's name inscribed on the lid.

Amenemhet V

Manetho gives his Ammenemes a reign of eight years while the Turin Canon gives a very specific nine years, three months and 27 days. A year ten is possible, but it is based upon the juxtaposition of two dates of two unnamed pharaohs. At present. the highest contemporary date we have for Amenemhet IV is a year 13 from an inscription found at Semna, at the Second Cataract.

References:

Dodson 2003 p. 97
Dodson and Hilton 2004 pp. 25, 90, 91, 92-93, 95, 96, 102, 104-105, 108-109
Fakhry 1952 pp. 39-41, and fig. 32
Gardiner 1959 pl. III, Col. VI.1
Gardiner 1961 p. 439
Gardiner and Peet 1952 pl. XI #35, XII #s 33-34, XVIII #57, XXXVI #118, XL, XLI #126, XLII #s 119, 127, XLIV A #s 128-129, XLV #122, XLVI #s 123, 123A, XLVII #s 124-125, XLVIII #121
Gardiner and Peet 1955 pp. 16, 24, 34, 35, 36, 37, 39, 43-44, 48, note f, 71-72 #s 33-35, 81 #57, 122-133 #s 118-130
Jidejian 1968 pp. 25, 26, 27
Lehner 1997 pp. 181, 184
Murnane 1977 pp. 13-20, 229
Newberry 1906 pp. 113 #22, 121 #38, pl. VI.20, IX.38
Peden 2001 pp. 32-33, 38, 42, 49
Petrie 1889 Numbers 273-275
Petrie 1978 p. pl. XIX # 12.7
Ryholt 1997a pp. 76, 91, 209-212, 214, table 47, 294-295
Sadek 1980 pp. 44-45 #21
Tufnell 1984 p. 364 #s 3091-3094, pl. LIII #s 3091-3094
Tyldesley 2006 pp. 70, 73-74
Valbelle and Bonnet 1996 pp. 11-12
Verbrugghe and Wickersham 1996 pp. 138, 196
Verner 1997 pp. 388, 432, 433
von Beckerath 1999 pp. 86 #7, 87 #7
Waddell 1940 p. 69

Amenemhet V — Dynasty XIII

Horus Name: Unknown

Nomen:

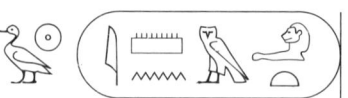

imn-m-ḥꜣt
Amenemhet

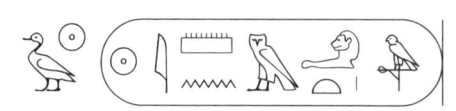

imn-m-ḥꜣt[rꜥ]
Amenemhet

Prenomen:

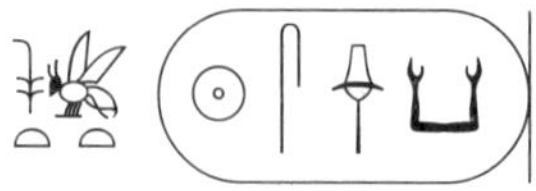

sḥm-kꜣ-rꜥ
Sekhemkare

Two Ladies: Unknown

Golden Falcon: Unknown

Length of Reign:	likely 3-5 years		
Tomb:	Pyramid at Dahshur(?)		
Mummy:	Unknown		
Consorts:	Unknown	**Variant Names:**	Ammenemes Re-Amenemhe
Manetho:	Not given		
King Lists:	T: (G 6.7; R 7.7; vB 6.7)		

The fourth pharaoh of Dynasty XIII, Amenemhet V is a shadowy figure at best. The only definite attestation for this king, aside from his listing in the Turin Canon, is a beautifully made statue from Elephantine, originally set up in the temple of the local goddess Satet. The body of the statue, minus the head, shoulders and arms, was discovered in the shrine of a temple built to honor a nomarch named Hekaib and is now in the Aswan Museum (No. 1318). The head and arms of the statue are in Vienna (Kunsthistoriches Museum, No. 37). A papyrus from el-Lahun in Central Egypt lists a year three and some months and days of a ruler whose prenomen was Sekhemkare and may refer to Amenemhet V, but might also belong to the pharaoh Sonbef, who bore the same prenomen (see also SEKHEMKARE). The Turin Canon originally gave a reign of three or four years.

References:
W. Davies 1981b p. 22
Dodson 2003 p. 97
Fay 1988 pp. 67-77, pl. 18-23
Gardiner 1959 pl. III, Col. VI #7
Gardiner 1961 p. 440 #6.7
Parkinson 1991 pp. 112 no. 38c
Ryholt 1997a pp. 71 fig. 10 Col. 7 #7, 73 table 17 #4, 74 Note 7/7, 80-82, 192 table 33, 209, 214-215 and tables 48 and 49 and note 738, 284 table 83, 337 File 13/4, 408 table 94 #4
von Beckerath 1999 pp. 88 #4, 89 #40

Amenemhet VI   Dynasty XIII

Nomen:

imny(s3)in-it.f(s3) imn-m-ḥ3t
(Ameny's Son, Intef's Son) Amenemhet

Amenemhet VII

Horus Name: *shr-t3wy*

Prenomen: *s'nh-ib-r'*
Seankhibre

Two Ladies: *nbty shm-h'w*

Golden Falcon: *bik nbw hk-m3't*

Length of Reign:	T: "...23 days"
Tomb:	Pyramid at Dahshur(?)
Mummy:	Unknown

Consorts:	Unknown	**Variant Names:**	None
Manetho:	Not given		
King Lists:	T: (G 6.10; R 7.10; vB 6.10)		

Probably the eighth pharaoh of Dynasty XIII, Amenemhet VI was, as evidenced by the filial nomina used in his cartouche, almost certainly the grandson of Amenemhet V and the son of a King's Son Intef, presumably a younger brother of the pharaoh Qemau. This would have made Amenemhet VI a cousin to king Hornedjheritef and perhaps to king Efni, whom Amenemhet VI succeeded.

Attestations for Amenemhet VI include two cylinder-seals from el-Mahamid el-Qibli, found some 40 km. south of Luxor, an architrave from a private tomb at Heliopolis, his name on a stele from Abydos and an inscription on an offering table from Karnak. He undoubtedly reigned from the old Dynasty XII capital, Itjtowy, in the Faiyum.

References:

Dodson 2003 p. 97
Gardiner 1959 pl. III, Col. VI #10
Gardiner 1961 p. 440 #6.10
Hayes 1939 p. 29 note 2
Hayes 1953 p. 342, 343 fig. 226
Helck 1983 p. 4 #7
Ryholt 1997a pp. 71 fig. 10 Col. 7 #10, 73 table 17 #8, 192 table 33, 207, 208 table 46, 214-215 and tables 48 and 49, 284 table 83, 338 File 13/8, 408 table 94
von Beckerath 1999 pp. 90 #7, 191 #7

Amenemhet VII   Dynasty XIII

Horus Name:

ḥry-tp-tꜣwy

Nomen:

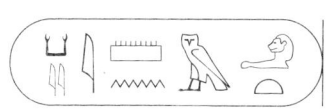

kꜣy(sꜣ) imn-m-ḥꜣt
(Kay's Son) Amenemhet

Prenomen:

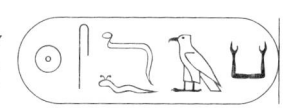

sḏfꜣ-kꜣ-rꜥ
Sedjefakare

sḏfꜣ-kꜣ-rꜥ
Sedjefakare

Two Ladies:

nbty nṯr-bꜣw

Golden Falcon:

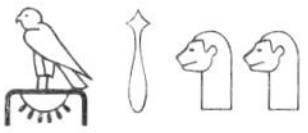

bik nbw ꜥꜣ-pḥti

Length of Reign:	Unknown
Tomb:	Unknown
Mummy:	Unknown

Consorts:	Unknown	Kay-Amenemhet
Manetho:	Not given	Ra-se-beq-ka
		Sebeka-ka-ra
King Lists:	T: (G 6.18; R 7.18)	Sebka-re(?)
Variant Names:	Ammenemes	

This king, who may have been the son of a much disputed ruler, Kay (see SEBKAY), is placed as the 20th pharaoh of Dynasty XIII by Ryholt, while von Beckerath places him as number 15. Recent scholarship places him at position 19.

Aside from his listing in the Turin Canon, Amenemhet VII is known from an inscribed block (possibly a barque stand) discovered at Medamud, about 3 miles north of Karnak; one cylinder-seal each from Kahun and Medinet el-Faiyum in Middle Egypt; four cylinder-seals from el-Mahamid el-Qibli, near Gebelein in Upper Egypt; two scarab-seals of unknown provenance; and a graffito found in the Saqqara tomb of Queen Khuit, the wife of Dynasty VI pharaoh Teti. It is interesting to note that nothing bearing any attestation to Amenemhet VII has been found north of Saqqara. He most likely ruled from the old Dynasty XII capital of Itjtowy in the Faiyum.

References:

Gardiner 1959 pl. III, Col. VI #18
Gardiner 1961 p. 440 #6.18
Gauthier 1907-17 vol. II p. 93 I and II and notes 1 and 2
Helck 1983 p. 1 #2
Newberry 1906 pp. 114 #2, 115 #6, pl. VII #s 2 and 6
Petrie 1891 pp. 245-246 and fig. 149
Petrie 1978 pl. XVIII, p. xviii 13.DE
Ryholt 1997a pp. 71 fig. 10 Col. 7 #18, 73 table 17 #20, 218-219 and tables 52 and 53, 317-318 319-320, 341 File 13/20, 408 #20
von Beckerath 1999 pp. 92 #15, 93 #15

Amenhotep I   Dynasty XVIII

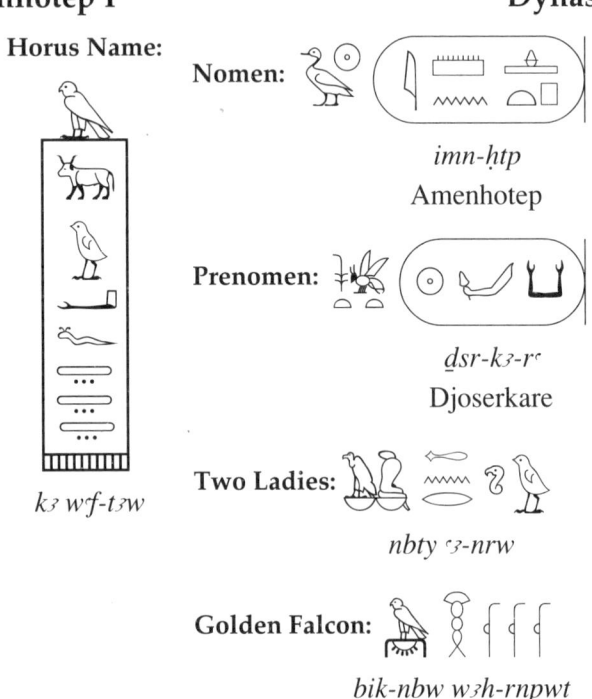

Horus Name:

kꜣ wꜥf-tꜣw

Nomen:

imn-ḥtp
Amenhotep

Prenomen:

ḏsr-kꜣ-rꜥ
Djoserkare

Two Ladies:

nbty ꜥꜣ-nrw

Golden Falcon:

bik-nbw wꜣḥ-rnpwt

Amenhotep I

Length of Reign:	21 years
Tomb:	Unknown
Mummy:	Royal cache at Deir el-Bahri Now at Cairo Museum: JE26211; CG61058

Consorts:	Meryetamen	**Variant Names:**	Amenophis Ammenophis Amonhotep Amunhotpe Djeserkare Zeserkara
Manetho:	Amenophthis (A) Ammenophis (E) Amophis (E)		
King Lists:	Ab: (67); S: (48)		

The son of his direct predecessor, the pharaoh Ahmose, Amenhotep I was the second ruler of Dynasty XVIII. While evidence is slight, it would appear that the two kings shared the throne for a short period, although it should be noted that several eminent scholars disagree. The coregency, if it occurred, might have lasted as long as six years. Upon the death of his father, the young king's mother, Ahmose-Nefertari, acted as regent for an undetermined period. It might have been as late as regnal year seven before Amenhotep reached his maturity. In year eight he was married to his sister, Meryetamen, thus establishing beyond doubt his right to the throne.

Years seven and eight saw military actions in Nubia. Although these expeditions have sometimes been described as shows of force to keep the "natives" in line, or efforts at consolidation, the biographies of several veteran soldiers who were involved in the actions make it clear that bloodshed was not uncommon. They speak of prisoners taken, slaves presented, and the hands of dead warriors given to Amenhotep as proof of the numbers slain. The young pharaoh was probably not in the actual thick of things, and only visited the battlefield to attend to the occasional ritual clubbing of an enemy chieftain. A stele at Aniba dated to the eighth regnal year records the bringing of tribute of gold and other exotic items to the king. At any rate, Amenhotep seems to have secured the boundary set by his father at the island of Sai, 100 km. south of the Second Cataract, and its series of fortresses. A statue and blocks inscribed with the king's name and the name of his mother, found on Sai, attest to a building project, very likely a small temple.

The biography of Ahmose Pennekhbet, one of the veterans mentioned above, tells of capturing three hands for Djoserkare during some sort of campaign in Libya. This is the only known reference to a Libyan campaign during this reign.

The king seems to have added to and/or restored the portico to the "Hathor Cave" in the temple of Hathor at Serabit el-Khadam in Sinai, as evidenced by the discovery of an inscribed lintel slab and

Amenhotep I

the fragment of what might have been a cornice. It has been suggested that Amenhotep I might have ventured into Western Asia as far as the river Euphrates, although the evidence is slight.

Except for the military actions mentioned above, the reign of Amenhotep I seems to have been peaceful and prosperous enough to allow for rather extensive building projects. At Abydos, the pharaoh was responsible for the construction of a limestone chapel dedicated to his father Ahmose and for some reconstruction to the temple of Osiris. At El Kab, the temple of Nekhbet was added to. At Karnak, he built an alabaster shrine or kiosk, a few small chapels and a replica of the "white chapel" of Senwosret I. All of these latter were dismantled and used as filler for the Third Pylon, built by Amenhotep III. Amenhotep I also added a gateway to the temple of Amen. Construction on the shrine was incomplete at the time of Amenhotep I's death and was completed by his successor, Thutmose I. Although some scholars believe that a short coregency may have existed between these two kings, the completion of the shrine by Thutmose is the sole evidence they offer.

Across the Nile from Thebes, at Deir el-Bahri, Amenhotep had repairs made to the temple of the Dynasty XI pharaoh Montuhotep II as well as building at the site a mud brick temple dedicated to himself and his mother. The temple was approached by walking between a series of statues of the king garbed as Osiris. A mortuary temple was constructed on the plain near the royal cemetery at Dra Abu el-Naga. The location of Amenhotep's tomb is a mystery. An inventory of royal tombs inspected during a spate of tomb robberies late in Dynasty XX records that Amenhotep I's tomb was inspected and found to be undisturbed, but the location given has been problematic, and to date no consensus has been reached on any of the three sites proposed.

Amenhotep and Ahmose-Nefertari were perhaps the founders of the tomb workmen's village at Deir el-Medina, where a temple dedicated to them was erected. Long after the builders' village was deserted, the pharaoh and his mother were worshipped in the Theban area as guardians of the necropolis; Sety I of Dynasty XIX built a temple to them. Their cult survived long into Dynasty XXV, a period of 800 years.

The mummy of Amenhotep I was one of those discovered in the Royal Cache at Deir el-Bahri. Because of the beautiful and intricate bandaging, it was decided not to unwrap the king. The royal mummy has, however, been X-rayed on several occasions, most recently in 1966.

In life, the king stood a little more than 1.8 m., tall for an ancient Egyptian. Estimates of age at death range from early twenties to late forties.

Amenhotep's length of reign is not known for certain. Various versions of Manetho give reigns of 20 years, 7 months to 24 years, while the highest year known from Egyptian sources is a regnal year 21. It has been suggested that Amenhotep I counted his reign beginning with the coregency he may have shared with his father. It has also been suggested that Amenhotep actually ruled 27 years, but didn't count the six years of joint rule. Whatever the length of rule, Amenhotep I celebrated a Sed Festival. The festival was mentioned in the biography of the Theban courtier Amenemhet, on the doorjambs of the pharaoh's limestone chapel at Karnak, and on a large lintel. Further evidence for the festival comes from inscribed blocks from the king's mortuary temple. Obviously, the celebration occurred prior to the thirtieth year of rule that was considered ideal.

References:

Björkman 1971 pp. 58-60
Bleiberg 2001 p. 71
Breasted 1906 vol. II pp. 17-18 §38-42, vol. IV p. 254 §513
Brier 1994 pp. 107, 262-264
Bryan 2000 pp. 218-219, 223-226
Carter 1916 p. 152
Derry 1934 pp. 47-48
Dodson and Hilton 2004 pp. 122, 123, 125, 126-129, 207
El Madhy 1989 pp. 26, 35, 37, 75, 76, 86, 87
Forbes 1994 pp. 14-24
Forbes 1998a pp. 618-619
Forbes 2005a pp. 27, 28-41
Gardiner 1961 pp. 443-444
Gardiner and Peet 1952 pl. LVI #s 172-173
Gardiner and Peet 1955 pp. 37, 55, 149 #s 171A-173
Grajetzki 2005 pp. 50-51
Grimal 1992 pp. 201, 202-207
Haring 2001 pp. 368-369
Harris and Weeks 1973 pp. 101,102, 128-130, 131, 132
Harris and Wente 1980
Ikram and Dodson 1998 pp. 79, 89, 91, ill. 88, 122, 157, 208 and ills. 265-266, 315, 316, 322

G. Johnson 2003/2004 pp. 54-70
Murnane 1977 pp. 114-115, 115, 230
Murnane 1981 p. 371, 374 and note 36, 375 and note 42
Partridge 1994 pp. 45, 62-65, 69, 76, 152, 155, 225
Peden 2001 pp. 81, 88, 134-135
Peet 1930 pp. 11, 37-38
Polz 1995 pp. 8-21
D. Redford 1967 p. 51, 72
Reeves and Wilkinson 1996 pp. 4, 15, 22-23, 88, 90, 91, 96, 195, 196, 203, 207
F. Schmitz 1978
G. Smith 1912 p. 18, pl. XIII
Strudwick 1999 pp. 51, 52, 54, 80, 97, 126, 127, 175, 184, 189, 190,
Tyldesley 2006 pp. 89, 91
Verbrugghe and Wickersham 1996 pp. 140, 198
Vittmann 1974 pp. 250-251
von Beckerath 1999 pp. 132 #2, 133 #2
Waddell 1940 pp. 100, 109, 111,113, 117, 115
Wente 1963 pp. 30-36
Wente 1980 pp. 239-241
R. Wilkinson 2000 pp. 143, 174, 189
Winlock 1942 pp. 135, 136, 208-209

Amenhotep II   Dynasty XVIII

Horus Name:

Nomen:

imn-ḥtp
Amenhotep

Prenomen:

ꜥꜣ-ḫprw-rꜥ
Aakheperure

kꜣ nḫt wr-pḥti

Two Ladies:

nbty wsr-fꜣw sḫꜥ-m-wꜣst

Golden Falcon:

bik-nbw iṯi-sḫm.f-m-tꜣw-nbw

Length of Reign:	26 years
Tomb:	Valley of the Kings: KV35
Mummy:	Tomb of Amenhotep II Now at Cairo Museum: JE26211; CG61069

Consorts:	Tiaa	**Variant Names:**	Amenophis Amonhotep Amunhotpe Okheperure
Manetho:	Amenophis (A, E, J) Amnophis (E)		
King Lists:	Ab: (71); S: (52-lost)		

The son of Thutmose III and, almost certainly, Queen Meryetre-Hatshepsut, Amenhotep II was the seventh pharaoh of Dynasty XVIII. He was evidently not the heir presumptive, but inherited the position after the death of a half-brother named Amenemhet. Unlike his sibling, Amenhotep II seems to have been quite healthy. On a stele erected near the Great Sphinx at Giza, he boasted of his prodigious physical strength: He claimed he could out-row 200 men (Manuelian has suggested that the king wasn't rowing, but steering the boat), and that no one else could draw his bow, but with it he was able to drive an arrow completely through each of four 7.5 cm. thick copper targets, while handling the reins of a chariot and team at full gallop. On a relief from the tomb of Min, mayor of This, a youthful prince Amenhotep (he is naked except for a skullcap) is shown at his archery practice, and a relief at Karnak shows him as a young man, reins tied around his waist, firing from a speeding chariot at what appears to be a copper target. The king even challenged his followers to an archery contest; no takers are recorded.

During the latter years of Thutmose III's reign, Amenhotep was made coregent and seems to have served as the junior ruler for between two and three years. He appears to have counted his regnal years from the inception of this joint rule. He also appears to have continued to carry out the eradication of all mention of his great aunt, Hatshepsut.

The Queen Mother, Meryetre Hatshepsut, evidently did not step down as "first lady" for quite some time after Amenhotep's ascension to the throne. Eventually (probably upon the death of Meryetre) Amenhotep's wife, Queen Tiaa, took her rightful place as consort. Tiaa was the mother of the future pharaoh, Thutmose IV.

Amenhotep II seems to have led three military expeditions to Asia. The first campaign, evidently begun early in the third year of the joint rule, was against an area in Syria known as Takhsy, which Redford describes as being between Kadesh and Damascus on the upper Orontes river. It was probably more the putting down of a revolt than a full-fledged war. It is likely that Thutmose III, who was almost certainly too old for active military duty at this point, died either while Amenhotep was absent, or soon after the younger king's return. Amenhotep referred to this expedition as his "first campaign" on some inscriptions. However, he also claimed as his "first campaign" a military action in Syria-Palestine during year seven, his first year as solo ruler. The year seven expedition appears to have been necessary to smash a widespread revolt. Amenhotep II led the victorious Egyptian army across the River Orontes and beyond, almost to Aleppo, at which point he halted and then retired, probably having accomplished his goal of putting the fear of Amen into the troublesome city-states. It has also been suggested that Amenhotep came up against the kingdom of Mitanni and proved lacking, either in an actual armed conflict or simply in a show of power, and so turned homeward. It has also been posited that conflict was averted or ended because some sort of treaty or understanding was reached between Mitanni and Egypt. Whatever actually happened near Aleppo, Amenhotep claimed to have returned to Egypt with 1,643 pounds of gold, 120,833 pounds of copper, 550 captive warriors, 240 women, 300 chariots and 210 horses. The third campaign, in year nine, was evidently a smaller affair centered around the area between Joppa and Tyre. Amenhotep II may have worked the turquoise mine at Serabit el-Khadim in Sinai; although no rock-cut inscriptions have been discovered, his prenomen has been found on fragments of decorated pillars as well as a fragment of inscribed vase and three inscribed menat amulets, all at the temple of Hathor.

Thutmose III did an excellent job of finally breaking the back of Nubian resistance, and Amenhotep II therefore inherited a relatively stable situation in the region, at least as far as the Fourth Cataract. Nonetheless, a military action by Amenhotep II seems to be indicated by an inscription in the shrine of the Viceroy of Kush, Usersatet, at Qasr Ibrim. It is interesting to note that early in his reign Amenhotep had the body of a rebel Asiatic chieftain brought all the way to Nubia, to be hung from the walls at Napata as a warning to would-be trouble makers. Attestations for Amenhotep II are numerous in Nubia and include (from south to north) fragments of a statue of the king as a sphinx or lion from Gebel Barkal, inscribed blocks reused by the Dynasty XXV Nubian pharaoh Taharqa on Argo Island, temple construction on the islands of Sai and Uronarti as well as at the Second Cataract fortress at Kumma, additions to the temple of Horus at Aniba, the temple of Min and Isis at Buhen, a temple to Amen-Re and Re-Horakhty built by Thutmose III and completed by Amenhotep II at Amada and a small rock-cut chapel on Sehel Island.

Amenhotep II built mightily in Egypt. From the Theban area south, attestations of construction activity include a small temple to Thoth at El Kab (later modified and enlarged by Ramesses II), inscribed blocks and a pair of obelisks from the island of Elephantine, a barque shrine at Tod for the god Montu, built by Thutmose III and restored or finished by Amenhotep II, and additions to the temple of Set at Ombos. From Thebes to the Delta area attestations include fragments of inscribed blocks, gateways, and other architectural elements from Medamud; inscribed jars from a foundation deposit at Dendera; a temple dedicated to Horemakhet (Horus of the Horizon) at Giza; an obelisk and inscribed blocks at Heliopolis and inscribed red granite blocks from Bubastis. A mention of monuments built for Amen and Horus at Nebesha and Tell Abu Sefa comes from the Louvre statue of the overseer of goldsmiths, Hatre.

The Theban area saw the largest concentration of attestations for Amenhotep II. At Karnak the king set up two obelisks, built an alabaster shrine, decorated the Eighth Pylon with scenes and texts, and built a Heb Sed Temple (modified and extended by Sety I). Other building activities are evidenced by a great many inscribed blocks reused as filler in the Third and Fourth Pylons, the temple of Khonsu, and a colonnade built by Taharqa. At Karnak North are inscribed blocks at the temple of Montu, a barque chapel built for the same deity, and Amenhotep's cartouches replacing those of Hatshepsut on the gateway of Thutmose I. At Luxor, Amenhotep seems to be responsible for a barque shrine for the god Amen as well as other architectural elements. Across the Nile, Amenhotep's mortuary temple (almost entirely destroyed) was slightly north of that of Ramesses II. Fragments of a red granite stele inscribed for Amenhotep II, probably from his mortuary temple, were found at Medinet Habu. The Hathor shrine at the temple of Thutmose III was completed by Amenhotep II.

In spite of robbers, the mummy of Amenhotep was found in his own tomb in the Valley of the Kings, KV35, when Victor Loret discovered the tomb in 1898. Priests of Dynasty XX had used the tomb as a cache for other royal and non-royal mummies. Since Amenhotep was the first pharaoh to have been discovered in his own tomb, it was decided to let the mummy remain. In 1901 modern tomb robbers broke into the tomb and rifled the mummy in a vain search for treasure. The king stayed in his tomb until 1931 when he was moved to the Cairo Museum. Like his father and his son to follow, Amenhotep II's mummy shows scabrous growths, especially evident on the mummy's chest The cause of these blemishes is unknown. At time of death Amenhotep II appears to have been in his mid- to late forties, with brown hair beginning to turn gray, and a bald spot. The mummy's length was 1.673 m.

The highest regnal date we have for Amenhotep II is the year 26, found on a jar fragment from the ruins of the king's mortuary temple. However, some scholars who identify Amenhotep II with Manetho's Amenophis have noted that Manetho's length of reign for his Amenophis is 30 years, 10 months. This longer reign, combined with the possibility that Amenhotep had two Sed festivals, has led a to the belief among a few Egyptologists that Amenhotep reigned for as long as 35 years.

References:

Brier 1994 pp. 111-117, 240, 267, 272, 275, 291, 295
Bryan 1998 pp. 27, 28-29, 30, 31-32, 32-39, 39-41
Bucaille 1990 pp. 17, 27, 28, 56-57, 63-64, 73, 116, 117-118, 135, 142, 157, fig. 17
Dodson and Hilton 2004 pp. 21, 23, 25, 123, 129, 130, 132-133, 134-135, 137-141, 207
El Madhy 1989 pp. 38, 39, 40, 84, 87, 88
Forbes 1992/1993a pp. 30-33, 86-87
Forbes 1997 pp. 36-52
Forbes 1998a pp. 59-87, 672-673
Gardiner and Peet 1952 pl. LX A-D
Gardiner and Peet 1955 pp. 163-164 #s 205 and 206
Grajetzki 2005 p. 53, 55

Harris and Weeks 1973 pp. 112, 113, 115, 116, 135, 136, 137, 138-139, 142, 157, 159, 166
Hassan 1937 pp. 129-134, pl. II
Ikram and Dodson 1998 pp. 38, 79, 84, 96, 132, 282, 285, 315, 316, 318, 324, ills. 330, 411, 413d, 415, 425
Lichtheim 1988 pp. 39-43
Manuelian 1987 pp. 32-40, 40-42, 42- 44, 45-56, 56 68, 68-83, 92-93, 191-214, 253-268
Manuelian 2006 pp. 413-429, 442
Murnane 1977 pp. 44-57
Partridge 1994 pp. 82-84
Peden 2001 pp. 68, 80, 84, 86 note 154, 90 and note 192
Petrie 1897 pp. 3, 4-6, 5, 21, pl. II #3, III #s 1-20, IV #s 9-29, V #s 1-12, XXII, XXIII
D. Redford 1965 pp. 107-122

Amenhotep III

D. Redford 1992 pp. 162-168,
Reeves and Wilkinson 1996 pp. 14, 25, 29, 37-38, 43, 47, 48, 69-70, 72, 79, 89, 91, 97-98, 100-103, 105-106, 108, 109, 113, 115, 120, 152, 155, 158, 179, 185, 191-192, 198-199, 203, 205, 207, 209
G. Smith 1912 pp. 36-38
Spalinger 2005 pp. 55, 78, 140-141, 144-145, 149, 170
Tyldesley 2006 pp. 89, 111, 112
Verbrugghe and Wickersham 1996 pp. 141, 199
von Beckerath 1999 pp. 132 #3, 133 #3
Waddell 1940 pp. 101, 113
R. Wilkinson 2000 pp. 119, 152, 181-182, 201, 203, 221, 223, 229

Amenhotep III   Dynasty XVIII

Horus Name:

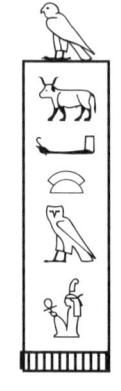

k3 nḫt ḥʿ-m-m3ʿt

Nomen:

imn-ḥtp ḥq3-w3st
Amenhotep (heqawaset)

Prenomen:

nb-m3ʿt-rʿ
Nebmaatre

Two Ladies:

nbty smn-hpw sgrḥ-t3wi

Golden Falcon:

bik nbw ʿ3-ḫpš

Length of Reign:	38 years
Tomb:	Valley of the Kings: WV22
Mummy:	Tomb of Amenhotep II Now at Cairo Museum: JE34560; CG61074

Consorts:	Gilukhepa Iset Sitamen Tadukhepa Tiye	**Manetho:**	Amenophis (A, E, J) Oros (A, E, J)

Amenhotep III

King Lists: Ab: (73); S: (54-missing)

Variant Names: Amenophis, Amonhotep, Amunhotpe, Immureya, Maat-Ra-neb, Mimmareya, Nebmare, Nibmuareya, Nimmureya, Ra-Maat-neb

The ninth ruler of Dynasty XVIII, Amenhotep III is, with the possible exception of Ramesses II, the best attested and documented of all the pharaohs of Egypt. Often referred to with the appellation "The Magnificent," Amenhotep III inherited an empire that stretched from Napata, at the Fourth Cataract of the Nile in Nubia, to Kadesh in northern Syria; his influence covered a territory half again as large. Egypt traded and maintained diplomatic relations with most of the Mediterranean and Aegean world, as well as with Babylon, Assyria, Mittani and the Hittites.

The son of Thutmose IV and a minor queen named Mutemwia, Amenhotep III ascended the throne upon the death of his father. As he was probably between ten and twelve years old at his accession, the young king would have been guided in his royal duties by a regent, or perhaps a council. Although there is no hard evidence to support it, it has been suggested that his mother, Mutemwia, served as regent.

In regnal year two, while he was still a young boy, Amenhotep married an equally young woman named Tiye. Her family, well-connected commoners, hailed from Akhmim, where her father was Prophet of the local deity Min. He was also "King's Lieutenant," and "Master of the Horse" under Thutmose IV, and therefore a person of some importance at court. Tiye's mother, Tjuya, was "Chief Lady of Amen's Harem," among other things. Later, Tiye's brother Anen became High Priest of Re at Karnak and Second Prophet of Amen. There can be little doubt that this family played a great part in shaping the formative years of Amenhotep III's reign, as illustrated by the special scarabs issued to commemorate the marriage of the king to Tiye. These large amulets give not only the titulary of the pharaoh and the name of his queen, but also the names of her parents. Such a thing had never happened in Egyptian history, and would never happen again. Yuya and Tjuya were also granted a tomb in the Valley of the Kings.

Amenhotep III also issued commemorative scarabs for lion hunting (he claims to have killed "with his own arrows" at least 102 lions in ten years), wild bull hunting, the building of a pleasure lake for Tiye, and the arrival, in regnal year ten, of the Mitannian princess Gilukhepa and her 317-woman retinue.

The conquests and foreign policy of Amenhotep's grandfather (Amenhotep II), and great-grandfather (Thutmose III) left their successors (Thutmose IV and Amenhotep III) with little need to pursue military action, though there were apparently two major exceptions: documentation exists of two significant military actions in Nubia. The first, led by the pharaoh himself in regnal year five, seems to have been the quelling of an uprising in Nubia. A second campaign after regnal year 30 was led by the viceroy of Kush.

Diplomatic relations with Egypt's neighbors were reinforced during this period with strategic royal marriages; Amenhotep took into his harem the Mitannian princess Gilukhepa, both a sister and daughter of the King of Babylon, and even a daughter of the king of Arzawa, in far off Asia Minor. Another princess of Mitanni, Tadukhepa, was sent to Egypt just before Amenhotep III's death; she would later marry his son, Amenhotep IV (Akhenaten).

In addition to these marriages and the one to Tiye, Amenhotep had at least two other wives, his daughters Iset and Sitamen. While brother-sister marriage was not uncommon among Egyptian kings (and to some slight extent among the nobility), father-daughter marriages were rare in the extreme. It has been suggested that another daughter of Amenhotep, the little-known Beketaten, may have been a child of the king and Sitamen.

Amenhotep III was evidently in constant communication with his allies, as was shown in the extensive foreign correspondence in the Amarna letters (see Glossary).

It is through these remarkable tablets, discovered in the late nineteenth century, that Egyptologists have been able to learn so much about Egypt's foreign relations during this period. Other evidence for widespread diplomatic relations comes from a statue base discovered in the ruins of the pharaoh's mortuary temple; it lists 14 cities, including Phaistos and Knossos on Crete, Mycenae and Thebes in Greece, and Troy (Illios) and Arzawa in Asia Minor. Fragments of faience plaques (probably originally nine plaques in total) from Mycenae bear the cartouche of Amenhotep III.

The influence of Amenhotep III's regime throughout the Levant and Syria-Palestine was extensive. There were six known Egyptian garrison towns, four on the coast and two inland. Aside from the military presence, trade between the regions was well-established. There were two major grain storage depots, and there is evidence that the Egyptians traded gold, small trinkets, stone and glassware for cedar, pine, copper, silver, bronze, wine and various oils.

Aside from his cartouche on some trade goods, attestations for Amenhotep in the Syria-Palestine region include dozens of scarabs (including many of the "commemorative" variety), beads, inscribed plaques, other small amulets, stelae, and small architectural elements. In Beth Shan, he built a migdol (fortress) and a temple dedicated to the god Mekal and the goddess Astarte. In Sinai, at the turquoise mines of Serabit el-Khadim, a fair number of attestations for Amenhotep III have been found, mostly at or near the temple of Hathor. These include two large stelae (which are dated to regnal year 36), half a dozen inscribed column fragments, several statue bases, fragments of statues and statuettes, vase fragments, fragments of menat amulets, fragments of a faience wand, a bust of Queen Tiye, and assorted scarabs.

Because of its key location protecting the southern border of Egypt and the abundance of coveted trade goods like gold, animal hides, and ivory, the Egyptians maintained a strong a presence in Nubia that has provided a wealth of attestations for Amenhotep III. In addition to adding to or restoring numerous temples, forts, and other structures, he built at least three new temples, including one at Sedeinga dedicated to Queen Tiye, one at Soleb dedicated to himself and the god Amen, and a rock-cut temple at el-Sabua.

The reign of Amenhotep III was almost certainly Egypt's "Golden Age." With the exception of the two Nubian campaigns, Egyptian military activity seems to have been limited to occasional troop replacements at the forts in Nubia and along the route from the Delta to Canaan, as well as the small units of troops attached to the few Egyptian settlements This long peace allowed unprecedented opportunity for both trade and building and resulted in great prosperity in the Egyptian economy.

The wealth acquired from trade and tribute allowed for a building boom unequalled in Egyptian history. Evidence of building activity in Egypt ranges from Bubastis and Athribis in the Delta to Aswan, at the Egyptian-Nubian border. These activities included a "harem" or pleasure palace in the Faiyum, and a huge new palace ("Palace of the Dazzling Sun Disk") at Malkata, on the west side of the Nile opposite Thebes. Near Malqata, as a gift to Tiye, Amenhotep caused an enormous "pleasure lake" to be dug. Stelae, inscriptions and statuary are to be found throughout Egypt.

In all this building, the gods of Egypt fared the best. The tomb-chapel and tomb of the first Apis bull were built at Saqqara. A great temple to Ptah, "Nebmaatre-United-with-Ptah," was built at Memphis. A temple known only from blocks reused by Ramesses III was constructed at Kom el-Ahmar. A group of colossal baboon statues were added to the temple of Thoth at Hermopolis, what appears to have been a large court was added to the temple of Thutmose III at Abydos, and other additions or repairs to temples were made throughout the Two Lands.

As the center for the worship of Amen-Re, chief god of the land, and the location of all pharaonic burials for more than 200 years, the Theban area received the greatest attention. At Karnak, among other things, Amenhotep III completed the decoration of a barque sanctuary that had been left unfinished at the death of his father. He also built the Third Pylon, added a decorated gate to the forecourt of the Fourth Pylon, added reliefs of himself to Pylon Five, and began, but did not live to finish, the Tenth Pylon. Several large statues of Amenhotep (at least one being more than 20m. tall) were set up in front of this pylon. North of the main Amen temple precinct, Amenhotep replaced an earlier structure with a new sandstone temple, also dedicated to Amen, and next to it a temple to the goddess Maat.

Amenhotep III

At Luxor, Amenhotep III had an earlier temple of Amen, built by Hatshepsut and Thutmose III, demolished and replaced with a new sandstone structure. Additions to the new temple were made on at least two later occasions, and the latest phase of construction was unfinished at the time of the king's death.

Across the Nile, on the west bank, Amenhotep erected his mortuary temple. It was the largest such monument ever constructed in Egypt (estimated to have covered about 91 acres), and was added to over a period of many years. The solar court alone was four times as large as the Luxor temple. Today it is almost completely gone, consisting mainly of rubble, but the two colossal seated statues built at the temple's entrance, today known as the Colossi of Memnon, still stand guard.

Amenhotep III's tomb, located in an offshoot of the Valley of the Kings known as the West Valley, has suffered greatly due not only to the ravages of time, but to the antiquities hunters of the nineteenth and twentieth centuries. Careful excavation and conservation have managed to preserve the remaining examples of wall paintings and text, as well as the pitifully few scraps left from the burial itself.

Amenhotep III celebrated three Sed Festivals (a fourth may have been in the planning stages) during the last quarter of his reign. These occurred in regnal years 30, 34, and 37.

Following pharaonic tradition, Amenhotep would have been worshipped as a demi-god until his death, whereupon he would have been completely deified. It has been suggested that at some point between the first and third Sed Festivals, Amenhotep's status was elevated to that of a full-fledged god, the earthly manifestation of the sun god Re.

Egyptologists have debated for more than a century the question of whether there was a coregency between Amenhotep III and his son Amenhotep IV (Akhenaten), and there is still no consensus on the issue. Theories range from ten to twelve years (Dodson and Johnson) to either a brief coregency (fewer than three years) or to no coregency at all (Redford). The uncertainty stems from the lack of any direct evidence and the presence of some indirect evidence. The absence of any double-dated monuments is striking, especially given the large number of documents and other attestations about both reigns. On the other hand, recent scholars have noted cultural similarities in the latter part of Amenhotep III's reign and Amenhotep IV's early regnal years. They note that the profound changes in religious and artistic styles that mark the reign of the son seem to have begun during the last years of the father's reign and, strikingly, Amenhotep III began at that time to identify himself more closely with the god Aten. While not conclusive, this evidence tends to support a coregency of some sort.

The highest regnal date known for Amenhotep III is year 38. This date is given on more than a dozen ostraca from the palace at Malkata.

Amenhotep III

The mummy identified as Amenhotep III was found, along with other royal mummies, in the tomb of Amenhotep II (KV35) in the Valley of the Kings. The body had been much damaged by tomb robbers, but the condition of the mummy is such as to show that in later life the pharaoh had been in poor health; he suffered from dental abscesses, caries, and tooth loss as well as obesity. His age at time of death seems to have been about fifty. The length of the body was 1.561 m.

References:

Berman 1998 pp. 1-25
Blankenberg-van Delden 1969
Brier 1994 pp. 90, 115, 119, 120, 177, 240, 267-269, 294-295
Bryan 2000 pp. 258, 260-271
Cline 1987 pp. 1-36
T. Davis 1907
Dodson 1995 pp. 89-96
Dodson and Hilton 2004 pp. 13, 14, 22, 29, 30, 36, 37, 130, 132-133, 134-135, 137-139, 142, 144-145, 145-146, 153, 154, 156-157, 182, 283 note 31, 285 note 105
El Madhy 1989 pp. 39, 54, 87, 88, 90, 135
Forbes 1990 pp. 52-57
Forbes 1992 pp. 24-34, 61
Forbes 1998a pp. 676-677
Gardiner and Peet 1952 pl. LIX, LXV, LXV A, LXXXIX
Gardiner and Peet 1955 pp. 38, 165-170 #s 210-222, 213 #426
Giles 1997
Grajetzki 2005 pp. 57-59
Hall 1913 pp. 170-195 #s 1713-1994, 271 #2647, 275-276 #s 2661-2675, 293 #2796, 300 #s 2852-2856
Harris and Weeks 1973 pp. 112, 140, 145
Ikram and Dodson 1998 pp. 40, 84, 88, 98, 101, 127, 170, 212, 214, 258, 260, 289, 315, 316, 318, 324, ills. 191, 363-364, pl. XVIII-XIX
W.R. Johnson 1991 p. 15-23, 6060-63, 65-66
W.R. Johnson 1996 pp. 65-82
Kozloff et al. 1992
Lacovara 1994 pp. 6-21
Loeben 1994 pp. 104-109
Moran 1992
Morkot 1990 pp. 323-337
Murnane 1977 pp. 123-169, 231-233
Murnane 2001 pp. 309-310
Newberry 1906 pp. 116 #3, 166 #s 26-30, 167-168 #s 1-12, 14-18, 170-172 #s 1-3, 173-178 #s 1,2, pl. VIII #3, XXX #s 26-32, XXXI #s 1-12, 14-18, XXXII #s 1-3, XXXIII #s 1,2
O'Connor and Cline 1998
Partridge 1994 pp. 118-120
Peden 2001 pp. 64, 65-67, 77, 84, 86, 90, 91, 95, 142-143
Petrie 1978 pl. XXXI-XXXV #s 18.9.1-18.9.168
Quibell 1908
D. Redford 1967 pp. 88-169
Reeves 1990b pp. 38-40
Reeves 2001 pp. 51-74, 75-80
Reeves and Wilkinson 1996 pp. 8, 21, 28, 29, 37, 40, 42, 45, 47, 54, 55, 58, 61, 71, 74, 76-77, 81, 84, 105, 110-117, 120, 128, 131, 161, 174, 176-177, 180, 182, 184, 191, 193, 199, 203, 207, 209, 210-211
Rowe 1936 pp. 127-136 #s 537-568, 178 #541, 217-218, 246-247 #s 41-44, pl. XIII-XVI #s 537-568, XIX #741, XXIV #SE 2 and 3, XXVII #s 41-44
G. Smith 1912 pp. 46-51, pl. XXXI-XXXV, C-CIII
Trad and Mahmoud 1995 pp. 40-50
Tyldesley 2006 pp. 115-123, 123-124
van Dijk 2000 pp. 260-271, 272-274
Verbrugghe and Wickersham 1996 pp. 141 and note 11, 159, 199
von Beckerath 1999 pp. 140-143 #9
Waddell 1940 pp. 103, 109, 113, 115, 117
R. Wilkinson 2000 pp. 188-189, 230-232

Amenmesse — Dynasty XIX

Horus Name:

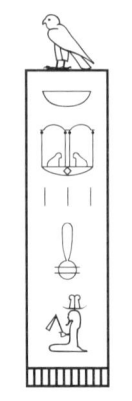

nb-ḥꜣbw-sd-mi-tꜣtnn

Nomen: imn-ms-sw ḥkꜣ-wꜣst
Amenmesses (heqawaset)

Prenomen: mn-mi-rꜥ stp.n-rꜥ
Menmire-setepenre

Two Ladies: nbty wr-biꜣwt-iptswt

Golden Falcon: bik-nbw ꜥꜣ ḥpš sꜣ wꜣst n ms.sw nswt bity nb tꜣwy

Length of Reign:	4 years
Tomb:	Valley of the Kings: KV10
Mummy:	Unknown

Consorts:	Baketwernel	**King Lists:**	None
Manetho:	Ammenemes (E) Ammenemnes (A)	**Variant Names:**	Amenmessu

Depending on which of several theories is correct, Amenmesse was either the fifth or sixth king of Dynasty XIX. His parentage is uncertain, although it appears that he was of royal blood. It is certain that his mother was named Takhat and that she was the daughter of a king. If she was the Takhat who was one of Ramesses II's daughters and wife to Sety II, then Amenmesse was a nephew to Merenptah and a son of Sety II.

The two principal theories on the successors of Merenptah, fourth king of Dynasty XIX, are that Amenmesse's reign directly followed that of Merenptah (placing him as fifth in the dynasty) or that Amenmesse succeeded Sety II (placing him sixth in the dynasty). Kitchen supports the view that Amenmesse was the fifth pharaoh, and that he usurped a throne intended to go to Merenptah's son, Sety II. The fact that Amenmesse buried Merenptah provides strong support for this theory, as the successor traditionally buried his predecessor. Kitchen further theorizes that Sety II may have been out of the area when his father died, which may have given Amenmesse the opportunity to take the throne. Dodson, however, posits a very different scenario, suggesting that Sety II directly succeeded Merenptah. This was clearly what was intended, as Sety II has the title Crown Prince on several statues. Dodson further suggests that Amenmesse usurped his father's throne, as Sety II's name disappears from the Theban records sometime after year two of his reign. Apparently, Sety II intended his successor to be another son, Prince Sety-Merenptah, and Amenmesse seized the throne to prevent his brother from becoming pharaoh. According to this theory, Amenmesse lost the throne in his fourth regnal year; what is not questioned is that Sety II at this point regained (or, in the previous theory, gained) the throne at this point.

Very few attestations for Amenmesse have survived. Whatever dynastic position Amenmesse occupied, it angered Sety II to such an extent that a *damnatio memoriae* was declared. Amenmesse's name was expunged from practically every item and monument that bore his name; this was done with such thoroughness that it has been remarked that Hatshepsut and Akhenaten were the only other pharaohs whose names were so viciously and thoroughly hunted down and erased.

A few items were missed during the purge. Within Egypt, most were found in the Theban area. These include, at Karnak, a few inscriptions in the Hypostyle Hall, a series of colossal statues, texts in the Temple of Amen-Re-Horakhty and various minor statues and usurpations. At Luxor, all that remained were the bases of two statues. Across the river at Deir el-Medina, two stelae survived; one shows the king offering an image of Maat to the Theban triad Amen, Mut, and Khonsu, the other the pharaoh receiving a sword from Amen. Inscriptions and other records were also found in the Small Temple and the Dynasty XVIII temple at Medinet Habu. A graffito, although the reading is questionable, may refer to a mortuary temple for Amenmesse, but to date no remains have been found. About 15 km. south of Thebes at Armant, Amenmesse's cartouches are cut into the pylon of Thutmose III at the temple of the god Montu. Further south at Tod, Amenmesse had his name carved into a barque shrine of Montu. To the north, a glazed vase inscribed with Amenmesse's cartouches was found at Riqqa, 45 km. south of Memphis, the farthest north that any reference to Amenmesse is found within Egypt.

Outside Egypt, a small shrine was erected to Amenmesse at Amara West in Nubia. Fragments of faience from a model naos at Timna in the Sinai Peninsula bear a damaged inscription that may include Amenmesse's prenomen. This scanty fragment has led one scholar to propose that Amenmesse was actually Moses, a theory not widely held in the Egyptological community.

Along with his other monuments, texts, and usurpations, Amenmesse's tomb in the Valley of the Kings was stripped of every mention of his name. At some point, part of the tomb was redecorated for Queens Takhat and Beketwernel, who were evidently interred there. Interestingly enough, some scholars believe that Amenmesse was never buried in the tomb. The tomb itself, reaching a length of 70 m., was never completed.

A fragment of a statue now in the Cairo Museum, probably belonging to Amenmesse, has recently been analyzed by Hardwick. He concludes that if this fragment is genuinely Amenmesse's, a complete titulary, including a full Golden Falcon name, can now be ascribed to this king.

As with his dynastic position, Amenmesse's length of reign is controversial; estimates range from three to five years, with the majority of scholars agreeing on four years. Nothing for certain is known about the circumstances under which he left the throne; he may have died, or been deposed by Sety II.

References:

Callender 2006 p. 50
Dodson 1985 pp. 7-11
Dodson 1995 pp. 133-137
Dodson and Hilton 2004 pp. 176-183, 192, 194, 286 note 130
Ertman 1993 pp. 38-46
Forbes 1993 pp. 55-56
Grajetzki 2005 p. 70
Hardwick 2006 pp. 255-260
Harris and Weeks 1973 pp. 158
Ikram and Dodson 1998 pp. 263, 315
Kitchen 1982 pp. 216
Kitchen 1987 pp. 23-25
Peden 2001 pp. 162-163 and note 166.
Reeves 1990b pp. 104-105
Reeves and Wilkinson 1996 pp. 24, 29, 37, 47, 51, 53, 54, 79, 150, 153, 155, 159, 191, 209-210
Schaden 1994 pp. 243-254
Tyldesley 2006 pp. 161-162
van Dijk 2000 p. 303
Verbrugghe and Wickersham 1996 pp. 143, 199
von Beckerath 1999 pp. 158 #5, 159 #5
R. Wilkinson 2000 p. 201

'Ammu   Dynasty XIV

Horus Name: Unknown   **Nomen:**

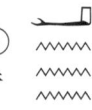

ʿamu

'Ammu

'Ammu

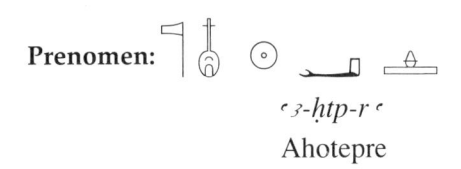

Prenomen: ꜥꜣ-ḥtp-rꜥ
Ahotepre

Two Ladies: Unknown

Golden Falcon: Unknown

Length of Reign:	Unknown
Tomb:	Unknown
Mummy:	Unknown

Consorts:	Unknown	**Variant Names:**	'Amu
Manetho:	Not given		
King Lists:	None		

Perhaps the fourth king of Dynasty XIV, 'Ammu is known from a great many scarab-seals. These have been found in Lachish and Tell el-Ajjul in Canaan, in Egypt in the Delta, at Abydos and at the fortress of Semna in Nubia. Although missing from the Turin Canon, 'Ammu is identified as a predecessor of the well-attested king Sheshi (see Dynastic King List) because of the unique seriation of his scarab-seals. Ryholt's suggestion that this king's name is probably of west Semitic origin is most likely correct; however, this does not mean that 'Ammu wasn't born in Egypt. The wide area of distribution of 'Ammu's seals should not lead one to assume that this king had any influence in those regions; like all rulers of Dynasty XIV, 'Ammu's sphere of influence was evidently restricted to the eastern Delta. However, the distribution of the seals does seem to point to extensive trade during this king's reign.

Von Beckerath would see the prenomen "Ahotepre" as a separate ruler in his XV./XVI. Dynastie and gives Ammu's prenomen as "Khawoserre," which in fact is the prenomen of the Dynasty XIV king, Qareh.

References:

Budge 1976 p. 99 (as Aamu(?), a prince)
Giveon 1985 pp. 60-61 #2
Hall 1913 p. 31 #283
Hayes 1959 pp. XIV, 7
Hornung and Staehelin 1976 p. 220 #149
Ryholt 1997a pp. 12 table 2 #8/29, 40-41, 44 table 11, 46-49, 50 table 12 D, 96, 98 #4, 100-101, 199 table 38, 299, 323-325, 364-366 File 14/4, 409 #4
Tufnell 1984 vol. II pp. 378 #s 3353 - 3355, 379 pl. LX #s 3353-3355
von Beckerath 1999 pp. 118 #s, j and p, 119 #s, j and p

'Anati — Dynasty XIV

Horus Name: Unknown

Nomen: ꜥa-na-ti — 'Anati

Prenomen: ḏdkꜣ-rꜥ — Djedkare

Two Ladies: Unknown

Golden Falcon: Unknown

Length of Reign:	Unknown
Tomb:	Unknown
Mummy:	Unknown

Consorts:	Unknown	**Variant Names:**	Nebennati
Manetho:	Not given		...nnat
King Lists:	T: (G 8.27; vB 8.27)		Djed...re ...ka[re?]

Perhaps the thirty-third king of Dynasty XIV, 'Anati is one of a group of kings known only from the Turin Canon. The fragmentary state of the papyrus allows for varying interpretations as to the positioning of some of the kings of this dynasty. However, 'Anati's place seems secure, as a recent study shows that two previously separated fragments of the papyrus should be joined. This places 'Anati firmly in his proper dynastic order. The exact transliteration of the nomen is debated; it appears the scribe transcribing the Turin Canon was unused to Semitic names and used the symbol ⌒ (nb) in place of ⌒ (ꜥ).

References:

Gardiner 1959 pl. III, Col. IX #29
Gardiner 1961 p. 442 #9.29 as "...ka[re?] Nebennati"
Ryholt 1997a pp. 17, 95 Col. 7.27, 98 #33, 380 File 14/33, 409 #33

von Beckerath 1999 pp. 110 #28, 111 #28

Anedjib   Dynasty I

Horus Name:

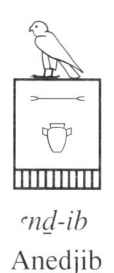

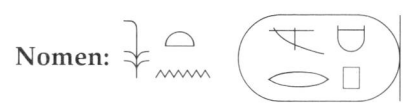

ꜥnḏ-ib
Anedjib

Nomen:

mr-biꜣ-p
Merbiape

mr-biꜣ-p
Merbiape

mr-biꜣ-pn
Merbiapen

Two Lords:

nbwy mr-pi-biꜣ

Golden Falcon: Unknown

Length of Reign:	10 years(?)
Tomb:	Abydos, Umm el Qa'ab, X
Mummy:	Unknown

Consorts:	Betrest(?)	**Variant Names:**	Adjib
Manetho:	Miebidos (A) Niebais (E)		Andjyeb Azab
King Lists:	Ab: (6); P; S: (1); T: (G2.17)		Enezib Merpibia

The sixth king of Dynasty I, Anedjib is one of the least documented rulers of that period. Only four sites, Saqqara, Helwan and Abydos in Egypt, and En Besor in Palestine, have yielded any mention of his name. Although Anedjib was the direct successor of

Anedjib

Den, as shown by the chronological listing of rulers found on a jar sealing discovered at Abydos and by inscribed stone vases from Saqqara, it is not known if Anedjib was related to his predecessor.

Anedjib's tomb at Abydos was one of the smallest of all the royal tombs and, even though the burial chamber was lined with imported wood, was of very poor construction. The tomb was surrounded by 63 subsidiary burials. To date, no funerary enclosure for Anedjib has come to light. By contrast, Tomb 3038 at Saqqara, which was evidently built during Anedjib's reign (for a high official named Nebitka) was of superb design and construction. What is most interesting about Nebitka's tomb was an eight-stepped structure contained within the superstructure; it is perhaps a precursor to Djoser's step pyramid. Tomb 1371 H.2 at Helwan, dated to Anedjib's reign by jar sealings as well as the royal name scratched on a large pottery jar, is also much superior to the king's tomb at Abydos.

Anedjib's reign appears to have seen the continuance of trade with Palestine. Two jar sealings of Anedjib are known from En Besor. Also, stone vessels bearing Anedjib's name, found in the galleries beneath Djoser's step pyramid, once held oil made from trees native to southern Palestine.

As with almost all of the Dynasty I pharaohs, the length of Anedjib's reign is unknown. Two fragments of stone vases, one from Abydos and one from Saqqara, mention a Sed Festival, so it is possible that this king reigned for at least 30 years. However, it is also possible that the festival was celebrated earlier than year 30. This could be for any number of reasons, the most probable being the king's physical decline, as evidenced by the poor construction and small size of his tomb at Abydos. In the latest reconstruction of the Palermo Stone, Wilkinson presents a strong argument for a reign of 10 years. Manetho gives Anedjib (under the name Miebidos, i.e., Merbiape) a rule of 26 years.

References:

Dodson and Hilton 2004 pp. 44, 45, 46, 48
Emery 1949-58 vol. I pp. 8-9, 82-94, pl. 21-35
Emery 1961 pp. 80-84
Gardiner 1959 pl. I, Col. II #17
Gardiner 1961 pp. 401, 430
Lacau and Lauer 1959 pp. 15-18, pl. 4 #s 19-21
Lehner 1997 pp. 80-81
Petrie 1900 pp. 5, 6, 19, 20, 39, pl. III, VI #s 1-8, VII #6, XXVI, XXVII, LXI, LXV, LXVI #s 1 and 2
Petrie 1901a pl. XLVIII # W 33 102
Petrie 1902b pp. 3, 5, 8, pl. V and XIV
Quibell 1934 p. 71
Rice 1999 p. 37
Saad 1969 pp. 18-20, 28, pl. 2-6, 16, 20
Schulman 1983 p. 250
Uphill 1984
Verbrugghe and Wickersham 1996 pp. 114, 132, 185, 188
von Beckerath 1999 pp. 40 #6, 41 #6
Waddell 1940 pp. 29, 31
T. Wilkinson 1999 pp. 78-79, 153-154, 275-276
T. Wilkinson 2000 pp. 79, 193-194, 256

'Ap...   **Dynasty XIV**

Horus Name: Unknown

Nomen: Unknown

Prenomen:

ip...
'Ap...

Two Ladies: Unknown

Golden Falcon: Unknown

Length of Reign:	Unknown
Tomb:	Unknown
Mummy:	Unknown

Consorts:	Unknown	**Variant Names:**	Apepi Ip...
Manetho:	Not given		
King Lists:	T: (G 9.16; R 10.15; vB 11.x+13)		

Perhaps the fifty-first king of Dynasty XIV, 'Ap... is one of a group of kings known only from the Turin Canon. The fragile state of the papyrus allows for varying interpretations as to the position of this king within Dynasty XIV (see "Turin Canon" in Glossary). Ryholt sees a possibility that this king's name should be restored as *'ap[p]* ("Apepi" or "Apophis") and therefore may be identified with a "King's Son, Apophis" for whom two seals are known. One of the seals shows the name "King's Son, Apepi" enclosed in a cartouche and also includes the epitaph (*di ʿnḫ*) "given Life"; the cartouche and epitaph were only used by kings or designated successors.

Von Beckerath would place this king in his XV./XVI. Dynastie.

References:

Gardiner 1959 pl. III, Col. IX #16
Gardiner 1961 p. 442 #9.16
Ryholt 1997a pp. 95 Col. 10.15, 98
   #51, 255, 380 File 14/51, 409 #51

von Beckerath 1999 pp. 120 #dd, 121 #dd

Apepi Dynasty XV

Horus Name:

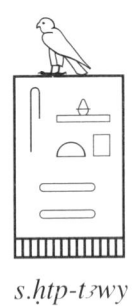

s.ḥtp-t3wy

Nomen: *ippi* — Apepi

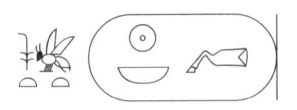

Prenomen: *˓3-ḳn-n-r˓* — Aaqenenre

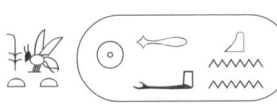

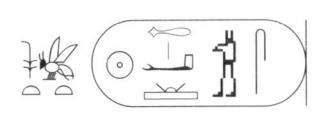

˓3-wsr-r˓ — Aawoserre

nb-ḥpš-r˓ — Nebkhepeshre

Two Ladies: Unknown

Golden Falcon: Unknown

Length of Reign:	Unknown
Tomb:	Unknown
Mummy:	Unknown

Consorts: Unknown

Manetho: Aphobis (A)
Aphôphis (A)
Apophis (E, J)

King Lists: T: (G 10.17; R 10.27)

Variant Names: Aakenenre

Apep
Aphôphis
Apopi
Auserre
Oa-qenen-ra
Ra-aa-qenen
Ra-oa-user

Apepi is the fifth ruler of Dynasty XV. His relationship to his predecessor Khyan is unknown, although Khyan was evidently not Apepi's father since two of Apepi's sisters are known and neither one bears the titles associated with royal daughters. It has been suggested that Apepi might have been a usurper, having seized the throne from Yanassi, the son of Khyan. However, this is pure conjecture.

During a reign likely to have been at least forty years, Apepi changed his prenomen on several occasions, which led earlier Egyptologists to believe that three separate kings named Apepi had held the throne. We do not know what prompted the name changes, though they usually occurred during or after an important political event. At any rate, attestations for Apepi, under his nomen or any one of the three prenomina, are found from Avaris and Bubastis in the Delta to Gebelein, just south of Thebes in Upper Egypt.

From Bubastis comes a doorjamb and two blocks of red granite bearing Apepi's nomen and Horus name that inform us that the king had built "many columns and a gate of 'brass'" for the temple of Bast. Of course, a great many attestations come from the site of Avaris, the Hyksos capital, including such items as an offering table, a shrine to the king's sister Tani (who is also known from an offering stand found at Medamud), and several sphinxes (including one of Amenemhet II) to whom Apepi had added his own name. The same is true for a pair of colossal statues of the Dynasty XIII ruler Imyremeshau, where the inscriptions added to the right shoulder of each read "The Good God, Aqenenre, Son of the Sun, Apepi, given life, beloved of Set." Other items attesting to Apepi in Lower Egypt include a portion of an inscribed jar from Tell el-Yahudiya, an inscribed red granite jar probably from Memphis and an electrum-handled dagger found on a mummy at Saqqara.

Although Dynasty XV's border did not extend any further south than Cusae, a little north of Abydos, attestations for Apepi's presence in Upper Egypt include an inscribed adze-blade from el-Mahamid Qibli, a vase found in a tomb at Dra Abu el-Naga and a lintel found at Gebelein that is inscribed with the prenomen Awoserre. Although Ryholt posits a Hyksos occupation of the Theban area based on the block from Gebelein, his time frame (one to two years) is probably not long enough for the construction of any sort of serious structure. Certainly there was a war between the Hyksos and the last two rulers of the Theban Dynasty XVII. It is likely that the adze-blade and vase were trophies captured from Apepi's army during this war and left by the Theban troops. The lintel may well have been brought home from Avaris by the triumphant Theban army.

During the last decade or so of his reign in Lower Egypt, Apepi had to contend with a series of uprisings led in succession by Theban rulers Seqenenre Taa, Kamose and Ahmose. When Ahmose finally drove him out of Egypt, Apepi evidently took refuge in the nearby fortress-city of Sharuhen, where he remained under siege until his death. More detailed narratives about the war are given in the entries for the Theban rulers mentioned above.

The Turin Canon gives Apepi a minimum of 40 years of rule. The papyrus is broken off after the four "tens" sign, so we are not sure how many numerals were originally recorded. The highest contemporary regnal year known is year 33, as recorded in the Rhind Mathematical Papyrus. Manetho gave his "Apophis" a reign of 61 years, following Africanus and Josephus (although, to be fair, it must be said that in Eusebius' version of Manetho, Apophis is given a reign of only 14 years).

References:

Bietak 2001 p
Bourriau 1976 p. 145
W. Davies 1981a p. 12 #1
Dawson 1925 pp. 216-217
Dodson and Hilton 2004 pp. 114, 115, 124
Fay 1996 pp. 9-23, pl. 1-50
Gardiner 1959 pl. III, Col. X.17
Gardiner 1961 p. 433
Gauthier 1907-17 vol. II p. 140 #5 IV
Goedicke 1986
Habachi 1972
Hall 1913 p. 33 #s295-297
Harvey 1994 p. 5
Hayes 1959 pp. 6-6, fig. 2
Hein 1994 pp. 148 #121, 149 #123, 152 #127, 153 #s128-129, 154 #s130-131, 155 #132, 156-158 #134, 167 #156, 240 #302
Helck 1983 pp. 55 #s 73-76, 56 #s 77-81, 57 #s 82 and 84, 57-58 #85
Lilyquist 1995 pp. 22-23 #s 2-5, 47-48 #B, 55 83 figs. 13-15, 84 fig. 16, 111 figs. 124-126
Naville 1891 pp. 22-23, pl. XXII.a, XXIII.b and .c
Newberry 1906 pp. 103 #I, 152 #s 30-35, 155 #s 30, 31-35, pl. I #1, XXIII #s 30-35, XXIV #s 34 and 35
D. Redford 1997 pp. 7 #s 32-44, 13-15 #s 68-70, 17-18 #74
Ryholt 1997a pp. 43, 48 fig. 6/b 119 and table 22, 125 table 23, 130, 131, 189-190, 201 and table 40, 308, 385-387 File 15/5, 410, table 96
Tufnell 1984 pp. pp. 382 #s 3434-3462, pl. XLII #s 3434
Verbrugghe and Wickersham 1996 pp. 139, 140, 157
von Beckerath 1999 pp. 114 #5, 115 #5
Waddell 1940 pp. 83, 91, 97, 99, 239

'Aper-'Anati   Dynasty XV

ḥḳ3-ḫ3swt ʿpr-ʿnti
(Ruler of Foreign Lands) 'Aper-'Anati

Length of Reign:	Unknown
Tomb:	Unknown
Mummy:	Unknown

Consorts:	Unknown	**Variant Names:**	Onta
Manetho:	Not given		Ontha
King Lists:	None		Useranat(?)

Ryholt has put forth the possibility that 'Aper-'Anati was the second, or at least a very early ruler of, the Hyksos' Dynasty XV, probably succeeding Semqen. He bases his theory upon the style and design of a single scarab of unknown provenance. Petrie, in his publication of the scarab, gives the name as Ontha and provides the interesting translation "Prince of the Desert, the Terror, Ontha."

References:

Dodson and Hilton 2004 p. 114
Martin 1971 p. 30 #318, pl. 41 #3
Petrie 1978 pl. XXI, Dyn XV #1
Ryholt 1997a pp. 121-123, 125, table 23, 127, 201 table 40, 383 File 15/2, 410, table 96

Tufnell 1984 p. 382 #3464, pl. LXII #3464
von Beckerath 1999 pp. 116 #b, 117 #b

Awibre (II)   Dynasty XIV

Horus Name:

Unknown   **Nomen:** Unknown

Prenomen:

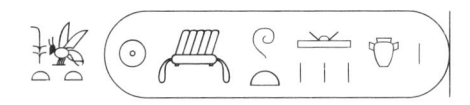

$ꜣw(t)$-ib-$rʿ$

Awibre

Two Ladies: Unknown

Golden Falcon: Unknown

Length of Reign:	Unknown
Tomb:	Unknown
Mummy:	Unknown

Consorts:	Unknown	**Variant Names:**	Auibre
Manetho:	Not given		
King Lists:	T: (G 8.12; R 9.12; vB 8.12)		

Ay

Perhaps the seventeenth king of Dynasty XIV, Awibre is one of a group of kings known only from the Turin Canon. The fragile state of the papyrus allows for varying interpretations as to the position of some of the kings of this dynasty. However, Awibre's place seems secure.

The roman numeral shown in parenthesis after the name is a modern convention used to differentiate between this king and Hor (I), a Dynasty XIII king with the same prenomen.

References:

Gardiner 1959 pl. III, Col. VIII #12
Gardiner 1961 p. 441 #8.12 as "Auibre"
Ryholt 1997a pp. 95 Col. 9.12, 98 #17, 198 table 37 and note 9/12, 379 File 14/17, 409 table 95 #17

von Beckerath 1999 pp. 108 #13, 109 #13

Ay   Dynasty XVIII

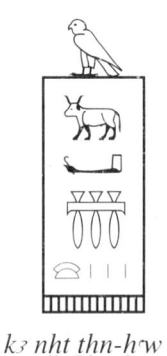

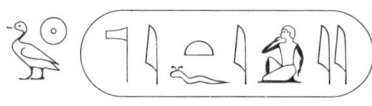

Horus Name:

k_3 nht thn-h'w

Nomen:

it-ntr iy
(God's Father) Ay

Prenomen:

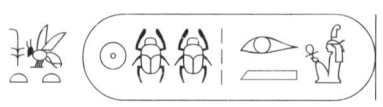

hpr-hprw-r' iri-m3't
Kheperkheperure-irimaat

Two Ladies:

nbty shm-phti dr-stt

Golden Falcon:

bik-nbw hk3-m3't shpr-t3wy

Length of Reign:	4 years
Tomb:	Valley of the Kings: WV23
Mummy:	Unknown

Consorts:	Tey	**King Lists:**	None
Manetho:	Acencheres (J)	**Variant Names:**	Ai
	Acherres (A, E)		Aye
	Akenkheres (J)		Eye
	Akherres (A, E)		

Ay was the fourteenth pharaoh of Dynasty XVIII. A former courtier and military man, Ay ascended the throne of Egypt upon the death of Tutankhamen. A commoner, Ay appears to have served every pharaoh from Amenhotep III to Tutankhamen, a period of at least forty years. Many scholars attribute his rise to prominence, probably during the latter years of Amenhotep III's reign, to being the brother of Queen Tiye. Though Ay built, added to, or perhaps only repaired a rock-cut shrine at Akhmim, the ancestral home of Tiye's family, this does not necessarily establish a familial relationship. Tiye's brother Anen is well known, but there is no mention of a second brother.

Irrespective of his familial background, Ay clearly maintained a close relationship with Akhenaten. Ay's other titles, as recorded in his unused tomb at Amarna (number 25), include the courtly "True Royal Scribe" and "Fan-bearer on the Right of the King." These titles are highly honorific, and were reserved strictly for intimates of the pharaoh. Another of his titles was "God's Father," perhaps implying that he was father-in-law to a king; e.g., he may have been Nefertiti's father. Furthermore, Ay's wife Tey bore the titles "Great Nurse Who Reared the Goddess and Nurse of the King's Great Wife Neferneferuaten Nefertiti" and "Greatly Praised of Waenre (Akhenaten)." Ay and Tey were literally "showered with gold" by the Royal Family, and in turn became "People of Gold." These titles, while not definitely proving a particular relationship, further reinforce the closeness of Ay and his wife to the royal family. It should be noted that Tey is nowhere referred to as Nefertiti's mother. If Ay was Nefertiti's father, Tey was probably his second wife.

Other evidence of Ay's closeness to Akhenaten was his tomb at Amarna which, had it been completed (for some reason all work on it ceased around regnal year nine) would have been the largest private tomb in the necropolis. The tomb was inscribed with the longest known example of the Hymn to the Aten, a prayer in poetic form very possibly written by Akhenaten himself. We have no idea of Ay's commitment to the new religion, but as a "survivor" during this unstable period, he probably accepted it with the same pragmatism that allowed him to return to the fold of Amen when times called for it.

Pragmatism came to the fore upon the death of Akhenaten in his regnal year 17. Predeceased by his coregent, Smenkhkare, Akhenaten seems to have elevated his Queen, Nefertiti, to the vacant position under the name Neferneferuaten. She may have survived him and served as coregent with the young Tutankhaten for a short period of time, although this is not certain. Whatever transpired early on, by regnal year 2 or 3, Tutankhaten had changed his name to Tutankhamen, forsaken Akhetaten for the ancient capital of Memphis, reinstated Amen in all his glory and reopened the temples of all the gods throughout the land. It is clear that the 10 or 12 year old pharaoh did not independently initiate this radical repudiation of his predecessor's "religious revolution," and it is likely that Ay and his eventual successor, Horemheb, played key roles in the direction of the young king's regime.

When Tutankhamen died, Ay succeeded to the throne even though Tutankhamen had apparently chosen General Horemheb to assume the throne. It is likely that Horemheb was out of Egypt, fighting the Hittites in northern Syria, when the young king died, and Ay may have taken advantage of the situation by claiming the throne. As was the custom, the new pharaoh officiated at his predecessor's funeral, and a scene in Tutankhamen's tomb shows Ay, wearing the blue crown of a king and the leopard skin mantle of a Sem-priest, performing the "opening of the mouth" (revitalizing) ceremony for the deceased ruler.

A ring bearing the cartouches of Ay and Tutankhamen's widow, Ankhsenamen, was found in the possession of an antiques dealer in Luxor in the early 1930s. This has led some scholars to speculate that Ay may have married Ankhsenamen upon the death of Tutankhamen, attaining the throne through this royal marriage. However, no other evidence for such a union has surfaced.

Ay, unquestionably an old man at his succession, ruled for only four years. During that time he continued the restorations of temples throughout Egypt. He also completed Tutankhamen's temple "The Mansion of Nebkheperure" at Karnak, where he added his titulary above that of his predecessor. Across the Nile, a little to the north of the later temple of Ramesses III at Medinet Habu, Ay built his mortuary temple. The temple, made of mud brick and sandstone, was usurped by Horemheb after Aye's death. Almost none of it survives. Colossal statues of Tutankhamen, usurped by Ay, were also re-inscribed for Horemheb.

Attestations for Ay outside of Egypt are extremely rare. There are a few scarabs from Syria-Palestine and alabaster vase fragments from Ashur in Iraq. In Nubia we have a lion bearing texts of Ay (and Tutankhamen) found at Temple B at Gebel Barkal, and a stele showing the king worshipping various deities from a small shrine at Gebel el-Shems, just south of Abu Simbel.

Ay apparently intended to pass the throne to his son Nakhtmin, but the son predeceased the father. Upon Ay's death, General Horemheb became pharaoh.

Ay's tomb in the Valley of the Kings may originally have been intended for Tutankhamen, although this is not certain. The tomb, some 60 m. deep, is not dissimilar to the tomb of Akhenaten at

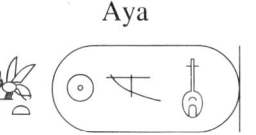

Amarna. Paintings in the burial chamber are very much like those in Tutankhamen's tomb, and it has been suggested that the same artist did both. All but two representations of Ay have been destroyed. These mutilations were probably done during Dynasty XIX, when all of the "Amarna Pharaohs," i.e., Akhenaten through Ay, were proscribed.

References:

Birrell 1997 pp. 11-18
Brier 1994 p. 269
Bryan 2000 pp. 261
Dodson and Hilton 2004 pp. 17, 142-147, 150, 151-154, 156-157, 167, 172, 256 note 115
Grajetzki 2005 pp. 63-64
Hall 1913 pp. 198 #s 1973, 1974, 280 #2708-2711
Harris and Weeks 1973 pp. 148-149
Ikram and Dodson 1998 pp. 73-74, 261, 315, 318, ills. 366c, pl. I
Krauss and Ullrich 1982 pp. 199-212
Martin 1991 pp. 35-98
Newberry 1906 pp. 168 #s 26, 29, 169 #34, pl. XXXI #s 26, 29, 34
Newberry 1932 pp. 50-52
Petrie 1978 pl. XXXVII 18.13. 1-10
Reeves 1990b pp. 70-72
Reeves and Wilkinson 1996 pp. 30, 37, 40, 42, 46, 47, 58, 77, 79, 116-117, 122, 124, 128-130, 182, 186-187, 191, 204, 207-210
Schaden 1992 pp. 92-115
Schaden 1994 pp. 39-64
Schaden 2000 pp. 88-111
Tyldesley 2006 pp. 139-140
van Dijk 2000 pp. 292-293, 295
Verbrugghe and Wickersham 1996 pp. 142, 180, 199
von Beckerath 1999 pp. 146 #13, 147 #13
Waddell 1940 pp. 103, 113, 117, 119
Weigall 1907 pp. 141-142
R. Wilkinson 2000 pp. 142, 164, 192

Aya Dynasty XIII

Horus Name: Unknown

Nomen: *iy* Aya

Prenomen: *mr-nfr-rꜥ* Merneferre

Two Ladies: Unknown

Golden Falcon: Unknown

Aya

Length of Reign:	T: "23 years, 8 months, 18 days"
Tomb:	Pyramid, location unknown, probably Memphis
Mummy:	Unknown

Consorts:	Ini	**Variant Names:**	Ay
Manetho:	Not given		Aye
King Lists:	T: (G 6.3; R 8.3; vB 7.3)		Iy
			Mernoferre

The ruler with the longest reign, not only for Dynasty XIII but for the entire Second Intermediate Period, Merneferre Aya would appear to be the thirty-second king of the dynasty, although Ryholt places him as thirty-third and von Beckerath and Dodson place him as twenty-seventh. He evidently bore no relationship to his predecessor, Sobekhotep VI, and most likely usurped the throne.

Attestations to Aya from Lower Egypt include a scarab-seal from Bubastis, two scarab-seals from Tell el-Yahudiya and the pyramidion (capstone) to his pyramid. The pyramid was most likely located in the Memphite area, but the pyramidion, which had been confiscated from "modern" robbers by the police at Faqus in 1911, near the ancient Hyksos Capital of Avaris, was undoubtedly moved to the delta by the Hyksos invaders.

Although over 58 scarab seals are known, including five from Lisht, two from Abydos and one from Coptos, as well as one cylinder-seal of unknown provenance, the only other inscribed object known is a single limestone block (possibly part of a lintel) discovered by Georges Legrain near the Sacred Lake at Karnak in 1908.

The dearth of material related to the reign of this pharaoh is certainly curious when one considers his almost 24 years of rule.

References:

Dodson 1994b p. 36 notes 90 and 92
Dodson 1994c p. 32
Dodson 2003 p. 104
Dodson and Hilton 2004 pp. 100, 106-108, 111, 120
Gardiner 1959 pl. III, Col. VII #3
Gardiner 1961 p. 44 #7.3
Habachi 1954 pp. 471-479
Helck 1983 p. 39 #50
Petrie 1906a pp. 10, 15, pl. IVA #B-4, IX #116
Quirke 2001a p. 261
Ryholt 1997a pp. 34, 35 fig. 2c, 36 fig. 3b and 5a, 38, 39, 40 table 10, 71 fig. 10, Col. 8 #3, 73 table 17 #33, 74 8/3, 77, 82, 91, 147, 192 table 33, 195, 233-235 and table 58, 354-356 File 13/33, 408 table 94 #33
Tufnell 1984 pp. 159-161, 181, 184-187, 200, 368-369 #s 3168-3183 and pl. LV-LVI
von Beckerath 1999 pp. 98 #27, 99 #27

Ba Dynasty II/III(?)

Horus Name:

bꜣ
Ba

bꜣ
Ba

Nomen:	Unknown
Two Ladies:	Unknown
Golden Falcon:	Unknown

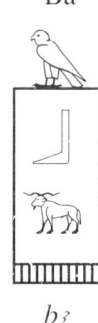

Length of Reign:	Unknown
Tomb:	Unknown
Mummy:	Unknown

Consorts:	Unknown	**Variant Names:**	None
Manetho:	Not given(?)		
King Lists:	None		

This king is known from a fragment of stone bowl found in a deposit in the corridors beneath Djoser's step pyramid at Saqqara. The fragment bears a representation of a single bird within a serekh. According to Egyptologist Nabil Swelim, a second serekh, containing the leg sign and a ram, was entered in the Register of Antiquities of the Chief Inspector of Saqqara (the "Saqqara Register") by Zakaria Goneim. Yet Quibell describes the find as being "written with a single bird sign."

It was long believed that an inscription found in the Wadi Maghara, in Sinai, belonged to the Horus Ba. It was incorrectly

Baufre

copied and is, in fact, an inscription of the Horus Sanakht of Dynasty III. The inscription is now in the Cairo Museum.

Von Beckerath lists the two serekhs as belonging to two different rulers: Ba and "Vogel"; this is highly unlikely.

References:

Dodson 1996 p. 20
Gardiner and Peet 1952 pl. IV
Gardiner and Peet 1955 pp. 55-56
Kahl et al. 1995 pp. 164-165
Lacau and Lauer 1959 p. 5 Inscriptions Royales Diverses #7, 54, pl. IV #7
Quibell 1934 p. 75
Saqqara Register S-10034
Sethe 1897 p. 6 note #4
Swelim 1983 pp. 182-183 iii, 185 #3, 220 iii, 224
von Beckerath 1999 pp. 46 #s, a and c, 47 #s, a and c
Weill 1908 p. 136 note 1
T. Wilkinson 1999 p. 82

Baufre   Dynasty IV

b3w.f-r
Baufre

Length of Reign:	Unknown
Tomb:	Giza Mastaba G7310 – 7320(?)
Mummy:	Unknown

Consorts:	Unknown	Bauefre
Manetho:	Not given	Rabauwf
		Rebaef
King Lists:	WH	Rebauf
Variant Names:	Bakare	

A section of graffito in the Wadi Hammamat shows a series of Dynasty IV royal names which lists three established kings, Khufu, Djedefre and Khafre, and two princes, Djedefhor and Baufre. All five names are enclosed within cartouches. A prince named Baufre is known to have existed during Dynasty IV; he is a son of Khufu who is cast as the narrator in one of the stories of magic found in the Westcar Papyrus. He was, as far as is known from direct evidence, never a king. However, a fragmentary list from Abusir gives what appears to be a list similar to the Hammamat group and, although the last cartouche is illegible except for the ☉ (r·) sign, it is preceded by the same cartouches as at Hammamat.

The graffito has been dated, based on paleography, to Dynasty XII of the Middle Kingdom. However, some Egyptologists would date it to the reign of Sobekhotep IV of Dynasty XIII due to the presence of a graffito of that king found nearby. It is interesting to note that during the Middle Kingdom there seems to have been a resurgence of interest in the Old Kingdom, and in Dynasty IV in particular. The Abusir list is probably from a private tomb dating to Dynasty XIX.

It has been suggested that Baufre might be equated with the owner of the unfinished pyramid at Zawiyet el-Aryan, a ruler whose very sketchy cartouche has been translated more than a dozen different ways, yet none of these translations come near to the reading "Baufre" (see BIKKA). It is much more likely that Baufre's tomb was Giza Mastaba G7310-7320.

References:

Drioton 1954 pp. 41-49
Lehner 1997 p. 138
Lichtheim 1975 p. 216
Parkinson 1991 pp. 47-48
D. Redford 1986 pp. 25 and note 87, 26, 237

Reisner 1942 p. 205
Rice 1999 p. 33
Verbrugghe and Wickersham 1996 pp. 190, 191 note 5
Verner 2001a p. 2419

Bebiankh   Dynasty XVI

Horus Name:
Unknown

Nomen:

bbi-ʿnḫ
Bebiankh

Prenomen:

s.wsr-n-rʿ
Sewoserenre

Two Ladies: Unknown

Golden Falcon: Unknown

Length of Reign:	T: 12 years
Tomb:	Unknown; probably at Dra Abu el-Naga
Mummy:	Unknown

Bebnum

Consorts:	Unknown	**Variant Names:**	Beb'anch Seuserenre
Manetho:	Not given		
King Lists:	K: (28); T: (G 11.8; R 11.8; vB 13.8)		

The ninth pharaoh of Dynasty XVI, Bebiankh's parentage is unknown, as is his relationship to his predecessor, Semenre.

A stele found at the mining site of Gebel el-Zeit on the Red Sea shows the king accompanied by Hathor, "Mistress of Galena" and Horus, "Master of the Deserts." The only other contemporary attestation is a dagger found at Naqada.

Some scholars place Bebiankh in Dynasty XVII, however his position in the Turin Canon puts him firmly in Dynasty XVI. The Canon also tells us that, directly after his reign, the throne was unoccupied for an unspecified number of days.

References:
Castel and Soukiassian 1985 pp. 291, 292, 293, pl. LXIV
Dodson and Hilton 2004 p. 116
Gardiner 1959 pl. IV, Col. XI #9
Gardiner 1961 p. 410 #11.8
Ryholt 1997a pp. 153 #11.8, 158, table 24, 159, 390 File 16/9, 410 table 97
von Beckerath 1999 pp. 126 #9, 127 #9

Bebnum   Dynasty XIV

Horus Name: Unknown

Nomen: *bbnm*
Bebnum

Prenomen: ...$k3$-[r^c]
...kare

Two Ladies: Unknown

Golden Falcon: Unknown

Length of Reign: Unknown

Tomb: Unknown

Mummy: Unknown

Consorts:	Unknown	**Variant Names:**	Babnem
Manetho:	Not given		Bebnem
King Lists:	T: (G 9.30; R 9.28; vB 8.28)		

Possibly the thirty-fourth king of Dynasty XIV, Bebnum is one of a group of kings known only from the Turin Canon. The fragile state of the papyrus allowed for varying interpretations as to the position of this king within Dynasty XIV (see "Turin Canon" in Glossary) until a recent study indicated that two previously separated papyrus fragments should be joined together, thus placing Bebnum firmly in his proper dynastic order.

References:

Gardiner 1959 pl. III Col. IX #30
Gardiner 1961 p. 442 #9.30 as
 "...ka[re?] Bebnem"
Ryholt 1997a pp. 24, 95 Col. 9.28, 98
#34, 380 File 14/34, 409 #34
von Beckerath 1999 pp. 110 #29, 111 #29

Bikka   Dynasty IV

bik-k₃
Bikka

Length of Reign:	Unknown; 2-4 years(?)
Tomb:	Unfinished pyramid at Zawiyet el-Aryan
Mummy:	Unknown

Consorts:	Unknown	Horka
Manetho:	Bicheris (A)	Khnemka
	Bikheris (A)	Maka
		Nebka
King Lists:	None	Neb(i)-Ka(i)
Variant Names:		Nebkare
	Aaka	Neferka
	Baka	Setka
	Bakare	Seth?ka
	Her-Kai	Wehemka

During excavations of an unfinished pyramid at Zawiyet el-Aryan, about four miles south of the Giza plateau, a number of stone blocks were uncovered. Many of these blocks bore the cartouches of

Bikka

an otherwise unknown king. The hieratic symbols were poorly painted in red ink and gave a royal name that has not been found elsewhere. As may be seen from this example,

and the list of variant spellings above, the name is difficult to read and open to many interpretations.

Structural likenesses between Bikka's unfinished pyramid and the pyramid of Djedefre at Abu Roash almost certainly date Bikka to the middle of Dynasty IV, although some scholars would place this king (as Nebka) in Dynasty III.

The granite, oval-shaped sarcophagus in the "Unfinished Pyramid" was sunk into a pit in the floor of what would have become the burial chamber. It is likely that the sarcophagus of Djedefre was also oval: Petrie found curved granite fragments in that king's burial chamber and believed them to be the remains of the royal sarcophagus. If, as seems probable, Djedefre owned an oval-shaped sarcophagus, it would constitute a second link with Bikka.

An interesting feature of the Unfinished Pyramid is that, although the monument was never completed, the sarcophagus was sealed. However, when opened, it was found to be empty. A similar situation occurred in the unfinished pyramid of the Dynasty III ruler Sekhemkhet.

Manetho gives his king Bicheris a reign of 22 years; Egyptologists usually opt for a year or two at most. The amount of work completed on the Unfinished Pyramid at Zawiyet el-Aryan would seem to indicate a reign of a few more than two years. If Manetho's king is to be identified with Bikka, we must discount almost two decades of reign. Scholars are uncertain about Bikka's placement in the dynasty: Edwards, Dodson and Hilton would place Bikka (as Baka or Setka) between Djedefre and Khafre, while Stadelmann, Verner and others see him ruling after Khafre and before Shepseskaf.

References:

Barsanti 1912 pp. 61-62
Barsanti and Maspero 1906
　pp. 257-286
Clayton 1994 p. 51
Dodson 2003 p. 60
Dodson and Hilton 2004 p. 55
Dunham 1978
Edwards 1993 pp. 146-147
Edwards 1994 pp. 98-100, 101, 104
Fakhry 1961b pp. 53-58
Lehner 1997 p. 129, 171
Maragioglio and Rinardi 1967
　pp. 1-29
Reisner 1931 p. 275
W. Smith 1971 pp. 5-9
Stadelmann 2001a p. 596
Swelim 1983 pp. 125 ff.
Verner 2001b p. 90
von Beckerath 1999 pp. 54 #5, 55 #5

Crocodile — Dynasty 00

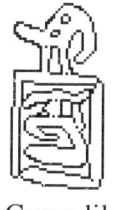

Crocodile

Length of Reign:	Unknown
Tomb:	Unknown
Mummy:	Unknown
Consorts:	Unknown
Manetho:	Not given
King Lists:	None
Variant Names:	Krokodil

The very existence of a Late Predynastic ruler named "Crocodile" is questionable. The only evidence for Crocodile is two serekhs, written cursively in ink on two stone jars found during the excavations carried out by Petrie at Tarkhan in middle Egypt. Petrie read the names as Ka(?) on one jar and Normer (Narmer) on the other. Kaplony reads the serekhs as being of Scorpion. Dreyer sees the name Crocodile on both examples.

Dreyer believes that Crocodile was contemporaneous with Narmer and may have been in contention for the throne, or perhaps an attempted usurper. Crocodile, providing he did exist, would seem to have had a limited amount of success in his bid for the throne; nothing is known of him beyond the two possible serekhs discussed above, from graves 315 and 1549 at Tarkhan, and a possible third serekh from grave 261 in that same cemetery. It has been suggested that this king also ruled the Faiyum.

References:

Adams and Cialowicz 1997 ill. 41
Dreyer 1992b pp. 259-263
Kaplony 1963 vol. III pl. 1, 2 and 8 #18
Petrie 1913 pp. 8, 9, 21, 26 Pl. XXXI.66
Petrie 1914 pp. 10, 11 PL. IX.3

De Dynasty 0

d
De

Length of Reign:	Unknown
Tomb:	Unknown
Mummy:	Unknown

Consorts:	Unknown	**Variant Names:**	None
Manetho:	Not given		
King Lists:	None		

The documentation for the existence of this king relies on a single inscription on a fragment of stone bowl, now in the Cairo Museum, found by the archaeologist Flinders Petrie. Petrie saw this "name" as either the Two Lords (nebwy) or Two Ladies (nebty) name of a previously unknown ruler. Whether or not this is the case is impossible to determine, since no other artifacts bearing this inscription have surfaced.

References:
Petrie 1900 pp. 6, 19 pl. XXXII.32

Dedumose SIP

Horus Name: Unknown **Nomen:**

ddw-ms
Dedumose

Prenomen: Unknown

Two Ladies: Unknown

Golden Falcon: Unknown

Length of Reign:	Unknown
Tomb:	Unknown
Mummy:	Unknown

Consorts:	Unknown	**Variant Names:**	Dedumes Dudumes
Manetho:	Not given(?)		
King Lists:	None		

The nomen Dedumose is found on the stele of a "king's son" named Horsekher that was purchased from a dealer at Edfu. It has been suggested that Horsekher may have been the grandson of this Dedumose, although granting the honorific title "King's Son" was a not uncommon practice at this time. Since the stele gives none of the rest of the ruler's titulary, it is impossible to say if the Dedumose mentioned is one of the two Dynasty XVI kings bearing this name. Englebach saw a strong stylistic resemblance between this stele and a stele of Dedumose I.

References:

Englebach 1921 pp. 189-190, pl. I Ryholt 1997a pp. 262, 402 File N/7
Helck 1983 p. 43 #58

Dedumose I Dynasty XVI

Horus Name:

wꜣḏ-ḥꜥ(w)

Nomen:

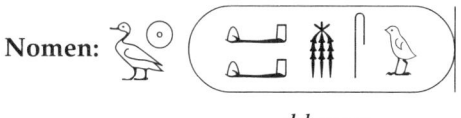

dd-msw
Dedumose

Prenomen:

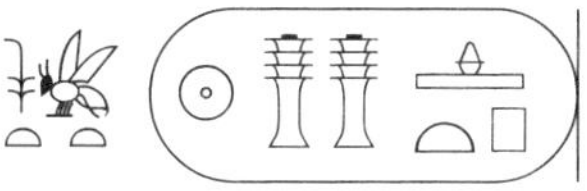

ḏd-ḥtp
Djedhotepre

Two Ladies:

nbty šd-tꜣwy

Golden Falcon:

bik nbw in-ḥtp

Dedumose II

Length of Reign:	Unknown
Tomb:	Unknown
Mummy:	Unknown

Consorts:	Unknown	Dudumesu
Manetho:	Not given	Ra-Zedui-Hetep
King Lists:	None	Uaz-kho
Variant Names:	Daduihetepre	

The only definite attestation for Dedumose I comes from the stele of a military commander named Khonsuemwaset found at Edfu. The inscription gives the king's full titulary and tells of his generosity toward the commander. Although Khonsuemwaset calls himself "King's Son" on the stele, it is undoubtedly an honorific title; ever since Dynasty XIII, as Redford points out, it had been the practice to bestow such a title upon favored individuals, "especially military commanders."

A stele purchased at Edfu gives the cartouche of a king named Dedumose, but none of the rest of the titulary is given and so it is impossible to say if it dates to Dedumose I or Dedumose II (see DEDUMOSE II). Englebach believed the stelae stylistically resemble each other.

References:

Barsanti 1908 pp. 1-2
Dodson and Hilton 2004 pp. 116, 117, 118, 120
Englebach 1921 pp. 189-190, pl. I
Helck 1983 pp. 41-42 #57, 43 #58
D. Redford 1997 pp. 2 #1, 3 #2
Ryholt 1997a pp. 156, 158, table 25 #A, 262, 289 table 86, 390-391 File 16/a, 410 table 97
von Beckerath 1999 pp. 100 #37, 101 #37

Dedumose II   Dynasty XVI

Horus Name:
Unknown   **Nomen:**

dd-msw
Dedumose

Dedumose II

Prenomen: *ḏd-nfr-rˁ*
Djedneferre

Two Ladies: Unknown

Golden Falcon: Unknown

Length of Reign:	Unknown
Tomb:	Unknown; probably at Dra Abu el-Naga
Mummy:	Unknown

Consorts:	Unknown	Dudumes
Manetho:	Unknown	Ra-Zed-Nefer
King Lists:	None	Zadneferre
Variant Names:	Dad-nefer-ra	

Dedumose II's parentage is not known for certain, but it is likely that he was the son of his predecessor and namesake, Dedumose I.

Attestations for this king are rare and range from Thebes south to Edfu, only some 80 km. distant from Dedumose's capital. Excavations at the Deir el-Bahri temple of the Dynasty XI pharaoh Montuhotep II have turned up two stone fragments, one bearing the nomen and the other the prenomen of Dedumose. Moving south, a stele at Gebelein gives the king's nomen and prenomen, and at El Kab a graffito etched into a fallen block of stone reads "Son of Re, Dedumose." The name is not in a cartouche and could actually belong to Dedumose I. At Edfu is the stele of Harseker; it gives a cartouche of Dedumose though, once again, we don't know to which Dedumose it refers.

Aside from the above-mentioned attestations, Petrie lists two scarabs that bear Dedumose's prenomen. (see DEDUMOSE).

References:

Dodson and Hilton 2004 pp. 116, 117, 118, 120
G. Fraser 1900 p. 9 #62
Helck 1983 pp. 43-44 #59
Naville 1910 pp. 12, 21, pl. XII #D
Peden 2001 p. 48 #ii
Petrie 1924 pp. 233-234

D. Redford 1997 p. 3 #3
Ryholt 1997a pp. 156-157, 158, table 25, 289 table 86, 306, 391 File 16/b, 410 table 97
von Beckerath 1999 pp. 100 #37, 101 #37

Den — Dynasty I

Horus Name: *dn* Den

Nomen: *ḫꜣsti* — Khasty

smt-y — Semty

Two Ladies: *nbty ḫꜣsti*

Golden Falcon: *(bik)-nbw i ꜥrt*

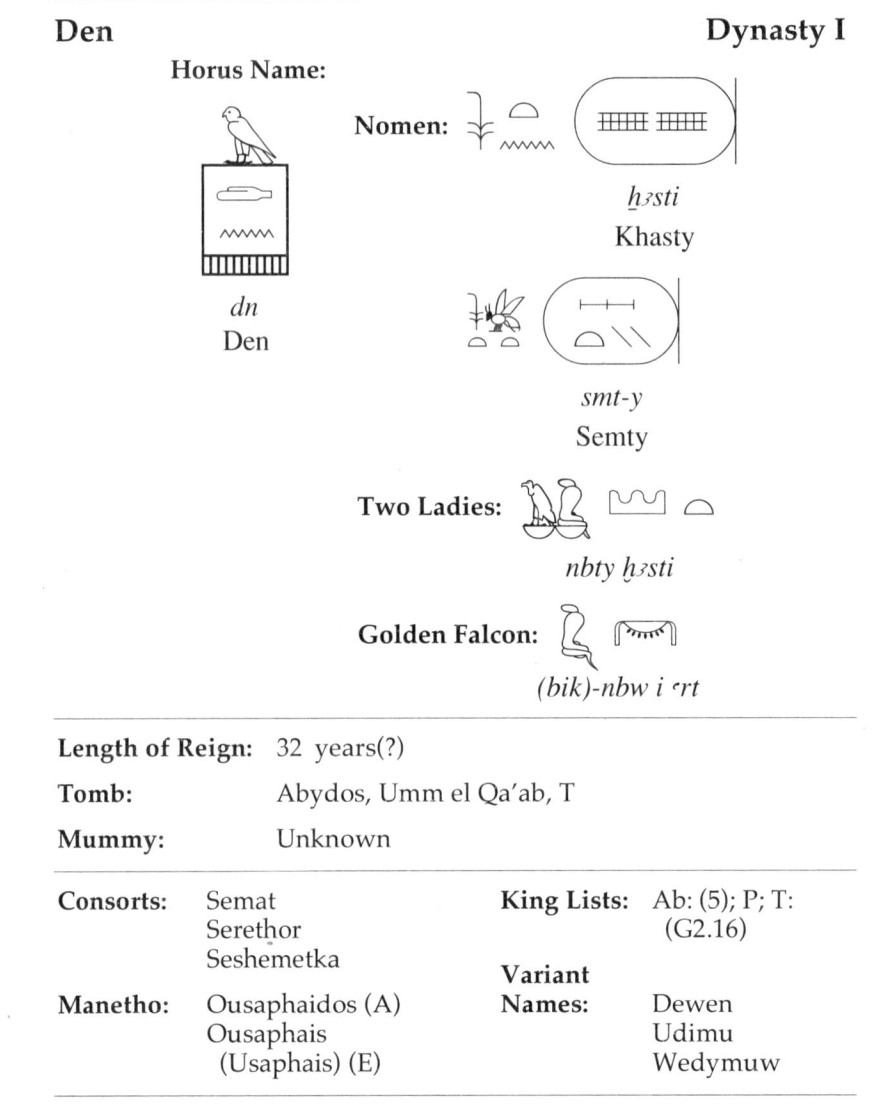

Length of Reign:	32 years(?)
Tomb:	Abydos, Umm el Qa'ab, T
Mummy:	Unknown

Consorts:	Semat Serethor Seshemetka	**King Lists:**	Ab: (5); P; T: (G2.16)
Manetho:	Ousaphaidos (A) Ousaphais (Usaphais) (E)	**Variant Names:**	Dewen Udimu Wedymuw

The fifth king of Dynasty I, Den was the son of Queen Merneith and, most likely, King Djet. Den seems to have inherited the throne at a very young age, Djet having died after a relatively short reign. It appears that Merneith acted as regent for some period of time during her son's youth (see MERNEITH).

Manetho gives Den a reign of only 20 years, which is certainly an underestimate. The main fragment of the Palermo Stone preserves 14 years near the middle to the end of the reign; Cairo Fragment Number Five preserves five years near the beginning. Estimates of the length of Den's reign vary from 41 to 45 years. Den lived long enough to celebrate two Sed Festivals; an entry on the main fragment of the Palermo Stone, which probably represents year 30 of the reign, lists one Sed Festival, and a fragment of a stone vessel found during a recent re-excavation of his tomb at Abydos lists a second. Since it is very likely that during this time in Egyptian history a king's Sed Festival did not occur until the thirtieth regnal year, and every third year thereafter, it follows that Den's reign was at least 33 years in length. An ebony label discovered by Petrie at Abydos and now in the British Museum might also show part of a Sed Festival, although this interpretation is disputed. Even if the label does represent such an event, it does not necessarily follow that it would represent a third festival.

It is in Den's reign that the royal title (*nswt-bity*), usually translated "King of Upper and Lower Egypt," first occurs. It was long believed that the double crown ⊲ + ⋎ = ⋎ first came into use at this time, however it now seems that it was in use earlier, in the reign of king Djet.

Den's reign was a time of great prosperity and many examples of foreign trade goods have been discovered that point to expansion into Asia. A serekh bearing Den's name has been found in Palestine at En Besor, where Egyptians may have had a small trading settlement. Petrie discovered Syro-Palestinian pottery in Den's tomb at Abydos. All together, some 81 such vessels have come to light from this source.

Evidence of military activity during Den's reign comes from several sources. Cairo Fragment Five of the Palermo Stone lists a "Year of the Smiting of the Asiatics" and a "Year of the Smiting of the Wolf(?) People." The Palermo Stone itself lists a "Year of the Smiting of the Troglodytes" and "the Smiting of Werka"; it would appear that all of these expeditions took place in Syria and Palestine. Likewise, five different labels from Den's tomb make mention of military action in the Syro-Palestine and Sinai regions.

Den's tomb contains several innovations, including the first example of stone pavement (pink granite from Aswan) and a stairway into the burial chamber. Surrounding the tomb were the burials of 121 retainers.

It is very likely that a funerary enclosure ascribed by Petrie to Den's mother and regent, Queen Merneith, actually belonged to the king, although he may have shared it with the queen. The enclosure was called "the seats of the gods" of king Den. This monument was surrounded by 80 subsidiary graves. Although Den would have been buried at Abydos, it is possible that he also had a funerary enclosure at Saqqara.

Tombs of high officials built at Saqqara during Den's reign or shortly thereafter include mastabas 3035, 3036 and 3506.

Djedefhor

References:

D. Arnold 1998 p. 34
Clagett 1989 pp. 71-74 and various notes
Dodson and Hilton 2004 pp. 44, 45, 46, 48-49
Dreyer 1990 p. 80 fig. 9, pl. 29d
Emery 1938
Emery 1949 vol. I pp. 5-6, 7, 71-81, pl. 14-20
Emery 1958 vol. III pp. 37-72, pl. 21-84
Emery 1961 pp. 73-80
Gardiner 1959 pl. I, Col. II #16
Gardiner 1961 pp. 401-402, 411, 430
Godron 1990
Petrie 1900 pp. 5, 11, 19, 21, 25, 28, 38, 40, 44, pl. III, V, X #s 11-14, XI #s 3-7 and 8-11, XII # 4, XIV-XVII, XXIV-XXY, LIX
Petrie 1901a pp. 9, 10, 25, 14, 25, 31, 33, 54, pl. VII #s 5-13, XVII #s 131-135, XVIII-XX, XXX, XL-XLI, LVI #s 5-6, LVII, LXII
Schulman 1983 pp. 249-250, 251
Spencer 1993 p. 66 fig. 45
Uphill 1984
Verbrugghe and Wickersham 1996 pp. 132, 188
von Beckerath 1999 pp. 38 #5, 39 #5
Waddell 1940 pp. 29, 31, 35
T. Wilkinson 1999 pp. 75-78, 158, 159, 212, 239-240
T. Wilkinson 2000 pp. 79, 103-104, 105-119, 240-247, 256

Djedefhor   Dynasty IV

$\underline{dd}.f$-$\underline{h}r[r\cdot]$ (sic)
Djedefhor

Length of Reign:	Unknown
Tomb:	Giza Mastaba G7210 - 7220
Mummy:	Unknown

Consorts:	Unknown	**Variant Names:**	Heru-ta-ta-f Hordedef Hordjedef Hordjedef[re]
Manetho:	Thamphthis(?) (A)		
King Lists:	WH; Abusir List		

Djedefhor, whose name has been found written within a cartouche on two "king lists" (one a graffito from the Wadi Hammamat and the other on a section of carved relief from Abusir), was a son of king Khufu. He was therefore a prince, but was almost certainly never a pharaoh.

The graffito bearing Djedefhor's name at Wadi Hammamat has been dated to Dynasty XII on paleographic grounds, although some scholars consider the carving to have been done during the time of the Dynasty XIII ruler Sobekhotep IV, since this king is named on a nearby carving. The Abusir list dates to Dynasty XIX.

Later generations remembered Djedefhor as a wise man. He was considered to be the author of a book of "Instructions" which some scholars date linguistically to the Old Kingdom, although others see it as dating to the Middle Kingdom. Papyrus Westcar contains a story in which Djedefhor brings a magician to court who foretells some of the future to Khufu. Djedefhor's name is linked with the great sage, physician and architect Imhotep in "The Harper's Song," which purports to have come from the tomb of one of the king Intefs of the early Middle Kingdom (and indeed may have), although of the two copies known, one is dated to the reign of Akhenaten of Dynasty XVIII and the other to the Ramessid Period (Dynasties XIX or XX).

As befitted the station of prince, Djedefhor was buried at Giza in a tomb near that of his father, Khufu.

References:
Lehner 1997 p. 138
Lichtheim 1975 pp. 5-7, 58-59, 196, 215, 217-219, 222

Djedefre   Dynasty IV

Horus Name:

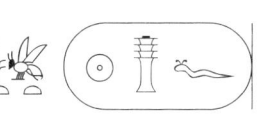

ḫpr

Nomen:

ḏd.f-rˁ
Djedefre

Two Ladies:

nbty ḫpr-m

Golden Falcon:

bik-nbw ḥrw

Length of Reign:	8 years
Tomb:	Pyramid at Abu Roash: "Djedefre Shines Like a Star"
Mummy:	Unknown
Consorts:	Hetepheres II Khentetka
Manetho:	Souphis II (A, E) Suphis II(?) (A, E)
King Lists:	Ab: (22); P; S: (18); T: (G 3.11)
Variant Names:	Djedefra Radjedef Redjedef

Djedefre

The son of Khufu and Queen Meritites, Djedefre is the third king of the dynasty. It is likely that he was not the chosen successor—that position seems to have belonged to an older brother, prince Kawab. Evidently, Kawab did not outlive his father, but the theory put forth many years ago by George Reisner and others, that Djedefre murdered Kawab, is totally without foundation. Djedefre was the legitimate successor and officiated at Khufu's funeral, as evidenced by his cartouche being on the limestone beams over Khufu's boat pit.

Djedefre's pyramid, identified by workmen's graffiti, was not located at Giza, as his father's had been. Instead, for unknown reasons, the pyramid was built at Abu Roash, some 8 km. (5 miles) north of the Giza plateau. It has been suggested that the king wanted his tomb nearer to Heliopolis, the center of the Solar Cult; Djedefre is the first pharaoh to use the "Son of Re" in his titulary.

The pyramid at Abu Roash may never have been completed. The reason for this was undoubtedly that Djedefre's rule was so short: the Turin Canon gives a reign of eight years, although a graffito found on a roofing block of one of Khufu's boat pits gives a year 11. Today the pyramid consists of a deep pit (23 x 10 m. wide and about 20 m. deep) reached by a sloping "access corridor" 49 m. long. The burial chamber was built into the pit and corridor. Had construction continued, the entire pit would have been lined with stone blocks. The superstructure of the monument, a central core of natural rock out-cropping to which masonry adheres, is only 10-12 m. high. However, a Franco-Swiss team that began excavating the site in 1995 has recovered a great many stone blocks from the original structure. They have also cleared the funerary chapel and the remains of a satellite pyramid. A causeway, some 1.5 kms. in length, leads from the complex to a valley temple; the temple has not been excavated.

Djedefre's pyramid, had it been completed, would have measured 106.20 m. square and 66 m. high. The structure would have been similar in size to the pyramid of Menkaure at Giza. A boat pit was on the east side of the monument.

Recent work in the Libyan Desert, southwest of the Dakhla Oasis, has found a carved cartouche of Djedefre at the site of a mining area. The material mined was a mineral powder apparently used as an ingredient in paint. On the opposite side of the Nile, Djedefre's name has been found in the gneiss quarry located in the Nubian Western Desert, about 65 km. from Abu Simbel.

A fragment of the Palermo Annals, now in the Cairo Museum, contains the records of one or two years in the reign of Djedefre, depending on which authority is cited. The text, much damaged and almost invisible to the naked eye, has been given various translations, no two agreeing.

Djedefre's funerary cult was revived for a period of time during Dynasty XXVI.

References:

Clagett 1989 p. 86
Dodson 2003 p. 59
Edwards 1994 p. 101
Gardiner 1959 pl. II, Col. III #11
Gardiner 1961 p. 434
Jánosi 1992 p. 52
Kanawati 2003 p. 2
Kuper and Förster 2003 pp. 25, 26, Cover
Lehner 1997 pp. 120-121
O'Connor 1995 p. 5
Peden 2001 p. 278
Stadelmann 2001a p. 596
Valloggia 2003 pp. 10-12
Verbrugghe and Wickersham 1996 pp. 135, 190
Verner 1997 pp. 156, 217-223, 462
Verner 2001b pp. 587-588
von Beckerath 1999 pp. 52 #3, 54 #3
Waddell 1940 p. 47
R. Wilkinson 2000 pp. 228-231

Djedkare   Dynasty V

Horus Name:

ḏd-ḫ ꜥw

Nomen:

issi
Isesi

Prenomen:

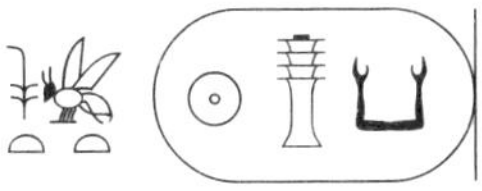

ḏd-kꜣ-rꜥ
Djedkare

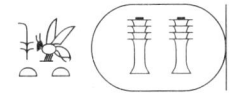

ḏd
Djed

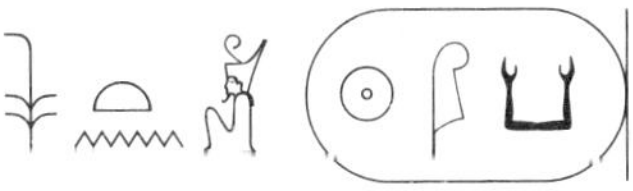

mꜣꜥt-kꜣ-rꜥ
Maatkare

Two Ladies:

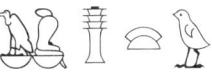

nbty ḏd-ḫ ꜥw

Golden Falcon:

bik-nbw ḏd

Djedkare

Length of Reign:	30-40 years
Tomb:	Pyramid at South Saqqara: "Beautiful is Isesi"
Mummy:	Part only. Qasr el-Aini: AI.491

Consorts:	Unknown	**Variant Names:**	Asosi
Manetho:	Tancheres (A) Tankheres (A)		Djadkere Izezi
King Lists:	Ab: (32); S: (31); T: (G 3.24)		Izozi

The eighth ruler of Dynasty V, Djedkare's parentage is uncertain. He has been described as the son of his predecessor Menkauhor, or perhaps that king's brother, or perhaps a cousin! But, whatever his parentage, his was a long and prosperous reign.

Trade and foreign contact certainly played an important role in Djedkare's reign. Attestations to continued Egyptian presence in Lebanon include an alabaster vase inscribed with the king's cartouche found at Byblos. Three, and possibly four, inscriptions bearing one or more of the king's names have been found at the copper and turquoise mines at Wadi Maghara in Sinai. Djedkare's nomen is found in a graffito at Tumas, some 150 km. south of Aswan.

An expedition to Punt was undertaken in this reign and a pigmy or dwarf was brought back as a very special gift to Djedkare. So rare and amazing was this little person that, when the Dynasty VI king Pepi II was informed that he too was about to receive a dwarf, he harkened back to the time of his predecessor and promised his official, Harkhuf, that "my majesty will do great things for you, more than was done…in the time of King Isesi…." Expeditions were also sent to the diorite quarries in the Western Desert of Lower Nubia.

Evidently not all relations with Egypt's neighbors were peaceful, if a scene from the tomb of the vizier Inti is to be believed—Egyptian troops storming and sacking an "Asian fortress."

Djedkare had a pyramid constructed at South Saqqara. Originally some 78.5 m. per side at the base and reaching a height of 50 m., the tomb was badly damaged by stone robbers in ancient times, although some of the original white limestone casing stones are still in place. The stone thieves destroyed the pyramid's chamber so thoroughly that only fragments of the sarcophagus, along with portions of canopic jars, remained of it; bits of the viscera, wrapped in pieces of linen, were discovered in conjunction with the jar fragments. Also in the burial chamber was almost half of a mummified body (including the left side of the face, parts of the skull with some skin and hair still attached, some of the chest and spine and portions of the left arm, hand and leg) which was almost certainly that of the king. The body was that of a man in his early fifties.

Djedkare did not construct a sun temple as had all of his dynastic predecessors except Menkauhor, but did have a mortuary temple and a valley temple, although neither to date has been properly excavated.

Djedkare's queen's name is unknown; a few scholars believe her to have been Meresankh IV, though that queen may have been the wife of Menkauhor. A smaller, though exquisitely designed, pyramid complex lies tangent to the northeast corner of the king's complex. Due to the proximity and fine workmanship, the pyramid and mortuary temple are believed to have been constructed for Djedkare's consort.

A series of papyri found at Abusir, at the sites of the pyramid complexes of the Dynasty V rulers Neferirkare (I) and Neferefre, date mostly to the reign of Djedkare. Written in early hieratic, they concern the supervision and running of funerary cults, everyday maintenance of pyramids and temples, letters, instructions regarding observance of religious festivals, inventories, etc.

The Abusir papyri mention a year of the twenty-first occurrence of the cattle count that, if the count was done on a biennial basis, would give Djedkare a reign of 39 to 40 years. This would come close to Manetho's 44 years. The Turin Canon gives Djedkare a reign of 28 years, which is perhaps closer to correct, as an alabaster vase, now in the Louvre, records a Sed Festival. Since the Sed was ideally celebrated in the king's thirtieth year of rule, it is fairly safe to give the king a reign of at least that many years, although the Sed Festival could be held by a monarch during any year of his choosing.

Probably due to a lacuna in the original source, the Turin Canon lists Djedkare as Djed. A scribal error is probably responsible for the king's name being given as Maatkare on the Saqqara list.

References:

Altenmüller 2001 pp. 600
Batrawi 1947 pp. 97-103
Brier 1994 pp. 247
Dodson 1994b pp. 9, 109 #s 2 and 2a, pl. IIIa
Dodson 2003 pp. 71-72, 125
Dodson and Hilton 2004 pp. 62, 64-65, 67-69
Gardiner 1959 pl. II, Col. III #24
Gardiner 1961 p. 435
Gardiner and Peet 1952 pl. IV #15, VII #13, VIII #14, IX #19(?)
Goedicke 2000 pp. 408-409
Ikram and Dodson 1997 pp. 92, 113, 278, 315, 317, 320-321
Lehner 1997 pp. 83, 147, 153-154, 158, 231
Lichtheim 1975 pp. 26-27
Ryholt 1997a p. 16
Spalinger 1994 pp. 299
Strouhal and Gaballa 1993 pp. 104-118
Verbrugghe and Wickersham 1996 pp. 136, 191
Verner 1997 pp. 141, 272-274, 323-332, 464
Verner 2002 pp. 142, 149
von Beckerath 1999 pp. 60 #8, 61 #8
Waddell 1940 p. 51
Weigall 1907 pl. LVIII
R. Wilkinson 2000 pp. 129-130

Djedkare Shemai   Dynasty VII/VIII

Horus Name:	Unknown
Nomen and Prenomen:	*ḏd-k₃-rʿ šmꜣi* Djedkare Shemai
Two Ladies:	Unknown
Golden Falcon:	Unknown

Length of Reign:	Unknown
Tomb:	Unknown
Mummy:	Unknown

Consorts:	Unknown	Variant Names:	Djedkare Schemai
Manetho:	Not given		Shemay
King Lists:	Ab: (44)		

The fifth king of Dynasty VII/VIII, Djedkare Shemai is known only from the Abydos King List. A lacuna is recorded in the Turin Canon where this Pharaoh would have been listed.

References:
Gardiner 1961 p. 437 #A 44
Ryholt 2000 pp. 96-97, 99 table 1
Sayce 1899b p. 111
von Beckerath 1999 pp. 66 #5, 67 #5

Djedkheperu   Dynasty XIII

Horus Name:

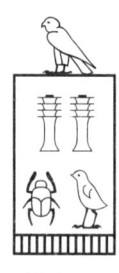

ḏd-ḫprw
Djedkheperu

Nomen: Unknown

Prenomen: *...k₃-rʿ* / ...kare

Two Ladies: *nbty ḏd-msw*

Golden Falcon:

bik (nbw) ꜥꜣ

Length of Reign:	Unknown		
Tomb:	Unknown		
Mummy:	Unknown		

Consorts:	Unknown	**Variant Names:**	Djedkheperew [...kare]
Manetho:	Unknown		
King Lists:	None		

The seventeenth ruler of Dynasty XIII, Djedkheperu was probably the son of the pharaoh Awibre Hor and brother and successor to the pharaoh Khabau. Aside from 10 seal-impressions found at Uronarti and one from Mirgissa (both Egyptian-garrisoned forts at the Second Cataract in Nubia) the only other known attestation for Djedkheperu comes from the tomb of the Dynasty I king Djer at Abydos. By Dynasty XIII, Djer's tomb had become identified as the tomb of Osiris, the god of the dead. Djedkheperu dedicated a large basalt sculpture showing Osiris lying on a bier. (The much-damaged royal titulary carved into the work was once identified as belonging to the Dynasty XIII king Khendjer, but recent study has shown the names as having belonged to Djedkheperu.)

References:

Dunham 1967 pp. 40: 28-11-319, 57: 29-1-314, 58: 30-2-19, 64: 4A, 160: 31-12-92

Ikram and Dodson 1998 p. 120

Ryholt 1997a pp. 70, 73 #17, 217 and notes 746 and 747, 218 and table 51, 219 table 52, 321-322 and table 93, 340 File 13/17, 408 #17

Djedkherure   Dynasty XIV

Horus Name: Unknown

Nomen: Unknown

Prenomen:

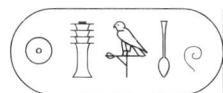

ḏd-ḫrw-rꜥ
Djedkherure

Two Ladies: Unknown

Golden Falcon: Unknown

Djed...re

Length of Reign:	Unknown
Tomb:	Unknown
Mummy:	Unknown

Consorts:	Unknown	**Variant Names:**	None
Manetho:	Not given		
King Lists:	T: (G 8.17; R 9.17; vB 8.17)		

Possibly the twenty-third king of Dynasty XIV, Djedkherure is one of a group of kings known only from the Turin Canon. The papyrus' fragmentary state allows for varying interpretations as to the positioning of some of the kings of this dynasty. However, Djedkherure's place seems secure.

References:
Gardiner 1959 pl. III, Col. VIII #17
Gardiner 1961 p. 441 #8.17
Ryholt 1997a pp. 95 Col. 9.17, 98 #23, 198 table 37 and note 9/16-17, 379 File 9/17, 409 #23

von Beckerath 1999 pp. 110 #18, 111 #18

Djed...re   Dynasty XIV

Horus Name: Unknown   **Nomen:** Unknown

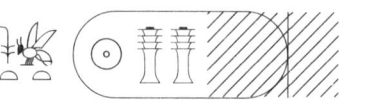

Prenomen:

ḏd-...re
Djed...re

Two Ladies: Unknown

Golden Falcon: Unknown

Length of Reign:	Unknown
Tomb:	Unknown
Mummy:	Unknown

Consorts:	Unknown	**Variant Names:**	None
Manetho:	Not given		
King Lists:	T: (G 9.9; R 10.9; vB 9.11)		

...djefare

Perhaps the forty-fifth king of Dynasty XIV, Djed...re is one of a group of kings known only from the Turin Canon. The papyrus' fragmentary state allows for varying interpretations as to the positioning of some of the kings of this dynasty. However, Djed...re's place seems secure.

References:
Gardiner 1959 pl. III, Col. IX #9
Gardiner 1961 pp. 442 #9,
Ryholt 1997a pp. 95 Col. 10.9, 98 #45, 380 File 14/45, 40 #45

von Beckerath 1999 pp. 112 #e, 113 #e

...djefare   Dynasty XIV

Horus Name: Unknown

Nomen: Unknown

Prenomen:

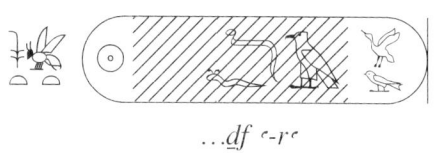

...*ḏf ꜥ-rꜥ*
...djefare

Two Ladies: Unknown

Golden Falcon: Unknown

Length of Reign:	Unknown
Tomb:	Unknown
Mummy:	Unknown

Consorts:	Unknown	**Variant Names:**	None
Manetho:	Not given		
King Lists:	T: (G 8.10; R 9.10, vB 8.10)		

Possibly the fifteenth king of Dynasty XIV, ...djefare is one of a group of kings known only from the Turin Canon. The papyrus' fragmentary state allows for varying interpretations as to the positioning of some of the kings of this dynasty. However, ...djefare's place seems secure.

Djehuty

References:

Gardiner 1959 pl. III, Col. VIII #10
Gardiner 1961 p. 441 #10
Ryholt 1997a pp. 95 Col. 9.10, 98 #15, 198 table 37, 379 File 14/15, 409 #15

von Beckerath 1999 pp. 108 #11, 109 #11

Djehuty   Dynasty XVI

Horus Name:

iṯ-m-nḫt

Nomen:

ḏḥwty
Djehuty

Prenomen:

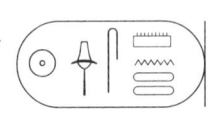

sḫm-rˁ s.mn-tȝwy
Sekhemre-sementowy

Two Ladies:

(nbty)...ḏḥwty (?)

Golden Falcon:

bik nbw wsr-ḫˁw

Length of Reign:	3 years
Tomb:	Unknown; probably at Dra Abu el-Naga
Mummy:	Unknown

Consorts:	Mentuhotep	Dhuti
Manetho:	Not given	Tahuti
		Tehuti
King Lists:	K: (1); T: (G 11.1; R 11.1)	Thuty
Variant Names:	Dhout	

The second pharaoh of Dynasty XVI, Djehuty's predecessor is unknown, the Turin Canon being much damaged at this point. Although some scholars would place this king in Dynasty XIII and others in Dynasty XVII, K.S.B. Ryholt has presented a strong case for Djehuty's inclusion in Dynasty XVI.

Almost no attestations for Djehuty have come to light. The few we have are from a limited area of Upper Egypt, namely from Ballas, some 45 km. north of Luxor, to Edfu, about 100 km. to the south, which seems to have been about the limit of Dynasty XVI's sphere of influence. Petrie discovered a single block at Ballas inscribed with the king's nomen and prenomen; a canopic chest inscribed with funerary formulae, the king's cartouche and an inscription telling us that the chest was given to the King's Great Wife, Mentuhotep, in whose tomb at Dra Abu el-Naga the chest was discovered; and an inscribed and painted block, found at Edfu.

It has been proposed that Djehuty's prenomen (as well as those of several other kings of this period) reflect the political and military situation at the time. Certainly Dynasty XVI was a time of unrest, due to the Hyksos rulers whose Dynasty XV was contemporary and hostile. Djehuty's prenomen $sḥm-rʿ-s.mn-tꜣwy$, "the Might of Re which (re-)establishes the Two Lands," might well have been wishful thinking.

The Turin Canon gives a reign of three years. No dated objects for this reign have been found.

References:

Dodson 1994b pp. 37-40, 43-46, 49, 148-149, pl. XI
Dodson and Hilton 2004 pp. 116, 117, 120
Gardiner 1959 pl. IV, Col. XI #1
Gardiner 1961 p. 442
Ikram and Dodson 1998 p. 254
Lilyquist 1995 pp. 59-61, 118 fig. 147
Petrie 1896a p. 8, pl. XLIII #4
Ryholt 1997a pp. 152, 153 fig. 14 #1, 158, table 24, 160, 259, 260. table 74, 305, 388 File 16/2, 410 table 97 #2
von Beckerath 1999 pp. 126 #4, 127 #4
von Falck 1985 pp. 15-23
Winlock 1924 pp. 269-271

Djer　　　　　　　　　　　　　　　　　　　　　　　　　　　Dynasty I

Horus Name:

ḏr
Djer

Nomen: *itti*
Iteti

Two Ladies: Unknown

Golden Falcon:
(bik)-nbw ni

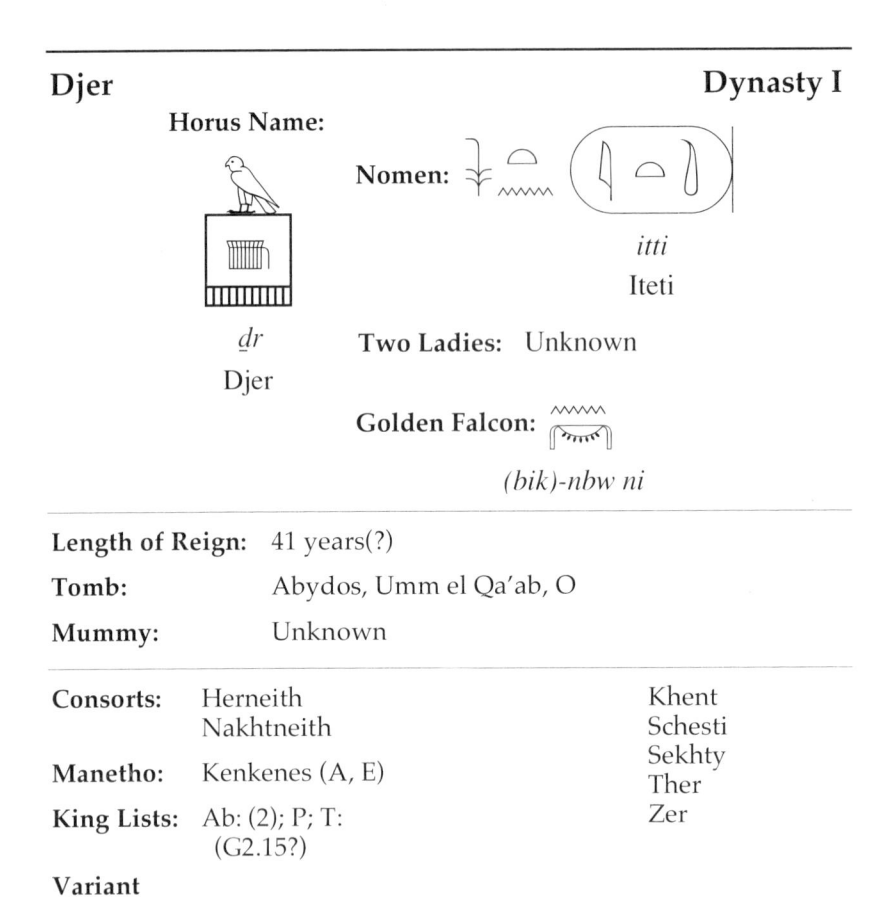

Length of Reign:	41 years(?)
Tomb:	Abydos, Umm el Qa'ab, O
Mummy:	Unknown

Consorts:	Herneith Nakhtneith	Khent Schesti Sekhty Ther Zer
Manetho:	Kenkenes (A, E)	
King Lists:	Ab: (2); P; T: (G2.15?)	
Variant Names:	Jer	

　　The third king of Dynasty I, Djer was the son of a lady named Khenthap and, probably, king Aha. Although we do not know how long Djer reigned, the Palermo Stone gives nine years and a portion of a tenth to a king who is usually given as Djer. Cairo Fragment Number One of the Palermo Stone gives an additional nine years with Djer's Horus, nomen and Golden Falcon names given, as well as the name of Djer's mother, Khenthap. It has been estimated that the stone originally listed about fifty years. Manetho gives a reign of 31 or 39 years, depending on the source. In any event, Djer's reign was undoubtedly a long one, as he celebrated at least one Sed Festival in or around his thirtieth year of rule. A seal impression from Djer's tomb at Abydos gives the earliest example of a king wearing both the Heb-sed robe and the crowns of Upper and Lower Egypt.

　　Judging from funerary goods found in Djer's tomb at Abydos and from mastaba tombs 2185 and 3471 at Saqqara, which are dated to his time, the reign must have been a time of prosperity. A magnificent collection of copper tools, vessels and weapons found in

Mastaba 3471 points to contact with Sinai. An entry on the main Cairo fragment of the Palermo Stone records an expedition to a land called Setjet (*stt*), a designation for western Asia in later times, but which probably refers to Sinai during this earlier period. This possibility is supported by the turquoise jewelry found in Djer's tomb, turquoise being one of the main items mined in the Sinai area. Expeditions to Palestine are also very likely. Whether these expeditions were of a warlike or peaceful nature is not known, but a great many items of Palestinian origin, particularly wine and oil, are attested to by pottery jugs and vases found in Djer's tomb.

Djer's foreign relations include what appears to be some sort of expedition against the Libyans, if an inscribed alabaster palette found at Saqqara is to be believed: it shows the king in the traditional pose of bashing in the skull of an enemy, and that enemy is wearing the outfit of a Libyan chieftain. For many years, an expedition into Nubia, reaching as far as Gebel Suleiman near the Second Cataract, was believed to have been conducted during Djer's reign. Evidence for this was an inscription thought to bear the king's name. However, it has been proven that the serekh is uninscribed and the accompanying petroglyphs are to be dated to the Predynastic Period.

Djer's Abydos tomb was much larger than those of either of his two predecessors. It was surrounded, according to Petrie's count, by some 326 (Emery gives 338) subsidiary burials of various retainers, artists and, chiefly, women, all of whom had been sacrificed in order to serve their king in the next world. A further 269 burials were discovered at the king's funerary enclosure, called "The Companion of the Gods," which was located about a mile's distance from the tomb. In the king's burial chamber, covered in bandages and hidden in a hole in the ruined wall, Petrie discovered a human arm wearing four of the most beautiful bracelets ever found in Egypt. Petrie believed the arm, undoubtedly because of the jewelry, to be that of a queen; but it might just as easily have been Djer's. The tomb had been gutted by fire, possibly as early as Dynasty II.

During the Middle Kingdom, Djer's tomb was thought to have been that of the god Osiris; evidently, the hieroglyph for Djer's Horus name ▭ (*dr*) was mistaken for the sign ▭ (*hnt*), "Khent," which was taken to stand for the local god Khentamentiu. This deity, whose name translates as "The First of the Westerners," "Westerners" being a euphemism for the dead, is well attested in the Early Dynastic Period; for example, the name of Djer's mother is Khenthap. There was a temple dedicated to Khentamentiu at Abydos at least as early as the Old Kingdom, and during that time the god began to be associated with Osiris, the god of the dead. Abydos became the cult center for Osiris, and an image of the god on a funerary bier was placed in Djer's tomb sometime during the Middle Kingdom, probably by the Dynasty XIII king Djedkheperu.

Djet

References:

Adams 1990 p. 4 and illustration 5 *
Adams and Cialowicz 1997 pp. 18, 45, 62
D. Arnold 1998 p. 34
Clagett 1989 pp. 68-71 and notes
Dodson 1997-98 pp. 37-47
Dodson and Hilton 2004 pp. 44-45, 46, 48
Edwards 1971 pp. 18-19
Emery 1949 vol. I pp. 13-70, pl. 1-13
Emery 1961 pp. 56-63
Gardiner 1959 pl. I, Col. II #12
Gardiner 1961 pp. 401, 430
Kemp 1966 pp. 13, 15, pl. VIII
Kemp 1967 pp. 25-26
Legge 1906 p. 16
O'Connor 1989 pp. 61-82
Petrie 1901a pp. 8, 14, 16-17, Pl. I, V-VI, 30, pl. XV, Pl. LVIII and LX
Petrie 1925a pp. 2, 4
Quibell 1923 pp. 15-17: pl. V-X
Quirke 1992 pp. 52-54
Ryholt 1997a p. 217
Spencer 1993 p. 81 Illustration 59
Troy 1986 pp. 94, 106, 152 # 1.5 and 1.6
Uphill 1984
Verbrugghe and Wickersham 1996 pp. 131, 187
von Beckerath 1999 pp. 38 #3, 39 #3
Waddell 1940 pp. 29, 31
T. Wilkinson 1999 pp. 71-73
T. Wilkinson 2000 pp. 79, 92-103, 186-193
Williams 1987 pp. 282-284

* Illustrations 5 and 6 have been accidentally reversed in this article so that Djer's label is 5 but the legend for it is under 6.

Djet   Dynasty I

Horus Name:

dt
Djet

Nomen:

itȝ
Ita

Two Ladies:

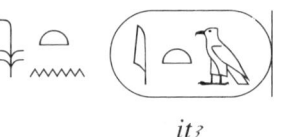

nbty itrti

Golden Falcon: Unknown

wȝd
Wadji

Length of Reign:	10-15 years(?)
Tomb:	Abydos, Umm el Qa'ab, Z
Mummy:	Unknown

Djet

Consorts:	Merneith(?)	Djaiti
Manetho:	Ouenephis (A)	Edjo
	Vavenephis (E)	"Snake"
		Uadji
King Lists:	Ab: (3); T:	Wadji
	(G2.15?)	Zet
Variant Names:	Djait	

The fourth king of Dynasty I, Djet was in all likelihood the son of king Djer and one of his queens, probably Herneith. Although Manetho gives Djet a reign of either 23 or 42 years, depending on the source, archaeological evidence consisting primarily of seals from Abydos points to a fairly short rule. Short or not, Djet's reign seems to have been as prosperous as that of his predecessors. Foreign relationships would appear to have continued, as a sealing of Djet's has been found at En Besor in Southern Palestine. Lapis lazuli found in Djet's tomb at Abydos as well as in a large mastaba tomb at Giza (Mastaba V), dating to Djet's time, certainly point to foreign trade, with lapis coming from as far away as the Pakistani-Iranian border. A serekh bearing Djet's name has been found in the Wadi Abbad, an important trade route from the Nile to the Red Sea. A copper adze and axe found in the subsidiary graves around Djet's tomb point to trade with, and possible expeditions to, Sinai. These weapons are good examples of the metal working of the time. Pottery of Palestinian origin has been found in tombs dated to Djet's reign at Tarkhan, Saqqara and Abydos, providing further evidence of foreign connections.

By Petrie's count, Djet's tomb at Abydos was surrounded by the graves of 174 retainers, and his funerary enclosure, about a mile away from the tomb, was surrounded by a further 154 graves (Emery gives the number as 161). As with all the tombs of Dynasty I, Djet's had been gutted by fire. Still, Petrie found a great many vases and other objects there.

A series of 12 "boat graves" has been discovered near Djet's funerary enclosure and it is very likely that they belong to this king. However, they still have not been excavated, and until they are the dating is only tentative.

Besides Mastaba V at Giza, which is definitely dated to Djet's reign and may have been a tomb built for his queen or mother, a mastaba tomb at Saqqara, number 3504, is also associated with this king. At Tarkhan, Petrie's discoveries included two or possibly three large mastabas (Numbers 1060, 2038, and 2050), probably belonging to government officials.

As may be seen from the list of variant spellings and the alternate name shown above, there is some question concerning the

Djoser

spelling of Djet's Horus Name. "Djet" is used in this encyclopedia because it is the more common rendering. However, an inscription cut into the rocks at Shatt el-Rigal, about 20 miles south of Edfu, shows a serekh with Djet's name given as W_3d, "Wadji." If the inscription is contemporary, it probably represents the way the name was pronounced. Another interesting thing about the Shatt el-Rigal carving is that the falcon perched above the serekh wears the double crown that, again if the carving were contemporary, would be the earliest example of the two crowns combined.

References:

Dodson and Hilton 2004 pp. 44-45, 46, 48
Emery 1949-58 vol. II pp. 5-127, pl. I-XXXVII
Emery 1961 pp. 69-73, figs. 83, 100, 146, pl. 2B, 8, 9,
Gardiner 1958 pp. 38-39
Gardiner 1959 pl. I, Col. II #15(?)
Gardiner 1961 pp. 401, 430
Kemp 1966 pp. 13, 15, pl. VIII
Legrain 1903b p. 221 and fig. 7
O'Connor 1989 pp. 57 and notes 14 and 15, 58-59, 61, 62, 78-81, fig. 1, fig. 19
O'Connor 1991 pp. 7, 10
Petrie 1900 pp. 4-6, 8-10, 16, 38, Pl. III, IV, X-XI, XIII, XVIII-XIX, XXXIII- XXXIV, LIX, LXI-LXIV
Petrie 1901a p. 38, pl. XXXVII-XXXVIII
Petrie 1907 pp. 3-6, pl. II-VI
Petrie 1913 pp. 13-18, pl. XV-XIX
Petrie 1914 pp. 3-9, pl. III 35, IV, XV, XVIII, XLVII
Petrie 1925a pp. 2-5, pl. III #s 7- 8, pl. IV #s1-4, V #s 5-7
Quibell 1934 p. 71
Schulman 1983 pp. 250-251
Uphill 1984
Verbrugghe and Wickersham 1996 pp. 113, 117, 132, 188
von Beckerath 1999 pp. 38 #4, 39 #4
Waddell 1940 pp. 29, 31
T. Wilkinson 1999 pp. 73-74, 164-165,
T. Wilkinson 2000 p. 73, 90, 107, 236, 256

Djoser   Dynasty III

Horus Name:

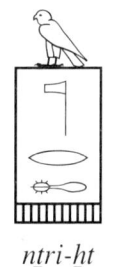

ntri-ht
Netjerikhet

Nomen:

dsr
Djoser

dsr s3
Djosersa

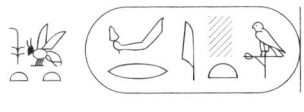

Djoser

dsr it(?)
Djoserit(?)

Two Ladies:

nbty ntri-ht

Golden Falcon:

nbw rˁ(?)

Length of Reign:	19-20 years	
Tomb:	Step Pyramid at Saqqara	
Mummy:	Part only. Qasr el-Aini. A1.490	
Consorts:	Hotephernebti	Netcherikhe
Manetho:	Sesorthos (E)	Neterikhet
		Nether-er-Inhet
	Sosorthus (E)	Nether-er-Khet
	Tosorthros (A)	Zeser
		Zoser
King Lists:	Ab: (16); P; S: (12); T: (G 3.5)	
Variant Names:	Doser	

The first pharaoh of Dynasty III, Djoser was the son of king Khasekhemwy, the last pharaoh of Dynasty II, and Queen Nimaathap, as attested to by the more than 100 seal-impressions bearing Djoser's name found in the queen's huge mastaba tomb at Beit Khallaf and the literally dozens of similar sealings from Khasekhemwy's tomb at Abydos.

It should be noted that the king's Horus name, Netjerikhet, was the name used on all contemporary attestations. However, king lists from later times give the name Djoser, or a variant of that name. Also, tourists from later dynasties left graffiti praising "Djoser's" monument. The Horus name and nomen of Djoser are found together in only one case, a stele on Sehel Island, just south of Aswan. The stele's text is, as Petrie called it, "a pious forgery,"

Djoser

having been composed in Ptolemaic times but claiming to have come from Dynasty III.

Both the Turin Canon and Manetho place Djoser as second pharaoh of Dynasty III, giving the pharaoh Nebka as the first. However, archaeological evidence certainly points to Djoser as first king of the dynasty. In particular, Djoser's serekh is found in Khasekhemwy's tomb: since it was very important in pharaonic tradition that the new king bury his predecessor, this is strong evidence that Djoser immediately succeeded Khasekhemwy. Further, the Saqqara king list also places Djoser as the direct successor to Khasekhemwy.

Why a dynastic change came about with Djoser's accession is not known. However, in the Turin Canon, Djoser's name is recorded in red ink, thus signifying an important change or event; that coupled with the archaeological evidence would tend to lock Djoser in place.

Djoser, as Netjerikhet, seems to be the earliest royal figure to have been carved at the turquoise mines at Maghara in Sinai. He is shown bashing in the head of an enemy, a "wretched sand-dweller." By Djoser's time, the picture of a pharaoh smiting his enemy had become something of a stereotypical representation. It is very doubtful that the king would have accompanied the expedition, although undoubtedly heads were bashed; these early expeditions were certainly military actions to one degree or another.

Djoser chose not to build his tomb in the royal cemetery at Abydos. Instead, he decided upon a site on the west side of the Nile, at the border of Upper Egypt and Lower Egypt, just above his capital city, Inebu-hedj (White Walls), usually referred to by its Greek name, Memphis. As architect he picked his vizier Imhotep, the Leonardo da Vinci of his day, the "Superintendent of All the King's Works," "High Priest of Heliopolis," builder, sculptor and "maker of stone vases," and physician. So famous was Imhotep that in later times he was deified and the Greeks identified him with their god of medicine, Aesculapius.

Imhotep's original design was for a large, square, stone mastaba. But the mastaba was elongated, and changed into a stepped structure, first four steps and finally six. The pyramid measured 121 x 109 m. on the sides and rose to a height of 62 m. Access to the burial and other underground chambers was gained from a shaft sunk in the temple floor. The burial chamber lay at the bottom of a 28 m. deep shaft. Entrance to the chamber was through the ceiling, the entrance-hole being sealed off by a massive stone plug. Once the body had been placed in the chamber, the plug was lowered into place and the shaft was filled with stone and covered by the temple's flooring blocks. Aside from the burial chamber, the pyramid's subterranean area is honeycombed with galleries, magazines, stairs and passages. In an eastern chamber were a series of panels, decorated with turquoise-colored tiles and bands of limestone that bore reliefs of Djoser in either the red or white crown. More than

40,000 stone vessels (plates, cups and such), many inscribed with the names of former rulers, were discovered in several shafts. There were also a series of shafts for burial of members of the royal family.

The pyramid was surrounded by a vast complex covering some 37 acres. The whole area was surrounded by a wall 10.5 m. tall and a total of 1,645 m. long. "Dummy" buildings were located inside this enclosure, including the Pavilions of the North and South and the Sed Chapels. Also, there is the "Southern Tomb" and its temple. This complex holds an almost exact replica of the tomb beneath the pyramid, down to the turquoise panels. We don't know who was supposed to occupy the burial chamber, if anyone. It has been considered a tomb for Djoser's ka, a substitute representing a tomb in the royal cemetery at Abydos, a representation of a Lower Egyptian tomb from Buto, or a tomb for the king's placenta. It has also been considered a substitute tomb used during the Sed Festival, and certainly that festival of renewal is represented: the reliefs of Djoser found in the galleries of the step pyramid and the Southern Tomb appear to show the king performing a ritual walk or run that was part of the renewal ceremony.

While clearing some of the burial chamber of the step pyramid in 1926, the Egyptologist B. Gunn found parts of a right hip and spine of a mummified body, and during further clearance of the chamber in 1934 Quibell and Lauer found parts of a chest, upper arm and a left foot (still in its wrapping and molded in plaster). All of the remains were skeletal with some small portions of skin adhering. Unfortunately, recent carbon dating places the remains some 2,000 years later than Djoser's time, somewhere between 762 BC to 251 BC. Also, the age range found for the remains is from 19 to fifty-something, indicating that two bodies had been commingled.

Aside from his remarkable pyramid and mortuary complex at Saqqara and the sealings from Abydos and Beit Khallif, Djoser is little attested in Egypt. A few seals have come from Elephantine, a few more have been found in private tombs at Saqqara, and fragments of relief come from a shrine built by Djoser at Heliopolis. The exact purpose of the shrine is not known; it might have had connections to the Sed Festival, or it might have been built to honor the Heliopolitan Ennead.

The Turin Canon gives Djoser a reign of 19 years, while Manetho gives a decade longer. Cairo Fragment 1 of the Palermo Stone appears to record a year 20.

References:

Brier 1994 pp. 242-243
Dodson 1998 pp. 28-33, 38, 39
Dodson 2003 pp. 40-43
Dodson and Hilton 2004 pp. 44, 45, 46, 47, 48
Firth and Quibell 1935
Gardiner 1959 pl. II, Col. III #5
Gardiner 1961 pp. 72-76, 433
Gardiner and Peet 1952 pl. I #2
Gardiner and Peet 1955 pp. 14, 17, 24, 26, 27, 52, 53-54
Garstang 1903 pp. 4, 8-11, 19, VI-X, XXVI
Giddy 1996 p. 30
Giddy 1997 p. 29
Goedicke 2000 pp. 399-404, 409-411

Double Falcon

Ikram and Dodson 1998 pp. 8, 22, 24, ill. 14, 109, 245, 252, 315, 317, 320, pl. IV
Kahl et al. 1995 pp. 7-127
Lacau and Lauer 1959, 1961, 1965
Lauer 1936-39
Lauer 1976 pp. 11, 12, 90-136, pl. VII, X-XII, XVII
Lehner 1997 pp. 84-93
Newberry 1909 pl. XXIII
Petrie 1901a pl. XXIV #211
W. Smith 1981 pp. 53-69
Strouhal et al. 1998 pp. 1103-1107
Verbrugghe and Wickersham 1996 pp. 134, 189
Verner 1997 pp. 45, 76, 105-140, 461
von Beckerath 1999 pp. 48 #2, 49 #2
Waddell 1940 pp. 43, 45
T. Wilkinson 1999 pp. 95-98

Double Falcon	Dynasty 00

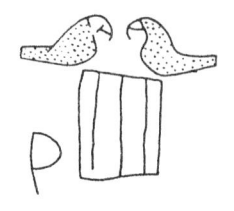

Double Falcon

Length of Reign:	Unknown
Tomb:	Unknown
Mummy:	Unknown

Consorts:	Unknown	**Variant Names:**	None
Manetho:	Not given		
King Lists:	None		

This early ruler's serekh has been found incised on pottery at Tell Ibrahim Awad, in the east-central Delta; el-Beda, in the extreme eastern Delta; and in the cemetery at Tura, on the east side of the Nile opposite Zawiyet el-Aryan. To date, no artifacts of this king have been found outside Lower Egypt and it is probably safe to assume that his sphere of influence was limited to that area.

However, trade with Upper Egypt undoubtedly occurred; note that el-Beda is located on the trade route to Sinai and Syria-Palestine, which makes cultural exchange more than likely.

The appellation "Double Falcon" is used because the reading of the hieroglyphs is uncertain.

References:
Cledat 1914 pp. 119-121, pl.XIII
Junker 1912 fig. 57.5
Kaiser 1964 fig. 7 a-d
Rothenberg 1979 p. 184
van den Brink 1992 fig. 8.1 p. 147
van den Brink 1996 table 1.5-6, fig. 1 IIa.5, table 5
Weill 1961 pp. 293-294

Efni   Dynasty XIII

Horus Name: Unknown

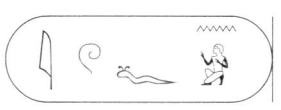

Nomen: *iw.f-n.i* / Efni

Prenomen: Unknown

Two Ladies: Unknown

Golden Falcon: Unknown

Length of Reign:	Unknown
Tomb:	Unknown
Mummy:	Unknown

Consorts:	Unknown	**Variant Names:**	Afnai Jewefni
Manetho:	Not given		
King Lists:	T: (G 6.9; R 7.9; vB 6.9)		

Probably the seventh king of Dynasty XIII, Efni is one of a group of kings known only from the Turin Canon. Although the papyrus' fragmentary state allows for varying interpretations as to the positioning of some of this dynasty's kings, Efni's place is secure.

References:

Gardiner 1959 pl. III, Col. VI #9
Gardiner 1961 p. 440 #6.9
Ryholt 1997a pp. 71 Col. 7.9, 73 #7, 197 #7, 214 table 48 and note 738, 215 table 49, 338 File 13/7, 408 table 94 #7
von Beckerath 1999 pp. 90 #6, 91 #6

H...

H...   Dynasty IX/X

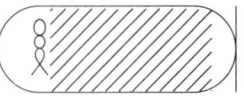

Horus Name: Unknown   **Nomen:**

ẖ...
H...

Prenomen: Unknown

Two Ladies: Unknown

Golden Falcon: Unknown

Length of Reign:	Unknown
Tomb:	Unknown
Mummy:	Unknown

Consorts:	Unknown	**Variant Names:**	None
Manetho:	Not given		
King Lists:	T: (4.26)		

    H... is one of the pharaohs who controlled an unknown amount of territory around Herakleopolis in Middle Egypt during the First Intermediate Period (see "Herakleopolitans" in Glossary). Attestations for the kings whose names are known are few; most are known only from the Turin Canon. Such is the case with H.... Based on his position in the Canon, he was the successor of the likewise ill-attested Shed...y. What familial relationship H... may have had with his predecessor is unknown.

References:
Gardiner 1959 pl. IV, Col. IV #26
von Beckerath 1999 pp. 72 #9, 73 #9

Hapu... (II)   Dynasty XIV

Horus Name: Unknown   **Nomen:**

ḥpw...[?]
Hapu...

Prenomen: (cartouche)

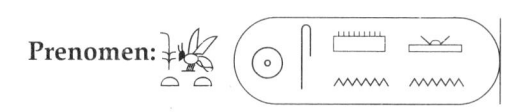

s.mn-n-rʿ
Semenenre

Two Ladies: Unknown
Golden Falcon: Unknown

Length of Reign:	Unknown
Tomb:	Unknown
Mummy:	Unknown

Consorts:	Unknown	**Variant Names:**	Hepu…
Manetho:	Not given		
King Lists:	T: (G 8.26; R 9.26; vB 8.26)		

Possibly the thirty-second king of Dynasty XIV, Hapu (II) is one of a group of kings known only from the Turin Canon. The fragile state of the papyrus allows for varying interpretations as to the position of the king within Dynasty XIV (see "Turin Canon" in Glossary). A recent study indicates that two previously separated fragments should be joined together, eliminating Semenenre as a separate ruler and making the name the prenomen of Hapu.

The roman numeral after this king's name is to differentiate between this king and another of the same name listed in the Turin Canon for this dynasty (see Appendix).

References:
Gardiner 1959 pl. III, Col. IX #28
Ryholt 1997a pp. 95 Col. 9.26, 98 #32, 380 File 14/32

von Beckerath 1999 pp. 110 #27, 111 #27

Hat-Hor   Dynasty 00

ḥꜣt-ḥrw
Hat-Hor

103

Hatshepsut

Length of Reign:	Unknown
Tomb:	Unknown
Mummy:	Unknown

Consorts:	Unknown	**Variant Names:**	Hati
Manetho:	Not given		
King Lists:	None		

Petrie's winter 1912-13 excavations at Tarkhan, south of modern Cairo on the western side of the Nile, yielded a pottery jar which bore a serekh with a hieroglyph. Petrie saw this as an archaic ideogram representing the forepart of a lion (Gardiner sign list Section F.4) which he translated as "Hati" or "Chief/Leader." The serekh, like other examples of this period, was crudely incised before the pottery was fired. As with other early serekhs, the Tarkhan example is not surmounted by the Horus falcon, but is nonetheless translated as "Hat-Hor." However, as with several other early serekhs, some scholars see this example as a crude writing of the name "Narmer."

References:

Fischer 1963a p. 44, fig. 2
Petrie 1914 p. 10, pl. VI. 2, pl. XX.1, pl. XXX. 74b, pl. XL. 1702

van den Brink 1996 p. 144, table 1.9, fig. 2 IIb.9

Hatshepsut   Dynasty XVIII

Horus Name:

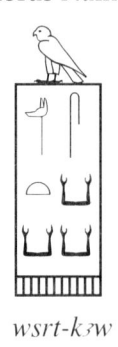

wsrt-k3w

Nomen:

h3t-špswt
Hatshepsut

Prenomen:

m3't-k3-r'
Maatkare

104

Hatshepsut

Two Ladies:

nbty wȝḏt-rnpwt

Golden Falcon:

bik-nbw nṯrt-ḥʿw

Length of Reign:	22 years, 6 months, 10 days
Tomb:	Valley of the Kings: KV20
Mummy:	Unknown

Consorts:	None	**Variant Names:**	Amesse
Manetho:	Amenses (E)		Hashepsowe
	Amensis (A)		Hatasu
	Amersis (A)		Hatchepsut
	Amessis (J)		Makare
King Lists:	None		Makere

The fifth pharaoh of Dynasty XVIII, Hatshepsut was the daughter of Thutmose I and his queen, Ahmose. She was married to her half-brother, Thutmose II, probably before either of them reached their majority. The marriage produced one daughter, Neferure, who would later be married to her half-brother, the future pharaoh Thutmose III. As queen to Thutmose II, Hatshepsut bore the titles King's Daughter, King's Sister, and King's Great Wife. She also held the title God's Wife of Amen (as had her mother and grandmother), and as such she was not only the wife of the king of Egypt, but also the consort of Amen, king of the gods.

Thutmose II died at about age thirty, leaving as heir to the throne a young son, perhaps not more than three or four years old. This son, named Thutmose after his father and grandfather (and thus known to us as Thutmose III) was the child of a minor wife or harem girl named Iset (Isis), and so to bolster his right to the throne, he may have been married to his half-sister Neferure. Hatshepsut filled the role of regent. However, that status changed dramatically a few years into the young king's reign (sometime between his regnal years two and seven; scholarly opinions are divided), when Hatshepsut declared herself pharaoh and coregent and backdated her reign to the accession of Thutmose III. The reason for her assumption of the throne is unknown, although countless pages of theories, as well as educated and uneducated guesses, have been written on the subject.

Hatshepsut

Certainly the love of power reared its head. Hatshepsut had been a powerful woman for many years; a number of scholars consider her to have been the true ruler of Egypt during the reign of Thutmose II. Evidently she thought so. She created a fictional coregency with her father, Thutmose I, and more or less ignored her marriage to Thutmose II (with whom she also claimed a coregency). The royal architect Ineni, who died before Hatshepsut declared herself pharaoh, had this to say about her regency: "Egypt was made to labor with bowed head for her, the excellent seed of the god, which came forth from him...the mistress of command, whose plans are excellent, who satisfies the Two Regions when she speaks."

Hatshepsut appears to have stepped rather easily to the throne, there probably being no real opposition. Her credentials were first-rate: the daughter of a pharaoh, the wife of a pharaoh, and the mother-in-law, aunt and recognized regent of a third pharaoh. Also, she was God's Wife of Amen, a title and position of great religious and political importance, and a virtual guarantee of support from the state god's priesthood, wealth, and power. The twelve-year-old Thutmose III was in no position to do other than accept Hatshepsut. Surprisingly, the partnership was quite successful, and although Hatshepsut was always the senior partner, as Thutmose grew into adulthood a certain division of power seems to have occurred. Hatshepsut appears to have been concerned with the actual running of the country, an extensive building program, and diplomatic relationships, while Thutmose was trained in the military and became a full-fledged commander. Had there been any animosity between the two rulers, it is difficult to believe that Hatshepsut would have allowed Thutmose to have had access to, let alone eventual command of, the army.

During her gradual assumption of the throne, Hatshepsut's image as represented on her various monuments and in texts began to change. As a queen under Thutmose II, during her regency with Thutmose III, and for an unknown time after claiming the throne, Hatshepsut was represented as a female, dressed in the proper queenly regalia. However, over a period of time the queenly garb and accoutrements gave way to those of a pharaoh, with first the nemes headdress, then the kilt; not long thereafter, Hatshepsut's breasts almost disappear from statuary and all other representations; finally there is the false beard. As pointed out by Forbes, it is doubtful if she went around naked to the waist, however "she doubtless would have donned whichever of Egypt's several crowns or headgear was appropriate to the particular event." After the assumption of pharaonic power, references to her in texts appear in either gender, often using both in the same inscription.

The building program undertaken by Hatshepsut was far and away the most extensive since Dynasty XII, some three hundred years earlier. Most of the construction was in the Theban area, especially at the temple of Amen at Karnak, where among other things, she installed a row of sphinxes (much extended during later reigns) and the Eighth Pylon (which was usurped by Amenhotep II). A beautiful little temple built of red quartzite, inscribed with the names and figures of both Hatshepsut and Thutmose III, was later demolished and the stone blocks reused as filler for other monuments. Two pair of obelisks were added, one of which still stands, measuring 29.5 m. tall. Hatshepsut also constructed a series of shrines along the processional way between the temples of Karnak and Luxor.

Across the Nile from Luxor and Karnak, Hatshepsut erected a small temple on the grounds of what would become the temple/palace of Ramesses III, where it stands today. Two tombs were built, one for her as queen (never completed) and one as king, the first being abandoned when she assumed the red and white crowns. At Deir el-Bahri, Hatshepsut's beautiful funerary temple, Djeser-Djeseru ("Holy of Holies"), was built next to the funerary temple of Dynasty XI ruler Montuhotep II. The three-tiered monument is arguably the most beautiful ancient structure to have survived. This remarkable temple continued to function in one form or another, finally ending up as a Coptic monastery until it was abandoned in the eighth century AD. Other attestations for Hatshepsut come from the island of Elephantine at Aswan, where a great many decorated blocks have been found, probably from a chapel. An inscribed lintel comes from El Kab. In Middle Egypt, in a desert area south of Beni Hassan, Hatshepsut built a temple to the lion-headed goddess Pakhet, known today as the Speos Artemidos. The temple bears inscriptions in which she claims to have vanquished the Hyksos—never mind that four kings and 75 years stood between!

Outside Egypt, the turquoise mines of Sinai were worked under Hatshepsut and Thutmose III as evidenced by a rock carving from Wadi Maghara. Dated to the year 16 of the joint rule, the carving shows the two pharaohs presenting wine and bread to the god Soped, Lord of the East, and Hathor, Lady of the Turquoise. From the mine at Serabit el-Khadim comes a variety of attestations, including remains of a hall added to the Hathor temple and dedicated to Soped by Hatshepsut and Thutmose, inscribed blocks, and stelae of the two kings dated to years 11 and 20.

The wealth of Nubia had been exploited since early in Dynasty XVIII, and Hatshepsut followed suit by leading a military expedition against the Kushites early in the joint rule (see below). She and Thutmose III were responsible for refurbishment of the joint temple of the Nubian god Dedwen and Dynasty XII pharaoh Senwosret III at Semna. At Buhen, Hatshepsut was responsible for the construction of a temple to Horus of Buhen. Other attestations to Hatshepsut's presence in Nubia come from Sai, Faras and Quban.

Although Hatshepsut referred to her reign as "years of peace," and earlier Egyptologists generally concurred, it seems that at least six military expeditions were conducted during her rule, two in Syria-Palestine and four in Nubia. Evidence is slight for the Asiatic

Hatshepsut

campaigns, but the petty city-states were constantly causing trouble, and it was perhaps more of a policing matter than a real campaign. It seems certain that Thutmose III commanded the second of the expeditions and that the important city of Gaza was captured. Hatshepsut's Nubian campaign is better attested. Fragments of inscriptions from her mortuary temple at Deir el-Bahri show scenes of fighting with Kushites, and a most interesting scene shows the god Dedwen leading to Hatshepsut a group of captive Nubian towns. A much-damaged text relates the usual story of Egypt in Nubia: "...a slaughter was made among them, the number (of dead) being unknown; their hands were cut off..." What is undoubtedly the same campaign is the topic of the graffito of the courtier Ty found on the island of Sehel, near Aswan. The text seems to give an eyewitness account of the hostilities, and informs us that Hatshepsut was there in person "overthrowing the Nubian nomads...destroying the land of Nubia." The stele of the official Djehuty informs us that he had seen Hatshepsut receiving captured booty on the battlefield. A graffito found at Tangûr, dated to year 12 of the joint monarchy, mentions a Nubian campaign led by Thutmose. Thutmose III also led an expedition to the region of Miu (location unknown, but probably up the Nile, beyond Napata), and finally a short campaign into Nubia in the twentieth year of the reigns, as evidenced by an inscription from Tombos and from a temple pylon at Armant. This latter campaign seems to have occurred just prior to Thutmose's expedition against Gaza.

A Sed festival was held for Hatshepsut during year 15 of her reign. These festivals were traditionally not held until the thirtieth year of a pharaoh's reign. The earlier date for Hatshepsut's festival may have been chosen to support her claims of coregencies during the reigns of Thutmose I and Thutmose II. However, there are other possible explanations, including the monarch's failing health, that might have been used to justify the timing of the festival.

Undoubtedly the most important event in the reign of Hatshepsut was the trading expedition sent to Punt in her ninth regnal year. The land, which seems to have been located on the southeast coast of Africa, probably in the Sudan/Eritrea region, was famous for its incense, spices, ivory, electrum, gold, animal hides, exotic animals, and other luxury items. The Egyptians were happy to trade for the beads and bronze weapons they had brought. The Deir el-Bahri temple was adorned with beautiful carvings depicting the land of Punt and its inhabitants and the myriad exotic people, animals and plant life that were loaded on five ships and brought back to Egypt, including a number of living trees to be planted at the temple.

Many courtiers held office under Hatshepsut, but the best known is undoubtedly the Chief Steward of Amen, Senenmut. Despite a humble birth, Senenmut was intelligent and talented enough to come to the attention of the royal family, and added to his many titles that of Steward of the God's Wife (Hatshepsut) and

Steward to the King's Daughter (Neferure). Almost half of the known statues of Senenmut show him in the company of Neferure. He said of himself, "I was the greatest of the great...guardian of the secrets of the king...with whose advice the Mistress of the Two Lands was satisfied." It has been suggested that he was the architect of the Deir el-Bahri temple; certainly figures of him have been found on some of the temple walls. Although it has been suggested, there is no evidence whatsoever for any sort of intimate relationship between Hatshepsut and Senenmut. Whatever his position, he is not heard of after Hatshepsut's 16th regnal year. Surprisingly, he seems to have been the possessor of two tombs, although neither one was ever finished, and almost certainly never occupied. His name was erased in many places and his red quartzite sarcophagus was smashed into more than 1200 pieces. The erasures of his name, the smashing of statues, etc., were almost certainly the work of Thutmose III and probably did not occur until many years after Senenmut's death.

The 21 years, 9 months given as the length of reign for Manetho's Amensis is extremely close to the 22 years, 6 months and 10 days given as the length of Hatshepsut's rule on a stele from Armant. She was interred in KV20. At some point she had had this tomb enlarged to accommodate the mummy and funerary equipment for her father, Thutmose I. He was later moved to tomb KV38 by Thutmose III, and Hatshepsut was left alone in KV20. We do not know how she died, although it was most likely from natural causes.

It has been suggested that a female mummy discovered by Howard Carter in KV60 (along with the mummy of Hatshepsut's wet nurse, In-Sitre), in the Valley of the Kings, may be the remains of the female pharaoh herself. The nurse's mummy was sent to the Cairo Museum, but the other mummy was left behind and the tomb reburied and the location lost until rediscovery by archaeologist Donald P. Ryan in 1989. The mummy is that of a short (1.55 m) obese woman, perhaps in her early fifties. The left arm is flexed across the chest and the position of the hand is such as to suggest that it may once have held an object, perhaps a scepter. This same positioning of hand and arm is known from the remains of other queens, which indicates that the KV60 mummy was royalty. The only body part that was certainly Hatshepsut's was an organ, either a liver or spleen, packed away in an ivory box, that had been discovered in the Royal Cache at Deir el-Bahri, but it was unclear if the organ came from the mummy.

However, two recent events strongly support the theory that the mummy found in KV60 is in fact Hatshepsut. The first was DNA testing of the mummy that revealed "similarities" with Hatshepsut's grandmother, but these similarities were insufficient to convince the scientific community. Second, a CT scan of the box containing the organ revealed a tooth, which has been matched by a Cairo University dentist with a gap in the mummy's jaw. On the basis of this additional evidence, Egyptian authorities are now convinced that Hatshepsut's mummy has been found.

Some years after Hatshepsut's death, late in his reign, Thutmose III ordered her name and image erased wherever found; the names of her father, Thutmose I, and her husband, Thutmose II, replaced hers. Her statues and the avenue of sphinxes at Deir el-Bahri were smashed to pieces and thrown into pits and gullies. Her obelisks were bricked up and her buildings at Karnak dismantled. The proscribing of her name and image occurred throughout Egypt. There are many theories as to the cause of what has been described as a *damnatio memoriae*, and as to why it was twenty years in coming. Perhaps the answer is simply that Thutmose was too busy dealing with the sudden weight of single rule, too busy building an empire, to deal with the bitterness and anger he must have felt at having been made to play second fiddle to his aunt for two decades. Amenhotep II, the son and successor of Thutmose III, continued his father's policy, defacing, demolishing or altering all images and inscriptions of Hatshepsut's that came to hand.

References:

Breasted 1906 vol. II pp. 142-143 §340-343
Brier 1994 pp. 88,90,264-267, 274
Bryan 1998 pp. 27-30, 31-32
Bryan 2000 pp. 235-243
Callender 1995/1996 pp. 16-27, 79-80
Carter 1917 pp. 107-118
T. Davis 1906
Dodson and Hilton 2004 pp. 14-17, 31, 86, 130-131, 132-133, 138, 176, 229-230, 283 note 11
Dorman 1988
Dorman 2006 pp. 39-68
Forbes 1998a p. 48
Forbes 2005a pp. 82-109, 110-129, 130-139
Gardiner 1961 pp. 443-444
Gardiner and Peet 1952 pl. XIV #44, LVI #s 176, 182, LVII #s 181, 187, LVIII #s 178, 179, 183, 184, LXI #180, LXII #191, LXXXII #340
Gardiner and Peet 1955 pp. 12, 13, 24, 28, 35, 36, 37, 38, 74 #44, 127, 129, 130, 150 # 174A, 151-155 #s 177-184, 156-157 #191, 201 #340
Goedicke 2004
Grajetzki 2005 p. 52
Habachi 1957 pp. 99-104
Harris and Weeks 1973 pp. 131, 133-136, 137
Hawass 2006 pp. 40-43
Ikram and Dodson 1998 pp. 37, 38, 84, 88, 89, 124, 160,210, 255, 258, 284, 315, 318, ills. 301, 354, 356, 360, 413b, 414, 430
Karkowski 1981
Manuelian 2006 p. 422
Murnane 1977 pp. 32-44, 115-116
Naville 1895-1908
Peden 2001 pp. 62, 71-73, 89-90
Petty 1997 pp. 44-53
Petty 2002/2003 pp. 49-57
Ratié 1979
D. Redford 1967 pp. 57-87
D. Redford 1992 pp. 149, 151-153
Reeves 1990b pp. 13, 17
Reeves and Wilkinson 1996 pp. 15, 16, 29, 31, 37, 47, 53, 54, 71, 75, 80, 91-95, 115, 150, 173, 180, 186-187, 191, 196, 204, 207-210
Robbins 1999 pp. 103-112
Ryan 1990 pp. 34-39, 58-59, 63
Teeter 1990 pp. 4-13, 56-57
Tefnin 1979
Tyldesley 1996
Tyldesley 2006 pp. 94-109
van Siclen 1989 pp. 85-86
Verbrugghe and Wickersham 1996 pp. 114, 140, 198
von Beckerath 1999 pp. 134 #5, 135 #5
Waddell 1940 pp. 111, 115, 241, 245
R. Wilkinson 2000 pp. 51, 56-57, 58-59, 139, 157, 175-178, 196, 219, 229, 239

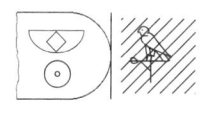

...hebre · Late SIP

Horus Name: Unknown
Nomen: Unknown
Prenomen: ḫb-rˁ
...hebre
Two Ladies: Unknown
Golden Falcon: Unknown

Length of Reign:	1-2 years
Tomb:	Unknown
Mummy:	Unknown

Consorts:	Unknown	**Variant Names:**	None
Manetho:	Not given		
King Lists:	T: (G fr. 163 #1; R 11.26)		

Due to the fragile condition of the Turin Canon, nothing beyond a partial name survives for this king. No contemporary attestations have been found. Ryholt suggests that ...hebre belonged to what Ryholt calls the "Abydos Dynasty," but there is no evidence to support such a dynasty.

References:
Gardiner 1959 pl. IV, Col. XI, fr. 163 #1

Ryholt 1997a pp. 153, fig. 14 #26, 165, table 26, 392 File Abyd/15

Heribre · Dynasty XIV

Horus Name: Unknown
Nomen: Unknown
Prenomen: ḥr-ib-rˁ
Heribre

Hor (I)

Two Ladies: Unknown

Golden Falcon: Unknown

Length of Reign:	Unknown
Tomb:	Unknown
Mummy:	Unknown

Consorts:	Unknown	**Variant Names:**	None
Manetho:	Not given		
King Lists:	T: (G 8.13; R 9.13; vB 8.13)		

Perhaps the eighteenth king of Dynasty XIV, Heribre is one of a group of kings known only from the Turin Canon. The fragmentary state of the papyrus allows for varying interpretations as to the positioning of some of the kings within this dynasty. However, Heribre's place seems secure.

References:

Gardiner 1959 pl. III, Col. 8. #13
Gardiner 1961 p. 441 #8.13
Ryholt 1997a pp. 95 Col. 9.13, 98 #18, 198 table 37, 379 File 14/18, table 95 #18

von Beckerath 1999 pp. 108 #14, 109 #14

Hor (I)   Dynasty XIII

Horus Name:

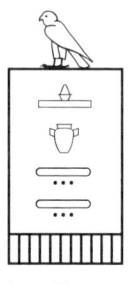

ḥtp-ib-tꜣwy

Nomen:

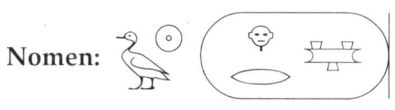

ḥr

Hor

ḥr

Hor

Prenomen:

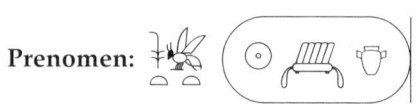

ꜣw(t)-ib-rꜥ

Awibre

Hor (I)

Two Ladies:

nbty nfr-ḥw

Golden Falcon:

bik nbw nfr-nṯrw

Length of Reign:	T: ..., x + 7 days
Tomb:	Shaft tomb at Dahshur
Mummy:	Skeleton, in Cairo Museum

Consorts:	Nubhotepi I	**Variant Names:**	Auibre Har
Manetho:	Not given		
King Lists:	T: (G 6.17; R 7.17; vB 6.17)		

The fifteenth ruler of Dynasty XIII, although von Beckerath places him as fourteenth, Hor seems to have been no relation to his predecessor, Ranisonb. He is therefore, most likely, a usurper, though whether he attained the throne through bloodshed is not known. In any event, his reign was probably of only a few months duration and, while listed in the Turin Canon, he was otherwise unknown until the French Archaeologist Jacques de Morgan discovered his tomb at Dahshur in 1894.

Hor's final resting place was a shaft tomb built near the northeast corner of the pyramid of the Dynasty XII ruler Amenemhet III. The original shaft had been cut for a member of Amenemhet's court. For Hor's burial the tomb was enlarged with the addition of a new stone burial chamber and an antechamber. Although the tomb had been pillaged at some point, it still contained a goodly portion of funerary objects including canopic equipment, a life-size wooden ka-statue of the king in its own shrine, a funerary mask stripped of its gilding, and a rotted coffin. Also found were other small statues, alabaster vases, wooden "dummy" vases, two stele, flails and scepters, wooden staves and pottery. The king's mummy had been desecrated and was nothing more than a skeleton. Anatomist Georges Fouquet pronounced the remains to be those of a man in his forties at time of death. There was no way to determine the cause of death. The skeleton is now in the Cairo Museum.

Other than the tomb and items therein, very few attestations to Hor have survived. An architrave bearing the cartouche of Hor and his immediate successor Khabau, found at Tanis in the Delta, was

...hor

probably originally at Memphis, but had been moved during the Hyksos Period. The juxtaposition of names on the architrave suggests a coregency between the two kings. Other attestations for Hor include an inscribed plaque now in the Berlin Museum (Berlin 7670) and an inscribed jar lid of unknown provenance.

References:

Cron and Johnson 1995a pp. 34-43
Cron and Johnson 1995b pp. 58-60
W. Davies 1981b p. 23 #s 7 and 8
Dodson 1994b pp. 115-116, pl. VII-VIII
Dodson 1994c pp. 29-31
Dodson 2000 pp. 13-14
Dodson 2003 pp. 99-100
Gardiner 1959 pl. III Col. VI #17
Gardiner 1961 p. 440 #6.17
Ikram and Dodson 1997 p. 21
Ikram and Dodson 1998 p. 321
Kaplony 1973 p. 14 #39, pl. 10 #39, pl. 22 #39
de Morgan 1895 pp. 88-106, pl. XXXIII- XXXVI, XXXVIII
Ryholt 1997a pp. 36 fig. 4 a, 39-40 and table #10, 62, 71 Col. 7.17, 73 #15, 81, 83, 192 table 33, 209, 216-219 and tables 51 and 52, 284 table 83, 318 and note 1099, 339-340 File 13/15, 408 table 94 #15
von Beckerath 1999 pp. 92 #14, 93 #14

...hor   Dynasty XIII

Horus Name: Unknown

Nomen:

...ḥr
...Hor

Prenomen:

...wbn-rꜥ
...webenre

Two Ladies: Unknown

Golden Falcon: Unknown

Length of Reign:	Unknown
Tomb:	Unknown
Mummy:	Unknown

Consorts:	Unknown	**Variant Names:**	None
Manetho:	Not given		
King Lists:	T: (G 7.15; R 8.23; vB 7.15)		

114

Perhaps the fifty-second ruler of Dynasty XIII, ...hor is one of a group of kings known only from the Turin Canon. Although the papyrus' fragmentary state allows for varying interpretations as to the positioning of some of the kings of this dynasty, recent study by K.S.B. Ryholt would tend to place ...hor securely in this position.

References:
Gardiner 1959 pl. III, Col. VII #15
Gardiner 1961 p. 441 #7.15
Ryholt 1997a pp. 71 Col. 8.23, 73 #53, 197 #53, 358 File 13/53

von Beckerath 1999 pp. 100 #39, 101 #39

Horemheb   Dynasty XVIII

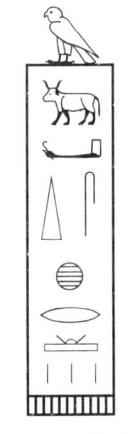

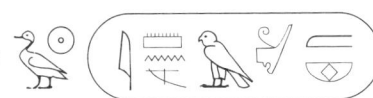

Horus Name:

k3 nḫt spd-sḫrw

Nomen:

ḥr-m-ḥ3b mry-imn
Horemheb (meryamen)

Prenomen:

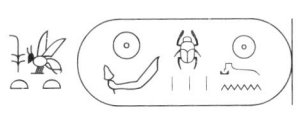

ḏsr-ḫprw-rʿ stp.n-rʿ
Djoserkheperure-setepenre

Two Ladies:

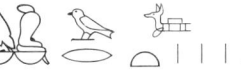

nbty wr-bi3wt-m-iptswt

Golden Falcon:

bik-nbw ḥrw-ḥr-m3ʿt sḫpr-t3wy

Length of Reign:	13–30 years
Tomb:	Valley of the Kings: KV57
Mummy:	Unknown

Horemheb

Consorts:	Mutnodjmet	**Variant Names:**	Harmhab
Manetho:	Armais (E)		Heruemheb
	Armesis (A)		Tcheser-
	Danaos (E)		kheperu-ra
	Danaus (E)		Zeser-kheperu-ra
	Harmais (J)		
King Lists:	Ab: (74); S: (55-missing)		

The fifteenth and final pharaoh of Dynasty XVIII, Horemheb bore no known relationship to his immediate predecessor Ay, nor to any of the previous kings of that dynasty. His parentage is unknown, although it is probably safe to assume that he was of rather humble origin. He seems to have come from Middle Egypt, and, although the town is disputed, the region around Herakleopolis is the most likely.

The first known attestations for Horemheb occur during the reign of Tutankhamen, under whom he held a staggering number of titles (an estimated 90). He undoubtedly achieved prominence based on his career in the military, which probably began during the reign of Akhenaten. He eventually rose to the post of commander general of the Egyptian army. It has been suggested that Horemheb might be identified with someone named Paatenemheb, whose name and titles were found on carved surfaces of an incomplete tomb (number 24) at Amarna. Work on the tomb had progressed only as far as a staircase and partial corridor before it was abandoned. Its tentative identification with Horemheb is based on the similarity of its and Horemheb's names and titles, in particular "Overseer of the Soldiery of the Lord of the Two Lands."

Horemheb's military background, as reflected in his tomb at Saqqara and in many of his titles, leaves no doubt that he commanded the entire Egyptian army. The tomb inscriptions indicate that his role in Tutankhamen's court went well beyond simply that of an important general; most likely, he was truly the "power behind the throne" of the boy king. Van Dijk points out that such titles as "Supreme Chief of the Land," and "Hereditary Prince and Count" provide convincing evidence of his powerful role. Most significantly, the designation "Eldest Son of Horus," a title applied only to the heir of a pharaoh, indicates that Horemheb was Tutankhamen's choice as his successor.

At the time of Tutankhamen's death, the Egyptian army was fighting against the Hittites in southern Syria; it is likely that Horemheb was leading this campaign and thus far from Egypt when the young king died. This provides a reasonable explanation for why it was Ay, rather than Horemheb, who became the next pharaoh.

Although some scholars have suggested that Horemheb usurped the throne upon the death of Ay, there is no direct evidence that such was the case. While Ay's throne may have been intended for his son Nakhtmin, who also bore the title "Eldest Son," Nakhtmin probably predeceased his father. Under the circumstances, Horemheb would have been the logical successor to Ay. Another possible tie between Horemheb and Ay is that Horemheb's second wife, Queen Mutnodjmet, may have been Nefertiti's sister, and thus possibly Ay's daughter (although this relationship is not secure). In addition, Ay's cartouche sealed the burial chamber of Horemheb's first wife, Amenia.

While there may have been no personal animosity between Ay and Horemheb, Horemheb eventually saw to it that Ay's name and image were destroyed wherever found, actually going so far as to open Ay's tomb in the Valley of the Kings and chip out the cartouches of the old pharaoh and the images of Ay and Queen Tey painted on the walls of the burial chamber. Ay's funerary temple, which might well have been usurped from Tutankhamen, was in turn taken over by Horemheb. In fairness to Horemheb, it must be said that Ay was not singled out: All of the "Amarna Pharaohs" (Akhenaten through Ay) were eventually anathematized, and Horemheb dated the beginning of his reign to the death of Amenhotep III, claiming an additional 30 or more years beyond his actual rule. Interestingly enough, Tutankhamen's tomb was not violated during this "purge."

Internal affairs in Egypt undoubtedly occupied a great deal of the new pharaoh's attention. Akhenaten's reign had proved disastrous for Egypt, and the reigns of Tutankhamen and Ay seem to have left a great deal to be done in order to stabilize the country. As exemplified by his "Legal Stele" at Karnak, Horemheb enacted a number of laws covering property rights (including commandeering of slaves), the reorganization of judicial and military administration and structure, illegal taxation, land and tax fraud, bribery, theft, and much more, down to and including stealing vegetables.

Undoubtedly foreign relations in Syria continued to be strained. The Hittites had moved as far south as Byblos, and therefore to territory previously held for generations by Egypt, and this certainly hurt the Egyptian economy; the port of Byblos was the major trade center for the region. This incursion into Egyptian territory was not reversed until the reign of Ramesses II.

Although Horemheb built throughout Egypt, the majority of his architectural attestations are to be found in the Theban area. He especially favored the temple of Amen at Karnak, and repairs and additions to it were many. His additions included Pylons Nine, Ten, and possibly the beginning of Two (although many scholars believe it was begun by Ramesses I), an avenue of sphinxes, and the initial construction of the great Hypostyle Hall. Work at Luxor included additions to the decorations of the processional colonnade, various textual additions and evidence of usurpation of some of Amenhotep III's cartouches.

Although Horemheb had been granted and completed a tomb in the Memphite cemetery now known as Saqqara during the reign of Tutankhamen, as pharaoh Horemheb ordered a new tomb built in the Valley of the Kings. This tomb, begun in regnal year seven, was never completed. In fact, progress was so slow that in year 13, when Queen Mutnodjmet died (perhaps in childbirth, since a baby's remains were found with the queen's skeleton), she was interred in the Memphite tomb. The Theban tomb, KV57, is over 100 m. in length, one of the largest in the Valley; although never completed, Horemheb was nonetheless interred there, as a number of artifacts from the burial attest.

The length of Horemheb's reign has long been in question. The highest certain date actually attested is a year 13 from a wine docket found in the Saqqara tomb. However, Redford has reported a year 16 given on a stone bowl of unknown provenance, now in the hands of a private collector. A graffito from the king's mortuary temple recording a year 27 has been interpreted as referring to the year of Horemheb's burial, and some scholars suggest a reign as long as 30 years. In any case, he was a very old man who died with no heirs. Prior to his death, he chose as his successor an army general named Paramesses, who became Ramesses I.

References:

Breasted 1906 vol. III pp. 22-33 § 45-67
Brier 1994 pp. 269-270
B. Davies 1995 pp. 77-83
T. Davis 1912
de Buck 1937 pp. 152-164
Dodson and Hilton 2004 pp. 17, 33, 142, 143, 144, 153, 156, 158, 160, 162, 179
El Madhy 1989 pp. 46, 51
Forbes 1998b pp. 31-44
Grajetzki 2005 p. 64
Hall 1913 pp. 198-200 #s 1975-1987, 281 #s 2713-2719
Harris and Weeks 1973 pp. 148, 149, 151
Hornung 2006 p. 209
Ikram and Dodson 1998 pp. 62, 84, 95, 98, 132, 216, 261, 315, 318, ills. 298, 366d, 413g, 420, 425
S. James 2001/2002 pp. 32-41
G. Johnson 2000 pp. 120-159
Martin 1989b
Martin 1991 pp. 35-97
Newberry 1906 p. 179 #s 1-8, pl. I #5, XXXIV #s 1-8
Petrie 1978 pl. XXXVIII #s 18.14.1-27
D. Redford 1974 pp. 6-23
Reeves and Wilkinson 1996 pp. 25-26, 30, 33, 36-38, 40, 42-43, 77-80, 108, 122, 125, 129-130, 133, 134-137, 147, 157, 186, 191-193, 204-205, 207
Strouhal and Callender 1992 pp. 67-75
Tyldesley 2006 p. 140
van Dijk 1996 pp. 29-42
van Dijk 2000 pp. 292-294
Verbrugghe and Wickersham 1996 pp. 108, 142, 159, 199
von Beckerath 1999 pp. 146 #14, 147 #14
Waddell 1940 pp. 103, 105, 109, 113, 117, 119

...hori Dynasty XIII

Horus Name: Unknown

Nomen:

...ḥr-i
...Hori

Prenomen:

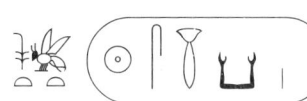

swḏ-kȝ-rʿ
Sewadjkare

Two Ladies: Unknown

Golden Falcon: Unknown

Length of Reign: T: "5 years,..., 8 days"

Tomb: Unknown

Mummy: Unknown

Consorts: Unknown

Manetho: Not given

King Lists: T: (G 7.7; R 8.7; vB 7.7)

Variant Names: None

Probably the thirty-sixth king of Dynasty XIII, ...hori is one of a group of kings known only from the Turin Canon. Although the papyrus' fragmentary state allows for varying interpretations as to the positioning of some of this dynasty's kings, ...hori's place seems secure.

References:

Gardiner 1959 pl. III, Col. VII #7
Gardiner 1961 p. 440 #7.7
Ryholt 1997a pp. 71 Col. 8.7, 73 #37, 192 table 33 197 #37, 356 File 13/37, 408 #37

von Beckerath 1999 pp. 98 #31, 99 #31

Hornedjheritef   Dynasty XIII

Horus Name: Unknown

Nomen:

qmꜣw sꜣ ḥr-nḏ-ḥr-it.f
(Qemau's son) Hornedjheritef

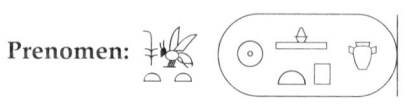

Prenomen:

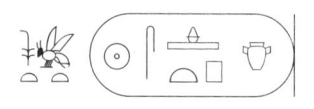

ḥtp-ib-rꜥ
Hotepibre

sḥtp-ib-rꜥ
Sehotepibre

Two Ladies: Unknown

Golden Falcon: Unknown

Length of Reign:	1 – 5 years possible
Tomb:	Unknown
Mummy:	Unknown

Consorts:	Unknown	**Variant Names:**	Harnedjheritef Iamu-Sahornedjheriotef Siharnedjheritef
Manetho:	Not given		
King Lists:	T: (G 6.8; R 7.8; vB 6.8)		

Hornedjheritef is probably the sixth pharaoh of Dynasty XIII, although he is listed as number nine by von Beckerath. He was most likely the son of his predecessor, Qemau, as is evidenced by the use of filiative nomina in his cartouche. Some scholars have assumed that the hieroglyphs in his cartouche were to be translated as ꜥm, "the Asiatic" or "Son of the Asiatic," and that Hornedjheritef was, in fact, of Asiatic origin. However, this does not make sense from a philological standpoint; in addition, Qemau was evidently a common Egyptian name during the late Middle Kingdom. Further "evidence" that Hornedjheritef was of foreign birth and therefore an

Asiatic is based on the finding of a single statue of this king at Qantir (Avaris). However, the statue was discovered along with statues of the Dynasty XII ruler Sobekneferu and these statues were undoubtedly moved from the Memphite area by the Dynasty XV Hyksos kings.

Aside from the statue discovered at Qantir, only one other positive attestation of Hornedjheritef is known: an inscribed block found at El-Atawla, near Asyut in Middle Egypt. A scepter found in a tomb at Ebla, and inscribed with what seems to be the prenomen Hotepibre, has been attributed to Hornedjheritef, but recent study of the scepter's poor workmanship and incorrectly placed hieroglyphs has cast considerable doubt on its origins.

Hornedjheritef's prenomen is given as Sehotepibre in the Turin Canon, but this is incorrect (probably due to a scribal confusion with Sehotepibre, the prenomen of the Dynasty XII ruler Amenemhet I). The correct version, as attested to by all surviving examples, is Hotepibre.

References:

W. Davies 1981b p. 22 #4
Gardiner 1959 pl. III, Col. VI #8
Gardiner 1961 p. 440 #6.8
Habachi 1954 pp. 460-461, pl. IX, X-XI
Hein 1994 p. 116 Catalogue #54
Helck 1983 p. 4 #s 8 and 9
Ryholt 1997a pp. 71 Col. 7.8, 73 #6, 80, 84-85 note 265, 192 table 33, 193, 208 and table 46, 209, 214 tables 48 and 49 and notes 737 and 738, 215 table 49, 284 table 83, 297, 320 and table 92, 321, 338 File 13/6, 408 table 94 #6
Ryholt 1997b pp. 97, 99, 100
Ryholt 1998b pp. 1-5
von Beckerath 1999 pp. 90 #9, 91 #9

Hotep   Dynasty VII/VIII

Horus Name: Unknown

Nomen: ḥtp
Hotep

Prenomen: ...-rʿ
...re

Two Ladies: Unknown

Golden Falcon: Unknown

Hotepkare

Length of Reign:	Unknown
Tomb:	Unknown
Mummy:	Unknown

Consorts:	Unknown	Hotpe
Manetho:	Not given	Noutirkere-Hotep
King Lists:	None	Ra Sa?
Variant Names:	Hetep	

This ruler, if he indeed held the throne, is known from a single graffito at the Shatt er Rigal, just north of Gebel Silsila in southern Upper Egypt. The crude carving shows two cartouches evidently belonging to a single individual. The cartouches are much weathered, and while it is possible to make out the name "Hotep" in one cartouche; the other name is more problematical and has been read in several different ways, no one of which has gained general acceptance by the scholarly community.

The carving seems to date to the First Intermediate Period, and probably Dynasty VII/VIII, although a date at some point in the Second Intermediate Period has been suggested. It is quite possible that Hotep was only a local official who gave himself the trappings of royalty during a period of internal strife and that he "reigned" concurrently with one of the pharaohs given in the Abydos lists.

References:

Gauthier 1907-17 p. 180
Legrain 1903a p. 220
Petrie 1902a p. 246
von Beckerath 1999 pp. 70 #e, 71 #e

von Bissing and Kees 1913 p. 18, fig. 1, fig. 4 #15
Winlock 1947 p. 61, pl. 35

Hotepkare   SIP

Horus Name:
Unknown

Nomen: Unknown

Prenomen:

ḥtp-k3-rˁ
Hotepkare

Two Ladies: Unknown

Golden Falcon: Unknown

...hotep[re?]

Length of Reign:	Unknown
Tomb:	Unknown
Mummy:	Unknown

Consorts:	Unknown	**Variant Names:**	Hetepkare
Manetho:	Not given		
King Lists:	None		

This name is known from a cylinder-seal whose provenance is unknown. Von Beckerath attributes this seal to Intef V of Dynasty XIII, whose prenomen is Sehotepkare, but as the seal is carved clearly and there is no room for an "S," von Beckerath's attribution is highly unlikely.

References:
Petrie 1978 pl. XVIII #13 DE
Ryholt 1997a pp. 72, 403 File P/3
von Beckerath 1999 pp. 94 #19, 95 #19

...hotep[re?]   SIP

Horus Name: Unknown

Nomen:
Prenomen: (see text)

...ḥtp [rˁ?]
hotep[re?]

Two Ladies: Unknown
Golden Falcon: Unknown

Length of Reign:	Unknown
Tomb:	Unknown
Mummy:	Unknown

Consorts:	Unknown	**Variant Names:**	None
Manetho:	Not given		
King Lists:	T: (?)		

This name is found on a stele that was discovered at Abydos and is now in the Vatican Museum. The name is so badly preserved that it is impossible to tell if it is a nomen or prenomen. Stylistically

Hotepsekhemwy

the stele would appear to date from Dynasty XIII. Ryholt suggests that, if the name is a nomen, it may belong to a Sobekhotep, a Neferhotep or Montuhotep V.

References:
Franke 1984 Dossier 230
Ryholt 1997a p. 404 File P/10
Simpson 1974 p. 22 ANOC 65.2, pl. 65.2

Hotepsekhemwy   Dynasty II

Horus Name:
Nomen:

bd3w
Bedjau

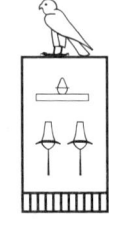

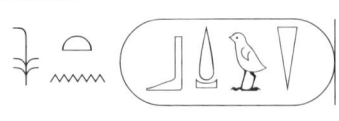

ḥtp-sḫmwi
Hotepsekhemwy

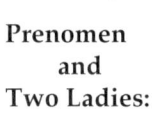

b3w-nṯr
Baunetjer

Prenomen and Two Ladies:

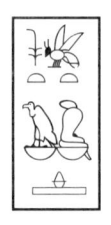

ḥtp
Hotep

Golden Falcon: Unknown

Length of Reign:	Unknown
Tomb:	Saqqara, Tomb "A" (near Step Pyramid complex)
Mummy:	Unknown

Consorts:	Unknown	**Variant Names:**	Bauneter Hetepsekhemui Hotep Ahaui
Manetho:	Boethos (A) Bokchos (E) Bokhos (E)		
King Lists:	Ab: (9)		

124

Although Hotepsekhemwy is the first king of Dynasty II, there is very little doubt that he was considered the legitimate successor of Qa'a, last ruler of Dynasty I. Jar-sealings from the latter's tomb at Abydos make it clear that Hotepsekhemwy was very much involved in the burial of his predecessor and, whether or not there was a familial relationship, it was traditionally the responsibility of the legitimate successor to the throne to bury the previous ruler. For this reason, it is difficult to see why a new dynasty was called into existence. The most likely reason appears to be that Qa'a died without a son to succeed him and that Hotepsekhemwy was either a relative or a noble powerful enough to seize the throne.

The name Hotepsekhemwy translates as "The Two Powers are at Peace" and this may refer to some form of social and/or political problem the new king had to overcome prior to or shortly after ascending the throne; certainly some of the royal tombs at Abydos were robbed and burned at this time. A strong possibility is that a usurper seized power for a short time after Qa'a's death and that Hotepsekhemwy was forced to quell an uprising and destroy the would-be king. If such was the case, it is possible that the usurper was an obscure ruler named Seneferka, whose meager remains are found only at Saqqara (see SENEFERKA). If there had been an unsuccessful rebellion in Lower Egypt, it would certainly account for the Horus name "The Two Powers are at Peace" and might even explain why Hotepsekhemwy abandoned the royal cemetery at Abydos in Upper Egypt in favor of burial at Saqqara. Of course, another reason for the relocation of the royal cemetery is that Hotepsekhemwy may have been a native of Lower Egypt. Memphis was undoubtedly the administrative center of Egypt from its founding (probably by the Dynasty I pharaoh, Aha). It is certainly true that powerful nobles and administrators resided there, as is evident from the magnificent mastaba tombs they built for themselves.

Hotepsekhemwy's tomb at Saqqara was discovered by Barsanti in 1901, during the excavation of the mortuary temple of the Dynasty V king Unas. The remains of the tomb consisted of an amazing series of underground chambers and galleries that stretched to a length of some 130 m. There was no trace of the tomb's superstructure, that having been removed during the building of a temple during Unas' reign. A great many jar-sealings bearing the name Hotepsekhemwy identified him as the tomb's owner. Also discovered were numerous jar-sealings of Nebre, Hotepsekhemwy's successor. The tomb has never been systematically studied. It is unknown if the king was buried there, although there is no reason to believe he was not.

Other attestations to the reign of Hotepsekhemwy include inscribed stone vessels from Djoser's Step Pyramid, two inscribed stone bowls discovered in the pyramid complex of the Dynasty IV king Menkaure and stone vessel fragments from the Abydos tombs of Dynasty II rulers Sekhemib/Peribsen and Khasekhemwy.

Probably the most important attestation discovered to date is the statue of a priest named Hotepdief who seems to have been responsible for the mortuary cults of Hotepsekhemwy and that king's two immediate successors, Nebre and Ninetjer. Hotepdief's statue presents the Horus names of the three rulers in what appears to be chronological order.

Manetho gives Hotepsekhemwy a reign of 38 years.

Hotepsekhemwy's personal name was Hotep. During much later times, when king-lists were being prepared and the sign for "Hotep," ⌂ (*ḥtp*), was transcribed from hieroglyphs into hieratic, it would appear that a series of scribal errors transformed the original name into Bedjau (as seen on the Abydos King List) and Baunetjer (as seen on the Saqqara king list and in the Turin Canon).

References:

Barsanti 1902 pp. 183-184
Budge 1976 p. 10 2. Hetep-Sekhemui II and IV
Clayton 1994 p. 27 color illustration
Dodson 1996 pp. 19-22 and sketch-plan on 21
Dodson and Hilton 2004 pp. 44-46, 49
Edwards 1971 p. 30
Emery 1961 pp. 91-92
Gardiner 1961 pp. 431, 432
Gardiner 1959 pl. I Col. II #20
Gunn 1928 p. 156, pl. 2
Lacau and Lauer 1959 pp. 12-13, pl. V #s 6 and 7, pl. 17 #s 79-83 pl. 10-12
Lacau and Lauer 1961 pp. 29-32, 39-40
Maspero 1902 p. 187 type no. 2 A
Petrie 1901a pp. 5, 6, 26 #s 8-11, 51 #s 8-11, pl. VIII #s 8-10
Quibell 1934 p. 7
Reisner 1931 p. 102-103, 122
Schulz and Seidel pp. 36-37
Stadelmann 1985 pp. 296 and 297 fig. 1
Verbrugghe and Wickersham 1996 pp. 132, 188
von Beckerath 1999 pp. 42 #1, 43 #1
Waddell 1940 p. 34, 35
T. Wilkinson 1999 pp. 82, 83-84, 91, 202, 207, 240-241

Hudjefa (I)   Dynasty II

Horus Name: None

Nomen: *ḥw-dfȝ*
Hudjefa

Prenomen: *ḥw-dfȝ*
Hudjefa

Two Ladies: None

Golden Falcon: None

Hudjefa (II)

Length of Reign:	None
Tomb:	None
Mummy:	None

Consorts:	None	**Variant Names:**	None
Manetho:	None		
King Lists:	S:(10); T:(3.2)		

A king named Hudjefa never existed. The word $ḥwdf$ in Egyptian meant something like "lacuna" and seems to have been used in the Turin Canon to show that the name of the ruler who filled that position in the king list had been lost. A cartouche in the Saqqara king list gives the "name" Hudjefa, probably because it was copied from a hieratic document and a scribal error occurred. The eleven years shown in the Turin Canon represent a gap in the records, rather than a reign or reigns of that length. This eleven year gap comes directly before Khasekhemwy, the last king of Dynasty II. Dodson has suggested that the missing name might be part of the titulary of the Horus Seneferka, though there is little evidence to support this idea. Furthermore, Seneferka's place in the dynasty is itself unknown; it has been suggested that he was actually a Dynasty I ruler (see SENEFERKA).

It should be noted that the Roman numeral I is a modern convention used to separate the Dynasty II "Hudjefa" from one listed for Dynasty III.

References:

Dodson 1996 p. 20
Edwards 1971 p. 35
Gardiner 1959 pl. II Col. III #2
Gardiner 1961 p. 431

Goedicke 1956 pp. 50-53
von Beckerath 1999 pp. 44 #8, 45 #45
T. Wilkinson 2000 pp. 55, 58, 73

Hudjefa (II)   Dynasty III

Horus Name: None   **Nomen:**

$ḥw$ df
Hudjefa

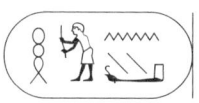

Huni

Prenomen: *ḥw-ḏfꜣ*
Hudjefa

Two Ladies: None
Golden Falcon: None

Length of Reign:	None
Tomb:	None
Mummy:	None

Consorts:	None	**Variant Names:**	None
Manetho:	None		
King Lists:	T: (3.7)		

A king named Hudjefa never existed. The word *ḥwdfꜣ* in Egyptian meant something like "lacuna" and seems to have been used in the Turin Canon to show that the name of the ruler who filled that position in the king list had been lost. The six years recorded in the Canon reflect a six year gap between known rulers, not a six year reign.

However, Dodson and Goedicke both point out that the word "sedjes" may also indicate a lacuna in the original source documents used to put together the Abydos list (see SEDJES). Both Dodson and von Beckerath equate Sedjes with Hudjefa (II).

References:

Dodson 1998 p. 28
Gardiner 1959 pl. II, Col. II #7
Gardiner 1961 p. 433

Goedicke 1956 pp. 50-53
von Beckerath 1999 pp. 44 #8, 45 #8

Huni   Dynasty III

Horus Name: Unknown   **Nomen:** *ḥwni*
Huni

Huni

niswt ḥwi
Nyswth

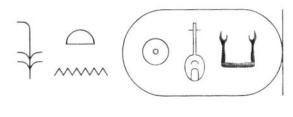

nfr-k3-rˤ
Neferkare

Two Ladies: Unknown

Golden Falcon: Unknown

Length of Reign:	24 years
Tomb:	Unfinished brick pyramid at Abu Roash(?)
Mummy:	Unknown

Consorts:	Meresankh I(?)	**King Lists:**	S: (15); T: (3.8)
Herodotus:	Asychis	**Variant Names:**	Hu
Manetho:	Achês (A) Akhes (A) Kerpheres (A)		

As with many rulers of Dynasty III, Huni's parentage is unknown. To complicate matters, even his name has caused problems among scholars. Some see the name as "Nysweth"(*niswt*), some as "King Hu" (, *niswt ḥ(wi)*), etc. Scholars seem to have agreed on "Huni" until more information becomes available.

The Turin Canon gives Huni a reign of 24 years. It is thus virtually certain that Huni built a tomb for himself. Recently, Egyptologist Nabil Swalim rediscovered the ruins of a pyramid that he was able to date to late Dynasty III; he, along with Dodson and others, believe it is very possibly Huni's burial place.

Probably intended as a step pyramid, the structure was made of mud brick and measured 215 m. to the side and a height of at least 107.5 m. What remains of the structure today is the core of natural rock, in which the burial chamber had been carved; the rest of the pyramid was carried away for building material.

This structure may also be the pyramid of a 2,200 year old tradition. When Herodotus visited Egypt in about 450 BC, he was told by priests that the successor of Mycerinus (Menkaure) was a king named Asychis who, wishing to out-do his forefathers, built a pyramid of brick and with a stone inset that read "Do not compare me to my disadvantage with the stone pyramids. I surpass them as far as Zeus the other gods...."

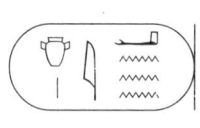

A series of seven small step pyramids, all dating to the end of Dynasty III/early Dynasty IV, were constructed from Seila, near Meidum, to the island of Elephantine. Seneferu's name is associated with the Seila pyramid and Huni's name is tentatively connected to the monument at Elephantine, the latter's name appearing on a granite cone found nearby. The remaining five structures may have been built by either or both pharaohs (see SENEFERU). None of the small step pyramids were ever used for burial purposes.

A cult of Huni seems to have survived for quite some time: a reference to his mortuary estate is mentioned on the Palermo Stone, during the reign of the Dynasty V king Neferirkare (I), 150 years after Huni's death.

The correlation between Manetho's kings and Huni is uncertain. Dodson equates Huni with Kerpheres, while Verbrugghe and Wickersham suggest Akhes, whom Dodson equates with Khaba.

Dodson makes a strong case that Huni should be equated with the cartouche of a king named Neferkare, who precedes Seneferu on the Abydos king list.

References:

Dodson 1998 pp. 35-36, 38, 39
Dodson 2003 pp. 47-48
Dodson and Hilton 2004 pp. 51, 52-53
Gardiner 1959 pl. II, Col. III #8
Gardiner 1961 pp. 75, 433
Goedicke 1956 pp. 18-24
Herodotus 1954 p. 183
Kahl et al. 1995 pp. 164-165
Meltzer 1971 pp. 202-203
Quirke 2001b pp. 122-123
Schäfer 1902 p. 40
Swelim 1987
Verbrugghe and Wickersham 1996 pp. 134, 190
Verner 1997 pp. 107, 152, 153, 166-167, 172
von Beckerath 1999 pp. 48 #6, 49 #6
Waddell 1940 p. 43
T. Wilkinson 1999 pp. 94, 100, 101, 103-105, 117, 118, 247, 254, 277-279, 330
T. Wilkinson 2000 pp. 54, 58, 150, 177-178

Iaib Dynasty XIII

Horus Name: Unknown **Nomen:**

iꜥ-ib

Iaib

Iaib

Prenomen: *wꜣh-ib-rꜥ*
Wahibre

Two Ladies: Unknown

Golden Falcon: Unknown

Length of Reign:	10+ years
Tomb:	Unknown
Mummy:	Unknown

Consorts:	Unknown	Ab-aa
Manetho:	Not given	Ia'yeb
		Ibiaw
King Lists:	T: (G 7.2; R 8.2; vB 7.2)	Ja'ib
		Ra-uah-ab
		Uah-ab-re
Variant Names:	Aa-ab	Yayebi

Probably the thirty-first king of Dynasty XIII, although Ryholt places him as thirty-second and von Beckerath places him as number 26.

While the Turin Canon records a reign of ten years, eight months and 28 days, very little evidence of Iaib's rule has been discovered. A scarab-seal bearing this king's prenomen, discovered at Byblos in Canaan, may indicate trade with that city, but it is the only foreign attestation known for Iaib and may represent nothing more than an isolated incident. Attestations in Egypt include a fragment of an inscribed cup from Kahun and a bead and possibly a seal-stamp from Lisht. Both sites are in the vicinity of the Faiyum, near the border between Lower and Middle Egypt. Excavations in Upper Egypt have turned up three cylinder-seals from el-Mahamid Qibli and a private funerary stele, found at Thebes, which bears his nomen. Eight scarab-seals are also known, but their provenances are unknown.

The lack of any attestations from Lower Egypt may indicate that Iaib's power did not extend beyond Middle Egypt. Bourriau suggests that the center of royal power, and therefore the capital of Egypt, had shifted to Thebes by Iaib's time.

Ibi

References:

Bourriau 1988 pp. 57-59, fig. 45
Budge 1913 p. 9, pl. 27
Gardiner 1959 pl. III, Col. VII #2
Gardiner 1961 p. 440 #7.2
Newberry 1906 pp. 115 #5, pl. VII #5
Petrie 1890 pl. X #72
Ryholt 1997a pp. 71 Col. 8.2, 73 #32, 192 table 33, 195, 197 table 36, #33, 353 File 13/32, 408 table 94 #32
Tufnell 1984 p. 368 #s 3168-3171, pl. LV #s 3168-3171
von Beckerath 1999 pp. 96 #26, 97 #26

Ibi   Dynasty XIII

Horus Name: Unknown

Nomen: *ibi*
Ibi

Prenomen: ...m3ˁt-rˁ
...maatre

Two Ladies: Unknown

Golden Falcon: Unknown

Length of Reign:	Unknown
Tomb:	Unknown
Mummy:	Unknown

Consorts:	Unknown	**Variant Names:**	Aba Iby
Manetho:	Not given		
King Lists:	T: (G 7.14; R 8.22; vB 7.14)		

Probably the fifty-first king of Dynasty XIII, Ibi is one of a group of kings known only from the Turin Canon. Although the papyrus' fragmentary state allows for varying interpretations as to the positioning of some of the kings of this dynasty, recent research by K.S.B. Ryholt strongly supports this position for Ibi.

References:

Gardiner 1959 pl. III, Col. VII #14
Gardiner 1961 p. 441 #7.14
Ryholt 1997a pp. 71 Col. 8.22, 73 #52, 197 #52, 358 File 13/52
von Beckerath 1999 pp. 100 #39, 101 #39

Imhotep   Dynasty VII/VIII or X(?)

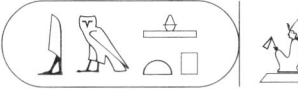

ii-m-ḥtp
Imhotep

Length of Reign:	Unknown
Tomb:	Unknown
Mummy:	Unknown

Consorts:	Unknown	**Variant Names:**	None
Manetho:	Not given		
King Lists:	None		

This king is known only from an inscription in the Wadi Hammamat. The text deals with a quarrying expedition led by the King's Son, Djaty, that included a work force of 2,350 men, a seemingly inordinate number for a routine quarrying project. The numbers may be exaggerated or may refer to the number of work days figured in man-hours. Another possibility is that an excessive number of men was sent on the expedition as a show of strength, perhaps indicating that the Wadi Hammamat was not under Imhotep's control. If the latter is the case, it might be that Imhotep ruled later than Dynasty VII/VIII, the period to which many scholars have assigned him, and may, in fact, have been a ruler of Herakleopolis during Dynasty X (see "Herakleopolitans" in Glossary). This would have put Imhotep at odds with the early Dynasty XI, centered at Thebes. It would also go far in explaining the references to fighting at the beginning of the Wadi Hammamat inscription.

References:
Breasted 1906 vol. I p. 175
Couyat and Montet 1912 pp. 103-104
   #206, pl. XXXIX

Gauthier 1907-17 vol. 1 pp. 143-144
Goedicke 1990 pp. 77-93
von Beckerath 1999 pp. 70 #d, 71 #d

Imyremeshau   Dynasty XIII

Horus Name: Unknown

Nomen:

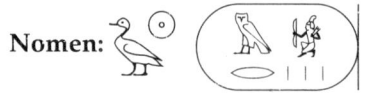

imy-r-mšˤw
Imyremeshau

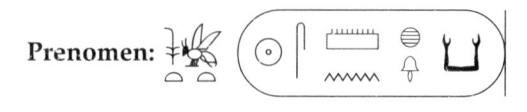

Prenomen:

smnḫ-ka-rˤ
Semenkhkare

Two Ladies: Unknown

Golden Falcon: Unknown

Length of Reign:	T: ..., X + 4 days
Tomb:	Unknown
Mummy:	Unknown

Consorts:	Unknown	**Variant Names:**	Emramescha' Mermeshau
Manetho:	Not given		
King Lists:	T: (G 6.21; R 7.21; vB 6.21)		

The twenty-second king of Dynasty XIII, Imyremeshau does not seem to have been related to his predecessor, Khendjer. It is very probable that Imyremeshau was a usurper, although it is unknown if the change in rulers was accomplished through political means only or, as some scholars believe, by a military takeover. In any case, the word (*imy-rˤ*), is not only a well-attested personal name, but also the military title of "General." Gardiner and Hayes transcribe this entry in the Turin Canon as "Semenkhkare the General," while von Beckerath brings up the interesting theory that the title is used as a name because the real name was a foreign one Egyptians could not pronounce.

Attestations for Imyremeshau are limited to a pair of monumental statues dedicated to Ptah, and therefore most likely originally from Memphis, found by Petrie at Tanis. The statues were probably moved to Tanis by the Hyksos (there is an inscription of the Hyksos ruler Aqenenre Apepi on the right shoulder of each), although they may have been moved by order of Ramesses II of Dynasty XIX (both statues bear inscriptions of his name). The two statues are now in the Cairo Museum (JE37466 and 37467). Davies has suggested that the torso of a statuette (JE54493) found during excavation of the pyramid of an unnamed XIII Dynasty ruler at South Saqqara might belong to Imyremeshau. The fragment is uninscribed and Davies' tentative dating of the piece "to [a] close successor of Khendjer" is based "on grounds of provenance." The only other item attributable to Imyremeshau is a white steatite bead with an inscription that reads "Semenkhkare [Imyremeshau] beloved of Sobek, Lord of Shedyt." The bead, which is unpublished, is in the British Museum (BM EA74185). Its reference to Shedyt would seem to indicate it is from that town, which was a center for the worship of the crocodile god Sobek and was located in the Faiyum, some miles south of Memphis.

Von Beckerath places Imyremeshau as the eighteenth pharaoh of Dynasty XIII while Ryholt sees him as the twenty-third.

References:

W. Davies 1981b p. 24 #s 13,14 and 15
Gardiner 1959 pl. III Col. VI #21
Gardiner 1961 p. 440 #6.17
Hayes 1973 p. 47
Helck 1983 p. 12 #18
Jéquier 1933b p. 67 and note 4
Petrie 1885 pp. 8-9, pl. III #s 17 A-C and XIII #6

Petrie 1889 p. 18 #17
Quirke 1991 p. 131
Ryholt 1997a pp. 71 Col. 7.21, 73 #23, 192 table 33, 221-222, 284 table 83, 342 File 13/23, 408 table 94 #23
Vassilika 1995 p. 201 #2
von Beckerath 1964 p. 52
von Beckerath 1999 pp. 94 #18, 95 #18

Ined   Dynasty XIII

Horus Name:

Unknown   **Nomen and Prenomen:**

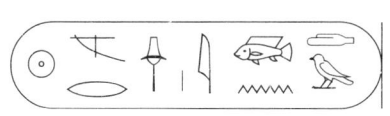

mr-sḫm-rʿ ind
Mersekhemre Ined

Prenomen:

mr-sḫm-rʿ
Mersekhemre

Two Ladies: Unknown

Golden Falcon: Unknown

Inek(?)

Length of Reign:	Unknown
Tomb:	Unknown
Mummy:	Unknown

Consorts:	Unknown	Variant Names:	Ind
Manetho:	Not given		
King Lists:	T: (G 7.6; R 8.6; vB 7.6)		

Probably the thirty-fifth king of Dynasty XIII, Ined is one of a group of kings known only from the Turin Canon. While the fragmentary condition of the papyrus allows for varying interpretations as to the positioning of some of these kings, Ined's position seems secure.

References:
Gardiner 1959 pl. III, Col. VII #6
Gardiner 1961 p. 440 #7.6
Ryholt 1997a pp. 71 Col. 8.6, 73 #36, 195, 197 #36, 356 File 13/36, 408 #36

von Beckerath 1999 pp. 98 #30, 99 #30

Inek(?)   Dynasty XIV

Horus Name:
   Unknown   **Nomen:** Unknown

Prenomen:

ink
Inek(?)

Two Ladies: Unknown

Golden Falcon: Unknown

Length of Reign:	Unknown
Tomb:	Unknown
Mummy:	Unknown

Consorts:	Unknown	**Variant Names:**	Ineb
Manetho:	Not given		Ink
King Lists:	T: (G 9.14; R 10.13; vB 11.x+11)		

Perhaps the forty-ninth king of Dynasty XIV, Inek is one of a group of kings known only from the Turin Canon. The papyrus' fragmentary state allows for varying interpretations as to the positioning of some of the kings of this dynasty. However, Inek's place seems secure. Inek's name has also been given as Ineb, the sign ⌐ (k) having been mistaken for the sign ⌐ (nb). It should be noted that von Beckerath would place Inek in his XV./XVI. Dynastie.

References:

Gardiner 1959 pl. III, Col. IX #14
Gardiner 1961 p. 442
J. Rose 1985 p. 76
Ryholt 1997a pp. 95 Col. 10.13, 98 #49, 380 File 14/49, 409 #49

von Beckerath 1999 pp. 120 #bb, 121 #bb

Ini I Dynasty XIII

Horus Name: Unknown

Nomen:

ini

Ini

Prenomen:

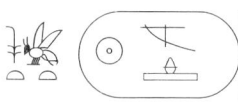

mr-ḥtp-rꜥ

Merhotepre

Two Ladies: Unknown

Golden Falcon: Unknown

Length of Reign:	T: "2 years, 3/4(?) months, 9 days"
Tomb:	Unknown
Mummy:	Unknown

Ini II

Consorts:	Unknown	Ani
Manetho:	Not given	Inai
		In(j)
King Lists:	T: (G 7.4; R 8.4)	Merhetepre
Variant Names:	Ana	

The son and direct successor to Aya, Ini I was probably the thirty-third king of Dynasty XIII, although he is placed as thirty-fourth by Ryholt and in the nebulous position of 28a by von Beckerath. Nothing of this king's reign is known and the only objects bearing his name are either non-contemporary ("The Juridical Stele," found at Karnak, which dates to the reign of Nebiryraw I of Dynasty XVI, and the Turin Canon) or of unknown provenance (a scarab-seal and an inscribed jar lid).

References:

Dodson and Hilton 2004 pp. 100, 106-107
Gardiner 1959 pl. III, Col. VIII #4
Gardiner 1961 p. 440 #7.4
Helck 1983 pp. 65-69
Kaplony 1973 p. 15 #40, pl. 10 #40, pl. 22 #40
Newberry 1906 p. 123 #21, pl. X #21
Quirke 2001a p. 263
Ryholt 1997a pp. 71 fig. 10, Col. 8 #4, 73 table 17 #34, 155, 192 table 33, 232, 233, 234, 235 and table 58, 284 table 83, 356 File 13/34, 408 table 94 #34
Tufnell 1984 pp. 181
von Beckerath 1999 pp. 98 #28a, 99 #28a

Ini II   Dynasty XIII

Horus Name: Unknown

Nomen:

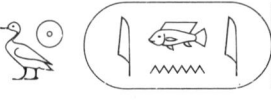

ini

Ini

Prenomen:

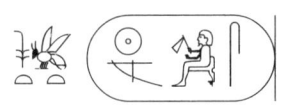

mr-šps-rˁ

Mershepsesre

Two Ladies: Unknown

Golden Falcon: Unknown

Length of Reign:	Unknown	
Tomb:	Unknown	
Mummy:	Unknown	
Consorts:	Unknown	Ani
Manetho:	Not given	Inai
King Lists:	T: (R 8.16?)	In(j)
Variant Names:	Ana	

The only evidence for this king is an inscription, giving both the nomen and prenomen, carved on the bottom half of a stone statue whose provenance was probably Karnak, and which is now housed in the Museo del Sannio in Benevento, Italy. Ini may be recorded in the Turin Canon (column 8.16, as reconstructed by Ryholt, column VII.21 according to Gardiner). If the partially preserved prenomen "Mer...re" in the Papyrus is in fact the listing for Mershepsesre, then Ini II would have been the forty-sixth king of Dynasty XIII (however, see NEFERHOTEP II). In any event, Ini II would have ruled towards the end of this dynasty.

References:
W. Davies 1981b pp. 28-29 #41
Dodson and Hilton 2004 p. 100
Gardiner 1959 pl. III, Col. VII #21
Helck 1983 p. 44 #61
Ryholt 1997a pp. 70, 72, 74 table 18, 358 File 13/a

von Beckerath 1963 pp. 4-5
von Beckerath 1999 pp. 104 #h, 105 #h (as Ini I)

In(tef)   Concurrent with Dynasty XI

Horus Name:

snfr-t3wy.f

Nomen: *s3 r˓ in*
(Son of Re) In

Prenomen: *q3-k3-r˓*
Qakare

In(tef)

Two Ladies: *nbty snfr-tꜣwy.f*

Golden Falcon: *bik-nbw nfr*

Length of Reign:	Unknown
Tomb:	Unknown
Mummy:	Unknown

Consorts:	Unknown	Haa-ka
Manetho:	Not given	Hakara
		Ho-ka-ra
King Lists:	None	In
		Kakare
Variant Names:		Ka-ku-Re
	An(tef)	Ra-qa-ka
	An(jotef)	Seanra
	An(yotef)	Wazkara
	En(yotef)	

Attestations for this "pharaoh" are known only from Lower Nubia, where 16 rock-carved inscriptions bearing his name have been found between Gudhi and Abu Simbel. The inscriptions vary from a single cartouche to a full titulary, but give no further information. It has long been posited that Qakare In(tef) was most likely a Nubian chieftain who had taken on pharaonic trappings at a time when Egyptian control over Nubia had waned, that is, either after the fall of the Old Kingdom and concurrent with the early Dynasty XI, during the troubled period at the end of Dynasty XI, or during the Second Intermediate Period.

It has been pointed out that In(tef) bears the same prenomen as a Dynasty VII/VIII pharaoh, Qakare Ibi, and the nomen of three pharaohs of the early Dynasty XI, and this could indicate a reign during that period. However, Zaba makes a strong case for the close of Dynasty XI/early Dynasty XII, which would also rule out the Second Intermediate Period date.

Although there are two other local "pharaohs" named on the rock carvings of Nubia (see IYIBKHENTRE and SEGERSENI), evidence is too sparse to indicate what, if any, connection these three may have had. Although the Horus name of Iyibkhentre is found carved next to the titulary of In(tef) at Toshka, this probably only means that space was available on that particular surface. It would be interesting to know which name was carved first.

References:

Budge 1908 vol. I p. 105-106
Gardiner 1961 p. 121
Grajetzki 2006 pp. 27-28
Hayes 1953 p. 167
Peden 2001 p. 24
Petrie 1924 vol. I p. 149

von Beckerath 1999 pp. 80 #a, 81 #a
Weigall 1907 pl. XXXIV #1, LIV #s 1,3,4,6, LXIV #s 4 and 8, LXV #1
Winlock 1947 p. 100
Zaba 1974 pp. 154-155 #141, 160-161 #149, 162-163, figs. 248, 249, 259

Intef — Dynasty XI

Horus Name: Unknown

Nomen: iry-pꜥt ḥꜣt in-it.f
(Hereditary Prince) Intef

Prenomen: Unknown

Two Ladies: Unknown

Golden Falcon: Unknown

Length of Reign: Unknown

Tomb: Unknown

Mummy: Unknown

Consorts: Unknown

Manetho: Not given

King Lists: K: (12); T: (G 5 1??)

Anjotef
Anyotef
Enyotef
Inyotef

Variant Names: Antef

Not a pharaoh at all, Intef was rather a nomarch of the Theban nome who is shown on Dynasty XVIII pharaoh Thutmose III's "chapel of royal ancestors" at Karnak. Although his name is not surrounded by a cartouche, and his title is given as "Count and Hereditary Prince," it is clear that Intef was considered, if not the founder, at least a key figure in the foundation of Dynasty XI. It is probable that this Intef should be equated with the Intef-aa (Intef the Elder, or the Great), son of Ikui, whose name is on a small gray-granite seated statuette found at Karnak and dedicated by Senwosret I: "Made by the King of Upper and Lower Egypt Kheper-ka-Re as his monument for his father Prince Intef the Elder...born of Ikui." The stele of the Gatekeeper Maat, a minor official from the reign of Montuhotep II, asks that a prayer be said for "In(tef) the Elder the son of Ikui." He is probably also the Intefi of the stele found by Mariette at Dra Abu el-Naga, "the Hereditary Prince, Count, Great Lord of the Theban Nome, satisfying the King as Keeper of the Gateway to the South, Great Pillar of him who makes his Two Lands to Live, the Chief Prophet...." A fragment of stele from Dendera mentions the "Great Prince of the Southland, Intef the Elder."

The king whom Intef served is unknown, but it was one of the Herakleopolitan rulers of Dynasty IX/X. Also, how much actual territory Intef controlled is unknown. Certainly he held some sort of sway over the land between Thebes and the southern border of Egypt at Aswan if the stele found at Thebes by Mariette is to be believed. It is also likely that he controlled the area north of Thebes to Coptos.

A few scholars have suggested that this Intef later claimed the throne and became Intef I, but there no evidence to support such a theory.

Gardiner believed that Intef was originally listed in the Turin Canon's column 5, number 12, a section missing from the much-damaged papyrus. This was pure speculation on his part.

References:

Clère and Vandier 1948 pp. 7-9 #s 11-14
Dodson and Hilton 2004 pp. 83, 84, 85, 88
Gardiner 1959 pl. II, Col. V #12
Gardiner 1961 pp. 117-118, 438
Gomaa 2001 pp. 468-469
Grajetzki 2006 pp. 10-11
Grimal 1992 p. 143
Habachi 1958 pp. 182, 183 fig. 4
Hayes 1953 pp. 148, 153-154 and fig. 91
Petrie 1924 pp. 136-137 and fig. 87
Seidlmayer 2000 p. 133
Strudwick 1999 p. 23
von Beckerath 1999 pp. 76 #2, 77 #2 (Combines the nomarch Intef with Intef I)
Winlock 1947 p. 5-6, pl. 2

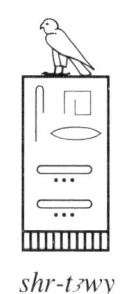

Intef I — Dynasty XI

Horus Name: *shr-t3wy* — Sehertowy

Nomen: *s3-rˤ in-it.f* (Son of Re) Intef

Prenomen: Unknown

Two Ladies: Unknown

Golden Falcon: Unknown

Length of Reign:	4-16 years
Tomb:	Saff-tomb at El-Tarif, "Saff el-Dawba"
Mummy:	Unknown

Consorts:	Unknown	Anjotef
Manetho:	Not given	Anyotef
		Enyotef
King Lists:	K: (13); T: (G 5.13; vB 5.13)	Inyotef
Variant Names:	Antef	

Most probably the son of Montuhotep I, Intef I is the true first king of Dynasty XI, and certainly the first Theban ruler to lay claim to a Horus name (though Montuhotep I received an honorific Horus name many years after his death). By taking a Horus name, Intef was declaring himself king of all Egypt, which probably didn't set well with rival nomarchs to the north, or with whichever Herakleopolitan ruler was also claiming to be pharaoh at the time. The sentiment expressed by Intef's Horus name, Sehertowy, "Pacifier of the Two Lands," was premature.

Aside from the ruins of his tomb at Thebes, no contemporary attestations for Intef I are known. However, recent work by the Theban Desert Road Survey has led to the discovery of an interesting hieratic graffito at the Gebel Tjauti in the Western Desert, northwest of Thebes. The inscription reads "the assault troops of the son of Re, Intef." It has been posited that the nomen and the soldiers belonged to Sehertowy Intef I, and that they were there in order to fight an action against Tjauti, nomarch of the Coptite nome (after whom the Gebel is named). An eroded stele erected by Tjauti perhaps supports

Intef II

this theory. It tells us that Tjauti had constructed a road by which to allow his people to cross the desert, "which the ruler of another nome had sealed off [when he came in order to] fight with my nome...." Without a doubt, the Tjauti inscription is referring to an Intef, but we cannot be sure of which one, although it would be either Intef I or his brother and successor, Intef II. The lack of a Horus name is unfortunate. Whoever the ruler, the defeat of Tjauti seems to have cleared the way for the eventual taking not only of Coptos, but everything as far north as Abydos, thus pushing Theban control some 250 km. northward.

Intef I's tomb, cut into the side of a hill at el-Tarif, opposite Thebes, is what is called a saff-tomb, after the Arabic word for "row," since a row of pillars fronts the tomb. What survives is a huge sunken courtyard (some 65 x 300 m.), backed by a colonnade, behind which is carved a mortuary chapel flanked by two chambers. The king's burial chamber is carved beneath the chapel.

Two blocks from the temple of Montu at Tod, dating to the reign of Montuhotep II, show that king with three kings named Intef; above each Intef is written his Horus name, thus giving the order of succession from Intef I to Montuhotep II. (Intef III's Horus name has broken away, but his place is secure.)

Although no dated material has survived, estimates for Intef's length of reign vary from four to sixteen years. The much-damaged Turin Canon has a gap at this point, and Intef I's name is lost.

References:

J.C. and D. Darnell 1997b p. 26
J.C. Darnell 2002 pp. 38-40, 42, pl. 5b and 26
Dodson 2003 p. 81
Dodson and Hilton 2004 pp. 80, 82, 83, 84, 85
Franke 2001 pp. 528, 529, 530
Gardiner 1959 pl. II, Col. V.12
Gardiner 1961 pp. 118, 438
Gomaa 2001 p. 469
Grajetzki 2006 pp. 11-13, 15
Habachi 1958 pp. 179, 182, 183 fig. 4
Habachi 1963 p. 46 fig. 22
Hayes 1953 pp. 148, 151
Lehner 1997 p. 165
Peden 2001 p. 17
Polz 2001 p. 386
Seidlmayer 2000 p. 134
Strudwick 1999 pp. 22-23, 24
von Beckerath 1997 p. 209
von Beckerath 1999 pp. 76 #2, 77 #2

Intef II   Dynasty XI

Horus Name:

Nomen: s3-rꜥ in-it.f ꜥ3

(Son of Re) Intef (ꜥ3)

wꜣḥ-ꜥnḫ

Prenomen: Unknown

Two Ladies: Unknown

Golden Falcon: Unknown

Intef II

Length of Reign:	49 years	
Tomb:	Saff-tomb at El-Tarif, "Saff el-Qasisiya"	
Mummy:	Unknown	
Consorts:	Neferu (II)	Anjotef
Manetho:	Not given	Anyotef
		Enyotef
King Lists:	K: (15); T:	Inyotef
	(G 5.14; vB 5.14)	Uah-onkh
		Wahonkh
Variant Names:	Antef	

The son of Montuhotep I and his Queen Neferu, Wahankh Intef II ascended the throne upon the death of his brother (or half-brother) Sehertowy Intef I. Intef II's familial relationships are revealed by an inscription on the base of a statue of his father that Intef II caused to be placed in the sanctuary of Heqaib at Elephantine, and by several blocks from the temple of Montu at Tod which show Intef II in a sort of "ancestor list," preceded by Intef I and followed by his successor, Intef III.

Intef II's consort was most likely a woman called Neferu, which would seem to be a diminutive for Neferukayet, a lady who is referred to as a king's daughter, a king's wife and a king's mother on the funerary stele of her Seal-bearer, "Sole Companion and Favorite...," Rediu-Khnum. She was likely the daughter of Montuhotep I and his wife Neferu, and therefore a sister as well as the wife of Intef II.

The "kingdom" Intef II inherited seems to have consisted of the first four nomes of Upper Egypt, from Thebes south to the Nubian border at Elephantine. Control of this area must have been stable enough to allow Intef to pursue interests to the north, where dwelt a rival claimant to the throne of Upper and Lower Egypt ruling from his capital at Herakleopolis, just south of the Faiyum. Of course, the "pharaoh" from Herakleopolis, of whose name we are unsure, claimed control of Egypt in its entirety, when in fact his southern border seems to have varied depending on the loyalty of the various southern nomes. Most definitely, that loyalty ceased completely at the Theban border.

Trouble with the Coptite nome, which bordered Theban territory to the north, was certain to erupt eventually, and it finally did either late in the reign of Intef I or early in the reign of Intef II. Possible evidence for the hostilities comes from Gebel Tjauti, on the west side of the Nile, northwest of Thebes and many kilometers west, and across the river from the Coptite capital at Khozam. A stele of the Coptite nomarch Tjauti (after whom the site is named) records a conflict between himself and "the ruler of another nome" in that area. Not far from the stele is a graffito which reads "the assault troops of the son of Re, Intef," which would seem to support the stele's text. Unfortunately, we don't know whether Intef I or Intef II is meant. Under whichever Intef it may have started, the conflict between Coptos and Thebes eventually led to the downfall of the Coptite nome, and Intef II took dominion over all land north to the border of Asyut, a total of more than 250 km. Stelae, such as those of the courtiers Hotepi from El Kab and Djari from Thebes, make prominent mention of troops and battle. On a stele from his funerary chapel, the king lauds his own acquisitions: "I captured the entire Thinite nome, I opened all her fortresses, I made her the Door of the North."

The rival pharaoh at Herakleopolis would not have been pleased by the Theban encroachment on his domain and there is mention of fighting with the "house of Khety" in an inscription of a Theban official named Djari. However, it seems as though the nome of Asyut became something of a buffer state and kept the two rival claimants to the throne separated. At any rate, open hostility would appear to have abated.

Although not many attestations remain from his reign, Intef tells us that he contributed to the temple of Montu at Karnak, and at Karnak a column bearing his name is the earliest known example of royal architecture from the temple of Amen. Intef also added chapels to the temples of Satet and Khnum at Elephantine, and from the same island comes a "stele" bearing his Horus name and nomen. Intef is also attested to by inscriptions of several officials such as the biographical stelae of Hotepi, the "sole friend" Djari and the "personal servant and chamberlain" Tjetji.

A hieroglyphic graffito of Intef II was discovered at Amada in Upper Nubia. It has been suggested that the carving might have been left by a military or commercial expedition, but the evidence is very slight indeed.

Intef II's tomb at El-Tarif was a saff tomb, an extended and enlarged version of that of Intef I, filled with many chambers and fronted by a double row of columns that faced a courtyard which measured some 70 x 250 m. This tomb was one of those royal tombs investigated by a royal commission during a spate of robberies almost nine hundred years later, during the reign of the Dynasty XX pharaoh Ramesses IX. The tomb was found intact with its stele, showing Intef with his hunting dogs, still in place.

Although Intef II's name is missing, the Turin Canon gives him a reign of 49 years. This is in keeping with the 50 years given on a stele from his tomb. A large statue fragment of a king in the Sed Festival costume, discovered in the sanctuary of Heqaib at Elephantine, may represent Intef II. It was one of a group of three statues, two of which bore Intef's cartouche, and all three were most likely carved by the same sculptor. In addition, Intef certainly reigned long enough to have held a Sed Festival.

References:

Allen 1976 pp. 1-29
D. Arnold 1976 pp. 19-22, pl. 11-13
Clère and Vandier 1948 pp. 9-11 #15, 14 #18
Dodson 2003 pp. 81-82
Dodson and Hilton 2004 pp. 82, 83, 84, 85, 88-89
Gabra 1976 pp. 45-56, pl. 14
Gardiner 1959 pl. II, Col. V.14
Gardiner 1961 pp. 118-119, 438
Gomaa 2001 p. 469
Grajetzki 2006 pp. 10, 11, 12-16, 19, 21, pl. XVIII
Grajetzki 2005 pp. 26-27
Grimal 1992 p. 298
Habachi 1958 pp. 176-180, 182, 183 fig. 4
Habachi 1963 p. 46-47 and fig. 22
Habachi 1985 pl. 189 a-d, 190 a-b, 191 and 192
Hayes 1953 pp. 151-152 and fig. 90
Lehner 1997 p. 167
Peden 2001 pp. 22-23
Peet 1930 p. 38
Petrie 1924 pp. 137-138 and fig. 88
Polz 2001 p. 386
Seidlmayer 2000 pp. 134-138
Strudwick 1999 pp. 22-23, 24, 93, 120
von Beckerath 1997 p. 209
von Beckerath 1999 pp. 76 #3, 77 #3
Winlock 1947 pp. 12-18, pl. 4

Intef III   Dynasty XI

Horus Name:

nḫt nb-tp-nfr
Nakhtnebtepnefer

Nomen:

sꜣ-rꜥ in-it.f
(Son of Re) Intef

Prenomen: Unknown

Two Ladies: Unknown

Golden Falcon: Unknown

Length of Reign:	8 years
Tomb:	Saff tomb at El-Tarif: "Saff el-Baqar"
Mummy:	Unknown

Consorts:	Iah		Anjotef
Manetho:	Not given		Anyotef
			Enyotef
King Lists:	K: (16?);		Inyotef
	T: (G 5.15)		
Variant Names:	Antef		

The third king of Dynasty XI, Nakhtnebtepnefer Intef III was the son of his immediate predecessor, Intef II. His father had reigned for 49 years, so it is likely that Intef III was at least a middle-aged man at the time of his accession to the Theban throne. He seems to have inherited a relatively peaceful kingdom, with some sort of uneasy (and probably unspoken) truce between Thebes and Herakleopolis having been in effect since at least the latter part of his father's rule.

Attestations for Intef III are few. It is known that he added to the temple of Satet at Elephantine, and there is a doorjamb from the sanctuary of Heqaib, also at Elephantine. Another doorjamb, this one from the tomb of the official Nakhty at Abydos, also bears Intef's name as king of Upper and Lower Egypt. The king is mentioned on stelae of officials such as the treasurer Tjetji, which speaks of the death of Intef II and the ascension to the throne of Intef III. Two blocks from the temple of Montu at Tod show the succession of kings from Intef I to Montuhotep II. The three Intef kings are identified by their Horus names, and while Intef III's Horus title is missing, his position in the line-up is certain. Also from the time of Montuhotep II comes a large rock carving at Wadi Shatt el-Rigal, showing that pharaoh facing Intef III, who is identified as his father.

Intef III's tomb at El-Tarif was a saff tomb, much in the style of the tomb of Intef II in that it has a great many rooms behind its facade as well as rooms to the left and right of the main structure. The courtyard is 75 m. wide, but the length is unknown.

Due to the fragmentary condition of the Turin Canon, Intef III's name has been lost. However, the length of his reign has survived; it is given as eight years.

References:

Dodson 2003 p. 82
Dodson and Hilton 2004 pp. 36, 82, 84, 85, 88-89
Gardiner 1959 pl. II, Col. V.15
Gardiner 1961 pp. 119-120, 438
Grajetzki 2006 pp. 15-17
Habachi 1958 pp. 182, 183 fig. 4
Habachi 1963 p. 46 fig. 22
Habachi 1985 pl. 190c

Lehner 1997 p. 165
Lichtheim 1975 pp. 90-93
Lichtheim 1988 pp. 42-46, 46-49
Polz 2001 p. 386
Seidlmayer 2000
von Beckerath 1997 p. 209
von Beckerath 1999 pp. 76 #4, 77 #4
Winlock 1947 p. 19, 62, 64, pl. 2, 12, 36

Intef IV   Dynasty XIII

Horus Name:

Unknown   **Nomen:**

in-it.f
Intef

Intef IV

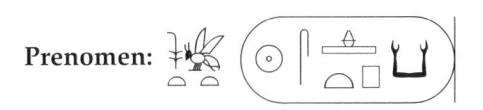

Prenomen: *s.ḥtp-k3-rʿ*
Sehotepkare

Two Ladies: Unknown

Golden Falcon: Unknown

Length of Reign:	T: "…+ 3 days"
Tomb:	Unknown
Mummy:	Unknown

Consorts:	Unknown	**Variant Names:**	Antef
Manetho:	Unknown		Anjotef
King Lists:	K: (23); T: (G 6.22; R 7.22; vB 6.22)		Anyotef Inyotef

Intef IV is probably the twenty-third king of Dynasty XIII, although Ryholt places him as the twenty-fourth king. The only contemporary attestation for Intef IV is the lower half of a seated statue found in the temple complex of the serpent goddess Renenutet at Medinet Madi in the Faiyum and now in the Cairo Museum (JE67834). Ryholt sees this pharaoh as the fifth ruler named Intef. Von Beckerath places Intef IV as the nineteenth ruler of Dynasty XIII.

References:

W. Davies 1981b p. 24 #16
Gardiner 1959 pl. III, Col. VI #22
Gardiner 1961 p. 440 #6.22
Ryholt 1997a pp. 71 Col. 7.22, 73 #24, 192 table 33, 342 File 13/24, 408 #24

von Beckerath 1999 pp. 94 #19, 95 #19

Intef V — Dynasty XVII

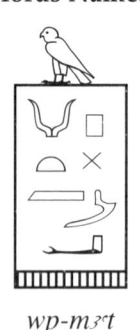

Horus Name: wp-m3't

Nomen: in-it.f 3 — Intef (the Elder)

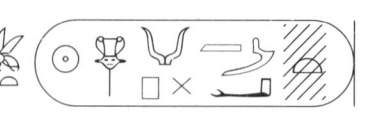

Prenomen: sḫm-rʿ-wp-m3't — Sekhemre-wepmaat

Two Ladies: Unknown

Golden Falcon: Unknown

Length of Reign:	Unknown
Tomb:	Dra Abu el-Naga
Mummy:	Unknown

Consorts:	Unknown		Anjotef
Manetho:	Not given		Anyotef
			Inyotef
King Lists:	None		Ra-seshes-up-maat
Variant Names:	Antef		Seshes-Ra-up-maat
	Antefaa		

The third ruler of Dynasty XVII, Intef V was the son of his immediate predecessor, Sobekemsaf I, and probably Queen Nubkhaes. He was also the older brother of his successor, Intef VI, as is evidenced by the appellation ⌒ (ꜥ), usually translated as "the Elder."

Beyond his familial relations, nothing is known about Intef V. His attestations are few and, with the possible exception of an adze blade whose provenance is unknown, relate directly to his burial.

The capstone from his pyramid at Dra Abu el-Naga has survived and its inscriptions give us his Horus name, prenomen and nomen, one to a side. On the fourth side is inscribed the titles and name of his mother; her titles remain but the name is gone. The pyramid itself, made of brick, does not seem to have survived, although two sarcophagi, those of Intefs V and VII remain. The coffins were retrieved by modern tomb robbers.

Intef V was buried by his successor and brother, Intef VI. His coffin was made "as a gift to him from his brother King Intef."

Ryholt gives this king as Intef VI.

References:

Budge 1913 p. 9, pl. 29
Dewachter 1985 p. 65
Dodson 1994c p. 33
Dodson 2000 pp. 17 and fig. 13, 19, 21
Dodson 2003 p. 107
Dodson and Hilton 2004 pp. 116, 117, 118
Ikram and Dodson 1998 pp. 10, 315,318

Lehner 1997 p. 188
Peet 1930 p. 38
Ryholt 1997a pp. 65, 167, 169, 170, 171, table 28, 176, 266, 267, 270-271 and table 79, 393-394 File 17/3, 410, table 98
von Beckerath 1999 pp. 128 #11, 129 #11 (as Intef VI)
Winlock 1924 pp. 234-237, pl. XIV and XV

Intef VI   Dynasty XVII

Horus Name:

nfr-ḫprw

Nomen:

in-it.f
Intef

Prenomen:

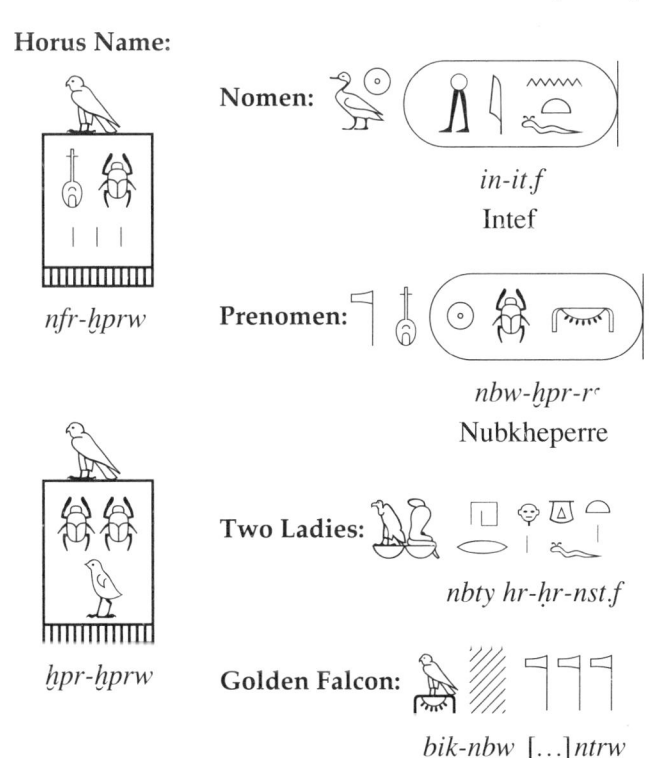

nbw-ḫpr-rˁ
Nubkheperre

ḫpr-ḫprw

Two Ladies:

nbty hr-hr-nst.f

Golden Falcon:

bik-nbw […]nṯrw

Length of Reign:	3+ years
Tomb:	Dra Abu el-Naga
Mummy:	Destroyed

151

Intef VI

Consorts:	Sobekemsaf B	Anjotef
Manetho:	Not given	Anyotef
		Inyotef
King Lists:	K: (27)	Ra-nub-kheper
Variant Names:	Antef	

The son of the pharaoh Sobekemsaf I and the brother and successor of king Intef V, Intef VI was the fourth ruler of Dynasty XVII. Based at Thebes, Intef VI's domain appears to have remained the same as at the beginning of the dynasty. This situation might indicate that hostility with the rival Dynasty XV had abated for a time.

Attestations for Intef VI are found only within the limits of the Theban state. He undertook restoration at Abydos and also built there extensively; several inscribed blocks, an architrave, a "relief," and an inscribed column have been found. Also from this site comes the stele of the treasurer Ahnefer, which shows Intef VI leading the official to the god Osiris. Lastly, from Abydos comes the stele of a King's Son, Nakht, which gives a regnal year three for the king.

From Coptos come inscribed stone blocks from a chapel and a royal decree that, like the Abydos stele, is dated to year three.

From the Theban area come the majority of attestations. A doorjamb and a graffito come from Thebes itself; from the royal cemetery at Dra Abu el-Naga we have the remains of the king's pyramid, a pair of obelisks (unfortunately lost in the Nile!), a sarcophagus, a silver diadem, inscribed linen fragments and a portion of a collar. From the Deir el-Bahri area come a wooden panel and graffiti bearing the king's nomen. From the temple of Ptah at Karnak comes a stele inscribed with his titulary.

Edfu has supplied the stele of the scribe Nakhthor, which bears Intef's nomen. Also, perhaps from the Edfu area, come bracelets, a signet ring, a pendant, and jewelry of Queen Sobekemsaf, which is also inscribed with Intef's name.

Intef's pyramid at Dra Abu el-Naga was discovered by Mariette in 1860 but, due to the lack of any publication, was lost again until its existence was rediscovered by Winlock in 1920. In 2001, the German Institute of Archaeology (DAI) began excavations in the area where Winlock had deduced the tomb would be and almost at once found the king's prenomen in a small private chapel. Shortly thereafter, the remains of Intef's pyramid were discovered. The pyramid, made of mud brick, had stood some 13 m. tall and had a base of 11 m. The burial chamber, which was fitted with a recess in the floor for the king's coffin, was at the bottom of a 7 m. shaft located just outside the southeast corner of the tomb. A portion of the pyramidion was also discovered.

In the sixteenth year of the Dynasty XX king Ramesses IX, rumors of tomb robbery led to an inspection of a series of tombs, one of which belonged to Intef VI. An attempt to bore into the pyramid was evidenced by a "tunnel" some 2 1/2 cubits deep in the north side of the tomb, but the thieves hadn't managed to gain entrance and the tomb was regarded as intact. We can only assume that the hole was filled in.

Intef's pyramid seems to have remained undisturbed until 1827, when it was discovered by local tomb robbers. A report written by Giovanni D'Athanasi, an agent employed by the British consul Henry Salt, who was "building" an Egyptian collection, tells us of the fate of Intef's mummy: "They discovered, placed around the head of the mummy, but over the linen, a diadem, composed of silver and beautiful mosaic work, its center being formed of gold, representing an asp...The Arabs...immediately proceeded to break up the mummy, as was their usual custom, for the treasures it might contain...."

References:

Andrews 1990 pp. 89 fig. 65, 153
Brier 1994 254-255
Budge 1913 p. 9, pl. 28
Budge 1922 p. 8, pl. 28
Dodson 1994b pp. 41 note 26, 42 note 35, 45 note 55
Dodson 2000 pp. 18, fig. 14, 19-20, 21, 22, 28
Dodson 2003 p. 108
Dodson and Hilton 2004 pp. 10, 147, 160, 254, 315, 318
Helck 1983 pp. 72 #105, 74 #107, 75-76 #108, 76 #109, 77 #12
Ikram and Dodson 1998 pp. 10, 315, 318
Peet 1930 p. 38
Petrie 1896b pp. 9-11, pl. VI #s 1-12, pl. VII and VIII
Petrie 1902b pp. 28, 41-42, pl. LV #3-5 and 8, LVII
Petrie 1903 pp. 35, pl. XXXII #s 3 and 4
Polz 2003 pp. 12-15
Polz and Seiler 2003
Ryholt 1997a pp. 167, 169, 171, table 28, 176, 266-268, 309, 394-395 File 17/4, 410, table 98 (as Intef VII)
von Beckerath 1999 pp. 124 #1, 125 #1 (as Intef V)
Winlock 1924 pp. 228-230, pl. XIV

Intef VII   Dynasty XVII

Horus Name:
Unknown   **Nomen:**

in-it.f3
Intef (3)

Intef VII

Prenomen:

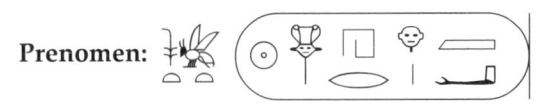

sḫm-rꜥ ḥr ḥr-mꜣꜥt
Sekhemre-herhermaat

Two Ladies: Unknown

Golden Falcon: Unknown

Length of Reign:	Unknown
Tomb:	Unknown; probably at Dra Abu el-Naga
Mummy:	Unknown

Consorts:	Haankhes(?)	Anjotef
Manetho:	Not given	Anyotef
		Inyotef
King Lists:	None	Ra-seshes-her-maat
Variant Names:	Antef	

The fifth pharaoh of Dynasty XVII, Intef VII's parentage is unknown, as is his relationship to his predecessor, Intef VI. Various scholars suggest that Intef VII may have been a brother, son or even brother-in-law to Intef VI. The only thing we know with a modicum of certainty is that Intef VII was buried in a coffin that had been inscribed with the name of his predecessor.

This coffin, the only attestation for Intef VII, was one of two coffins purchased by the French Egyptologist Auguste Mariette at Luxor in 1854 (the other was the coffin of Intef V). The coffin has been described as "undertaker's stock," or "a private coffin, hurriedly adapted to hold the body of King Sekhemre-heruhirmaet Inyotef (VII)." Wherever the coffin came from originally, it had been inscribed with the nomen of Intef VI (which was written slightly differently from the other Intefs) which was changed to fit the writing of Intef VII. The prenomen, Sekhemre-herhermaat, was written across the coffin's chest in ink—a hasty job at best!

Ryholt posits a coregency between the two Intefs. He cites the fact that VI's original coffin was outfitted for VII, which would imply that VI outlived (and buried) VII. This was not a case of usurpation, since Intef VI had another coffin made for his eventual use.

Ryholt numbers Intef VII as VIII.

References:
Dodson 2000 pp. 19, 21
Dodson 2003 p. 107
Dodson and Hilton 2004 pp. 116, 117, 118, 120
Ryholt 1997a pp. 167 and note 602, 171 table 28, 176 note 628, 266-268, 395 File 17/5, 410, table 98
von Beckerath 1999 pp. 128 #12, 129 #12
Winlock 1924 pp. 267, pl. XXI

I...re   Dynasty XIV

Horus Name: Unknown

Nomen: Unknown

Prenomen:

i...rˁ
I...re

Two Ladies: Unknown

Golden Falcon: Unknown

Length of Reign:	Unknown
Tomb:	Unknown
Mummy:	Unknown

Consorts:	Unknown	**Variant Names:**	A...re
Manetho:	Not given		Ya
King Lists:	T: (G 8.23; R 9.23; vB 8.23)		

Possibly the twenty-ninth king of Dynasty XIV, I...re is one of a group of kings known only from the Turin Canon. The papyrus' fragmentary state allows for varying interpretations as to the positioning of some kings of this dynasty. However, I...re's place seems secure. Gardiner ignores the hieroglyph ☉ (*rˁ*) and sees the name as Ya. Von Beckerath also ignores the ideogram for *rˁ* and gives the partially preserved name as A....

References:
Gardiner 1959 pl. III, Col. VIII #23
Gardiner 1961 p. 441 8.23
Ryholt 1997a pp. 95 Col. 9.23, 98 #29, 380 File 14/29, 409 #29
von Beckerath 1984 pp. 75 #24, 160 XIV Dynasty #24, 213 #24

Iry-Hor   Dynasty 0

iri-ḥrw
Iry-Hor

Length of Reign:	Unknown
Tomb:	Abydos, B 0/1/2
Mummy:	Unknown

Consorts:	Unknown	Irj-Hor
Manetho:	Not given	Ra
King Lists:	None	Ro
Variant Names:	Iri (-Hor)	

    This early ruler was discovered by Petrie during the excavation of tomb complex B1/2 at Abydos in 1899. While there has been some question in the past as to whether the "name" found on pottery in the complex is in fact the name of a king, the most recent interpretations of the data support Petrie's original thesis that Iry-Hor was a king.

    Petrie read the hieroglyphs of the name (a falcon standing above the mouth symbol) as "King Ro." More recently the name has been given as Iry-Hor.

    Re-excavation of B1/2 in the 1990s led to the uncovering of an adjoining section, B0. This enlargement of the original complex and the complex's positioning make it almost certain that B0/1/2 is part of the sequence of king's tombs which slightly pre-date the royal tombs of Dynasty I.

    Although Iry-Hor's name has been associated exclusively with Abydos, it is possible that he is also represented by a seal impression found in tomb Z 401 at Zawiyet el-Aryan.

References:

Dreyer et al. 1996 pp. 11-81
Hendrickx 1999 p. 241
Kaiser 1982 pp. 230-235
Kaplony 1963 vol. III pl. 7.13
Legge 1904 p. 128
O'Brien 1996 pp. 131-132
Petrie 1900 pl. XLIV. 2-9
Petrie 1902a pp. 3, 6
Petrie 1902b pp. 4-5
Petrie 1903 p. 26
Petrie 1905 p. 283
Spencer 1993 p. 57
van den Brink 1996 p. 146, figs. 3 III.14 and IVa.22 pl. 31.a-b
von Beckerath 1999 pp. 36 #x+1, 37 #x+1
T. Wilkinson 1993 pp. 241-243
T. Wilkinson 1999 p. 55
Willoughby 1988 pp. 44, 73

Isu   Dynasty VII/VIII

Horus Name: Unknown

Nomen: *isw* — Isu

Prenomen: Unknown

Two Ladies: Unknown

Golden Falcon: Unknown

Length of Reign: Unknown
Tomb: Unknown
Mummy: Unknown

Consorts: Unknown
Manetho: Not given
King Lists: None
Variant Names: Asu

Isu is perhaps not a king at all. Arthur Weigall found a much weathered and, in places, illegible carving north of Gebel Silsila in 1908. It contained an inscription that dealt with a King's Son Isu-Ankh (*isw-ꜥnh*), which led Weigall to posit a ruler named Isu, since the name is compounded with a cartouche.

References:
von Beckerath 1999 pp. 70 #g, 71 #g
Weigall 1908 p. 110

Ity   Dynasty IX/X(?)

ity
Ity

Iyibkhentre

Length of Reign:	Unknown
Tomb:	Pyramid called "Glory of Ity," location unknown
Mummy:	Unknown

Consorts:	Unknown	**Variant Names:**	None
Manetho:	Not given		
King Lists:	None		

This king is known only from an inscription carved into the rocks of the Wadi Hammamat, on the principal trade route from Coptos to the Red Sea. The inscription is dated to the first year of Ity's reign and concerns an expedition to acquire a finer grade of stone for the king's pyramid, the "Glory of Ity."

Some scholars would equate Ity with either king Teti or king Userkare of Dynasty VI. Goedicke finds it "tempting" to equate Ity with king Djer of Dynasty I. None of these identities is convincing. Structural idiomatics of the text of the inscription would appear to point to Dynasty X (see "Herakleopolitans" in Glossary). However, it should be noted that von Beckerath places him in Dynasty VII/VIII and Gardiner offers a theory that would place Ity as a contemporary of Dynasty VI.

The location of Ity's pyramid is unknown, although Grdseloff would place it at Saqqara.

References:

Breasted 1906 vol. I p. 174
Couyat and Montet 1912 pp. 94
Gauthier 1907-17 vol. 1 pp. 144-145
Goedicke 1990 pp. 65-76
Goyon 1957 p. 42, pl. XLVII and XLVIII
Grdseloff 1939 pp. 393-396
Spalinger 1994 p. 313
Verner 1997 p. 322
von Beckerath 1999 pp. 70 #c, 71 #c

Iyibkhentre   Concurrent with Dynasty XI

Horus Name:

grg-t3wy.f

Nomen: Unknown

Prenomen:

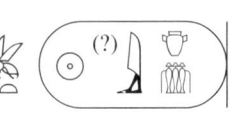

i(y)-ib-ḫnt-rˤ
Iy(?)ibkhentre

Two Ladies: Unknown

Golden Falcon: Unknown

Length of Reign:	Unknown	
Tomb:	Unknown	
Mummy:	Unknown	

Consorts:	Unknown	I-khent-yeb-Re'
Manetho:	Not given	Ijibchentre
King Lists:	None	Ra-...-ab-khent
		Ra-ab-khent
Variant Names:	Ker(?)-taui-f	

The "pharaoh" is attested to only in Lower Nubia, where three rock-carvings bear his name. In two cases the name Iyibkhentre is accompanied by his Horus name, and in the third case only the Horus is given.

Iyibkhentre is one of three Nubian chieftains who seem to have declared themselves kings of Upper and Lower Egypt, despite the fact that their sphere of influence only covered a portion of Lower Nubia (see In(tef) and Segerseni). We do not know if these rulers were related in any way, or if they succeeded each other. Also, the period in which they held sway is uncertain, though it had to have been at a time when Egyptian control was minimal or nonexistent. The most likely time would have been after the fall of the Old Kingdom and concurrent with the early Dynasty XI, or at the troubled period at the end of that dynasty, with evidence slightly favoring the latter date.

References:

Budge 1908 vol. II p. 105
Grajetzki 2006 p. 27
Hayes 1953 p. 167
Peden 2001 p. 24
Petrie 1924 vol. I p. 238

von Beckerath 1999 pp. 80 #b, 81 #b
Weigall 1907 pl. XXXII unnumbered, XLIX #1, L #1, LXV #1
Zaba 1974 p. 162

Iytjenu Dynasty VII/VIII

Horus Name: Unknown

Nomen:

iytnw
Iytjenu

Prenomen: Unknown

Two Ladies: Unknown

Golden Falcon: Unknown

Ka

Length of Reign:	Unknown
Tomb:	Unknown
Mummy:	Unknown

Consorts:	Unknown	**Variant Names:**	Aïtnou Iytenu
Manetho:	Not given		
King Lists:	None		

There is a single attestation for this possible king: a false door belonging to a priestess of Hathor named Satlytjenu (*s3t-iy-tnw*), [cartouche], discovered by C.M. Firth during the 1922-23 excavations at Saqqara. Since the name is compounded within a cartouche, Fischer posits a previously unknown pharaoh.

References:
Fischer 1963b pp. 35 note 2, 36, pl. VI von Beckerath 1999 pp. 70 #h, 71 #h
Gauthier 1923 p. 198

Ka   Dynasty 0

k3
Ka

Length of Reign:	Unknown
Tomb:	Abydos B 7/9
Mummy:	Unknown

Consorts:	Unknown	**Variant Names:**	Sechen Sekhen
Manetho:	Not given		
King Lists:	None		

Discovered at Abydos by Petrie, this early ruler dates to the period directly before Narmer. It is not known whether Ka ruled in Upper Egypt only or was, in fact, king of the entire country. His name has been found in the northeastern Delta at Tell Ibrahim Awad, at Abydos, and at Helwan and Tarkhan, cemeteries just south of modern Cairo. A fragmentary clay pot bearing the partially preserved serekh of Ka has been recently discovered at the site of Lod, about ten miles southeast of Tel Aviv.

The royal tomb at Abydos, believed by Petrie to be B 7 only, but now known to include B 9, contained a great many cylinder-shaped jars which bore the serekh of Ka, written in ink with a brush.

Petrie misread some of the symbols that sometimes accompanied the royal serekh and mistakenly gave Ka a second name, Ap. He also gave Ka a queen, Ha. In actuality, Ka's other names have yet to be discovered and his queen is also unknown. It should be noted that Kaplony would translate the king's Horus name as "Sechen." Also, as shown above, the position of the "ka" sign could shift.

References:

Kaiser 1982 p. 263 fig. 14
Kaplony 1958 pp. 54-57
O'Brien 1996 pp. 131, 132
Petrie 1901a pp. 4,5, 14, 19, 30, 48 pl. II.1, XIII. 89 and LIX
van den Brink and Braun 2002 pp. 173-174 and figs. 1 and 2

von Beckerath 1999 pp. 36 #x+2, 37 #x+2
T. Wilkinson 1999 pp. 22, 55, 57-58, 125, 234

Kakemetre   Dynasty XIV

Horus Name:
  Unknown   **Nomen:** Unknown

Prenomen:

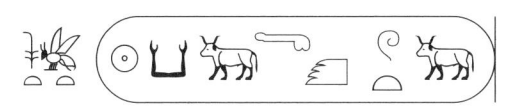

k3-kmt-r'

Kakemetre

Two Ladies: Unknown

Golden Falcon: Unknown

Length of Reign:	Unknown
Tomb:	Unknown
Mummy:	Unknown

Consorts: Unknown

Manetho: Not given

King Lists: T: (G 8.21; R 9.21; vB 8.21)

Variant Names: Kakemure

Kamose

Possibly the twenty-seventh king of Dynasty XIV, Kakemetre is one of a group of kings known only from the Turin Canon. The papyrus' fragmentary state allows for varying interpretations as to the positioning of some of the kings of this dynasty. However, Kakemetre's place seems secure.

References:

Gardiner 1959 pl. III, Col. VIII #21
Gardiner 1961 p. 441
Ryholt 1997a pp. 95 Col. 9.21, 98 #27, 380 File 14/27, 409 #27

von Beckerath 1999 pp. 110 #22, 111 #22

Kamose   Dynasty XVII

Horus Name:

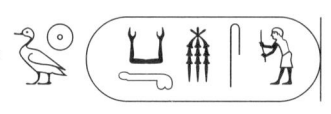

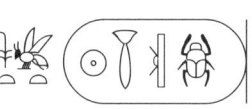

ḫʿ-ḥr-nst.f

Nomen: *k3-ms*
Kamose

Prenomen: *w3ḏ-ḫpr-rʿ*
Wadjkheperre

nfr-ḫ3b-t3wy

Two Ladies:  *nbty wḥm-mnw*

Golden Falcon: 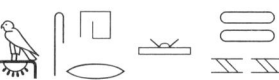 *bik-nbw shr-t3wy*

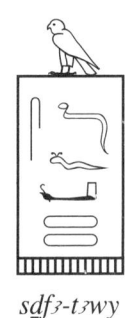

sḏf3-t3wy

162

Length of Reign:	3+ years
Tomb:	Pyramid at Dra Abu el-Naga
Mummy:	Destroyed

Consorts:	Ahhotep II	**Variant Names:**	Kames Uatch-keper-re
Manetho:	Not given		
King Lists:	None		

The ninth and last king of Dynasty XVII, Kamose was probably the son of the pharaoh Senakhtenre Taa and therefore the brother of king Seqenenre Taa. This would have made him the uncle of Ahmose, the first king of Dynasty XVIII, although some scholars believe that he was a son of Seqenenre and the older brother of Ahmose. No matter the relationship, he was Seqenenre's immediate successor and so inherited the empty title of Lord of the Two Lands and much strife. Seqenenre Taa had died violently, almost certainly in battle against the Hyksos Dynasty XV to the north. To the south, the ruler of Kush was allied with the Hyksos and was threatening the Theban state's southern border.

A pair of stelae erected at Karnak by order of Kamose supplies us with all we know about his ensuing war against the Hyksos and Kushites, and while much of the first stele is lost, we have a hieratic copy of a large part of it inscribed on a writing board found by Howard Carter in 1908. Dated to regnal year three, the combined texts tell us how Kamose sailed north to lay waste the lands under Hyksos domination: "I fared downstream in might to overthrow the Asiatics ... my brave army in front of me like a breath of fire...." Egyptians who had collaborated with the Hyksos fared no better: "...I was upon him as it were a hawk...I overthrew him, I razed his wall, I slew his people...."

Having reached the Hyksos capital, Avaris, and come so close to the walls as to be able to hurl taunts at the Hykos king Apepi, Kamose seems to have been content with wreaking havoc on the lands and dwellings that surrounded the city. No effort was made toward a real siege, and within a short while Kamose led the army south, back to Thebes. We don't know what prompted the pharaoh's pullout; perhaps having burned the crops of his enemy he needed to get his soldiers back home where they could harvest the Theban crops. Or perhaps it was the interception of a Hyksos messenger carrying a request from Apepi for aid from the Kushites that sent Kamose home to look after his southern border at Elephantine. Whatever the reason, Kamose returned home proclaiming himself a great victor; and so he probably was. Certainly he added the 200 km. stretch of land between Abydos and Cusae to the Theban sphere of interest. Additionally, he had done enough damage to Apepi to stop that ruler from following the Theban army in its retreat. (It should be noted that a few scholars believe that Kamose never reached Avaris and, in fact, stopped at Cusae, and that the greater part of the tale given on the stelae is nothing more than bombast.)

Kamose must have felt secure enough about the Hyksos situation to turn his eyes toward Lower Nubia, which he certainly wanted to control. How large a force was sent is unknown, but it must have been substantial to have gotten as far as the Middle Kingdom fortress at Buhen, near the Second Cataract, where some restoration was undertaken and where some sort of administration was probably put together. A stele dated to Kamose's third regnal year has been found at Buhen and a second stele, belonging to an army officer named Ahmose, bears a cartouche that has been much damaged but has been credited by some to Kamose. This cartouche may actually belong to his successor, Ahmose.

Several scholars have suggested that at some point Kamose had taken the younger Ahmose as a coregent. The two names are certainly found together on rock inscriptions at Arminna and at Toshka, but nowhere else to date. Ryholt points out that, for the graffiti bearing the two names to truly reflect a coregency, a second Nubian campaign would have been necessary. Ryholt's support for a coregency is based primarily on "epigraphic criteria," which "suggests that the names of these two kings were engraved at the same time." It can be dangerous to place too much weight upon the calligraphy of much damaged and eroded graffiti.

Kamose probably did not live to see a fourth year of rule. How he met his death is unknown. He was buried beneath a small brick pyramid at Dra Abu el-Naga. His tomb was found intact when inspected during the tomb robbery scandal of late Dynasty XX. Eventually the tomb was considered unsafe and the king's mummy, in its stripped-down coffin, ended up hidden in a pile of rubble, where it was discovered in 1857. On Kamose's arm was tied a gold and silver dagger. The excavators (Auguste Mariette and Heinrich Brugsch) claimed that the mummy crumbled to dust when the coffin lid was opened. Much more likely, as pointed out by Brier, the mummy was treated none-too-gently in order to extract its amulets, scarab and pectoral and then was simply discarded.

As may be seen above, Kamose changed his Horus name three times in his three years on the throne.

References:

Carnarvon and Carter 1912 pp. 4, 36-37, pl. XXVII-XXVIII
Dodson 2000 pp. 21-22
Dodson and Hilton 2004 pp. 114, 122, 124,126-127, 128-129
Gardiner 1916 pp. 95-110, pl. XII-XIII
Gardiner 1961 pp. 165-168
Habachi 1972
Hall 1913 p. 303 #2885
Hein 1994 pp. 272-273 #382, unnumbered color plate, 273-275
Helck 1983 pp. 82-90 #119, 99 #121
Ikram and Dodson 1998 pp. 10, 77, 118, 315, 318
Karkowski 1981 pp. 93 #14, pl. VI #14
Lehner 1997 p. 189
Newberry 1906 p. 156 #s 1 and 2, pl. XXVI #s 1 and 2
Peden 2001 pp. 56-57, 88
Peet 1930 p. 39

Petrie 1978 pl. XXIII 17.O1 and 17.O.2
D. Redford 1986 pp. 39, 43, 45, 48 #12, 51 #24
D. Redford 1997 pp. 13-15, #s 67-69
Ryholt 1997a pp. 146, 170, 171 table 28, 171-174, 175-180, 181, 182-183, 272-274, 306, Notes 1067 and 1068, 309, 325-327, 398-400, File 17/9, 410, table 98
H.S. Smith 1976 pp. 8-9, 228, pl. II #1.488, pl. LVIII #1.488
Trigger 1976 p. 104 and fig. 35
Vandersleyen 1971 pp. 61-62, 62-64
von Beckerath 1999 pp. 130 #15, 131 #15
Weigall 1907 p. 127, pl. LXV #4
Winlock 1924 pp. 259-265, pl. XXI

Khaba   Dynasty III

Horus Name:

ḫʿ-bꜣ
Khaba

Nomen: Unknown

Two Ladies: Unknown

Golden Falcon: Unknown

Length of Reign:	5-6 years
Tomb:	Zawiyet el-Aryan. The "Layer Pyramid"
Mummy:	Unknown

Consorts:	Unknown	**King Lists:**	None
Manetho:	Achês (A) Akhes (A) Mesôchris (A) Mesokhris (A)	**Variant Names:**	Chaba Khoba

Another pharaoh of Dynasty III about whom almost nothing is known, Khaba's position in the dynasty is uncertain, although he seems to be the direct predecessor of the dynasty's last king, Huni. It has been suggested that Khaba might have been Huni's Horus name, but there is no evidence for such a speculation and, in fact, the recently discovered serekh of a pharaoh named Qahedjet is a much more likely candidate.

Scholars are divided as to the identification of Khaba in Manetho's Dynasty III. Verbrugghe and Wickersham equate this king with Manetho's Mesôchris, while Dodson and others see him as Manetho's Achês.

About 6 kilometers south of Giza, at Zawiyet el-Aryan, lies an incomplete step pyramid known as the Layer Pyramid, due to the technique used in its construction. Originally 84 m. to the side, Lehner has estimated that when complete, the structure would have been five-stepped and would have had a height of 42 to 45 m.; other scholars have suggested as many as seven steps. However, the pyramid was never completed, and today is about 17 m. high. The substructure of the tomb has been described as "so similar to Sekhemkhet's that there can be little doubt that scarcely any time elapsed between the two." Unfortunately, not one inscription has been found in the tomb. In fact, nothing was found in the tomb: the entire substructure was empty, not even containing a sarcophagus. The structure has been attributed to Khaba based solely on stone bowls inscribed with that king's serekh, found in a mastaba (Z500) located near the pyramid.

Aside from the unfinished pyramid and the stone bowls at Zawiyet el-Aryan, contemporary attestations for Khaba are rare. They consist of a seal impression from Elephantine, a seal impression from Hierakonpolis, a serekh inscribed on an alabaster bowl found in the mortuary temple of the Dynasty V pharaoh Sahure at Abusir, two inscribed stone bowls of unknown provenance and a portion of a cylinder seal, also of unknown provenance.

Khaba's length of reign is unknown. While it is dangerous to speculate too much, when the unfinished state of his pyramid and dearth of attestations are considered, his rule seems to be short, perhaps no more than six years.

References:

Arkell 1956 p. 116
Arkell 1958 p. 120
Dodson 1998 pp. 35, 38, 39
Dodson 2003 pp. 46-47
Dunham 1978
Gardiner 1961 p. 74-75
Kahl et al. 1995 pp. 153-161
Kaplony 1963 vol. III pl. 132 #805
Lehner 1997 p. 95
Petrie 1978 p. viii #2?, pl. VIII #2? (as Kho-bau)
Verbrugghe and Wickersham 1996 pp. 134, 189
Verner 1997 pp. 107, 148-151
von Beckerath 1999 pp. 50 #b, 51 #b
Waddell 1940 p. 43
T. Wilkinson 1999 pp. 99-101

Khabau   Dynasty XIII

Horus Name:

Nomen: Unknown

Prenomen:

$ḫ^c-b3w$
Khabau

$sḫm-r^c-ḥw-t3wy$
Sekhemrekhutowy

Two Ladies:

nbty whm-dd

Golden Falcon:

bik-nbw 'nh-rnptw

Length of Reign:	Unknown
Tomb:	Unknown
Mummy:	Unknown

Consorts:	Unknown	**King Lists:**	None
Manetho:	Not given	**Variant Names:**	Khabaw

According to Ryholt, Khabau was the sixteenth ruler of Dynasty XIII, succeeding the short-lived king Hor. Von Beckerath would place Khabau at the third position in the dynasty. His name is not given in the Turin Canon or any other king list. Khabau, whose nomen is unknown, would appear to be a son of Hor, and very possibly that king's coregent, if the association of their names on an architrave found at Tanis is taken into account. Fragments of another architrave of Khabau were discovered by Naville at Bubastis, not far to the southeast of Tanis. Both architraves were very likely moved to Tanis and Bubastis from the Memphite area during Hyksos times.

Further attestations for Khabau are a cylinder-seal found at el-Mahamid el-Qibli, just south of Thebes; four seal-impressions from Uronarti, a fortress in Nubia at the Second Cataract; and a seal impression from Mirgissa, another fortress at the Second Cataract.

Khabau's authority would have certainly extended from Memphis to Aswan and in all probability included the western Delta and Nubia at least to the Second Cataract. He probably reigned for only a year or two. His burial would have taken place in the Memphite area and may well have been a simple shaft tomb, much like his predecessor Awibre Hor.

References:

Budge 1914 p. 7 #284 (as Sobekhotep I), pl. XVIII #284
Dunham 1967 pp. 38: 28-11-234, 57: 29-1-314, 58: 30-2-19, 64: 3A
Naville 1891 p. 15, pl. XXXIII
Petrie 1978 p. 23 (as Sobekhotep I), pl. XVIII 13.15.1

Ryholt 1997a pp. 70, 73 table 17 #16, 216-217, 218 and table 51, 219 table 52, 284 table 83, 318, 321-322 and table 93, 340 File 13/6, 408 table 94 #16
von Beckerath 1999 pp. 88 #3, 89 #3

Khaenptah SIP

Horus Name: Unknown

Nomen: Unknown

Prenomen: Unknown

Two Ladies: Unknown

Golden Falcon:
bik-nbw ḫʿn-ptḥ
Khaenptah

Length of Reign:	Unknown
Tomb:	Unknown
Mummy:	Unknown

Consorts:	Unknown	**Variant Names:**	Sekhenptah
Manetho:	Not given		
King Lists:	None		

This name is from a single cylinder-seal of unknown provenance, made of blue-green steatite. The seal gives an otherwise unknown Golden Falcon name, yet offers no clue as to the rest of the titulary. Originally in the Timmins Collection, the seal now seems to have been lost, as it is reportedly not in the Metropolitan Museum of Art with the rest of the collection. Ryholt, who reads the name "Sekhaenptah," considers the possibility that, because of the reference to the Memphite deity Ptah, the name might belong to the Dynasty XIII king Sankhptahi. Newberry dates the seal to "about the end of the Middle Kingdom."

References:

Newberry 1905 p. 105 (k)
Newberry 1907 p. 12, pl. I #13

Ryholt 1997a pp. 404-405 File G/1

Khafre   Dynasty IV

Horus Name:

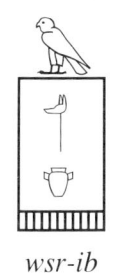

Nomen:

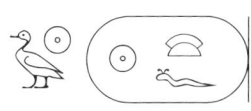

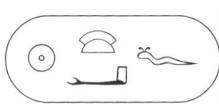

ḫʿ.f-rʿ
Khafre

wsr-ib

ḫw.f-rʿ
Khafre

Two Ladies:

nbty wsr-m

Golden Falcon:

bik-nbw nṯr-sḫm

Length of Reign:	25 years(?)
Tomb:	Pyramid at Giza: "Great is Khafre"
Mummy:	Unknown

Consorts:	Hekenuhedjet(?)
	Hetepheres II(?)
	Khamerer-
	  nebti I(?)
	Meresankh II(?)
	Meresankh III
	Per[senet](?)
		Herodotus:
		
		Manetho:
			Chefren
			Chephren
			Khephren
			
			Suphis II (A, E)
			Souphis II(?)
			  (A, E)

Khafre

King Lists:	Ab: (23); S: (19); T: (G 3.12)	Khufukaf Rakhaef Rekhaef
Variant Names:	Khafkhufu	

The son of Khufu and one of his consorts, a lady named Henutsen, Khafre was the fourth king of Dynasty IV. Khafre was evidently a younger son of Khufu and came to the throne after the death of his older brother, the pharaoh Djedefre. He also married his brother's widow, Hetepheres II, who was the daughter of Khufu and therefore Khafre's sister or half-sister. It seems likely that Khafre was originally named Khufukhaf ($hwfw$-hf) and built the double mastaba G 7130-40 in the East Cemetery at Giza. If such is the case, Khufukhaf changed his name to Khafre in honor of the sun god, and imitated his brother-predecessor in using the title "Son of Re," which was forevermore included in the Royal Titulary.

Attestations for Khafre have been found as far from Egypt's borders as Ebla, in Syria, where alabaster vases bearing his name were discovered. His name has also been found on fragments of stone vessels during the excavations at the Temple of Baalat-Gebal at Byblos.

Khafre chose to build his pyramid complex near that of his father, at Giza. The pyramid itself was only slightly smaller than that of Khufu, the sides measuring 215.25 m. at the base and the height measuring 143.5 m., but the tomb was built upon a plateau with a slightly higher elevation than Khufu's pyramid, making Khafre's pyramid seem taller. The Khafre complex included a huge mortuary temple, the largest built to date; it was the first to include all of the architectural and religious elements that would be standard in future temples throughout Egyptian history.

The so-called Valley Temple lay about 410 m. east of the mortuary temple, connected to it by a causeway. This structure, built of megalithic blocks of granite, once housed 23 life-sized (and larger) seated statues of the king, some of which were discovered in a pit at the temple and are now in the Cairo Museum.

Next to the Valley Temple lies the Great Sphinx. The Sphinx, an amazing sculpture measuring 74 m. in length and 20 m. in height, has been called "the most immense sculpture ever made by man." Its head and body are carved from a large out-cropping of granite, the paws being of brick. Due to its proximity to Khafre's temple, and the Dynasty XVIII "dream stele" of Thutmose IV which arguably credits it to Khafre, the Sphinx has long been ascribed to Khafre. However, this identification has been challenged by Stadelmann, who has presented an interesting theory that the features of the Sphinx represent Khufu. Dodson mentions the very unlikely possibility of the Sphinx having been carved in the Archaic Period, and also a chance that the monument may have been "completely recarved," perhaps during the reign of the Dynasty XII pharaoh Amenemhet II.

A large inscribed block from Khafre's mortuary temple at Giza has been found built into the pyramid of the Dynasty XII pharaoh Amenemhet I at Lisht. An inscribed block from Bubastis, and now in the British Museum, attests to a Dynasty IV temple located at that city.

The Greek historian Herodotus, who identifies Khafre as Khufu's brother, tells us that Khafre (Chephren) "was no better than his predecessor; his rule was equally oppressive." Supposedly, like Khufu, Khafre kept the temples closed, allowing no worship, thus forcing the land into "greatest misery." Herodotus would have us believe that the Egyptians hated Khafre and Khufu so much that even as late as his time (ca. 480 BC) they preferred not to mention their names. No matter what may or may not have been believed to be true in 480 BC, Khafre's mortuary cult may have been maintained as late as the Middle Kingdom. Graffiti at Giza informs us that a cult dedicated to Khafre was "revived" during Dynasty XXVI, and a stele (no. 291) from the Serapeum at Saqqara informs us that during the reign of the Persian king Darius I (522-486 BC), a cult to Khafre was in existence.

The length of Khafre's reign is unknown. His regnal years are lost from the Turin Canon. Herodotus gives him 56 years and Manetho 66. The highest date known from contemporary evidence is a "Year of the 13th. occurrence." This may refer to a year 13 or to a year 26, depending on whether or not a biennial cattle count was taken. The general consensus among scholars is that Khafre probably reigned about 25 years.

References:

Dodson 2003 pp. 60-62
Dodson and Hilton 2004 pp. 50, 52-53, 54, 55-58, 59, 60-61
Gardiner 1959 pl. II, Col. III #12
Gardiner 1961 pp. 80-82, 434
Goedicke 1971 pp. 23-24
Herodotus 1954 pp. 179-180
Hölscher 1912
Jidejian 1968 p. 17
Jánosi 1992 p. 52
Jordan 1998
Kanawati 2003 p. 2
Lehner 1997 pp. 122-132
Malek 2000 p. 248
Naville 1891 pp. 5, 8, 9, pl. XXXII B
O'Connor 1995 p. 5
D. Redford 1986 p. 62 note 225
D. Redford 1992 p. 41
Siliotti 1997 pp. 58-67
Spalinger 1994 pp. 286-288
Stadelmann 2001a p. 596
Stadelmann 2001b pp. 307-310
Verbrugghe and Wickersham 1996 p. 190, 191 note 5
Verner 1997 pp. 156-157, 223-234, 463
Verner 2001b p. 588
von Beckerath 1999 pp. 54 #4, 55 #4
Waddell 1940 p. 47

Khakare Dynasty XIV

Horus Name: Unknown

Nomen: Unknown

Prenomen:

ḫʿ-kꜣ-rʿ
Khakare

Two Ladies: Unknown

Golden Falcon: Unknown

Length of Reign:	Unknown
Tomb:	Unknown
Mummy:	Unknown

Consorts:	Unknown	**Variant Names:**	...ka[re?] Kha...re
Manetho:	Not given		
King Lists:	T: (G 8.24; R 9.24; vB 8.24)		

Possibly the thirtieth king of Dynasty XIV, Khakare is one of a group of kings known only from the Turin Canon. The papyrus' fragmentary state allows for varying interpretations as to the position of some of the kings of this dynasty. However, Khakare's place seems secure since a recent study indicates that two previously separated fragments of the papyrus should be joined together, thus placing Khakare firmly in his proper dynastic order.

References:

Gardiner 1959 pl. III Col. VIII #24 as "Kha...re"
Gardiner 1961 p. 441 8.24
Ryholt 1997a pp. 95 Col. 9.21, 98 #30, 380 File 14/30, 409 #30

von Beckerath 1999 pp. 110 #25, 111 #25

Khakherure   Dynasty XIV

Horus Name: Unknown

Nomen: Unknown

Prenomen:

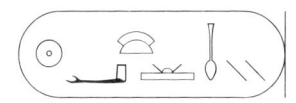

ḫ'-ḥrw-r'
Khakherure

ḫ'-ti(t)-r'
Khatyre

Two Ladies: Unknown

Golden Falcon: Unknown

Length of Reign:	Unknown
Tomb:	Unknown
Mummy:	Unknown

Consorts:	Unknown	**Variant Names:**	Kha-kherewre
Manetho:	Not given		Khatire
King Lists:	T: (G 8.2; R 9.2; vB 8.2)		Khatyre

Perhaps the seventh king of Dynasty XIV, Khakherure is one of a group of kings known only from the Turin Canon. The canon's fragmentary state allows for varying interpretations as to the positioning of some of the kings of this dynasty. However, Khakherure's place seems secure. There is some argument as to whether or not the spelling given in the Turin Canon is accurate. The name is usually given as Khatyre, however that transliteration is certainly faulty and it seems likely that the original copyist of the papyrus mistook the hieroglyph (*ti*) for (*hrw*).

Khamudi

References:

Gardiner 1959 pl. III, Col. VIII #2
Gardiner 1961 p. 441 #8.2 as "Khatyre"
Ryholt 1997a pp. 95 Col. 9.2, 98 #7, 198 table 37, 378 File 14/7, 409 table 95 #7

von Beckerath 1999 pp. 108 #3, 109 #3

Khamudi   Dynasty XV

Horus Name: Unknown   **Nomen:**

(*ḥḳ3-ḫ3swt*) *ḫ3mwdi*
(Ruler of Foreign Lands) Khamudi

Prenomen:

ḥtp-ib-rˁ
Hotepibre

Two Ladies: Unknown

Golden Falcon: Unknown

Length of Reign:	1-11(?) years
Tomb:	Unknown
Mummy:	Unknown

Consorts:	Unknown	**Variant Names:**	Chamudi Ḥamudi Khondy
Manetho:	Not given		
King Lists:	T: (G 10.20; R 10.28; vB 11.6)		

According to the Turin Canon, Khamudi was the final ruler of Dynasty XV, the sixth king of the dynasty, and the last "Hyksos Pharaoh." His relationship to his predecessor, Apepi, is unknown.

Khamudi inherited the throne at a very bad time. It is generally believed that Apepi, after a long, drawn-out war with the Theban rulers Seqenenre, Kamose and Ahmose, was finally forced out of Egypt and into the fortress of Sharuhen, in southern Palestine. Khamudi seems to have inherited a throne but not a kingdom. The siege of Sharuhen lasted several years (the inscription is damaged at this spot, and the number has been read as anywhere between three and six years). Khamudi probably never set foot in his Egyptian "kingdom" after his succession to the throne.

Aside from the Turin Canon, Khamudi's attestations amount to two scarab-seals found at Jericho and another seal of unknown provenance (the latter unpublished). A cylinder-seal inscribed with a cartouche

has sometimes been read as Khamudi, $ḥ(ꜣ)mw$-di, but Ryholt believes that this is incorrect, that the cartouche actually reads

and that a more accurate transliteration is $k(ꜣ)$-n-d-y, Kandy, and therefore belongs to an unidentified king.

The Turin Canon does not give the regnal years for Khamudi. Ryholt has suggested a single year. Bietak asserts that a "year eleven" of an unnamed king found on the reverse side of the Rhind mathematical papyrus must belong to Khamudi, because the opposite side is firmly dated to the reign of Apepi.

References:

Bietak 2001 p. 140
Gardiner 1959 pl. III, Col. X.20
Gardiner 1961 p. 442 #10.20
Petrie 1924 vol. I p. 123
Petrie 1978 p. XIX "Khondy", pl. XIX "Khondy"
Rowe 1936 pp. 5 #18, pl. I #18
Ryholt 1997a pp. 43, 48 fig. 6/b, 119 and table 22, 125 table 23, 130 note 458, 201 table 40, 309, 387-388 File 15/6, 410, table 96
Tufnell 1984 pp. 356 #2873, 364 #3097, pl. XLIX #2873, LIII #3097
von Beckerath 1999 pp. 114 #6, 115 #6
Ward 1970 p. 69

Khamure   Dynasty XIV(?)

Horus Name: Unknown

Nomen: Unknown

Prenomen:

$ḫꜥ$-mw-$rꜥ$
Khamure

Two Ladies: Unknown

Golden Falcon: Unknown

Kha...re

Length of Reign:	Unknown
Tomb:	Unknown
Mummy:	Unknown

Consorts:	Unknown	**Variant Names:**	Kho-Ra
Manetho:	Not given		
King Lists:	None		

Khamure is known from two scarab-seals, both of unknown provenance. His position within Dynasty XIV is uncertain. He is not listed in the Turin Canon. Tufnell reads the name as "Ammu," but this is incorrect. The latter reading should not be confused with the well-attested king Ammu who probably belongs to the early part of Dynasty XIV.

References:
Newberry 1906 p. 150 #30, pl. XXI #30
Petrie 1978 pl. XXII K. Kho-Ra #'s 1 and 2, Catalogue p. xxii K. Kho-ra
Ryholt 1997a pp. 51 and note 138, 52 table 13, 99 table 20 #e, 381 File 14/e
Tufnell 1984 p. 378 #3361, 379 pl. LX #3361

Kha...re   SIP

Horus Name: Unknown

Nomen: Unknown

Prenomen:

ḫꜥ...rꜥ
Kha...re

Two Ladies: Unknown

Golden Falcon: Unknown

Length of Reign:	Unknown
Tomb:	Unknown
Mummy:	Unknown

Consorts:	Unknown	**Variant Names:**	None
Manetho:	Not given		
King Lists:	None		

This name is known from a colossal statue discovered by Petrie at Tanis. Petrie believed the name to be the prenomen of (Usertsen II) Senwosret II of Dynasty XII. Ryholt believes the name to date to Dynasty XIII and suggests that the statue may have originally come from Memphis. If the prenomen is from Dynasty XIII, it may well belong to one of four kings: Sobekhotep II (Khaankhre), Neferhotep I (Khasekhemre), Sobekhotep IV (Khaneferre) or Sobekhotep VI (Khahotepre). The present location of the statue is unknown.

References:

Petrie 1885 pp. 6, 15, pl. II #6a and 6b, unnumbered plan 2 pos. #84

Petrie 1888 p. 16 #6
Ryholt 1997a p. 404 File P/8

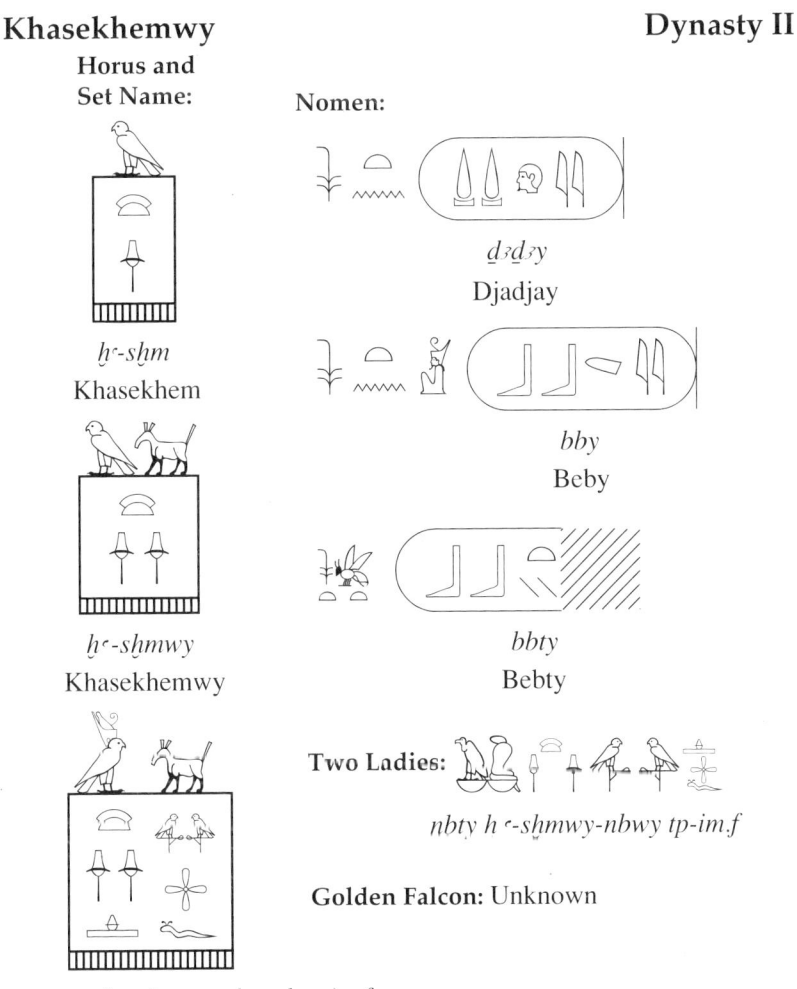

Khasekhemwy Dynasty II

Horus and Set Name:

hʿ-shm
Khasekhem

hʿ-shmwy
Khasekhemwy

hʿ-shmwy-nbwy htp-im.f
Khasekhemwy-nebwyhotepimef

Nomen:

dȝdȝy
Djadjay

bby
Beby

bbty
Bebty

Two Ladies:

nbty hʿ-shmwy-nbwy tp-im.f

Golden Falcon: Unknown

Khasekhemwy

Length of Reign:	18 - 27 years
Tomb:	Abydos, Umm el Qa'ab, V
Mummy:	Unknown

Consorts:	Nimaathap	**Variant Names:**	Khasekhem Khasekhemui
Manetho:	Cheneres (A) Kheneres (A)		
King Lists:	Ab: (14); P; S: (11); T: (G 3.3)		

The last king of Dynasty II, Khasekhemwy ascended the throne as the Horus Khasekhem. Sometime during his reign, he changed his name to Khasekhemwy, often adding the epithet Nebwyhotepimef. Some earlier Egyptologists believed that Khasekhem and Khasekhemwy were two different kings, but on linguistic grounds it appears the names belong to one person.

Our understanding of the political situation in Egypt during Dynasty II is quite incomplete. Several ephemeral kings are known, but their actual place in the dynasty is questionable. Most of the established rulers are known from attestations in either Upper or Lower Egypt, but not from both. It is possible that there were several "kings" at the same time. The changing of the Horus name Khasekhem ("The Power has Appeared") to Khasekhemwy ("The Two Powers have Appeared") may well represent a reuniting of the Two Lands. The epithet Nebwyhotepimef, "The Two Lords are at Peace in Him," would tend to support such a view, the "Two Lords" representing Upper and Lower Egypt. When the name changed from Khasekhem to Khasekhemwy, the Horus Falcon suddenly found itself sharing top billing with Set. It has been suggested that Khasekhem may have been responsible for the overthrow of his predecessor, Peribsen; since Peribsen had replaced the Horus falcon with the Set animal, Khasekhem added Set to his serekh as a sign of his having complete control of Egypt.

Certainly, Khasekhem's reign saw its share of fighting. A fragment of a stele found during Quibell and Green's excavations in the Horus Temple area at Hierakonpolis shows a victory of some sort in Nubia. The same excavation uncovered three stone vessels bearing inscriptions that read "victory over the papyrus people, unification of Egypt" that tend to add weight to the identification of Khasekhem with Khasekhemwy. Also found were two statues, the bases of which bear the name Khasekhem, that show scenes that commemorate a victory over Lower Egypt in which 47,209 northerners were slain (although these numbers were undoubtedly inflated). It would have been at this point that Khasekhem's name change occurred.

A large funerary enclosure built by Khasekhem at Hierakonpolis would certainly seem to indicate that this king originally planned to be buried there and not at Abydos; however, no trace of a tomb has ever been found at Hierakonpolis.

Attestations of Khasekhem are limited to Hierakonpolis, with the exception of one inscribed diorite bowl that was found at Djoser's Step Pyramid complex at Saqqara.

Attestations for Khasekhemwy are found from Hierakonpolis in Upper Egypt to Byblos on the coast of Lebanon. A fragment of stone vessel, discovered in the Egyptian temple area at Byblos, bears the king's name along with the hieroglyphs for "given life." This vessel may have reached Byblos at a later date, but it is just as likely that it represents trade between Egypt and the Levant at this point in history. Two seal-impressions from Khasekhemwy's funerary enclosure at Abydos give the earliest known example of the title "Overseer of Foreign Land," which seem to point toward a good deal of activity outside Egypt's borders during this reign.

Khasekhemwy is represented at Saqqara by fragments of an inscribed stone bowl found in Djoser's step pyramid complex and by an inscription from private tomb S3043.

Whatever the political situation in Egypt during Khasekhemwy's reign, he was responsible for the construction of the largest of the Archaic Period tombs at Abydos; the burial chamber of this tomb represents the largest use of dressed stones to this date. Khasekhemwy's funerary enclosure at Abydos (known today as the Shunet ez-Zebib) is the largest ever to be constructed.

Artifacts of this reign discovered at Abydos include a scepter made from precious stone with bands fashioned from gold, limestone vases covered in sheets of gold, and vessels made of copper.

References:

Ayrton et al. 1904 pp. 3, 4, 40, pl. IX #9
Dodson 1995 pp. 18-21
Dodson and Hilton 2004 pp. 44-46, 48
Edwards 1971 pp. 32-35
Emery 1961 pp. 98-103
Farag 1980 pp. 77-79
Firth and Quibell 1935 vol. I p. 141 fig. 22
Gardiner 1959 pl. II, Col. III #3
Gardiner 1961 pp. 416-420, 431, 432
Grdseloff 1944 pp. 299-301
Hoffman 1991 pp. 348-354
Kaplony 1963 vol. I p. 160-163, vol. III pl. 72 #269, pl. 78 m #291
Lacau and Lauer 1959 pp. 10 #18, Pl. 3 #18
Lacau and Lauer 1961 pp. 44-45
Petrie 1901a pp. 6, 12, 13, 14, 27, 28, 31, 51, pl. IX, XXIII-XXIV, XLV #s 22-80, LVII #s 3-6, LVIII, LXIII
Quibell and Petrie 1900 p. 5, 11, pl. II, XXXVI-XLI
Quibell and Green 1902 pp. 2, 10, 11, 28, 29, 31, 33, 34, 35, 39, 44, 47, 48, 50 pl. XXIII, LVIII, LIX, LXV
Reeves 2000 pp. 97-99
Troy 1986 pp. 95, 106, 111
Verbrugghe and Wickersham 1996 pp. 133, 189
von Beckerath 1984 pp. 49 #9, 158 II Dynastie #9, 175 #9
Waddell 1940 p. 37
T. Wilkinson 1999 pp. 91-94, 142-143, 127, 129, 160, 180, 245, 246
T. Wilkinson 2000 pp. 130-138, 248-251, 256

Khayu   Predynastic

ḫȝiw
Khayu

Length of Reign:	Unknown
Tomb:	Unknown
Mummy:	Unknown

Consorts:	Unknown	**Variant Names:**	Iucha
Manetho:	Not given		Khaau
King Lists:	P		Tesau

Khayu is one of a group of nine kings known only from the Palermo Stone. Each name is followed by a representation of a squatting king wearing the crown of Lower Egypt. Whether these names are to be taken as historic personages or mythic "ancestors" is not known.

References:

Clagett 1989 pp. 66, 97-98
Edwards 1971 pp. 3-4
Gardiner 1961 pl. III

O'Mara 1979 p. 5
T. Wilkinson 2000 pp. 62, 85-86
von Beckerath 1999 pp. 72 #6, 73 #6

Khendjer   Dynasty XIII

Horus Name:

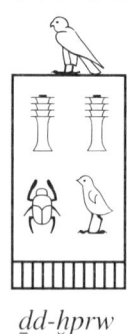

ḏd-ḫprw

Nomen:

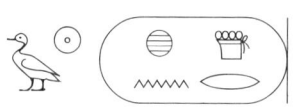

ḫnḏr
Khendjer

Prenomen:

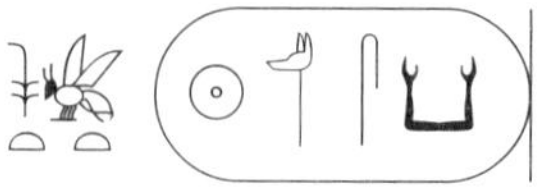

wsr-kȝ-rʿ
Userkare

Khendjer

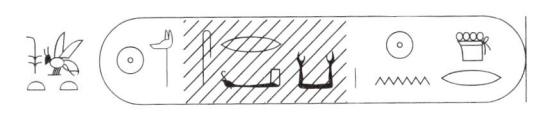

wsr-[kꜣ]-rꜥ ny-ḏr-rꜥ
Userkare Nydjerre

Two Ladies:

nbty ḏd-msw

Golden Falcon: Unknown

Length of Reign:	5+ years	
Tomb:	Pyramid at South Saqqara	
Mummy:	Unknown	
Consorts:	Sonbhenas I(?)	Khenzer
Manetho:	Not given	Ouserkara
		Userkare
King Lists:	T: (G 6.20; R 7.20; vB 6.20)	Woserkare
Variant Names:	Chendjer	

Probably the twenty-first king of Dynasty XIII, although Ryholt sees him as twenty-second and von Beckerath as the seventeenth, Khendjer succeeded Wegaf. It has been suggested that the two kings were coregents, although the evidence for this is slight at best and open to interpretation. Furthermore, Khendjer is a Semitic name and it seems unlikely that Wegaf, whose name is Egyptian, would have shared his throne with a foreigner. Verner has posited that Khendjer may have been a commander of Semitic mercenaries serving in Egypt. Whatever the situation, we know that Khendjer reigned at least into his fifth year; this is documented by a control note on a block from his pyramid. The inscribed pyramidion, though much damaged, still survives and may be seen in the Cairo Museum (JE53045).

Khendjer's pyramid, which is located at South Saqqara, was excavated by Gustave Jéquier from 1929 through 1931. The structure, now a ruin only 1 m. high, once stood 37.35 m. tall and had a base measurement of 52.5 m. (172.2 ft.). The pyramid was of mud brick faced with limestone. The burial chamber, which was located underground, proved to have been made from one very large single block of quartzite with places cut into the floor for the sarcophagus

Khentkaues (I)

and canopic jars. The ruins of a mortuary temple were found on the pyramid's east side and remains of a chapel on the north side. At the northeast corner of the tomb stood a much smaller subsidiary pyramid which contained burial chambers for two of the king's wives; a fragment of canopic jar names one wife, Sonbhenas.

Further attestations for Khendjer include three statuettes found at the Saqqara pyramid complex and now in the Cairo Museum (JE53668, 9.12.30.1 and 9.12.30.2); three cylinder-seals from Athribis in the delta; a tile from Lisht, just south of Memphis; an inscribed axe-blade whose provenance is unknown; several scarab-seals whose provenance is unknown; foundation deposits; and a stele from Abydos.

Due to a scribal error, Khendjer's name is given incorrectly in the Turin Canon: ☉ (r՝) is used instead of the proper ⊜ (ẖ).

References:

F. Arnold 1990 pp. 176-181 Kh1-Kh 20
Dodson 1994b pp. 33, 35, 116 #21, pl. Xd
Dodson 1994c p. 28, 29
Dodson 2000 pp. 10 fig. 8, 11-12, 14
Dodson 2003 p. 101-102, 135
Gardiner 1959 pl. III, Col. VI #20
Gardiner 1961 p. 440 #6.7
Helck 1983 p. 7-8 #12
T. James 1974 p. 62 #144, pl. XL #144
Jéquier 1933b pp. 3-38 and fig. 21, pl. I-XII
Kaplony 1973 p. 26 #62, pl. 14 #62 and 25 #62
Lehner 1997 pp. 186-187
Murnane 1977 pp. 25, 229-230
Ryholt 1997a pp. 17, 36 fig. 4 b, 39, 40 and table 10, 80 and Note 244, 81, 71 fig. 10 #20, 73 table 17 #22, 209, 193, 220-221 table 54 and notes 761, 284 table 83, 342 File 13/22, 408 table 94 #22
Verner 1997 pp. 426, 439-440
von Beckerath 1999 pp. 94 #17, 95 #17

Khentkaues (I)   Dynasty V

A large monument on the Giza plateau (LG100) has been identified as belonging to Khentkaues (I), a queen from early in Dynasty V. There is sufficient controversy about this queen that Egyptologists routinely refer to "the Khentkaues problem" when discussing her. While numerous theories have emerged about the implications of her unusual tomb and the meaning of the inscriptions found therein, scholars are nowhere near consensus about the role of this queen in Egyptian history.

There is certainly evidence that Khentkaues was no ordinary queen. Her tomb was once supposed to belong to Shepseskaf, the last ruler of Dynasty IV. However, when the tomb was excavated in 1932, it was discovered that the structure was not a pyramid at all, but rather a two-stepped monument, something between a mastaba and a pyramid that was unlike any traditional Egyptian tomb of the era. The excavation also revealed evidence that the tomb's owner was not Shepseskaf, but Queen Khentkaues. The titles inscribed for Khentkaues included

nswt-bity mwt-msw-bity
King of Upper and Lower Egypt and Mother of a King of Upper and Lower Egypt
or
mwt-nswty-bitwy
Mother of Two Kings of Upper and Lower Egypt

Of the two possible translations, the first is certainly unique for a queen of that period. This has led some scholars to speculate that for some time period Khentkaues acted as the ruler, perhaps as a regent for her son Sahure, second king of Dynasty V. Other evidence to support this thesis can be found in illustrations inside the tomb, which show her bearded, wearing what may be a uraeus, with her left arm in a "kingly pose," and holding something which may be a flail.

The most that can be said with relative certainty is that there was a Queen Khentkaues (I) in Dynasty V who was the mother of the pharaohs Sahure and Neferirkare (I), that she was probably the wife of Userkaf, and her unusual tomb reflects her great importance in the early years of Dynasty V.

References:

Dodson and Hilton 2004 pp. 61-65
Tyldesley 2006 pp. 52-54
Verner 1994 pp. 116-121
Verner 1995 pp. 165-170
Verner and Callender 1997 pp. 28-35

Khety I   Dynasty IX/X

Horus Name:

mry-ib-tꜣwy

Nomen:

ḥty
Khety

Prenomen:

mry-ib-rꜥ
Meryibre

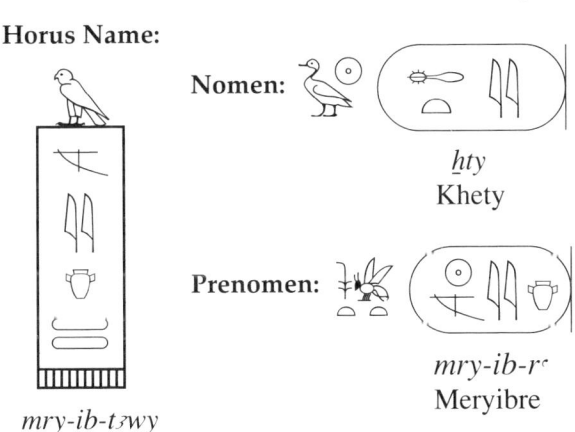

183

Khety I

Two Ladies: *nbty mry-ib-tꜣwy*

Golden Falcon: *bik-nbw mry*

Length of Reign:	Unknown
Tomb:	Unknown
Mummy:	Unknown

Consorts:	Unknown	**King Lists:**	None
Manetho:	Akhthoes (A) Ochthois (E)	**Variant Names:**	Akhtoy

Khety I is one of the pharaohs who controlled an unknown amount of territory around Herakleopolis in Middle Egypt (see "Herakleopolitans" in Glossary). Attestations for the kings whose names are known are few; most are known only as names from the Turin Canon. Although Khety I's name is missing from the Canon, he is known from a small number of other attestations.

Generally considered the first pharaoh of Dynasty IX/X (although without real proof, other than a reference in Manetho), Khety I was probably the nomarch of Herakleopolis in Middle Egypt. With the decentralization of power at the end of Dynasties VII/VIII, Khety seized the throne and declared himself king of Upper and Lower Egypt, a title adopted by his 17 (or possibly 18) successors, but hotly contested by the nomarchs of Thebes, and probably by a great many other regional authorities. According to Manetho, Khety's rise to power was violent; the historian relates that he was "more terrible than his predecessors" and "wrought evil things." Manetho also tells us that Khety eventually went insane and was killed by a crocodile (although the two events, if they happened at all, may have happened separately).

Among the few physical remnants of the reign are an inscribed ebony staff, fragments of a copper brazier, fragments of an ivory box found at Lisht, and possibly a scarab inscribed with his prenomen. Based on graffiti found at Aswan formerly read as Meryibre and Khety, Egyptologists once concluded that Khety had conquered all of Upper Egypt. However, it was later determined that the names on the rock were those of private individuals unrelated to this pharaoh. It is likely that Khety I's rule never extended beyond Abydos.

References:

Lorton 1987 pp. 22-28
Peden 2001 p. 14 note 2
Petrie 1978 pl. X #9.1
Verbrugghe and Wickersham 1996 pp. 137, 194

von Beckerath 1999 pp. 74 #e, 75 #e
Waddell 1940 p. 61

Khety II   Dynasty IX/X

Horus Name: Unknown

Nomen:

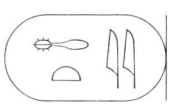

ḫty
Khety

Prenomen:

wsḥ-ks-rꜥ
Wahkare

Two Ladies: Unknown

Golden Falcon: Unknown

Length of Reign:	Unknown
Tomb:	Unknown
Mummy:	Unknown

Consorts:	Unknown	**Variant Names:**	Akhtoy
Manetho:	Not given		
King Lists:	T: (4.21)		

Khety II is one of the pharaohs who controlled an unknown amount of territory around Herakleopolis in Middle Egypt (see "Herakleopolitans" in Glossary). Attestations for the kings whose names are known are few; most are known only as names from the Turin Canon.

Based on his position in the Turin Canon, Khety II is the successor of a ruler whose name is given as Neferkare. What relationship they might have had, if any, is unknown.

It has been suggested that Khety II might be the author of a famous piece of Egyptian literature, *Instructions to Merykare*, but there is no real evidence to support it.

Khety III

Aside from the Turin Canon, Khety II's only attestation seems to be a decorated coffin found at el-Bersha that was inscribed with Khety's prenomen, Wahkare. The coffin belonged to a courtier named Nefri. Why Wahkare's name is inscribed upon it is unknown; perhaps the coffin was usurped at some time after the king's death.

References:
Dodson and Hilton 2004 p. 80
Gardiner 1959 pl. II, Col. IV #23
Gardiner 1961 p. 112

Lorton 1987 p. 25
von Beckerath 1999 pp. 72 #6, 73 #6

Khety III   Dynasty IX/X

Horus Name:
Unknown

Nomen:

ht[y s3(?)] nfr-k3-r'
Khety Neferkare

Prenomen: Unknown

Two Ladies: Unknown

Golden Falcon: Unknown

Length of Reign:	Unknown
Tomb:	Unknown
Mummy:	Unknown

Consorts:	Unknown	**Variant Names:**	Akhtoy
Manetho:	Not given		
King Lists:	T: (4.23)		

Khety III is one of the pharaohs who controlled an unknown amount of territory around Herakleopolis in Middle Egypt (see "Herakleopolitans" in Glossary). Attestations for the kings whose names are known are few; most are known only as names from the Turin Canon. Such may be the case with this king, although there is one possible additional item. A literary work traditionally ascribed to the predecessor of Merykare (Khety V, if Dodson's chronology is accepted) could, instead, be the work of Khety III. This work, entitled *Instructions to Merykare*, gives fatherly advice to the pharaoh about how to handle his kingdom. Khety III's successor, Khety IV, had a prenomen of Mery...re, and may have been the intended recipient of the advice.

Khety III is the successor of a ruler whose name is preserved in the Turin Canon as Senen.... What relationship these kings might have had, if any, is unknown.

References:
Gardiner 1959 pl. II, Col. IV #23

Khety IV   Dynasty IX/X

Horus Name: Unknown

Nomen: Unknown

Prenomen:

mry-...-(rꜥ) ḥty
Mery...(re) Khety

Two Ladies: Unknown

Golden Falcon: Unknown

Length of Reign:	Unknown
Tomb:	Unknown
Mummy:	Unknown

Consorts:	Unknown	**Variant Names:**	Akhtoy
Manetho:	Not given		
King Lists:	T: (4.24)		

Khety IV is one of the pharaohs who controlled an unknown amount of territory around Herakleopolis in Middle Egypt (see "Herakleopolitans" in Glossary). Attestations for the kings, whose names are known, are few; most are known only as names from the Turin Canon. Such may be the case with this king, although there is one possible additional item. A literary work traditionally ascribed to the predecessor of Merykare (Khety V, if Dodson's chronology is accepted) could, instead, be the work of Khety III. This work, entitled *Instructions to Merykare*, gives fatherly advice to the pharaoh about how to handle his kingdom. Khety IV, whose prenomen was Mery...re, may have been the intended recipient of the advice.

Khety IV is the successor of a ruler whose name is given in the Turin Canon as Khety III. What relationship these kings might have had, if any, is unknown.

Khety V

References:
Gardiner 1959 pl. II, Col. IV #24
von Beckerath 1999 pp. 72 #7, 73 #7

Khety V		Dynasty IX/X
Nomen and Prenomen:		

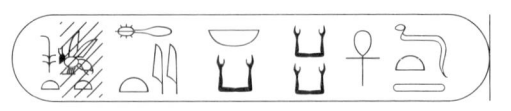

ni-swt-bit ḫty nb-kȝw-rˁ ˁnḫ ḏt
Nebkaure Khety

Horus Name:	**Two Ladies:** Unknown
Unknown	**Golden Falcon:** Unknown

Length of Reign:	Unknown
Tomb:	Unknown
Mummy:	Unknown

Consorts:	Unknown	**Variant Names:**	Akhtoy
Manetho:	Not given		
King Lists:	None		

Khety V is one of the pharaohs who controlled an unknown amount of territory around Herakleopolis in Middle Egypt (see "Herakleopolitans" in Glossary). Due to the great damage the Turin Canon has suffered, Khety V's name is missing from that text, however it would appear that he ruled quite late in the dynasty, perhaps as the penultimate ruler.

Although few attestations survive for the reign, there is one definite literary reference to Khety V in classic Egyptian Literature. *The Eloquent Peasant*, a tale written during the Middle Kingdom, refers to "King Nebkaure, the justified." As Nebkaure is considered Khety V's prenomen, it is safe to conclude that the tale is set in this reign. A second literary attribution has traditionally been ascribed to the predecessor of Merykare—Khety V, if Dodson's chronology is accepted. This work, entitled *Instructions to Merykare*, gives fatherly advice to the pharaoh about how to handle his kingdom. However, it is possible that this work should be attributed to Khety III, as his successor, Khety IV, had a prenomen of Mery...re which may well have actually been Merykare.

Other than the tales mentioned above, Khety V is known from an inscribed weight and a scarab found by Petrie at Tell el-Rabata in the Delta.

References:
Dodson and Hilton 2004 pp. 80-81
Lichtheim 1975 pp. 169-184
Newberry 1912 p. 123
Petrie 1906a pl. XXXIIA
Petrie 1978 pl. X #9.2 (as Khety II)
von Beckerath 1999 pp. 74 #d, 75 #d

Khufu   Dynasty IV

Horus Name:

mḏdw

Nomen:

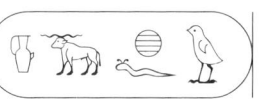

ḫwfw
Khufu

ḫnmw-ḫwfw
Khnum-khufu

Two Ladies:

nbty mḏd-r

Golden Falcon:

bik-nbw ḥrw

Length of Reign:	23 years
Tomb:	Great Pyramid at Giza: "Khufu's Pyramid which is at the Place of Sunrise and Sunset"
Mummy:	Unknown

Consorts:	Henutsen Meritites	**Manetho:**	Souphis (I) (A, E) Suphis
Herodotus:	Cheops		

Khufu

King Lists: Ab: (21); P; S: (17); T: (G [3.10]) Khnum-khufwey Khufwey

Variant Names: Khnum-khufu

The second king of Dynasty IV, the son of Seneferu and Queen Hetepheres, Khufu is remembered today as Cheops, builder of the Great Pyramid at Giza. The Greek historian Herodotus, visiting Egypt in about 451 BC, was told by his Egyptian guides that Cheops had been a cruel tyrant who had closed the temples and enslaved the people to force them to work on his pyramid. They further alleged that Cheops was so debased that he turned his own daughter toward a life of prostitution in order to acquire the stones to build his tomb. Her price: one stone per client.

Manetho, the Egyptian historian of the third century BC, refers to the builder of the Great Pyramid as Suphis and tells us that this king reigned for 63 years and was arrogant towards the gods until he thought better of his actions and wrote a religious book.

In actuality, very little is known about Khufu, or Khnum-Khufu as he was also called. Obviously we can conclude that he was a ruler powerful enough to command the construction of the Great Pyramid. This monument to himself covered 13 acres and rose to a burnished point 481 feet high. It consisted of some 2,300,000 blocks of dressed stone, each weighing an average of 2.5 tons.

Perhaps there was a kernel of truth in the stories told to Herodotus, that Khufu was indeed an unpopular ruler. As magnificent as it is, the Great Pyramid is the only monument of Khufu still standing today. There are a number of decorated blocks from his adjoining funerary temple (now long gone) which were discovered at the site of the pyramid and temple at Lisht of the Dynasty XII ruler Amenemhet I. These blocks, adorned with the various names of Khufu and bits and pieces of relief, a few others at Giza, and blocks at Tanis and Bubastis in the Delta, are all the known remains of Khufu's building endeavors. Other than the Great Pyramid and these remnants, the man who built the most famous building in history is today only represented by a three inch tall ivory statuette discovered at Abydos, and now housed in the Cairo Museum.

Several years of Khufu's reign would appear to be recorded on some of the Cairo fragments of the Palermo Stone.

Khufu's name is found at the Hat Nub Quarries, near El Amarna in Central Egypt, as well as on the island of Sehel at the First Cataract, and as far south as the diorite quarries near Abu Simbel in Nubia. Farther afield, the turquoise mines at Wadi Maghara in Sinai once bore an inscription with Khufu's name as testimony to an expedition he sent.

An axe head bearing Khufu's cartouche, discovered at the mouth of the Adonis River near Byblos in Syria, points toward trade with that region. At Byblos, Khufu is attested on fragments of alabaster vessels found during the excavation of the Temple of Baal-Gebal.

The tomb of Khufu's mother, Hetepheres, was discovered in 1925 during excavations conducted by American Egyptologist George Reisner of the Harvard-Boston expedition. The tomb, located at the bottom of a shaft on the east side of the Great Pyramid, contained a selection of funerary objects as well as day-to-day items. The queen's sarcophagus was there, and it was empty. Hetepheres' "tomb" may have been a cache containing all that remained of the queen's burial goods. The queen's original burial place is unknown, but it was probably near her husband's pyramid at Dahshur.

In 1954, excavations at Giza revealed two undisturbed sealed pits, each of which contained a complete cedarwood boat which had been taken apart to fit into its pit. One ship, reassembled from over 1,200 separate pieces, measured 43.3 m. long. These ships were intended for Khufu's use in the afterlife.

Although the Turin Canon gives Khufu a reign of 23 years, the size and number of building projects undertaken during his time make this short a reign almost impossible. If the year date for Khufu as given in the Turin Canon is based upon biennial cattle counts, his reign would have been a more plausible 45-50 years. (It should be mentioned that the Turin Canon gives the number of years of Khufu's reign where his name undoubtedly once appeared. However, the actual name of Khufu has been destroyed.)

References:

Bennett 1966 p. 175
Clagett 1989 pp. 85-86
Dodson 1995 pp. 29-32
Dodson 2003 pp. 56-67
Edwards 1993 pp. 98-121
Gardiner 1959 pl. II, Col. III.10 (name lost)
Gardiner 1961 pp. 79-80, 434
Goedicke 1971 pp. 8-23
Hart 1991 pp. 89-104
Herodotus 1954 pp. 179-180
Jánosi 1992 pp. 52, 55
Jenkins 1980
Jidejian 1968 p. 17
Kuper and Förster 2003 pp. 25-28
Lehner 1985
Lehner 1997 pp. 108-119
Reisner 1955
Spalinger 1994 pp. 283-285
Verbrugghe and Wickersham 1996 pp. 134-135, 190
Verner 1997 pp. 154-156, 189-217, 462
Verner 2001b pp. 586-587
von Beckerath 1999 pp. 52 #2, 53 #2
Waddell 1940 pp. 46, 49
T. Wilkinson 2000 pp. 215-216, 222-226, 236-237

Khui   Dynasty VII/VIII

Horus Name:
Unknown   **Nomen:**

ḫwi
Khui

Prenomen: Unknown

Two Ladies: Unknown

Golden Falcon: Unknown

Length of Reign:	Unknown
Tomb:	Pyramid at Dara
Mummy:	Unknown

Consorts:	Unknown	**Variant Names:**	Khuwi Khuy
Manetho:	Not given		
King Lists:	None		

This king is unknown except for a single cartouche discovered in a private tomb at Dara in central Egypt and dated to the First Intermediate Period by pottery style. It is doubtful that he reigned over all of Egypt; he was probably no more than a local noble who assumed a pharaonic role.

A much-ruined brick structure near the tomb, at first considered to be a mastaba, but now believed to be the ruins of a pyramid, is thought to belong to Khui. This ruin, which at present stands about 4 m., has a base length of some 130 m., making it the second largest brick pyramid ever built. (The largest is a brick pyramid at Abu Roash, perhaps belonging to Huni of Dynasty III.)

References:
Baines and Málek 1980 p. 141
Dodson 2003 p. 79
Kamal 1912 pp. 128-129
Lehner 1997 pp. 164-165
Swelim 1987 pp. 71-72
Verner 1997 pp. 379-380
von Beckerath 1999 pp. 70 #f, 71 #f

Khuiqer Dynasty XIII/?

Horus Name:

Nomen: ḫwi-kr
Khuiqer

mrwt(i)

Prenomen: Unknown

Two Ladies: Unknown

Golden Falcon: Unknown

Length of Reign:	Unknown
Tomb:	Unknown
Mummy:	Unknown

Consorts:	Unknown	Chuiqer
Manetho:	Unknown	Ra-u-aqer
King Lists:	None	Ua-qer-ra
Variant Names:	Chui-oqre	

    This king is known from a single block discovered by Petrie at Abydos. Petrie believed the inscription dated to the Dynasty XIV, but also considered the possibility that Khuiqer might belong to Dynasty VII. Ryholt opts for a First Intermediate Period date while Franke would place the king in the "Abydos Dynasty." Von Beckerath sees Khuiqer as belonging to Dynasty XIII, although he is unable to place the king's exact position within that dynasty.

References:

Franke 1988 p. 259
Leahy 1989 p. 59
Petrie 1903 p. 34-35 pl. XXXI, Pl. XXXII #1
Ryholt 1997a pp. 163 note 595, 334 note 1134

von Beckerath 1964 pp. 70, 233 XIIIC
von Beckerath 1999 pp. 106 #p, 107 #p

Khyan   Dynasty XV

Horus Name:

ink-idbw

ḥḳꜣ-ḫꜣswt ḫyꜣn
(Ruler of Foreign Lands) Khyan

Nomen:

ḫyꜣn
Khyan

Prenomen:

s.wsr-n-rꜥ
Sewoserenre

Two Ladies: Unknown

Golden Falcon: Unknown

Length of Reign:	ca. 40 years
Tomb:	Unknown
Mummy:	Unknown

Consorts:	Unknown	**Variant Names:**	Khayan
Manetho:	Iannas (J)		Khian
	Staan (A)		Seuserenre
King Lists:	T: (R 10.26)		

Probably the fourth ruler of Hyksos' Dynasty XV, Khyan's relationship with his predecessors is unknown. However, it is known that Khyan followed Sakir-Har in adding the Egyptian Royal Titulary to his original title "Ruler of Foreign Lands." Sakir-Har had used the Horus, Two Ladies and Golden Falcon names; going his direct predecessor one better, Khyan added the nomen and prenomen.

More than a dozen scarab-seals and three cylinder-seals bearing the title *ḥḳꜣ-ḥaswt*, Ruler of Foreign Lands, are known for Khyan. Most are of unknown provenance; however, we do have one each from two Hyksos strongholds at Ezbet Rushdi and Tell el Yahudiya, and one from Giza. Of particular interest is a scarab-seal of this group, mounted in gold, found at Gezer in Palestine.

Attestations in Egypt for Khyan as pharaoh, i.e., objects bearing all or parts of the royal titulary as opposed to simply the Ruler of Foreign Lands title, are not uncommon. They include a stele carved for the King's Son, Yanassi, from Tell el-Dab'a; a ka-statue from Bubastis, usurped from a Middle Kingdom pharaoh; an inscribed block from Gebelein; scarab-seals from Tell el Yahudiya; a cylinder-seal from Saqqara and a more than a dozen scarab-seals of unknown origin, some of them mounted in gold.

Outside Egypt, excavations at Tell Zaft in southern Palestine have yielded a seal impression. Farther afield, a sculpted lion found at Baghdad bears Khyan's prenomen, a fragment of an obsidian perfume jar inscribed with this pharaoh's cartouches was discovered at the Hittite city of Hattusas (Bogazköi, Turkey) and, from the palace at Knossos, Crete, comes the lid of an alabaster jar inscribed with the pharaoh's cartouches. It is likely that the lion found in Baghdad represents spoil carried away from Egypt at some later date. At least one scholar has suggested that the vase fragment from Turkey and the jar lid from Crete were all that remained of gifts from Khyan to the kings of the Hittites and Minoans as "tokens of personal and dynastic interest in establishing friendly relations." Other scholars point out that, except for the "Minoan" style frescoes found at Tell el-Dab'a, no evidence of any sort of Cretan presence has been found at the site; certainly no examples of Minoan pottery have come to light there. The same is true for the Hittites: no attestations of their presence have been found. The Bogazköi fragment and the lid from Knossos might well have arrived at their final destinations after years of being passed along.

It has been suggested that the inscribed block found on the grounds of the temple of Hathor at Gebelein, some 30 km. to the south of Thebes, may indicate that at one point Khyan was in control of all Upper Egypt. However, one block does not a temple build, and it is possible that the block was one of many brought south to be reused after the defeat of the Hyksos. It is interesting to note that Khyan's successor, Apepi, is represented at Gebelein by a single architrave (although an axe-blade bearing Apepi's prenomen was found at el Mahamid Qibli, just a few km. north of Gebelein).

Khyan's length of reign is unclear. Manetho, as per Africanus, gives Staan a reign of 50 years, and in Josephus' version of Manetho, Iannes receives the same length, plus one month. The Turin Canon is of little help since, not only has Khyan's name been lost, but the length of reign is incomplete and may have been anything from 10 to 40 years. No contemporary date for this king is known.

References:

Ben-Tor 1989 p. 49 #6
Bietak 1981 pp. 63-71
Budge 1914 p. 7 #340, pl. XVIII #340

Dodson and Hilton 2004 pp. 114-115
Gardiner 1961 pp. 443
Görg 1981 pp. 71-73

Mekh

Giveon 1965 pp. 202-204
Hein 1994 pp. 149 #124, 150 #125, 155-156 #133, Color pl. 125
Helck 1983 pp. 54 #s 70-72, 55 #74, 145 #154
Lilyquist 1995 pp. 22 #1, 46 #A, 82 fig. 12, 111 fig. 123
Martin 1971 pp. 91-92 #s 1169-1181a, pl. 40 #s 28-35, pl. 41 #5, pl. 42a #7, pl. 46 #s 1-3
Mellink 1995 pp. 85-89
Newberry 1906 pp. 46, fig. 23, 115 #s 7 and 10, pl. VII #s 7 and 10, 151 #s 20-26, pl. XXII #s 20-26, 198, pl. XLIV #6
D. Redford 1997 p. 6-7 #s 26-31
Ryholt 1997a pp. 41, 42-43, 48, fig. 6c, top row, 50, table 12, 119 and table 22, 120-121, 124-125, table 23, 128-129, 130 note 458, 131, 143, 149, 201 and table 40, 304, 383 File 15/4, 410 table 96
Tufnell 1984 pp. 370 #s 3207-3220, pl. LVI #s 3207-3220, 382 #3459, pl. LXII #3458
Verbrugghe and Wickersham 1996 pp. 139, 197
von Beckerath 1999 pp. 114 #4, 119 #4
Waddell 1940 p. 83, 91
Winlock 1947 p. 146, pl. 21 (2nd row)…maatre

Mekh   Predynastic

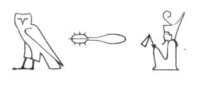

mḫ
Mekh

Length of Reign:	Unknown
Tomb:	Unknown
Mummy:	Unknown

Consorts:	Unknown	**Variant Names:**	Imichet
Manetho:	Not given		Mekha
King Lists:	P		Menkhe

Mekh is one of a group of nine kings known only from the Palermo Stone. Each name is followed by a representation of a squatting king wearing the crown of Lower Egypt. Whether these names are to be taken as historic personages or mythic "ancestors" is not known.

References:

Clagett 1989 pp. 66, 97-98
Edwards 1971 pp. 3-4
Gardiner 1961 pl. III

O'Mara 1979 p. 5
T. Wilkinson 2000 pp. 62, 85-86, 88

Menkare   Dynasty VII/VIII

Horus Name:
Unknown   **Nomen:**

mn-k3-r'
Menkare

Prenomen: Unknown

Two Ladies: Unknown

Golden Falcon: Unknown

Length of Reign:	Unknown
Tomb:	Unknown
Mummy:	Unknown

Consorts:	Unknown	**Variant Names:**	None
Manetho:	Not given		
King Lists:	Ab: (41)		

The second ruler of Dynasty VII/VIII, Menkare is known only from the Abydos King List. There is a lacuna in the Turin Canon where Menkare would have been listed. A glazed steatite cylinder seal, now in the British Museum, bears the inscription "The Good God, Lord of the Two Lands, Menkare." Although some scholars believe the seal's inscription to refer to Menkare of Dynasty VII/VIII, others believe that seal may bear a corruption of Menkaure of Dynasty IV. In any case, the seal was most likely carved during Dynasty XXVI, some 17 centuries later.

References:

Gardiner 1961 p. 437 #A41
Hall 1913 p. 272 #2650
Kaplony 1981 vol. II pp. 427-428, pl. 113 #1, 114 #s 1 & 2

Petrie 1902a pp. 86, 104-105
Ryholt 2000 pp. 91, 93, 96-97, 99 table 1
von Beckerath 1999 pp. 66 #2, 67 #2

Menkauhor — Dynasty V

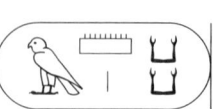

Horus Name: *mn-ḥ ꜥw*

Nomen: *ikꜣw-ḥr* — Akauhor

Prenomen: *mn-kꜣw-ḥr* — Menkauhor

Two Ladies: Unknown

Golden Falcon: *bik-nbw ḥḏ*

Length of Reign:	8 years
Tomb:	Pyramid at North Saqqara(?): "Divine of Places"
Mummy:	Unknown

Consorts:	Meresankh IV(?)	**Variant Names:**	Hor-A-Kau Ikaouhor Menkaouhor
Manetho:	Mencheres (A) Menkheres (A)		
King Lists:	Ab: (31); S: (30); T: (G 3.23)		

The seventh king of Dynasty V, Menkauhor is of unknown parentage. To date, nothing has been found to associate him with any of his predecessors, although it has been suggested, on very shaky grounds, that his father may have been Niuserre. Even his wife, Meresankh IV, is uncertain, her possible connection being based upon the closeness of her tomb to a pyramid that might have belonged to Menkauhor.

Very few attestations for this king have survived. A "rough stele" bearing the king's cartouche comes from Mastaba 904 at Saqqara. From the Serapeum at Saqqara come two inscribed stone blocks (originally from the XVIII Dynasty tombs of two high officials) both of which bear likenesses and cartouches of Menkauhor. Also from Saqqara is an alabaster statue of the king dressed in the ceremonial robe associated with the Sed Festival. A cylinder seal bearing Menkauhor's Horus name comes from the funerary complex of Niuserre at Abusir.

Menkauhor's sun temple, "The Horizon of Re," has not been found. It was probably located at Abu Gurob, but may never have been completed, or later kings may have used it as a quarry.

A small rock carving bearing Menkauhor's cartouche found at Wadi Maghara attests to an Egyptian presence at those copper and turquoise mines during this reign.

Menkauhor evidently chose not to be buried at Abusir, where his dynastic predecessors had built their pyramids. To date, we are not sure where his tomb is located, although a number of scholars suggest North Saqqara, to the east of the funerary complex of the Dynasty VI pharaoh Teti.

A pyramid at North Saqqara, known locally as the "Headless Pyramid," and among Egyptologists as "Lepsius XXIX" (after Karl Richard Lepsius, the German Egyptologist who first noted it), is considered a likely contender for the tomb of Menkauhor. Completely covered in sand, this structure, which has never been properly excavated or studied, has a base measurement somewhere in the neighborhood of 65 x 68 m. Firth, who cleared the ruin and did a cursory examination in 1930, found the burial chamber which contained an intact lid and broken sarcophagus made of "very fine blue-grey hard stone." Firth believed the pyramid to have belonged to the Dynasty IX/X(?) ruler Ity, but later exploration of the site places the structure in Dynasty V. However, it should be noted that Malek sees the pyramid as having belonged to Merykare, also of Dynasty IX/X.

The Turin Canon gives Menkauhor a reign of eight years while Manetho records nine. While a statue of the king in the costume reserved for a Sed Festival was found at Saqqara, there is no reason to assume the reign was longer than eight to nine years.

References:

Berlandini 1979 pp. 3-28
Borchardt 1907 p. 132
de Rougé 1866 pp. 98-99, pl. VI
Dodson 2003 pp. 71, 79
Dodson and Hilton 2004 pp. 62, 64-65, 66-69
Gardiner 1959 pl. II, Col. III #23
Gardiner 1961 p. 435
Gardiner and Peet 1952 pl. VII #12
Gardiner and Peet 1955 pp. 25, 28, 44 Note b and fig. 2
Lehner 1997 pp. 150, 165

Ockinga 2000 pp. 129-130
Petrie 1924 pp. 89-90
Quibell 1909 p. 24
Verbrugghe and Wickersham 1996 pp. 112, 136, 191
Verner 1997 pp. 188, 271-272, 321, 322-324, 464
Verner 2000b pp. 594-595
Verner 2002 pp. 33, 59, 84
von Beckerath 1999 pp. 58 #7, 59 #7
Waddell 1940 p. 51

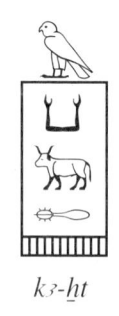

Menkaure — Dynasty IV

Horus Name: kȝ-ḫt

Nomen: mn-kȝw-rˁ — Menkaure

Two Ladies: nbty kȝ

Golden Falcon: (bik) nbw nṯr

Length of Reign:	T: 18 years(?)
Tomb:	Pyramid at Giza: "Menkaure is Divine"
Mummy:	Unknown

Consorts:	Khamerernebti II Rekhetre(?)	**King Lists:**	Ab: (24); P; S: (20); T: (G 3.14?)
Herodotus:	Mykerinos Mycerinus	**Variant Names:**	None
Manetho:	Mencheres (A) Menkheres (A)		

The builder of the third pyramid at Giza, Menkaure was the son of the pharaoh Khafre and an unknown consort. He is the canonical fifth pharaoh of Dynasty IV. However, it is possible that a son of the earlier king, Djedefre, may have held the throne for several years between the reigns of Khafre and Menkaure (see BIKKA). Whatever his position, Menkaure cemented his right to the throne by marrying his sister, or half sister, Khamerernebti.

Not a great deal is known about the reign of Menkaure. That he followed in the tradition of his predecessors and continued trade with Syria-Palestine is evidenced by the discovery of alabaster fragments bearing his cartouche in the Temple of Baalat-Gebal at Byblos. Recently a graffito of Menkaure's cartouche has been found in the Eastern Desert, in the remote Wâdi Sheikh Ali. This would seem to indicate that the king sent at least one stone-cutting expedition to this region.

Menkaure's pyramid is the smallest of the three king pyramids at Giza, measuring 103 m. at the base and 65 m. tall. As pointed out by Mark Lehner, the base of Menkaure's pyramid is less than one quarter that of Khufu's and contains only 10 percent of the total mass of Khufu's tomb. Menkaure's pyramid and its temples were left incomplete at the king's death and were completed, albeit in brick, by his successor Shepseskaf.

When Menkaure's pyramid was opened in 1827, the burial chamber was found to contain a finely carved basalt sarcophagus. Also found was the lid of a wooden anthropoid coffin inscribed with Menkaure's name and human remains that included the legs and lower torso and a foot. Unfortunately, the stone sarcophagus was lost at sea while being transported to the British Museum. The wooden sarcophagus has proved to date to the XXVI Dynasty and the human remains have been carbon-14 dated to the fifth century AD.

Dozens of statues and statuettes of Menkaure, many broken, some unfinished, and some complete, were discovered during excavations conducted at Giza by G.A. Reisner for the Joint Expedition of Harvard University and the Boston Museum of Fine Arts. The sculptures represent Menkaure alone as well as with an unnamed queen, the goddess Hathor, and goddesses of various nomes. The work is superb and stands with the finest examples of Egyptian sculpture.

A cult to Menkaure was established as late as Dynasty XXVI.

Herodotus' description of his king Mycerinus is more than twice as long as the information he offers on Cheops (Khufu) and Chephren (Khafre) combined. The Greek historian tells us that Menkaure reversed Khufu's and Khafre's policies of oppression of the temples. Herodotus also informs us that Menkaure received an oracle from the priests in the city of Buto telling him that he had only six years to live; being exceedingly clever, the king ordered that lamps burn 24 hours a day, thus giving him twelve years instead of six.

How long Menkaure's reign lasted is unsure, but certainly not the 63 years Manetho gives. A much damaged compartment on the Palermo Stone records the number of months and days of the king's last year, but the number of years is missing. The king's name is missing from the Turin Canon, but a regnal date of at least eighteen years is recorded in the position where Menkaure's name most likely would have appeared; the papyrus is much frayed and it is possible that an additional ten years might have been recorded. Contemporary or near contemporary dates recorded for this pharaoh are, for the most part, questionable and consist of a few quarry marks, graffiti and two tomb inscriptions. The highest date given is a "Year of the 11th. occurrence," which, if it refers to Menkaure, might

Men...re

mean a year 22, if the biennial cattle count was in effect. A rule of 18 to 28 years is possible.

References:

Aldred 1965 pp. 111, Ill. 110, 112-115
Brier 1994 pp. 244-245
Clagett 1989 p. 86
Dodson 2003 pp. 62-63
Dodson and Hilton 2004 pp. 50, 52-53, 55, 55-56, 58-59, 61
Gardiner 1959 pl. II, Col. III #14
Gardiner 1961 pp. 82-83, 434
Hawass 1995 pp. 232-245
Hawass 2001 pp. 378-379
Herodotus 1954 pp. 180-183
Ikram and Dodson 1998 pp. 246-248, 314, 317, 320
Jánosi 1992 pp. 52, 55
Jidejian 1968 pp. 17, 19
Lehner 1997 pp. 134-137
Manuelian 1990/1991 pp. 15-17
Meyer 1983 p. 81
Peden 2001 p. 7, 278
Reisner 1931
Spalinger 1994 pp. 288-291
Stadelmann 2001a pp. 596-597
Verbrugghe and Wickersham 1996 pp. 109, 135, 190
Verner 1997 pp. 157, 242-254, 463
Verner 2001b p. 588
von Beckerath 1999 pp. 54 #6, 55 #6
Waddell 1940 pp. 47
T. Wilkinson 2000 p. 149

Men...re   Dynasty XIV

Horus Name: Unknown

Nomen: Unknown

Prenomen:

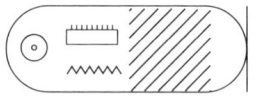

mn...rˁ

Men...re

Two Ladies: Unknown

Golden Falcon: Unknown

Length of Reign:	Unknown
Tomb:	Unknown
Mummy:	Unknown

Consorts:	Unknown	**Variant Names:**	Men[ib]re Menibre
Manetho:	Not given		
King Lists:	T: (G 9.8; R 10.8; vB 9.80)		

Perhaps the forty-fourth king of Dynasty XIV, Men...re is one of a group of kings known only from the Turin Canon. The papyrus' fragmentary state allows for varying interpretations as to the positioning of some of the kings of this dynasty. However, Men...re's place seems secure. There is some disagreement as to the transliteration of this king's name, with von Beckerath seeing ◯ | (*ib*) in the fragment of papyrus bearing the name, while Gardiner and Ryholt do not.

References:
Gardiner 1959 Col. IX #8
Gardiner 1961 p. 442 9.8
Ryholt 1997a pp. 95 Col. 10.8, 98 #44, 380 File 14/44, 409 #44

von Beckerath 1999 pp. 112 #d, 113 #d

Merdjefare   Dynasty XIV

Horus Name:
Unknown   **Nomen:** Unknown

Prenomen:

mr-dfɜ-rˁ
Merdjefare

Two Ladies: Unknown

Golden Falcon: Unknown

Length of Reign:	Unknown
Tomb:	Unknown
Mummy:	Unknown

Consorts:	Unknown	**Variant Names:**	None
Manetho:	Not given		
King Lists:	T: (G 8.5; R 9.5; vB 8.5)		

Possibly the tenth king of Dynasty XIV, Merdjefare is one of only a handful of kings of Dynasty XIV to have left any attestation beyond the Turin Canon. His name is recorded on a stele of the royal seal-bearer and treasurer Ranisonb found at Saft el-Hinna in the southeastern Delta.

Ryholt has suggested that Merdjefare may perhaps be the prenomen of one of two ephemeral kings, Wazad or Sheneh; this however is conjecture.

203

Merenhor

References:
Gardiner 1959 pl. III, Col. VIII #5
Gardiner 1961 p. 441
Ryholt 1997a pp. 61, 95 Col. 9.5, 97, 98 #10, 198 table 37, 379 File 14/10
von Beckerath 1999 pp. 108 #6, 109 #6
Yoyotte 1989 pp. 17-63

Merenhor   Dynasty VII/VIII

Horus Name: Unknown

Nomen:

mr.n-ḥr
Merenhor

Prenomen: Unknown

Two Ladies: Unknown

Golden Falcon: Unknown

Length of Reign:	Unknown
Tomb:	Unknown
Mummy:	Unknown

Consorts:	Unknown	**Variant Names:**	None
Manetho:	Not given		
King Lists:	Ab: (46)		

The seventh pharaoh of Dynasty VII/VIII, Merenhor is known only from the Abydos King List. A lacuna is recorded in the Turin Canon where he would have been listed.

References:
Gardiner 1961 p. 437 #A 46
Ryholt 2000 pp. 96-97, 99 table 1, 379 file 14/10
von Beckerath 1999 pp. 66 #7, 67 #7

Merenptah   Dynasty XIX

Horus Name:

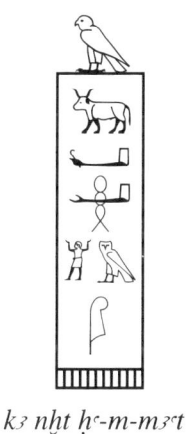

kꜣ nḫt hꜥ-m-mꜣꜥt

Nomen:

mry.n-ptḥ ḥtp-ḥr-mꜣꜥt
Merenptah (hotephermaat)

Prenomen:

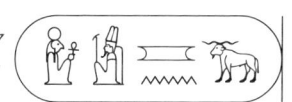

bꜣ-n-rꜥ mry-imn
Baenre-meryamen

Two Ladies:

nbty ḥꜥi-mi-ptḥ-m-ḫnw-ḥfnw

Golden Falcon:

bik-nbw nb-snḏ ꜥꜣ-šfit

Length of Reign:	Unknown
Tomb:	Valley of the Kings: KV8
Mummy:	Tomb of Amenhotep II Now at Cairo Museum: JE34562; CG61079

Consorts:	Bintanath (II)(?) Isetneferet (II)	**Variant Names:**	Amenophath Ammenephthes Ammenephthis Merneptah
Manetho:	Not given		
King Lists:	None		

The fourth ruler of Dynasty XIX, Merenptah was the son of Ramesses II and Queen Isetneferet. The new pharaoh was an old man upon his accession, being Ramesses' thirteenth surviving son. He outlived twelve of his brothers, four of whom had been given the

205

Merenptah

title Crown Prince before him. Merenptah's promotion to heir apparent occurred in about regnal year 55, when Ramesses was probably almost 80 years of age. We know from his mummy that the old king suffered greatly from arthritis of the hip, arteriosclerosis, and severe dental abscesses (all of which he passed on to Merenptah). There is every reason to believe that he was in almost continual pain. It is almost certain that Merenptah became what Kitchen calls "the king's right-hand-man." Although he was never formally named coregent, he undoubtedly was, for all practical purposes, ruler of Egypt long before he formally ascended to the throne.

Evidently the early part of Merenptah's reign ran smoothly, but within a few years the situation changed dramatically. In regnal year two or three he found it necessary to send a military force into Canaan. The cities of Ashkelon, Gezer, and Yenoam fell to the Egyptian army, and the name Israel is listed among the peoples vanquished. Undoubtedly the death of Ramesses II emboldened the various cities and tribes to revolt, but the real cause of the flare-up was the incursion of migrating peoples into that area. These peoples, part of a mass wave of various tribes and cultures, had fled famine and invading tribes as crops failed and cities and kingdoms such as Mycenae and Troy had fallen. In their quest for survival, these displaced masses seem to have formed into a loose coalition which the Egyptians referred to as "the Sea People." Traveling by land and sea, these marauders pillaged and burned as they went. The Hittite Empire, once Egypt's greatest threat and rival, was reeling from the force of the invasion, and would never recover. Ugarit and other cities in Syria-Palestine fell. It is a testament to the organization and abilities of the Egyptian army that it was able to retake and hold its possessions where so many others had failed.

However, Merenptah's troubles were far from over. In regnal year five, the Libyans, in tandem with a group of the Sea People, attempted an invasion of Egypt's western Delta, evidently laying siege to and/or bypassing the forts Ramesses II had erected there. A great battle between the invaders (who had brought their entire families, possessions and livestock with them) and the Egyptians ensued, perhaps near the ancient city of Buto. According to inscriptions at Karnak, the battle lasted for six hours, and when it ended the Egyptians were victorious. The Karnak inscription tells us that the Libyan leader fled so quickly that he left his sandals behind. He also left behind six dead sons, whose phalli were cut off along with those of more than 6,100 Libyans and 2,300 of the Sea People. These grim trophies were presented to Merenptah, for according to the inscription, they were "carried off to the place where the king was."

A revolt in Lower Nubia also erupted, evidently at almost the same time as the Libyan invasion, raising a suggestion that the Libyans and the Nubians may have acted in collusion. This is certainly possible, as lines of communication were open via the string of oases in the Western Desert. (It is interesting to note that the same route was attempted by Hyksos messengers trying to reach Nubian allies during the reign of Kamose, three centuries earlier.) Whatever the circumstance, the Egyptian army, most likely under the command of the Viceroy of Kush, was able to put down the affair in a relatively short time. Brutality was the order of the day, and while the numbers of slain and captive Nubian warriors is not given, it is recorded that many were taken to Egypt and dealt with in the cruelest manner. Some were burned alive, others were blinded, or had their hands or ears cut off. These latter were then shipped back to Nubia, where they were left to fend for themselves. On the stele that records the campaign, at the temple at Amada, in Lower Nubia, we are reassured that there would never be another Nubian rebellion.

The remaining five or so years of Merenptah's reign seem to have been a time of peace for Egypt and it is likely that the majority of the king's building activities were carried out during that period. As with some of the monuments built by Ramesses, work was hastily done. Merenptah, undoubtedly well aware of his age, wanted as many projects as possible completed before his death. This is certainly the case with his mortuary temple in Western Thebes, which was mostly built of stone pilfered from the nearby temple of Amenhotep III. Not far away, in the Valley of the Kings, Merenptah built his tomb.

Aside from his mortuary temple, no new building projects at Thebes seem to be attributable to Merenptah. At Karnak, scenes and texts were added to already existing structures, and cartouches were usurped. The situation at Luxor Temple is much the same.

However, away from the Theban area, Merenptah mounted extensive building programs. He seems to have built extensively at Memphis, where he was responsible for a temple to the god Ptah. He also built a new palace, part of which was made of stones inscribed with the name of Ramesses II. Merenptah also usurped statues of Ramesses II and the Dynasty XII pharaoh Amenemhet III. At Saqqara, two sphinxes of Merenptah were found near the Serapeum. At Hermopolis in Middle Egypt, Merenptah began a small sanctuary for Amen, which his son, Sety II, completed. Farther south, at Abydos, Merenptah added images and texts to the cenotaph of his grandfather Sety I, as well as that king's temple. For good measure, Merenptah added his cartouches to the temple of Ramesses I, and cartouches and text to the temple of Ramesses II. A Hathor shrine at Dendera was usurped from the Dynasty XI pharaoh, Montuhotep III. South of Thebes, Merenptah built a small rock-cut chapel at Gebel Silsila.

Outside of Egypt, bits and pieces of inscribed pottery and scarabs have been found in Palestine. The temple of Hathor at the turquoise mines of Serabit el-Khadim, in Sinai, have yielded fragments of inscribed pottery, vases, and wands as well as an inscribed doorjamb, fragments of at least one stele, and a sphinx. In

Merenptah

Nubia he seems to have been content with adding his cartouches, bits of text and the occasional image to temples at Dongola, Amara West, Buhen, Serra East, Amada and el-Sabua.

Merenptah apparently died sometime in his tenth regnal year, when he was between 60 and 70 years old. He was succeeded by his son, Sety II.

The mummy of Merenptah was discovered in the tomb of Amenhotep II (KV35) in the Valley of the Kings. The body, much damaged by tomb robbers, is that of an old man who suffered arthritis and arteriosclerosis. The pharaoh had bad teeth, and many were missing. It is likely that he was overweight. The height of the body was 1.714 m. Because of the mummification process, the mummy was encrusted with sodium chloride; the salty remains at one time led some scholars to the absurd conclusion that the mummy was that of the pharaoh of the Exodus, covered in salt because the pharaoh had drowned in the Red Sea.

References:

Brier 1994 pp. 272-273
Brock 1992 pp. 122-140
Bucaille 1990 pp. viii-xviii, 10, 27, 28, 57, 58-59, 61-62, 63, 84-87, 90-91, 93-94, 95, 98-99, 102, 103-104, 109-111, 116, 118, 121-124, 127, 131, 136-138, 144-145, 148-150, 156-160, 165, 200, figs. 8, 20, 21, 22, 23, 29, 34, 36, 39, 40, 42, 45
B. Davies 1997 pp. 151-172, 173-188, 189-194
Dodson and Hilton 2004 pp. 22, 158, 160-161, 170, 171, 176, 178, 182, 196, 283 note 31
Drews 1993 pp. 5, 6, 19-20, 48-49, 79, 158, 200, 215-216
El Madhy 1989 pp. 84, 88, 90, 91
Forbes 1993 pp. 52-56
Forbes 1998a pp. 678-681
Gardiner and Peet 1952 pp. 183-184 #s 265-267A
Gardiner and Peet 1955 pl. LXIX and LXXIII
Grajetzki 2005 p. 70
Harris and Weeks 1973 pp. 112, 155, 156-158
Ikram and Dodson 1998 pp. 42, 96, 121, 127, 228, 252, 261, 263, 265, 266, 288, 315, 326, 327, ills. 41, 368-370, 371-372
Kitchen 1982 pp. 72, 89, 100, 103, 112-113, 207, 215-216
Manassa 2003
Partridge 1994 pp. 159-161
Reeves 1990b pp. 95-98
Reeves and Wilkinson 1996 pp. 24-25, 30, 35, 37-38, 40, 47, 51, 53-54, 72, 81, 84, 140, 147-150, 152, 156, 160, 199, 201, 202, 207, 209
G. Smith 1912 pp. 65-70, pl. XLV-XLIX
Spalinger 2005 pp. 178, 202-203, 229, 235-237, 238, 239, 241-243, 267
Tyldesley 2000 pp. 16, 57, 65, 132, 133, 152, 153, 166, 181, 182, 185-189, 190
Tyldesley 2006 pp. 160
von Beckerath 1999 pp. 156-159 #4
R. Wilkinson 2000 pp. 106, 113, 140, 148, 161, 187-188, 208, 221

Merenre I   Dynasty VI

Horus Name: ꜥnḫ-ḫꜥw

Nomen: nmti-m-sꜣ.f — Nemtyemsaf

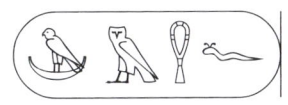

Prenomen: mr-n-rꜥ — Merenre

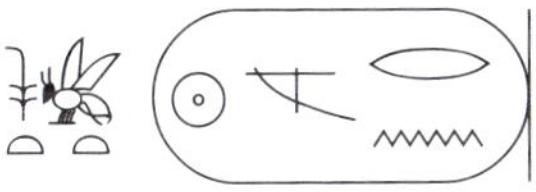

Two Ladies: nbty ꜥnḫ-ḫꜥw

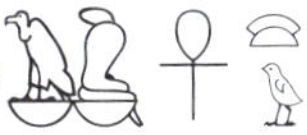

Golden Falcon: bikw-nbw

Length of Reign:	6-7 years
Tomb:	Pyramid at South Saqqara: "The Perfection of Merenre Appears"
Mummy:	Found in pyramid. Now in Cairo Museum

Consorts:	Unknown	**Variant Names:**	Antiemdjaf
Manetho:	Menthousouphis (A)		Antyemsaf
	Methusuphis (A)		Mernere
King Lists:	Ab: (37); S: (35); T: (G [4.4]); SSA		

The son of Pepi I, Merenre was the fourth pharaoh of Dynasty VI. He was a child of Pepi I's middle age, after he had married two sisters, both named Ankhenespepi (also known as Ankhesemeryre). Ankhenespepi I was Merenre's mother, while Ankhenespepi II was the mother of Merenre's half-brother and eventual successor, Pepi II.

Merenre I

Attestations for Merenre are few. His Horus name and Nomen are found on an inscription from the alabaster quarries at Hatnub, and his Horus name, Two Ladies, Golden Falcon and Nomen are found on a stele at the Wadi Hammamat. That Merenre built at Abydos is confirmed by the finding there of inscribed blocks. Merenre is mentioned in the tomb of the nomarch Ibi, at Deir el-Gebrawi.

The smaller of two copper statues found at Hierakonpolis has often been identified as being Merenre, but there is no proof for such an assignment.

Stelae at Aswan record a visit there by the king in his fifth regnal year. They tell us that the chiefs of the powerful Nubian tribes of Irtjet, Medjay and Wawat "all did obeisance and gave great praise." Certainly Merenre's interest in Nubia was intense. He commissioned the cutting of five canals at Aswan, thus avoiding the cataract and making shipping, both north and south, easier. Weni, a courtier who had served Teti and Pepi I, was the man responsible not only for cutting the canals, but also for constructing boats to haul back granite for Merenre's pyramid at Saqqara. Another courtier, Harkhuf, led three expeditions into Nubia, "as far as the western corner of heaven."

Merenre's pyramid at South Saqqara was of the same dimensions as those of his father and grandfather, a height of 52 m. and a base that was 79 x 79 m. Pyramid texts were found in the pyramid's interior. The sarcophagus contained the mummy of a young man, still wearing the side-lock of youth. The mummy was almost intact (although the upper front teeth were missing, as was the lower jaw). Most scholars believe the mummy to be an intrusive burial from a much later dynasty.

The Turin Canon, much damaged as it is, lacks the name of the king at this point in time, but gives a reign of 44 years. This is rather implausible, since we know that Pepi II was Merenre's younger half-brother and just a child when he inherited the throne. The highest dates known from contemporary attestations come from one of the stelae at Aswan, which gives a very clear date of "Year 5, 2nd. Month of Shomu, 28th Day" (although Spalinger reads it as "Year of the 3rd occurrence, etc.") and from the inscription from Hatnub, which reads "Year after the 5th occurrence." If the cattle count ("occurrence") was done biennially, Merenre's highest year would be year 11, but if the count was done annually, the highest count we have is year 6. Manetho gives Merenre, his Menthusuphis, a reign of seven years.

References:

Anthes 1928 pp. pl. 5, #VII
Brier 1994 p. 247
Couyat and Montet 1912 p. 58 #60
N. Davies 1902 pp. 21-22, pl. XXIII
Dodson 1994b pp. 13, 111 #6, pl. IIb
Dodson 2003 pp. 26, 76, 128
Dodson and Hilton 2004 pp. 70, 71, 72-73, 74
Forbes 1997 pp. 83-85
Gardiner 1961 pp. 99-101, 436
Ikram and Dodson 1998 pp. 81-82 and illustration 78, 250, 315, 317, 321
Lehner 1997 pp. 15, 31, 55, 83, 156, 158, 159, 160-162, 248, 332, 341, 359-361, 367

Peden 2001 pp. 7-8, 10
Petrie 1902b pp. 27, 41, pl. LIV
Quibell and Green 1902 pp. 27-28, 33, 34, 45, pl. L-LVI
Ryholt 2000 pp. 13-14, Notes #s 21-22, 24, and table 3, 91
Verbrugghe and Wickersham 1996 pp. 136, 192
Verner 1997 pp. 40, 248, 341, 359-361, 367
von Beckerath 1999 pp. 62 #4, 63 #4
Waddell 1940 p. 53

Merenre II Dynasty VI

Horus Name:
Unknown

Nomen:

nmti-m-s3.f
Nemtyemsaf

Prenomen:

mr-n-rˁ nmti-m-s3.f
Merenre-Nemtyemsaf

Two Ladies: Unknown

Golden Falcon: Unknown

Length of Reign:	1 year
Tomb:	Unknown
Mummy:	Unknown

Consorts:	Unknown	Antyemsaf
Manetho:	Menthesouphis (A)	Mehti-em-saf Mernere
King Lists:	Ab: (39); T: (G [4.6?])	Mirnire-Mihtimsaf
Variant Names:	Antiemdjaf	

The sixth pharaoh of Dynasty VI, Merenre II was the son of the long-lived Pepi II. Due to Pepi's long reign, it is likely that Merenre was not the first-born and that older brothers had died before their father. Such a situation occurred during Dynasty XIX: Ramesses II

Merhotepre

ruled for an incredible 67 years; his successor, Merenptah, had been predeceased by twelve older brothers. Merenre's mother, Neith A, may have been Pepi II's half-sister and queen; if that is the case, it is likely that, as with Merenptah, Merenre II would have been an old man. It is unlikely that a pyramid was ever begun for him.

A son of Pepi II, one Nemtyemsaf, is known from a stele found near the pyramid of Queen Neith. He is most likely Merenre II.

For many years, scholars have tried to tie Merenre II to the story found in Herodotus in which Queen Nitocris takes revenge on the murderers of her brother (allegedly Merenre). As is explained in the entry for Netjerkare Siptah, "Queen Nitocris" did not exist.

Although Merenre's name is lost, the Turin Canon preserves a length of "one year, one month" for his reign.

References:

Altenmüller 2001 p. 604
Dodson and Hilton 2004 pp. 70, 72-73, 73-74, 74, line drawing, 77
Gardiner 1961 p. 436
Herodotus 1954 p. 166
Jéquier 1933a pp. 55-56
Ryholt 2000 pp. 91
Verbrugghe and Wickersham 1996 pp. 136, 192
von Beckerath 1999 pp. 64 #6, 65 #6
Waddell 1940 p. 55

Merhotepre SIP

Horus Name:
Unknown   **Nomen:** Unknown

Prenomen:

mr-ḥtp-rˁ
Merhotepre

Two Ladies: Unknown

Golden Horus: Unknown

Length of Reign:	Unknown
Tomb:	Unknown
Mummy:	Unknown

Consorts:	Unknown	**Variant Names:**	None
Manetho:	Not given		
King Lists:	K: (50)		

This prenomen is found in the Karnak King List, on a cylinder-seal probably from the Medinet el-Faiyum and on a stele from

Abydos. The name undoubtedly belongs to either Sobekhotep V or Ini, both of Dynasty XIII and both having the prenomen Merhotepre.

References:
Budge 1968 p. 127
El-Alfi 1991 p. 34 #50 (as *Mry-htp-rˁ*)
Helck 1983 pp. 40 #53

Ryholt 1997a pp. 402-403 File P/1
Yoyotte 1957 p. 86 #1q

Merkare   Dynasty XIII

Horus Name: Unknown

Nomen: Unknown

Prenomen:

mr-kȝ-rˁ
Merkare

Two Ladies: Unknown

Golden Falcon: Unknown

Length of Reign:	Unknown
Tomb:	Unknown
Mummy:	Unknown

Consorts:	Unknown	**Variant Names:**	None
Manetho:	Not given		
King Lists:	T: (G 7.23; R 8.18; vB 7.23)		

Possibly the forty-seventh king of Dynasty XIII, Merkare is one of a group of kings known only from the Turin Canon. While the papyrus' fragmentary state allows for varying interpretations as to the positioning of some of the kings of this dynasty, recent research by K.S.B. Ryholt strongly supports this position for Merkare.

References:
Gardiner 1959 pl. III, Col. VII #23
Gardiner 1961 p. 441 #7.23
Ryholt 1997a pp. 71 Col. 8.18, 73 #48, 197 #48, 357 File 13/48

von Beckerath 1999 pp. 100 #47, 101 #47

Merkheperre Dynasty XIII

Horus Name: Unknown

Nomen: Unknown

Prenomen:

mr-ḫpr-rꜥ
Merkheperre

Two Ladies: Unknown

Golden Falcon: Unknown

Length of Reign:	Unknown
Tomb:	Unknown
Mummy:	Unknown

Consorts:	Unknown	**Variant Names:**	Mercheperre Ra-mer-kheper
Manetho:	Not given		
King Lists:	T: (G 7.22; R 8.17; vB 7.22)		

Very likely the forty-sixth ruler of Dynasty XIII, although placed as forty-seventh by Ryholt, attestations for this king are practically nonexistent. Aside from his prenomen given in the Turin Canon, Merkheperre's name is to be found on a small weight of unknown provenance, and a scarab now in the British Museum, although Ryholt argues that the scarab "lacks any royal attributes."

References:

Dodson and Hilton 2004 p. 100
Gardiner 1959 pl. III, Col. VII #22
Gardiner 1961 p. 441 #7.22
Hall 1913 p. 21 #200
Petrie 1933 p. 37 #3
Ryholt 1997a pp. 71 fig. 10, Col. 8 #17, 73 table 17 #47, 357 File 13/47
Tufnell 1984 p. 370 #3206 and pl. LVI
von Beckerath 1999 pp. 100 #46, 101 #46

Merneith   Dynasty I

Horus Name: Unknown   **Nomen:** *mr-nt* Merneith

Two Ladies: Unknown

Golden Falcon: Unknown

Length of Reign:	Unknown
Tomb:	Abydos, Umm el Qa'ab, Y
Mummy:	Unknown

Consorts:	Djet	Merneit
Manetho:	Not given	Meryet-nit
		Meryt-neith
King Lists:	None	
Variant Names:	Meritneith	

Queen Merneith has long been a mysterious figure in the history of Egypt and it is only recently that her role in Dynasty I politics has begun to be understood; even her sex has been questioned. When Petrie first cleared her tomb at Abydos in the winter of 1899-1900, he believed that he had discovered a new king. As recently as 1971 I.E.S. Edwards wrote "If Mer(it)neith was a woman..." in mentioning her in a chapter on the early dynastic period written for the *Cambridge Ancient History*. It is now certain that Merneith was, indeed, a woman. On a jar sealing recently found in the tomb of king Den, the hieroglyphs for "king's mother" follows her name; also, she is given as Den's mother on Fragment Five of the part of the Palermo Stone in the Cairo Museum. It is now believed that Merneith probably acted as a regent, Den having been too young to rule at the time of his accession to the throne upon the death of king Djet. It is very likely that Djet was Den's father, and so it follows that Merneith was a consort and probably chief queen of Djet.

The same sealing mentioned above gives the succession of every Dynasty I king from Narmer to Den, and so is a very important piece of historic evidence. What makes it doubly important is that after Den's name is the name of Merneith: this sealing shows, without a doubt, that the Queen Mother was considered a ruler of Egypt, at least during Den's lifetime. A similar sealing from the tomb of king Qa'a, last ruler of Dynasty I, lists the succession for the entire period but omits Merneith, which probably means that after her son's death she was relegated back to the position of a royal consort. Nonetheless, it seems certain that Neithhotep was the first woman in the history of Egypt to have been considered powerful enough to be treated as a ruler, regent though she may have been, and accorded some of the ruler's prerogatives.

One of the ruler's prerogatives Merneith was accorded was burial in the cemetery at Abydos reserved strictly for kings. Her tomb at Abydos was quite as sumptuous and well-constructed as any tomb in the royal cemetery. It was identified by two large stelae bearing Merneith's name, but not in a serekh. Like the kings of this dynasty, Merneith's tomb is surrounded by subsidiary burials, in her case 41 of them. She may also have possessed a funerary enclosure near all the other such monuments, about a mile from her tomb at Umm el Qa'ab. This structure, which was surrounded by 80 burials of sacrificed retainers, may have been hers alone; however, it is just as likely that the enclosure was either shared by her and her son or that it belonged to Den alone.

Merneith's name is also associated with mastaba 3503 at Saqqara; jar sealings bearing her name have been found there. However, it appears that 3503 was the tomb of a high official named Seshemka.

References:

Dodson and Hilton 2004 pp. 45, 46, 48, 65
Lehner 1997 pp. 77, 78, 79
Newberry and Wainwright 1914 pp. 154-155
O'Connor 1989 p. 51, 57 note 16, 58, 73
Petrie 1900 pp. 11, 17, 19, 36, 37, pl. *Frontpiece*, III, V, XX-XXIII, XXXVII, #s15-28, LIX, LXIV-LXV
Petrie 1925a pp. 1, 2, 3, pl. XV, XVIII
Spencer 1993 p. 82, figs. 60 and 61
Troy 1986 pp. 106, 107-108, 139, 152 #1.7
Uphill 1984
T. Wilkinson 1999 pp. 74-75, 239
T. Wilkinson 2000 pp. 103-105

Mer...re   Dynasty XIII

Horus Name: Unknown

Nomen: Unknown

Prenomen:

$[m]r$-...-r^c

Mer...re

Two Ladies: Unknown

Golden Falcon: Unknown

Length of Reign:	Unknown		
Tomb:	Unknown		
Mummy:	Unknown		
Consorts:	Unknown	**Variant Names:**	None
Manetho:	Not given		
King Lists:	T: (G 7.21; R 8.16)		

This fragmentary prenomen is known only from the Turin Canon. Mer...re is probably the forty-fifth king of the dynasty. He may be an otherwise unknown king or may be a name that belongs to either Ini Mershepses or Neferhotep Mersekhemre, both of whom reigned in the latter part of Dynasty XIII.

References:

Gardiner 1959 pl. III, Col. VII #21
Gardiner 1961 p. 441 #7.21
Ryholt 1997a pp. 71 Col. 8.16, 73 #46, 357 File 13/46

von Beckerath 1999 p. 101 #42-43
"names lost"

Mersekhemre SIP

Horus Name: Unknown

Nomen: Unknown

Prenomen:

mr-shm-rʿ
Mersekhemre

Two Ladies: Unknown

Golden Falcon: Unknown

Length of Reign:	Unknown		
Tomb:	Unknown		
Mummy:	Unknown		
Consorts:	Unknown	**Variant Names:**	None
Manetho:	Not given		
King Lists:	K: (41)		

Mery...[hathor?]

This prenomen is found on the Karnak King List and undoubtedly belongs to either Ined or Neferhotep II, both of Dynasty XIII and both having the prenomen Mersekhemre.

References:
Budge 1968 p. 127
El-Alfi 1991 p. 33 #41 (as *S<u>h</u>m-mry-r·*)
Ryholt 1997a p. 403 File P/2

Mery...[hathor?]   Dynasty IX/X

Horus Name: Unknown   **Nomen:**

mry...[ḥwt-ḥr?]
Mery...[Hathor?]

Prenomen: Unknown

Two Ladies: Unknown

Golden Falcon: Unknown

Length of Reign:	Unknown
Tomb:	Unknown
Mummy:	Unknown

Consorts:	Unknown	**Variant Names:**	Mery...(?)
Manetho:	Not given		
King Lists:	None		

Mery...[hathor?] is known only from a single, much-damaged graffito at the travertine quarries of Hatnub in Middle Egypt. It is generally assumed that he was one of the Herakleopolitan pharaohs who controlled an unknown amount of territory around Herakleopolis in Middle Egypt (see "Herakleopolitans" in Glossary), although this by no means certain. Likewise in question is his name: the squatting figure in the cartouche is too worn for proper identification; when taken into account at all, it is considered probable that it represents the goddess Hathor.

References:
Anthes 1928 p. 14 inschr. IX and note 1, pl. VII (top)
von Beckerath 1999 pp. 74 #b, 75 #b

Merykare   Dynasty IX/X

Horus Name: Unknown

Nomen: Unknown

Prenomen:

mry-k3-r˓
Merykare

Two Ladies: Unknown

Golden Falcon: Unknown

Length of Reign:	Unknown
Tomb:	Pyramid at Saqqara: "Flourishing are the abodes of Merykare"
Mummy:	Unknown

Consorts:	Unknown	**Variant Names:**	Merikara
Manetho:	Not given		
King Lists:	None		

Merykare is one of the pharaohs who controlled an unknown amount of territory around Herakleopolis in Middle Egypt (see "Herakleopolitans" in Glossary). Due to the great damage suffered by the Turin Canon, Merykare's name is missing from that text; however, it would appear that he ruled quite late in the dynasty, perhaps as the final ruler.

There is evidence that Merykare led at least one campaign against his Theban contemporaries, probably at the time of Montuhotep II. An inscription found in the tomb of a nomarch named Khety (of no known relationship to the Herakleopolitan royal family) refers to Merykare leading an armed fleet up the Nile as far as the border of Asyut in Middle Egypt. Another inscription, found in the tomb of the nomarch's father, Tefibi, also refers to an engagement with the Thebans. However, it is not known whether this engagement took place during the reign of Merykare or one of his predecessors. Perhaps in recognition of the support of the nomarchs of Asyut, Merykare ordered the restoration of the temple of the god Wepwawet.

In addition, a literary attribution has traditionally been ascribed to Merykare's predecessor (Khety V, if Dodson's chronology is accepted). This work, entitled *Instructions to Merykare*, gives fatherly advice to the pharaoh about how to handle his kingdom. However, it is possible that this work should be attributed to Khety III, as his successor, Khety IV, had a prenomen of Mery...re, which might actually have been Merykare.

The ruins of a pyramid (L.XXIX) built just to the east of the pyramid of Teti of Dynasty VI at North Saqqara may have belonged to Merykare. Called the "Headless Pyramid" locally, the structure is completely destroyed. Recent reconstruction of a fragile bit of text found near the ruin may indicate that the structure was once occupied by Merykare. If so, Dodson has suggested that this king's burial was a usurpation, since he sees the pyramid's design as more appropriate to Dynasty V, and possibly belonging to Menkauhor. Excavations indicate that the pyramid had been occupied at some point. It should be noted that a mortuary cult for Merykare was active at Saqqara, and that some texts appear to indicate that the cult shared its priesthood with that of Teti.

References:

Breasted 1906 vol. I pp. 180-183, 183-187
Dodson 2003 pp. 71, 79
Dodson and Hilton 2004 pp. 80-81
Franke 2001 p. 530
Grajetzki 2006 pp. 8-9
Hayes 1953 p. 144
Lehner 1997 p. 165
Lichtheim 1975 pp. 97-109
Lorton 1987 pp. 22, 26
Seidlmayer 2000 pp. 139, 145
Verner 1997 pp. 324, 376
von Beckerath 1999 pp. 74 #f, 75 #f

Merytowy SIP

Horus Name:

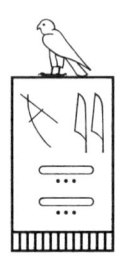

mry-tꜣwy
Merytowy

Nomen: Unknown

Prenomen: Unknown

Two Ladies: Unknown

Golden Falcon: Unknown

Length of Reign:	Unknown
Tomb:	Unknown
Mummy:	Unknown

Consorts:	Unknown	**Variant Names:**	None
Manetho:	None		
King Lists:	None		

This Horus name was found on a seal-impression from the Middle Kingdom fort at Uronarti in Nubia. The context in which the impression was found would seem to indicate that it belongs to a Dynasty XIII king who ruled prior to Awibre Hor.

References:

Dunham 1967 pp. 53 # 29-1-125, 64 #1A

Ryholt 1997a pp. 321-322, 404 File H/1

Montuemsaf   Dynasty XVI

Horus Name: Unknown

Nomen:

mntw-m-s3f
Montuemsaf

Prenomen:

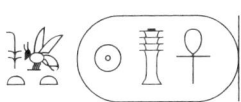

dd-'nh-r'
Djedankhre

Two Ladies: Unknown

Golden Falcon: Unknown

Length of Reign:	Unknown
Tomb:	Unknown; probably at Dra Abu el-Naga
Mummy:	Unknown

Consorts:	Unknown	**Variant Names:**	Dedui-ankh-ra Mentemsaf Mentuemsaf
Manetho:	Not given		
King Lists:	None		

Montuemsaf's parentage is not known, nor is his relationship to his probable predecessor, Dedumose II.

Attestations for Montuemsaf are few: an inscribed block from Gebelein, a bronze axe-blade of unknown provenance inscribed "The good god, Djedankhre, given life," and two scarab-seals, also of unknown provenance.

References:

W. Davies 1981b pp. 43 #101, pl. 18 #101, 31 #101

Dodson and Hilton 2004 p. 116

Montuhotep I

Newberry 1906 pp. 123 #s 25 and 26, pl. X #s 25 and 26
Ryholt 1997a pp. 156-157, 158, table 25, 391 File 16/c, 410 table 97
Tufnell 1984 p. 370 #s 3202 and 3203: pl. LVI #s 3202 and 3203
von Beckerath 1999 pp. 102 #b, 103 #b

Montuhotep I — Dynasty XI

Horus Name:

tpi-ˁ
Tepya

Nomen: *mnṯw-ḥtp* Montuhotep

Prenomen: Unknown

Two Ladies: Unknown

Golden Falcon: Unknown

Length of Reign:	Unknown
Tomb:	Unknown
Mummy:	Unknown

Consorts:	Neferu (I)	Mentehotpe
Manetho:	Not given	Menthotpe
		Menthuhotepo
King Lists:	K: (13); T: (vB 5.12)	Mentuhotep
		Mentuhotep-aa
Variant Names:	Mentehotep	Monthhotep
		Montjuhotep

The "ancestors" list of Thutmose III at Karnak gives Montuhotep, Horus Tepya, as the successor to "Hereditary Prince" Intef. We do not know what, if any, relationship existed between these two individuals, although it is very possible that they were father and son. The Horus name Tepya means "the Ancestor," and this has led scholars to believe that the name was a later addition, an honorific title bestowed upon Montuhotep as a founder of the dynasty. Likewise, the cartouche surrounding the name Montuhotep was honorific. The statue of one Montuhotep-aa (Montuhotep the Elder) found in the sanctuary of Heqaib at Elephantine, and almost certainly the Montuhotep of Thutmose III's list, bears the name, along with the title "Gods' Father" and several epithets all enclosed in a cartouche. During the Middle Kingdom, the term "God's Father" seems to have referred to the non-royal father of a king. In this case, the inscription "Gods' Father" (plural possessive) indicates that he was the father of more than one king. Because Intef II dedicated the statue, he must have been one of the kings. The other king Montuhotep sired was almost certainly Intef I.

Despite the honorifics, Montuhotep was almost certainly master of no more than the Theban nome and the three nomes from Thebes south to the border with Nubia at Elephantine. His power to the north stopped at the border to the Coptite nome.

Montuhotep's actual name is missing from the Turin Canon, because of damage to it.

References:

Dodson and Hilton 2004 pp. 36, 82, 83, 84, 85, 88
Grajetzki 2006 p. 11
Habachi 1958 pp. 176-179, figs. 2 and 3, pl. Ic and IIIb
Habachi 1985 pp. 109-110 and no. 97, pl. 187 a-d, 188 a-b
Strudwick 1999 p. 23
von Beckerath 1999 pp. 76 #1, 77 #1

Montuhotep II　　　　　　　　　　　　Dynasty XI

Horus Name:

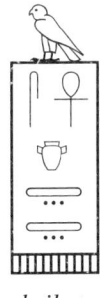

s'nḫ-ib-t3wy

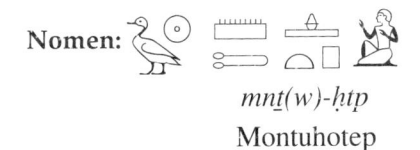

Nomen: *mnṯ(w)-ḥtp*
Montuhotep

Prenomen: Unknown

Two Ladies: Unknown

Golden Falcon: Unknown

Horus Name:

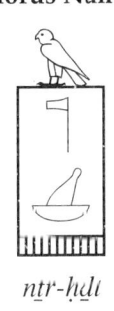

nṯr-ḥḏt

Nomen: *mnṯw-ḥtp*
Montuhotep

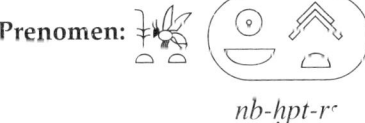

Prenomen: *nb-ḥpt-rʿ*
Nebhepetre

Montuhotep II

Two Ladies:  *nbty nṯr-ḥḏt*

Golden Falcon: Unknown

Horus Name: *smꜣ-tꜣwy*

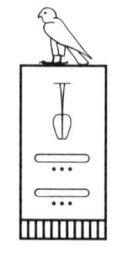

Nomen:  *mnṯw-ḥtp* — Montuhotep

Prenomen: 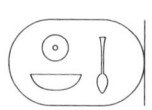 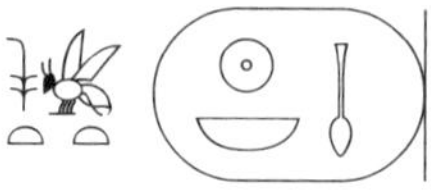 *nb-ḥpt-rꜥ* — Nebhepetre

Two Ladies: 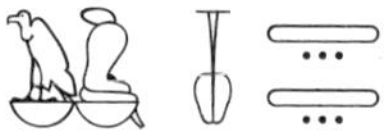 *nbty smꜣ-tꜣwy*

Golden Falcon:  *bik-nbw ḳꜣi-šwti*

Length of Reign:	51 years
Tomb:	Temple-Tomb at Deir el-Bahri: "Glorious art the places of Nebhepetre"
Mummy:	Unknown
Consorts:	Ashayt Henhenet Kawit(?) Kemset(?) Neferu Sadeh Tem
Manetho:	Not given
King Lists:	Ab: (57); K: (25); S: (37); T: (5.16)
Variant Names:	Mentehotep Mentehotpe Menthotep Menthuhotep Mentuhotep Monthhotep Montjuhotep

The fifth pharaoh of Dynasty XI, Montuhotep II was the direct successor of his father, Intef III, and Queen Iah. Montuhotep II was considered by the ancient Egyptians to have been one of their three most important rulers, along with Menes and Ahmose, each venerated for his role in unifying the Egyptian people.

Although Montuhotep II, like his three immediate predecessors, considered himself to be the ruler of Upper and Lower Egypt, the truth was very different. While Montuhotep, with his capital at Thebes, controlled Egypt from its southern border at Aswan to perhaps Asyut in Middle Egypt, a rival pharaoh, one of the Herakleopolitan kings (see Glossary), held sway from Asyut north, his capital being perhaps at Memphis. It has been suggested that some sort of uneasy truce had existed between the two rival powers, but this was to end some time before Montuhotep's regnal year 14, when the rival pharaohs clashed. How long the war lasted is unknown, since no inscriptions directly related to the conflict have survived. However, a rough timeline may be inferred by the several changes made to Montuhotep's titulary over the passage of time.

Prior to his reign, none of the Theban pharaohs' titularies consisted of more than a Horus name and nomen, and such was the case with Montuhotep II up to his year 14, after which he began making changes in his titulary. The first change, which occurred some time between regnal years 14 and 39, was a change in his Horus name and the addition of a Two Ladies name and a prenomen. The addition of these names reflected a significant change (or, perhaps, wishful thinking) about the extent of his rule. Many scholars have inferred from the move toward a complete titulary that Montuhotep II actually had become the ruler of Upper and Lower Egypt, and thus had finally reunited the kingdom. The final change, which occurred by year 39, was the adoption of the Horus name Smatowy ("who united the two countries") and the addition of a Golden Falcon name. It is safe to assume that by this point in the reign he had defeated his Herakleopolitan opponents and was in the process of reunifying Egypt. This was undoubtedly a long process, as the country had been divided for at least a century.

Another problem that Montuhotep II faced was re-establishing the vast bureaucracy that made a united Egypt possible. To a large extent, he created and filled key positions with trusted Thebans. Simultaneously, he began the process of regaining dominion over the various nomes, which in many cases had become more or less independent city-states, some of the nomarchs going so far as to date events based on their own "regnal years." This process continued throughout the early reigns of Dynasty XII. However, at some point, Montuhotep must have felt secure enough to begin sending expeditions into Nubia. The border between the two countries seems to have been secure during the preceding few dynasties, but Egypt had lost control of her greatest cash cow, and in fact, there appears to have been a group of Nubian chieftains who claimed the title of

Montuhotep II

pharaoh. Although records are scarce, what remains makes it clear that Montuhotep was able to push as far south as Buhen at the Second Cataract. There is slight evidence that he may have been responsible for the initial founding of a settlement there, perhaps even the beginning phases of construction of the fort that eventually guarded that point on the river.

Evidence for a pharaonic presence in Asia during the reign is limited to broken bits of fragmentary inscriptions and decorated blocks, which may or may not represent actual occurrences. A statue base inscribed with Montuhotep II's prenomen, along with the prenomina of Montuhotep III, Amenemhet I and Senwosret I, has been found at Serabit el-Khadim in Sinai, but this is merely a votive object, and obviously dates to the reign of Senwosret I. It is not impossible, but rather unlikely, that Montuhotep II had time for "clubbing the eastern lands, striking down the hill countries, trampling the deserts, enslaving the Nubians..., the Libyans, and the Asiatics" while in the midst of a civil war that lasted for a generation. All that can be confirmed is that a trading expedition did bring home a shipment of cedars from Lebanon.

Attestations for Montuhotep II are primarily found in Upper Egypt, although a recently discovered temple near Qantir in the eastern Delta may date to his reign. At Abydos, evidence for building activity includes a number of inscribed and decorated blocks of a shrine. There is a small chapel at the temple of Hathor in Dendera, and decorated blocks and lintels attest to building activities at Deir el-Ballas, Hermonthis, and El Kab. At Tod, Montuhotep repaired and rebuilt the temple of Montu; he built a chapel and monumental doorway at Gebelein, and added a chapel to the temple of Satis at Elephantine.

Montuhotep II's greatest building achievement was his mortuary temple-tomb built on the west bank of the Nile. This magnificent structure, built into the cliffs at Deir el-Bahri, has been described as "a gigantic Saff tomb" by Lehner, who also points out that the entire complex was not only the royal tomb, but also a temple to the deified king, Montu, and Amen-Re. Beginning at a valley temple, a long causeway leads to the main structure which is built in tiers, culminating in a hypostyle hall that ended in a sanctuary. Cut beneath the hall, and leading at a downward angle for 125 meters, is a corridor ending in the king's burial chamber. Also buried within the temple structure were Montuhotep's two principal queens, Neferu and Tem, as well as several minor wives and concubines, some of whose burials were found almost intact. Alas, such was not the case with the pharaoh, whose tomb was empty.

References:

D. Arnold 1974
D. Arnold 1979
D. Arnold 1981
Callender 2000 pp. 149-155
Dodson 2003 pp. 82-84, 129
Dodson and Hilton 2004 pp. 36, 79, 82-83, 84, 85-89, 123
Gardiner and Peet 1952 pl. XXII
Gardiner and Peet 1955 pp. 39, 86 #70

Grajetzki 2005 pp. 26-29
Grajetzki 2006 pp. 18-23
Naville 1895-1908
Naville 1907
Peden 2001 pp. 18-20, 23-25

Petrie 1903 pl. XXIV, XXV, LIV
Tyldesley 2006 pp. 66-68
Verner 1997 pp. 381-382, 388-395, 465
von Beckerath 1999 pp. 78 #5, 79 #5

Montuhotep III   Dynasty XI

Horus Name:

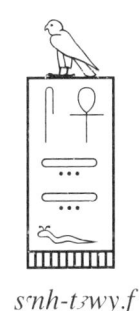

s'nh-t3wy.f

Nomen:

mntw-htp
Montuhotep

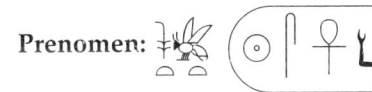

Prenomen:

s'nh-k3-r'
Seankhkare

Two Ladies:

nbty s'nh-t3wy.f

Golden Falcon:

bik-nbw htp

Length of Reign:	12 years
Tomb:	Unknown
Mummy:	Unknown

Consorts:	Imi(?)	Mentehotpe
Manetho:	Not given	Menthotep
		Mentluhotep
King Lists:	Ab (58); K: (30);	Mentuhotep
	S (38); T (5.17)	Monthhotep
		Montjuhotep
Variant Names:	Mentehotep	Senekhkere

The sixth ruler of Dynasty XI, Montuhotep III was the direct successor of his father, Montuhotep II, and Queen Tem. The new pharaoh was probably not a young man upon his accession, and in

227

Montuhotep III

his 12 year reign he continued the administrative and military reconstruction of a unified Egypt begun during his father's half-century of rule. He also followed his father's example by building or adding to temples at Abydos, where he seems to have made additions to the temple of Osiris-Khentamentiu and built a small chapel. He ordered work on the temples of Montu at Armant and at Tod, and there is evidence of architectural work at Elephantine (a beautifully executed relief). Also, like his father, the Theban area saw the most building activity, including a sanctuary at Medinet Habu, and a temple to Horus built on "Thoth Hill," an escarpment rising some 400 meters high, located north of the Valley of the Kings. The temple, much ruined, was built of mudbrick, and contains what some scholars believe to be the actual burial chamber of Montuhotep III, although this is far from certain. A large, incomplete tomb not far from Deir el-Bahri was once considered by some scholars to belong to Montuhotep III, but it is now believed that the structure was begun and then abandoned by Amenemhet I of Dynasty XII.

Montuhotep III's reign was noted for the exceptional quality and beauty of its building projects; later Middle Kingdom artisans strove to emulate the standards set during that time.

Montuhotep III's name is found in the offering formula inscribed on the remains of a statuette of a man and his wife found at Qantir, in the east Delta; he is not otherwise attested to in Lower Egypt.

A rock-cut inscription left by the Chief Steward Henenu in the Wadi Hammamat records an expedition to Punt in Montuhotep III's regnal year eight. This is the earliest known excursion to the "God's Land" during the Middle Kingdom. Henenu led a force of 3,000 men 145 km. (90 miles) through the dry wadi, digging 14 wells along the way. When the force reached the Red Sea, Henenu saw to the building of ships, built from wood transported all the way from the Nile. The expedition was a success, and a pack train of donkeys heavily laden with the riches of Punt returned to Egypt. On the journey back through Wadi Hammamat, Henenu, though encumbered by the pack train, saw to the cutting of stone blocks destined to become statuary in one or more of the pharaoh's various temple building projects.

Aside from the expedition to Punt, there is no real evidence for Montuhotep III's presence outside Egypt; this is perhaps simply due to a lack of preservation of attestations. A statue base inscribed with Montuhotep III's prenomen and the prenomina of Montuhotep II, Amenemhet I and Senwosret I, was found at Serabit el-Khadim in Sinai. However, this is merely a votive object, and obviously can't have been carved until at least the reign of Senwosret I.

A queen named Imi is given as the mother of Montuhotep III's successor Montuhotep IV at Wadi Hammamat. It is possible that she was the wife of Montuhotep III, although she is not called King's Wife, only King's Mother. Her son, Montuhotep IV, may have borne no relationship to his predecessor.

References:
Breasted 1906 vol. I pp. 208-210
Callender 2000 pp. 155-156, 157, 179
Couyat and Montet 1912 pp. 81-84, pl. XXXI
Dodson and Hilton 2004 pp. 82, 83, 84, 86-87, 92, 98, 141
Gardiner and Peet 1952 pl. XXII
Gardiner and Peet 1955 pp. 39, 86 #70
Jeffreys 1993 pp. 68-72
Grajetzki 2006 pp. 23-25, 29-30, 90-91, 92, 95
Tyldesley 2006 p. 68
von Beckerath 1999 pp. 80 #6, 81 #6
Vörös 1998
Vörös 2003 pp. 547-556

Montuhotep IV   Dynasty XI

Horus Name:

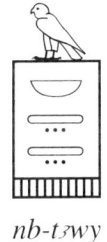

nb-t3wy

Nomen:

mntw-htp
Montuhotep

Prenomen:

nb-t3wy-rˤ
Nebtowyre

Two Ladies:

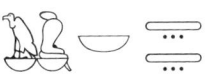

nbty nb-t3wy

Golden Falcon:

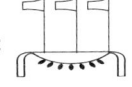

(bik)-nbw ntrw

Length of Reign:	2 years?
Tomb:	Unknown
Mummy:	Unknown

Consorts:	Unknown	Mentehotpe
Manetho:	Not given	Mentehotep
		Mentehotpe
King Lists:	None	Monthhotep
		Montjuhotep
Variant Names:	Menthotep	Neb-towi-re

229

Montuhotep IV

The last ruler of Dynasty XI, Montuhotep IV is an enigmatic figure. No monument bears his name. A single scarab inscribed with his prenomen is of Dynasty XVIII make. He is not named on any king lists; interestingly, the Turin Canon records seven kingless years where his name would be expected. This has led some scholars to conclude that he might have been a usurper; certainly his paternity is unclear. His mother's name, Imi, is known from a single inscription found at Wadi Hammamat.

Quarrying expeditions to Wadi Hammamat occurred in Montuhotep IV's first and second regnal years, as did expeditions to the amethyst mines at Wadi el-Hudi, some 25 km. south-east of Aswan. The inscriptions at el-Hudi are the earliest evidence of pharaonic activity at the site. The "year 2" recorded at both locations is the highest date known for Montuhotep. It is interesting to note that the Hammamat inscriptions also record Montuhotep's Sed festival, a celebration which was ideally held after a reign of 30 years, but could be enacted at any time when a ritualistic renewal of vitality or power was needed.

An inscription from Ayn Soukhna records an expedition of 3,000 men returning to Egypt laden with turquoise from Sinai.

The end of Montuhotep's reign is as mysterious as its beginning. His celebration of a Sed festival so early in the reign might indicate that he was already an old man at his accession. He may have died soon after, or even during the jubilee. A much more likely possibility is that Montuhotep IV was overthrown in a *coup d'état* some time shortly after his second year on the throne. The new pharaoh and founder of Dynasty XII, Amenemhet, is most probably to be identified with Montuhotep's vizier of the same name. He is prominently featured on four of the nine inscriptions at Wadi Hammamat, in which he modestly informs us that he was supervisor of "that which heaven gave, the earth creates and the Nile brings...." A fragment of slate bowl found at Lisht bears Montuhotep's nomen and partial Horus name on one side and the Horus name of Amenemhet I on the other. Based on this fragment several scholars have proposed a coregency between the two pharaohs.

References:

Abd el-Raziq et al. 2002 pp. 40-41, #4
Breasted 1906 vol.I pp. 211-216 § 434-453
Callender 2000 p. 156
Couyat and Montet 1912 pp. 77-78 #110, 79-81 #113, 97-98 #191, 98-100 #192, pl. XXIX, XXXVI, XXXVII
Dodson and Hilton 2004 pp. 82-83, 85, 87, 88, 90, 92
Fakhry 1952 pp. 19-23, figs. 14-19, pl. VI.A & .B, VII.A & .B, VIII.A
Gardiner 1961 p. 438
Goyon 1957 pp. 76-81 #s 52-60, pl. XVIII-XX
Hayes 1953 p. 167 and fig. 102
Lichtheim 1975 pp. 113-115
Murnane 1977 p. 227-228
Peden 2001 pp. 22, 25-26
Petrie 1978 pl. XI #s 1-4
Sadek 1980 pp. pp. 4-14
Tidyman 1995 pp. 103-109
von Beckerath 1999 pp. 80 #7, 81 #7
Ward 1978 pp. 12-13 and fig. 2
Winlock 1947 pp. 54-57

Montuhotep V   Dynasty XIII

Horus Name:
Unknown

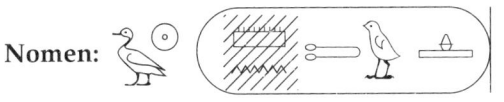

Nomen: *mnṯw-ḥtp*
Montuhotep

Prenomen: *s.wḏ'-r'*
Sewadjare

Two Ladies: Unknown

Golden Falcon: Unknown

Length of Reign:	Unknown
Tomb:	Unknown
Mummy:	Unknown

Consorts:	Sitmut(?)	Menthuhotep
Manetho:	Not given	Mentuhotep
		Monthhotep
King Lists:	T: (R 8.20)	Montjuhotep
		Sewadjre
Variant Names:	Menthotpe	

Probably the forty-ninth king of Dynasty XIII, although Ryholt places him fiftieth and von Beckerath lists him as unplaced and makes him Montuhotep VI. In any case, Sewadjare Montuhotep certainly seems to have ruled near the very end of the dynasty. The only positive attestation for this king comes from a single fragment of relief found at the site of the Dynasty XI temple of Nebhepetre Montuhotep II at Deir el-Bahri. The coffin of the "eldest son of the king," Herunefer, now in the British Museum, gives the father's nomen as Montuhotep, but the prenomen is absent. Ryholt opts for Montuhotep V, but Dodson and Hilton believe the coffin to have belonged to the son of Merankhre, that is, Montuhotep VI of Dynasty XVI.

References:
B. Davies 1995 p. 147 #31
Dodson and Hilton 2004 pp. 100, 117, 118, 120, 284 note 93, 291
Naville 1907 p. 3, 68, pl. XII #i

Ryholt 1997a pp. 236-237, 357 File 13/50, 408 table 94 #50
von Beckerath 1999 pp. 104 #i, 105 #i, (as Montehotpe VI)

Montuhotep VI   Dynasty XVI

Horus Name: Unknown

Nomen:

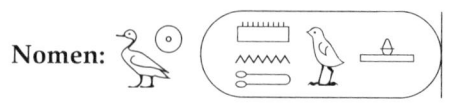

mntw-ḥtp
Montuhotep

Prenomen:

mr-ʿnḫ-rʿ
Merankhre

Two Ladies: Unknown

Golden Falcon: Unknown

Length of Reign:	Unknown
Tomb:	Unknown
Mummy:	Unknown

Consorts:	Sitmut(?)	Menthuhotep
Manetho:	Not given	Mentuhotep
		Monthhotep
King Lists:	None	Montjuhotep
Variant Names:	Menthotpe	

    Perhaps the fourteenth king of Dynasty XVI, Montuhotep VI's parentage is unknown, as is his relationship to his predecessor, Montuemsaf. There is no doubt that he was of Theban origin.

    Only two attestations for Montuhotep VI have been discovered; both are statuettes. The first, found at Karnak, is a seated figure, missing the head and feet. The inscription gives the king's nomen and prenomen and a dedication to the god Sobek. The second statuette, whose provenance is unknown, shows the king standing. His nomen and prenomen are present, but the dedication is missing.

A fragment of wooden coffin of an "Eldest King's Son" named Herunefer bears the cartouche of a king whose nomen was Montuhotep, but since no prenomen remains it is impossible to assign a definite identification to the Montuhotep in question, although the texts from the *Book of the Dead* found on the coffin may link it to the latter half of Dynasty XVI. If this date is correct, the "Senior Queen" Sitmut named on the fragment would be the wife of Montuhotep VI and Herunefer would be his son. Ryholt dates the coffin to the time of Montuhotep V of Dynasty XIII.

References:

W. Davies 1981b p. 28 #s 39 and 40, 33 notes 33 and 33
Dodson and Hilton 2004 pp. 116, 117, 118, 120

Ryholt 1997a pp. 158, table 25, 236-237 and table 60, 391 File 16/d, 410 table 97

Montuhotepi   Dynasty XVI

Horus Name:
Unknown

Nomen:

mntw-ḥtp-i
Montuhotepi

mntw-ḥtp-i
Montuhotepi

Prenomen:

s.ꜥnḫ-n-rꜥ
Seankhenre

Two Ladies: Unknown

Golden Falcon: Unknown

Length of Reign: 1 year
Tomb: Unknown; probably at Dra Abu el-Naga
Mummy: Unknown

Montuhotepi

Consorts:	Unknown	Mentuhotepi
Manetho:	Not given	Monthhotepi
		Sewadjenre
King Lists:	K: (59); T: (G	Sewahenre
	11.4; R 11.4)	Swadj[en?]re
Variant Names:	Menthotpe	

The fifth king of Dynasty XVI, Montuhotepi's parentage is unknown, as is his relationship with his predecessor, Neferhotep III. Certainly Neferhotep and Montuhotepi had one thing in common—a constant state of unrest, skirmishes and perhaps even outright battles with the Hyksos kings of Dynasty XV. A stele from Karnak confirms that the king was a native of Thebes and that Thebes was "mistress of the entire land, city of triumph." There are references to driving back "foreign lands." The king's might over his enemies is likened to Sakhmet, in her aspect as a goddess of death and destruction; like Sakhmet, Montuhotepi terrorizes and kills with his "flaming breath." The term "foreign lands" may be a euphemism for the Hyksos, although it has been suggested that Thebes may have engaged in hostilities with the Nubians at this time.

Two limestone sphinxes, one bearing the nomen and the other the prenomen of Montuhotepi, were found at Edfu in the temple of Horus during excavations in 1924.

A scarab-seal of unknown provenance, which may bear Montuhotepi's prenomen, is the only other contemporary attestation for this pharaoh. This scarab, which has never been drawn or photographed for publication, has been read variously as Sewahenre, Sewadjenre and most recently as Seankhenre.

Montuhotepi's prenomen, Seankhenre, as given in the Turin Canon is unclear, and was once read as Sewadjenre. Recent research would seem to verify that Seankhenre is the correct reading. The Canon gives a reign of only one year.

It should be noted that von Beckerath places this pharaoh (as Montuhotep VII) as the fifth ruler of Dynasty XVII.

References:

W. Davies 1981b pp. 30-31 #s 51 and 52 (as Mentuhotpe VII)
Dodson and Hilton 2004 pp. 116, 117, 120
Gardiner 1959 pl. IV Col. XI #4
Gardiner 1961 p. 442 #11.4
Gauthier 1931 pp. 1-6
Helck 1983 p. 64 #97 (as Menthuhotep VI)
Petrie 1978 p. 36
D. Redford 1992 p. 112
D. Redford 1997 p. 9 #50
Ryholt 1997a pp. 153 #11.4, 154, 155, 158, table 25, 159, 261, 388-389 File 16/5, 410, table 97
von Beckerath 1999 pp. 126 #5, 127 #5 (as Mentuhotpe VII)

Montuwoser   SIP

Horus Name:
Unknown   **Nomen:**

mntw-wsr
Montuwoser

Prenomen: Unknown

Two Ladies: Unknown

Golden Falcon: Unknown

Length of Reign:	Unknown
Tomb:	Unknown
Mummy:	Unknown

Consorts:	Unknown	**Variant Names:**	Mentu-user
Manetho:	Not given		Mentuwoser
King Lists:	None		Monthwoser

King Montuwoser is known from two stone blocks bearing his cartouche. These blocks were probably found during excavations carried out for Lord Dufferin in 1860 at the temple built by Montuhotep II at Deir el-Bahri. The blocks are the only definite evidence of this king's existence; he is otherwise unattested. A stele of the Dynasty XVI king Montuhotepi lists a "King's Son" named Montuwoser, but it is likely that this is a different individual who never succeeded to the throne, and who may not have actually been the son of a king. If "King's Son" Montuwoser was the king Montuwoser, it is remotely possible that he was Semenre, the third successor of Montuhotepi, whose nomen is unknown and who ruled some two dozen years after Montuhotepi (see SEMENRE).

References:

Budge 1914 p. 7, pl. 18
Edwards 1965 p. 26 #5
Ryholt 1997a p. 261, 400 File N/2

Vernus 1989h pp. 147 line 17, 153 ao) and ap)
Vernus 1990 p. 221

...mosre   Dynasty XIII

Horus Name:
Unknown   **Nomen:** Unknown

Prenomen: ...*ms*[*rˁ*]
...mosere

Two Ladies: Unknown

Golden Falcon: Unknown

Length of Reign:	Unknown
Tomb:	Unknown
Mummy:	Unknown

Consorts:	Unknown	**Variant Names:**	...mose
Manetho:	Not given		
King Lists:	T: (G 7.13; R 8.21)		

Probably the fiftieth king of Dynasty XIII, ...mosre is one of a group of kings known only from the Turin Canon. The fragmentary condition of the papyrus has caused the loss of most of this king's name, but recent studies by K.S.B. Ryholt strongly support this position for ...mosre.

References:
Gardiner 1959 pl. III, Col. VII #13
Gardiner 1961 p. 441 #7.13
Ryholt 1997a pp. 71 fig. 10, Col. 8

#21, 73 #51, 197 #51, 357 File 13/51

Narmer — Dynasty I

Horus Name: n'r-mr / Narmer

Nomen: mni / Meni

Two Ladies: nbty mn

Golden Falcon: Unknown

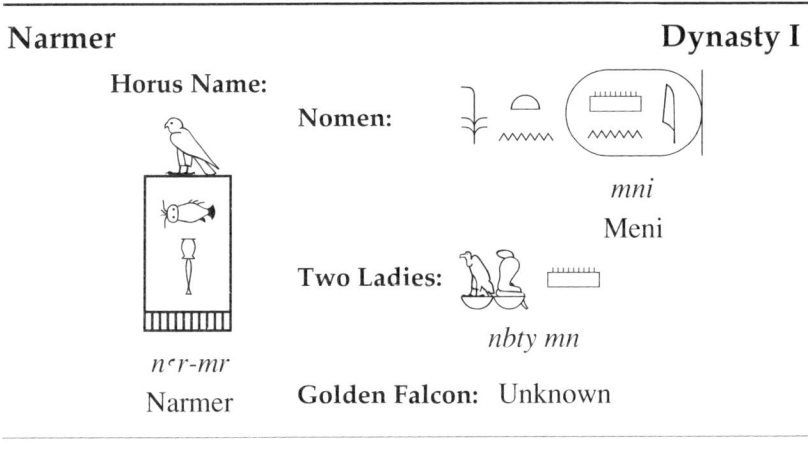

Length of Reign:	Unknown
Tomb:	Abydos, Umm el Qa'ab, B 17/18
Mummy:	Unknown

Consorts:	Neithhotep	**Variant Names:**	Men...
Herodotus:	Menes		Mer-Nar
Manetho:	Menes (A, E, J)		Merunar
King Lists:	Ab: (1); T: (G2.11) (as Meni)		Nar Narmeru

Because of the famous ceremonial palette bearing his name and image, Narmer is without a doubt the best known of the early rulers of Egypt. Although his position as first king of Dynasty I was questioned in the past, excavations at Abydos in 1985 by the German Archaeological Institute uncovered a clay seal impression which gives the succession of the first five kings and one queen of Dynasty I: Narmer heads the list. This would seem to support Narmer's identification with the Menes listed in Manetho's History of Egypt. Although subject to an alternate interpretation (see AHA), it would appear that an ivory label found in the tomb of Queen Neith-hotep at Naqada bears the Two Ladies name Men in a context that also points toward Narmer.

Manetho (as transcribed by various chroniclers) tells us that Menes reigned for 30, 60 or 62 years, and that he led his army across a frontier, thereby winning glory. He was later killed by a hippopotamus. Herodotus informs us that Menes founded the city of Memphis. Whether any of this information pertains to Narmer is unknown. We do know that the ancient Egyptians considered a king named Meni to be the first ruler of a united Egypt. His name is found on the Abydos King List and also on the Turin Canon. The name Meni in a cartouche is not known before Dynasty XVIII.

Narmer's chief claim to fame, the Narmer Palette, was discovered in a deposit in the temple area at Hierakonpolis (ancient Nekhen) about 80 kilometers south of Luxor. Narmer, wearing the white crown of Upper Egypt, is shown on one side of the palette about to club a defeated foe who is represented by a symbol for a papyrus marsh. On the other side of the stone, Narmer, wearing the red crown of Lower Egypt, is shown inspecting the bodies of two lines of decapitated foes. Until recently, the general consensus among Egyptologists has been that the Narmer Palette bears a record of the conquest of Lower Egypt by Upper Egypt. However, archaeological research conducted in the Delta has led some scholars to believe that the unification came some time before Narmer's reign. They assert this palette commemorates either victories over desert tribesmen or Libyans who had invaded the western Nile Delta, or simply a "mopping up" action by Narmer of some still-resistant Lower Egyptian factions.

A decorated macehead bearing Narmer's name, from the same deposit as that holding the Narmer Palette, appears to show a wedding ceremony. This is usually interpreted as the wedding of Narmer to Neith-hotep, presumably a lady of some standing and, Neith being a Lower Egyptian goddess, probably from the Delta.

While no large monuments attributable to Narmer have been found north of Tarkhan, which is some distance south of ancient Memphis, pottery bearing his serekh has been found in the east Delta at Tell Ibrahim Awad and Manshiyet Abu Omar. This pottery may have been made at or near the locations where it was discovered or it may represent trade goods.

Narmer's name is the earliest ruler's name to be discovered at Saqqara; it is on a porphyry bowl in a deposit of stone vessels beneath Djoser's step pyramid.

Foreign trade was not unknown during this reign. The king's serekh has been found carved into the rocks in the Wadi-el-Qash on the Coptos-Quseir trade route. In Palestine, Narmer's name has been found at Tel Erani, Tel Gat, Tel Arad, Small Tel Malhata, Tel Halif terrace, Tel Lod, Gezer and other locations. The pottery on which the royal name has been found is of Egyptian workmanship and probably represents trade goods as opposed to items brought into the area during military occupation. Indeed, there is evidence to suggest that Egyptian traders lived amongst the local population during Narmer's time. There is no evidence of Egyptian military occupation under this ruler.

References:

Dodson 1995 pp. 12-14
Dodson and Hilton 2004 pp. 44-46
Emery 1961 pp. 43-49
Fairservis 1991 pp. 1-20
Gardiner 1961 pp. 403-405
Gophna 1987 pp. 14-16
Herodotus 1954 pp. 165-166
Mark 1997 pp. 104, 111-112
Millet 1990 pp. 53-59
Petrie 1900

Petrie 1901a
Spencer 1993 pp. 52-56, 76-77
Uphill 1984
van den Brink and Braun 2002 pp. 174-180 and figs. 3-7
Verbrugghe and Wickersham 1996 pp. 131, 187

von Beckerath 1999 pp. 36 #x+4, 37 #x+4
Waddell 1940 pp. 21 ff.
T. Wilkinson 1999 pp. 67-70
T. Wilkinson 2000 pp. 47, 72, 187

Nebdjefare   Dynasty XIV

Horus Name: Unknown

Nomen: Unknown

Prenomen:

nb-df_3-r ʿ
Nebdjefare

Two Ladies: Unknown

Golden Falcon: Unknown

Length of Reign:	Unknown
Tomb:	Unknown
Mummy:	Unknown

Consorts:	Unknown	**Variant Names:**	None
Manetho:	Not given		
King Lists:	T: (G 8.7; R 9.7; vB 8.7)		

Perhaps the twelfth king of Dynasty XIV, Nebdjefare is one of a group of kings known only from the Turin Canon. The papyrus' fragmentary state allows for varying interpretations as to the positioning of some of the kings of this dynasty. However, Nebdjetare's place seems secure.

References:
Gardiner 1959 pl. III, Col. VIII #7
Gardiner 1961 p. 441
Ryholt 1997a pp. 95 Col. 9.7, 98 #12, 198 table 37, 379 File 14/12, 09 table 95 #12

von Beckerath 1999 pp. 108 #8, 109 #8

Nebfawre　　　　　　　　　　　　　　　　　Dynasty XIV

Horus Name: Unknown　　**Nomen:** Unknown

Prenomen:

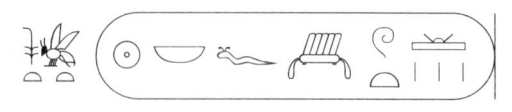

nb-fꜣw-rꜥ
Nebfawre

Two Ladies: Unknown

Golden Falcon: Unknown

Length of Reign:	Unknown
Tomb:	Unknown
Mummy:	Unknown

Consorts:	Unknown	**Variant Names:**	Nebfaure
Manetho:	Not given		
King Lists:	T: (G 8.3; R 9.3; vB 8.3)		

Possibly the eighth king of Dynasty XIV, Nebfawre is one of a group of kings known only from the Turin Canon. The papyrus' fragmentary state allows for varying interpretations as to the positioning of some of the kings of this dynasty. However, Nebfawre's place seems secure.

References:

Gardiner 1959 pl. III, Col. VIII #3
Gardiner 1961 p. 441
Ryholt 1997a pp. 95 Col. 9.3, 98 #8, 198 table 37, 379 File 14/8, 409 #8

von Beckerath 1999 pp. 108 #4, 109 #4

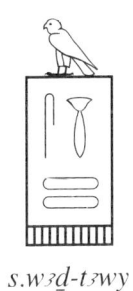

Nebiryraw I — Dynasty XVI

Horus Name: *s.wȝḏ-tȝwy*

Nomen: *nb-iry-r-ȝw* — Nebiryraw

Prenomen: *s.wȝḏ-n-rʿ* — Sewadjenre

Two Ladies: *nbty nṯr-ḫprw*

Golden Falcon: *bik nbw nfr-ḥʿw*

Length of Reign:	26 years
Tomb:	Unknown; probably at Dra Abu el-Naga
Mummy:	Unknown

Consorts:	Unknown	Nebiriau
Manetho:	Not given	Nebirieraw
		Suah-n-ra
King Lists:	K: (33 or 59); T: (G 11.5; K 11.5; vB 13.6)	Suat'en-ra
		Suazenra
		Swaz-en-re
Variant Names:	Neberaw	

The sixth pharaoh of Dynasty XVI, Nebiryraw's parentage is unknown, as is his relationship to his predecessor, Montuhotepi. However, unlike Montuhotepi's one year, Nebiryraw held the throne for a long reign of 26 years.

Nebiryraw I

It is tempting to see Nebiryraw's reign as a time more peaceful, and perhaps more prosperous, than had been known since the beginning of the Dynasty. Two scarab-seals found at Lisht are the farthest north of any attestation for any pharaoh of Dynasty XVI that has been discovered. Perhaps these scarabs ended up so far from Thebes through trade, although they may represent booty from a conflict between the Hyksos and the Thebans.

From within the Dynasty XVI sphere of influence come several attestations. A beautiful ivory-handled, copper-bladed dagger, inscribed with Nebiryraw's prenomen, was found in a grave at Hiw (Hu). At Qift (Coptos), Petrie found a scarab in the foundation deposit of a temple built by Thutmose III some 150 years after Nebiryraw's reign. A stele, now known as the "Juridical Stele," was found at Karnak.

Nebiryraw is the only king of this dynasty to have attestations from Nubia. Two scarab-seals come from Gennari, one from the fortress at Faras and another from Mirgissa. Ten more scarabs, all of unknown provenance, are in museum collections in London, Berlin, Paris and Cairo. Exactly how the seals got to Nubia is unknown. Ryholt suggests "permanently stationed officials," which is possible, but since Nebiryraw's seals are the only attestations for all of Dynasties XVI and XVII until Kamose, it is perhaps more likely that the scarabs were obtained by limited trade or by military action.

A bronze statuette of unknown provenance but dated to the Ptolemaic Period bears the prenomen of this pharaoh as well as that of his likely successor, Neferkare(?) Nebiryraw II. It is unknown why such obscure rulers would be remembered 1,500 years after their deaths.

References:

Dodson and Hilton 2004 pp. 116, 117, 118
Gardiner 1959 pl. IV, Col. XI #5
Gardiner 1961 p. 442 #11.5
Hall 1913 p. 22 #210
Hayes 1953 p. fig. 226
Hayes 1959 p. 11 fig. 1
Helck 1983 pp. 65-69 #98
Karkowski 1981 pp. 92-93 #13, pl. VI #13
Mace 1922 pp. 14 #5, pl. III #5
Petrie 1889 pl. 11 #s 333-336
Petrie 1901b pp. 52 #82, pl. XXXII #17
Petrie 1978 p. 23, pl. XIX 14.69.1-5
Quirke 2001a p. 263
D. Redford 1986 p. 55 #27
Ryholt 1997a pp. 153 #11.5, 155, 158, table 25 and 11/6, 159 and note 582, 162, 261, 289, table 86, 389-390 File 16/6, 410, table 97
von Beckerath 1999 pp. 126 #6, 127 #6

Nebiryraw II   Dynasty XVI

Horus Name: Unknown   **Nomen:**

nb-iri-r-ȝw

Nebiryraw

Nebiryraw II

Prenomen:

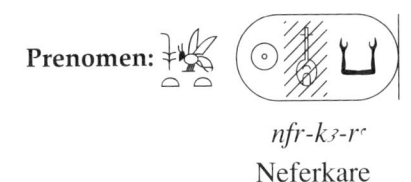

nfr-k3-rˁ
Neferkare

Two Ladies: Unknown

Golden Falcon: Unknown

Length of Reign:	Unknown
Tomb:	Unknown; probably at Dra Abu el-Naga
Mummy:	Unknown

Consorts:	Unknown	**Variant Names:**	Neberaw Nebiriau Nebirieraw Nebitau…
Manetho:	Not given		
King Lists:	T: (G 11.6; R 11.6; vB 13.7(?))		

A local Theban ruler, and the successor of the well-attested Nebiryraw I, Nebiryraw II is known only from the Turin Canon. The relationship to his predecessor is unknown, although Ryholt suggests that Nebiryraw II may have been his son. Certainly Nebiryraw I reigned long enough (26 years according to the Turin Canon) to have had adult heirs.

No contemporary attestations have been found for this king. However, a small bronze statuette of the god Harpocrates dated to the Ptolemaic Period gives the prenomen of Nebiryraw I (Sewadjenre) and the prenomen Neferkare, which might very likely belong to Nebiryraw II, although this is only speculation. It is interesting to think that these obscure rulers were remembered more than 1,500 years after their deaths.

The Turin Canon list Nebiryraw as Nebitau…, probably due to a scribal error.

References:
Dodson and Hilton 2004 pp. 116-118
Gardiner 1959 pl. IV, Col. XI #6
Gardiner 1961 p. 442 #11.6
D. Redford 1986 p. 55 #27
Ryholt 1997a pp. 153 fig. 14 #6, 155, 158, table 24, 159, 261, 289
table 86, 390 File 6/7, 410 table 97 #7
von Beckerath 1999 pp. 126 #7, 127 #7

Nebmaatre   Dynasty XVII(?)

Horus Name:
Unknown   **Nomen:** Unknown

Prenomen:

nb-mꜣꜥt-rꜥ
Nebmaatre

Two Ladies: Unknown

Golden Falcon: Unknown

Length of Reign:	Unknown
Tomb:	Unknown
Mummy:	Unknown

Consorts:	Unknown	**Variant Names:**	None
Manetho:	Not given		
King Lists:	None		

This prenomen is known from a bronze axe-head discovered at Mostagedda, near Asyut in Central Egypt and from a black steatite lion amulet of unknown provenance. In Petrie's opinion, the lion was too roughly made to belong to Amenhotep III (whose prenomen was also Nebmaatre) and suggested that it might belong to the Dynasty XIII ruler Ibi, whose prenomen is given as …maatre (*…mꜣꜥt-rꜥ*) in the Turin Canon. However a trace of a vertical stroke visible in the lacuna before the preserved symbols of the name precludes there being a ⌒ (*nb*) sign.

Ryholt sees Nebmaatre as belonging to Dynasty XVII, in an unplaced position, presumably on the grounds that the axe-head mentioned above was discovered in a Pan grave. The Pan-grave people were Nubian mercenaries employed by the Theban kings of Dynasty XVII to fight against the Dynasty XV Hyksos invaders. It is believed that the Theban rulers of the period provided weapons such as this battleaxe to the Pan.

Von Beckerath places Nebmaatre in his Dynasty XV/XVI.

References:

Brunton 1937 pp. 117, 127, 128, 131, pl. LXXIV #9
W. Davies 1981b p. 43 #102, pl. 18 #102, pl. 31 #102
Petrie 1978 p. 23, pl. XIX # 13.41

Ryholt 1997a pp. 168, 171, 179 and note 643, 400 File 17/a
Taylor 1991 p. 26 fig. 28
von Beckerath 1999 pp. 118 #o, 119 #o

Nebnennu — Dynasty XIII

Horus Name: Unknown

Nomen:

nb.n-nw
Nebnennu

Prenomen:

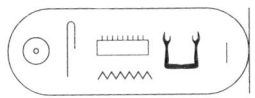

s.mn-k3-rˁ
Semenkare

Two Ladies: Unknown

Golden Falcon: Unknown

Length of Reign:	T: "..., 22 days"
Tomb:	Unknown
Mummy:	Unknown

Consorts:	Unknown	**Variant Names:**	Nebennu Nebnun
Manetho:	Not given		
King Lists:	T: (G 6.11; R 7.11; vB 6.11)		

Nebnennu was possibly the ninth ruler of Dynasty XIII. Aside from his prenomen recorded in the Turin Canon, Nebnennu's only attestation is a stele, bearing both his nomen and prenomen, discovered at the galena mines at Gebel el-Zeit on the Gulf of Suez.

Ryholt has pointed out Nebnennu's seeming lack of royal connections and concludes that this king was unrelated to his predecessors.

References:

Castel and Soukiassian 1985 p. 290, pl. LXII
Gardiner 1959 pl. III, Col. VI #11
Gardiner 1961 p. 440 #6.11
Ryholt 1997a pp. 71 Col. 7.11, 73 #9, 78 and note 236, 192 table 33, 209 and note 714, 338 File 13/9, 408 table 94 #9
Ryholt 1997b p. 97, 98, 99-100
von Beckerath 1999 pp. 90 #8, 91 #8

Nebre   Dynasty II

Horus Name:

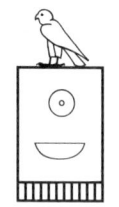

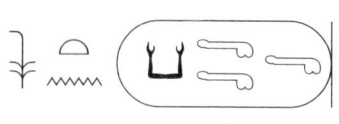

Nomen: $k\!_3\text{-}k\!_3w$
Kakau

nb-rˁ
Nebre

Two Ladies: Unknown

Golden Falcon: Unknown

Length of Reign:	Unknown
Tomb:	Saqqara (Location unknown)
Mummy:	Unknown

Consorts:	Unknown	**King Lists:**	Ab: (10); S: (4); T: (G2.21)
Manetho:	Choös (E) Kaiechos (A) Kaiekhos (A) Kechoos (E) Khoös (E)	**Variant Names:**	Raneb Reneb

Nebre was the second king of Dynasty II, as is shown on a statue of the priest, Hotepdief, where Nebre's name is recorded between those of Hotepsekhemwy and Ninetjer. His tomb, which is very likely at Saqqara, has not yet been discovered, but it is probably to be found south of the Step Pyramid complex of Djoser, not far from the tombs of kings Hotepsekhemwy and Ninetjer. A funerary stele bearing Nebre's name, which evidently came from the Saqqara area, was purchased from an antiquities dealer in 1960 and is now in the Metropolitan Museum of Art in New York City.

A great many jar-sealings of Nebre's were found in the tomb of Hotepsekhemwy, implying that Nebre was responsible for his predecessor's burial. Another possibility, though unlikely, is that Nebre appropriated the tomb completely.

Other attestations of Nebre from the Memphite area are stone vessels inscribed with his name from Djoser's complex, one of which, though bearing the serekh of king Ninetjer, mentions an estate of Nebre. A stone bowl discovered during excavations at the site of the Dynasty IV king Menkaure's temples at Giza has the name Nebre inscribed over a partially erased serekh of Hotepsekhemwy.

Beyond the Memphite area there is very little evidence of Nebre's reign. A stone bowl from the tomb of Sekhemib/Peribsen at Abydos was originally inscribed with the name of Nebre's palace, but was erased and replaced with the name of Ninetjer. A "little steatite plaque" inscribed with Nebre's name was discovered at a tomb-site at El Kab. Of more interest is a serekh of Nebre carved on the rocks in the western desert behind Armant, near an ancient trade route to the western oases; Wilkinson sees this as representing a possible expedition out of the Nile valley. There is also a possibility of a serekh of Nebre near Wadi Hammamat in the eastern desert, although the inscription is difficult to read.

Manetho gives a reign of 39 years.

Some Egyptologists give the name Nubnefer (nbw-nfr) as part of Nebre's titulary, yet there is not the slightest bit of evidence to support this assignment (see NUBNEFER).

References:

Clayton 1994 p. 27 color illustration
Dodson 1996 p. 22 and illustration
Edwards 1971 p. 30
Emery 1961 pp. 92-93
Firth and Quibell 1935 vol. I p. 121 #s10 and 11, vol. II pl. 89 #s10 and 11
Gardiner 1959 pl. I Col. II #21
Gardiner 1961 pp. 431, 432
Lacau and Lauer 1959 pp. 13 #58, 14 #77, pl. 11 # 58, pl. 16 # 77
Petrie 1901a pp. 6, 7, 26 #12, 51 #12, pl. VIII #12
Quibell 1898 p. 7
Reisner 1931 pp. 102 #1, 103 #15, 122
Verbrugghe and Wickersham 1996 pp. 133, 188
von Beckerath 1999 pp. 42 #2, 43 #2
Waddell 1940 pp. 35, 37
T. Wilkinson 1999 pp. 84, 169, 173, 240, 242, 263, 282, 292, 333
Winkler 1938 pl. XI #s 4 and 5

Nebsenre   Dynasty XIV

Horus Name: Unknown

Nomen: Unknown

Prenomen:

nb-sn-r ʿ

Nebsenre

Two Ladies: Unknown

Golden Falcon: Unknown

Length of Reign:	Unknown
Tomb:	Unknown
Mummy:	Unknown

Nedjemibre

Consorts:	Unknown	**Variant Names:**	Ranebsen
Manetho:	Not given		
King Lists:	T: (G 8.14; R 9.14; vB 8.14)		

Perhaps the nineteenth king of Dynasty XIV, Nebsenre is one of only a handful of kings of that dynasty to have left any attestation beyond the Turin Canon. His name has been found on a jar whose provenance is, unfortunately, unknown.

References:

Gardiner 1959 pl. III, Col. VIII #14
Gardiner 1961 p. 441 #8.14
Kaplony 1973 p. 15, pl. 10 #23
Ryholt 1997a pp. 95 Col. 9.14, 98 #19, 198 table 37, 379 File 14/19, 409 #19

Ryholt 2000 p. 97
von Beckerath 1999 pp. 108 #15, 109 #15

Nedjemibre   Dynasty XIII

Horus Name: Unknown

Nomen: Unknown

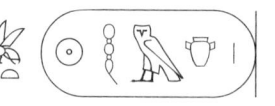

Prenomen:

nḏm-ib-rꜥ

Nedjemibre

Two Ladies: Unknown

Golden Falcon: Unknown

Length of Reign:	T: "0 years, 7 months, …"
Tomb:	Unknown
Mummy:	Unknown

Consorts:	Unknown	**Variant Names:**	None
Manetho:	Not given		
King Lists:	T: (G 6.14; R 7.14; vB 6.14)		

This king is known only from the Turin Canon. According to Ryholt's reconstruction of the Canon, Nedjemibre is the twelfth king of Dynasty XIII. Von Beckerath sees Nedjemibre as the eleventh ruler of the dynasty.

References:

Gardiner 1959 p. 16 V 14 b: pl. III, Col. VI #14
Gardiner 1961 p. 440 #6.14
Ryholt 1997a pp. 71 Col. 7.14, 73 #12, 74 note 7/14, 192 table 33 and note 7/14, 339 File 13/12, 408 table 94 #12
von Beckerath 1999 pp. 90 #11, 91 #11

Neferefre — Dynasty V

Horus Name:

nfr-ḫʿw

Nomen:

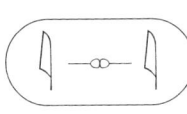

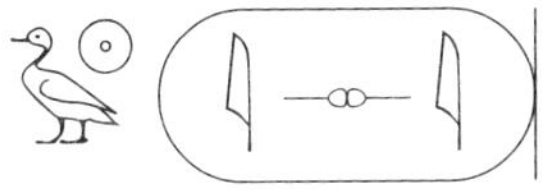

isi
Isi

Prenomen:

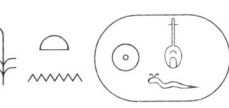

nfr.f-rʿ
Neferefre

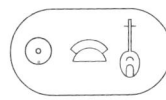

ḫʿ-nfr-rʿ
Khaneferre

Two Ladies:

nbty nfr-m

Golden Falcon:

(bik) nbw nṯr-nfr

Neferefre

Length of Reign:	2-3 years
Tomb:	Pyramid at Abusir: "The Bas of Neferefre are Divine"
Mummy:	Found in the pyramid at Abusir

Consorts:	Unknown	**Variant Names:**	Neferre Ranefer Raneferef Reneferef
Manetho:	Cheres Kheres		
King Lists:	Ab: (29); S: (29); T: (G [3.21])		

The fourth king of Dynasty V, Neferefre is almost certainly to be identified with the eldest son of Neferirkare (I) and Khentkaues, Neferre (Ranefer); even though the Saqqara king-list gives the nebulous ruler Shepseskare the fourth position, archaeological evidence favors Neferefre. Entries for Dynasty V in the Turin Canon are much damaged and Neferefre's name is missing (as is that of Shepseskare), and though it has been generally assumed that Neferefre occupied Gardiner's column III.21, there is absolutely no basis for such an assumption. Neferefre might very well have occupied III.20.

Further evidence supporting Neferefre as the direct successor of Neferirkare (I) is the placement of their pyramids, located at Abusir, in relation to each another. There is strong reason to believe that the pyramids of Sahure, Neferirkare and Neferefre were built in chronological order, just as the pyramids at Giza had been.

Neferefre's pyramid, originally identified by a hieratic graffito found on a stone block at the monument's center, had never been completed, and up until the graffito was discovered it was known only as the "Unfinished Pyramid." Undoubtedly the early death of the king brought the building of the pyramid to a halt, and the tomb was completed as a square based mastaba-like structure. The finished product measured some 65.5 m. square and rose to a height of 7 m., with its flat roof made of packed mud and gravel. The tomb was much damaged by stone robbers, and thieves plundered the burial chamber and carried off most of the sarcophagus, which they had first smashed to pieces. During excavations, fragments of four alabaster canopic jars and other stone containers were recovered.

Also discovered during excavations were portions of the king's body, found in the burial chamber of his pyramid; they include the mummified left hand; the left clavicle, still covered with skin; a fragment of skin probably from part of the forehead and upper eyelid; a skin fragment from a left foot and various other bones. Chronometrical dating adds credence to the remains having belonged to Neferefre. The king's age at death was somewhere between 20 and 23 years old.

Manetho gives his king Cheres a reign of 20 years, which is obviously too long. The Turin Canon gives a damaged "X + 1" years for a king whose name is missing and may, in fact belong to the little-known Shepseskare, evidently Neferefre's successor. The highest date attested from archaeological sources for this ruler are from builders' graffiti which mention "year of the first cattle count," which would correspond to regnal year two if the count occurred every other year. Verner believes that year two, or possibly year three, was the highest Neferefre attained. Von Beckerath has suggested that the king ruled for eleven years, however this view has few supporters.

Although a temple complex grew up around Neferefre's pyramid, the sun temple named "Re's Offering Table" has yet to be found. Half a dozen clay seal impressions showing the Horus name of the little-known king Shepseskare have been found in Neferefre's mortuary temple and it has been suggested that Shepseskare continued the building's construction which, if true, would certainly go a long way towards proving that he succeeded Neferefre. A great many statues of the king have been recovered from the temple complex. No causeway or valley temple was ever built.

Scribal error would seem to be responsible for Neferefre's name being given as Khaneferre in the Saqqara king-list.

References:

Altenmüller 2001 p. 599
Bares 2000 p. 10
Dodson 2003 pp. 68-69
Dodson and Hilton 2004 pp. 62, 64, 66
Gardiner 1959 pl. II, Col. III #21
Gardiner 1961 p. 435
Lehner 1997 pp. 66, 142, 150, 146-148, 235
Posener-Kriéger 1991 pp. 293-304, pl. 38
Spalinger 1994 p. 298 and note 60
Strouhal et al. 2003 pp. 480-481
Strouhal and Vyhnánek 2000 pp. 551-560, pl. 98-109
Verbrugghe and Wickersham 1996 pp. 136, 191
Verner 1997 pp. 55, 58, 96-97, 148, 269-270, 282, 296-297, 306-311, 395, 464
Verner 2000a pp. 10, 551-560, 562, 563, 565-566, 570-571, 575-576 figs. 1 and 2
Verner 2001b p. 587, 588-589, 595-597
Verner 2002 pp. 43, 54, 55, 58, 59, 108, 111-133, 138, 148-150
von Beckerath 1997 pp. 153-155, 188
von Beckerath 1999 pp. 58 #5, 59 #5
Waddell 1940 p. 51
R. Wilkinson 2000 p. 124

Neferhotep SIP

Horus Name: Unknown **Nomen:**

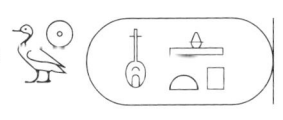

nfr-ḥtp
Neferhotep

Neferhotep I

Prenomen: Unknown

Two Ladies: Unknown

Golden Falcon: Unknown

Length of Reign:	Unknown
Tomb:	Unknown
Mummy:	Unknown

Consorts:	Unknown	**Variant Names:**	None
Manetho:	Not given		
King Lists:	T:(?)		

This name, without any prenomen, is found on a stele discovered at Abydos and on two bronze vessel lids found at Tell ed-Dab'a (Avaris) which might originally have come from Thebes. Helck attributes the Abydos stele to king Neferhotep I, but this is mere conjecture. Ryholt suggests that the two bronze lids might date to the time of Neferhotep III and represent booty carried off from Thebes by the Hyksos king Apepi; however, this is only a theory. These pieces might date to any of the three Neferhoteps known to have ruled during the Second Intermediate Period.

References:

Bietak 1970 pp. 33-34, pl. XVIII c) and d)
Bietak 1986 pl. XXXV b
Helck 1983 p. 30 #34
Ryholt 1997a pp. 400-401 File N/3

Neferhotep I   Dynasty XIII

Horus Name:

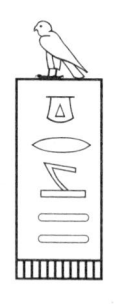

grg-t3wy

Nomen:

nfr-ḥtp
Neferhotep

Prenomen:

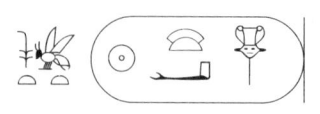

ḫꜥ-sḫm-rꜥ
Khasekhemre

Neferhotep I

Two Ladies: [hieroglyphs]

nbty wp-mȝʿt

Golden Falcon: [hieroglyphs]

bik nbw mn-mrwt

Length of Reign:	T: "11 years, 1-4 months, …"
Tomb:	Unknown
Mummy:	Unknown

Consorts:	Senebsen	**Variant Names:**	Neferhotpe Ra-Kha-Seshes
Manetho:	Not given		
King Lists:	K: 37; T: (G 6.25; R 7.25; vB 6.25)		

Neferhotep I was probably the twenty-sixth pharaoh of Dynasty XIII, although Ryholt places him as twenty-seventh and von Beckerath as twenty-second. Neferhotep was unrelated to his predecessor, Sobekhotep III, and was, like that king, a usurper. He was the son of the God's Father Haankhef and the Lady Kemi, both commoners, and was most likely born at Thebes. The entry in the Turin Canon includes Haankhef's name, a very high honor for a commoner. Neferhotep had two younger brothers, Sihathor and Sobekhotep IV; both would eventually act as his coregent, and Sobekhotep IV would succeed him. The three brothers' grandfather had been an officer in the military and it may be that the military had a hand in raising Neferhotep I to the throne.

Neferhotep I is one of the best documented rulers of the Second Intermediate Period, with attestations ranging from Byblos in Canaan to the Second Cataract forts at Buhen and Mirgissa in Nubia. This would seem to indicate that Dynasty XIII at least still had access to trade routes through the eastern Delta, although Dynasty XIV would have been in power there at this time. A single scarab of Neferhotep I has been found at Tel el-Yahudiya. Attestations for Neferhotep in Nubia are scant and consist of some pieces of jewelry at Buhen and a seal-impression from Mirgissa.

Neferhotep's capital continued to be Itjtowy at the opening of the Faiyum. There are a few finds from the Faiyum area, including a seated statuette of the king dedicated to the gods Sobek and Horus of Shedet. The statuette, discovered at Medinet el-Faiyum (Bologna Museo Civico, KS 1799), attests to Neferhotep's presence, but finds become much more plentiful the further south one looks. Excavations at Abydos over the years have uncovered two stelae (Cairo JE35256 and JE6307), one of which was usurped from a predecessor, Khutowyre Wegaf, as well as an inscribed block and several scarab-seals.

A stele from the Wadi Hammamat (now lost) inscribed for Sobekhotep IV and giving Neferhotep I's cartouche next to and of the same size as that of Sobekhotep, has been put forth by some scholars as evidence for the coregency of these two kings. Others, while agreeing with the coregency theory, see the inscription as purely honorific: the inscription makes it quite clear that Neferhotep was dead when the stele was carved. Another joint inscription of the two brothers comes from Karnak. Under any circumstance, the two kings were co-rulers for an unspecified period of time, and Sobekhotep IV did indeed succeed to the throne.

Between Thebes and Aswan we have no fewer than eleven rock-carved inscriptions for Neferhotep I, seven of which are found on the island of Sehel. The carvings vary from simple cartouches to family lists to scenes such as that of the pharaoh being given the sign of life from the goddess Anukis.

The family of Neferhotep is known from lists carved at Sehel and Philae. The Philae list gives us the names of the king's parents and brothers, Sihathor and Sobekhotep IV. The list from Sehel gives the same familial group, and adds the name of Neferhotep's queen, Senebsen, his son Haankhef and daughter Kemi. Both lists declare Sihathor as dead. Two carvings from Sehel show Neferhotep in close proximity with the Dynasty XII pharaoh, Senwosret III, a ruler evidently much admired by the king.

Attestations of unknown provenance include more than fifty scarab-seals, a cylinder-seal and a small amulet in the shape of a scepter dedicated to the god Sobek.

Neferhotep's son, Haankhef, most likely died young. For unknown reasons (though it is possible that Neferhotep I was not a young man at his accession) the pharaoh chose his younger brother, Sihathor, as a coregent. However, Sihathor died while still coregent, and was succeeded as coregent by Neferhotep's second brother, Sobekhotep IV, who became pharaoh at Neferhotep's death.

References:

W. Davies 1981b p. 25 #s 19-21
Delia 1991/1992 pp. 7-8, pl. 1
Dodson and Hilton 2004 pp. 31,36, 100, 101, 105, 106-107, 108-109, 112
Gardiner 1959 pl. III Col. VI.25
Gardiner 1961 p. 440 6.25
Habachi 1950 pp. 501-507
Habachi 1981 pp. 77-81
Helck 1983 pp. 19 #27, 20 #30, 21-29 #32, 30 #s 33-35
Leahy 1989 pp. 41-60, pl. VI and VII #1
Newberry 1906 p. 122 #5, pl. X #5
Peden 2001 pp. 48, 50
Ryholt 1997a pp. 34, 35 fig. 1 c and d, 71 Col. 7.25, 73 #27, 77 note 230, 87 note 277, 192 table 33, 225 and notes 787-791, 226-228, 229, 230, 231 table 56, 240, 284-286 and table 83 and note 1032, 345-348 File 13/27, 408 table 94 #27
Simpson 1969 pp. 154-158, pl. VIIa
von Beckerath 1999 pp. 96 #22, 97 #22

Neferhotep II — Dynasty XIII

Horus Name: Unknown

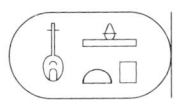

Nomen: *nfr-ḥtp* — Neferhotep

Prenomen: *mr-sḫm-rˁ* — Mersekhemre

Two Ladies: Unknown

Golden Falcon: Unknown

Length of Reign:	Unknown
Tomb:	Unknown
Mummy:	Unknown

Consorts:	Unknown	**Variant Names:**	None
Manetho:	Not given		
King Lists:	T: (G 7.21; R 8.16)		

Neferhotep II is attested to by two statues discovered by Legrain at Karnak in 1903 that are now in the Cairo Museum (CG's 42023 and 42024). It is possible that this king may be identified with "Mer…re," who, in Ryholt's reconstruction of the Turin Canon, occupies column 8 #16. This would place Neferhotep II toward the end of Dynasty XIII, possibly as the Dynasty's forty-sixth ruler (however, see INI II).

References:

Gardiner 1959 pl. III, Col. VII #21
W. Davies 1981b pp. 27-28 #s 34 and 35
Reeves 2000 pp. 118-120
Ryholt 1997a pp. 70, 72, 73 #46, 74 table 18, 358 File 13/b, 408 table 94

von Beckerath 1999 pp. 98 #30a, 99 #30a

Neferhotep III — Dynasty XVI

Horus Name: 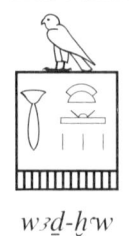
wꜣḏ-ḫw

Nomen: 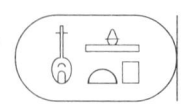 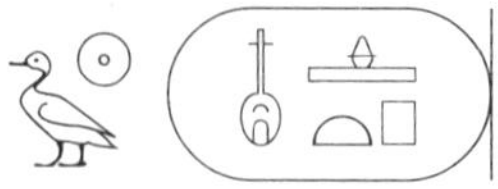
nfr-ḥtp
Neferhotep

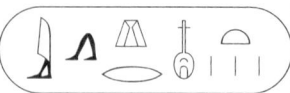

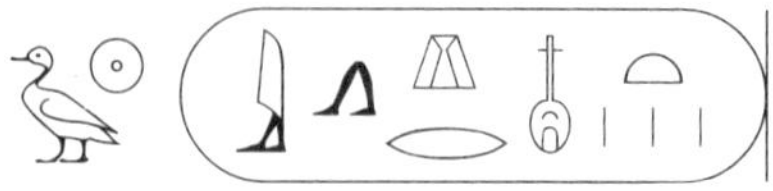

iy-ḫr-nfrt
Iykhernefert

Prenomen: 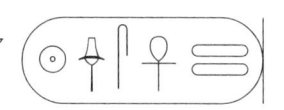
sḫm-rꜥ-s.ꜥnḫ-tꜣwy
Sekhemre-seankhtowy

Two Ladies: 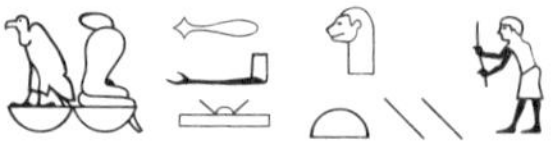
nbty ꜥꜣ-pḥty

Golden Falcon: 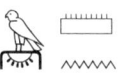
bik nbw mn...

Length of Reign:	1 year
Tomb:	Unknown; probably at Dra Abu el-Naga
Mummy:	Unknown

Consorts:	Unknown		Ikhernofret
Manetho:	Not given		Nofrehotpe
King Lists:	T: (G 11.3; R 11.3)		Sekhemre
			Se'onkhtowy
Variant Names:	Ijchernofre		

The parentage of Neferhotep, fourth pharaoh of Dynasty XVI, is unknown, as is his relationship to his predecessor, Sobekhotep VIII. Some scholars have placed Neferhotep in Dynasty XIII, but the most recent research places him in Dynasty XVI.

As with the other kings of this dynasty, with the exceptions of Nebiryraw I and Bebiankh, no contemporary attestations have been discovered outside of the Theban sphere of influence (an area along the Nile from Hiw in the north to Edfu in the south, a distance of about 200 km.). The kings of Dynasty XVI controlled less than one quarter of Egypt.

A stele found at Karnak tells of great troubles during Neferhotep's reign, the "slaughter against them that had attacked [him]" and that the king "pacified...rebellious foreign lands." It is very likely that some fighting did occur with the rival Hyksos Dynasty XV, and the reference to foreign lands is most likely a euphemism for the Hyksos. The stele also suggests that times were lean and the king "entered his city with sustenance preceding him." It is interesting to note that Neferhotep adopted a second nomen, Iykhernofer, which translates as "He who comes bearing good things."

Other than the Karnak stele, attestations for Neferhotep III are few; they include a lintel and a few blocks found at El Kab, and a stele mentioning his name from Gebelein.

References:

Capart 1938 p. 625 #3
Dodson and Hilton 2004 p. 116
Gardiner 1959 pl. IV, Col. XI #3
Gardiner 1961 p. 442
Helck 1983 p. 44 #60, 45 #62
D. Redford 1984 p. 99
D. Redford 1992 p. 112

Ryholt 1997a pp. 151, 152, 153 #11.3, 155, 158, table 24, 305, 306, 388
File 16/4, 410, table 97
Vernus 1989a pp. 129-135, pl. I
von Beckerath 1999 pp. 102 #c, 103 #c

Neferibre Dynasty XIV

Horus Name: Unknown

Nomen: Unknown

Prenomen:

nfr-ib-r ʿ
Neferibre

Two Ladies: Unknown

Golden Falcon: Unknown

Neferirkare (I)

Length of Reign:	Unknown
Tomb:	Unknown
Mummy:	Unknown

Consorts:	Unknown	**Variant Names:**	None
Manetho:	Not given		
King Lists:	T: (G 8.22; R 9.22; vB 8.22)		

Perhaps the twenty-eighth king of Dynasty XIV, Neferibre is one of a group of kings known only from the Turin Canon. The papyrus' fragmentary state allows for varying interpretations as to the positioning of some of the kings of this dynasty. However, Neferibre's place seems secure.

References:
Gardiner 1959 pl. III, Col. VIII # 22
Gardiner 1961 p. 441 #8.22
Ryholt 1997a pp. 95 Col. 9.22, 98 #28, 380 File 14/28, 409 #28

von Beckerath 1999 pp. 110 #23, 111 #23

Neferirkare (I) — Dynasty V

Horus Name:

wsr-ḫʿw

Nomen: *k₃k₃i*
Kakai

Prenomen: *nfr-iri-k₃-rʿ*
Neferirkare

Two Ladies: *nbty ḫʿ-m*

Golden Falcon: *(bik) nbw sḥmw*

Neferirkare (I)

Length of Reign:	11 years(?)		
Tomb:	Pyramid at Abusir: "The Ba of Neferirkare"		
Mummy:	Unknown		
Consorts:	Khentkaues II	**King Lists:**	Ab: (28); S: (27); P; T: (G [3.19])
Manetho:	Nephercheres (A) Nepherkheres (A)	**Variant Names:**	None

The third ruler of Dynasty V, Neferirkare (I) was probably the brother of his predecessor, Sahure, although some Egyptologists believe the two to have been son and father, respectively. However, a relief discovered in Sahure's mortuary temple was found to have been recut so that a figure standing near to Sahure was endowed with royal insignia and renamed Neferirkare. Verner points out that a fair amount of the identification of Neferirkare as Sahure's brother is based on this relief and that the recutting "concerned only the upgrading of his status" and not the replacement or usurpation by Neferirkare of a previous contender for the throne, perhaps Sahure's eldest son Netjerirenre. For whatever reason, Neferirkare succeeded to the throne of Egypt.

Little is known about Neferirkare's reign. The main fragment of the Palermo Stone preserves regnal year one and a portion of year eleven, but these entries deal only with religious endowments and tell us nothing of trade or conquest. A single piece of the stone known as the London Fragment may possibly belong to the king's second regnal year. A graffito from the core of Neferirkare's pyramid gives what may be a year sixteen; however, the reading is doubtful. Manetho gives Neferirkare, as Nepherkheres, a reign of twenty years, which is certainly too high.

Neferirkare's pyramid at Abusir, at first called "Kakai is a Ba," was originally a six-stepped structure that was enlarged to eight, and then enlarged once more and converted to a true pyramid. The final structure measured 104 m. square and would have stood about 72 m. high had it been completed. The king died and the pyramid was left rough with only a few of the lower levels of the red granite casing stones properly in place.

Neferirkare's mortuary temple, like his pyramid, went through several changes and enlargements. Also, once a final design had been decided upon, the construction was suddenly hurried. Stone gave way to mud brick; even the foundations were brick. It has been suggested that the sudden rush was due to the illness and subsequent death of the king; certainly, even with corner-cutting and haste, the temple was unfinished at the time of the king's death. The temple was eventually completed by two of his successors, Neferefre and Niuserre. For whatever reason, the temple, which had been begun in stone, was completed in wood and mud brick. Even the columns inside the temple's interior stone walls were wooden.

Two large wooden boats were buried in pits next to the pyramid, one at the north side and one at the south. The south pit was excavated. Sad to relate, the boat had crumbled to nothing.

The *Abusir Papyri*, a collection of papyri discovered over a period of time in Neferirkare's mortuary temple, have provided invaluable information on a great many aspects of the operation of such a temple and the funerary complex in general. Although cached in Neferirkare's temple, the majority of the papyri actually dated to the reign of Djedkare Isesi, eighth pharaoh of Dynasty V.

No valley temple or causeway for Neferirkare was ever constructed. However, a sun temple called "Place of Re's Pleasure" was built, although its location has never been found. It is possible that it was dismantled and the stone reused by later kings.

Evidence of Egyptian presence in Nubia is represented by seals and ostraca of Neferirkare and other Dynasty IV and V kings at Buhen, at the Second Cataract. From Byblos in Lebanon come the remains of an alabaster bowl bearing Neferirkare's name.

References:

Altenmüller 2001 p. 598
Borchardt 1909
Clagett 1989 pp. 92-95
Dodson 2003 pp. 67-68,124
Dodson and Hilton 2004 62, 64-66, 68, 69
Emery 1963 pp. 116, 119, fig. 2 #A5-46
Gardiner 1959 pl. II, Col. III #19
Gardiner 1961 pp. 87, 435
x 2000 pp. 475-479
Lehner 1997 pp. 144-145, 152,
Spalinger 1994 pp. 297-298, 314

Verbrugghe and Wickersham 1996 pp. 135, 191
Verner 1991 pp. 411-418
Verner 1997 pp. 54-56, 93-96, 291-297, 297-301
Verner 2000a pp. 562, 563
Verner 2000b pp. 590-591, 592, 595
Verner 2002 pp. 43, 48,49, 50, 52-54, 62, 75, 97, 108-114, 135-151
von Beckerath 1999 pp. 56 #2, 57 #2
Waddell 1940 p. 51
R. Wilkinson 2000 p. 123
T. Wilkinson 2000 pp. 172-180, 252

Neferirkare (II)   Dynasty VII/VIII

Horus Name:

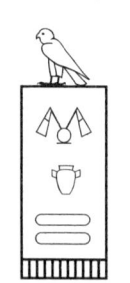

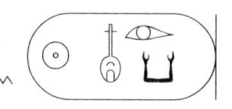

dmd-ib-tȝwy
Demedjibtowy

Nomen:

nfr-iri-kȝ-rʿ
Neferirkare

Prenomen: Unknown

Two Ladies: Unknown

Golden Falcon: Unknown

Length of Reign:	T: " 1 year, 6 months..."
Tomb:	Unknown
Mummy:	Unknown

Consorts:	Unknown	**Variant Names:**	None
Manetho:	Not given		
King Lists:	Ab: (56); T: R 5.13)		

Neferirkare (II) was the seventeenth king of Dynasty VII/VIII according to the Abydos List, and Ryholt's recent reconstruction of the Turin Canon would seem to agree with that placement. The only other attestation for this king is a single decree issued under his Horus name, Demedjibtowy, for the temple of the god Min at Coptos.

References:
Altenmüller 2001 p. 604
Gardiner 1961 p. 437 #A 56
Hayes 1946 pp. 6, 20, 21, 23

Ryholt 2000 pp. 91, 99 table 1
von Beckerath 1999 pp. 68 #17, 69 #17, pg. 70#b, pg. 71#b

Neferkahor   Dynasty VII/VIII

Horus Name: Unknown

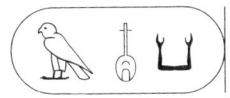

Nomen: *nfr-k3-ḥr*
Neferkahor

Prenomen: Unknown

Two Ladies: Unknown

Golden Falcon: Unknown

Length of Reign:	Unknown
Tomb:	Unknown
Mummy:	Unknown

Consorts:	Unknown	**Variant Names:**	None
Manetho:	Unknown		
King Lists:	Ab: (50)		

Neferkamin

The eleventh king of Dynasty VII/VIII, Neferkahor is known from the Abydos King List as well as from a black serpentine cylinder seal of unknown provenance. A lacuna is recorded in the Turin Canon where this pharaoh would have been listed.

References:
Gardiner 1961 p. 437
Kaplony 1981 vol. II p. 435, pl. 114

Ryholt 2000 pp. 96-97, 98, 99 table 1

Neferkamin   Dynasty VII/VIII

Horus Name: Unknown

Nomen and Prenomen:

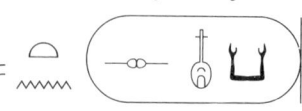

nfr-k3-mn
Neferkamin

Prenomen:

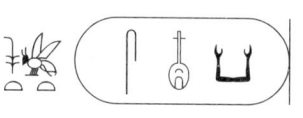

s.nfr-k3
Seneferka

Two Ladies: Unknown

Golden Falcon: Unknown

Length of Reign:	Unknown
Tomb:	Unknown
Mummy:	Unknown

Consorts:	Unknown	**Variant Names:**	Seneferka Sneferka
Manetho:	Not given		
King Lists:	Ab: (47)		

The eighth king of Dynasty VII/VIII, Neferkamin is known only from the Abydos King List. A lacuna is recorded in the Turin Canon where this pharaoh would have been listed.

Neferkamin's name has been given as Seneferka by some Egyptologists and in the Abydos Lists of both Sety I and Ramesses II. The reason for the difference in transliteration and translation is that the ⟶, normally (*s*), could take the place of the ⟷, an ideogram for the god Min (*mn*). Either version may be correct.

Neferkamin Anu

References:
Gardiner 1957 pp. 496 #34, 503 #22
Gardiner 1961 p. 437 #A 47
Hayes 1946 p. 23 note 1

Ryholt 2000 pp. 96-97, 98, 99 table 1
von Beckerath 1999 pp. 66 #8

Neferkamin Anu   Dynasty VII/VIII

Horus Name: Unknown

Nomen:

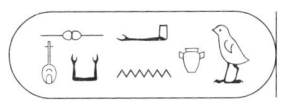

nfr-k3-mn ʿnw
Neferamin Anu

Prenomen:

nfr
Nefer

Two Ladies: Unknown

Golden Falcon: Unknown

Length of Reign:	Unknown
Tomb:	Unknown
Mummy:	Unknown

Consorts:	Unknown	**Variant Names:**	Nefer
Manetho:	Not given		Nefer<kamin>
King Lists:	Ab: (52); T (G 4.10; R 5.9; vB 4.9)		Nufe Seneferka-Anu Sneferka-Anu

Neferkamin Anu was the thirteenth king of Dynasty VII/VIII, according to the Abydos King List, and Ryholt's recent reconstruction of the Turin Canon would seem to agree with that placement. Gardiner, writing before the reconstruction of the papyrus, places this king (as Nufe) in his column IV, in the tenth position, and gives him a reign of 2 years, 1 month and 1 day, which is actually the reign of his immediate successor, the pharaoh Qakaure Ibi. Other than the king lists, we have no attestations for Neferkamin Anu.

It should be noted that transliteration of Neferkamin Anu's name has the same issues as that of his predecessor, Neferkamin: the hieroglyph —∞— (*s*) was sometimes used to replace the ⊂∞⊃ (*mn*).

Neferkare

References:

Gardiner 1959 pl. II, Col. IV #10
Gardiner 1961 p. 437 #A 52
Ryholt 2000 pp. 91, 97, 98, 99 table 1

von Beckerath 1999 pp. 68 #13, 69 #13

Neferkare   Dynasty II

Horus Name: Unknown   **Nomen:**

nfr-k3-rʿ
Neferkare

nfr-k3
Neferka

Two Ladies: Unknown

Golden Falcon: Unknown

Length of Reign:	Unknown
Tomb:	Unknown
Mummy:	Unknown

Consorts:	Unknown	**King Lists:**	S (8)
Manetho:	Nephercheres (A) Nepherkheres (A)	**Variant Names:**	Aka Neferka

Neferkare is known from the Saqqara king list and the Turin Canon. Gardiner sees him as probably being fictitious because Dynasty II is too early for the reference to Re to be included in a name. Gardiner evidently overlooked Nebre. Wilkinson points out the fact that other than the mention of Neferkare in the Saqqara and Turin lists, there is no contemporary evidence for this king's existence, and refers to him as a "shadowy" ruler at another point in his book. Dodson equates Neferkare with Sekhemib/Peribsen.

The variant spelling of Aka for Neferka comes from Gardiner's misreading of the name in the Turin Canon. The papyrus, being in hieratic, was transcribed into hieroglyphs before transliterating, and it would appear Gardiner read the sign (∴) when it is actually (*nfr*).

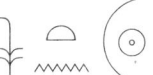

As with other "shadowy" kings of this period, attempts to equate Neferkare with a well-attested pharaoh, in this case Sekhemib/Peribsen, must remain guesswork until hard evidence comes to light.

Manetho gives Neferkare (his Nepherkheres) a reign of 25 years and informs us that in his reign there was a story that the Nile ran with water and honey for 11 days.

References:

Barta 1981 pp. 12, 15, 19
Edwards 1971 p. 35
Emery 1961 p. 98
Dodson 1996 p. 20
Gardiner 1959 p. 15 note II 25, pl. I Col. II #25

Gardiner 1961 pp. 416, 416, 431
Verbrugghe and Wickersham 1996 pp. 111-112, 133, 189
von Beckerath 1999 pp. 44 #6, 45 #6
Waddell 1940 pp. 37, 39
T. Wilkinson 2000 pp. 55, 58, 73

Neferkare   Dynasty VII/VIII

Horus Name: Unknown

Nomen: *nfr-k3-rʿ*
Neferkare

Prenomen: Unknown

Two Ladies: Unknown

Golden Falcon: Unknown

Length of Reign:	Unknown
Tomb:	Unknown
Mummy:	Unknown

Consorts:	Unknown	**Variant Names:**	None
Manetho:	Not given		
King Lists:	Ab: (42)		

The third king of Dynasty VII/VIII, Neferkare is known only from the Abydos King List. A lacuna is recorded in the Turin Canon where Neferkare would have been listed.

References:

Gardiner 1961 p. 437 #A 42
Petrie 1978 pl. X #s 4 or 6

Ryholt 2000 pp. 96-97, 99 table 1
von Beckerath 1999 pp. 66 #3, 67 #3

Neferkare — Dynasty IX/X

Horus Name: Unknown
Nomen: Unknown

Prenomen:

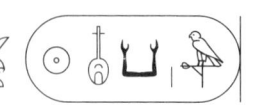

nfr-k₃-rˁ
Neferkare

Two Ladies: Unknown
Golden Falcon: Unknown

Length of Reign:	Unknown
Tomb:	Unknown
Mummy:	Unknown

Consorts:	Unknown	**Variant Names:**	None
Manetho:	Not given		
King Lists:	T: (4.20)		

Neferkare is one of the pharaohs who controlled an unknown amount of territory around Herakleopolis in Middle Egypt (see "Herakleopolitans" in Glossary). Attestations for the kings whose names are known are few; most are known only as names from the Turin Canon. Such would seem the case with this king; however, it is possible that he is mentioned in the tomb of the nomarch Ankhtifi of Mo'alla, in Upper Egypt.

References:

Dodson and Hilton 2004 p. 80
Doret 2001 pp. 94-96
Gardiner 1959 pl. II, Col. IV #20
Gardiner 1961 pp. 111, 112
Lorton 1987 pp. 23, 26
von Beckerath 1999 pp. 72 #3, 73 #3

Neferkare Khendu — Dynasty VII/VIII

Horus Name: Unknown
Nomen:

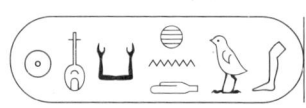

nfr-k₃-rˁ ḫndw
Neferkare Khendu

Neferkare Neby

Prenomen: Unknown

Two Ladies: Unknown

Golden Falcon: Unknown

Length of Reign:	Unknown
Tomb:	Unknown
Mummy:	Unknown

Consorts:	Unknown	Variant Names:	Neferkare Chendu
Manetho:	Not given		
King Lists:	Ab: (45)		

The sixth king of Dynasty VII/VIII, Neferkare Khendu is known from the Abydos King List. A lacuna is recorded in the Turin Canon where Khendu would have been listed. It has been suggested that a very crudely inscribed cylinder-seal bearing a cartouche reading ⟨cartouche⟩ (ḫndy) belongs to this ruler.

References:
Frankfort 1926 p. 92 and fig. 6
Gardiner 1961 p. 437 #A 45
Ryholt 2000 pp. 96-97, 99 table 1
von Beckerath 1999 pp. 66 #6, 67 #6

Neferkare Neby — Dynasty VII/VIII

Horus Name: Unknown	Nomen and Prenomen: ⟨cartouche⟩

nfr-k₃-rʿ nby
Neferkare Neby

Two Ladies: Unknown

Golden Falcon: Unknown

Length of Reign:	Unknown
Tomb:	Pyramid at Saqqara(?): "Enduring of Life"
Mummy:	Unknown

Consorts:	Unknown	Variant Names:	Nebi
Manetho:	Not given		Neferkare II
King Lists:	Ab: (43)		Neferkare Nebi

Neferkare Pepi-Sonb

The fourth monarch of Dynasty VII/VIII, Neferkare Neby would seem to have been a son of Pepi II. A stele located in the tomb of Pepi's wife, Ankhenespepi IV, at Saqqara lists her son, Neferkare, and even gives the name of his pyramid. Other than the Abydos King List, Neferkare Neby is known only from his mother's stele. The Turin Canon records a lacuna where Neferkare's name would appear.

Although we know the name of Neferkare's pyramid, its location has not been discovered, but it was most likely at Saqqara.

References:

Dodson and Hilton 2004 pp. 70, 73, 74, 76
Gardiner 1961 p. 437 #aA 43
Jéquier 1933a pp. 52-54 and fig. 31
Ryholt 2000 pp. 96-97, 99 table 1
Sayce 1899b p. 111
Verner 1997 pp. 369-370
von Beckerath 1999 pp. 66 #4, 67 #4

Neferkare Pepi-Sonb — Dynasty VII/VIII

Horus Name: Unknown

Nomen and Prenomen:

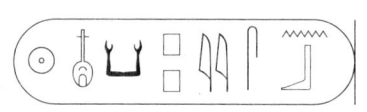

nfr-k₃-rˁ ppy-snb
Neferkare Pepi-Sonb

Prenomen:

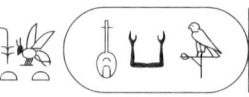

nfr-k₃-rˁ ḥrd
Neferkare Khered...

Two Ladies: Unknown

Golden Falcon: Unknown

Length of Reign:	Unknown
Tomb:	Unknown
Mummy:	Unknown

Consorts:	Unknown		Neferka Khered-Sonb
Manetho:	Unknown		Neferka<re>
King Lists:	Ab: (51) T: (G 4.9; R 5.8; vB 4.8)		Neferka<re> Pepi-Sonb
Variant Names:	Neferka		

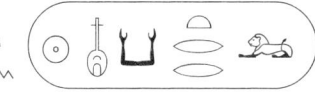

The twelfth ruler of Dynasty VII/VIII, Neferkare Pepi-Sonb is known from the Abydos King List and the Turin Canon. The Canon shows the king's name as Neferka Khered..., dropping the "re" and confusing "Pepi-Sonb" with "Khered." The error may have been caused by damage in the original text or a misreading by the copyist. However, due to the Turin reading, Neferkare has sometimes been called "Neferkare the Younger" and even "Neferkare Junior," the hieroglyph 𓐍, (ḥrd) being translated as "child," "young," etc.

K.S.B. Ryholt's recent reconstruction of the Turin Canon gives us regnal dates for several pharaohs of Dynasty VII/VIII; however, damage to the papyrus leaves us only knowing that Neferkare Pepi-Sonb ruled for at least one year and some months and days.

References:

Gardiner 1957 p. 443 #17
Gardiner 1959 pl. II, Col. IV.9
Gardiner 1961 pp. 436, 437 #A 51
Sayce 1899b p. 111

Ryholt 2000 pp. 91, 93-94, 99 table 1: 99-100
von Beckerath 1999 pp. 68 #12, 69 #12

Neferkare Tereru   Dynasty VII/VIII

Horus Name: Unknown	**Nomen and Prenomen:**	
		nfr-kȝ-rꜥ trrw
		Neferkare Tereru
Two Ladies: Unknown		
Golden Falcon: Unknown		

Length of Reign:	Unknown
Tomb:	Unknown
Mummy:	Unknown

Consorts:	Unknown	**King Lists:**	Ab: (49)
Manetho:	Not given	**Variant Names:**	Telulu

The tenth king of Dynasty VII/VIII is known from the Abydos King List and his name probably appears on an inscribed cylinder seal. A lacuna is recorded in the Turin Canon where this pharaoh would have been listed. Some scholars once believed Tereru to have been an Asiatic name, but there is no evidence to support that theory and most Egyptologists have long since disregarded it.

Neferkaseker

References:
Frankfort 1926 p. 92 and fig. 6
Gardiner 1961 p. 437
Petrie 1978 p. 17, pl. X #7.10
Ryholt 2000 pp. 96-97, 99 table 1
von Beckerath 1999 pp. 68 #10, 69 #10

Neferkaseker   Dynasty II

Horus Name: Unknown   **Nomen:**

nfr-k3-skr
Neferkaseker

nfr-k3-skr
Neferkaseker

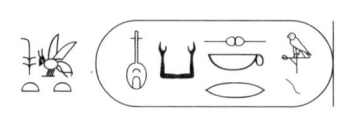

Two Ladies: Unknown
Golden Falcon: Unknown

Length of Reign:	8 years
Tomb:	Unknown
Mummy:	Unknown

Consorts:	Unknown	**King Lists:**	S: (9); T: (G3.10)
Manetho:	Sesochris (A, E) Sesokhris (A, E)	**Variant Names:**	Neferkasokar

Although this king is listed in the Turin Canon and the Saqqara King List, there is no contemporary evidence to prove his existence (however, see below). This has led some Egyptologists to cast doubt upon his entries in the Saqqara and Turin lists. Gardiner considers Neferkaseker to be one of several rulers (along with Hudjefa and Beby) to be of northern Egyptian origin and writes that "they were real occupants of the throne whose claims to recognition were deemed by Manetho and his forerunners to be superior to those of certain pharaohs from the south...." There was civil strife during parts of Dynasty II; it is possible that Neferkaseker was of Lower Egyptian origin and a rival claimant to the throne. However, it is just as likely that his name is to be identified as part of the titulary of one of the known kings of that dynasty.

There is a seal that gives the name Neferkaseker twice in cartouches. If the seal is contemporary, and from the treatment of the hieroglyphs it looks to be, this would be the earliest example of a pharaoh's name so enclosed. The seal reads: "The King of Upper and Lower Egypt, Neferkaseker, beloved of the gods, Neferkaseker."

It is of interest to note that Neferkaseker seems to be mentioned in a Roman Period demotic papyrus having to do with the planning and construction of temples.

Manetho gives Neferkaseker a reign of 48 years and claims his physical height to have been 5 cubits and 3 palms (about eight and a half feet).

References:

Barta 1981 p. 12, 15, 19
Gardiner 1959 p. 15 note #1, pl. II Col. III #1
Gardiner 1961 pp. 416, 431
Kaplony 1981 vol. IIA pp. 1-2, vol. IIB table 1
M. Smith 1980 pp. 173-174
Verbrugghe and Wickersham 1996 pp. 133, 189
von Beckerath 1999 pp. 44 #7, 45 #7
Waddell 1940 pp. 37, 39, 41
T. Wilkinson 2000 pp. 55, 58, 73

Neferkauhor   Dynasty VII/VIII

Horus Name:

nṯr-bꜣw

Nomen:

pw(?)...ḥpw
Pu(?)...hapi

ḫw-w-ḥpw
Khuwihapi

Prenomen:

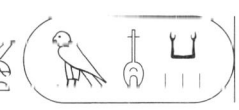

nfr-kꜣw-ḥr
Neferkauhor

Two Ladies: Unknown

Golden Falcon: Unknown

Neferkaure

Length of Reign:	T: "2 years, 1 month, 1 day"	
Tomb:	Unknown	
Mummy:	Unknown	

Consorts:	Unknown	Chuwihapi
Manetho:	Not given	Ka(?)-pu-ib(i)(?)
		Khuihapy
King Lists:	Ab: (55); T: (R 5.12)	Neferkawhor
Variant Names:	Chui...(?)	

The sixteenth pharaoh of Dynasty VII/VIII, Neferkauhor is listed in the Abydos king-list; Ryholt's reconstruction of the Turin Canon gives him a reign of just a little over two years. The only other attestations are a series of eight decrees the king caused to be placed in the temple of Min at Coptos during the first year of his reign. These decrees, seven of which were issued on one day, tell us that the king's eldest daughter, Nebyet, was married to the vizier Shemay and that the pharaoh had endowed the chapels of the two with mortuary priests. The decrees also tell us that the family of Shemay was given special consideration and its members were appointed to very important offices. We also learn that the king was concerned about inventories at the temple of Min.

References:

Altenmüller 2001 p. 604
Dodson and Hilton 2004 pp. 70, 73
Franke 2001 pp. 527, 528, 529
Gardiner 1961 p. 437 #A55
Hayes 1946 pp. 5-6, 12-20, 21, 22-23, pls. III and IIIa, IV and IVa, V

Jéquier 1931 p. 38 fig. 3
von Beckerath 1999 pp. 68 #16, 69 #16

Neferkaure   Dynasty VII/VIII

Horus Name:

$ḥr$-...

Nomen: Unknown

Prenomen:

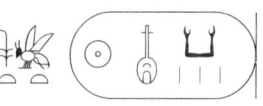

nfr-$k3w$-r^c
Neferkaure

Two Ladies: Unknown

Golden Falcon: Unknown

Length of Reign:	T: "4 years, 2 months, 0 days"		
Tomb:	Unknown		
Mummy:	Unknown		
Consorts:	Unknown	**Variant Names:**	Kha'-[bau(?)] Neferkawre
Manetho:	Not given		
King Lists:	Ab: (54); T: (R 5.11)		

The Abydos king-list places Neferkaure as fifteenth ruler of Dynasty VII/VIII and the recent reconstruction of the Turin Canon by K.S.B. Ryholt gives this pharaoh a reign of just over four years. Aside from these lists, Neferkaure is known for his issuance of a decree concerning offerings to the temple of Min at Coptos. The decree is much damaged, and only a portion of the king's serekh survives. The inscription was dated to this pharaoh's fourth regnal year.

References:

Altenmüller 2001 p. 604
Gardiner 1961 p. 437 #A 54
Hayes 1946 pp. 5, 11-13, 23, pl. s III and IIIa top

Ryholt 2000 pp. 91, 99 table 1
von Beckerath 1999 pp. 68 #15, 69 #15

Neferneferuaten   Dynasty XVIII

Horus Name: Unknown

Queen:

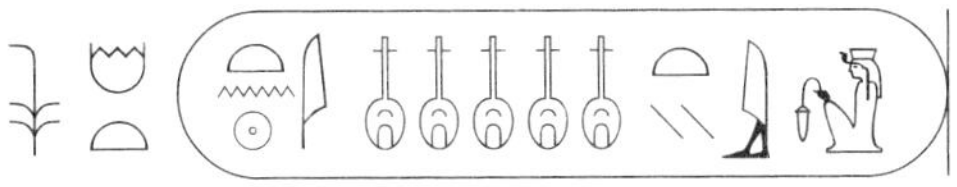

nfr-nfrw-itn nfrt-ii-ti
Neferneferuaten Nefertiti

Nomen:

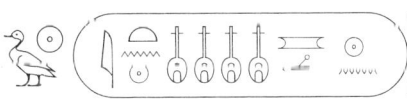

nfr-nfrw-itn mry-wʿ-n-rʿ
Neferneferuaten (merywaenre)

Prenomen:

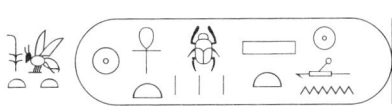

ʿnḫt-ḫprw-rʿ-mryt-wʿ-n-rʿ
Ankhetkheperure-mer(y)etwaenre

Neferneferuaten

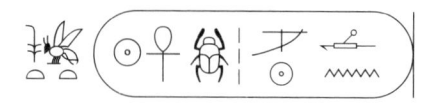

ʿnh-ḫprw-rʿ-mry-wʿ-n-rʿ
Ankhkheperure-merywaenre

Two Ladies: Unknown

Golden Falcon: Unknown

Length of Reign:	3+ years
Tomb:	Amarna
Mummy:	Unknown

Consorts:	Akhenaten	**Variant Names:**	Nefertiti
Manetho:	Not given		
King Lists:	None		

Most likely the twelfth pharaoh of Dynasty XVIII, the name Neferneferuaten is known from a graffito in the tomb of Pere at Thebes (TT139). The graffito is dated to regnal year three of a king called Ankhkheperure Neferneferuaten. This king has generally been equated with Akhenaten's shadowy coregent Smenkhkare, whose prenomen was Ankhkheperure. However, there is abundant circumstantial evidence, and increased scholarly support, for the alternative interpretation that Aekhnaten's Chief Queen Nefertiti, who added Neferneferuaten to her name, assumed the role of coregent toward the end of Akhenaten's reign.

Around year two or three of Akhenaten's reign, Nefertiti added a cartouche giving the name Neferneferuaten with the epithet *mery-Waenre*, "Beloved of Waenre"—in other words, "Beloved of Akhenaten." In the latter part of his reign, Akhenaten almost definitely had a coregent named Neferneferuaten with the prenomen Ankhkheperure, a prenomen also used by Smenkhkare. This is undoubtedly the source of the confusion about the length of Smenkhkare's coregency and the identity of Neferneferuaten. As the *mery-Waenre* epithet is found only in conjunction with *both* Neferneferuaten and Ankhkheperure, and is never found in conjunction with Smenkhkare's prenomen, the most logical conclusion is that Nefertiti was the pharaoh Neferneferuaten.

The Ankhkheperure mentioned above in a graffito dating to regnal year three includes the epithet mery-Waenre, and thus is more logically identified with Neferetiti than Smenkhkare. This identification would also go far in solving the problem of the supposed "disappearance" of Nefertiti after Akhenaten's regnal year

12: she did not die, nor was she "disgraced"; rather, she changed her name and became coregent with her husband.

Dodson and others postulate that Neferneferuaten's coregency continued after the death of Akhenaten and into the early years of the reign of Tutankhamen.

References:
Do. Arnold 1996
Dodson Forthcoming pp. 1-13
Ertman 1992 pp. 50-55
Ertman 2001/2002 pp. 26-28
Freed et al. 1999
S. James 2001/2002 pp. 32-41
Reeves 2001 pp. 172-
Samson 1978
Samson 1982 pp. 61-67
Tyldesley 1998

Nefertum...re — Dynasty XIV

Horus Name: Unknown

Nomen: Unknown

Prenomen:

nfr-tm...-rˁ
Nefertum...re

Two Ladies: Unknown

Golden Falcon: Unknown

Length of Reign:	Unknown
Tomb:	Unknown
Mummy:	Unknown

Consorts:	Unknown	**Variant Names:**	Kanefertemre Nefertemre
Manetho:	Not given		
King Lists:	T: (G 8.19; R 9.19; vB 8,19)		

Possibly the twenty-fifth king of Dynasty XIV, Nefertum...re is one of a group of kings known only from the Turin Canon. The papyrus' fragile state allows for varying interpretations as to the positioning of some of the kings of this dynasty. However, Nefertum...re's place seems secure.

References:
Gardiner 1959 pl. III, Col. VIII #19
Gardiner 1961 p. 441 #8.19
Ryholt 1997a pp. 95 Col. 9.19, 98 #25, 198 table 37, 379 File 14/25, 409 table 95 #25
von Beckerath 1999 pp. 110 #20, 111 #20

Neheb *n-hb* Neheb — Predynastic

Length of Reign:	Unknown
Tomb:	Unknown
Mummy:	Unknown

Consorts:	Unknown	**Variant Names:**	Ni-heb
Manetho:	Not given		
King Lists:	P		

Neheb is one of a group of nine kings known only from the Palermo Stone. Each name is followed by a representation of a squatting king wearing the crown of Lower Egypt. Whether these names are to be taken as historic personages or mythic "ancestors" is not known.

References:

Clagett 1989 pp. 66, 97-98
Edwards 1971 pp. 3-4
Gardiner 1961 pl. III
O'Mara 1979 p. 5
T. Wilkinson 2000 pp. 62, 85-86, 87

Nehsy — Dynasty XIV

Horus Name: Unknown

Nomen: *nḥsi* Nehsy

Prenomen: *ʿ3-sḫ-rʿ* Asehre

Two Ladies: Unknown

Golden Falcon: Unknown

Length of Reign:	Unknown		
Tomb:	Unknown		
Mummy:	Unknown		
Consorts:	Unknown	**Variant Names:**	Nehasi Nehesi
Manetho:	Not given		
King Lists:	T: (G 8.1; R 9.1; vB 8.1)		

Possibly the sixth king of Dynasty XIV, Nehsy seems to have been the son of King Sheshi and Queen Tati, the latter probably a Nubian, or at least of Nubian descent, which is undoubtedly the reason for Nehsy's name, i.e., "The Nubian."

It would appear that Nehsy was not originally intended to be the successor to the throne, but only achieved this position upon the death of an elder brother, prince Ipqu.

Four scarab seals, one from Semna in Nubia and three of unknown provenance, point to the likelihood that Nehsy served as a coregent to his father, Sheshi, for an unknown period of time.

Nehsy is one of the few kings of Dynasty XIV to have left attestations beyond the Turin Canon. Aside from the scarab-seals mentioned above, he is also represented by some two dozen other such seals from various locations, two stele from Tell Habwe in the eastern Delta, several fragments of pillars and a stone block at Avaris (Tell ed-Dab'a). Another item of interest is a statue dedicated by Nehsy to the god Set, Lord of Avaris, which was moved from that city to Tell el Muqdam (the Greek Leontopolis), some miles away, and usurped by the Dynasty XIX king Merenptah.

It is possible that Nehsy's memory survived for some time after his death, as several locations in the Delta bore names such as "The Mansion of Pinehsy" and "The Place of the Asiatic Pinehsy," Pineshy being a Late Egyptian rendering of Nehsy; Nehsy did indeed come from a Canaanite background.

Special Note: Gardiner and Ryholt position Nehsy as the first ruler of Dynasty XIV according to the Turin Canon, whereas von Beckerath and Bietak see him as the second ruler of that dynasty. The Turin Canon is much damaged and therefore open to interpretation; however, it would appear that the likeliest positioning does show Nehsy as representing the first king for this dynasty. It is possible that the compilers of the Turin Canon believed or knew that Nehsy was the first Dynasty XIV ruler to have used Avaris as his capital and concluded that he was therefore its founder. The number of architectural remains from that area attributable to Nehsy would seem to support such a theory.

Nerikare

References:

Bietak 1970 pp. 255-256 and pl. XVIIIa
El Maksoud 1983 pp. 3-5 and pl. I
El Maksoud 1989 pp. 173-186
Helck 1983 p. 48 #66
Gardiner 1959 pl. III, Col. VII #1
Gardiner 1961 p. 441 #8.1
Ryholt 1997a pp. 43, 51, 52 table 13, 57, 56 fig. 9, 94, 96-97, 95 Col. 9.1, 98 #6, 198 table 37, 252-253, 299-300, 376-378 File 14/6, 409 #6
Sourouzian 1989 p. 95 #48
von Beckerath 1999 pp. 108 #2, 109 #2

Nerikare   Dynasty XIII

Horus Name: Unknown

Nomen: Unknown

Prenomen:

nry-k3-rˤ
Nerikare

Two Ladies: Unknown

Golden Falcon: Unknown

Length of Reign:	6 years(?)
Tomb:	Unknown
Mummy:	Unknown

Consorts:	Unknown	[Kheper?]kare
Manetho:	Not given	Ner(?)kare
		Nerikare
King Lists:	T: (lacuna)	[Si?]kare
Variant Names:	Djefakare	

Nerikare is known from a graffito marking the height of the Nile near the fortress at Semna in Nubia, and dated to his first regnal year. Ryholt believes that Nerikare's name is also to be read in a much-damaged cartouche found in another graffito, also at Semna. However, the central hieroglyph in the second cartouche is much disputed: Ryholt sees it as (*nry*) and therefore equates it with Nerikare; other scholars have read the sign as (*ḫpr*) and (*s3*). To confuse matters even more, Hintze and Reineke have misread the central hieroglyph in the dated cartouche as (*df3*). This king is also known from a fragment of stele found at Thebes, but now seemingly lost.

Although there is a lacuna in the Turin Canon at this point, Ryholt has demonstrated through the dating of the graffiti at Semna that Nerikare should be listed as the third ruler of Dynasty XIII, evidently the successor to the pharaoh Sonbef.

References:

Dunham and Janssen 1960 p. 132, R.I.S. 9, pl. 93D
Gabolde 1990 pp. 213-222
Helck 1983 p. 13 #19
Hintze and Reineke 1989
Peden 2001 p. 51
Ryholt 1997a pp. 73 #3, 192 table 33 and note 7/6, 195, 197 #3, 318-319, 320 table 92, 337 File 13/3 and notes 1 and 2, 408 table 94 #3
Ryholt 2000 p. 977
von Beckerath 1999 pp. 106 #r, 107 #r

Netjerkare Siptah   Dynasty VII/VIII

Nomen:

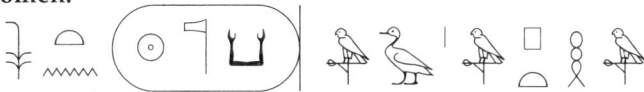

nṯr-k3-rꜥ s3-ptḥ
Netjerkare Siptah

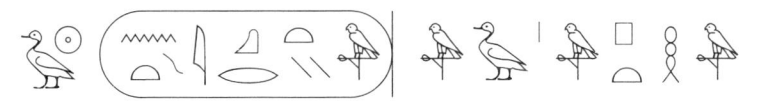

nt-ikrti s3-ptḥ
Neitiqerty Siptah

Horus Name: Unknown

Prenomen: Unknown

Two Ladies: Unknown

Golden Falcon: Unknown

Length of Reign: T: "…years, …months,…days"

Tomb: Unknown

Mummy: Unknown

Consorts: Unknown

Manetho: Nitocris (A, E)

King Lists: Ab: (40); T (G 4.7 or 8; R 5.7; vB 4.7)

Neterkare
Nitacrit
Nitocris
Nitokerty
Nitokris

Variant Names: Neitiqerty

Nikare

Since the time of Herodotus, a queen named Nitocris has been put forth as a pharaoh reigning in late in Dynasty VI. Manetho calls her "...the noblest and loveliest of the women of her time...braver than all the men of her time," and also ascribes the third pyramid at Giza to her. For many years Nitocris has been identified with the king Neitiqerty (see above nomen) listed in the much-damaged Turin Canon, although Newberry posited that she was to be equated with Neith, a queen of Pepi II. However, a recent reconstruction of the Canon by K.S.B. Ryholt, based on a comparison of fibers in the various pieces and fragments of the papyrus, would appear to prove that no woman named Nitocris, or Neitiqerty, was ever a pharaoh. The new placement of fragments gives us Siptah as a nomen for Neitiqerty, which is a male name. It is easy to see how Neitiqerty was bastardized into Nitocris; it is a bit more difficult to follow the transition from Netjerkare to Neitiqerty, but such seems to be the case.

According to the Turin Canon, Netjerkare was the immediate successor of Merenre Nemtyemsaf II of late in Dynasty VI, but whether he was related to his predecessor is unknown. He is sometimes listed as the first king of Dynasty VII, although it is now generally agreed that the ephemeral kings of Dynasties VII and VIII are run together and usually counted as the latter, ignoring Dynasty VII. He is given here as the first pharaoh of Dynasty VII/VIII.

Aside from his mention in the Turin Canon and the Abydos King List, Netjerkare is known from a single attestation: a copper tool of unknown usage and unknown provenance, now in the British Museum, bears his prenomen.

References:

Gardiner 1959 pl. II, Col. IV #8
Gardiner 1961 pp. 102, 436, 437 #A 40
Herodotus 1954 p. 166
T. James 1961 p. 38, pl. XII #4
Newberry 1943 pp. 51-54
Ryholt 2000 pp. 91, 92-93, 96, 97, 98, 99-100, 99 table 1

Verbrugghe and Wickersham 1996 pp. 101 and note 24, 117 note 57, 136, 192, 193 note 7
von Beckerath 1999 pp. 64 #7, 65 #7, 66 #1, 67 #1
Waddell 1940 pp. 55, 57, 221

Nikare   Dynasty VII/VIII

Horus Name: Unknown

Nomen and Prenomen:

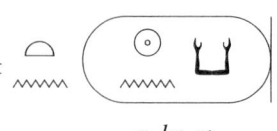

n-$k\!з$-r^c

Nikare

Two Ladies: Unknown

Golden Falcon: Unknown

Ninetjer

Length of Reign:	Unknown		
Tomb:	Unknown		
Mummy:	Unknown		
Consorts:	Unknown	**Variant Names:**	Nykare
Manetho:	Not given		
King Lists:	Ab: (48)		

The ninth king of Dynasty VII/VIII, Nikare is known only from the Abydos King List, although a faience cylinder-seal which seems to bear his name is known to exist. A lacuna is recorded in the Turin Canon where this pharaoh would have been listed.

References:
Gardiner 1961 p. 437 #a 48
Kaplony 1981 vol. II p. 433, pl. 114
Petrie 1978 pl. X #7.9

Ryholt 2000 pp. 96-97, 98, 99 table 1
von Beckerath 1999 pp. 66 #9, 67 #9

Ninetjer   Dynasty II

Horus Name:

ni-nṯr
Ninetjer

Nomen:

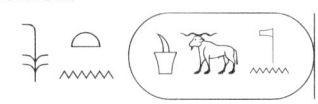

b3-nṯr-n
Banetjeren

b3-nṯrw
Banetjeru

Ninetjer

Nomen and Two Ladies:

ni-nṯr
Ninetjer

Two Ladies:

nbty ni-nṯr

Golden Falcon:

(bik) nbw rn

Length of Reign:	40 years
Tomb:	Saqqara Tomb "B" (South of Djoser complex)
Mummy:	Unknown

Consorts:	Unknown	Baneteru
Manetho:	Binothris (A) Biophis (E)	Neteren Neterymu Netjeren
King Lists:	Ab: (11); P; S: (5); T: (G 2.22)	Ninutjer Nutjeren Nyneter
Variant Names:	Baneteren	

Ninetjer, the third king of Dynasty II, is one of the best known rulers of the entire dynasty. The Palermo Stone's entire surviving fourth register is devoted to Ninetjer and gives a record of 16 years (years 6 through 21) of his reign. The main Cairo Fragment of the Palermo Stone gives us a further nine years, although exactly where in the reign they fall is unknown. Ninetjer's Horus name, along with those of Hotepsekhemwy and Nebre, is found on the statue of the mortuary priest Hotepdied, confirming the succession for the first part of the dynasty.

Ninetjer

If the Palermo Stone and its main Cairo Fragment are to be trusted, Ninetjer ruled for about forty years. A long reign is certainly implied by an inscription found on a stone vessel from Djoser's Step Pyramid; it gives a "seventeenth occasion" of the biennial cattle count, i.e., the thirty-fourth year of rule. Although we have no direct proof, such a long reign would see Ninetjer celebrating at least one Sed Festival. In favor of this likelihood is a statuette of Ninetjer (provenance unknown), now in the Georges Michailides Collection, that shows the king wearing the body-hugging robe commonly associated with this ceremony.

Egyptologist Selim Hassan discovered Ninetjer's tomb during his 1937-38 excavations at Saqqara. He described the tomb, which was sealed by two limestone blocks, as "being cut in the rock and having an area of several acres and forming a kind of labyrinth." Although sealed, the tomb had certainly been entered, as it was found to contain "some thousands" of Late Period mummies and mummy cases. The tomb is located about 130 m. east of the tomb of Hotepsekhemwy.

The Memphite region contains numerous attestations to Ninetjer. Three mastaba tombs of highly placed courtiers at Saqqara (tombs S2171, S2302 and S2498) have yielded jar-sealings. Jar-sealings were also found in an elite mastaba near Giza, and across the Nile in a tomb located in the cemetery of Helwan.

Except for several inscribed stone bowls (one showing Ninetjer's name inscribed over that of his predecessor, Nebre), found by Petrie in the tombs of Peribsen and Khasekhemwy at Abydos, there are no attestations for Ninetjer beyond the Memphite area. This has led some Egyptologists to theorize that the earliest kings of Dynasty II were based entirely in Lower Egypt and that a dynastic struggle might have begun in Ninetjer's time. However, outside of a reference on the Palermo Stone to "hacking up Shemre, hacking up Ha" (both thought to be Lower Egyptian sites), there is little or no evidence to support any sort of dynastic struggle during this reign. It has been postulated that Ninetjer's "attack on a northern town" was responsible for the outbreak of a civil war between Upper and Lower Egypt. But, since Ninetjer seems to have ruled from Memphis and was, like his predecessors Hotepsekhemwy and Nebre, buried at Saqqara, it is difficult to understand why he would have hacked up towns located in the north. It is interesting to note that Dodson and Clagett both point out that the term translated as "hacking" may also refer to the digging of foundations. So it is possible that the Palermo Stone leaves a record of the founding of the towns(?) Shemre and Ha. Still, dynastic troubles do seem to have occurred toward the end of Ninetjer's reign, as is evidenced by the accession to the throne of the ephemeral rulers Weneg and Sened.

References:

Clagett 1989 pp. 130-131 note 60.
Clayton 1994 p. 27 Color illustration statue of priest Hotepdied
Firth and Quibell 1935 vol. I p. 136, vol. II pl. 105#2
Gardiner 1959 pl. I Col. II #22

Niuserre

Gardiner 1961 pp. 415, 431, 432
Hassan 1938 p. 521
Lacau and Lauer 1959 pp. 6 #3, pl. V #3, pl. 13-16
Lacau and Lauer 1961 pp. 33-38
Lacau and Lauer 1965 pp. 88 no. 273, fig. 172, 89 no. 274, fig. 173
Lauer 1936-39 pp. 13, 16
Petrie 1901a pp. 6, 7, 26, 51, pl. VIII #s 13 and 13
Petrie 1907 p. 7
Quibell 1923 pp. 23-24, 29-30, 44-45, pl. XV #3 and XVII #3
Quibell 1934 p. 7
Reisner 1931 pp. 103a, 122
Saad 1951 p. 17: pls. XII.a, XII.b and XIII.a
Simpson 1956 pp. 45-49
Verbrugghe and Wickersham 1996 pp. 111, 133, 188
von Beckerath 1999 pp. 42 #3, 43 #3
Waddell 1940 p. 37
T. Wilkinson 1999 pp. 85-87, 240-242
T. Wilkinson 2000 pp. 59, 79, 119-129, 204-206

Niuserre   Dynasty V

Horus Name:

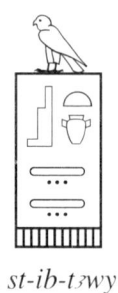

st-ib-t3wy

Nomen:

ini
Ini

Prenomen:

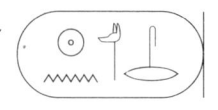

n-wsr-r˓
Niuserre

Two Ladies:

nbty st-ib

Golden Falcon:

bik-nbw nṯr

Length of Reign:	11-34 years(?)
Tomb:	Pyramid at Abusir: "The Places of Niuserre are Enduring"
Mummy:	Unknown

Consorts:	Reptynub	**Variant Names:**	Any
Manetho:	Rathures (A)		Neuserre
	Rhathoures (A)		Newoserre
King Lists:	Ab: (30); T: (G [3.22])		Nyuserra

The sixth ruler of Dynasty V, Niuserre was the son of the pharaoh Neferirkare (I) and Queen Khentkaues II, and the brother of the pharaoh Neferefre. There seems to have been a problem with the succession during Dynasty V, evidently between the immediate families of the brothers, and pharaohs Sahure and Neferirkare (I); because of this, Neferefre was succeeded by a son of Sahure(?) named Shepseskare. Niuserre came to the throne after Shepseskare's very short reign.

Like many pharaohs before him, Niuserre maintained contact with Egypt's eastern neighbors; a fragment of an alabaster vase inscribed with his name has been found at the temple of Baalat-Hathor in the port city of Byblos in Lebanon. Also from Byblos comes a bust of Niuserre. At the copper and turquoise mines at Wadi Maghara in Sinai, a large carved tablet (now in Cairo Museum) showed the king bashing in the head of an Asiatic. To Egypt's south, a seal-impression of Niuserre's Horus name was discovered at Buhen in Nubia.

Niuserre's pyramid is located between those of his father, Neferirkare (I), and his uncle, Sahure, at Abusir. With sides measuring 78.5 m. and a height of 50 m., the tomb was almost exactly the image of Sahure's, a slightly steeper angle adding 2 m. to its height. The pyramid's core was a seven-stepped structure that was filled in and cased with fine white limestone. The pyramid's burial chamber was originally lined with white limestone and pink granite, but stone robbers removed the great majority of the stone. The burial chamber and its antechamber were almost completely destroyed.

A mortuary temple located on the east side of the pyramid was built in an unusual "L" shape to avoid destroying several earlier mastabas. This mortuary temple connected to a causeway that led to a valley temple; both had been usurped from Neferirkare (I) Excavators recovered a great deal of beautifully carved relief work. Also found were blocks bearing the name of Sahure's sun temple, which had been usurped by Niuserre; this temple has never been found and may have been demolished and its stone reused.

Niuserre's sun temple, the "Delight of Re," was located near that of Userkaf's, at Abu Gurob, just a little north of Abusir. Originally built of brick, but later rebuilt in stone, the temple structure took the form of a valley temple connected by a causeway to an upper temple. The upper temple contained a gigantic truncated obelisk, some 36 m. high, which stood upon a base that was some 20

m. tall. The upper temple contained beautiful reliefs showing, among other things, Niuserre's Sed Festival.

There is some dispute as to the length of Niuserre's reign. The Turin Canon is much damaged and part of the record of the king's reign has been lost. All that survives is the number eleven and it is possible that as many as an additional 23 years could have been recorded. The fact that Niuserre celebrated a Sed Festival, and that such a festival was supposed to occur in the thirtieth year of the reign, does not necessarily imply that the king actually held the throne for that length of time. The Sed Festival was concerned with renewing vitality and power, and a ruler could order the festival any time he felt it was needed. Certainly Manetho's 44 years is too high by at least a decade.

Niuserre's funerary cult continued into Dynasty XII, long after the other kings of Dynasty V were forgotten. Some 1,200 years after Niuserre's death. Ramesses II of Dynasty XIX had Niuserre's sun temple restored.

References:

Bares 2000 pp. 2, 5
Borchardt 1907
Bothmer 1971
Kees 1928
Daoud 2000 p. 199, 204
Dodson 2003 p. 70
Dodson and Hilton 2004 pp. 60, 62, 64-65
Edel and Wenig 1974
Emery 1963 pp. 116-120 and fig. 2 #C4-1
Gardiner 1959 pl. II, Col. III #22
Gardiner 1961 p. 435
Gardiner and Peet 1952 pl. VI
Gardiner and Peet 1955 pp. 21, 26, 28, 58, 59-60
Goedicke 2000 p. 408
Kees 1928
Lehner 1997 pp. 60, 142, 146, 148-149, 151-153, 230
Malek 2000 pp. 245-246, 255
Ryholt 1997a p. 13, note 21
Smolarikova 2000 pp. 68-71
Verbrugghe and Wickersham 1996 pp. 114, 136, 185, 191
Verner 1997 pp. 73, 124-125, 269-271, 309, 311-314, 316-321, 324, 464
Verner 2002 pp. 33, 43, 55, 58-62, 76-85, 108, 137, 151, 166, 168, 228-229
von Beckerath 1999 pp. 58 #6, 59 #6
von Bissing 1905
von Bissing and Kees 1923
Waddell 1940 p. 51
R. Wilkinson 2000 pp. 20-21, 120, 123

Nubnefer   Dynasty II

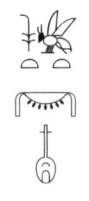

nbw-nfr
Nubnefer

Length of Reign:	Unknown
Tomb:	Unknown
Mummy:	Unknown

Consorts:	Unknown	**Variant Names:**	None
Manetho:	Not given(?)		
King Lists:	None		

This king is known from fragments of two schist bowls discovered near the Step Pyramid of Djoser at Saqqara during the 1923-24 digging season. The pieces were found at the bottom of a shaft discovered while excavations were being carried out on two mastabas thought to be the tombs of princesses who were probably members of Djoser's harem.

The two bowls bore the same inscriptions: "King of Upper and Lower Egypt, Nubnefer" and "The Mansion 'Enduring of Life'."

Gardiner, von Beckerath and Edwards all consider Nubnefer to have been the (*nswt-bity*) name for Horus Nebre. There is absolutely no proof to support this view. Edwards also considers the possibility that Nubnefer may have been the *nswt-bity* name of Horus Ninetjer; however, it is established that Ninetjer's *nswt-bity* name was Ninetjer.

References:

Edwards 1971 p. 30
Firth 1924 p. 126
Firth and Quibell 1935 pp. 75, 121, Pl. 89 #s 10 and 11
Gardiner 1961 p. 432
Gunn 1928 pp. 153, 160-161 A.15 and A 16, pl. II #s 7 and 8
Lacau and Lauer 1959 pp. 6, 48, Pl. VI #s 3 and 4
von Beckerath 1999 pp. 42 #2 E, 43 #2 E
T. Wilkinson 1999 p. 89
T. Wilkinson 2000 p. 203

Nuya   Dynasty XIV

Horus Name:
Unknown

Nomen:
nw-y
Nuya

Prenomen: Unknown

Two Ladies: Unknown

Golden Falcon: Unknown

Ny-Hor

Length of Reign:	Unknown
Tomb:	Unknown
Mummy:	Unknown

Consorts:	Unknown	Variant Names:	None
Manetho:	Not given		
King Lists:	None		

Nuya is known from a single scarab-seal, the provenance of which is unknown. His position within Dynasty XIV is uncertain. Ryholt, the only scholar to suggest that Nuya is a ruler of this or any dynasty, bases his claim on the seriation of royal scarab-seals. Hornung and Staehelin read the name as "Chian" i.e., "Khayan," a ruler of Dynasty XV, although this is most certainly wrong.

References:
Hornung and Staehelin 1976 p. 218 #140
Ryholt 1997a pp. 52 table 13, 96, 99
table 20a, 101 and note 331, 381
File 14/a

Ny-Hor   Dynasty 00

ni-ḥrw
Ny-Hor

Length of Reign:	Unknown
Tomb:	Unknown
Mummy:	Unknown

Consorts:	Unknown	Variant Names:	Nu-Hor
Manetho:	Not given		
King Lists:	None		

Attestation for the existence of this early ruler comes from the cemetery at Tura. During excavations carried out there by Junker in 1909-10, two graves were found to contain examples of this king's serekh. Neither of the two serekhs was surmounted by the Horus falcon, but the name is generally given as Ny-Hor. It should be noted, however, that some scholars see these serekhs as a crude attempt at writing the name of Narmer.

References:
Fischer 1963a fig. 3 c-d
Junker 1912 fig. 57.3-4
Kaiser 1964 fig. 7 h-i

van den Brink 1996 table 1.7-8, fig. IIb.6, table 5

Palmanthoes   Fictitious

The Jewish historian Artapanus of Alexandria, writing during the Ptolemaic Period, informs us that Palmanthoes became pharaoh upon the death of his father, Pharethothes.

Palmanthoes supposedly treated the Jews very poorly and evidently used them to build the city of Saïs in the Nile delta, where he also founded a temple. This ruler, according to Artapanus, established a shrine at Heliopolis.

Artapanus places him in Dynasty XIII, but Palmanthoes is a fictional king.

References:
Collins 1985 p. 898 and notes 3b-d

Pantjeny   Dynasty XIII/?

Horus Name: Unknown

Nomen: $p(3)$-n-tny
Pantjeny

Prenomen: shm-r^c-hw-$t3wy$
Sekhemrekhutowy

Two Ladies: Unknown

Golden Falcon: Unknown

Length of Reign:	Unknown
Tomb:	Unknown
Mummy:	Unknown

Pe-Hor

Consorts:	Unknown	Penthen
Manetho:	Not given	Pentjeny
King Lists:	None	Pentini
Variant Names:	Pantini	

This king is attested to by a single stele, discovered by Petrie at Abydos and now in the British Museum (EA630). The stele was carved for the "King's Son, Djehutya (Tahuti-aa)" and the "King's Daughter, Hotepneferu"; one was or both were a child of Pantjeny.

Ryholt places Pantjeny in the "Abydos Dynasty" because the stele was discovered at Abydos and the name $p(3)$-n-$ṯny$ may be translated "He of Thinis." (Thinis was located a few miles north of Abydos and in the same nome.) Von Beckerath sees Pantjeny as ruling early in Dynasty XIII.

Von Beckerath would identify Pantjeny's prenomen, Sekhemrekhutowy, with a series of Nile records found at the Second Cataract fort of Semna. However, Ryholt would seem to have proved that the inscriptions date to the reign of Sobekhotep I, whose prenomen is also Sekhemrekhutowy.

References:

Budge 1913 p. 9 pl. XXVI, pl. 26
Helck 1983 pp. 2-3 #4
Petrie 1903 pp. 34 #55, 44 pl. XXXI, pl. XXXI
Ryholt 1997a pp. 163 and note 593, 165 table 27, 264, 304, 316-317 and table 91, 319-320, 392 File Abyd/b
von Beckerath 1999 pp. 88 #3, 89 #3

Pe-Hor   Dynasty 00

p-$ḥrw$
Pe-Hor

Length of Reign:	Unknown
Tomb:	Qustul, L 2(?)
Mummy:	Unknown

Consorts:	Unknown	**Variant Names:**	None
Manetho:	Not given		
King Lists:	None		

Excavations at Qustul Cemetery L in Lower Nubia have yielded what some scholars consider an early Horus name. Read as Pe-Hor, the "name" is scratched into an already-fired jar and consists of a crudely incised bird standing atop what may be the hieroglyph for "p." Below these two signs is what might be a "ka" sign. It is evidently not a part of the name.

The quality of the inscription on the Qustul jar is similar to that on some of the jars from the B Cemetery at Abydos and has been read as "Iry-Hor" by some Egyptologists. However, Pe-Hor would have lived several generations earlier and several hundred miles south of Iry-Hor's territory.

It should be borne in mind that the inscription may not be a name, but simply a mark of royal ownership.

References:

Adams 1985 pp. 185-192
von der Way 1993 pp. 99, 101, 118 note 850
Williams 1980 pp. 12-21
Williams 1986 pp. 149, 164, table 40, 42, pl. 76-77
Williams 1987 pp. 19 f.

Pepi   SIP

Horus Name: Unknown

Nomen: *ppy*
Pepi

Prenomen: Unknown

Two Ladies: Unknown

Golden Falcon: Unknown

Length of Reign:	Unknown
Tomb:	Unknown
Mummy:	Unknown

Consorts:	Unknown	**Variant Names:**	Pepy Phiops
Manetho:	Not given		
King Lists:	None		

Pepi I

This nomen is found on a scarab of unknown provenance now in the Metropolitan Museum of Art. Ryholt believes the scarab's decoration suggests that it be dated to the Second Intermediate Period.

References:

Newberry 1907 p. 15, pl. IV #51
Newberry 1913 pp. 117-118, pl. XXX #3

Ryholt 1997a p. 400 File N/1
Winlock 1947 pl. 21 row 3 #3

Pepi I   Dynasty VI

Horus Name:

Nomen:

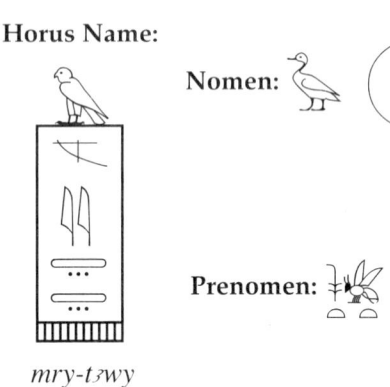

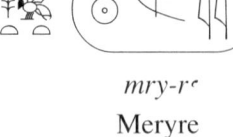

ppy
Pepi

Prenomen:

nfr-s3-ḥr
Nefersahor

mry-tзwy

mry-rˁ
Meryre

Two Ladies:

nbty mry-ḫt

Golden Falcon:

bik-nbw ḥrw

Length of Reign:	35 years.
Tomb:	Pyramid at Saqqara: "The Perfection of Meryre is Established"
Mummy:	Hand; present location unknown

Pepi I

Consorts:	Ankhenespepi I Ankhenespepi II Inenet-inti Mehaa Meritites IV Nebwenet Nedjeftet	**King Lists:** **Variant Names:**	Ab: (36); S: (34); T: ([4.3]); SSA Hor-nefer-hen Merire Pepy Phiops
Manetho:	Phios (A) Phius (A)		Piopi Pipi

The son of Teti and his consort Iput, Pepi I was the third pharaoh of Dynasty VI, having been preceded by the little-known king Userkare. It has been suggested that Userkare was a usurper, perhaps a son of Unas, last king of Dynasty V. Others posit that Userkare was an older brother of Pepi who held the throne only during Pepi's minority, or that he was Teti's legitimate heir and successor, but he died without issue, thus passing the kingship to Pepi. Manetho tells us that Teti was assassinated; if true, it might explain an interloper (Userkare?) claiming the throne.

However rocky the beginning of Pepi's rule might have been, it is doubtful that the new king was prepared for the attempt upon his life, allegedly by one of his queens, that occurred in the early years of his reign. We do not know the exact year, nor have we the name of the queen, but we do have the autobiography of the man who judged her: Weni, leader of troops, architect, judge and eventual governor of Upper Egypt. Sadly, we don't know the outcome of the trial. It has also been suggested that there was a second attempt on Pepi's life, but that would have happened much later in his life; this is only supposition on the part of a few scholars.

Despite early problems, the reign of Pepi I appears to have been one of the most prosperous of the entire Old Kingdom. Petrie wrote: "This king has left more monuments, large and small, than any other ruler before the XIIth. Dynasty." Whether Petrie was right is hard to say, but Pepi I built at Bubastis, Saqqara, Abydos, Dendera, and Elephantine, i.e., the entire length of Egypt. Numerous non-architectural attestations also exist: a decree at Dahshur, inscriptions at the Hatnub quarries, a decree at Coptos, graffiti at Wadi Hammamat, a graffito at El Kab, graffiti at Silsila, rock inscriptions at Elephantine and more such inscriptions in Nubia, at Sehel and at Tumas.

Many smaller items are also known; these include statuettes, cylinder-seals, vases, plaques and scarabs. A magnificent pair of statues of an adult and a young person striding, made of beaten copper, comes from Hierakonpolis. One suggestion is that this group represents Pepi and his son, the future pharaoh Merenre; another is that it represents Pepi as a child and as an adult.

Pepi I

Somewhere around regnal year ten, Pepi changed his prenomen from Nefersahor to Meryre. The reason for the change is disputed.

Pepi was very active outside of Egypt. His name has been found on fragments of alabaster vases in the temple of Baalat-Gebal at Byblos—in fact, three dozen inscriptions bearing the names of Pepi I and Pepi II have been found there. An additional eight other fragments inscribed with Pepi I's cartouche come from Byblos, but are otherwise of unknown provenance.

Two inscriptions at Wadi Maghara in Sinai would indicate that the turquoise mines there were again in use during Pepi's reign, for the first time since the reign of Dynasty V king Djedkare Isesi, a century earlier.

Military actions were certainly not uncommon under Pepi: the courtier Weni tells us that he personally led five, possibly six, military expeditions against the "Sand-dwellers," i.e., the Bedouin peoples living to the north of Sinai.

While we have graffiti giving Pepi's names and the names of expedition leaders from Sehel and Tumas, military action in Nubia during this reign seems to have been slight. Weni used Nubian mercenaries in his battles with the "Sand-dwellers."

Pepi I had his pyramid built at Saqqara. When the tomb was completed, it measured 79 m. to the side and 52 m. tall. Today it is a mass of rubble some 10 m. high. The interior of the pyramid was inscribed with large sections of the Pyramid Texts and was much damaged. In the rubble was found a mummified hand. The canopic chest, still intact with fragments of the jars and a package of internal organs, sat in a recess in the burial chamber floor.

Pepi had at least five and possibly six pyramids constructed for his wives. The pyramid of Queen Ankhenespepi II is inscribed with examples of the Pyramid Texts, the first queen to be so honored. Recently found reliefs from Saqqara have turned up a new queen for Pepi, the lady Nedjeftet.

The length of Pepi's reign is much disputed. Manetho gives him a reign of 53 years; the Turin Canon gives him 20 years. A builders' inscription found on a block within the king's pyramid references Pepi's thirty-second cattle count. If the count was done biennially, Pepi's reign would be at least 64 years. However, it is more than likely that the cattle count was done annually during Dynasty VI, giving a reign of at least 32 years.

Pepi celebrated a Sed Festival, although three different dates are given for it!

References:

Anthes 1928 pl. 4 #s III-IV, pl. 5 #V
Baud and Dobrev 1995 pp. 23-92
Couyat and Montet 1912 pp. 59-60 #s 62 and 63
J.C. and D. Darnell 1997a p. 26
J.C. Darnell 2002 pp. 28-29, pl. 18
Dobrev 2003 pp. 174-177
Dodson 1994b pp. 12, 13, 110 #s 5 and 5a1, pl. IIIb
Dodson 2003 pp. 26, 75, 127
Dodson and Hilton 2004 pp. 19, 35, 70-71, 72-73, 74, 76-78
Gardiner 1961 p. 436
Gardiner and Peet 1952 pl. VII #16

Goyon 1957 pp. 53-56 #s 19(J), 20(J), 21(L), pl. VI-VIII
Hall 1913 pp. 263-265 #s 2602-2605
Hayes 1946 p. 4 (a)
Ikram and Dodson 1997 pp. 82, 278, 315, 315, 317, 321
Jidejian 1968 pp. 19, 20
Kanawati 2003 pp. 4, 169-182
Lehner 1997 pp. 19, 22, 31, 33, 55, 83, 105, 156, 157-160, 161, 163, 234
Lichtheim 1975 pp. 18-2
Naville 1891 pp. 5-7, 50, pl. XXXII
Peden 2001 pp. 5, 7-8, 10, 12
Quibell and Green 1902 pp. 27-28, 33, 34, 45, pl. L-LVI
Quibell and Petrie 1900 p. 45, pl. XLV
Spalinger 1994 pp. 303-306
Verbrugghe and Wickersham 1996 pp. 136, 192
von Beckerath 1999 pp. 62 #3, 63 #3
Waddell 1940 p. 53
Weigall 1907 pp. 108-109, pl. LVII-LVIII
Verner 1997 pp. 351-359, 360

Pepi II　　　　　　　　　　　　　　　　　　Dynasty VI

Horus Name:

nṯr-ḫ ʿw

Nomen:

ppy
Pepi

Prenomen:

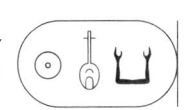

nfr-kꜣ-rʿ
Neferkare

Two Ladies:

nbty nṯr-ḫ ʿw

Golden Falcon:

bik-nbw sḥm

Length of Reign:	90+ years(?)
Tomb:	Pyramid at South Saqqara: "Neferkare is Established and Alive"
Mummy:	Unknown

Consorts:	Ankhenespepi III	Iput II
	Ankhenespepi IV	Neith A
		Udjebten

Pepi II

Manetho:	Phiops (A, E)	Piopi
King Lists:	Ab: (38); S: (36); T: (G [4.5])	Pipi
Variant Names:	Pepy	

The fifth ruler of Dynasty VI, Pepi II was the son of Pepi I and his queen Ankhenespepi II, and was the half-brother of his immediate predecessor, Merenre I. It also appears that one of Pepi II's wives, Ankhenespepi III, was the daughter of Merenre I. Two other wives of Pepi II, Neith A and Iput II, were his sisters.

Pepi seems to have attained the throne at a very young age; according to Manetho, he was only six years old. In fact, we have a copy of a letter the young king wrote to the nobleman Harkhuf concerning a dancing dwarf or pygmy that was being brought back from the Nubian kingdom of Yam as a gift for Pepi. The letter is dated in Pepi's second regnal year. The young king is very excited to be receiving such a wonder and also very concerned about the dancer's welfare: "Come northward to court immediately....My majesty desires to see this dwarf more than all the gifts of Sinai and of Punt...appoint excellent people who shall be beside him...take care lest he fall in the water...when [he] sleeps at night appoint excellent people who shall sleep beside him in his tent; inspect him ten times a night." Pepi's mother was regent during this period.

Many attestations for Pepi II have been found at Byblos in Lebanon, primarily at the temple of Baalat-Gebal. An inscription at Wadi Maghara shows that the Sinai mines were still being exploited early in Pepi's reign (second cattle count). His would be the last such expedition until Dynasty XII.

Nubia was much in Egypt's mind during Dynasty VI. The letter from the king to Harkuf quoted above was on the event of that explorer's return from his third expedition to the lands beyond Egypt's border at the island of Elephantine. Harkuf's successor, Pepinakht (called Heqaib) made two expeditions to Nubia where he had been ordered to "hack up Wawat and Irtjet." Certainly a great many goods came from Wawat, Yam and other such Nubian "kingdoms." We don't know how much of the gold and other riches pouring into the royal treasuries from Nubia were acquired through trade and how much through warfare, but assuredly much blood was spilled, many rapes committed and many towns and villages looted and burned.

In Egypt itself, Pepi's name has been found in inscriptions at the tin-mining area at Gebel El Mueilha in the eastern desert and at the Hatnub quarries near Amarna. At Elephantine is a stele mentioning his second Sed Festival. The temple at Coptos has yielded relief sculptures of the king, and his name is found in many private tombs from Aswan to Saqqara. Pepi also ordered repair of Niuserre's funerary complex, and seems to have ordered similar work at Menkaure's mortuary temple at Giza.

Pepi II chose to build his pyramid at South Saqqara, not far from those of his father and older brother. As in keeping with some sort of dynastic tradition, Pepi's pyramid measured 79 m. to the side, but was one m. taller than the previous buildings, standing 53 m. Today the pyramid is a low mound of rubble. Inside the pyramid, the ceilings are painted with stars and many of the walls were inscribed with examples of the Pyramid Texts. The mortuary temple, built against the pyramid's east side, was connected by a long causeway to Pepi's valley temple. Cut into the inner walls of the causeway are well-executed reliefs showing the typical scenes, such as the king harpooning a hippopotamus and, as a lion, trampling his enemies. Reliefs from the temples and corridor show the king bashing in the head of a Libyan chieftain (most likely merely a conventional scene—it is doubtful Pepi ever fought a Libyan!). The pyramids of three of Pepi's queens, Ankhenespepi III, Udjebten and Iput II (all bearing Pyramid Texts) are located around his complex.

Though Pepi II came to the throne at a very early age and reigned for many years, the exact length is open to some discussion. Manetho, who is usually not particularly trustworthy, is more or less in agreement with the Turin Canon, giving a reign of 94 years, while the Canon gives "90 + x" years. The highest dated contemporary attestation comes from a much-damaged decree found at the pyramid site of Queen Udjebten and gives us a thirty-third cattle count. If the cattle count was done biennially, it would give us a regnal year 66. Pepi celebrated at least three Sed Festivals. In favor of the highest year possible is the evidence for the loss of royal authority and centralized government to various local dynasties toward the end of the reign.

Pepi was succeeded by several sons, beginning with Merenre II, none of whom ruled for more than a year or two. Dynasty VI faded into a nebulous period of Egyptian history known as the First Intermediate Period.

References:

Anthes 1928 pp. 19-23, pl. X #s 3,4,5, XI #6, XII #s 7 and 8
Dodson 1994b pp. 13, 14, 111 #7
Dodson 2003 pp. 76-77, 128-129
Dodson and Hilton 2004 pp. 70-71, 72-73, 74, 76-78
Gardiner 1959 pl II, Col. IV #5
Gardiner 1961 pp. 101, 436
Gardiner and Peet 1952 pl. IX #19
Gardiner and Peet 1955 p. 28
Goedicke 1988 pp. 111-121
Hayes 1946 pp. 4-5 (b-g)
Ikram and Dodson 1998 pp. 82, 250, 315, 317
Jéquier 1928b
Jéquier 1933a
Jéquier 1936-40
Jidejian 1968 pp. 19, 20, 22
Peden 2001 pp. 4, 7-10, 63, 98 note 249
Petrie 1896b p. 4, pl. V #s 7 and 8
D. Redford 1992 pp. 56-61, 64
Rothe et al. 1996 pp. 97-100, figs. 31, 32, 35
Ryholt 2000 pp. 91
Verbrugghe and Wickersham 1996 pp. 136, 192
Verner 1997 pp. 40, 67, 80, 141, 248, 338, 339, 341, 342, 355, 359, 360, 362-366, 367-372, 373, 376
von Beckerath 1999 pp. 64 #5, 65 #5
Waddell 1940 p. 55

Pharethothes — Fictitious

According to the Jewish historian Artapanus of Alexandria, Pharethothes was king of Egypt during Dynasty XIII, when the Hebrews under Abraham arrived in Egypt. Supposedly Abraham, during his 20 year stay, taught the king astrology. Although Abraham returned to "Syria," many of the Hebrews elected to remain in Egypt.

As pointed out by J.J. Collins, Pharethothes is without doubt a fictitious name, a combination of Pharaoh and Thoth.

References:
Collins 1985 p. 897 and notes 1c-1e

...pu — Predynastic

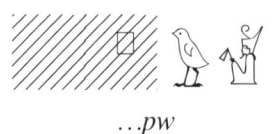

...*pw*
...pu

Length of Reign:	Unknown
Tomb:	Unknown
Mummy:	Unknown

Consorts:	Unknown	**Variant Names:**	None
Manetho:	Not given		
King Lists:	P		

...pu is one of a group of nine kings known only from the Palermo Stone. Each name is followed by a representation of a squatting king wearing the crown of Lower Egypt. Whether these names are to be taken as historic personages or mythic "ancestors" is not known.

References:
Clagett 1989 pp. 66, 97-98
Edwards 1971 pp. 3-4
Gardiner 1961 pl. III
O'Mara 1979 p. 5
T. Wilkinson 2000 pp. 62, 85-86

Qa'a — Dynasty I

Horus Name: k3-ʿ / Qa'a

Nomen: ḳbḥ / Kebh

ḳbḥw / Kebhu

Two Ladies: nbty k 3-ʿ

nbty sn

nbty sn

Golden Falcon: Unknown

Length of Reign:	33 years
Tomb:	Abydos, Umm el Qa'ab, Q
Mummy:	Unknown

Consorts:	Unknown	**Variant Names:**	Ka'a Qa Qaa Qay-a
Manetho:	Bienekhes (A) Oubienthis (E) Vibenthis (E)		
King Lists:	Ab: (8); P; S: (2); T: (G2.19)		

Qa'a was the eighth and probably the last king of Dynasty I. However, two ephemeral Horus names which may date to the end of this period, though both known only from Saqqara, seem to have been inscribed on several stone vessels originally bearing Qa'a's name (see SENEFERKA and BA). Some scholars have seen the usurpation of these few stone vessels as proof that a certain degree of political unrest followed Qa'a's death. This would seem to be pinning a great deal on very little evidence. The fact that Hotepsekhemwy, first king of Dynasty II, was apparently responsible for Qa'a's burial would likely indicate a peaceful transition between the two dynasties, if indeed there was a transition—Manetho's dynastic divisions do not always make sense.

Qa'a's tomb and funerary enclosure were the last royal funerary structures built at Abydos until the latter part of Dynasty II. Excavations carried out in recent years indicate that the tomb was constructed over a long period of time. This, coupled with the discovery of a stone bowl at Saqqara which mentions Qa'a's second Sed Festival, would seem to indicate a fairly long reign. Manetho gives this king a rule of 26 years.

While the royal tomb has undergone excavation and re-excavation, Qa'a's funerary enclosure seems to be buried beneath the Coptic village of Deir Sitt Damiana, where it is forever safe from archaeological disturbance; all we know about it is its name: "The Mound of the Gods." The tomb itself was surrounded by only 26 subsidiary burials, the smallest group in all of Dynasty I.

Two large mastaba tombs at Saqqara, Tombs 3505 and 3500, are associated with Qa'a's reign. Tomb 3505 belonged to a high official, Merka, whose funerary stele lists a great many of his titles, giving evidence of the sophistication that writing had attained by Qa'a's time. The owner of 3500 is unknown, but a jar sealing consisting of a row of Qa'a's serekh alternating with the phrase "ruling in the (king's) heart" may indicate the tomb of a consort or another important member of the royal family or court. Tomb 3500 also yielded four subsidiary graves.

Rock carvings of Qa'a's serekh have been found near El Kab, near the village of Naga el-Oqbiya (about 10 km. north of El Kab) and along the southern edge of the Wadi Hellal. These serekhs probably represent the sending of expeditions into the eastern desert and the Red Sea Hills, no doubt in search of gold and other precious minerals or, in the case of the Wadi Hellal, as a military or trading venture. It seems very likely that Qa'a was active to some extent in the Syria-Palestine area: An ivory gaming-rod from his tomb at Abydos is engraved with a picture of a bound prisoner who is identified as coming from Syria-Palestine (Stt); a small hoard of pottery vessels was also discovered from the same locale.

Qa'a's first regnal year, marking his accession to the throne, is recorded on the main Cairo fragment of the Palermo Stone. Various labels from his tomb record the foundation of a temple or other religious structure, gathering of timber, and the tours of the king about the country; two labels record the running of the Apis bull.

References:

D. Arnold 1998 p. 34
Dodson and Hilton 2004 pp. 44, 48
Emery 1949-58 pp. 5-36, 98-109,
    Pl. 1-39, 114-125
Emery 1961 pp. 86-90, 90
Gardiner 1959 pl. I, Col. II #19
Gardiner 1961 pp. 401, 430
Huyge 1984
S. Johnson 1990 pp. 55-58
Petrie 1900 pp. 5, 6, 14-16, 17, 26, 39,
    pl. XL-XLIII, XXXI, XXXVI, LX,
    LXVI #s 5 and 6, LXVII
Spencer 1993 pp. 83-84, 93, 97,
    fig. 62
Uphill 1984
Verbrugghe and Wickersham 1996
    pp. 132, 188
von Beckerath 1999 pp. 40 #8, 41 #8
Waddell 1940 pp. 29, 33, 35
T. Wilkinson 1999 pp. 80-82, 83, 239,
    300
T. Wilkinson 2000 pp. 58, 193, 201-
    202

Qahedjet   Dynasty III

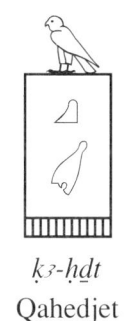

kꜣ-ḥḏt
Qahedjet

Length of Reign:	Unknown
Tomb:	Unknown
Mummy:	Unknown

Consorts:	Unknown	**Variant Names:**	Kahedjet
Manetho:	Not given		
King Lists:	None		

This Horus name was unknown until recently. In 1967, the Louvre purchased a limestone stele which bore the name Qahedjet. Although the stele's original provenance is unknown, it is likely to have come from Saqqara. The style and quality of work points to a period near the end of Dynasty III. The Horus name Qahedjet may belong to Huni, last ruler of this dynasty (see HUNI), or may represent a distinct king.

Aside from giving a new Horus name, the stele is important because it shows the earliest known example of a god, Horus, embracing a pharaoh.

Qakare Ibi

References:
Kahl et al. 1995 p. 164-165
Vandier 1968 pp. 16-22
von Beckerath 1999 pp. 50 #c, 51 #c
Vandier 1968 pp. 16-22
T. Wilkinson 1999 pp. 104
Ziegler 1990 pp. 54-57

Qakare Ibi   Dynasty VII/VIII

Horus Name: Unknown

Nomen:

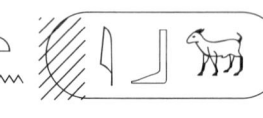

ib(i)
Ibi

Prenomen:

q3(i)-k3-rʿ
Qakare

Two Ladies: Unknown

Golden Falcon: Unknown

Length of Reign:	T: "2 years, 1 month, 1 day"
Tomb:	Pyramid at Saqqara
Mummy:	Unknown

Consorts:	Unknown	Ibi
Manetho:	Not given	Iby
King Lists:	Ab: (53); T: (G 4.11; R 5.10; vB 4.10)	Kakare Kakaure Ka?kaure Qaikare
Variant Names:	Aba	Qakaure

The Abydos King List places Qakare Ibi as the fourteenth pharaoh of Dynasty VII/VIII, and Ryholt's recent reconstruction of this part of the Turin Canon supports this position. The only other attestation for this king is a small ruined pyramid near the pyramid of Dynasty VI pharaoh Pepi II at Saqqara. The pyramid, excavated by Jéquier between the years 1929 and 1931, originally measured 31.5 m. square at the base; its height and angle are unknown. The ruins at the time of excavation were only 3 m. tall. The underground burial chamber was reached by a passage lined with limestone and both the passage and the burial chamber were inscribed with chapters from the Pyramid Texts. These texts are the latest examples to come to light so far. On the pyramid's eastern side lie the ruins of a mud brick mortuary chapel.

References:

Altenmüller 2001 p. 604
Dodson 2003 p. 78
Franke 2001 p. 527
Gardiner 1959 pl. II, Col. IV #11
Gardiner 1961 p. 436, 437 #A53
Jéquier 1935
Lehner 1997 pp. 31,
Ryholt 2000 pp. 91, 99 table 1
Verner 1997 pp. 40, 141, 362, 377-378, 465
Verner 2001a p. 93
von Beckerath 1999 pp. 68 #14, 69 #14
R. Wilkinson 2000 p. 130

Qareh   Dynasty XIV

Horus Name: Unknown

Nomen:

ka-r-$ḥ$

Qareh

Prenomen:

$ḫ^c$-wsr-r^c

Khawoserre

Two Ladies: Unknown

Golden Falcon: Unknown

Length of Reign: Unknown

Tomb: Unknown

Mummy: Unknown

Consorts: Unknown

Manetho: Not given

King Lists: None

Variant Names: Nebuahab
Qar
Shub

Possibly the third king of Dynasty XIV, Qareh is known from some thirty scarab-seals, only one of whose provenance is secure (Jericho in Canaan). Qareh, whose name translates as "the bald one," is dated by Ryholt to the early part of this dynasty based on scarab-seal seriation. Like all rulers of Dynasty XIV, Qareh held sway over the eastern Delta. Whether he was of Canaanite origin or simply of Canaanite descent is not known.

Qemau

References:
Newberry 1906 p. 150 #s 23 and 24, pl. XXI #s 23 and 24
Petrie 1978 p. xxii 16.G, pl. XXII G
Ryholt 1997a pp. 44 table 11, 96, 101 and note 329, 199 table 38, 299, 323-325, 409 #3
Ryholt 1998a pp. 194-200
von Beckerath 1999 pp. 120 #z, 121 #z

Qemau   Dynasty XIII

Horus Name: Unknown

Nomen: Unknown

Prenomen:

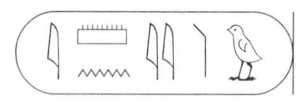

imny (sꜣ)ḳmꜣw
(Ameny's Son) Qemau

Two Ladies: Unknown

Golden Falcon: Unknown

Length of Reign:	Unknown
Tomb:	Pyramid at South Dahshur
Mummy:	Unknown

Consorts:	Unknown	Ameny Kemau
Manetho:	Not given	Ameny Qemau Aminikimau
King Lists:	T? (lacuna)	Kemau
Variant Names:	Ameny-Amu	

Qemau is probably the fifth ruler of Dynasty XIII (although von Beckerath lists him as unplaced). Ryholt presents a solid argument for Qemau having been the son of his direct predecessor, Amenemhet V, as evidenced by the use of filiative nomina in his cartouche.

Qemau's name is missing from the surviving fragments of the Turin Canon and, beyond his pyramid, only two attestations for his existence are known: fragments of four inscribed canopic jars found in the pyramid, and a small plaque-like object of unknown provenance. It has been suggested that the plaque might be a modern forgery.

Qemau's pyramid at South Dahshur was discovered in 1957 but not properly investigated and published until 1968. The superstructure, which originally measured about 50 square m., is much ruined and a great deal of damage has occurred to its underground corridors and chambers. Qemau's burial chamber was carved from a single block of quartzite, similar to the burial chamber of Amenemhet III's pyramid at Hawara.

Although attestations of this king are limited to his pyramid, there is no reason to believe that he did not rule over the whole of Egypt, with the exception of a small section of the eastern Delta which was evidently held by the early rulers of Dynasty XIV.

References:

Dodson 1987 pp. 36 fig. 1, 37 fig. 2, 38 fig. 3a, 39 fig. 3b, 40 and Note 7, 43
Dodson 1994b pp. 30, 32, 33, 36, 114, pl. Xa
Dodson 1994c pp. 27-28, 30, 31
Dodson 2000 pp. 8-14
Dodson 2003 p. 98
Edwards 1993 p. 229
Fischer 1987 p. 49 and fig. 5
Lehner 1997 pp. 185, 187
Maragioglio and Rinardi 1968 pp. 325-338
Ryholt 1997a pp. 73 #5, 81-82, 208 table 46, 214 and table 48, 215 and table 49: 284 table 83, 337 File 13/5, 408 table 94 #5
Ryholt 1997b pp. 96 table 1, 97-99, 100
Ryholt 1998b pp. 1-2
Swelim and Dodson 1998 pp. 319-334, pl. 54 and 55
Verner 1997 pp. 187, 437-438
von Beckerath 1999 pp. 102 #e, 103 #e

Ramesses I   Dynasty XIX

Horus Name:

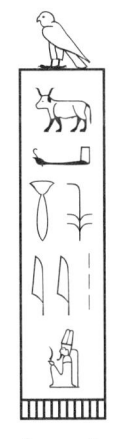

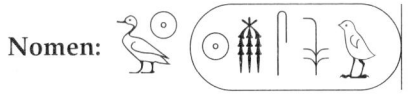

ka nḫt wȝḏ-nsyt

Nomen:

rʿ-ms-sw
Ramesses

Prenomen:

mn-pḥti-rʿ
Menpehtire

Ramesses I

Two Ladies: nbty ḫʿ-m-nsw-mi-itm

Golden Falcon: bik-nbw smn-mꜣʿt-ḫt-tꜣwy

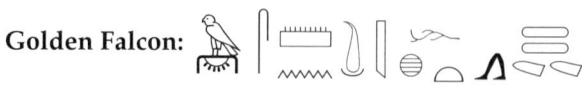

Length of Reign:	2 years
Tomb:	Valley of the Kings: KV16
Mummy:	Unknown

Consorts:	Sitre	**Variant Names:**	Paramesses Piramesses Pramesses Rameses Ramessu
Manetho:	Ramesses (J) Rapses (J) Rhamesses (A)		
King Lists:	Ab: (75); S: (56-missing)		

Late in his reign, the aging and evidently childless pharaoh Horemheb chose as coregent and successor to his throne Paramesses, a man who had served as diplomat, general, commander of the fortress of Sile, and vizier. Horemheb's choice assumed the name Ramesses, and became the first pharaoh of Dynasty XIX. He was a native of Avaris, in the eastern Delta, the son of a soldier named Sety who had been a Commandant of Troops as far back as the reign of Akhenaten. Because of his father's military stature, it was not surprising that Ramesses came to the attention of and won favor with Horemheb. The coregency probably only lasted for a few months, terminating upon the death of Horemheb. Ramesses promptly appointed his own adult son, also named Sety, as coregent, so there were perhaps only a few weeks of independent rule in a reign that lasted no more than two years.

Ramesses I appears to have been very well aware that with the death of Horemheb all ties to the pharaohs of Dynasty XVIII had been severed. As founder of a new dynasty, Ramesses harkened back to the founder of Dynasty XVIII, Ahmose, and chose as his prenomen the name Menpehtire "Enduring of Might is Re," which reflected the prenomen of Ahmose, Nebpehtire "Lord of Might is Re." The Horus names were also intentionally similar.

There was very little foreign activity during Ramesses' reign. He is known to have sent an expedition to the turquoise mines at Serabit el-Khadim in Sinai (the first known since regnal year 36 of

Ramesses I

Amenhotep III), and a foray into Canaan led by Sety that may well have been just a bit of saber-rattling to let the always troublesome city states know there was a new pharaoh to deal with. Nubia offered no problems and about the only attestation we have for Ramesses I in that region is a stele from Buhen listing new temple endowments, dated to year two of his reign.

Major attestations for Ramesses I are not plentiful due to the shortness of his reign, and are almost exclusively found in the Theban area. He may have begun the Second Pylon and the Hypostyle Hall at Karnak, but both were completed by his son and grandson. Since there was no time to build a mortuary temple for Ramesses, Sety added a chapel dedicated to his father to the temple he built at Dra Abu el-Naga.

A male mummy from a privately owned museum in Niagara Falls, Canada, was purchased for the Michael C. Carlos Museum at Emory University, Atlanta, Georgia and went on display in 2003. The mummy, that of a balding, late-middle-aged man who would have stood a little over 1.6 m. tall and whose arms were crossed over the chest, is believed by some to be the remains of Ramesses I; the identification is based upon the mummy's crossed arms and its profile's similarity to that of Sety, Ramesses I's son. Also, the embalming technique appears to be late Dynasty XVIII or early Dynasty XIX. The mummy was returned to Egypt.

References:

Brand 1998a pp. 46-57
Brier 1994 pp. 107, 108, 270
Dodson and Hilton 2004 pp. 17, 36, 123, 158, 159, 160-162, 171, 173, 174, 175
El Madhy 1989 pp. 35, 90
Forbes 1992/1993b pp. 30-33, 86-87
Forbes 1998a pp. 28, 29, 56
Forbes 2004 pp. 30-31
Gardiner and Peet 1952 pls. LXVIII-LXIX
Gardiner and Peet 1955 p. 174 #s 244 and 245
Gardiner 1961 pp. 247-249
Gibson 2000/2001 pp. 18-29
Gibson-Kirwin 1992/1993 p. 37
Grajetzki 2005 p. 65
Harris and Weeks 1973 pp. 151
Ikram and Dodson 1998 pp. 226, 261, 263, 315, 318, 325, ill. 288
G. Johnson 2000/2001 pp. 62-75
Kitchen 1982 pp. 15-20
Murnane 1977 pp. 182-183, 234
Peden 2001 pp. 113 and note 329, 146
Reeves 1990b pp. 91-92, 246
Reeves and Wilkinson 1996 pp. 36-37, 47, 58-59, 72, 78, 130, 134-135, 137-138, 143, 195-197, 203, 207
M. Rose 2003 pp. 18-25
Spalinger 2005 pp. 172, 176, 177, 184, 192, 193
Trope and Lacovara 2003 pp. 45-51
Tyldesley 2006 pp. 142
van Dijk 2000 pp. 294-295
Verbrugghe and Wickersham 1996 pp. 142, 159, 199
von Beckerath 1999 pp. 148 #1, 149 #1
Waddell 1940 pp. 103, 109, 113
R. Wilkinson 2000 p. 174
Winlock 1937

Ramesses II   Dynasty XIX

Horus Name:

kꜣ nḫt mry-mꜣꜥt

Nomen:

rꜥ-ms-sw mry-imn
Rameses (meryamen)

Prenomen:

wsr-mꜣꜥt-r stp.n-rꜥ
Usermaatre-setepenre

Two Ladies:

nbty mk-kmt-ḫꜣswt

Golden Falcon:

bik-nbw wsr-rnpwt ꜥꜣ-nḫtw

Length of Reign:	67 years
Tomb:	Valley of the Kings: KV7
Mummy:	Royal Cache at Deir el-Bahri Now at Cairo Museum: JE26214; CG61078

Consorts:	Bintanath (I)		Miamûn (J)
	Henutmire		Ramesses (A, E)
	Isetneferet (I)		Rampses (J)
	Maathorneferure		Rhamessês
	Meryetamen		Miamoun (J)
	Nebettawy		Rhampses (E)
	Nefertari		Rhapsakes (A)
	Sutererey		
		King Lists:	Ab2: (last row)
Diodorus:	Osymandias	**Variant**	
Manetho:	Aegyptus (E)	**Names:**	Rameses
	Harmessês		Ramessu

Ramesses II

The son of the pharaoh Sety I and Queen Tuia, Ramesses II was the third king of Dynasty XIX. He succeeded his father after having served as Prince Regent for perhaps as long as six years; for the last two years he may have served as coregent. He was most certainly born during the latter years of the reign of the pharaoh Horemheb, last king of Dynasty XVIII, and was probably in his early twenties when he assumed the throne. By that time he had gained considerable military experience, having accompanied his father on a campaign against a Libyan invasion of Egypt's western Delta and on a major campaign against the Hittites in which the Egyptian army recaptured Kadesh (although it was soon lost again). Also, in Sety's year 13, the young prince led an expedition of his own to quell a minor uprising in Nubia, and not long after that was called upon to chastise a horde of Mediterranean pirates, the Sherden, who had raided the eastern Delta. Shortly thereafter, Sety died, probably in the palace at Avaris. He was taken south to be buried in his tomb in the Valley of the Kings at Thebes, where Ramesses was officially crowned pharaoh in the temple of Amen at Karnak.

Egypt's days of empire were all but finished by the time Ramesses II inherited the throne. While Horemheb and Sety I had managed to reconquer a portion of the former holdings in Syria-Palestine that had been lost during the Amarna Period, the Hittites held most of northern Syria and had recently destroyed Egypt's powerful ally, Mitanni. The loyalty of Egyptian vassals in these areas was questionable in most cases, and the Hittites found it politically expedient to foment as much trouble as possible among the always bickering petty princes. In response to the unrest, Ramesses led at least six separate campaigns in Syria-Palestine between his fourth and twenty-first regnal years. While Ramesses claimed a great victory against the Hittites at Kadesh in year five, this particular campaign in actuality culminated in a near-disastrous rout by the Hittite forces; the timely arrival of Egyptian reinforcements made retreat possible and probably saved the pharaoh's life. The Egyptians returned rapidly to Egypt; taking advantage of this situation, many of the city states rebelled. Ramesses was forced to return again and again, sometimes fighting the Hittites, sometimes the local "kings." Eventually, Ramesses was able to re-establish enough control that he was able to place garrisons of Egyptian soldiers, as well as governors and other officials, in a number of principalities. Thus the tribute could continue to be delivered to Egypt every year. Peace came only when the Hittites, beleaguered by the Assyrians, finally signed a treaty with Egypt in year 21 of Ramesses' reign. This allowed Ramesses a firmer hand on his "vassals," and eventually garnered him two Hittite princesses as wives.

The turquoise mines at Serabit el-Khadim in Sinai were worked during this reign and stelae, inscribed blocks, fragments of small statues and other inscribed remains are common.

Ramesses II

Nubia, as always, remained a cash cow, supplying gold, exotic woods, animals, incense, and slaves. The land had evidently remained quiet since Ramesses' punitive campaign as a prince under Sety I. However, a revolt in the territory of Irem sprang up and was ruthlessly crushed in or about Ramesses' regnal year 20. This also seems to have been used as something of a training expedition for several of the Egyptian princes, including Merenptah, who would succeed his father some 47 years later.

Ramesses built extensively in Nubia, his first effort being a small rock-cut temple at Beit el-Wali, just south of Aswan, built in honor of his victory as Crown Prince. Other temples were built at el-Sebua, Serra East, el-Derr, Amara West, and of course the magnificent temple at Abu Simbel, with its smaller temple dedicated to Queen Nefertari and the goddess Hathor. At most of the temples Ramesses was worshipped as a god, usually in conjunction with Amen.

If the reign of Amenhotep III was the Golden Age of ancient Egypt, the 67 year reign of Ramesses might be called the Gilded Age. In place of a vast and wealthy empire enriched by constant tribute and the spoils of great victories, Ramesses led a country constrained by a web of treaties and trade agreements. Despite his pretensions of power and glory, Ramesses' Egypt lacked the greatness of his predecessors. In addition to greatly exaggerating his military prowess, Ramesses also aspired to be a great builder, in particular to outdo Amenhotep III. He wanted a larger palace, larger statues, and more temples than any preceding pharaoh, and he wanted them built in his lifetime. He "achieved" this goal by erecting a series of often huge, sometimes shoddily built temples from Upper Nubia to the eastern Delta. He further glorified himself by usurping many existing temples from his most prominent forebearers, with a particular focus on those built by Amenhotep III and the classical period pharaohs of Dynasty XII. Ramesses further expanded his legacy by taking at least eight wives (some of them his daughters) and by fathering more than 100 children.

A partial list of buildings constructed or added to by order of Ramesses II during 67 years on the throne will give some idea of the vast effort expended by the tens of thousands of men, free and slave, involved in the cutting and hauling of the stone, as well as the masons, architects, and endless bureaucracy needed to oversee dozens of projects over scores of years. An entire city, meant to be Ramesses' new capital, Pi-ramesses, was built near the Summer Palace at Avaris, in the eastern Delta. A temple to Hathor was built at Memphis, and at Crocodilopolis in the Faiyum a temple to Sobek was added to and extended. In Middle Egypt, at Ihnasya el-Medina the temple to the god Herishef was enlarged, a temple was built at el-Shiek Ibada, and a pylon was added at el-Ashmunein. At Abydos, Ramesses built a small limestone temple near the temple of Osiris, a cenotaph temple, and he completed the cenotaph of Sety I. Additions were made to the temple of Hathor at Dendera, the temple of

Nekhbet at El Kab, and the temple of Khnum at Elephantine. A rock-cut temple was built at Gebel Silsila. This was all in addition to the seven major temples built in Nubia.

Of course, much of the most spectacular work was done in the Theban area. The temple of Amen at Karnak received, among other things, an avenue of ram-headed sphinxes (120 in total), a massive gateway, and a pair of obelisks. Ramesses also finished the decorations to the great Hypostyle Hall of Sety I. This was done by adding scenes of some of the highlights of Ramesses' reign, including his own coronation, the "victory" at Kadesh, and the Hittite treaty, as well as by usurping some of Sety's cartouches; the final touch was naming the temple "Glorious is Ramesses in the Domain of Amen." At the temple at Luxor, he completed Sety's forecourt and pylon (adding, of course, scenes from Kadesh), and usurped colossal statues and two obelisks (among other things).

Across the Nile, Ramesses completed his father's mortuary temple at Dra Abu el-Naga and built his own, known today as "The Ramesseum." Unlike some of Ramesses II's building projects, his mortuary temple was carefully constructed over a period of 20 years. When complete, the temple was huge, and included two hypostyle halls, a barque shrine, a palace, vast numbers of storage magazines, and quarters for staff and servants. The temple, dotted by colossal statues of the pharaoh, was beautifully carved with reliefs of Ramesses and various deities, as well as the ubiquitous scenes of the battle at Kadesh.

Ramesses II's tomb in the Valley of the Kings, while not the longest (at a little over 80 m.), is probably the largest, covering an area of about 820 square m., mostly due to the very large size of the burial chamber and associated auxiliary chambers. The decorations, although much destroyed or missing completely, are of a high quality, though not to be compared with the magnificent works to be seen in the tomb of his principal wife, Queen Nefertari, in the Valley of the Queens (QV66).

Ramesses II also provided for the afterlife of his sons. A massive multilevel tomb in the Valley of the Kings (KV5) contains dozens and dozens of chambers intended for the burials of the various princes. Although the tomb is much destroyed due to flooding, erosion and vandalism, it is still possible to see several scenes of Ramesses and various sons (there were more than 50) before the gods.

Beginning in regnal year 30 and ending in year 66, Ramesses II celebrated a total of 14 Sed Festivals. He died a few months into his sixty-seventh year on the throne. He was succeeded by his thirteenth eldest son, Merenptah; all older sons had died during his long reign.

The mummy of Ramesses II, found in the Royal Cache at Deir el-Bahri, was 1.733 m. in length, and revealed the king to have been at least 80 years old at death, and perhaps as old as 90. The pharaoh suffered from abscesses and was missing a great many teeth. He also suffered from arthritis in his hip and severe arteriosclerosis. His last years were undoubtedly painful.

Ramesses III

References:

Brier 1994 pp. 90, 107, 108, 172, 194-207, 219, 270-272, 276, 300
Bucaille 1990 pp. vii-x, xii-xv, xvii, xviii, 5, 6, 9, 10, 5, 6, 9, 10, 17-18, 21, 27, 28, 56, 59-60, 63, 64, 75, 78-80, 94-98, 100-107, 112-114, 122, 129, 135, 142-152, 163-228, figs. 2, 3, 6, 30, 33, 35 36, 43, 44, 48
Dodson and Hilton 2004 pp. 14-16, 22, 23, 29, 33, 34, 137, 146, 158-176, 179, 183, 186, 188, 186, 188, 198, 284 note 52, 285 notes 125 and 128
El Madhy 1989 pp. 11, 27, 31, 37, 50, 51, 72, 75, 82, 84, 87, 88, 89, 90, 132-133, 166
Forbes 1998a pp. 636-641
Gardiner 1960
Gardiner 1961 p. 445
Gardiner and Peet 1952 pls. LXV A, LXVIII-LXXII
Gardiner and Peet 1955 pp. 174 #244, 176-181 #s 250-261, 181-183 #s 263-264
Grajetzki 2005 pp. 66-69
Harris and Weeks 1973 pp. 101, 112, 153-156
Hawass 2000
Ikram and Dodson 1998 pp. 42, 45, 91, 95, 96, 121, 128, 216, 235, 252, 261, 263, 266, 288, 315, 318, 325, ills. 39, 122-123, 288
Murnane 1977 pp. 57-87
D. Redford 1992 pp. 181-191
Reeves 1990b pp. 94-95
Reeves and Wilkinson 1996 pp. 8, 21, 23-24, 26, 35, 36-37, 42, 45, 51, 53-54, 56, 60, 80, 84, 86, 88, 106, 109, 115, 125, 138, 140-148, 150, 162, 172, 191, 194-197, 201, 203, 206-207, 209-210
Sanchez 2003 pp. 58-65
Schmidt 1973
Tyldesley 2006 pp. 144, 145-159
Partridge 1994 pp. 154-158
G. Smith 1912 pp. 59-65, pl. XLII-XLIV
Verbrugghe and Wickersham 1996 pp. 142, 159, 162, 180, 199
von Beckerath 1999 pp. 152-157 #3
Waddell 1940 pp. 103, 109, 117, 119
Weeks 1992 pp. 99-121
Weeks 1998
R. Wilkinson 2000 pp. 59-60, 106, 108, 111, 115, 137, 138, 139-140, 144-146, 149, 155, 157-158, 160, 166, 168, 173-174, 182-186, 203, 208, 211, 217, 219-220, 221-222, 223-228, 228-229
Zuhdi 1997/1998 pp. 60-73

Ramesses III   Dynasty XX

Horus Name:

kꜣ nḫt ꜥꜣ-nyst

Nomen:

rꜥ-ms-sw ḥkꜣ-iwnw
Ramesses (hekaiunu)

Prenomen:

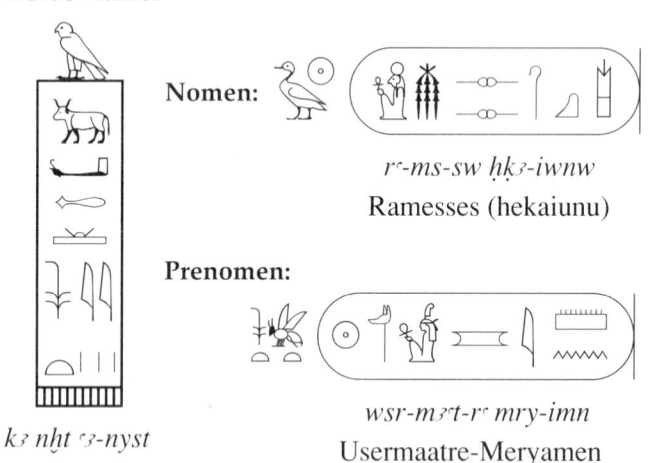

wsr-mꜣꜥt-rꜥ mry-imn
Usermaatre-Meryamen

Ramesses III

Two Ladies: *nbty wr-ḥȝbw-sd-mi-tȝtnn*

Golden Falcon: *bik-nbw wsr-rnpwt-mi-itm*

Length of Reign:	32 years
Tomb:	Valley of the Kings: KV11
Mummy:	Royal cache at Deir el-Bahri Now at Cairo Museum: JE26208b; CG61083

Consorts:	Iset Tiye	**Variant Names:**	Rameses Ramessu Usimare
Manetho:	Not given		
King Lists:	None		

The second pharaoh of Dynasty XX, Ramesses III was the son and successor of Setnakht and Queen Tiye. Ramesses was almost certainly an adult at the time of his succession, perhaps as old as 30. He may have been an officer in the Egyptian army, although there is no real evidence to back such a supposition. It is possible that he was coregent with his father, as a chapel in the "Sanctuary of Ptah," near Deir el-Medina, was evidently decorated by the two kings, and their figures and cartouches are juxtaposed on two panels of relief and a lintel found there. Also, there is a scarab, now in the British Museum (No. 17134), on which the prenomina of Setnakht and Ramesses are found together.

Setnakht, an interloper who claimed the throne at the collapse of Dynasty XIX, had ruled for only two years. His reign was not nearly long enough to make sense of the chaos and corruption that had undoubtedly run rampant during the ephemeral reigns preceding his takeover. It seems likely that the first several years of Ramesses' reign were thus taken up with administrative duties and the rebuilding of central authority. That Ramesses' administrative structure was made sound is perhaps proven by the quick response of the Egyptian army to an emergency in the western Delta.

Just a little more than two decades prior to Ramesses III's reign, the pharaoh Merenptah of Dynasty XIX had been forced to repel an invasion of Libyan tribes. That confederation of tribes had returned to the western Delta, and Ramesses, in his fifth regnal year, led an army of infantry and chariots against them. Reliefs from the pharaoh's mortuary temple at Medinet Habu show us the various tribes and the columns of Egyptian soldiers who opposed them. If the numbers of the slain and captured Libyans are any indication (and if there is any truth in them), the invasion must have been huge; the captives are given as 1,000, while the dead are given as an amazing 12,535. The piles of severed hands and penises cut as trophies from the dead tribesmen are carved on the temple walls for the entire world to see, as is Ramesses returning in his chariot. The pharaoh is shown basking in the glory of Amen; piled on the chariot's floor, surrounding his feet, are amputated hands, destined to be displayed on city and temple walls.

An even more serious danger arose in regnal year eight, when an invasion by land and sea threatened Egypt's very existence. Called the "Sea People," a vast wave of humanity made up of various tribes and nationalities had spread across Greece, the Aegean islands, Anatolia and Syria-Palestine. The mass migration was caused by many things including natural disasters (earthquakes, volcanic eruptions and drought) and the breakdown of central authority in all of the areas mentioned above. By the time Egypt confronted these peoples (which included the Philistines), the Hittite empire had fallen, as had Cyprus, Amurru, Arzawa, Carchemesh and all the city-states in Syria-Palestine. Ramesses III, in no position to be the aggressor, seems to have taken a defensive position. In either southern Canaan or at the Egyptian border, his forces drove the invaders back. At the same time, a sea battle of sorts took place, evidently in the northeastern Delta. The Egyptian Navy, such as it was, confronted a fleet of enemy vessels and trounced them thoroughly, while Ramesses personally directed the battle from the shore.

In year eleven, another attack on Egypt's western Delta was launched by a new Libyan tribal coalition. As before, Egyptian troops were able to repulse them. Enemy losses as recorded at Medinet Habu came to 2,175 dead and 2,052 prisoners.

Ramesses III also claimed a military campaign against the Hittites and against the Nubians. The majority of scholars consider these expeditions bogus. Reliefs and texts for the Hittite campaign were lifted from the mortuary temple of Ramesses II and the Hittite empire had ceased to exist very early in Ramesses III's reign, if not before. The Nubian war seems to have never been fought, as the battle scenes found at Medinet Habu were made up of conventional representations taken from earlier reliefs. These fictions have led some scholars to doubt all of Ramesses' campaign records.

From regnal year 12 until year 29, Egypt seems to have been allowed to remain at peace. During this period at least one expedition each was sent to the turquoise mines at Serabit el-Khadim, the copper mines at Timna (both in Sinai), and the distant land of Punt, for incense and other exotic items. Neither did Ramesses neglect Nubia. Attestations for activity in that land have been found at Gebel Barkal, Sai Island, Kawa, Amarah West, Aniba, Soleb Semna, Buhen, Faras, Qasr Ibrim, and other sites.

Despite the loss of perhaps all of Egypt's foreign holdings in Syria-Palestine, the country was exceedingly wealthy, and this allowed Ramesses III to spend vast fortunes on the construction of new temples and monuments and the refurbishing of the old. Evidence of building activities include the construction of a temple of Sutekh (the Syrian version of Set) at Piramesses, a new palace and temple at Tell el Yahudiya, a chapel to Mnevis at Heliopolis, a way station for the temple of Ptah at Memphis, and other buildings, statuary, and stelae at Ashmunein, Asyut, Abydos, Dendera, Coptos, El Kab, and Elephantine. As with all New Kingdom pharaohs, the vast majority of building activity centered around the Theban area. A great deal of construction was done at Karnak, including a small temple to Amen, a temple to Khonsu and additions, inscriptions and repairs throughout the entire temple complex. Across the Nile, Ramesses built his great mortuary temple "United with Eternity" at Medinet Habu. The vast area was not just the temple itself, but a great complex of temples, shrines, a palace, priests' quarters, soldiers' barracks and storage magazines; a great wall surrounded the whole. Almost the entire complex was decorated with beautifully executed reliefs, and it is from these and the Harris Papyrus that we gather most of what we know of Ramesses' wars and accomplishments. Ramesses' tomb in the Valley of the Kings (KV11) was originally begun for Setnakht, but was abandoned by that king after only three chambers had been dug. Ramesses had the tomb expanded until its length was 125 m. long. The tomb is beautifully decorated throughout.

Trouble seems to have dogged Ramesses' last years. The loss of a great deal of Syria-Palestine, and the yearly tribute therefrom, had undoubtedly affected the Egyptian economy adversely, as had the constant drain caused by continuous building projects and temple donations: an estimated one-third of all cultivable land belonged to temple estates, and of that, 75 percent was owned by the god Amen. This led to an imbalance in the delicate distribution of power between church and state, which further weakened an economy already plagued by the effects of corruption. Increased grain prices and consequent reductions in grain rations for the workers led to history's first known labor disputes, as the tomb builders went on a series of organized strikes in year 29. In that same year, an unnamed vizier led a revolt against the pharaoh that led to a siege of the city of Athribis. By the time of the king's Sed Festival celebration in year 30, a series of low inundations had caused grain shortages and famine, tomb robbery was rampant, and Libyan rebels dared to harass the west bank at Thebes in year 28.

A short time later, on the anniversary of his thirty-second year as pharaoh, assassins struck at Ramesses. The attempt was instigated by Tiy, a minor queen seeking to put her son on the throne. Although Ramesses survived for about three weeks, he died on the fifteenth day of the third month of summer, presumably from inflicted wounds. Despite the efforts of the conspirators, prince Ramesses (later Ramesses IV) succeeded to the throne after seeing to the funeral of his father.

The mummy of Ramesses III was found in the Royal Cache at Deir el-Bahri. When it was partially unwrapped, the mummy proved to be the well-preserved body of a man probably in his mid-sixties at the time of death. No discernible cause of death could be found. He was obese in life and stood a little taller than the 1.683 m. that his mummy measured.

References:

Brier 1994 pp. 91, 267, 268, 275-276, 277
Dodson 1995 pp. 142-147, 148, 150, 159, 209, 216
Dodson 1997 pp. 29-43
Dodson and Hilton 2004 pp. 31, 33, 165, 179, 184, 185, 186-190, 192-194, 196, 198, 205, 209, 238
Drews 1993 pp. 4-6, 19, 21, 48, 50-53, 153-154, 158-161, 210-211, 222, 223
Edgerton and Wilson 1936
El Madhy 1989 pp. 37, 86, 98, 115, 136
Forbes 1998a pp. 642-645
Gardiner and Peet 1952 pl. LXXIII
Gardiner and Peet 1955 pp. 116, 186-187 #s 272-273
Grajetzki 2005 pp. 74-75
Grandet 1993
Hall 1913 pp. 231-235 #s 2306-2343
Harris and Weeks 1973 pp. 160, 161-164, 167
Ikram and Dodson 1998 pp. 49, 63, 73, 226, 263-265, 315, 318, 327, ills. 371-372
Lesko 1980 pp. 83-86
McIntyre 1990 pp. 12-17, 60-63
Montet 1981 pp. 235-236
Murnane 1977 pp. 185-186
Partridge 1994 pp. 171-173
Peden 1994a pp. 7-68, 187-224
Peden 1994b pp. 1-13, 14, 16, 18-22, 78-79
Peden 2001 pp. 86, 120, 121-122, 124, 127, 128, 130, 131, 166, 182-187
S. Redford 2002
Reeves 1990b pp. 115, 116
Reeves and Wilkinson 1996 pp. 16, 21, 23-24, 25-27, 29-30, 36-37, 45, 51, 53-54, 55, 56, 61-62, 64, 69, 72, 77, 79-80, 130, 143, 145-147, 150, 154, 159-161, 165-166, 169, 191, 193, 195, 196, 199, 200, 203, 205-209
Siliotti 1996 pp. 62-63, 124-128
G. Smith 1912 pp. 84-87, pl. L-LII
Strudwick 1999 pp. 86-87, 89-90
Tyldesley 2006 pp. 167-171
van Dijk 2000 pp. 304-306
von Beckerath 1999 pp. 164-167 #2
R. Wilkinson 2000 pp. 44, 45, 50-51, 61, 67-68, 71, 77, 78, 84, 93, 95, 106, 156
Zuhdi 2001/2002 pp. 42-52

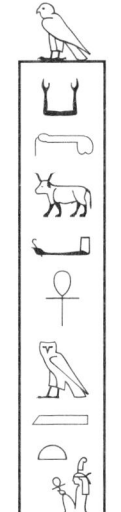

Ramesses IV — Dynasty XX

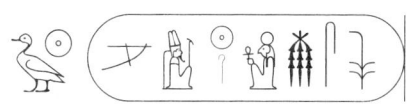

Horus Name:

kꜣ nḫt ꜥnḫ-m-mꜣꜥt

Nomen: *rꜥ-ms-sw ḥkꜣ-mꜣꜥt mry-imn*
Ramesses (hekamaat-meryamen)

Prenomen: *wsr-mꜣꜥt-rꜥ stp.n-imn*
Usermaatre-setepenamen

ḥkꜣ-mꜣꜥt-rꜥ stp.n-rꜥ
Hekamaatre-setepenre

Two Ladies: *nbty mk-kmt wꜥf-pdt-9*

Golden Falcon: *bik-nbw wsr-rnpwt wr-nḫtw*

Length of Reign:	6 years
Tomb:	Valley of the Kings: KV2
Mummy:	Tomb of Amenhotep II Now at Cairo Museum: JE34597; CG61084

Consorts:	Duatentopet	Ramessu
Manetho:	Not given	Usimare-setepenre
King Lists:	None	
Variant Names:	Rameses	

317

Ramesses IV

The third king of Dynasty XX, Ramesses IV was the son of Ramesses III and Queen Iset. Although Ramesses IV was the fifth son of Ramesses III, the four older princes had died, and he apparently became crown prince in year 22 of his father's reign. Unlike most princes of Egypt, Ramesses IV's career prior to his succession to the throne is relatively well documented. He is shown in reliefs in his father's temple in the Amen temple complex at Karnak and his father's mortuary temple at Medinet Habu. His tomb as prince, located in the Valley of the Queens (QV53), has survived, though in a much-damaged state. He is also known from the tomb of Amenopet (Theban Tomb 148), where he is shown participating in the investiture of that worthy courtier as high priest of the goddess Mut. He is further known from a fragment of inscribed stone lintel, perhaps from Piramesses in the Delta, and a graffito from the temple of Amenhotep III at Soleb in Nubia.

Ramesses IV's titles include Hereditary Prince, Royal Scribe and "Generalissimo." It is probably safe to assume from the latter appellation that he was active in the military. It has been suggested that the prince may have done a tour of duty in Nubia during year five of Ramesses III's reign, but this is far from certain.

Ramesses IV inherited the throne upon the death of his father in the latter's thirty-second regnal year. Ramesses III had evidently fallen victim to an assassination plot hatched by a minor queen, Tiy, who desired to see her son, Pentaweret, become pharaoh. Ramesses III apparently died a few weeks after the attack, but as Pentaweret did not become pharaoh, the plot ultimately failed. A trial was held and Pentaweret and eight others were allowed to commit suicide; two dozen more suffered either mutilation or execution. The actual sentence given to Tiy is unknown, but she was almost certainly condemned to death.

As if an assassination attempt were not enough, Ramesses IV inherited a number of other problems. Whether through graft and corruption or simply poor management, the grain rations for the tomb workers at Deir el-Medina were repeatedly late during the first 18 months or so of the reign. Such problems had led to labor strikes during the reign of Ramesses III, and there is no reason to think that things were any different under his son. Also, the Theban area seems to have been visited by unwelcome guests in the form of Libyan tribesmen who may have taken over the oases of Kharga, Dakhla, and Farafra. Libyans had also migrated into the eastern Delta and were undoubtedly troublesome. Also, the treasury was certainly feeling the pinch of the reduction of trade and tribute from a large part of Syria-Palestine. A much-damaged stele found at Amarah West in Nubia, which internal evidence seems to date to Ramesses IV's third regnal year, appears to have recorded a sea battle and some other conflict, perhaps a battle at night. These engagements may have been in response to another incursion of the Sea People, fought on land and water as in the reign of Ramesses III.

Attestations for Ramesses IV in the Levant amount to only a few scarabs coming from Tell el-Fara South, Tell es-Safi, Tell Zakariya, and Tel-Aphek. On the other hand, activity in Sinai continued unabated, and as many as five expeditions to the turquoise mines at Serabit el-Khadim (the last in regnal year five) seem likely. Ramesses added a chapel at the temple of Hathor. Surviving reliefs show the pharaoh offering to Amen(?) and Hathor. Other objects from the temple area include an inscribed doorjamb, a statue of Thoth bearing the king's cartouches, a stone block bearing a relief of the king's head, and a doorjamb usurped from Thutmose III. Although mining activities were probably carried out at the copper mines of Timna, Ramesses IV is represented by nothing more than a few bits of glazed fragments found in that area.

Nubia seems to have remained firmly in Egyptian hands. While no Nubian building projects during the reign are known, attestations from there include a stele dated to year three found at Amarah West (mentioned above), as well as bits of inscriptions and graffiti from Gerf Hussein, Aniba, Qasr Ibrim, Buhen, and Dorginarti, among other places.

A great deal of building activity in Egypt began immediately upon Ramesses' accession to the throne. Stone was needed for a variety of projects and quarries would have been kept busy. The quarries in the Wadi Hammamat were visited four times in the first three years of the reign. The largest expedition, the fourth, employed (according to the stele that commemorated the event) a force of 9,268 men, of whom 900 are recorded as having died. Unfortunately, not many of Ramesses IV's buildings survive; most may not have gotten beyond the first stages of construction. The Papyrus Wilbour mentions temples in the Faiyum, in the vicinity of Minya, and another, possibly at Herakleopolis. An obelisk at Heliopolis, along with a set of cartouches on a pylon and an inscribed column from the temple of Ramesses II, suggest building activity there.

Early in his reign Ramesses IV had his titulary cut into the central doorway of a pylon at the temple of Sety I at Abydos. The same thing was done on a pylon of the temple of Ramesses II. Also at Abydos, inscribed plaques, evidently from a foundation deposit, indicate that Ramesses IV at least began a structure of some sort there. This may have been a cenotaph, but more likely was a chapel or small temple. Two large stelae record the pharaoh's desire for a long reign; one of them asks for a reign twice as long as that of Ramesses II, amounting to 134 years.

Although a few scraps of inscribed material come from Tod, Armant and Edfu, Ramesses IV's main attestations were found in and near Thebes. At Karnak, Ramesses IV added his titulary to the base of a colossal statue of Ramesses II and to inscriptions carved on some of the columns in the Great Hypostyle Hall. He also added his name to an obelisk of Thutmose I, and a set of texts to the Fourth Pylon. Texts were also added to Pylons VI, IX and X, and to the courts of Pylons VIII and IX. Ramesses' name was carved on two

Ramesses IV

statues of Thutmose III. Additions of his name and/or texts occurred at the temples of Mut, Maat and Montu, as well as the temple of Ramesses III. At Luxor Temple, a number of texts were inscribed on the walls of the "Long Colonnade." Texts were also added to the temple of Khonsu. Across the Nile, Ramesses IV had his titulary cut into some of the columns and colonnades at the mortuary temple of Ramesses II (the Ramesseum). At the mortuary temple of his father at Medinet Habu, Ramesses IV added texts extensively to Pylons I and II, various courts, the East Gate Tower and Pavilion, and more. Foundation deposits and a small number of inscribed stone blocks are all that remain of a temple Ramesses IV began, but most likely never completed, just north of Hatshepsut's temple at Deir el-Bahri. Another small temple was at least begun near the temple of Amenhotep III; nothing remains of it today.

It should be noted that Ramesses IV changed his prenomen from Usermaatre-setepenamen to Hekamaatre-setepenre during his second regnal year.

The tomb of Ramesses IV, KV2, lies about 100 m. north of the tomb of Ramesses II in the Valley of the Kings. The tomb had stood open since antiquity, and was empty. However, excavations at its entrance, first by Davis in 1905/1906 and later by Carter in 1920, turned up a number of very crudely made ushabtis of Ramesses, as well as various ostraca, one of which gave a sketch plan of the tomb's entrance. Interestingly enough, a very detailed plan of the tomb is to be found on a papyrus now in the Turin Museum. The decorations of the tomb are beautifully preserved and consist of chapters of the *Book of the Dead* and other sacred texts.

Ramesses IV did not live to reign twice as long as Ramesses II, as was his prayer recorded on the stele from Abydos. He seems to have held the throne for not much more than six years. It is possible that he was sickly and aware that his time was short: he doubled the number of royal tomb workers at Deir el-Medina and the tomb is relatively small, about 80 m. long.

The mummy of Ramesses IV was discovered in the tomb of Amenhotep II (KV35), in the Valley of the Kings. The body was that of an almost bald-headed man of indeterminate age; estimates vary from mid-twenties to early fifties. The mummy's length is 1.604 m.

References:

Breasted 1906 vol. IV § 416-456
Brier 1994 pp. 115, 173, 240, 276
Bucaille 1990 pp. 7, 55, 116, 118-120, 122
T. Davis 1908 pp. 6-7, 8
Dodson 1995 pp. 148-149, 209, 216
Dodson 1997 pp. 32-33, 35-37
Dodson and Hilton 2004 pp. 32, 123, 184, 186-187, 188-190, 192-194
El Madhy 1989 pp. 39, 86
Forbes 1998a pp. 688-689
Gardiner and Peet 1952 pl. LXV A, LXX-LXXII, LXXIV-LXXVII
Gardiner and Peet 1955 pp. 16, 187-192 #s 274-288
Hall 1913 pp. 235-237 #s 2344-2365
Harris and Weeks 1973 pp. 163, 164-166
Ikram and Dodson 1998 pp. 121, 264, 289, 315, 318, 327-328, ills. 373-374, 388
Partridge 1994 pp. 174-176
Peden 1994a pp. 69-72, 81-100, 133-174, 195-210
Peden 1994b

Ramesses V (Amenhirkopshef I)

Peden 2001 pp. 124-126, 130 note 458, 131-132, 198, 203-204, 245
Petrie 1978 pp. 28 #59, 38, pl. XLV, 20.2 #s 1-12
Reeves 1990b pp. 115-117
Reeves and Wilkinson 1996 pp. 24, 26-27, 28-29, 31, 37, 42, 45, 50-51, 53-54, 63, 68-69, 73, 84, 159, 162-164, 170, 173, 198-199, 201, 203, 207

Rowe 1936 p. 197 #833, pl. XXI #833
G. Smith 1912 pp. 87-90, pl. LIII-LIV, LVII
Strudwick 1999 pp. 90, 114
Tyldesley 2006 p. 171
van Dijk 2000 pp. 306-307
von Beckerath 1999 pp. 166-169 #3
R. Wilkinson 2000 pp. 181, 190

Ramesses V (Amenhirkopshef I)   Dynasty XX

Horus Name:

kꜣ nḫt mꜣʿt

Nomen:

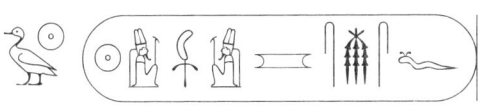

rʿ-ms-sw imn-(ḥr)-ḫpš.f
Ramesses Amenhirkopshef

Prenomen:

wsr-mꜣʿt sḫpr-n-rʿ
Usermaatre-sekheperenre

Two Ladies: Unknown

Golden Falcon:

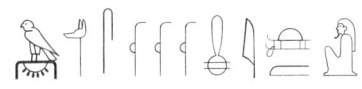

bik-nbw wsr-rnpwt-mi-itn

Length of Reign:	5 years
Tomb:	Valley of the Kings: KV9
Mummy:	Tomb of Amenhotep II Now at Cairo Museum: JE34566; CG61085

Consorts:	Henutwati Tawerettenru	**Variant Names:**	Rameses Ramessu Usimare-sekheperenre
Manetho:	Not given		
King Lists:	None		

321

Ramesses V (Amenhirkopshef I)

The fourth pharaoh of Dynasty XX, Ramesses V was the only son of Ramesses IV and his consort, Duatentopet. His original name was Amenhirkopshef, but he added "Ramesses" to his name when he became pharaoh. He inherited the throne at an extremely unstable and corrupt time in Egyptian history, and attestations for his reign are few. In keeping with the time, a papyrus dated to this reign (Turin 1887) deals with charges of embezzlement and theft in the temple of Khnum at Elephantine. Another important papyrus dated to this reign, Papyrus Wilbour, has proved invaluable to the study of the agricultural and tax structures of ancient Egypt. Written documents aside, attestations in Egypt consist of a rock-cut stele from the sandstone quarries at Gebel Silsila in Middle Egypt, a few scattered graffiti, and a handful of scarabs; from the Theban area come a dedication stele near Pylon IV of the Temple of Amen at Karnak (usurped by Ramesses X), a few inscribed blocks at the site of an unfinished temple begun by Ramesses IV near Deir el-Bahri, and an unfinished tomb begun by Ramesses V and completed by his successor, Ramesses VI.

In Sinai, Ramesses V is known to have continued working the turquoise mines at Serabit el-Khadim and the copper mines at Timna. With the exception of these mines, any sort of Egyptian control in western Asia seems to have ended by the close of the reign. Whatever military units might have remained at the end of the reign of Ramesses IV were certainly recalled by the time of the death of Ramesses V.

In Nubia, at the fortress of Buhen, Ramesses V's nomen and prenomen, juxtaposed with those of his father, were discovered on an inscribed column in Dynasty XX in addition to the temple of Horus (often referred to as the South Temple), built by Hatshepsut. Based on this inscription, Caminos mentions the interesting possibility of a coregency between the two kings, but much more evidence would be needed before such a possibility could be seriously considered.

As mentioned above, the tomb Ramesses V had begun in the Valley of the Kings, incomplete at the time of his death, was finished by his successor and uncle, Ramesses VI. The new pharaoh may have buried Ramesses V in the tomb, and had himself interred there upon his own death. However, many scholars believe Ramesses V might not have shared the tomb with Ramesses VI, but instead was buried elsewhere; perhaps in a hastily constructed, undecorated tomb.

The mummy of Ramesses V was found in the tomb of Amenhotep II (KV35), in the Valley of the Kings, where it had been moved in Dynasty XXI. Age at death is not known, but probably the king was in his mid-twenties. The face had been painted with red ochre, which did little to hide the small nodules that also covered his neck and chest, probably from smallpox. Other problems included an enlarged scrotum, due to an inguinal hernia, and an ulcer in the right groin; even the king was not immune to the ailments of the time. The mummy measured 1.726 m. in length.

References:

Amer 1985 pp. 66-67
Brier 1994 pp. 115, 173, 276
Bucaille 1990 pp. 5, 6, 54-55, 56, 73, 96, 111-112, 116, 118-120, 122, figs. 5. 6, 16, 46, 47
Caminos 1974 vol. I pp. 43-44, pl. 55
Dodson 1995 pp. 149, 209, 216
Dodson 1997 p. 37
Dodson and Hilton 2004 pp. 184, 186-187, 190, 192-194
El Madhy 1989 pp. 38, 39
Gardiner 1941-48
Gardiner and Peet 1955 p. 192 #289
Hall 1913 pp. 237-238 #s 2366-2370
Harris and Weeks 1973 pp. 166-167
Ikram and Dodson 1998 pp. 84, 121, 127, 315, 318, 328, ill. 97
Newberry 1906 p. 184 #25, pl. XXXVI #25

Partridge 1994 pp. 177-179
Peden 1989 pp. 41-45 and plate
Peden 1994b pp. 76-77
Peden 2001 pp. 123 note 458, 205
Petrie 1889 p. 54 #1682
Petrie 1906b pp. 108, 143-144, fig. 149 #s 12 and 20
Petrie 1978 pl. XLVI 20.3 #s 1-17
Randall-MacIver and Woolley 1911 pp. 17, 32
Reeves 1990b pp. 117-119
Reeves and Wilkinson 1996 pp. 24, 37, 45, 51, 53-54, 159, 164-165, 191, 198, 199, 201, 203, 207
G. Smith 1912 pp. 90-92, pl. LV-LVII
Tyldesley 2006 p. 171
von Beckerath 1999 pp. 168 #4, 169 #4

Ramesses VI (Amenhirkopshef II) Dynasty XX

Horus Name:

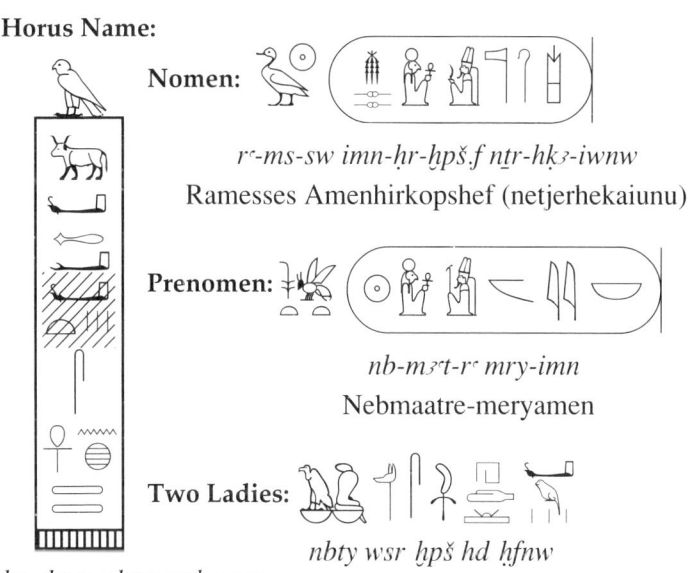

k₃ nḫt ʿ₃-nḫtw s'nḫ-t₃wy

Nomen:

rʿ-ms-sw imn-ḥr-ḫpš.f nṯr-ḥḳ₃-iwnw

Ramesses Amenhirkopshef (netjerhekaiunu)

Prenomen:

nb-m₃ʿt-rʿ mry-imn

Nebmaatre-meryamen

Two Ladies:

nbty wsr ḫpš hd ḫfnw

Golden Falcon:

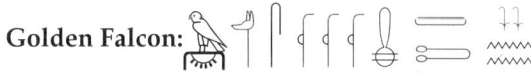

bik-nbw wsr-rnpwt-mi-t₃ṯnn

Ramesses VI (Amenhirkopshef II)

Length of Reign:	8 years
Tomb:	Valley of the Kings: KV9
Mummy:	Tomb of Amenhotep II Now at Cairo Museum: JE34562; CG61086

Consorts:	Iset Nubkhesbed	King Lists:	None
Manetho:	Not given	Variant Names:	Rameses Ramessu

The fifth king of Dynasty XX, Ramesses VI was born Amenhirkopshef II; he was the son of Ramesses III and the full brother of Ramesses IV. He adopted the name Ramesses when he took the throne after the death of his nephew and predecessor, Ramesses V, who evidently died childless.

Ramesses VI inherited a throne troubled by the corruption and instability that had plagued the reigns of his two immediate predecessors. While it was once believed that Ramesses VI had violently seized the throne during a civil war, this theory has been supplanted; recent scholarship indicates that the transition from Ramesses V to Ramesses VI was not problematic, but that the Theban area during that period was under siege from both Libyan raiders and groups of lawless Egyptian "bandits." A statue of Ramesses VI found at Karnak showing the king grasping a cowering Libyan, as well as similar statues located throughout Egypt, might commemorate the king's ousting of these troublesome pests. A much-damaged triumphal scene carved on the vestibule of Pylon II at Karnak may represent the same "victory," although no portrayal of the enemy (beyond upraised hands) has survived. There is no evidence of any military action outside Egypt during this reign.

Attestations for Ramesses VI in Egypt include statues from Tanis, Bubastis, and Coptos, an Apis burial, an inscribed gateway at Memphis and a stele from Coptos. However, the largest number of attestations to survive come from the Theban area. Apart from the statue and the relief on Pylon II, Ramesses VI's contributions to the temple at Karnak are, for the most part, nothing but usurpations, e.g., his name being carved over that of Ramesses IV on processional routes. Across the Nile, Ramesses VI continued work on the temple site near Deir el-Bahri begun by Ramesses IV and V. The temple was never finished, and nothing remains except scattered, broken blocks bearing bits of inscriptions of the three different rulers. There is also the king's tomb, discussed below.

Scarabs of Ramesses VI have been found at Gezer, Gaza, and Beth Shemesh, and an inscribed bronze statue base was discovered at Megiddo. No other evidence of an Egyptian presence in Syria-Palestine is known for the remainder of Dynasty XX. Certainly, all

Ramesses VI (Amenhirkopshef II)

Egyptian garrisons had been abandoned prior to the end of Ramesses VI's reign, if not before.

Ramesses VI was also the last pharaoh of Dynasty XX to leave attestations at the turquoise mines of Serabit el-Khadim. These included a stele usurped from an unknown king and an inscribed pillar from the temple of Hathor. Also found were a section of glazed bracelet and a fragment of inscribed vase. His regime was also apparently the last to mine copper at Timna.

Egyptian control of Nubia seems to have remained stable during the reign, though there are few attestations for Ramesses VI. These include graffiti at Aniba, Amarah West, and possibly at Qasr Ibrm, and cartouches carved in the temple of Ramesses II at Wadi es-Sabua. His cartouches have been found as far south as the Third Cataract.

Ramesses appears to have reigned three months into his eighth year, and was buried with all the pomp and splendor available at the time. His tomb in the Valley of the Kings was originally meant for Ramesses V, but remained incomplete at that pharaoh's death. The completed tomb consisted of 11 chambers, of which probably only the first four were completed by Ramesses V. As Ramesses V was not buried until the second year after his death, it is likely that Ramesses VI completed a tomb meant for both kings prior to placing his predecessor's body within it. This interpretation is supported by the fact that inscriptions relating to Ramesses V are found only in the first four corridors; the elaborate decorations of the next seven chambers are all related to Ramesses VI. Ramesses VI's tomb is a showpiece, and is considered one of the finest in the Valley of the Kings. Ironically, the construction debris from this tomb, tossed down the hillside, concealed the entrance to Tutankhamen's tomb, thus protecting it from pillaging and desecration for thousands of years. In contrast, Ramesses VI's tomb was accessed by thieves fewer than two decades after his burial (during regnal year nine of Ramesses IX).

The mummy of Ramesses VI was found in the tomb of Amenhotep II (KV35) in the Valley of the Kings. When unwrapped, the body proved to have been hacked to bits and had to be put back together as well as possible. Parts of the body were missing completely, and body parts from other people (a woman's right hand and another man's hand and arm) were included in the wrappings. It was impossible to estimate age, or even height.

References:

Amer 1985 pp. 66-70
Brier 1994 pp. 115, 173, 276, 278
Bucaille 1990 pp. 19, 116-118, figs. 12, 49
Delia 1993 p. 75
Dodson and Hilton 2004 pp. 31, 32, 184, 186-187, 188-189, 190, 192
Drews 1993 p. 19
El Madhy 1989 pp. 27, 39, 45, 84
Forbes 1998a pp. 692-693
Gardiner and Peet 1952 pl. LXIX, LXII, LXXIII
Gardiner and Peet 1955 pp. 38, 39, 192 #s 290-293
Harris and Weeks 1973 pp. 167-168
Ikram and Dodson 1998 pp. 63, 122, 226, 264, 265, 315, 318, 328, ill. 40, pl. IX

Ramesses VII (Itamen)

Janssen 1978 pp. 45-46
Newberry 1906 p. 184 #s 26 and 28, pl. XXXVI #s 26 and 28
Partridge 1994 pp. 179-182
Peden 1994a pp. 259-263
Peden 2001 pp. 127, 130, 132, 205-206 note 453
Petrie 1906b pp. 90, 108, 143, 149, fig. 149 #13
Petrie 1978 pl. XLVI, 20.4 #s 1-8
D. Redford 1992 pp. 290 and note 26, 291
Reeves 1990b pp. 117-119
Reeves and Wilkinson 1996 pp. 21, 22, 27, 29, 31-32, 37, 53-54, 62, 63, 69, 71-72, 79, 81, 84, 109, 115, 124, 151, 154, 159, 164-169, 170, 191-192, 199, 207-209
Rowe 1936 p. 197 #834, pl. XXI #834
G. Smith 1912 pp. 92-94, pl. LVIII-LIX
Strudwick 1999 pp. 90, 114, 115, 132
Tyldesley 2006 p. 171
von Beckerath 1999 pp. 170 #5, 171 #5

Ramesses VII (Itamen)   Dynasty XX

Horus Name:

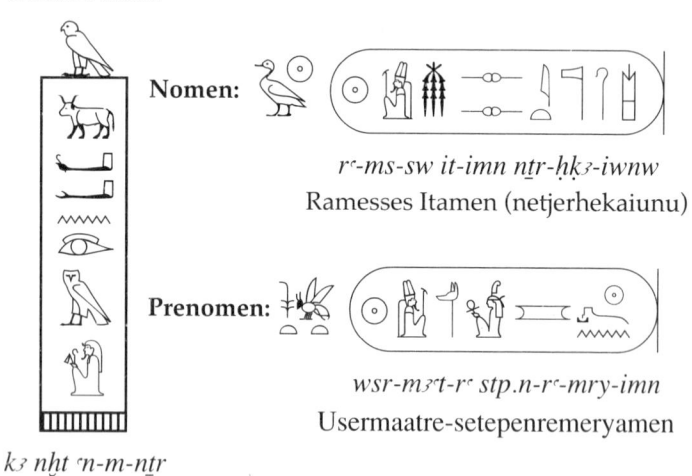

k3 nḫt ʿn-m-nṯr

Nomen:

rʿ-ms-sw it-imn nṯr-ḥḳ3-iwnw
Ramesses Itamen (netjerhekaiunu)

Prenomen:

wsr-m3ʿt-rʿ stp.n-rʿ-mry-imn
Usermaatre-setepenremeryamen

Two Ladies:

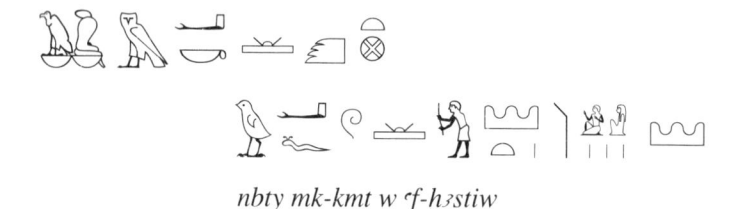

nbty mk-kmt wʿf-ḫ3stiw

Golden Falcon:

bik-nbw wsr-rnpwt-mi-itm

Ramesses VII (Itamen)

Length of Reign:	8 years
Tomb:	Unknown
Mummy:	Unknown

Consorts:	Unknown	Ramessu Usimare-setepenre-meryamen
Manetho:	Not given	
King Lists:	None	
Variant Names:	Rameses	

The sixth pharaoh of Dynasty XX, Ramesses VII was the son of his direct predecessor, Ramesses VI, and that ruler's wife, Nubkhesbed. Named Itamen at birth, he adopted the name Ramesses upon accession to the throne. The country he inherited had been troubled for some time. Corruption and graft seem to have been rampant. Inflation had forced grain prices to rise. There were labor strikes. Libyan raiders occasionally harassed the area around Thebes, and had invaded the Delta twice. All Egyptian holdings in Syria-Palestine had been lost. The turquoise and copper mines in Sinai were abandoned, probably due to lack of funds to finance the expeditions. On the other hand, Nubia seems to have remained under Egyptian control, although Ramesses VII's name is found only at Kawa. And Ramesses did send expeditions to mine gold and galena in the eastern desert during years one and two of his reign.

Although Ramesses VII held the throne for eight years, very few attestations to the reign have been found in Egypt. Much of this is probably due to difficulties in archaeological excavation of the Delta, where the chief residence of the pharaoh was located at Piramesses. He is mentioned at Tell el-Yahudiya, Heliopolis (where he was responsible for the burial of a sacred Mnevis Bull), and El Kab, and graffiti dating to his reign have been found on Sehel Island at Aswan. He is further known from a collection of papyri of unknown provenance, now held in the Turin museum.

In the Theban area, Ramesses VII is known almost exclusively from usurpations of inscriptions of previous kings at Karnak, graffiti in the mortuary temple of Ramesses II, an inscribed lintel from Deir el-Medina, and his tomb in the Valley of the Kings. The tomb, one of the smallest royal tombs in the valley, is decorated with excerpts from the *Book of the Earth*, the *Book of Gates*, and other such religious texts. The sarcophagus was actually a pit sunk in the floor, the lid being an inverted sarcophagus box made of stone. Two niches cut into the tomb wall appear to have been for canopic jars. When the tomb was cleared in the 1980s, all that was found were a few broken ushabtis, one each of calcite, faience and wood, as well as ostraca, at least four of which were "trial pieces" for scenes decorating the walls of the tomb.

No mummy for Ramesses VII is known, although four faience cups bearing his nomen and prenomen were found near the Royal Cache at Deir el-Bahri. It is possible that the pharaoh may be one of the unidentified mummies from the cache.

Through the mid-1950s, many Egyptologists confused the prenomina of Ramesses VII and Ramesses VIII. Thus, citations and dynastic king lists from some early works show these pharaohs in reverse order.

References:

Brier 1994 p. 278
Brock 1995 pp. 47-67
Dodson 1994b pp. 75-76
Dodson and Hilton 2004 pp. 184, 186-187, 188-191, 194
Eyre 1980 pp. 168-170
Gauthier 1907-17 vol. 3 pp. 202-204 #s I-IX
Hayes 1959 pp. 375 fig. 235, 376 (as Ramesses VIII)
Ikram and Dodson 1998 pp. 265, 289, 315, 319, ills. 55, 375
Kitchen 1972 pp. 182-194
Newberry 1906 p. 184 #27, pl. XXXVI #27
Peden 1994a pp. 101-106
Peet 1925 pp. 72-75
Petrie 1889 pl. XX #s 1686-1688
Petrie 1978 pl. XLVI 20.5
Reeves 1990b p. 119
Reeves and Wilkinson 1966 pp. 19, 37, 40, 51, 53-54, 115, 159, 166-167, 209
Ventura 1983 pp. 271-277
von Beckerath 1999 pp. 170-173 #6

Ramesses VIII (Sethirkopshef)   Dynasty XX

Horus Name:

Unknown

Nomen:

rˁ-ms-sw sth̠-ḥr-ḫpš.f mry-imn
Ramesses Sethirkopshef (mry-imn)

Prenomen:

wsr-mꜣʿt-rˁ ꜣḫ.n-imn
Usermaatre-akhenamen

Two Ladies: Unknown

Golden Falcon: Unknown

Ramesses VIII (Sethirkopshef)

Length of Reign:	1 year		
Tomb:	Unknown		
Mummy:	Unknown		
Consorts:	Unknown	**Variant Names:**	Rameses Ramessu
Manetho:	Not given		
King Lists:	None		

The seventh pharaoh of Dynasty XX, Ramesses VIII was the son of Ramesses III. He was therefore an uncle of his direct predecessor, Ramesses VII, whose only child (also named Ramesses) had predeceased him. Ramesses VIII, whose name before his assumption of power was Sethirkopshef, was probably in his sixties when he became king. He reigned for only a year and what few attestations are known come only from the Theban area. These consist of an inscribed plaque, his princely name, titles and cartouche at Medinet Habu, and a graffito from the tomb chapel of the priest Kynebu (TT113). Scarabs once thought to have named Ramesses VIII are now believed by Kitchen and Yoyotte to be "statue-cult scarabs" of Ramesses II.

Given Ramesses VIII's short tenure as pharaoh, he would not have had time to complete a tomb elaborate enough for his own interment. The location of his tomb and mummy are unknown. However, Belzoni discovered tomb KV19, which belonged to Ramesses IX's son Montuhirkopshef. Edwin Brock determined that this tomb had originally been intended for prince Sethirhkopshef, but that the Set-animal symbol had been replaced with the falcon of Montu. The tomb was presumably abandoned when the prince became pharaoh.

Through the mid-1950s, many Egyptologists confused the prenomina of Ramesses VII and Ramesses VIII. Thus, citations and dynastic king lists from some early works show these pharaohs in reverse order.

References:
Amer 1981 pp. 9-12
Ayrton 1908 pp. 20-29
Brier 1994 p. 278
Dodson 1997 pp. 40, 41
Dodson and Hilton 2004 pp. 32, 184, 186-187, 188-189, 190, 192, 194
Hall 1913 pp. 238 #s 2372-2374
Hayes 1959 pp. 375 fig. 235, 376 (as Ramesses VII)
Peden 2001 pp. 119-120
Reeves 1990b p. 119
Reeves and Wilkinson 1996 pp. 167, 179
von Beckerath 1999 pp. 172 #7, 173 #7

Ramesses IX (Khaemwaset I) — Dynasty XX

Horus Name:

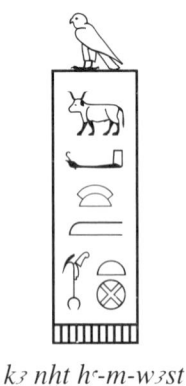

kꜣ nḫt ḫꜤ-m-wꜣst

Nomen:

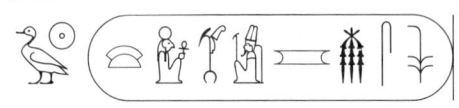

rꜤ-ms-sw ḫꜤ-(m)-wꜣst mry-imn
Ramesses Khaemwaset (meryamen)

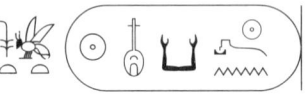

Prenomen:

nfr-kꜣ-rꜤ stp.n-rꜤ
Neferkare-setepenre

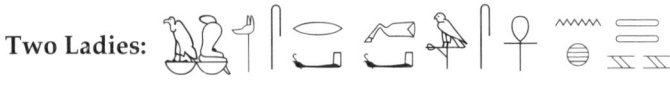

Two Ladies:

nbty wsr-ḫpš sꜤnḫ-tꜣwy

Golden Falcon:

bik-nbw wsr-rnpwt-mi-rꜤ

Length of Reign:	18 years
Tomb:	Valley of the Kings: KV6
Mummy:	Royal cache at Deir el-Bahri Now at Cairo Museum: No acquisition number

Consorts:	Baketwernel (II)(?)	**Variant Names:**	Rameses Ramessu
Manetho:	Not given		
King Lists:	None		

The eighth king of Dynasty XX, Ramesses IX's relationship to his predecessor, Ramesses VIII, is uncertain, but he seems to have been a grandson of Ramesses III. If so, then Ramesses VIII would have been his uncle. Whatever his familial relationships, the kingdom he inherited was rife with problems.

Among the difficulties plaguing the reign, the most serious included inflated grain prices around Thebes, Libyan raiders from the Western Desert, tomb robbers, labor strikes, and riots. The continued growth in the power of the Priesthood of Amen, already seen to be a problem because of the priests' increased landholdings during the reign of Ramesses III, diverted key resources from government control and contributed to the instability of the era. The priesthood became so powerful during this period that at one point the high priest of Amen, Amenhotep, actually had himself depicted on two reliefs at Karnak in the same scale as Ramesses IX.

Almost all of the surviving information about the reign comes from Upper Egypt around the Theban area; records in this region have tended to be better preserved and excavated than in Lower Egypt. From the temple of Amen at Karnak we have inscribed walls and a doorway in the southern part of the court between Pylons Three and Four, fragments of scenes in Court I, north of Pylon Seven, and in Court II, located between Pylons Seven and Eight. Also from the temple come a sandstone porch and lintel and fragments of several stelae. Ramesses IX also usurped a space on an alabaster barque shrine built by the Dynasty XVIII pharaoh Thutmose III. Across the Nile from Karnak, a short inscription dated to regnal year seven comes from the Medinet Habu temple of Ramesses III, as do painted fragments from that temple's west fortified gate.

The royal tomb, located in the Valley of the Kings, was evidently incomplete at the time of the king's death, and the last of the completed chambers was enlarged to become the burial chamber. No sarcophagus was used for the burial, and the king's coffins were lowered into a pit and covered by a (now missing) stone slab. Most of the tomb's decoration was hurriedly, and none too carefully, finished. Large sections of the tomb were left unplastered.

A few pieces of funerary equipment from Ramesses IX's burial are preserved in the Salt collection at the British Museum. These include several wooden ushabtis, statuettes and a life-sized "ka" statue. A clearing operation carried out in 1888 uncovered dozens of ostraca, some bearing rough drawings. Also discovered was a set of wooden runners, either for a shrine, or perhaps part of the sledge that carried the mummy to the tomb.

A few attestations for Ramesses IX have been discovered in the Memphite region, including the top half of a stele dated to regnal year 13, and the burial of an Apis Bull. From Heliopolis came fragments of a kneeling statue, a statue making offerings, an offering table, and an inscribed gateway made for the king's son, Nebmaatre, the High Priest of Re.

A papyrus dated to Ramesses IX's second regnal year records a military campaign against the Shosu Bedouins at an unknown location in the Eastern Desert near the Red Sea coast. The "Strong

Ramesses IX (Khaemwaset I)

Arm of Pharaoh," in company with Amen-Re, was triumphant in what was almost certainly a minor policing action.

At Dakhla Oasis in the Western Desert, Ramesses IX restored the temple of Mut, which was either a Dynasty XVIII or XIX structure.

Attestations for Ramesses IX in Nubia are found in several locations. Beginning at Gebel Barkal at the Fourth Cataract and progressing northward, the locations include the temple of Ramesses II at Amarah West, where his name has been found in the Inner Court, the Hypostyle Hall, and on the jambs of the West Gate. At Buhen, inscriptions found on the remains of a doorjamb have led some scholars to suggest that Ramesses IX was "invoked as a god" there. The king's name is also found at Quban, and the names of officials of the reign are found at Serra East, Buhen, Semna West, Sai Island and the temple of Ramesses II at Abu Simbel.

During the reign of Ramesses IX, there were rumors about a rash of tomb robberies in the royal cemeteries of western Thebes. Beginning in regnal year 16, there was a royal commission established to investigate the rumors. It was found that unsuccessful attempts had been made to enter several tombs, and the robbers had succeeded in violating the tomb of Queen Aset, the wife of Ramesses III, in the Valley of the Queens. In addition, the Dra Abu el-Naga tomb of Dynasty XVII king Sobekemsaf I and his queen, Nubkhas, had been completely looted. Many of the tomb robbers were caught, and admitted to burning the mummies after removing all valuables from the tomb. The thieves were tried, convicted, and executed.

Discovered in the Royal Cache at Deir el-Bahri, the mummy of Ramesses IX was much damaged by tomb robbers. It has never been properly unwrapped or examined physically. X-rays indicate an age at death of 35-40 years.

References:

Abitz 1992 pp. 165-185
Aldred 1955 pp. 3-8
Amer 1982 pp. 11-15
Brier 1994 pp. 118, 253, 278
Dodson and Hilton 2004 pp. 184-185, 186-187, 188, 191-194
Dodson and Reeves 1988 pp. 223-226
El Madhy 1989 pp. 26, 27, 37
Forbes 1998a pp. 646-647
Grimal 1992 pp. 289-290
Ikram and Dodson 1998 pp. 265, 315, 319, 329
Kitchen 1984 pp. 127-134
Peden 1994a pp. 73-76, 107-110, 175-180, 225-244, 245-258, 259-264
Peden 2001 pp. 118, 130 note 458, 132-133, 187-188, 189 note 357, 223-224, 268 note 10, 205-206 note 453
Peet 1930
Reeves 1990b pp. 119-120, 186, 250
Reeves and Wilkinson 1996 pp. 32-33, 37, 47, 51, 53, 54, 60, 63, 69, 72, 78, 84, 88, 117, 120, 159, 165, 168-171, 173, 190-193, 196, 203, 206-207
H.S. Smith 1976 p. 97 #484, pl. XIII #2, LXXIII #2
Tyldesley 2006 p. 171
von Beckerath 1999 pp. 172 #8, 173 #8

Ramesses X (Amenhirkopshef III)   Dynasty XX

Horus Name:

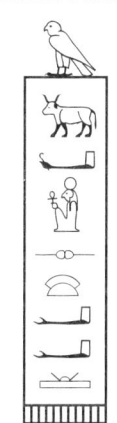

Nomen:

rꜥ-ms-sw imn-(ḥr)-ḫpš.f mry-imn
Ramesses Amenhirkopshef (meryamen)

Prenomen:

ḫpr-mꜣꜥt-rꜥ stp.n-rꜥ
Khepermaatre-setepenre

Two Ladies: Unknown

kꜣ nḫt sḫꜥ-n-rꜥ   **Golden Falcon:** Unknown

Length of Reign:	10 years
Tomb:	Unknown
Mummy:	Unknown

Consorts:	Tyti(?)	**Variant Names:**	Rameses Ramessu
Manetho:	Not given		
King Lists:	None		

The ninth king of Dynasty XX, Ramesses X's relationship to his immediate predecessor, Ramesses IX, is unknown and, although he evidently reigned for ten years, practically nothing is known of him. Attestations are all but nonexistent, and consist of a few minor usurpations at Karnak, including a stele usurped from a former pharaoh (name lost). He is also mentioned on inscribed fragments at Aniba, in Nubia. His tomb in the Valley of the Kings has never been seriously investigated, and except for its first chamber, it is clogged with debris. Years one to three of his reign are referenced in three papyri now at a museum in Turin, Italy.

References:

Bierbrier 1975 p. 251
Brier 1994 p. 278
Dodson and Hilton 2004 pp. 184-186, 186-187, 188, 191, 194
Hall 1913 p. 238 #s 2375-2378
Ikram and Dodson 1998 pp. 63, 315
Reeves 1990b pp. 135, 138 note 65, 120, 259, 274, 290
Reeves and Wilkinson 1996 pp. 29, 35, 37, 53-54, 71, 159, 170, 172, 187, 191, 208-209
Tyldesley 2006 p. 171
von Beckerath 1999 pp. 174 #9, 175 #9

Ramesses XI (Khaemwaset II) — Dynasty XX

Nomen:

rʿ-ms-sw ḫʿ(m)-wꜣst mrr-imn nṯr-ḥḳꜣ-iwnw
Ramesses Khaemwaset
(mereramen-netjerheqaiunu)

Horus Name:

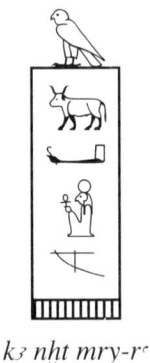

kꜣ nḫt mry-rʿ

Prenomen:

mn-mꜣʿt-rʿ stp.n-ptḥ
Menmaatre-setepenptah

Two Ladies:

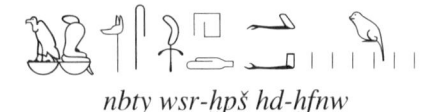

nbty wsr-ḫpš ḥd-ḥfnw

Golden Falcon:

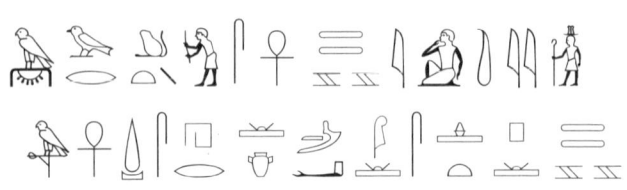

bik-nbw wr-pḥti sʿnḫ-tꜣwyity ḥrw-ḥ-mꜣʿt sḥtp-tꜣwy

Length of Reign:	29-30 years
Tomb:	KV4
Mummy:	Unknown

Consorts:	Tentamen(?)	**Variant Names:**	Rameses Ramessu
Manetho:	Not given		
King Lists:	None		

Ramesses XI (Khaemwaset II)

The tenth and final pharaoh of Dynasty XX, Ramesses XI's relationship to his predecessor, Ramesses X, is unknown. It has been suggested that he was a son of either Ramesses IX or X, but this is nothing more than conjecture. In any case, Ramesses XI inherited a troubled kingdom. Egypt had been steadily deteriorating since the reign of Ramesses III, a span of some fifty years. Inflation, famine, labor strikes, tomb robbery, and harassment by the Libyan tribes of the Western Desert had become commonplace, almost regular occurrences. Graft and corruption were rampant. All of Egypt's control in southwest Asia was long gone, and control of Nubia was shaky at best. By the time of Ramesses XI's death, Egypt had permanently lost its military, economic, and political presence in Nubia.

Another problem long besetting Egypt was the power wielded by the Temple of Amen and its priesthood. By the reign of Ramesses IV, the combined temples of Egypt controlled one-third of all arable land, and the Temple of Amen claimed three-quarters of that. By the start of Ramesses XI's reign, the power of the priesthood was much greater.

Midway through Ramesses XI's reign, a series of events began to unfold that ultimately led to the collapse of Dynasty XX. As a result of widespread civil unrest and marauding Libyans, the Viceroy of Nubia, Panehsy, marched into Thebes to restore order, perhaps under orders from the pharaoh. Panehsy assumed the office of "overseer of the granaries" in order to ensure provisions for his men while occupying the troubled city. This brought Panehsy into conflict with the high priest Amenhotep and ultimately led to a siege of the high priest's fortified temple at Medinet Habu. Ultimately, Panehsy appears to have led a rebellion against the king, eventually marching all the way into Lower Egypt. He was driven back to Nubia, perhaps by General Piankh (who was probably the son-in-law of General Hrihor). After Panehsy was driven out, Hrihor's position was cemented when Ramesses elevated him to the position of High Priest of Amen.

In regnal year 19, Egypt was essentially divided between two rulers, Hrihor in the south and General Smendes in the north, both technically subjects of Ramesses. Egypt was declared to be in a renaissance ("repeating of births"). The new regime was designated as year one, and Hrihor assumed many of the trappings of the kingship, including the full titulary of a pharaoh, at least on the wall-reliefs of the temple to Khonsu he built at Karnak. While Ramesses XI remained technically pharaoh, he was at this point perhaps a mere puppet, and he remained in either Memphis or Piramesses, far from the main center of power in Thebes.

Hrihor died in year seven of the renaissance, about five years before the death of Ramesses XI. During the remaining years of Ramesses' nominal reign, Upper Egypt was actually under the control first of Piankh, followed by Piankh's son, Pinudjem I.

Ramesses XI (Khaemwaset II)

Ramesses XI's death marked the end of Dynasty XX and of what scholars refer to as the New Kingdom. General Smendes then became the first pharaoh of Dynasty XXI.

Attestations for Ramesses XI are almost non-existent. Outside of Egypt, we have graffiti from Buhen and Aniba in Nubia. In Egypt we have the burial of an Apis bull during his rule recorded at Memphis. From Memphis also comes an inscribed block. A fragment of wooden furniture was found at Saqqara. A votive stele from Abydos gives a regnal date of year 27. At Thebes he added a hypostyle hall to the temple of Khonsu at Karnak, and seemingly in conjunction with Hrihor, a court and pylon to the same temple. Several papyri dated to Ramesses XI's reign have been discovered. These deal primarily with a spate of robberies of royal and private tombs at Thebes.

Ramesses XI began construction of a tomb in the Valley of the Kings, but the project was abandoned unfinished for some unknown reason. Where the pharaoh was buried is also unknown. It is not impossible that he was hurriedly interred in a small, still undiscovered tomb somewhere in the Valley. But a more likely reason for KV4's abandonment would be that the pharaoh died at Memphis or Piramesses, and was buried in Lower Egypt. Wherever the burial eventually took place, it is interesting to note that in a rule of three decades the royal tomb remained unfinished. Ramesses' mummy has never been found, or at least never identified.

References:

Breasted 1906 vol. IV pp. 299-307 §608-626
Brier 1994 pp. 91, 278
Dodson 2000 pp. 135-139, 140
Dodson and Hilton 2004 pp. 184-186, 186-187, 188, 191-194, 196, 200, 206, 209
El Madhy 1989 pp. 98, 136
Harris and Weeks 1973 pp. 108, 168, 169, 170, 171
Ikram and Dodson 1998 pp. 63, 95, 315
Peden 1994a pp. 111-114, 181-186, 265-270, 271-276, 277-280
Peden 2001 pp. 129, 130 note 458, 133, 232, 233 note 618
Peet 1930
Reeves 1990b pp. 121-123
Reeves and Wilkinson 1996 pp. 29, 30, 37, 43, 50-51, 53, 59, 73, 76, 84, 94, 98, 172-173, 175, 177, 183, 188, 190-192, 204, 208-209
Tyldesley 2006 p. 171
von Beckerath 1999 pp. 174 #10, 175 #10

Ranisonb   Dynasty XIII

Horus Name: Unknown   **Nomen:** Unknown

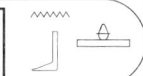

Prenomen:

rn(i)-snb
Ranisonb

Two Ladies: Unknown

Golden Falcon: Unknown

Length of Reign:	4 months
Tomb:	Unknown
Mummy:	Unknown

Consorts:	Unknown	**Variant Names:**	Ranisonbe Rensonb
Manetho:	Not given		
King Lists:	T: (G 6.16; R 7.16; vB 6.16)		

Ranisonb is probably the fourteenth king of Dynasty XIII. Other than the mention of this king's nomen in the Turin Canon, his sole attestation comes from a note found in the papers of Percy E. Newberry. It mentions Newberry having seen, at a Cairo antique shop, an inscribed bead giving the name "Ranisonb" and a filial nominative "(son of) Amenemhet, who gives life." Ryholt suggests that Ranisonb's father might have been Amenemhet VI, but he also considers the possibility that one of three other predecessors—Sehotepibre (Ryholt's Sehotepibre II), Sewadjkare I or Nedjemibre—whose nomina are unknown, might also have fathered this king.

References:

Gardiner 1959 pl. III, Col. VI #16
Gardiner 1961 p. 440 #6.16
Ryholt 1997a pp. 71 Col. 7.16, 73 #14, 192 table 33, 208 table 46, 216, 339 File 13/14, 408 table 94 #14
Ryholt 1997b pp. 95-96
von Beckerath 1999 pp. 92 #13, 93 #13

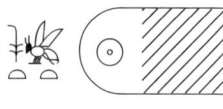

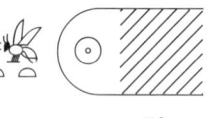

...re

...re   Dynasty XIII

Horus Name: Unknown   **Nomen:** Unknown

Prenomen: ...rʿ
...re

Two Ladies: Unknown

Golden Falcon: Unknown

Length of Reign:	Unknown
Tomb:	Unknown
Mummy:	Unknown

Consorts:	Unknown	**King Lists:**	T: (R 8.26)
Manetho:	Not given	**Variant Names:**	None

...re is probably the fifty-fifth king of Dynasty XIII. Due to the fragile condition of parts of the Turin Canon, nothing beyond the partial name "re" survives from this king's listing.

References:
Ryholt 1997a pp. 73 Col. 8.26, 358 File 13/5-6

...re   Dynasty XIV

Horus Name: Unknown   **Nomen:** Unknown

Prenomen: ...rʿ
...re

Two Ladies: Unknown

Golden Falcon: Unknown

Length of Reign:	Unknown
Tomb:	Unknown
Mummy:	Unknown

Consorts:	Unknown	**Variant Names:**	None
Manetho:	Not given		
King Lists:	T: (G 8.15; R 9.15)		

Possibly the twenty-first king of Dynasty XIV. Due to the fragile condition of the Turin Canon, nothing beyond the partial name "re" survives from this king's listing. This is one of four kings in this dynasty for whom "re" is the only identifier. The other three are all located in column G9/R10.

References:

Gardiner 1959 pl. III, Col. VIII #15
Gardiner 1961 p. 444 #8.15

Ryholt 1997a pp. 95 Col. 9.15, 98 #21, 379 File 14/21

...re   Dynasty XIV

Horus Name: Unknown

Nomen: Unknown

Prenomen:

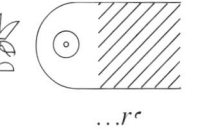

...rꜥ
...re

Two Ladies: Unknown

Golden Falcon: Unknown

Length of Reign:	Unknown
Tomb:	Unknown
Mummy:	Unknown

Consorts:	Unknown	**Variant Names:**	None
Manetho:	Not given		
King Lists:	T: (G 9.1; R 10.1)		

Possibly the thirty-seventh king of Dynasty XIV. Due to the fragile condition of parts of the Turin Canon, nothing beyond the

...[re]

partial name "re" survives from this king's listing. This is one of four kings in this dynasty for whom "re" is the only identifier. Of the others, two are also located in column G9/R10 and one in column G8/R9.

References:
Gardiner 1959 pl. III, Col. IX #1
Ryholt 1997a pp. 95 Col. 10.1, 98
   #s 35-42

...[re]   Dynasty XIV

Horus Name: Unknown

Nomen: Unknown

Prenomen:
...[rʿ]
...[re]

Two Ladies: Unknown

Golden Falcon: Unknown

Length of Reign:	Unknown
Tomb:	Unknown
Mummy:	Unknown

Consorts:	Unknown	**Variant Names:**	None
Manetho:	Not given		
King Lists:	T: (G 9.5; R 10.5)		

Perhaps the forty-first king of Dynasty XIV. Due to the fragile condition of parts of the Turin Canon, nothing beyond the partial name "re" survives from this king's listing. This is one of four kings in this dynasty for whom "re" is the only identifier. Of the others, two are located in column G9/R10 and one in column G8/R9.

References:
Gardiner 1959 pl. III, Col. IX #5
Ryholt 1997a pp. 95 Col. 10.5, 98
   #s 35-42

...[re] — Dynasty XIV

Horus Name: Unknown

Nomen: Unknown

Prenomen:

...[rˁ]
...[re]

Two Ladies: Unknown

Golden Falcon: Unknown

Length of Reign:	Unknown
Tomb:	Unknown
Mummy:	Unknown

Consorts:	Unknown	**Variant Names:**	None
Manetho:	Not given		
King Lists:	T: (G 9.6; R 10.6)		

Perhaps the forty-second king of Dynasty XIV. Due to the fragile condition of parts of the Turin Canon, nothing beyond the partial name "re" survives from this king's listing. This is one of four kings in this dynasty for whom "re" is the only identifier. Of the others, two are also located in column G9/R10 and one in column G8/R9.

References:

Gardiner 1959 pl. III, Col. IX #6
Ryholt 1997a pp. 95 Col. 10.6, 98 #s 35–42

Rehotep — Dynasty XVII

Horus Name:

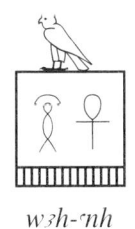

wзḥ-ˁnḫ

Nomen:

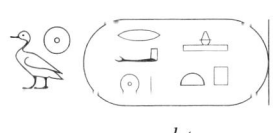

rˁ-ḥtp
Rehotep

341

Rehotep

Prenomen: *sḫm-rꜥ-wꜣḥ-ḫꜥw*
Sekhemre-wahkhau

Two Ladies: *nbty wsr-rnpwt*

Golden Falcon: *bik-nbw wꜣḏ-* [...]

Length of Reign:	1+ years
Tomb:	Unknown; probably at Dra Abu el-Naga
Mummy:	Unknown

Consorts:	Unknown	Rahotpe
Manetho:	Not given	Rehotpe
King Lists:	K: (54)	Sekhem-uah-kha-ra
Variant Names:	Rahotep	Sekhemre Wa-ka'-u

The first king of Dynasty XVII, Rehotep's parentage is unknown, as is his relationship to his predecessor, the Dynasty XVI pharaoh Senwosret IV, although it seems likely that there was no connection between them. Rehotep claimed the Theban throne at a time when king after petty king of Dynasty XVI had ruled at Thebes, at least 16 in a span of only 60-70 years. He inherited the remains of a disaster. The Hyksos kings of Dynasty XV had harassed and fought the contemporaneous Dynasty XVI and, at some point, had invaded the Theban rump state, looting and destroying temple and palace alike. For whatever reasons, the Hyksos rulers withdrew from the Theban territory and Rehotep was able to claim territory as far as Abydos, some 75 km. further north than Dynasty XVI's border at Hiw (Hu). A great deal of restoration was needed and it is certain that Rehotep ordered such work attended to at temple sites at Abydos and Coptos. At Abydos, he had the enclosure walls of the temple of Osiris restored.

On a stele from Coptos, Rehotep informs us that, at the temple of Min, the "gates and doors are fallen into ruin"; naturally the king set things right and assures us that nothing was ever destroyed during his reign. The stele also tells us that the king was the uniter of Upper and Lower Egypt as well as a guardian of the people who never slept. Rehotep, of course, was not the uniter of the Two Lands, but by good fortune or some military expertise, his reign saw the Theban Kingdom expanded by some 25 percent.

A bow found at Coptos bears a dedication by Rehotep to the "King's Son" Ameny. Whether Ameny was the bodily son of Rehotep or the term was honorific is unknown.

The stele of the chamberlain Seankhptah found at Abydos is dated to the king's first regnal year. This is the only regnal date known for Rehotep.

Vandersleyen would place Rehotep in Dynasty XIII, although his argument is slim and has been rejected by most scholars.

References:
Budge 1913 p. 9, pl. 24
Clère 1982 pp. 60-68, pl. IV-VI
Dodson and Hilton 2004 pp. 116, 117, 118-120
Helck 1983 pp. 59-60 #87, 60-61 #88
Petrie 1896b pp. 12-13, pl. XII #3
D. Redford 1997 p. 8 #s 45 and 46
Ryholt 1997a pp. 146, note 525, 168, 169, 171 table 28, 265-266, 309, 392-393 File 17/1, 410, table 98
B. Schmitz 1977 pp. 216-217
Vandersleyen 1993 pp. 189-191
von Beckerath 1999 pp. 124 #2, 125 #2

Sahure   Dynasty V

Horus Name:

nb-ḫꜥw

Nomen:

sꜣḥw-rꜥ
Sahure

sꜣḥw-rꜥ
Sahure

Two Ladies:

nbty nb-ḫꜥw

Golden Falcon:

(bik) nbw nṯrw

Sahure

Length of Reign:	12 years
Tomb:	Pyramid at Abusir: "The Ba of Sahure Appears"
Mummy:	Unknown

Consorts:	Neferethanebty	**Variant Names:**	None
Manetho:	Sephres (A)		
King Lists:	Ab: (27); S: (26); T: (G [3.18])		

The second pharaoh of Dynasty V, Sahure was probably the son of Userkaf and Khentkaues I, although a few scholars believe him to have been Userkaf's brother or half-brother.

For unknown reasons, Sahure chose to forsake both Saqqara and Giza and build his pyramid at Abusir, a short distance from the sun temple of Userkaf at Abu Ghurab. The pyramid, which measured 78.5 m. per side and rose to a height of about 48 m., was built on a foundation of several layers of limestone blocks which themselves were laid on the bare earth. The pyramid's core was constructed using blocks of rough-cut stone held together with mud. When completed, the pyramid was encased with dressed blocks of white limestone which were brought from a quarry not far distant, on the opposite side of the Nile.

Today the pyramid is much ruined both externally and internally. Stone robbers carried off the casing blocks and destroyed most of the pyramid's interior. Even the sarcophagus was smashed and carried away; only one small fragment was found in the much-damaged burial chamber.

The pyramid complex also contains a small subsidiary pyramid.

Sahure's mortuary temple is considered by many scholars to be the most sophisticated such structure to have been built up until that time and was, indeed, the model for all future Old Kingdom temples of this type. The temple's open courtyard was surrounded by 16 huge columns made of pink granite and inscribed with the king's titulary. The walls of the temple and the 235 m. causeway leading down to the valley temple were once covered with an estimated 10,000 square m. of beautifully executed carved reliefs. Subjects of these reliefs included scenes of victorious military expeditions: the king clubbing a Libyan chieftain, the goddess Seshat recording booty captured in Libya, various gods escorting captives, wildlife, and much more. Some 1,100 years later, probably initiated by Thutmose IV of Dynasty XVIII, a part of Sahure's mortuary temple was used as a cult center for the goddess Sekhmet, here called "Sekhmet of Sahure." Other New Kingdom pharaohs connected with the cult included Horemheb of Dynasty XVIII and Sety I of Dynasty XIX.

Sahure constructed a sun temple, as had Userkaf, but the site has not been found. A decorated block from this temple was discovered embedded in a wall of the mortuary temple of the later pharaoh, Niuserre. Lehner posits that Sahure's sun temple along with several other such temples might have been used as quarries by their successors. The temple was called "Field of Re."

Although his name has been lost, the number of years for Sahure's reign has been preserved in the Turin Canon as 12. The Palermo Stone records what appears to be the first nine months of a year 13. Altogether, the Palermo Stone and its Cairo fragments have preserved years 2, 3, 5, 6 and the partial year 13. Manetho records a reign of 13 years.

Contact with foreign countries was prevalent during this reign. An expedition was sent to the land of Punt in year 13 and brought back to Egypt 80,000 measures of myrrh among many other things. Also during year 13, an expedition to the copper and turquoise mines at Wadi Maghara in Sinai returned with 6,000 measures of copper. Sahure marked the Egyptian presence there with two carvings, one of which shows the pharaoh "smiting the Asiatics." Contact with the Levant is represented by reliefs in the king's mortuary temple that show ships returning from a venture loaded with "Asiatics" and their children. An alabaster bowl bearing Sahure's name was found during excavations of the temple of Baalat-Gebal in the city of Byblos, on the sea coast in Lebanon.

In Nubia, Sahure's cartouche appears among the graffiti at Tumas and a stele of him was found at the diorite quarries in the western desert near Abu Simbel. Seals bearing his name have been found as far south as Buhen, at the Second Cataract.

References:

Altenmüller 2001 p. 598
D. Arnold 1998 p. 67
Bares 2000 pp. 5, 7-9
Borchardt 1910, 1913
Clagett 1989 pp. 90-92
Dodson 2003 pp. 22, 66-67
Dodson and Hilton 2004 pp. 18, 60-62, 64-65, 66, 68-69
Emery 1963 p. 119, fig. 2 #Z3-3
Gardiner 1959 pl. II, Col. III #18
Gardiner 1961 p. 435
Gardiner and Peet 1952 pl. IV #8, pl. VII #9
Gardiner and Peet 1955 pp. 29
Jidejian 1968 p. 17
Lehner 1997 pp. 60, 142-144, 149 150, 152, 162, 223, 229, 233
Marcus 2002 pp. 408, 410
Pankhurst 1984 p. 6
Rzepka 2000 p. 522
W. Smith 1971 pp. 182-183
Spalinger 1994 pp. 296-297
Verbrugghe and Wickersham 1996 pp. 135, 191
Verner 1997 pp. 280-290, 463
Verner 2000a pp. 588-589
Verner 2000b pp. 590-597
Verner 2002 pp. 42-61, 82-83
von Beckerath 1999 pp. 57 #2, 58 #2
Waddell 1940 p. 51
Weigall 1907 p. 108, pl. LVII and LVIII
R. Wilkinson 2000 pp. 84, 121-122
T. Wilkinson 2000 pp. 159 171, 220-221

Sakir-Har   Dynasty XV

Horus Name: Unknown

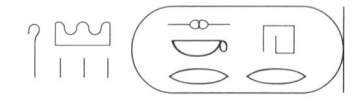

ḥqꜣ-ḫꜣswt skr-ḥr
(Ruler of Foreign Lands) Sakir-Har

Two Ladies:

nbty ṯz-pḏwt

Golden Falcon:

bik-nbw iri-tꜣš.f

Length of Reign:	Unknown
Tomb:	Unknown
Mummy:	Unknown

Consorts:	Unknown	**Variant Names:**	Sakarher
Manetho:	Not given		
King Lists:	None		

Sakir-Har is the first Hyksos ruler of Dynasty XV for whom a contemporary attestation is known. Ryholt considers him to be perhaps the third ruler of the dynasty, having been preceded by Semqen and 'Aper-'Anati. The attestation consists of the greater section of a damaged doorjamb found at the Hyksos Capital of Avaris (Tell el-Dab'a, in the eastern Delta) inscribed with a Horus name (unfortunately lost), Two Ladies name, a Golden Falcon name and the personal name Sakir-Har. The latter is not the formal nomen of the standard pharaonic titulary, usually preceded by , Son of Re, but the Hyksos title , Ruler of Foreign Lands. To date, Sakir-Har is the first known Hyksos ruler to adopt any portion of the traditional Egyptian titulary; he is also the earliest Hyksos ruler attested at Avaris.

References:

Hein 1994 pp. 150-152, Catalogue #126
Ryholt 1997a pp. 119-120, 123-124, 125 and table 23, 127-128, 201
table 40, 304, 383 File 15/3, 410, table 96
von Beckerath 1999 pp. 116 #d, 117 #d

Sanakht   Dynasty III

Horus Name:

s3-nḫt
Sanakht

Nomen:

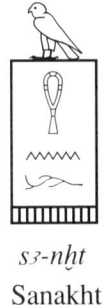

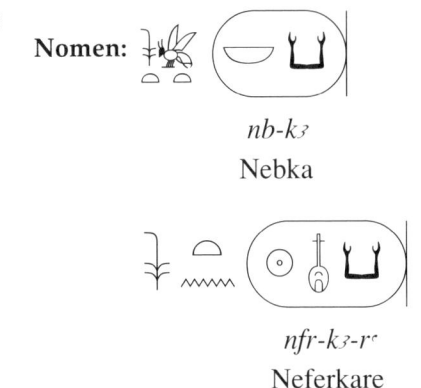

nb-k3
Nebka

nfr-k3-rˁ
Neferkare

Two Ladies: Unknown

Golden Falcon: Unknown

Length of Reign:	3-6 years
Tomb:	Unknown
Mummy:	Unknown

Consorts:	Unknown	**King Lists:**	Ab: (15); S: (14); T: (G 3.7)
Manetho:	Necherôchis (E) Necherôphês (A) Nekherokhis (E) Nekherophes (A)	**Variant Names:**	Hen-Nekht Sa-Nekht Zanakht

One of the most enigmatic rulers of Dynasty III, Sanakht's position in that dynasty is far from clear. His parentage is unknown, as is his relationship to other kings of the dynasty. The Turin Canon places him, under his nomen, Nebka, directly after Khasekhemwy, the last pharaoh of Dynasty II, and directly before Djoser of Dynasty III. The Abydos List agrees with the Canon, as does Manetho. However, the Saqqara List has Nebka (as Nebkare) succeeding Sekhemkhet, and therefore the third king of Dynasty III. Also, a tale found in the Papyrus Westcar places Nebka after Djoser.

Archaeological evidence tends to agree with the Saqqara List and the papyrus. Sanakht played little or no part in the burial of Khasekhemwy, yet that almost certainly would have been an obligatory duty for the successor to perform in order to fulfill all of

Sanakht

the rituals involved with ascending to the throne. Instead, dozens of seal-impressions of Djoser's have been found in Khasekhemwy's tomb. Likewise, tomb K1 at Beit Khallaf, which was built for Khasekhemwy's wife, Nimaathap, has yielded not one mention of Sanakht, but more than 100 examples of Djoser's Horus name. Interestingly enough, tomb K2, which sits 300 m. to the north of Nimaathap's mastaba, has given us some two dozen sealings of Sanakht.

Sanakht's equation with Nebka is based on a single seal-impression discovered by Garstang in 1902. The sealing is much damaged, but what is left shows the serekh of Sanakht next to a fragment of cartouche that gives a bit of glyph that appears to be part of the archaic form of the symbol for *ka*, ⊔. Speculations on the size of the cartouche when complete seem to agree that the best fit would be the sign *nb*, ⌣. This fragment is the earliest known use of the cartouche, it not becoming a regular part of the titulary until the reign of Huni, last king of Dynasty III.

Further attestations for Sanakht in Egypt amount to two seal impressions from Djoser's North Temple at Saqqara and a single impression from Elephantine.

Sanakht's burial site is unknown. Garstang believed the king to have been buried in tomb K2 at Beit Khallaf. The tomb contained remains of a wooden coffin and the better part of the skeleton of an adult male. Other scholars believe that the original mastaba, which evolved into the step pyramid at Saqqara, was Sanakht's tomb, usurped by Djoser. It has also been suggested that a much-damaged brick structure at Abu Roash (called "el-Deir") may have been this king's final resting place.

Sanakht's serekhs and incised figures, one showing the king in the usual "smiting" pose, were found at the turquoise mines at Wadi Maghara in Sinai, placed near those of Djoser and Sekhemkhet, probably his direct predecessors.

Manetho gives his king Necherôchis a reign of 28 years. Not one regnal date for the names Sanakht or Nebka has been discovered. However, a short reign seems likely, probably not more than a few years.

References:

Dodson 1998 pp. 30, 33, 38, 39
Dodson 2003 p. 44
Gardiner 1961 pp. 74-75
Gardiner and Peet 1952 pl. I #4, pl. IV #3
Gardiner and Peet 1955 pp. 21, 24, 29, 53, 54-56
Garstang 1903 pp. 3, 11-14, 24-25, Pl. XVII, XIX, XXIII
Kahl et al. 1995 pp. 139-151
Spencer 1993 pp. 100-101 and fig. 77, 104
Verbrugghe and Wickersham 1996 pp. 134, 189
Verner 1997 pp. 105, 116, 134, 139
Waddell 1940 p. 41, 43
von Beckerath 1999 pp. 48 #1, 49 #1, 50 a, 51 a

Sankhptahi   Dynasty XIII

Horus Name: Unknown

Nomen: s.ʿnḫ-ptḥ-i
Sankhptahi

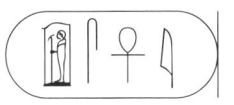

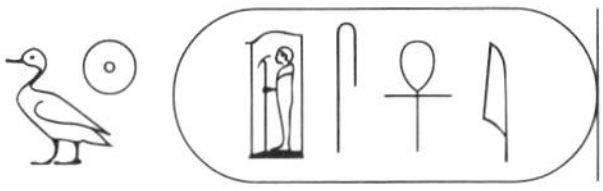

Prenomen: s.ḥḳ-n-rʿ
Seheqenre

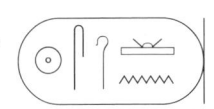

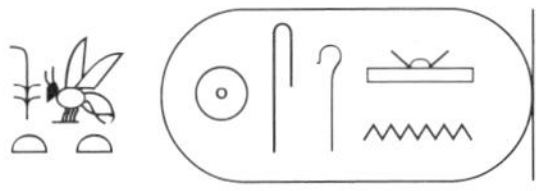

Two Ladies: Unknown

Golden Falcon: Unknown

Length of Reign:	Unknown
Tomb:	Unknown
Mummy:	Unknown

Consorts:	Unknown	**Variant Names:**	Se'anchptah Seankhptah
Manetho:	Not given		
King Lists:	T: (R 8.25)		

Probably the son of the pharaoh Se...kare, Sankhptahi would appear to be the fifty-fourth ruler of Dynasty XIII, although Ryholt would place him fifty-fifth and von Beckerath simply lists him as unplaced. In Ryholt's recent reconstruction of the Turin Canon, he is placed in column 8 #25.

A stele of unknown provenance, most likely from the Memphite area, contains a list of members of a royal family. A King's Son name ([s.ʿnḫ]ptḥi) is given and it is probably safe to assume that this prince is the future pharaoh Sankhptahi. A second stele, also probably from Memphis, dates to year one of Sankhptahi's reign. On the strength of these stelae, it has been suggested that this king was born in and probably ruled from Memphis.

References:

Dodson and Hilton 2004 pp. 100, 106-107, 108
Lange and Schäfer 1908 no. 20600
Ryholt 1997a pp. 69, 71 fig. 10, Col. 8 #25, 73 table 17 #55, 238-239, 284 table 83, 358 File 13/55, 408 table 94 #55
Sotheby's 1988 Lot 78
von Beckerath 1999 pp. 106 #q, 107 #q

Scorpion   Dynasty 00/0

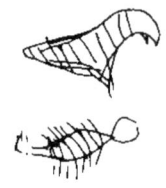

Length of Reign:	Unknown
Tomb:	Unknown
Mummy:	Unknown

Consorts:	Unknown	**Variant Names:**	Selk
Manetho:	Not given		Selkh
King Lists:	None		Skorpion

This is the only known attestation of a ruler called "Scorpion" in conjunction with a Horus hawk. The name appears to be part of a "tableau" recently discovered in Gebel Tjauti, slightly to the west of the ancient city of Nekhen (Naqada). The tableau has been interpreted as a record of a victory by Scorpion of Abydos over a rival city, probably Nekhen. If this interpretation is correct, the rock drawing at Gebel Tjauti probably shows one of the earliest steps in the unification of Egypt. However, it should be borne in mind that this reading of the "tableau" is only one of many possible interpretations.

While it is possible that the Horus Scorpion shown at Gebel Tjauti is a newly discovered ruler, it is more likely that the graffito represents one of the two known king Scorpions (see SCORPION I and SCORPION II). If this is the case, the most likely candidate is Scorpion I.

References:

J.C. and D. Darnell 1997a pp. 70-72
J.C. Darnell 2002 pp. 18-19, pl. 9-11
Friedman and Hendrickx 2002 pp. 10-18, 10 illustration

Peden 2001 pp. 1-2
M. Rose 2002 pp. 54-55

Scorpion I   Dynasty 00

Scorpion
Scorpion I

Length of Reign:	Unknown		
Tomb:	Abydos, U-j		
Mummy:	Unknown		

Consorts:	Unknown	**Variant Names:**	Selk
Manetho:	Not given		Selkh
King Lists:	None		Skorpion

Although the name "Scorpion" never appears in a serekh, it is the general consensus among Egyptologists that a ruler, and more likely two rulers, bore that name.

Scorpion I (Roman numerals are for convenience of identification only) is known from pottery jars, some painted with the ideogram for "scorpion" and discovered in Tomb U-j at the Umm el-Qa'ab cemetery in Abydos. Cemetery U is thought to contain the tombs of very early rulers or chieftains of the Abydos area. How extensive these rulers' sphere of influence may have been is impossible to tell, but Tomb U-j contained more than 400 clay vessels imported from southern Palestine, which would indicate at least a widespread trade pattern.

Tomb U-j, discovered in 1988 during excavations carried out by the German Institute of Archaeology, is large, measuring 9.1 m. by 7.3 m. and consisting of 12 chambers. Besides the imported vessels mentioned above, the tomb also contained remnants of a wooden shrine, inscribed bone labels, bits of gaming pieces, a wide variety of Egyptian pottery (this includes wavy-handled pots, plates, bread molds, etc.), and, most interesting of all, a "heka" or "crook" scepter made of ivory. This latter item would seem to be proof of a royal interment.

References:

J.C. and D. Darnell 1997a pp. 70-72
Dreyer 1992a
Dreyer 1993a pp. 33 fig. 4, 34-35, 49-56

Dreyer 1998
Shaw and Nicholson 1995 p. 254

Scorpion II   **Dynasty 0**

Scorpion
Scorpion II

Scorpion II

Length of Reign:	Unknown
Tomb:	Hierakonpolis. Locality 6, Tomb 1(?)
Mummy:	Unknown

Consorts:	Unknown	**Variant Names:**	Selk
Manetho:	Not given		Selkh
King Lists:	None		Skorpion

This king is known only from fragments of several large limestone maceheads found by Quibell and Green during excavations at Hierakonpolis in the 1896-98 seasons. The fragments were found in what they referred to as the "main deposit" in the temple precinct area. Although the excavators' records leave a lot to be desired, it is possible, on stylistic grounds, to date the Scorpion macehead to late protodynastic times.

It is likely that this king was Narmer's direct predecessor. Some Egyptologists see Scorpion as a possible rival of Narmer, ruling in Hierakonpolis while Narmer ruled at Abydos. This latter theory has not gained a lot of support; still, it must be noted that no record of Scorpion II has been found at Abydos (see SCORPION I).

One fragment of a Scorpion macehead shows a ruler wearing the white crown of Upper Egypt; he holds a mattock, and seems to be officiating at some sort of ground-breaking ceremony. In the register above the king, there is a row of standards; from each hangs a dead bird. What this all means is open to debate.

Another fragment of macehead shows Scorpion wearing the red crown and seated beneath a canopy. Before him is a falcon clutching an object that is now gone, but which undoubtedly was a tether attached to a human head, much as on the Narmer Palette.

Whether Scorpion was king of a united Egypt is unknown.

As with Scorpion I, this king's name is not found in a serekh.

References:

Arkell 1963 pp. 31-35
Baumgartel 1966 pp. 9-13
W. Davis 1992 pp. 224-229
Hoffman 1982 pp. 43-47
Hoffman 1991 pp. 129, 313, 316
Kaplony 1965 p. 132-167
Quibell and Petrie 1900 pl. XXV, XXVIc
Quibell and Green 1902 p. 41
Rice 1990 p. 103
Shaw and Nicholson 1995 p. 254
von Beckerath 1999 pp. 36 #x+3, 37 #x+3
Yurco 1998 pp. 85-86, 88, 90, fig. 1

Seankhibre   Dynasty XIV

Horus Name:
Unknown   **Nomen:** Unknown

Prenomen:

sʿnḫ-ib-rʿ
Seankhibre

Two Ladies: Unknown

Golden Falcon: Unknown

Length of Reign:	Unknown
Tomb:	Unknown
Mummy:	Unknown

Consorts:	Unknown	**Variant Names:**	S'ankhibre
Manetho:	Not given		
King Lists:	T: (G 8.18; R 9.18; vB 8.18)		

Perhaps the twenty-fourth king of Dynasty XIV, Seankhibre is one of a group of kings known only from the Turin Canon. The papyrus' fragile state allows for varying interpretations as to the positioning of some of the kings of this dynasty. However, Seankhibre's place seems secure.

References:

Gardiner 1959 pl. III, Col. VIII #18
Gardiner 1961 p. 441 #8.18
Ryholt 1997a pp. 95, Col. 9 #18, 98 #24, 198 table 37, 379 File 14/24, 409 table 95 #24

von Beckerath 1999 pp. 110 #19, 111 #19

Sebkay   Dynasty XIII

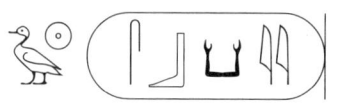

Horus Name: Unknown
Nomen: *sbk₃y* — Sebkay

Prenomen: Unknown

Two Ladies: Unknown

Golden Falcon: Unknown

Length of Reign:	Unknown
Tomb:	Unknown
Mummy:	Unknown

Consorts:	Unknown	Ra-se-beq-ka
Manetho:	Not given	Seb
		Sebek-ka-ra
King Lists:	T: Lacuna	Sebkai
Variant Names:	Kay	Sebekai
		Sebka-re(?)

This name is known only from the inscription on a single "magical" wand found by Randall-MacIver and Mace at Abydos in 1901 that is now in the Cairo Museum (JE34988 [CG9433]). Since publication of the excavation report in 1902, it has been suggested that Sebkay was a hitherto unknown pharaoh of Dynasty XIII or that the name should be read *sdf₃-k₃[r]*, "Sedjefaka[re]," evidently a misreading of ⌐ (*b*) as 𓆓 (*df₃*), the prenomen of Amenemhet VII. Ryholt believes the cartouche holds the names of two kings, Seb and Kay, but actually belongs to Kay, Seb being the father, and thus making this cartouche an example of filiative nomina. Ryholt also points out that the cartouche is preceded by 𓇓 and 𓅭, a combination denoting a ruler's nomen that is peculiar to the Second Intermediate Period; therefore the name cannot be a prenomen. While Ryholt's theory is not universally accepted, it is possible that his case is bolstered by the cartouche of Amenemhet VII, (*k₃y(s₃) imn-m-h₃t*) "(Kay's Son) Amenemhet." If "Kay" is an example of a filiative nomina, then it would hold that Seb and Kay were two individuals and that Kay is the father of Amenemhet VII (see AMENEMHET VII).

Although there is no record of this ruler (or rulers) in the Turin Canon, Ryholt believes that Seb and Kay were not included because of a lacuna in the original records used by the scribe who transcribed the papyrus. While von Beckerath views Sebkay's position in Dynasty XIII as unknown, Ryholt places his Seb and Kay in the eighteenth and nineteenth reigns of that dynasty.

References:

Gauthier 1907-17 vol. 3 p. 93 and note 3
Quirke 1986 pp. 206-207
Quirke 1991 pp. 129-130
Randall-MacIver 1902 pp. 69, 87 pl. XLIII Tomb 78, 92 pl. LIV, 100 #78, pl. XLIII #D78

Ryholt 1997a pp. 70, 208 and table 46, 218-219 and table 52, 340 File 13/18, 340-341 File 13/19, 408 table 94 #s 18 and 19
von Beckerath 1999 pp. 106 #o, 107 #o

Sedjes   Dynasty III

Horus Name: Unknown

Nomen: *sḏs*
Sedjes

Two Ladies: Unknown

Golden Falcon: Unknown

Length of Reign:	Unknown
Tomb:	Unknown
Mummy:	Unknown

Consorts:	Unknown	**King Lists:**	Ab: (18)
Manetho:	Mesôchris (A) Mesokhris (A) Sephouris (A) Sêphuris (A)	**Variant Names:**	Sezes

This name is known only from the Abydos king list. Dodson would equate Sedjes with Manetho's Sêphuris, while Verbrughee and Wickersham favor Mesôchris. Dodson also posits an identification of Sedjes with Nebkare, although it seems more likely that the name Nebkare was a variant spelling of the nomen Nebka and actually belongs to the pharaoh Sanakht (see SANAKHT). However, Dodson and Goedicke both point out that the word

Se...enre

"sedjes" may indicate a lacuna in the original source documents used to put together the Abydos list.

Dodson also equates Sedjes with Hudjefa (II) (see HUDJEFA (II)). Hudjefa, as pointed out by Goedicke, is not the name of a king but, much like the word "sedjes," is a term meaning "lacuna."

References:

Dodson 1998 pp. 28, 38, 39
Gardiner 1961 p. 433
Goedicke 1956 p. 50
Verbrugghe and Wickersham 1996
   pp. 134, 189

von Beckerath 1999 pp. 48 #4, 49 #4
Waddell 1940

Se...enre   Dynasty XIII

Horus Name: Unknown

Nomen: Unknown

Prenomen:

s...-n-[rʿ]
Se...enre

Two Ladies: Unknown

Golden Falcon: Unknown

Length of Reign:	Unknown
Tomb:	Unknown
Mummy:	Unknown

Consorts:	Unknown	**Variant Names:**	None
Manetho:	Not given		
King Lists:	T: (R 8.27)		

This fragmentary prenomen, known only from the Turin Canon, may represent an otherwise unknown ruler or it may well be that the name belongs to either Sekhaenre or Senebmiu Sewahenre. Se...enre is probably the fifty-sixth king of Dynasty XIII.

References:

Ryholt 1997a pp. 71 Col. 8.27, 72,
   73 #57, 358 File 13/57

Segerseni — Concurrent with Dynasty XI

Horus Name: Unknown

Nomen: 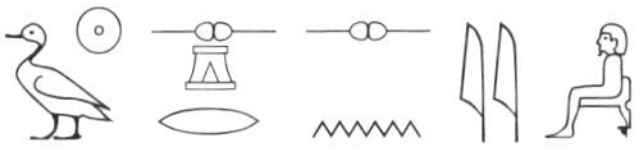 *sgrsny* — Segerseni

Prenomen: 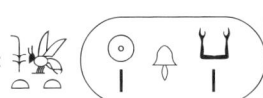 *mnḫ-kȝ-rˁ* — Menkhkare

Two Ladies: Unknown

Golden Falcon:  *bik-nbw ˁnḫ*

Length of Reign:	Unknown
Tomb:	Unknown
Mummy:	Unknown

Consorts:	Unknown	Uaz-ka-ra
Manetho:	Not given	Uthkere
		Wadjkare
King Lists:	None	Wadj-ku-Re
		Zegerzenti
Variant Names:	Sekherseny	

This "pharaoh" is known from a single inscription found at Umbarakab in Lower Nubia. Roughly carved and badly weathered, it has led to some confusion regarding the reading of Segerseni's throne name; it has sometimes been rendered as Wadjkare, the (*wḏ*) being mistaken for the (*mnḫ*).

Segerseni is one of three Nubian chieftains who seem to have declared themselves kings of Upper and Lower Egypt, despite the fact that they only "ruled" a section of Nubia and had no ties to Egypt whatsoever (see IN(TEF) and IYIBKHENTRE). We do not know if these rulers were related in any way. Also, the period in

Sehebre

which they held sway is uncertain, though it had to have been a time when Egyptian control in Nubia was at a minimum or nonexistent. The most likely time would have been after the fall of the Old Kingdom and concurrent with early Dynasty XI, or at the troubled period at the end of that dynasty, with evidence slightly favoring the latter date.

References:

Gardiner 1961 p. 121
Grajetzki 2006 p. 27
Grimal 1992 pp. 159, 160
Hayes 1953 p. 167
Petrie 1924 vol. I p. 122 #VII.A
von Beckerath 1999 pp. 80 #c, 81 #c
Weigall 1907 p. 261, pl. XIX #2
Weigall 1925 p. 261 #16
Winlock 1947 p. 100
Zaba 1974 p. 162

Sehebre   Dynasty XIV

Horus Name: Unknown

Nomen: Unknown

Prenomen:

sḥb-rʿ
Sehebre

Two Ladies: Unknown

Golden Falcon: Unknown

Length of Reign:	Unknown
Tomb:	Unknown
Mummy:	Unknown

Consorts:	Unknown	**Variant Names:**	Sehabre
Manetho:	Not given		
King Lists:	T: (G 8.4; R 9.4; vB 8.4)		

Perhaps the ninth king of Dynasty XIV, Sehebre is one of a group of kings known only from the Turin Canon. The papyrus' fragile state allows for varying interpretations as to the positioning of some of the kings of this dynasty. However, Sehebre's place seems secure.

Ryholt has suggested that Sehebre may be the prenomen of one of two ephemeral kings, Wazad or Sheneh. This, however, is merely speculation.

References:

Gardiner 1959 pl. III, Col. VIII #4
Gardiner 1961 p. 441 #8.4
Ryholt 1997a pp. 95 Col. 9 #4, 97: 98 #9, 198 table 37, 379 File 14/9, 409 #9

von Beckerath 1999 pp. 108 #5, 109 #5

Sehotepibre   Dynasty XIII

Horus Name:

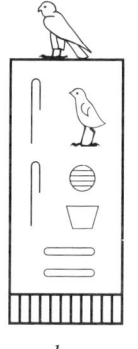

swsḫ-tȝwy

Nomen: Unknown

Prenomen:

sḥtp-ib-rʿ
Sehotepibre

Two Ladies: Unknown

Golden Falcon: Unknown

Length of Reign:	T: "...1-4 months, 27 days..."
Tomb:	Unknown
Mummy:	Unknown

Consorts:	Unknown	**Variant Names:**	Seusekhtowy Sewesekhtowy
Manetho:	Not given		
King Lists:	T: (G 6.12; R 7.12; vB 6.8)		

The Turin Canon places Sehotepibre as the tenth ruler of Dynasty XIII. We do not know if he was related to the royal family or a usurper, as his predecessor Nebnennu usurped the throne. Certainly, Sehotepibre continued Nebnennu's operations at the galena mines on the Red Sea at Gebel el-Zeit, as evidenced by a stele bearing his prenomen.

Sehotepibre certainly maintained relations with the important city of Byblos, on the coast of Lebanon, as attested to by a lapis-lazuli cylinder-seal found in that city. The seal gives his prenomen and is dedicated to Hathor, Lady of Byblos. Also inscribed on the cylinder, in cuneiform, is the name Yakin-Ilu; he was perhaps the Governor of Byblos.

Seka

References:

Giveon 1974b pp. 163
Helck 1983 p. 19 #28
Mey et al. 1980 pp. 304-305 and fig. 1 (1), pl. 80
Pinches and Newberry 1921 pp. 196-199, pl. XXXII

Ryholt 1997a pp. 71 Col. 7.12, 73 #10, 87 and note 278, 192 table 33, 340 File 13/10, 408 table 94 #10
Ryholt 1997b pp. 99-100

Seka — Predynastic

skȝ
Seka

Length of Reign:	Unknown
Tomb:	Unknown
Mummy:	Unknown

Consorts:	Unknown	**Variant Names:**	None
Manetho:	Not given		
King Lists:	P		

Seka is one of a group of nine kings known only from the Palermo Stone. Each name is followed by a representation of a squatting king wearing the crown of Lower Egypt. Whether these names are to be taken as historic personages or mythic "ancestors" is not known.

References:

Clagett 1989 pp. 66, 97-98
Edwards 1971 pp. 3-4
Gardiner 1961 pl. III

O'Mara 1979 p. 5
T. Wilkinson 2000 pp. 62, 85-86

Se...kare — Dynasty XIII

Horus Name: Unknown

Nomen: Unknown

Prenomen:

s...-kȝ-rʿ
Se...kare

Two Ladies: Unknown

Golden Falcon: Unknown

Length of Reign:	Unknown		
Tomb:	Unknown		
Mummy:	Unknown		

Consorts:	Unknown	**Variant Names:**	Re...ka
Manetho:	Not given		
King Lists:	T: (G 7.16; R 8.24; vB 7.16)		

Probably the fifty-third ruler of Dynasty XIII, Se...kare is one of a group of kings known only from the Turin Canon. Although the papyrus' fragmentary state allows for varying interpretations as to the positioning of some of the kings of this dynasty, recent research by K.S.B. Ryholt strongly supports this position for Se...kare. Se...kare is probably the prenomen of king Senebmiu, or maybe all that remains of the prenomen Sekhaenre.

References:

Gardiner 1959 pl. III, Col. VII #16
Gardiner 1961 p. 441 #7.16
Ryholt 1997a pp. 71 Col. 8 #54, 73 #54, 197 #54, 358 File 13/54

von Beckerath 1999 pp. 100 #40, 101 #40

Sekhaenre   Dynasty XIII

Horus Name: Unknown

Nomen: Unknown

Prenomen:

s.ḫꜥ-n-rꜥ
Sekhaenre

Two Ladies: Unknown

Golden Falcon: Unknown

Length of Reign:	Unknown
Tomb:	Unknown
Mummy:	Unknown

Sekhemib/Peribsen

Consorts:	Unknown	**Variant Names:**	None
Manetho:	Not given		
King Lists:	T: (R 8.27?)		

This king may be represented in the Turin Canon by the partially preserved prenomen Se...enre, in which case he is perhaps the fifty-seventh king of Dynasty XIII (however, see SE...ENRE). Attestations for this king amount to three fragmentary stone blocks bearing incomplete cartouches of his prenomen found by Naville during excavations at the temple of Montuhotep II at Deir el-Bahri.

References:

Budge 1914 p. 7: pl. 18 43130
Naville 1907 p. 68, pl. XII j.
Naville 1910 p. 12, pl. X e
Ryholt 1997a pp. 70, 74 table 18, 359
    File 13/d

von Beckerath 1999 pp. 100 #44, 101 #44

Sekhemib/Peribsen   Dynasty II

Horus Name:

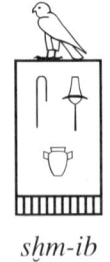

shm-ib
Sekhemib

Nomen:

shm-ib pr-n-m3ʿt
Sekhemib-Perenmaat

Two Ladies:

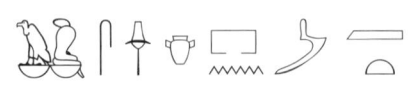

nbty shm-ib pr-n-m3ʿt

Golden Falcon: Unknown

Sekhemib/Peribsen

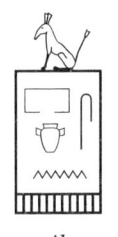

Set Name: pr-ib.sn / Peribsen

Nomen: pr-ib.sn / Peribsen

Two Ladies: nbty pr-ib.sn

Golden Falcon: Unknown

Length of Reign:	10-12 years
Tomb:	Abydos, Umm el Qa'ab, P
Mummy:	Unknown

Consorts:	Unknown	**King Lists:**	None
Manetho:	Chaires (A) Khaires (A)	**Variant Names:**	Peryebsen

Originally known as Sekhemib or Sekhemib-perenmaat, and later changing his name to Peribsen, this king is perhaps the most enigmatic ruler of one of the most confusing dynasties of Egyptian history. While it is not universally accepted that Sekhemib and Peribsen were the same person, the majority of scholars agree that this was probably the case.

The political situation in Egypt at the time of Sekhemib's ascension may have been very unstable. The half-dozen rulers to precede him in Dynasty II had evidently ruled from Memphis exclusively and, giving up the tradition of Dynasty I, had even constructed their tombs at Saqqara instead of at Abydos. Whether these kings ruled all of Egypt is difficult to say. Undoubtedly there was friction between the north and south, but there is no hard evidence to support an outright civil war at this time.

We have no way of knowing if Sekhemib, as he was originally called, was related to any of the previous kings of Dynasty II, or whether he was born in Upper or Lower Egypt. It has been suggested that he may have been a descendant of a Dynasty I king who reclaimed the Egyptian throne. We do not know how much of Egypt he controlled. It has been suggested that he may have ruled in Upper Egypt only; it has also been suggested that he was, as Peribsen, able to reunite the country. Another theory has him ruling concurrently with Dynasty II's last king, Khasekhemwy.

Sekhemib/Peribsen

On several broken stone vessels from the Step Pyramid complex, the name Sekhemib-perenmaat appears with the epithet "tribute (or conqueror) of foreign land(s)." Apart from these stone bowls, Sekhemib is also mentioned on a sealing discovered at the site of an Old Kingdom town at Elephantine and on an alabaster bowl of unknown origin. Sealings of this king were also found in both the tomb and funerary enclosure of Peribsen at Abydos.

Exactly why or when Sekhemib changed his name to Peribsen is unknown. Most puzzling of all, however, is why he removed the Horus falcon from his serekh and replaced it with the dog-like figure of the god Set. Some Egyptologists see this change of titular deities as being responsible for the later Egyptian myth "The Contendings of Horus and Set"; this is conjecture only. There is some evidence to support the connection of early pharaohs with Horus and Set; for instance, the Dynasty I ruler Anedjib, instead of bearing the Two Ladies (the goddesses Wadjet and Nekhbet) name as part of his titulary, used the Two Lords (Horus and Set).

Some of the sealings from Peribsen's tomb bear the inscription "tribute (or conquerer) of Setjet." Setjet ($S\underline{t}t$) usually refers to Syria-Palestine, but the determinative for a town, ⊗, instead of a country, ⌒, found on these sealings probably indicates a town in Egypt as being the conquered area. This town has been identified as Sethroë in the northeast Delta and was, in fact, a cult center for the god Set. Wilkinson considers the possibility that this town was added to Egypt proper and the Set cult begun there during Peribsen's reign.

The tomb of Peribsen, excavated at the turn of the century by Petrie, contained a number of sealings giving the name Peribsen as well as that of Sekhemib-perenmaat. The location of the Sekhemib seals, found at the tomb's entrance, has led a few scholars to believe that Sekhemib was the successor of Peribsen and was responsible for his burial. There were no subsidiary burials around the tomb.

Aside from the tomb at Abydos, Peribsen also had a funerary enclosure constructed alongside similar enclosures of pharaohs of Dynasty I.

Attestations of Peribsen's presence in Upper Egypt, aside from the funerary buildings at Abydos, include a sealing discovered on the island of Elephantine and a seal discovered during the excavation of Mastaba K1 at Beit Khallaf. A fragment of a stone vessel bearing Peribsen's serekh was also found in the Abydos tomb of the Dynasty I queen and regent Merneith. This latter find was undoubtedly intrusive, probably deposited in the tomb during the less-than-scientific excavation of the area by Amelineau in the late 1890s.

Although buried at Abydos, Peribsen's mortuary cult at Saqqara was still being maintained during Dynasty IV, some 150 years later.

References:

Amélineau 1899
Ayrton et al. 1904 pp. 1-5, pl. VII, IX #3
Dodson 1995 pp. 18-19
Dodson 1996 pp. 24-26
Dreyer in Kaiser et al. 1987 pp. 107-108, 109 fig. a., pl. 15a.
Edwards 1971 pp. 31-32, 33-34
Gardiner 1961 p. 416, 417-418, 419, 432
Grdseloff 1944 pp. 294-295, 296—299
Lacau and Lauer 1959 pp. 6, pl. V #8, pl. 18 #s 87-94
Lacau and Lauer 1961 pp. 41-43
Petrie 1901a pp. 11-12, 39, 31, 53, pl. XXI #s 164-177, XXII #181, XXXI, LXI tomb P
Quirke 1990 p. 45
Sharp 2001 pp. 65, 67
Shaw and Nicholson 1995 p. 220
Verbrugghe and Wickersham 1996 pp. 133, 188
von Beckerath 1999 pp. 44 #a and b, 45 #a and b
Waddell 1940 p. 37
T. Wilkinson 1999 pp. 89-90, 90-91, 244-245
T. Wilkinson 2000 pp. 74, 202, 203

Sekhem(?)kare Dynasty VII/VIII

Horus Name: Unknown

Nomen: Unknown

Prenomen:

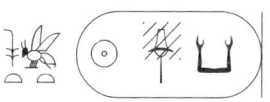

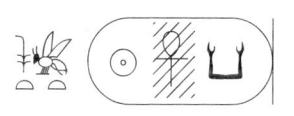

sḫm(?)-kꜣ-rꜥ
Sekhem(?)kare

ꜥnḫ(?)-kꜣ-rꜥ
Ankh(?)kare

Two Ladies: Unknown

Golden Falcon: Unknown

Length of Reign:	Unknown
Tomb:	Unknown
Mummy:	Unknown

Consorts:	Unknown	**Variant Names:**	Ankhkare
Manetho:	Not given		
King Lists:	?		

Sekhemkare

The only attestation for this king comes from a fragment of papyrus found at Elephantine. The fragment, written in hieratic script, is difficult to read and the cartouche shown may contain the name Sekhemkare or Ankhkare.

References:
Erman 1911 pp. 9 pl. Vb P 10523 [0] 285, 10 pl. V Berl. 0.285

von Beckerath 1999 pp. 70 #a, 71 #a

Sekhemkare   SIP

      Horus Name: **Nomen:** Unknown
      Unknown

                        Prenomen:

                                  $s\underline{h}m$-$k\jmath$-r^c
                                  Sekhemkare

                   Two Ladies: Unknown

                   Golden Falcon: Unknown

Length of Reign:	Unknown
Tomb:	Unknown
Mummy:	Unknown

Consorts:	Unknown	**Variant Names:**	None
Manetho:	Not given		
King Lists:	T: (?)		

This prenomen is found on a cylinder seal from Athribis(?), a scarab seal whose provenance is unknown, a statue of a vizier named Khnemes whose provenance is also unknown and a papyrus from Kahun. The papyrus is dated to a regnal year 3, month 3 of Akhet, day 25 of a king Sekhemkare. Parkinson would date the papyrus to the reign of Amenemhet V, whose prenomen was Sekhemkare; however, this dating is not proven. Aside from an otherwise unknown king, which is unlikely, this prenomen probably belongs to one of two kings from Dynasty XIII, Sonbef Sekhemkare or Amenemhet Sekhemkare, or to a Dynasty XIV ruler whose damaged prenomen, Sekhem...re, is found in the Turin Canon.

References:
Helck 1983 p. 3 #5
Parkinson 1991 p. 112 #38c
Petrie 1978 pl. XVIII #13.2

Ryholt 1997a p. 403 File P/5
Tufnell 1984 p. 366 #3098, pl. LIV #3098

Sekhemkhet   Dynasty III

Horus Name:

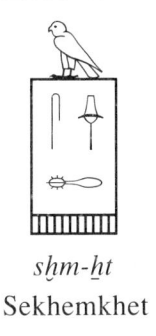

Nomen:

dsr-tti
Djoser-Teti

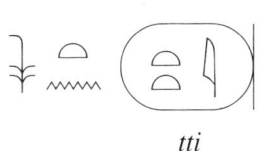

sḥm-ḥt
Sekhemkhet

tti
Teti

dsrti
Djoserty

Two Ladies:

nbty dsrt(i)ˁnḥ

Golden Falcon: Unknown

Length of Reign:	6 years
Tomb:	Unfinished step pyramid at Saqqara
Mummy:	Unknown

Consorts:	Unknown	**Variant Names:**	None
Manetho:	Tosertasis (A)		
King Lists:	Ab: (17); S: (13); T: (G 3.6)		

Probably the second pharaoh of Dynasty III, Sekhemkhet's very existence was unknown until the 1950s. The nomen, Djoserty, was known from the Turin Canon, but had not been matched up with a Horus name, and since Horus names were the only names used on contemporary attestations at that time, Djoserty was left hanging. All that began to change in 1952 when Egyptologist Zakaria Goneim

Sekhemkhet

began excavations just southwest of the pyramid complex of Djoser at Saqqara. Here he discovered the outlines of an enclosure wall much the same height and length of Djoser's enclosure wall. Inside the walls they discovered the ruins of the first level of what was intended to become a seven-stepped pyramid.

The pyramid, whose base was 120 m. square, would have stood about 72 m. tall if completed, almost 10 m. higher than Djoser's pyramid. However, only the first "step" of the monument, which rose to a height of 8 m., was ever completed. The underground structure of the tomb was rough-hewn for the most part. There were galleries and passages that yielded hundreds of stone bowls, urns and vases, and a small but beautiful selection of gold jewelry, including some 21 bracelets and armlets, a wand and a beautifully crafted cosmetics box in the shape of a bivalve shell. Also found were gold spacer-bars for jewelry, faience and carnelian beads, and a needle and tweezers made of electrum. Excavations also yielded many jar sealings with the Horus name Sekhemkhet.

The burial chamber, a rectangular room about 24 x 5 m., with a height of 5 m., had never been completed and was, in fact, not much more than a cave. In the northern part of the chamber lay an alabaster sarcophagus whose lid was not on top, but was a sliding panel at one end; the panel was sealed, the sarcophagus having not been opened in over 4,500 years. It proved to be empty, leaving scholars baffled. A body was, however, discovered in the "South Tomb," a limestone mastaba just 20 m. south of the pyramid. Found were the remains of a wooden coffin and the skeleton of a child (probably a boy) about two years old, perhaps Sekhemkhet's son.

Other than his pyramid, its surrounding complex and a single seal-impression from Elephantine, Sekhemkhet is known only from an inscription found at the turquoise mines at Wadi Maghara, in Sinai, where there are three carvings of the pharaoh, one wearing the red crown and two the white. One of the latter carvings is shown bashing in the head of a local chieftain. Prior to the discovery of Sekhemkhet, the name was given as Semerkhet (a king of Dynasty I), although most scholars were uncomfortable with that reading.

The Turin Canon gives Sekhemkhet a reign of only six years, and considering the unfinished state of his pyramid and the dearth of attestations, this does not seem out of line.

References:

Dodson 1998 pp. 33-34, 38, 39
Dodson 2003 pp. 44-45
Dodson and Hilton 2004 pp. 44, 48
Gardiner 1959 pl. II, Col. III #6
Gardiner 1961 p. 74, 433
Gardiner and Peet 1952 pl. I (a)
Gardiner and Peet 1955 pp. 14, 17, 24, 25, 27, 43, 53, 57
Giveon 1974a pp. 17-20
Goneim 1956
Goneim 1957
Kahl et al. 1995 pp. 129-137
Lauer 1976 pp. 137-140
Lehner 1997 pp. 62, 82, 83, 94, 95, 154, 156, 215,
Verbrugghe and Wickersham 1996 pp. 134, 190
Verner 1997 pp. 107, 141-142, 143-148,
von Beckerath 1999 pp. 48 #3, 49 #3
Waddell 1940 p. 43
T. Wilkinson 1999 pp. 98-99

Sekhemre... SIP

Horus Name:
Unknown

Nomen: Unknown

Prenomen:

sḫm...rˁ
Sekhemre...

Two Ladies: Unknown

Golden Horus: Unknown

Length of Reign:	Unknown		
Tomb:	Unknown		
Mummy:	Unknown		
Consorts:	Unknown	**Variant Names:**	None
Manetho:	Not given		
King Lists:	T: (?)		

This partial prenomen is known from a small fragment of a stele discovered by Petrie at Qurneh during the winter 1908-09 excavation of that site. A second partial cartouche had also been discovered by Petrie during continuing excavations at Abydos. The Abydos cartouche was found on the base of a statue of the Dynasty XII ruler Senwosret I, it having been a later addition. Petrie considered the Qurneh fragment to have been "of a stele of one of the Antefs, Ra-seshes-her-maat or Ra-seshes-up-maat." These prenominia were given to Antef I and Antef III of Dynasty XI in the 1902 version of *A History of Egypt* vol. I. It would appear that Petrie's identification was quite premature; both of these kings belong to Dynasty XVII (see INTEF V and INTEF VII). Sehkemre... was undoubtedly the prenomen of a king of Dynasty XIII, either a partial prenomen of Sobekhotep I (Sekhemrekhutowy), Khabau (also Sekhemrekhutowy), Sobekhotep III (Sekhemresewadjtowy) or one of several rulers of this dynasty whose prenominia are unknown.

References:
Petrie 1902a pp. 28-29, pl. LVIII
Petrie 1902b pp. 124, 125, 127, 129-130
Petrie 1909 p. 12, pl. XXX #4
Ryholt 1997a p. 404 File P/7

Sekhem...re   Dynasty XIV

Horus Name:
Unknown   **Nomen:** Unknown

Prenomen:

sḫm...-rˁ
Sekhem...re

Two Ladies: Unknown

Golden Falcon: Unknown

Length of Reign:	Unknown
Tomb:	Unknown
Mummy:	Unknown

Consorts:	Unknown	**Variant Names:**	None
Manetho:	Not given		
King Lists:	T: (G 8.20; R 9.20; vB 8.20)		

Perhaps the twenty-sixth king of Dynasty XIV, Sekhem...re is one of a group of kings known only from the Turin Canon. The papyrus' fragile state allows for varying interpretations as to the positioning of some of the kings of this dynasty. However, Sekhem...re's place seems secure.

References:

Gardiner 1959 pl. III, Col. VIII #20
Gardiner 1961 p. 441 #8.20
Ryholt 1997a pp. 95 Col. 9.20, 98 #26, 379 File 14/26, 409 #26

von Beckerath 1999 pp. 110 #21, 111 #21

...sekhem[re?] SIP

Horus Name: Unknown

Nomen: Unknown

Prenomen:

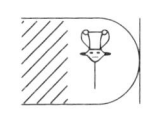

...s*ḫm*[*r‛*?]
...sekhem[re?]

Two Ladies: Unknown

Golden Falcon: Unknown

Length of Reign:	Unknown
Tomb:	Unknown
Mummy:	Unknown

Consorts:	Unknown	**Variant Names:**	Ra-Kho-Seshes
Manetho:	Not given		
King Lists:	T: (?)		

This partial name comes from a large blue bead, of unknown provenance, now in the Petrie Museum at University College, London. Petrie dated the bead to the reign of Neferhotep I of Dynasty XIII, but it might as easily belong to several other kings of that dynasty, including Sonbef (Sekhemkare), Amenhotep V (Sekhemkare) and Ined (Mersekhemre).

References:
Petrie 1925b pl. XXIV #13.21.7
Ryholt 1997a p. 404 File P/9

Sekhemre-shedwaset   Dynasty XVI

Horus Name: Unknown
Nomen: Unknown

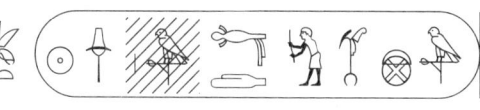

Prenomen:

sḫm-rʿ-šd-wȝst
Sekhemre-shedwaset

Two Ladies: Unknown
Golden Falcon: Unknown

Length of Reign:	Unknown
Tomb:	Unknown; probably at Dra Abu el-Naga
Mummy:	Unknown

Consorts: Unknown
Manetho: Not given
King Lists: T: (G 11.9; R 11.9)
Variant Names: None

The tenth king of Dynasty XVI, this king is known only from the Turin Canon. While no contemporary record of Sekhemre-shedwaset is known, it may be safely assumed that his power did not extend much beyond the area around Thebes. His name translates as "The Might of Re which rescues Thebes," and may mean that some fighting with the Hyksos had taken place, although this is pure speculation. He should not be confused with Dynasty XVII king Sobekemsaf I, whose prenomen was also Sekhemre-shedwaset.

References:

Dodson and Hilton 2004 p. 116
Gardiner 1959 pl. IV, Col. XI #9
Gardiner 1961 p. 442

Ryholt 1997a pp. 153, fig. 14 #9, 158, table 24, 390 File 16/10, 410 table 97 #10

Sekhemrekhutowy SIP

Horus Name: Unknown

Nomen: Unknown

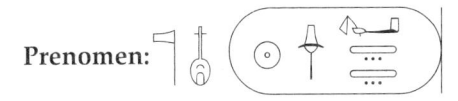

Prenomen:

sḫm-rʿ-ḫw-tꜣwy
Sekhemrekhutowy

Two Ladies: Unknown

Golden Falcon: Unknown

Length of Reign:	Unknown
Tomb:	Unknown
Mummy:	Unknown

Consorts:	Unknown	**Variant Names:**	None
Manetho:	Not given		
King Lists:	T: (?)		

This prenomen is found on a dozen cylinder-seals from various locations, and a prism, a bead and two scarabs, all of unknown provenance. While it is not impossible that one or more of these artifacts belong to a previously unknown ruler, it is much more likely that they are to be dated to Dynasty XIII rulers Sobekhotep I and/or Khabau, both of whom had the prenomen Sekhemrekhutowy. Many of the references given below attribute this prenomen to one or more of the Sobekhoteps, but the name Sekhemrekhutowy as found on the above mentioned items stands alone; no other elements of a titulary are given.

References:

Budge 1968 p. 127
El-Alfi 1991 p. 32 #36
Hall 1913 p. 270 #s 2641, 2642 and 2643
Hayes 1939 p. 29 note 2
Matouk 1972 pp. 37 #214, 182 #213
Newberry 1906 p. 115 pl. VII #4, 122 pl. X #1
Petrie 1925a pl. XXIV 13.15.5
Petrie 1978 p. XVIII #13.15.2, pl. XVIII # 15 Sobekhotep 2
Ryholt 1997a pp. 403-404 File P/6

Sekheperenre   Dynasty XIV

Horus Name:
Unknown   **Nomen:** Unknown

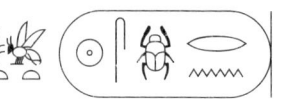

Prenomen:

sḫpr-n-rˁ
Sekheperenre

Two Ladies: Unknown

Golden Falcon: Unknown

Length of Reign: Unknown
Tomb: Unknown
Mummy: Unknown

Consorts:	Unknown	**Variant Names:**	Skheperenre
Manetho:	Not given		
King Lists:	T: (G 8.16; R 9.16; vB 8.16)		

Perhaps the twenty-second king of Dynasty XIV, Sekheperenre is one of only a handful of kings of that dynasty to have left any attestation beyond the Turin Canon. His name is found on a scarab-seal, now in the Ashmolean, whose provenance is unknown.

References:

Gardiner 1959 pl. III, Col. VIII #16
Gardiner 1961 p. 441 #8.16
Ryholt 1997a pp. 51, 52 table 13, 95 Col. 9.16, 98 #22, 198 table 37 and note 9/16-17, 379 File 14/22, 409 #22

Tufnell 1984 p. 382 #3465, 383 pl. LXII #3465
von Beckerath 1999 pp. 110 #17, 111 #17

Semenre — Dynasty XVI

Horus Name: Unknown

Nomen: Unknown

Prenomen:

s.mn-rˁ
Semenre

Two Ladies: Unknown

Golden Falcon: Unknown

Length of Reign:	Unknown
Tomb:	Unknown; probably at Dra Abu el-Naga
Mummy:	Unknown

Consorts:	Unknown	**Variant Names:**	Semenenre Semenmedjat(?)re
Manetho:	Not given		
King Lists:	T: (G 11.7; R 11.7; vB 13.7)		

The eighth king of Dynasty XVI, Semenre's parentage is unknown, as is his connection to his predecessor, Nebiryraw II. He is listed in the Turin Canon; his only other known attestation is an axe-blade, inscribed with his name, now in the Petrie Museum and of unknown provenance.

It should be noted that a few scholars would place Semenre in Dynasties XIII or XVII, though his position in the Canon definitely places him in Dynasty XVI.

References:

W. Davies 1981a pp. 177-178, pl. XXI #2
Dodson and Hilton 2004 p. 116
Ryholt 1997a pp. 158, table 24, 390 File 16/8, 410 table 97 #8

von Beckerath 1999 pp. 126 #8, 127 #8

Semerkhet — Dynasty I

Horus Name:

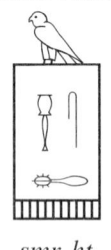

smr-ḫt
Semerkhet

Nomen:

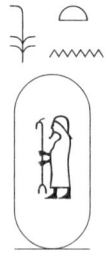

iri-nṯr
Iri-netjer
(also "Priestly Figure")

smsm
Semsem

Two Ladies:

nbty iri-nṯr

Golden Falcon: Unknown

Length of Reign:	9 years
Tomb:	Abydos, Umm el Qa'ab, U
Mummy:	Unknown

Consorts:	Unknown	**Variant Names:**	Mersekha Semenptah
Manetho:	Semempses Memphses (A, E)		
King Lists:	Ab: (7); P; T: (G 2.18)		

The seventh king of Dynasty I, Semerkhet's entire reign seems to be preserved on the Cairo Fragment I of the Palermo Stone, which states that his mother was a lady named Baterits or Betrest, but does not give his father, though he was probably Anedjib, Semerkhet's predecessor. As with most of the entries on the Palermo Stone, those of Semerkhet tell us nothing of real historic value; they record various appearances of the king, Nile heights, the making and dedications of statues of gods and religious festivals.

There has been some question as to the legitimacy of Semerkhet's accession to the throne. It is a fact that his tomb contained stone vessels that were originally inscribed with the name of Anedjib, erased and then recarved with the name of Semerkhet. However, stone vessels found beneath Djoser's step pyramid, carved with a chronological list of the last four kings of Dynasty I (Den, Anedjib, Semerkhet and Qa'a) certainly present a strong argument against a usurpation theory.

Semerkhet's reign may have seen some difficulties. Manetho states that "In his reign a very great calamity befell Egypt." While Manetho is a questionable source at best, it is certainly true that trade with Palestine was much reduced, although a small hoard of Palestinian clay vessels was discovered in Semerkhet's tomb. For a long time it was believed that a rock tablet carved in the Wadi-Maghara in Sinai represented a military invasion of that region by Semerkhet, but the name on the carving has been shown to have belonged to the obscure Dynasty III king Sekhemkhet.

Although no examples of monumental tomb construction at Saqqara come from Semerkhet's reign, his tomb at Abydos is of finer construction than that of Anedjib, his immediate predecessor. The tomb is surround by 69 subsidiary graves. An interesting innovation employed at the tomb is having the royal burial chamber and the subsidiary graves covered by the same roofing, proving that the courtiers buried around the tomb were interred at the same time as the king; thus, it is a pretty clear-cut example of ritual murder. It has been suggested that a structure often referred to as the "Western Mastaba," which stands near the funerary enclosures of Merneith/Den, may well be the enclosure of Semerkhet.

It is during this reign that the 𓎟𓏏 (*nbty* or Two Ladies) name became a permanent and separate part of the royal titulary. It had been used sporadically before this time, almost always in conjunction with the 𓇓𓏏 (*nswt-bity*) name; in fact, both the *nswt-bity* and *nbty* were usually the same.

As though archaeological problems were not enough, there are various transliterations and translations for Semerkhet's prenomina and Two Ladies name. In the past, "Priestly Figure" and/or "Semenptah" have been used, and there is some possibility that both of these translations are correct. The prenomen "Semsem" certainly is similar to "Semenptah," the priestly figure in the cartouche from the Abydos List is likely to be a priest of the god Ptah, and Manetho's "Semempses" is close to "Semenptah." However, recently "Iri-netjer" has been the preferred reading of the name.

References:

Clagett 1989 pp. 74-76
Dodson and Hilton 2004 pp. 44-46
Emery 1961 pp. 84-86, 199
Gardiner 1959 pl. I, Col. II #19

Semqen

Gardiner 1961 pp. 401, 430 (both entries as Semempses)
Gardiner and Peet 1952 pl. I #1a
Kaplony 1963 vol. I pp. 473-474
Lacau and Lauer 1959 pp. 9-12
Petrie 1900 pp. 5, 13-14, 24-25, 26, 42, 44, pl. VI #s 9-11, VII, XII #1, XXVIII, XXXV-XXXVI, LX, LXVI-LXVII
Rice 1999 p. 37
Spencer 1993 pp. 66-67, fig. 46
Uphill 1984
Verbrugghe and Wickersham 1996 pp. 117 note 57, 132, 188
von Beckerath 1999 pp. 40 #7, 41 #7
Waddell 1940 pp. 29, 33, 35, 215
T. Wilkinson 1999 pp. 79-80, 158, 159, 203, 207
T. Wilkinson 2000 pp. 193, 194-195, 195-200

Semqen   Dynasty XV

ḥkȝ-ḫȝswt smkn
(Ruler of Foreign Lands) Semqen

Length of Reign:	Unknown
Tomb:	Unknown
Mummy:	Unknown

Consorts:	Unknown	**Variant Names:**	Šamuqēnu Sem-ken
Manetho:	Not given		
King Lists:	None		

Ryholt has considered the possibility that Semqen may have been the first, or at least a very early, ruler of the Hyksos' Dynasty XV. His placing of Semqen is based upon the design of a single scarab found at the site of the Hyksos settlement at Tell el-Yahudiya in the Delta, made of brown steatite and inscribed with the title *ḥkȝ-ḫȝswt*, which is usually translated as "ruler of foreign lands," followed by the name Semqen. Ryholt makes it perfectly clear that he is only putting forth a possibility, and warns against assuming that the term *ḥkȝ-ḫȝswt*, even if dated securely to a Dynasty XV date, necessarily represents a ruler of that dynasty.

References:

Dodson and Hilton 2004 p. 114
G. Fraser 1900 p. 24 #179, pl. VII #179
Hornung and Staehelin 1976 pp. 223-224 #166
Martin 1971 p. 113 #1453, pl. 10 #26
Newberry 1906 p. 152 #10, pl. XXIII #10
Petrie 1978 pl. XXI, Dyn. XV #2
Ryholt 1997a pp. 121-123, 125 table 23, 127, 201 table 40 383, File 15/1, 410, table 96
Tufnell 1984 p. 382 #3463, pl. LXII #3463
von Beckerath 1999 pp. 116 #c, 117 #c

Senaaib   Dynasty XIII/?

Horus Name:

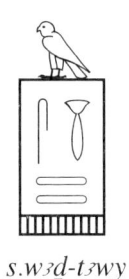

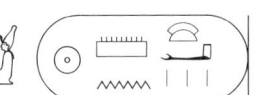

Nomen: *sn˓-ib*
Senaaib

s.w3d-t3wy

Prenomen: *mn-ḫ˓w-r˓*
Menkhaure

Two Ladies: Unknown

Golden Falcon: Unknown

Length of Reign:	Unknown
Tomb:	Unknown
Mummy:	Unknown

Consorts:	Unknown	Sennaib
Manetho:	Not given	Snaaib
		Snaiib
King Lists:	None	
Variant Names:	Sena'aib	

This king is known only from a stele discovered at Abydos and now in the Cairo Museum (CG20517) which gives us the Horus name, nomen and prenomen of this ruler. Ryholt places Senaaib in the "Abydos Dynasty" but von Beckerath places him near the end of Dynasty XIII.

References:

Helck 1983 p. 47 #64
Malaise 1981 p. 280
Ryholt 1997a pp. 163 and note 593, 165 table 27, 392 File Abd/c

von Beckerath 1999 pp. 104 #j, 105 #j

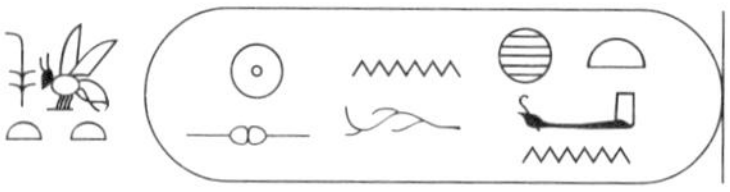

Senakhtenre   Dynasty XVII

Horus Name: Unknown

Nomen: *t3-ˁ3ˁ-3*
Taa (the Elder)

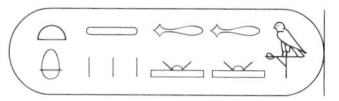

Prenomen: *s.nḫt-n-rˁ*
Senakhtenre

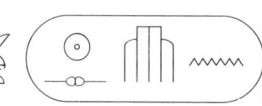

s.ḫnt-n-rˁ
Sekhentenre

Two Ladies: Unknown

Golden Falcon: Unknown

Length of Reign:	Unknown.
Tomb:	Dra Abu el-Naga
Mummy:	Unknown

Consorts:	Tetisheri	Taa-a
Manetho:	Not given	Ta'o
King Lists:	K: (26)	Te'o
Variant Names:	Taa	

The seventh king of Dynasty XVII, Senakhtenre is a shadowy figure whose parentage is unknown, as is his connection, if any, with his predecessor, Sobekemsaf II. In fact, no contemporary attestations for this pharaoh have been found. We know that he existed because of his inclusion on the Karnak king list, where his prenomen appears next to that of his successor, Seqenenre. He is also listed on an offering table from Thebes which dates to Dynasty XIX and his cartouche appears in a tomb dated to the reign of Ramesses II, although the name is given incorrectly as Sekhentenre.

During the reign of Ramesses IX, rumors of robbery prompted an inspection of some of the royal pyramid-tombs at Dra Abu el-Naga. Two of the inspected tombs were listed as having belonged to two rulers, each having the name Seqenenre Taa. The odds of two successive pharaohs bearing the exact same nomen and prenomen are astronomical; most likely, a scribal error occurred either during the actual tomb inspection, or when the field notes were later transcribed and the prenomen Senakhtenre was recorded as Seqenenre. However, Ryholt posits that Seqenenre may have had two pyramid-tombs for some unknown reason and therefore there is only one Tao. He suggests that Senakhtenre's nomen was Siamen and gives a stamp-seal inscribed with that name in a cartouche as possible evidence:

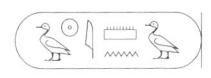

(s3) s3-imn

The stamp was found in a tomb at Dra Abu el-Naga along with a seal "virtually identical in workmanship" which gives the name Seqenenre. Another possibility is that the seal belonged to a son of the pharaoh Ahmose, also named Siamen, whose name enclosed in a cartouche appears in a scene from the tomb of Anhur-khau (TT359, reign of Ramesses IV) at Thebes. Seqenenre was most probably Siamen's grandfather; finding their names together seems at least as likely as Ryholt's theory.

The nomen Taa-a is sometimes translated "the Brave," however, it has been suggested that "the Elder" might be more accurate.

References:

Dodson and Hilton 2004 pp. 118-119, 122-123, 126-127
Ikram and Dodson 1998 p. 207 illustration 263,
Newberry 1906 p. 89, fig.s 95 and 96
Peet 1930 p. 38
Petrie 1889 #754

D. Redford 1986 pp. 43, 48 #12, 50 #23
Ryholt 1997a pp. 171 table 28, 272, 278-280, 396-396, File 17/7, 410, table 98
von Beckerath 1999 pp. 128 #13, 129 #13

Senebmiu   Dynasty XIII

Horus Name: **Nomen:**
Unknown

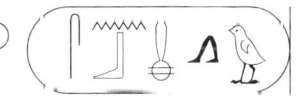

snb-mi-iw
Senebmiu

Senebmiu

Prenomen: *s.wꜣḥ-n-rꜥ*
Sewahenre

Two Ladies: Unknown

Golden Horus: Unknown

Length of Reign:	Unknown
Tomb:	Unknown
Mummy:	Unknown

Consorts:	Unknown	**Variant Names:**	Senebmaui Sonbmijew
Manetho:	Not given		
King Lists:	K: (49); T: (R 8.26?)		

This king may be represented in the Turin Canon by the partially preserved prenomen Se...enre, in which case he might be the fifty-seventh ruler of Dynasty XIII (However, see SEKHAENRE).

Attestations for Senebmiu are few; all come from Upper Egypt, in the vicinity of Thebes, which points to the fact that by this reign Lower Egypt, and possibly Middle Egypt, were no longer under the control of Dynasty XIII. Senebmiu's nomen and prenomen were discovered on one side of a small naos found during excavations of the temple of Montuhotep II at Deir el-Bahri. A staff bearing this king's prenomen, inscribed for the "Treasurer of the King of Upper and Lower Egypt...Sonbnay" was discovered in a now-lost tomb at Qurna, on the west side of the Nile, opposite Karnak temple. Finally, a fragment of a stele bearing Senebmiu's nomen was found at Gebelein near Thebes, and is now in the British Museum (BM EA24895).

References:

Berlev 1974 pp. 106, 111, pl. XXVIII
Budge 1914 p. 7, pl. 18 no. 24898
Dodson 1994b p. 38 note 10

Naville 1910 pp. 12, 21, pl. X c
Ryholt 1997a pp. 71, 72, 74 table 18, 358 File 13/c

Sened   Dynasty II

Horus Name: Unknown

Nomen:

snd
Sened

sndi
Senedi

snḏ
Senedji

Two Ladies: Unknown

Golden Falcon: Unknown

Length of Reign:	Unknown
Tomb:	Unknown
Mummy:	Unknown

Consorts:	Unknown	**Variant Names:**	Sendi Senedji
Manetho:	Sethenes (A)		
King Lists:	Ab: (13); S: (7); T: (G 2.24)		

Although Sened is given in the Abydos, Saqqara and Turin king lists, there is only one contemporary attestation to prove his existence. Other than the king lists, this ruler is mentioned in two Dynasty IV sources. an inscription in the Saqqara tomb of the mortuary priest Sheri and on a fragment of a stone block from the mortuary temple of Khafre at Giza.

Sheri was the "Overseer of the Priests of Sened" and also of another Dynasty II ruler, Peribsen. It is interesting that this obscure ruler's mortuary cult was still active some 150 years after his death. The inscribed stone from Khafre's temple was undoubtedly part of a reworked block, taken from an unknown site. The inscription

Seneferka

consists of Sened's name, not surrounded by a cartouche, preceded by the [glyph] title.

Sened was probably interred at Saqqara, yet no trace of his tomb has been found.

References:

Edwards 1971 pp. 20, 31
Gardiner 1959 pl. I, Col. II #24
Gardiner 1961 pp. 415, 431, 432
Steindorff, in Hölscher 1912 p. 106
Verbrugghe and Wickersham 1996
    pp. 112, 133, 188

von Beckerath 1999 pp. 42 #5, 43 #5
Waddell 1940 p. 37
T. Wilkinson 1999 pp. 88-89, 242
T. Wilkinson 2000 pp. 54, 59, 74, 79

Seneferka   Dynasty I/II(?)

Horus Name:

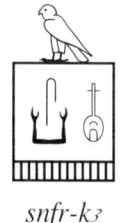

snfr-k3
Seneferka

Nomen: Unknown

Two Ladies: Unknown

Golden Falcon: Unknown

Length of Reign:	Unknown
Tomb:	Unknown
Mummy:	Unknown

Consorts:	Unknown	**Variant Names:**	Neferseka Sekanefer Sneferka
Manetho:	Not given(?)		
King Lists:	None		

Seneferka is attested to by a serekh found on a fragment of a stone vessel discovered on the surface during the excavation of Saqqara Tomb 3505 and by another serekh on a stone bowl discovered under Djoser's Step Pyramid, also at Saqqara. Exactly when this king reigned is unknown; however, the serekh discovered at Djoser's pyramid was carved over a partially erased serekh of king Qa'a, the last legitimate ruler of Dynasty I. Obviously Seneferka followed Qa'a, but the usurpation of the bowl does not necessarily mean that Seneferka followed him directly. Saqqara Tomb 3505 is dated to the reign of Den, the fifth king of Dynasty I, but since the vase fragment bearing the serekh was found on the surface, it is useless for dating purposes.

Recent excavations at the tomb of Qa'a at Abydos show that he was most likely interred by Hotepsekhemwy, first king of Dynasty II; this would make Hotepsekhemwy the direct successor of Qa'a, leaving no place for Seneferka at the end of Dynasty I. It has been suggested that an ephemeral king, perhaps Seneferka, ruled for an unknown time earlier in Dynasty I, between kings Aha and Djer. However, there is little or no evidence for this theory, and two seal impressions from Abydos, one giving the succession between Narmer and Den and the other the succession from Narmer to Qa'a, seem to negate the theory completely. Dodson would place Seneferka near Dynasty II's end, directly before Khasekhemwy. Wilkinson suggests "Seneferka" might have been "an alternative Horus name" which Qa'a used for a brief time.

It is not impossible that Seneferka was a short-lived usurper who ruled from Memphis for a short time and whom Hotepsekhemwy deposed.

References:

Dodson 1996 pp. 20, 30 note #6
Dreyer 1993b p. 11
Edwards 1971 p. 29
Emery 1949-58 vol. III pp. 11, 31-32 B #1, pl. 28a and b, pl. 38 #1
Kaplony 1968 p. 33-34, pl. 3, 20
Kemp 1966 p. 22
Lacau and Lauer 1959 p. 15 #86, Pl. 17 #86, 40 #86 and note 1
Spencer 1993 p. 64 fig. 43
Swelim 1974 pp. 67-77, pl. I and Chronological table
von Beckerath 1999 pp. 46 #b, 47 #b
T. Wilkinson 1999 p. 82, 209
T. Wilkinson 2000 p. 114

Senefer...re — Dynasty XIV

Horus Name: Unknown

Nomen: Unknown

Prenomen:

snfr...re
Senefer...re

Two Ladies: Unknown

Golden Falcon: Unknown

Length of Reign: Unknown
Tomb: Unknown
Mummy: Unknown

Seneferu

Consorts:	Unknown	**Variant Names:**	Senefer[ka?]re
Manetho:	Not given		
King Lists:	T: (G 9.7; R 10.7; vB 9.9)		

Perhaps the forty-third king of Dynasty XIV, Senefer…re is one of a group of kings known only from the Turin Canon. The papyrus' fragile state allows for varying interpretations as to the positioning of some of the kings of this dynasty. However, Senefer…re's place seems secure.

References:

Gardiner 1959 pl. III, Col. IX #7
Gardiner 1961 p. 441 #9.7 as "Senefer[ka?]re"
Ryholt 1997a pp. 95 Col. 10 #7, 98 #43, 380 File 14/43, 409 #43

von Beckerath 1999 pp. 112 #c, 113 #c

Seneferu   Dynasty IV

Horus Name:

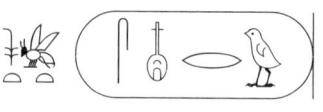

nb-m3't

Nomen: snfrw
Sneferu

Two Ladies: nbty nb-m3't

Golden Falcon: bik-nbw

Length of Reign:	24 years
Tomb:	Dahshur: (The Bent Pyramid) "The Southern Shining Pyramid"
	Dahshur: (The North or Red Pyramid) "The Shining Pyramid"
	Pyramid at Meidum: "Rises in Splendor"
Mummy:	Qasr el-Aini Hospital

Consorts:	Hetepheres I	**Variant Names:**	Senefru
Manetho:	Soris (A)		Senofru
King Lists:	Ab: (20); P; S: (16); T: (G 3.9; vB 3.9)		Snefru
			Snofru

Seneferu may have been the son of the pharaoh Huni and that ruler's queen, Meresankh I. Present knowledge of the period gives no hint of a dynastic rift, but for some reason Seneferu was considered the first king of Dynasty IV and it is with his reign that Egypt formally enters the period known as the Old Kingdom.

Seneferu is listed on various king lists, including the Abydos list, the Saqqara list, the Palermo Stone and the Turin Canon. The Palermo Stone has preserved what would seem to be regnal years 12(?) through 15(?), although it is evident that records of Seneferu's reign probably filled the entire sixth and seventh registers of the stone. Year 13(?) records "smiting Nubia," although it is unknown whether an action was actually fought, or whether the term implied some sort of ritual re-enactment. The stone records the taking of 7,000 prisoners of both sexes and some 200,000 sheep and goats. Wilkinson draws attention to the fact that Seneferu also had ordered the construction of a structure called "The wall of the south and north-land (called) 'the mansions of Sneferu'." He suggests that this might be a reference to the building of border fortifications, and might specially refer to the earliest fortress at Buhen, in Lower Nubia. Also mentioned in years 13, 14 and 15 are references to the importation of large quantities of pine wood (forty shiploads of this wood in year 13 alone) and the building of one pine and 63 cedar "royal" boats. Obviously trade with Byblos, which supplied virtually all of the wood, was in full swing.

A fragment of the Palermo Stone now in the Cairo Museum, dated to late in Seneferu's reign, records plunder of 1,100 "live captives" and 23,000(?) sheep and goats taken in Libya.

Expeditions were also sent to Sinai; two carved reliefs at Wadi Maghara attest to Egyptian presence at the turquoise mines there. In both reliefs, the king is shown clubbing a Bedouin; the scenes do not necessarily represent any military action, but may simply be idealized representations.

Although difficult to believe, all evidence points to Seneferu's having built three major pyramids and possibly as many as seven small step pyramids. Evidently, the first of these pyramids to be built was at Meidum, at the entrance to the Faiyum area in Middle Egypt. Originally conceived as a seven-stepped monument, the builders enlarged the structure to eight steps; the stepped structure was then filled in to form a true pyramid measuring 144 m. square and 92 m.

tall. The tomb was completed by regnal year 14, although it has been suggested that the original version ended as a step pyramid and the filling-in process occurred some years later in the reign. Today the tomb is a "bizarre, truncated pyramid" standing about 65 m. high and surrounded by huge mounds of stone rubble, the victim of many generations of stone robbery. Remains of a mortuary chapel were discovered on the pyramid's east side. No sarcophagus was found in the pyramid's burial chamber, which would seem to indicate that no burial took place there. There was one small subsidiary pyramid, now completely destroyed.

Two pyramids belonging to Seneferu were constructed at Dahshur. The "Bent Pyramid" seems to have been the first of the two under construction. Its odd name comes from the angle of the pyramid changing from its originally planned 60 degrees to 55 degrees, and then, at the height of 45 m., to an angle of only 45 degrees. This change may have been needed because the pyramid was built on a foundation of clay rather than stone, or possibly because of concern for possible damage to one or both burial chambers. The pyramid measured 189.43 m. square at the base and stood 105 m. tall. A small, open mortuary chapel was attached to the east side of the tomb. A roofless causeway led to a magnificently decorated valley temple, the only one of its kind so far discovered. A small subsidiary pyramid was located to the south of the king's pyramid. No evidence to support a burial has been discovered in either pyramid.

Seneferu's second pyramid at Dahshur is some 4 km. to the north of the Bent Pyramid. Today it is known as the "Red Pyramid" because of the color of the stone used in its construction. The structure measured 220 m. square and reached a height of 104 m. This pyramid has the lowest angle of any Egyptian pyramid, most likely due to fears created during the modification of the Bent Pyramid. It is also the first true pyramid to have survived relatively intact, missing only the casing stones.

A series of seven small step pyramids, running from Seila near Meidum to the island of Elephantine, may have been built during Seneferu's reign. The method of construction and architectural elements places these pyramids in late Dynasty III/early Dynasty IV; Seneferu's name has been found on a stele at the monument at Seila. Similarity in construction has led some scholars to give credit for all of the buildings to Seneferu. The discovery of a granite conical object bearing the name of Seneferu's father, Huni, near the pyramid at Elephantine has led other scholars to credit all of the monuments, with the exception of Seila, to Huni.

Charred human remains and wrappings discovered among the debris in one of the chambers of the Red Pyramid may perhaps belong to Seneferu. These incomplete remains belonged to a man of "rather small size" past middle age.

The exact length of Seneferu's rule is not certain. The Turin Canon gives him 24 years, yet some scholars believe that he may have reigned far longer. We have graffiti from the Red Pyramid that give dates of a "Year of the 24th occurrence...," which refers to the cattle census that was usually taken every two years. But during Seneferu's time, we cannot be sure the census was taken biennially. If the cattle count was every two years, Seneferu ruled about 48 years; if not, the Turin Canon is correct with its recording of 24 years.

Seneferu was married to his sister, Hetepheres; their son Khufu would succeed to the throne.

Seneferu was well treated by history. He was remembered as a wise ruler and figured in many literary works, including the *Instructions of Kagemni*, which tells of his succession to the throne, in *The Prophecies of Neferti*, where he is remembered as a "beneficent king," and in a "tale of wonder" from Papyrus Westcar, where he seeks a release from his boredom. The funerary cult of the king, whose center was located at the valley temple of the Bent Pyramid at Dahsur, continued well into the Middle Kingdom. During the reign of Amenemhet III of Dynasty XII, Seneferu became a local saint at Sinai, where he was identified with the god Horus.

References:

Batrawi 1951 pp. 435-440, pl. I & II
Clagett 1989 pp. 82-84
Dodson 2003 pp. 49-56
Dodson and Hilton 2004 pp. 18, 45, 50-52, 51, 52-53, 57-58, 60-61
Fakhry 1959
Fakhry 1961a
Fakhry 1961b pp. 63, 67-68, 70, 71-97
Gardiner 1959 pl. II, Col. III #9
Gardiner 1961 pp. 77-79, 434
Gardiner and Peet 1952 pl. II #5, IV #6
Gardiner and Peet 1955 pp. 56-57
Ikram and Dodson 1998 pp. 92, 111, 315, 317, 320
Jánosi 1992 p. 52
Kanawati 2003 p. 2
Lehner 1997 pp. 97-105, 245
Lichtheim 1975 pp. 58, 59-60, 139-140, 215-216
Malek 2000 pp. 253-254, 256
Spalinger 1994 pp. 281-283
Verbrugghe and Wickersham 1996 pp. 104 note 33, 134, 190
Verner 1997 pp. 153-154, 159-168, 174-189, 461-462
Verner 2001b p. 586
Ventura 1985 pp. 281-283
von Beckerath 1999 pp. 52 #1, 53 #1
Waddell 1940 p. 47
Weeks 2001 p. 422
T. Wilkinson 2000 pp. 140-146, 232-236, 251

Senen...   Dynasty IX/X

Horus Name: Unknown   **Nomen:**

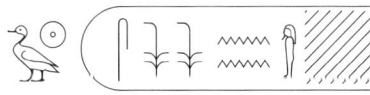

snn...

Senen...

Prenomen: Unknown

Two Ladies: Unknown

Golden Falcon: Unknown

Senwosret I

Length of Reign:	Unknown
Tomb:	Unknown
Mummy:	Unknown

Consorts:	Unknown	**Variant Names:**	Senne...
Manetho:	Not given		
King Lists:	T: (4.22)		

Senen... is one of the pharaohs who controlled an unknown amount of territory around Herakleopolis in Middle Egypt (see "Herakleopolitans" in Glossary). Attestations for the kings whose names are known are few; most are known only as names from the Turin Canon. Such is the case with this king.

Senen... is the successor of a ruler whose name is given as Khety in the Turin Canon, and is probably to be identified with Wahkare Khety II. What relationship they might have had, if any, is unknown.

References:
Gardiner 1959 pl. II, Col. IV #22
von Beckerath 1999 pp. 72 #5, 73 #5

Senwosret I   Dynasty XII

Horus Name:

ꜥnḫ-mswt

Nomen:

s-n-wsrt
Senwosret

Prenomen:

ḫpr-kꜣ-rꜥ
Kheperkare

Two Ladies:

nbty ꜥnḫ-mswt

Senwosret I

Golden Falcon:

bik-nbw ʿnḫ-mswt

Length of Reign:	45 years
Tomb:	Pyramid at Lisht: "Senwosret Beholds the Two Lands"
Mummy:	Unknown

Consorts:	Neferu (III)	**Variant Names:**	Senusert Senusret Sesostris Usertsen
Manetho:	Sesonchosis (A, E) Sesonkhosis (A, E)		
King Lists:	Ab: (60); S: (40); T: (G 5.21)		

The son of Amenemhet I and his queen, Neferitatjenen, Senwosret I had been a coregent with his father for ten years when the elder king was assassinated by his own bodyguards. It is likely that there had been a certain amount of civil unrest during Amenemhet's rule; it is safe to assume that there were rivals for the throne, and that a coregency was considered the best way to assure that Senwosret would hold it at his father's passing. A literary work of the late Middle Kingdom, *The Story of Sinuhe*, asserts that Senwosret was at the western border of Egypt, on his way home from a successful war with a Libyan tribe, the Tjehenu, when he received word of his father's death. Naturally "the hawk flew" to the palace and since Senwosret held the throne for another 35 years, it appears that the plot failed, unrest was stamped out, and many heads rolled. On the other hand, Senwosret rewarded loyalty by appointing those he trusted to high positions, e.g., the two Djefa-Hapi's at Asyut, and most importantly, Sarenput, who as governor at Elephantine was responsible for Egypt's southern border.

Once stability had been restored, Senwosret set to work building, restoring and adding to temples and other structures throughout the land. Examples of building projects, beginning at Aswan, include a rebuilding in limestone of the Dynasty XI mud-brick temple of the goddess Satet; inscribed blocks from the nearby Heqaib sanctuary; stone blocks from Kom Ombo, Edfu, and Esna inscribed with the cartouche of a pharaoh named Senwosret (almost certainly belonging to Senwosret I); an offering table and inscribed brick from Hierakonpolis; major construction at the temple of Montu at Tod; and inscribed blocks from the temple of Montu at Armant.

Senwosret I

Construction work on the temple of Amen at Karnak began sometime after year 22 of the reign. Although almost nothing from the Middle Kingdom temple survives, Senwosret's kiosk, sometimes referred to as the "white chapel," has been reconstructed, and is a lovely little building with beautifully cut examples of some of the finest art ever produced in Egypt.

The temple of Min at Coptos received attention under Senwosret I, as is evidenced by the finding of relief fragments bearing his cartouches—not in context, but in the vicinity of the temple. It should be noted that a fragment of relief containing the name of Amenemhet I was discovered with the Senwosret reliefs, which might be evidence of the two kings building together during the coregency.

Although Petrie discovered foundation deposits and a doorjamb, not much else remains of Senwosret's additions to the temple of Osisis at Abydos; however, excavations showed that a great deal of the earlier temple had been demolished to make way for the new building.

At El-Atawla, opposite Asyut, additions were made to the temple of Nemty. From the Faiyum comes a large (almost 13 m. tall) round-topped stele or obelisk found at Abgig, and of course there was the completion of Amenemhet I's pyramid and funerary complex, not to mention Senwosret's own tomb and complex.

An obelisk still standing at Heliopolis is almost all that remains of Senwosret's additions to the temple of Atum. We also have inscribed blocks from Bubastis. A statue of Senwosret from Tanis and another from Alexandria were moved there, probably from Heliopolis, by Merenptah in Dynasty XIX. While not numerous, scarabs are known for Senwosret.

Egypt's interest in the gold, ivory, and potential slaves of Nubia, pursued by Montuhotep II and Amenemhet I, was continued under Senwosret I. Two stelae found in the fortress of Buhen, at the Second Cataract, date to Senwosret I's regnal year five. We do not know what the stelae were meant to memorialize, but they predate the military invasion of year 29/9 of the father-son rule by about four years. Under any circumstance, the rape of Nubia continued unabated, as attested to by the campaigns of Senwosret I. The campaign in year 18 appears to have been the most successful, giving Egypt control over all of Lower Nubia and setting the boundary at the Second Cataract, where a series of forts were built at Buhen as well as at Aniba, Kubban, and Ikkur. Still in Nubia, but just barely, the Wadi el-Hudi amethyst mines, some 25 miles southeast of Aswan, were visited by expeditions sent by Senwosret in years 17, 20, 22, 23, 24 and 29. An undated stele from the same location lavishes these words of praise upon Senwosret: "The good god who slays the tribesfolk…who makes an end of Nubian hordes, who lops off heads of disaffected tribes…."

As with Nubia, Senwosret I followed his father's interests in the turquoise mines of Sinai. From the temple of Hathor at Serabit el-Khadim comes an undated stele and an inscribed lintel, the earliest architectural element found at the site. Also from the temple comes a base upon which three statues once stood, a central statue of Amenemhet I, flanked on each side by a statue of Senwosret I. Inscriptions from another statue group, probably dedicated by Senwosret I, give the name of the dedicator along with those of Montuhotep II, Montuhotep III and Amenemhet I. A fragment of white limestone from Byblos, on the coast of Lebanon, bears an engraving of Isis and of Senwosret's cartouche.

Expeditions to the Wadi Hammamat occurred in years 2, 16 and 38, and at least three expeditions (years 2, 16 and 31) went to the quarries at Hatnub. The Hammamat inscription of year 38 boasts a force of 17,000 people arriving there.

Senwosret chose to have his funerary complex built at Lisht, not far from that of his father. Evidence from control notes found on blocks from the pyramid show that construction didn't begin until the pharaoh's tenth regnal year. The pyramid, which today is a mound of rubble standing about 20 m. high, originally measured 61 m. tall with base of 105 x 105 m. The pyramid was constructed by building a series of retaining walls which decreased in size as they rose, the spaces between the walls being filled with blocks of cut stone and stone fragments cemented together. The whole was then enclosed in casing stones of white limestone. The tomb's entrance, once covered by a small chapel, is in the middle of the north side at ground level; a tunnel slopes downward to the burial chamber that has never been explored, since it lies beneath the water table and is flooded. The complex itself featured, aside from the cult temple, a mortuary temple and cult pyramid. All these buildings were surrounded by a stone wall which was decorated on the inward-facing sides with a series of bas-reliefs giving Senwosret's Horus name, prenomen or nomen every 5 m. Outside this inner enclosure wall were nine small subsidiary pyramids, built for the King's Great Wife Neferu and lesser wives and daughters. A causeway led from the mortuary temple to the valley temple (location unknown). The inner walls of the causeway were decorated, and every 10 cubits was a niche that held a nearly life-sized statue of the king, those on the north side wearing the red crown and those on the south the white crown. A goodly number of statues and relief work have survived from the complex and show a high degree of artistic achievement.

An inscription from the quarries at Hatnub and another from the "white chapel" at Karnak record a Sed festival celebrated in Senwosret's year 31. Manetho gives his Sesonkhosis (Sesostris) a reign of 46 years. The Turin Canon records a reign of 45 years, plus an unknown number of months. It has been suggested that a stone bowl inscribed with a "year 46" found at Elephantine may belong to Senwosret I, but it might also date to Amenemhet III, who reigned for 46 years and who also left inscriptions at Elephantine.

Senwosret I

References:

Anthes 1928 pp. 76-78, #49, pl. 31
D. Arnold 1988
D. Arnold 1992
F. Arnold 1990 pp. 65-155
Berman 1986 pp. 173-213
Callender 2000 pp. 160-162
Couyat and Montet 1912 pp. 64-66 #87, 84 #117, 85-86 #123, pl. XX
Dodson 2003 pp. 12, 86-87, 129, 130-131
Dodson and Hilton 2004 pp. 90, 92-93, 96-98
Fakhry 1952 pp. 23-24, 25, 29, 30, figs. 20-27, pl. VIII.B, IX-XIII, XIII.A
Forbes 1991/1992 pp. 12-18
Gardiner 1959 pl. II, Col. V.21
Gardiner 1961 p. 43
Gardiner and Peet 1952 pl. XIX #s 64, 66, 67, XX #65, XXI #s 68, 71, XXII #70
Gardiner and Peet 1955 pp. 34, 36, 38, 55, 84-86 #s64-70
Goyon 1957 pp. 81-85 #61, 86-88, 89, 89-90, pl. XIX-XXI, XXIII-XXIV, XXVI
Grajetzki 2005 p. 30
Grajetzki 2006 pp. 36-45, 107, 134-135
Habachi 1975 pp. 27-37
Hall 1913 pp. 7-10 #s 69-99
G. Johnson 2002
Lehner 1997 pp. 169, 170-173, 226-227
Lichtheim 1975 pp. 135-139, 139-145, 222-235
Murnane 1977 pp. 2-5 and note 20
Naville 1891 pl. XXXIV #d
Obsomer 1995
Peden 2001 pp. 20, 35-36, 38-40, 44-45, 68
Petrie 1903 pp. 6-7, 16-17, 20, 33, 43, pl. XXVI, LVI, LXII
Petrie 1978 p. 19 #38, pl. XII, 12.1 #s 1-36
Sadek 1980 pp. 16-36 #s 6-15, 84-92 #s 143-147
Sadek 1985 pp. 1-4 #s 153-154
H.S. Smith 1976 pp. 13-14 #882, 61-63, pl. IV #4, LIX #3
Seyfried 1984 pp. 247-253
Tufnell 1984 p. 360 #s 3001-3030, pl. LI #s 3001-3030
Tyldesley 2006 pp. 72
Verbrugghe and Wickersham 1996 pp. 138, 196
Verner 1997 pp. 384-385, 399-406, 465
von Beckerath 1999 pp. 82 #2, 83 #2
Waddell 1940 p. 67, 69, 71
Zaba 1974 pp. 109-115

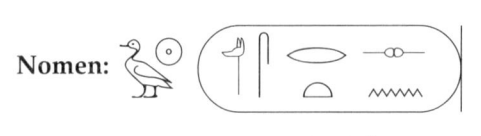

Senwosret II   Dynasty XII

Horus Name:

sšmw-t3wy

Nomen:

s-n-wsrt
Senwosret

Prenomen:

ḫʿ-ḫpr-rʿ
Khakheperre

Two Ladies:

nbty šri-m3ʿt

Senwosret II

Golden Falcon: bik-nbw ḥtp-ntrw

Length of Reign:	8+ years
Tomb:	Pyramid at Lahun: "The Power of Senwosret"
Mummy:	Unknown

Consorts:	Khenemetnefer-hedjet-Weret (I) Neferet (II)	**Variant Names:**	Ra-kho-kheper Senusert Senusret Sesostris Usertsen
Manetho:	Not given		
King Lists:	Ab: (62); S: (42); T: (G 5.23)		

The fourth ruler of Dynasty XII, Senwosret II's relationship to his predecessor is unclear. While it is generally assumed that he was a son of Amenemhet II, there doesn't seem to be any real evidence to support that assumption. However, Senwosret II was married to Amenemhet's daughter, Neferet (II), and seems also to have been elevated to the throne as a coregent in about year 32/33 of the senior king. The joint rule lasted for three years, until Amenemhet's death in his regnal year 35.

The development of the Faiyum area seems to have been of prime importance to Senwosret II. During his reign, a dyke was constructed and a series of canals were dug to divert water from Lake Moeris, thus reclaiming a large amount of land for farming. Settlements began to spring up and the area prospered. The pharaoh ordered monuments built, such as a sanctuary at Qasr es-Sagha; most of these monuments were never finished, as the pharaoh died before they could be completed. However, the development of the Faiyum continued throughout Dynasty XII.

Not a great many attestations for Senwosret II are known. A black granite statue of the king was found at Hierakonpolis and two granite statues of Queen Neferet were discovered at Tanis, although they had probably been brought from elsewhere, perhaps by Ramesses II. Stones plundered by Ramesses from Senwosret's pyramid chapel at Lahun were used in construction at Ihnasya el-Medina (Herakleopolis). A stele dated to year one comes from Wadi Gasus, on the Red Sea coast; an inscription near Aswan is double-dated years 35/3 of the coregency. An inscription commemorating an expedition in year two comes from the Wadi Hammamat (given incorrectly as year 11 by Couyot and Montet). The king is named in

Senwosret II

tombs of noblemen, the nomarch Khnumhotep at Beni Hassan, and the nomarch Djehutymose at Deir el-Bersha.

From the temple of Hathor at the turquoise mines at Serabit el-Khadim in Sinai comes a headless, kneeling statuette of a king, inscribed with the Horus name and nomen of Senwosret II.

Nubia, at least as far as the Second Cataract, seems to have been peacefully exploited. A small sandstone stele from the diorite mines at Toshka gives a year eight.

Senwosret II chose to have his pyramid and its complex built at Lahun, at the entrance to the Faiyum basin. This decision was almost certainly made because of the pharaoh's interest in the area. The pyramid, today a huge pile of mud brick, originally stood 49 m. tall and measured 106 m. to the side. The structure was built much like that of Senwosret I, his probable grandfather, in that a series of stone walls was constructed and then filled with mud bricks, the entire structure then being encased in white limestone. An interesting innovation was a trench cut into the rock around the tomb, which was filled with stones and acted as a run-off for water, thus helping to keep the subterranean chambers free from the flooding that occurred in the pyramids of Amenemhet I and Senwosret I. The entrance to the pyramid was located to the south-east, and was hidden beneath the tomb of a princess. All previous pyramids of the dynasty had entrances in the middle of the north side, hidden beneath a chapel. A shaft 16 m. deep let out into a passage, interrupted at one point by a well (depth unknown) on the other side of which the passage continues at a slight angle upward. After passing a side tunnel and then passing through a large room, one enters the burial chamber in which lies a red granite sarcophagus and an offering table dedicated to Osiris and Anubis. The side passage mentioned above runs around the burial chamber. Robbers long ago emptied the tomb, but excavators did find a gold uraeus, most likely from a statue, and a pair of leg bones that may well belong to Senwosret II.

Senwosret's funerary complex is surrounded by a wall of mud brick. The wall encloses the king's pyramid, as well as a smaller pyramid most likely for the queen, eight mastabas, and a series of princesses tombs on the southeast side. In one of these, that of Sithathoriunet, was found not only her sarcophagus and canopic jars but golden rings, necklaces, pectorals, a headband and much more. A small temple, once beautifully decorated with painted reliefs, was robbed for its stone in the time of Ramesses II. While no causeway has been excavated, a valley temple stood about 1.5 km. to the east. Excavators at the temple turned up a number of important papyri covering a great many subjects, from religion to works on astronomy and medicine to business dealings, to name a few. Most date to the reign of Senwosret III. Near the temple was discovered the workmen's "town," today called Kahun, an area that, even though much destroyed, still covered more than 18 acres and showed the remains of 2,145 houses. Estimates for the population run from 5,000 to 8,000 people.

Although the Turin Canon gives Senwosret II a reign of 19 years, the highest regnal year known from a contemporary source is the eighth year given on the stele from the quarries at Toshka in Lower Nubia.

References:

Budge 1913 p. 6, pl. VII
Callender 2000 pp. 164-165
Couyat and Montet 1912 pp. 72-73, pl. XXVI
Dodson 2003 pp. 89-91, 132
Dodson and Hilton 2004 pp. 90, 91, 93, 94
G. Fraser 1900 p. 5 #30
Gardiner 1959 pl. III, Col. V.23
Gardiner 1961 p. 439
Gardiner and Peet 1952 pl. XXII #79
Gardiner and Peet 1955 p. 89 #79
Grimal 1992 pp. 166-167
Grajetzki 2006 pp. 49, pl. XV
Hall 1913 pp. 10-11 #s 96,108, 265 #2610
Ikram and Dodson 1998 pp. 251, 279, 315, 318, 321, 352 #346
Lehner 1997 pp. 57, 171, 173, 175-176, 179, 226, 229, 231
Murnane 1977 pp. 7
Newberry 1906 pp. 111-112 #s 1, 6-8, 119 #s 19, 20, 23, pl. VI #s 1, 6-8, IX #s 19, 20, 23
Petrie 1889 #s 223-232
Petrie 1924 pp. 175-183
Petrie 1978 pl. XII, 12.4 #s 1-15
Stone 1997 pp. 91-99
Tufnell 1984 p. 362 #s 3033-3048
Tyldesley 2006 pp. 72, 76-77
Verbrugghe and Wickersham 1996 pp. 196
Verner 1997 pp. 386, 409-415, 419, 465
von Beckerath 1999 pp. 84 #4, 85 #4

Senwosret III   Dynasty XII

Horus Name:

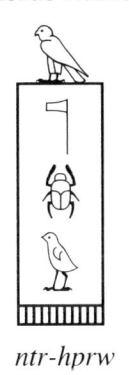

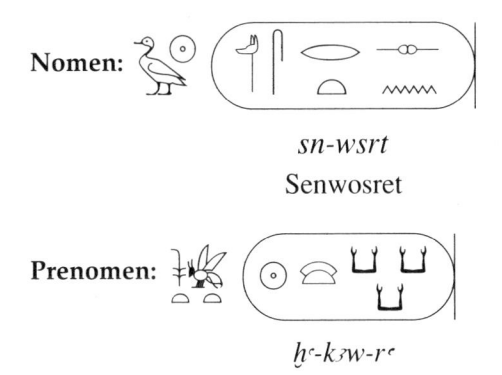

ntr-hprw

Nomen:

sn-wsrt
Senwosret

Prenomen:

hꜥ-kꜣw-rꜥ
Khakaure

Two Ladies:

nbty nṯr mswt

Senwosret III

Golden Falcon:

bik-nbw ḫpr

Length of Reign:	39 years		
Tomb:	Pyramid at Dahshur: "Pure is Senwosret"		
Mummy:	Unknown		
Consorts:	Khnemet-neferhedjet-Waret (II) Kho-kau-ra Meretseger(?) Neferthenut Sherit Sithathoriunet	**King Lists:** **Variant Names:**	Ab: (63); S: (43); T: (G 5.24) Khekure Kho-kheper-ra Senusert Senusret Usertsen
Manetho:	Sesostris (A, E, H)		

The fifth ruler of Dynasty XII, Senwosret III seems to have been the son of his predecessor, Senwosret II, and Queen Khenemetneferhedjet-Waret (I). It has been suggested that father and son might have shared the throne for a time. Coregencies were common in this dynasty, but the evidence rests on a single scarab and is not very convincing.

Senwosret III is well attested in Egypt. At the First Cataract region we have a statue from Biga Island. From the island of Sehel come graffiti dated to year eight, recording the clearance and repair of a canal which the king dedicated to the goddess Anukis, but named after himself: "Beautiful are the Ways of Khakaure." Also on Sehel, Senwosret either did extensive repairs to an existing temple of Anukis, or built it completely. From the shrine of Heqaib on Elephantine comes the bottom half of a seated statue. Statues are known from Hierakonpolis. Building activities are known from Tod. From the temple of Montu at Armant comes a doorway and wall, from the temple of Amen at Luxor comes an offering table, and from the temple at Karnak come five statues of the pharaoh, two of them over 2.75 m. tall. Six statues of the king, much damaged, were found at the temple of Montuhotep II at Deir el-Bahri. From Medamud come reliefs and the remains of about two dozen statues. Inscribed blocks have been found at Herakleopolis. In the Delta we have an architrave and statue from Tanis (probably transported from someplace else by Ramesses II), doorjambs from Khatana, and architraves and jambs from Bubastis. In the Faiyum region, a number of papyri dating to this reign were found in the workmen's village

(Kahun) and valley temple of Senwosret II. Senwosret III continued the irrigation and reclamation work begun by his father in the Faiyum, and he had extensive works at Abydos and Dahshur, discussed below.

A rock inscription at the alabaster quarries at Hatnub records a mining expedition under Senwosret III, but unfortunately the date is lost. Mining expeditions were sent to Wadi Hammamat in years 13 and 14.

From the Hathor cave at Serabit el-Khadim in the Sinai comes the lower portion of a statue of the pharaoh; also from Serabit comes a much-worn stele probably attesting to an expedition during Senwosret III's reign.

The stele of the military officer Khusobek informs us that Senwosret III launched a military campaign against *skmm* (Sekmem?), an unidentified city in Syria-Palestine (Retjenu), capturing it and laying waste to the general vicinity.

Senwosret took special interest in Nubia (Kush, Wawat, etc.) and sent the Egyptian army against the hapless tribes in regnal years 8, 10, and 19. His final boundary seems to have been set in the region about 150 kilometers to the south of the Second Cataract, where a series of forts were constructed—Semna South, Semna, Kumma, Uronarti, Shalfak and Askut.

Senwosret III had his pyramid and funerary complex built at Dahshur, just northeast of the Red Pyramid of Seneferu and the pyramid of Amenemhet II. The pyramid, now a great heap of crumbling mud bricks, which looks a lot like a scaled down Vesuvius, once stood 78 m. tall, with a base of 105 x 105 m. Unlike any pyramid ever built in Egypt, Senwosret's monument was built directly onto the sand and gravel, a stepped structure built entirely of mud brick, bonded together with packed sand rather than mortar. Limestone casing blocks, dovetailed together, covered the brick work. The entrance to the pyramid was located on its west side, north of center, a few meters from the monument and hidden beneath the paving stones that covered the area between the pyramid and its surrounding wall. The opening led to a corridor that sloped downward beneath the pyramid, turning several times and passing through several rooms before coming to the burial chamber. The chamber itself was built of granite which was, for reasons unknown, whitewashed. At one end of the room stands an empty red granite sarcophagus and an empty niche for the canopic jars. This has led many scholars to believe that the king might never have been interred at Dahshur, but instead was buried at Abydos.

Senwosret's pyramid was flanked on the north by four small pyramids and on the south by three. Beneath the southwestern-most pyramid is a passageway that leads beneath the king's pyramid to the burial chamber of Queen Weret, where human bones were found among fragments of stone, wood and pottery. Beneath the king's pyramid, on the northern side, lay a series of chambers and niches containing 12 sarcophagi, intended for the burial of princesses. When the galleries were opened in 1894, the excavator found hundreds of pieces of golden jewelry, some inlaid with semi-precious stones, belonging to princesses Mereret and Sit-Hathor.

Senwosret's building of a tomb at Abydos seems related to the rise in popularity of the god Osiris, Lord of the Underworld. It was believed that the god was buried at Abydos; in fact, the remains of the tomb of a Dynasty I pharaoh, Djer, were thought to belong to Osiris. Naturally, it was desirous to be buried near the god. The tomb itself was below ground, reached by a long tunnel that burrowed beneath the cliff terrace. The entrance to the tomb was beneath the huge court that made up part of the large funeral complex. The mortuary temple was located 700 m. from the complex.

Manetho informs us that his Sesostris (III) stood more than 6.4 meters tall, and that by his ninth year on the throne he had subdued all of Asia and a good deal of Europe. Herodotus also reports the military exploits and conquests of the pharaoh, recording how Sesostris led his troops as far as India!

Although Senwosret III's name is missing from the Turin Canon, a portion of his reign survives and reads, "30…years," which indicates a reign that lasted anywhere between 31 and 39 years. However, since no date higher than a year 19 was known from contemporary attestations, scholars have long questioned the regnal length given in the Canon.

The most powerful support of the longer regnal length is found in several relief fragments from the South Temple at Dahshur and an inscribed lintel from the temple of Montu at Medamud. These fragments depict the celebration of a Sed Festival by Senwosret III. At this time in Egyptian history, the first Sed Festival is not known to have been held before the thirtieth regnal year, so he must have been king for at least three decades, which is consistent with the Turin Canon. The absence of a date higher than year 19 is explained by W. K. Simpson, who argues definitively that year one of Amenemhet III's reign came directly after year 19 of Senwosret III's reign. Apparently, there was a lengthy coregency between the two, and during this period all dated material reflected regnal dates of the younger king.

The 1994 excavations by the Pennsylvania-Yale Expedition at Senwosret III's temple complex at Abydos unearthed a stone fragment that mentions a regnal date of year 39. This may provide evidence that Senwosret III's coregency extended for two decades. However, in the absence of other supporting material, this is highly questionable.

References:

Anthes 1928 pp. 17, pl. 8#XIII
D. Arnold 2002 pp. 44-45
Arnold and Oppenheim 1995 pp. 44-56
Breasted 1906 vol. I pp. 302-306 §676-687
Couyat and Montet 1912 pp. 49-51, pl. XIV
Delia 1995 pp. 18-33
Dodson 2003 pp. 91-93, 133
Dodson and Hilton 2004 pp. 19, 25-26, 28,

Gardiner 1959 pl. I, Col. V.24
Gardiner 1961 p. 439
Gardiner and Peet 1952 pl. XXII, XXV
Gardiner and Peet 1955 pp. 90 #s 81 and 82
Goyon 1957 pp. 90-91 #s 68-69, pl. XVII
Grajetzki 2005 pp. 32-34
Grajetzki 2006 pp. 51-58, 95-97
Habachi 1985 pl. 195-196
Herodotus 1954 pp. 166-168
Lehner 1997 pp. 101, 171, 177-179, 183, 190, 191, 226
Murnane 1977 pp. 9, 228
Oppenheim 1995
Peden 2001 pp. 35-36, 38, Note 81, 39-41
Randall-MacIver 1902 pp. 57-60, pl. XX-XXI
Tyldesley 2006 pp. 73, 76-77
Verbrugghe and Wickersham 1996 pp. 138, 196
Verner 1997 pp. 187, 386-388, 414, 416- 421, 465
von Beckerath 1999 pp. 84 #5, 85 #5
Waddell 1940 p. 67-69, 71-72
Wegner 1995 pp. 58-71
Wegner 1996 pp. 249-279

Senwosret IV Dynasty XVI

Horus Name:

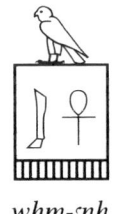

wḥm-ʿnḫ

Nomen:

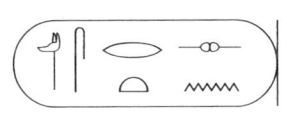

s-n-wsrt
Senwosret

Prenomen:

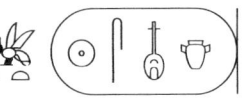

s.nfr-ib-rʿ
Seneferibre

Two Ladies:

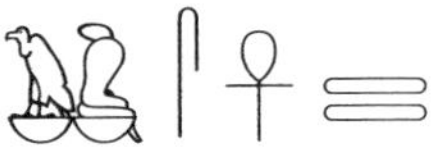

nbty s.ʿnḫ-t3wy

Golden Falcon:

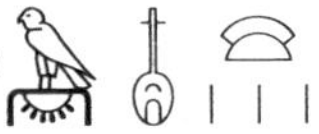

bik nbw nfr-ḫʿw

Length of Reign:	Unknown
Tomb:	Unknown; probably at Dra Abu el-Naga
Mummy:	Unknown

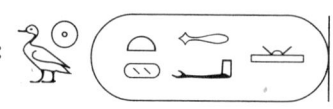

Seqenenre

Consorts:	Unknown	Senusert
Manetho:	Not given	Senusret
		Usertsen
King Lists:	K: (42 or 60)	
Variant Names:	Ra-Senefer-Ab	

Perhaps the fifteenth and last ruler of Dynasty XVI, Senwosret IV's parentage is unknown, as is his relationship to his predecessor, Montuhotep VI. He was without a doubt of Theban origin. Contemporary attestations for this king have been found no farther north than Karnak, which may mean that the dynasty's control of its northern boundary had been lost, or it may simply be that nothing to date has been found.

Attestations for Senwosret found at Karnak are 1) the greater part of a colossal red granite statue, inscribed with the king's full fivefold titulary and a dedication to Amen-Re, and 2) a much damaged stele dated to the king's first regnal year. South of Thebes, we have an inscribed block (whose present location is unknown) and a lintel from Edfu which bears only the nomen Senwosret and may or may not belong to Senwosret IV. Lastly, a dagger of unknown provenance, inscribed with the nomen Senwosret, may date to this king's reign.

References:

Bourriau 1988 pp. 54 illustration 53, 67-68
W. Davies 1981b p. 28 #38
Dodson and Hilton 2004 p. 116
Helck 1983 pp. 40 #55, 41 #56
Ryholt 1997a pp. 158, table 25, 306, 391, 410 table 97

Seqenenre — Dynasty XVII

Horus Name: ḥꜥ-m-wꜣst

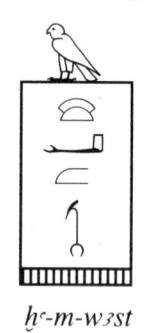

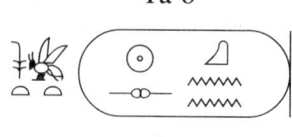

Nomen: tꜣ-ꜥꜣ — Taʿo

Prenomen: sḳn-n-rꜥ — Seqenenre

Two Ladies: Unknown

Golden Falcon: Unknown

Length of Reign:	5 years	
Tomb:	Dra Abu el-Naga	
Mummy:	Royal Cache at Deir el-Bahri Now at the Cairo Museum: JE26209; CG61051	
Consorts:	Ahhotep I Inhapy Sitdjehuty	Sekenenre Sequenenre Taa Ta'o Te'o
Manetho:	Not given	
King Lists:	K: (25)	
Variant Names:	Saqnounri	

The eighth ruler of Dynasty XVII, Seqenenre is almost certainly the son of his predecessor, Senakhtenre Taa and that king's queen, Tetisheri. Contemporary attestations for Seqenenre's reign are few and most are of unknown provenance. All securely attested finds come from the Theban area, with the exception of an inscribed lintel, found at Deir el-Ballas, some 50 km. to the north of Thebes, that carries the only known example of Seqenenre's cartouche preceded by the title "King of Upper and Lower Egypt."

From the Royal Cache at Deir el-Bahri we have the king's sarcophagus and mummy. From Dra Abu el-Naga comes a throwing stick inscribed with the king's nomen and the name of an otherwise unknown "King's Son," Tjuiu (which is perhaps only an honorific title). Also from Dra Abu el-Naga comes a stamp-seal bearing the king's prenomen. A *Book of the Dead*, found in Tomb 47 in the Valley of the Queens, states it belonged to the "King's Daughter and King's Sister, Ahmose, begotten by the Good God, Seqenenre," who is most likely the future Queen Ahmose-Nefertari, wife of Ahmose, first king of Dynasty XVIII. A fragment of jar purchased at Qurneh is inscribed with the king's Horus name and nomen. There is also an inscribed scribe's palette. Unprovenanced attestations include an inscribed jar-lid, an axe-blade, a pendant and a pair of silver sphinxes.

Seqenenre's name has been found in several tombs at Thebes, none of them contemporary with that pharaoh. These tombs date from the early part of Dynasty XVIII (the reign of Ahmose or Amenhotep I) to the reign of Ramesses IX of late Dynasty XX, a span of some five hundred years. Obviously, later generations considered Seqenenre Taa a very important king. Seqenenre's pyramid-tomb at Dra Abu el-Naga was inspected during the reign of Ramesses IX and found to be undisturbed.

The Theban rump-state seems to have held an uneasy truce with the contemporary Hyksos Dynasty XV. Some small amount of trade may have been conducted, but it is very likely that tribute in

Seqenenre

the form of taxes was flowing down the Nile to the east Delta city of Avaris, the Dynasty XV capital. Apepi, the Hyksos king at this time, considered himself, and almost certainly was, supreme overlord of Egypt in its entirety. The "kings" at Thebes were vassals who were undoubtedly resentful of their status. Such conditions couldn't be maintained and eventually, probably during Seqenenre's reign, open hostilities erupted.

While we will probably never know what single event finally brought about the outbreak of war, a tale written down in Ramesside times (Papyrus Sallier I) gives us an idea of the tension that was building up between Apepi and Seqenenre. The story is simply that Apepi wanted to pick a fight with the ruler of Thebes and, after much deliberation, decided to insult Seqenenre by demanding that the hippopotamus pool at Thebes be done away with because the noise from the beasts was keeping the Hyksos ruler awake! Certainly a rather silly thing to start a war over, especially because Seqenenre agreed to move the hippopotami. Unfortunately, at this point in the story the papyrus breaks off, so we do not know what the story says happened next. Goedicke posits that what has long been translated as "hippopotamus pool" should actually refer to re-claimed land occupied by mercenaries, i.e., "troops loyal to Seqenenre in the area east of Thebes." If this were the case, certainly Seqenenre would be concerned; Apepi was ordering him to divest Thebes of her allies. Goedicke believes that Seqenenre's agreement to do as Apepi has ordered is a clever ruse: he would move his paid warriors, not to their own homeland, but instead toward the Hyksos king and his capital.

Seqenenre's mummy is that of a man of between 35 and 40 years of age at time of death. He is estimated to have been 1.702 m. tall. The pathetic remains present proof of violence. The skull was fractured by axe blows that left gaping holes; the nose was smashed; there was a spear wound to the left cheek and another on the right side of the head. Even more disturbing, the hands are grotesquely twisted, the lips are pulled back and the teeth are clenched in a horrible grimace of agony.

References:

Bietak and Strouhal 1974 pp. 29-52, 78
Dodson and Hilton 2004 pp. 114, 122, 123, 126-127, 128-129
Forbes 1998a pp. 598-599
Gauthier 1907-17 vol. II pp. 157 #VI
Goedicke 1986
Hein 1994 p. 240 #302
Ikram and Dodson 1998 pp. 10, 117-118, 315, 318, 321
Kaplony 1973 pp. 15 #42, pl. 11 #42, 26-27 #63, pl. 14 #63
Lilyquist 1995 p. 23 #6, 84 fig. 17
Newberry 1906 p. 89 fig. 95
Partridge 1994 pp. 31-34
Partridge 2002 pp. 188-189
Peet 1930 p. 38
Petrie 1889 #759
Petrie 1924 vol. II p. 6 fig.s 1 and 2, 7-10 #XVII. 7

D. Redford 1986 pp. 43, 48 #12, 50-51 #23, 51 #24, 60
D. Redford 1997 pp. 17-18
Ryholt 1997a pp. 171 table 28, 176 note 628, 177, 257, 276-278, 304, 397-398 File 17/8, 410, table 98

G. Smith 1912 pp. 1-6, pl. I-III
Strudwick 1999 pp. 127
von Beckerath 1999 pp. 128-131 #14
Zuhdi 2000/2001

Se...re Khety   Dynasty IX/X(?)

Horus Name: Unknown

Nomen:

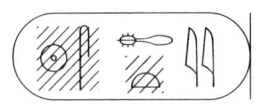

$s...\text{-}[r\text{'}] \underline{h} [t] y$

Se...re Khety

Prenomen: Unknown

Two Ladies: Unknown

Golden Falcon: Unknown

Length of Reign:	Unknown
Tomb:	Unknown
Mummy:	Unknown

Consorts:	Unknown	**Variant Names:**	Se...re Akhtoy
Manetho:	Not given		
King Lists:	Not given		

Se...re Khety is known only from a single, much-damaged graffito at the travertine quarries of Hatnub, in Middle Egypt. It is generally assumed that he was one of the Herakleopolitan pharaohs who controlled an unknown amount of territory around Herakleopolis in Middle Egypt (see "Herakleopolitans" in Glossary), although this is by no means certain. The nomen Khety, which was a very popular royal name during Dynasties IX/X, and only during that period, would seem to support the probability of such placement.

References:
Anthes 1928 p. 14 inschr. Xb, pl. 6
von Beckerath 1999 pp. 74 #c, 73 #c

Seth (I) — Dynasty XIII

Horus Name: Unknown

Nomen and Prenomen:

...ib[rˁ] stḫ
...ib-[re?] Seth

Prenomen:

mr-ib-rˁ
Meribre

Two Ladies: Unknown

Golden Falcon: Unknown

Length of Reign:	T: "..., 6 days"
Tomb:	Unknown
Mummy:	Unknown

Consorts:	Unknown	**Variant Names:**	Set
Manetho:	Not given		
King Lists:	T: (G 6.23; R 7.23; vB 6.23)		

This king may have been the twenty-fourth ruler of Dynasty XIII, although von Beckerath would place him as the twentieth. He probably usurped the throne from his predecessor, Intef IV.

Other than the Turin Canon, no certain attestations for Seth are known to exist. Ryholt suggests that a stele discovered at Abydos and now in Cairo (JE35256) once bore Seth's nomen, prenomen and Horus name. The stele, dated to year four, was usurped by king Neferhotep I. However, Leahy presents strong evidence that the stele was erected by the pharaoh Wegaf. Medamud, just northeast of Luxor, has yielded a great many architectural remains which probably originally belonged to Seth but were usurped by his successor, Sobekhotep III.

References:

Gardiner 1959 pl. III, Col. 6 #23
Gardiner 1961 p. 440 #6.23
Helck 1983 pp. 13-14 #s 20-21
Randall-MacIver 1902 p. 84 pl. XXIX
Ryholt 1997a pp. 71 Col. 7.23, 73 #25, 192 table 33, 285-286, notes 1031-1033, table 83, 342 File13/25, 408 #25
von Beckerath 1999 pp. 94 #20, 95 #20

Setnakht   Dynasty XX

Horus Name:

kꜣ nḫt wr-pḥti

Nomen: *stẖ-nḫt mrr-imn*
Setnakht (mereramen-re)

Prenomen: *wsr-ḫꜥw-rꜥ stp.n-rꜥ*
Userkhaure-setepenre

Two Ladies: *nbty twt-ḫꜥw mi-tꜣtnn*

Golden Falcon: *bik-nbw sḫm-ḫpš dr[rḳi]iw.f*

Length of Reign:	2 years
Tomb:	Valley of the Kings: KV14
Mummy:	Unknown

Consorts:	Hemdjert(?) Sitre(?) Tiy-Mereniset	**Variant Names:**	Sethnakhte Woserkhaure-setepenre
Manetho:	Not given		
King Lists:	None		

The first pharaoh of Dynasty XX, Setnakht's parentage is unknown, though it has been suggested he may have been a son or grandson of Ramesses II. His name, compounded as it is with the god Set, may indicate a familial relationship with the clan of Sety I. It might also indicate an origin in the east Delta, where Set was especially worshipped. Whatever his antecedents, Setnakht came to the throne at a very unsettled time. The two dozen years since the death of Ramesses II had seen the reigns of five pharaohs, two of whom seem to have usurped the throne. The last of these, a queen named Tawosret, had seized the throne upon the death of her stepson, Sety II (for whom she had been regent) and declared herself pharaoh. She was assisted in her rule by a "chancellor" named Bay, a gentleman of Syrian stock, considered by many scholars to have been the power behind Tawosret. At some point in her second or third regnal year, Tawosret and "the Upstart Syrian" were deposed and Setnakht claimed the throne.

Written more than thirty years after the event, the Papyrus Harris tells us that the new pharaoh "set in order the entire land, which had been rebellious; he slew the rebels who were in the land of Egypt; he cleansed the great throne of Egypt." A stele from Elephantine, dated to Setnakht's second and final regnal year, tells us that Setnakht had driven out rebels and captured the gold and silver with which they had intended to hire Asiatic mercenaries in order to gain control of the Two Lands. We do not know how accurately conditions were depicted in these texts; Setnakht's role may have been embellished to enhance his stature as pharaoh, a literary device commonly employed throughout pharaonic Egyptian history. As the king's principal function was to maintain "maat" (order, right, continuity) in the land, attributing these victories to Setnakht would have been consistent with pharaonic tradition. But it should be noted that these were troubled times, and a series of weak and ineffectual kings had seemingly allowed centralized power to slip through their fingers to such an extent that a foreign interloper had become the power behind the throne. Corruption was undoubtedly rampant, and minor rebellions may have occurred. However, the situation was not so bad as to interfere with the sending of an expedition to the turquoise mines at Serabit el-Khadim in Sinai. Setnakht's name has also been found at Amarah West, at the Third Cataract in Nubia.

Egypt was stable enough to allow the beginning of the construction of his tomb in the Valley of the Kings (KV11), which Setnakht abandoned prior to its completion. In its stead, he chose to occupy and modify the existing tomb of Tawosret and Sety II (KV14), expanding it into one of the largest tombs in the valley. Other than these tombs, there are very few attestations for Setnakht. In fact, he is virtually unknown aside from a stele at Medinet Habu (shared with his son, Ramesses III), a few scarabs and usurpations of several items such as a stele of Sety II, also from Medinet Habu, and a column from Memphis.

Probably not a young man at his accession, Setnakht seems to have died after a rule of just a little over two years. His son Ramesses III succeeded him.

It has recently been suggested that the mummy of Setnakht may have been found, but not recognized, in the cache of royal and semi-royal mummies found in the tomb of Amenhotep II (KV35) in the Valley of the Kings. The pharaoh's coffin was there, the overturned lid holding the body of an unnamed woman (possibly the queen Tawosret), and the bottom holding the mummy of Merenptah.

Reeves and Wilkinson have posited that a mummy found in a large (more than 2 m.) model barque may have been Setnakht's remains, since this was the only adult male body without identification. However, we cannot be certain the mummy was that of an adult, or male for that matter; it was never studied, and was smashed to bits by modern tomb robbers before it could be removed to Cairo. The robbers also stole the barque.

References:

Breasted 1906 vol. IV p. 198-200 §398-400
Brier 1994 pp. 274, 275
Dodson 1995 pp. 139, 141-142, 209, 216
Dodson and Hilton 2004 pp. 184, 186-187, 188, 191-194, 196, 200, 206, 209
Forbes 1993 p. 74
Forbes 1998a pp. 71, 75, 643, 678, 686, 687
Gardiner and Peet 1952 pl. LXXIII
Gardiner and Peet 1955 pp. 34, 186 #271
Hall 1913 pp. 231 #s 2301-2306
Ikram and Dodson 1998 pp. 226, 264, 315, 318, 326, 327, ill. 388

Kitchen 1982 p. 217
Murnane 1977 p. 235
Newberry 1906 pl. XXXVI #s 15-16
Peden 2001 pp. 130 note 458, 166, 184-185
Petrie 1978 p. xlv 19.10, pl. XLV
Reeves 1990b pp. 109-111
Reeves and Wilkinson 1996 pp. 24, 32, 37, 53, 54, 64, 150, 157-161, 199, 207, 209, 211
Tyldesley 2006 p. 165
von Beckerath 1999 pp. 164 #1, 165 #1

Sety I   Dynasty XIX

Horus Name:

Nomen:

sthy mry.n-ptḥ
Sety (merenptah)

Prenomen:

mn-mꜣʿt-rʿ
Menmaatre

kꜣnḫt ḫʿ-m-wꜣst sʿnḫ-tꜣwy

Sety I

Two Ladies: nbty wḥm-mswt sḫm-ḫpš dr-pdt 9

Golden Falcon: bik-nbw wḥm-ḫʿw wsr-pdwt-m-tꜣwy-nbw

Length of Reign:	11-14 years
Tomb:	Valley of the Kings: KV17
Mummy:	Royal Cache at Deir el-Bahri: Now at Cairo Museum: JE26213; CG61077

Consorts:	Tuia	**Variant Names:**	Men-ma-re Setui
Manetho:	Sethos (A, E, J) Aigyptos (J)		
King Lists:	Ab: (76); S: (57- missing)		

Sety I, the second king of Dynasty XIX, was the son of Ramesses I and his consort, probably Sitre. However, it should be noted that on the famous "Year 400 Stele" found at Tanis, Sety's mother is called Tia. It has been suggested that the two names refer to the same woman, but there is no real evidence one way or the other. In any case, Sety was evidently Ramesses I's only son.

Ramesses I originally came to the throne as coregent with his predecessor, Horemheb. Shortly after the death of Horemheb, Ramesses appointed Sety as coregent. Within less than a year, Ramesses had died and Sety found himself sole ruler of the Two Lands.

Like his father, Sety seems to have believed that the new dynasty meant new beginnings, and his Two Ladies name refers to him as a bringer of renaissance. His titulary also referred to him as "Strong-armed, Subduing the Foe," and "Mighty of Bows in All Lands."

The bellicose epithets of his titulary reflected more than Sety's wishful thinking. He had been a career army officer during the reign of Horemheb, perhaps serving in Syria-Palestine at some point; he certainly commanded a military action in that region as crown prince or coregent of Ramesses I. It is safe to assume that he was well aware of the squabbles and small-time wars that plagued the various city-states which made up Egypt's interests in that area, and was prepared to strike at the first excuse. Within months of his sole assumption of power, a confederation of Bedouin tribes (the Shosu) of Palestine rebelled. Sety led a force into the area: "His majesty marched against them like a fierce-eyed lion, making them carcasses...overturned in their own blood...." Once these tribes had been put down, Sety dealt with several warring petty city-states in a similar way. The victorious pharaoh ordered a stele to be set up in the city of Beth Shan, the text of which warned future miscreants that they were up against a great warrior king whose "heart is gratified at the sight of blood," who "loves the moment of crushing (the foe)," who "leaves them no heirs." Having put the fear of Amen, Set, and Re into the dissidents of the region, the king returned to Egypt.

Sety was back in Palestine-Syria again within a year to quell unrest among the city-states, and the Egyptian army campaigned from Canaan, north along the coast of Phoenicia, perhaps to Tyre, and also inland into the province of Upi. A victory stele was set up at Tell es-Shihab, between Damascus and Beth Shan, and a second stele at Beth Shan. Finally, another sweep of the coast brought the king once again to Tyre, then as far north as Simyra. On the road home, Sety stayed long enough in Byblos to order the felling of some of the famous cedar trees to be used for the construction of a river-barge and flagpoles for the temple of Amen at Thebes. Another stele proclaiming Sety's victories was set up at Tyre.

In two campaigns, Sety I had regained control of about half of the land lost during the Amarna Period. He had also pushed Egyptian control to the border of the Hittite Empire, and this necessitated a third campaign. The outcome of the battles (or perhaps only skirmishes) between Egypt and Hatti is uncertain, although an understanding between Sety I and the Hittite king Mursilis II was reached. This allowed Sety the time to lead a campaign against Libyan interlopers in the western Nile Delta.

In regnal year five or six Sety I again led his army to Syria. Breaching any Egyptian-Hittite agreement that might have been in place, Sety conquered the Amurru, then pushed all the way to the city of Kadesh, which soon fell. A triumphant stele was set up in the vanquished city, and then Sety led the victorious troops home, never to return. The dust from the retiring army had hardly settled when the Hittites reclaimed the lost territory. Most likely both Sety and the new king of Hatti, Muwatallis II, realized that a stalemate had been reached, as a treaty was negotiated.

Once the problems in Syria-Palestine had been settled, Sety was allowed two or three years of peace before trouble in Nubia began. In regnal year eight, the people of the area called Irem had threatened revolt and needed to be quelled. The whole affair was evidently not much more than a policing action and was handled by army commanders in conjunction with the Viceroy of Kush, Sety being more concerned with domestic issues at home. In year ten, Sety sent his son, the future Ramesses II, to quell a small uprising in Lower Nubia, and shortly after that, to deal with a much more serious problem: preventing an invasion of the Delta by a group of "warriors of the sea," the Sherden. They were repulsed, and Sety was able to

Sety I

spend the rest of his reign in peaceful pursuits. During these latter days of Sety's reign, trade with foreign lands, along with tribute exacted from conquered peoples, probably increased to near the point it had enjoyed during the empire's "golden age," the reigns from Thutmose III through Amenhotep III. Sety's primary goal as pharaoh had always been to reconstitute the Egyptian empire as it had existed during that era, prior to its dissolution under the rule of Akhenaten. He came close to achieving this goal.

Between wars and in the quieter second half of his rule, Sety made it his business to build and restore temples throughout Egypt and Nubia. A hypostyle hall, similar to that at Karnak though on a smaller scale, was added to the temple of Amen at Gebel Barkal in Nubia. Other examples of attestations from Nubia include stelae at Qasr Ibrim, Wadi Halfa, and Buhen, a temple at Sesebi, as well as repairs and additions to other monuments in the area. He was also responsible for reopening the gold mines east of Edfu and the construction of a small rock-cut temple (at Wadi Mia) and the digging of wells there. In addition to the gold mines mentioned above, Sety I also sent expeditions to the turquoise mines at Serabit el-Khadim in Sinai (where he added to the temple of Hathor) and to the copper mines at Timna, in the Wadi Arabah region, 150 km. northeast of the turquoise mines.

In Egypt, Sety I was responsible for repairs and reconstruction of temples throughout the land as well as additions to the temples of Re at Heliopolis, Ptah at Memphis, Set at Avaris, the Speos Artemidos near Beni Hasan and at Amada He also built at Abydos, where his great temple, called the "Memnonium" by the Greeks, is still a very imposing and beautiful monument. The temple, dedicated not only to the deified Sety I, but also to the deities Ptah, Re-Horakhty, Amen, Osiris, Isis and Horus, contains seven chapels dedicated to the gods just mentioned, as well as smaller chapels to Nefertem and Ptah-Seker. Certainly ancestor veneration was a very important part of the temple program, as evidenced in the "ancestor list" inscribed on a wall of the passageway that connects the innermost of the two hypostyle halls to a wing containing the chapels of Nefertem and Ptah-Seker. Behind the temple buildings lies the "Osireion," a magnificent underground cenotaph that Sety shared with Osiris.

A great many attestations for Sety I come, naturally enough, from the Theban area. At Karnak, Sety continued the hypostyle hall begun by either Horemheb or Ramesses I and it is from its beautifully carved reliefs that we have the record of Sety's foreign wars. Across the Nile, near Dra Abu el-Naga, Sety built his mortuary temple, "Glorious Sety in the West of Thebes," a magnificent structure which included a hypostyle hall, a row of sphinxes, and a chapel dedicated to the memory and worship of Ramesses I. This temple was completed by Ramesses II. Sety's tomb in the Valley of the Kings was discovered by Belzoni in 1817. The tomb is almost certainly the finest decorated of all the Theban royal tombs, as well as being, to quote Reeves and Wilkinson, "the longest, deepest and most completely finished of all the tombs in the valley."

At some point, perhaps as early as his seventh regnal year, Sety I officially named Ramesses II as Prince-Regent with all of the considerations, including his own palace, wives and concubines, and it is very likely that an actual coregency was begun some time after regnal year nine, lasting for about two years.

The length of Sety's reign is disputed The highest actual regnal year known to date is the year 11 given on the king's stele at Gebel Barkal, but lengths of up to 19 years have been suggested based on some versions of Manetho. It is interesting to consider that, depending on which version of Manetho you choose to follow, his "Sethos" may have reigned for 19, 51, 55, or 59 years.

The mummy of Sety I was discovered in the Royal Cache at Deir el-Bahri. Ill-used by tomb robbers, the mummy's head had become separated from the body; nonetheless, it is the best preserved of any of the royal mummies' heads. In life, Sety stood 1.665 m. tall. No agreement has been reached on the king's age at death, and estimates vary from 35 to 50 years old.

References:

Brand 1998a pp. 46-57, 62-68
Brand 1998b pp. 58-61
Breasted 1906 vol. III p. 47 § 88
Brier 1994 pp. 107, 108, 158, 172, 201, 267, 268, 270, 271, 272, 275
Bucaille 1990 pp. xi, 12, 27, 28, 73, 84-85, 97, 103, 112, 116, 135, 146, 147, 167, pl. 31-32, 38
Calverly et al. 1933-38
Caulfield 1902
Dodson and Hilton 2004 pp. 15, 36, 158-165, 170, 173, 175, 208, 283 note 10
El Madhy 1989 pp. 31, 35, 37, 87, 88, 90, 132-133, 140, 152
Forbes 1998a pp. 632-635
Gardiner and Peet 1952 pl. LXII, LXVIII, LXIX
Gardiner and Peet 1955 pp. 34, 38, 44, 174-177 #s 246-250
Grimal 1992 pp. 246-250
Grajetzki 2005 pp. 66-66
Harris and Weeks 1973 pp. 100, 112, 151-153, 154, 164
Ikram and Dodson 1998 pp. 41, 73, 116, 122, 226, 261, 263, 315, 318, 325, ills. 1, 38, 69, 93, 126, 286, 427
Kitchen 1982 pp. 19-41
Murnane 1977 pp. 57-87, 234
Murray 1903
Partridge 1994 pp. 151-153
D. Redford 1992 pp. 180-182
Reeves 1990b pp. 92-94
Reeves and Wilkinson 1996 pp. 4, 8, 12, 20, 24, 26, 36-37, 42, 45, 48, 53, 58-59, 60, 62, 64, 69, 71-72, 78-79, 86, 88, 130-131, 136, 137-139, 142-143, 148, 150-151, 164, 166, 183, 188, 196-197, 200, 203-204, 207-210
G. Smith 1912 pp. 57-59, pl. XXXVIII, XL-XLI
Spalinger 2005 pp. 187-201
Tyldesley 2006 pp. 143-145
Verbrugghe and Wickersham 1996 pp. 143, 159, 161, 162, 1999
von Beckerath 1999 pp. 148-153 #2
Waddell 1940 pp. 103, 105, 111, 121, 129, 149, 151
R. Wilkinson 2000 pp. 9, 36, 50, 55, 59, 75, 87, 143, 146-148, 157-158, 161, 173-174, 189, 204, 208, 221, 238

Sety II   Dynasty XIX

Horus Name:

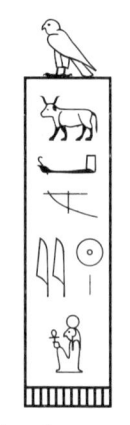

Nomen:

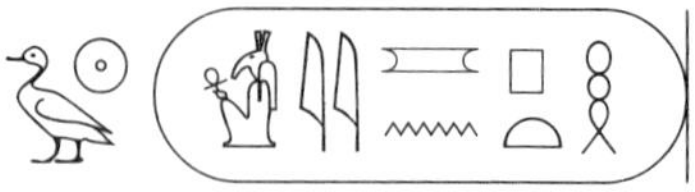

stẖy mry.n-ptḥ
Sety (merenptah)

Prenomen:

wsr-ḫprw-rꜥ mry-imn
Woserkheperure-meryamen

kꜣ nḫt mry-rꜥ

Two Ladies:

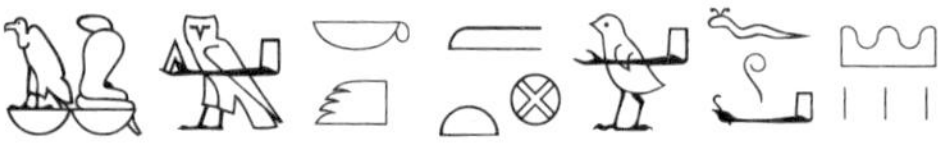

nbty mk-kmt wꜥf-ḫꜣswt

Golden Falcon:

bik-nbw ꜥꜣ-nrw-m-tꜣwy-nbw

Length of Reign:	6 years
Tomb:	Valley of the Kings: KV15
Mummy:	Tomb of Amenhotep II Now at Cairo Museum: JE34561; CG61081

Consorts:	Takhat Tawosret	**Variant Names:**	Sethos Seti Setui
Manetho:	Not given		
King Lists:	None		

Sety II was a son of Merenptah, the fourth king of Dynasty XIX. He assumed the throne during a troubled time, and the evidence about his place in the royal succession is scanty and sometimes contradictory. This has led to some disagreement among Egyptologists about whether to place him as the fifth king (directly following Merenptah) or the sixth (after his son, Amenmesse).

Sety II

Kitchen believes that Sety, although designated Crown Prince, did not assume the throne upon the death of his father. He suggests that Sety may have been out of the area when Merenptah died, and that Amenmesse usurped the throne in Sety's absence. Dodson, on the other hand, proposes the theory that Sety II succeeded his father, was deposed by Amenmesse, and reclaimed the throne after a few years of the usurper's reign (see Amenmesse). In any case, Sety made it quite clear that he was not happy about Amenmesse's term as king; as soon as the opportunity arose, he declared a *damnatio memoriae* and excised Amenmesse's name from almost all monuments and records in the kingdom, including his tomb in the Valley of the Kings.

It is not known if Amenmesse died or was deposed in a palace coup (a civil war is most unlikely). There is nothing in the surviving records to indicate violence toward Amenmesse's faction (which included the High Priest of Amen, Roma Roy), although many of them, Roma Roy included, found themselves replaced when Sety assumed the throne. On the other hand, Sety's treatment of his predecessor's monuments was telling.

Once he had vented his spleen on Amenmesse's memory and usurped his texts and statues, Sety began a serious building program. At Karnak he added a barque shrine for Amen, Mut and Khonsu, erected a pair of obelisks, as well as several stelae. Texts were added to already existing inscriptions. Inscriptions left by Amenmesse in the Hypostyle Hall were usurped by Sety, as were several statues. Many new statues, some of them of colossal proportions, and at least one sphinx were commissioned. He also repaired the Heb Sed Temple of Amenhotep II. At Luxor, an inscribed block shows Sety offering lettuces (considered an aphrodisiac) to Amen. Also from Luxor come stelae, bases of columns, and a few texts.

Across the Nile, a tomb for Sety II was begun in the Valley of the Kings (KV15). A second tomb, KV14, was also begun, presumably intended for his queen, Tawosret. In all likelihood, neither tomb was complete at the time of Sety's death, and he may have originally been buried in KV14. KV15 was hastily decorated, and remains in the tomb have led Egyptologists to believe that Sety was eventually interred there. The king's mortuary temple has not been located, although it is possible that he began the temple later used for Tawosret and Siptah.

The few attestations outside the Theban area include evidence of building activity as far north as the royal residence at Pi-ramesses. In the eastern Delta, the Temple of Ptah at Memphis has yielded fragments of inscribed columns and texts. Also from the Memphite area comes a granite statue of the pharaoh being worshipped by a baboon. At Hermopolis, Sety completed a sanctuary of Amen that had been started by Merenptah. A rock-cut stele in the Wadi Hammamat records a mining expedition in Sety's fifth regnal year; another pictures Sety before Min, Horus, and Isis. A fragment of inscribed column was found reused in the pavement of the South Kiosk of the temple of Montu at Medamud. Sety's name was added to the pylon built by Thutmose III at another temple of Montu at Armant. A stele dated to regnal year two was erected in the Great Speos temple of Horemheb at Gebel Silsila.

Outside Egypt, at Serabit el-Khadim in Sinai, scenes of Sety were added to the pylon of Thutmose III at the temple of Hathor. Also, inscribed fragments of faience from a vase, a menat, a bowl, a cup and a bracelet have been discovered.

Attestations for Sety II in Nubia are more numerous, and include an inscribed block from the temple of Isis at el-Dakka, a cartouche usurped from Ramesses II at that king's temple at Beit el-Wali, fragments of a stele from the temple of Amen-Re and Re-Horakhty at Amada, text and a cartouche cut into the temple of Ramesses II at Abu Simbel, and a stele of Sety smiting an enemy. Sety also added his cartouche to a doorjamb of Thutmose III in the South Temple at Buhen.

After reigning a few months over six years, Sety II died and was succeeded by his son, Siptah.

The mummy of Sety II was discovered in a cache of royal mummies in the tomb of Amenhotep II (KV35) in the Valley of the Kings. The body was that of a man, probably in his mid-thirties, with dark brown hair and a height of 1.640 m. The body, while well mummified, had suffered greatly at the hands of tomb robbers; the head was separated from the body, as were both arms. The right forearm and hand are missing completely.

References:

Brier 1994 pp. 111, 115, 116, 173, 272-273, 274, 275
Bucaille 1990 pp. 116, 118
Callender 2006 pp. 50-52
Couyat and Montet 1912 p. 49 #46, XIV
Dodson 1999 p. 131
Dodson and Hilton 2004 pp. 176-183, 283 note 31, 285 note 127, 286 note 131
El Madhy 1989 pp. 39, 90
Forbes 1998a pp. 682-683
Forbes 1998c pp. 65-69
Gardiner and Peet 1952 pl. LXIII
Gardiner and Peet 1955 pp. 38, 158-159 #194, 185 #268, 185 #269
Goyon 1957 pp. 109-110 #95, pl. XXXII

Harris and Weeks 1973 pp. 158-159, 164
Ikram and Dodson 1998 pp. 84, 148, 263, 315, 318, 326, ills. 368, 371-372
Partridge 1994 pp. 161-164
Peden 2001 pp. 109-110, 163-165, 177-178 note 278
Reeves 1990b pp. 103-104
Reeves and Wilkinson 1996 pp. 24, 26, 30, 32, 37-38, 47, 68, 72, 150, 152-154, 157-158, 165, 191, 199, 201, 203, 207
G. Smith 1912 pp. 73-81, pls. XLIV-XLVI
Tyldesley 2006 pp. 163-166
von Beckerath 1999 pp. 158-161 #6
R. Wilkinson 2000 pp. 140, 156

Sewadjkare I Dynasty XIII

Horus Name: Unknown

Nomen: Unknown

Prenomen:

sw3d-k3-rˁ
Sewadjkare

Two Ladies: Unknown

Golden Falcon: Unknown

Length of Reign:	Unknown
Tomb:	Unknown
Mummy:	Unknown

Consorts:	Unknown	**Variant Names:**	Swadjkare
Manetho:	Not given		
King Lists:	T: (G 6.13; R 7.13; vB 6.13)		

Probably the eleventh ruler of Dynasty XIII, Sewadjkare is one of a group of kings known only from the Turin Canon. Although the papyrus' fragmentary state allows for varying interpretations as to the positioning of some of the kings of this dynasty, Sewadjkare's place seems secure.

References:
Gardiner 1959 pl. III, Col. VI #13
Gardiner 1961 p. 440 #6.13
Ryholt 1997a pp. 71 Col. 7.13, 73 #11, 197 #11, 339 File 13/11, 408 table 94 #11
von Beckerath 1999 pp. 90 #10, 91 #10

Sewadjkare II — Dynasty XIV

Horus Name: Unknown

Nomen: Unknown

Prenomen:

swȝd-kȝ-rʿ
Sewadjkare

Two Ladies: Unknown

Golden Falcon: Unknown

Length of Reign:	Unknown
Tomb:	Unknown
Mummy:	Unknown

Consorts:	Unknown	**Variant Names:**	Swadjkare
Manetho:	Not given		
King Lists:	T: (G 8.6; R 9.6; vB 8.6)		

Possibly the eleventh king of Dynasty XIV, Sewadjkare is one of a group of kings known only from the Turin Canon. The papyrus' fragile state allows for varying interpretations as to the positioning of some of the kings of this dynasty. However, Sewadjkare's place seems secure.

The Roman numeral shown in parenthesis after the name is a modern convention used to differentiate this king from a Dynasty XIII king who is also known only from this prenomen.

References:

Gardiner 1959 pl. III, Col. VIII #6
Gardiner 1961 p. 441 #8.6
Ryholt 1997a pp. 95 Col. 9.6, 98 #11, 198 table 37, 200 table 39 #11, 379 File 14/11, 409 #11

von Beckerath 1999 pp. 108 #7, 109 #7

Sewadj...re   SIP

Horus Name:
Unknown

Nomen: Unknown

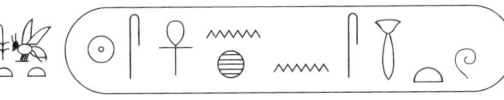

Prenomen: *sw3ḏ...rꜥ*
Sewadj...re

Two Ladies: Unknown

Golden Falcon: Unknown

Length of Reign:	Unknown
Tomb:	Unknown
Mummy:	Unknown

Consorts:	Unknown	**Variant Names:**	None
Manetho:	Not given		
King Lists:	T: (?)		

This prenomen is found on a block from Tod (about 20 miles south of Luxor). It may represent an otherwise unknown king, but more likely it is the prenomen of one of three Dynasty XIII rulers, Sewadjkare, Hori Sewadjkare or Se...kare, or of a Dynasty XIV king whose prenomen is also Sewadjkare.

References:
Bisson de la Roque 1937 p. 127 #1035
Ryholt 1997a p. 403 File P/4

Sewadjtu   Dynasty XIII

Horus Name:
Unknown

Nomen and Prenomen: *sꜥnḫ-n-rꜥ s.w3ḏ.tw*
Seankhenre Sewadjtu

Two Ladies: Unknown

Golden Falcon: Unknown

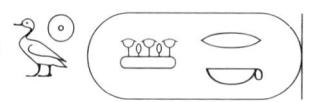

Sharek

Length of Reign:	T: "3 years, 2-4 months, ..."
Tomb:	Unknown
Mummy:	Unknown

Consorts:	Unknown	**Variant Names:**	S'ankhre'ens-wadjtu Sewadjtew
Manetho:	Not given		
King Lists:	K: (33); T: (G 7.5; R 8.5; vB 7.29)		

Sewadjtu was most likely the thirty-fourth pharaoh of Dynasty XIII, although Ryholt opts for thirty-fifth and von Beckerath for twenty-ninth. Beyond the Turin Canon, Sewadjtu is unknown. Ryholt suggests that the king's prenomen may have been misread when copied from the hieratic of some precursor of the Turin Canon to the hieroglyphs of the Karnak king-list; he posits that one of the two "Sewadjenres" listed in the latter may, in fact, represent Sewadjtu.

References:

Dodson and Hilton 2004 p. 100
Gardiner 1959 pl. III, Col. VII #5
Gardiner 1961 p. 440 #7.5
Ryholt 1997a pp. 71 fig. 10, Col. 8 #5, 73 table 17 #35, 192 table 33, 356 File 13/35, 408 table 94 #35
von Beckerath 1999 pp. 98 #29, 99 #29

Sharek   SIP

Horus Name: Unknown   **Nomen:** [cartouche]

š-r-k
Sharek

Prenomen: Unknown

Two Ladies: Unknown

Golden Falcon: Unknown

Length of Reign:	Unknown
Tomb:	Unknown
Mummy:	Unknown

Consorts:	Unknown	**Variant Names:**	Shalek
Manetho:	Saites (A) Salitis (J)		
King Lists:	None		

This king is known only from a priest's ancestor list from Memphis and is most likely fictitious. Von Beckerath has suggested that Sharek is the nomen of the Manetho's Dynasty XV ruler Salitis, but there is no evidence to support this theory.

References:
Borchardt 1935 pp. 96-112, pl. 2 and 2a
Ryholt 1997a p. 402 File N/10

von Beckerath 1999 pp. 120 #x and note 1, 121 #x

Sharu   Dynasty III/IV

šꜣrw
Sharu

Length of Reign:	Unknown		
Tomb:	Unknown		
Mummy:	Unknown		
Consorts:	Unknown	**Variant Names:**	Shaaru Shairu
Manetho:	Not given		
King Lists:	None		

This name was discovered in 1895, near El Kab, in Upper Egypt. It is a portion of a graffito which also includes the Dynasty IV ruler Khufu. The name Sharu is seen on each side of the name Khufu, all

421

Shed...y

scratched into a sandstone cliff at the edge of the desert. The Sharu names are enclosed in rectangles that resemble serekhs more than cartouches. Each is surmounted by dual representations of Horus standing on a "Nub" (*nb*), the hieroglyph for gold. One Horus wears the crown of Upper Egypt, the other the crown of Lower Egypt. The whole effect is that of a combination Horus and Golden Falcon name.

No other evidence for Sharu's existence has been found. If he ever lived, his dynastic position would probably be early in Dynasty IV, as his name is found adjacent to Khufu's.

References:
Green 1903 pp. 215-216
Petrie 1924 vol. I p. 55
Sayce 1899a pp. 108-110
Sayce 1904 p. 93

Shed...y   Dynasty IX/X

Horus Name: Unknown

Nomen: 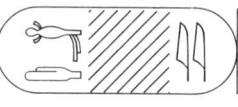 *šd...y* / Shed...y

Prenomen: Unknown

Two Ladies: Unknown

Golden Falcon: Unknown

Length of Reign: Unknown
Tomb: Unknown
Mummy: Unknown

Consorts: Unknown
Manetho: Not given
King Lists: T: (4.25)

Variant Names: None

Shed...y is one of the pharaohs who controlled an unknown amount of territory around Herakleopolis in Middle Egypt (see "Herakleopolitans" in Glossary). Attestations for the kings whose names are known are few; most are known only as names from the Turin Canon. Such is the case with this king.

Shed...y is the successor of Khety IV, a ruler whose name is preserved as Mery...(re) Khety and known only from the Turin Canon. What relationship these two kings might have had, if any, is unknown.

References:
Gardiner 1959 pl. II, Col. IV #25
von Beckerath 1999 pp. 72 #8, 73 #8

Sheneh   Dynasty XIV

Horus Name: Unknown   **Nomen:**

š-n-ḫ

Sheneh

Prenomen: Unknown

Two Ladies: Unknown

Golden Falcon: Unknown

Length of Reign:	Unknown
Tomb:	Unknown
Mummy:	Unknown

Consorts:	Unknown	**Variant Names:**	Shens Shenes
Manetho:	Not given		
King Lists:	None		

Sheneh is represented by only three scarab-seals, none of whose provenance is known. Though Sheneh's position in Dynasty XIV is unknown, the border decoration on one of his seals (now in Moscow) is a rope design. Although such a design was in use during Dynasty XIII, the only other known examples in Dynasty XIV come from scarab-seals of Sheshi, the fifth ruler of that dynasty, and his son Ipqu. It is likely that Sheneh ruled early in Dynasty XIV, and that his prenomen is perhaps preserved in the Turin Canon, but with his nomen lost due to the Canon's poor condition.

This king's name has usually been translated as "Shenes" due to a misreading of the epithet "given life."

Sheneh would have ruled over a part of the eastern Delta.

References:
Newberry 1906 p. 124 #28, pl. X #28
Ryholt 1997a pp. 51, 52 table 13, 96-97, 99 table 20, 101, 381 File 14/b
Ryholt 1998a p. 197 note 16

Tufnell 1984 p. 384 #s 3481 and 3482, pl. LXIII #3481 and 3482
von Beckerath 1999 pp. 120 #aa, 121 #aa

Shenshek   Dynasty XIV

Horus Name: Unknown

Nomen: *šnšk*
Shenshek

Prenomen: Unknown

Two Ladies: Unknown

Golden Falcon: Unknown

Length of Reign:	Unknown
Tomb:	Unknown
Mummy:	Unknown

Consorts:	Unknown	**Variant Names:**	None
Manetho:	Not given		
King Lists:	None		

Shenshek is known from a single scarab-seal found at Tell ed-Dab'a in the eastern Delta. His position within Dynasty XIV is uncertain, but it is likely that his prenomen is listed in the Turin Canon. Ryholt suggests the possibility of either Sehebre or Merdjefare as Shenshek's prenomen, but this is uncertain.

Bietak would see the name on the scarab as variant of the name of King Sheshi, but this is unlikely; it is much more likely that Shenshek was a separate ruler.

References:
Bietak 1991 pp. 52, 53 fig. 18 #6160
Hein 1994 p. 145
Ryholt 1997a pp. 52 table 13, 96-97, 99 table 20, 101 and note 337, 381
File 14/c

Shepseskaf   Dynasty IV

Horus Name:

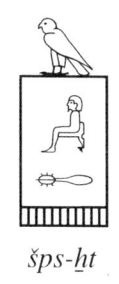

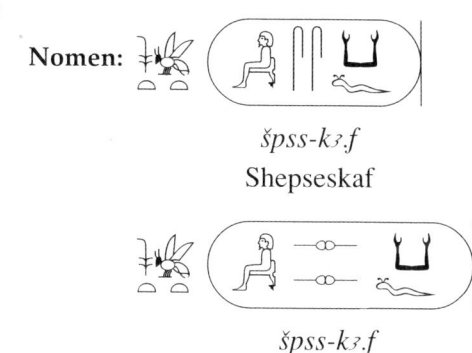

šps-ḫt

Nomen: *špss-k3.f* — Shepseskaf

špss-k3.f — Shepseskaf

Two Ladies: *nbty šps*

Golden Falcon: Unknown

Length of Reign:	T: "four years"
Tomb:	South Saqqara, Mastabat el-Fara'un: "Shepseskaf is Pure"
Mummy:	Unknown

Consorts:	Bunefer(?) Khentkaus I(?)	**King Lists:**	Ab: (25); P; T: (G 3.15)
Manetho:	Sebercheres (A) Seberkheres (A)	**Variant Names:**	None

Shepseskaf's parentage is in question. Some scholars believe him to have been the son of his predecessor, Menkaure, while others believe him to have been that king's brother, and thus the son of Khufu. In any case, he succeeded Menkaure and is the last canonical ruler of Dynasty IV.

Shepseskaf was responsible for the completion of Menkaure's funerary monuments at Giza, which he finished by using brick instead of stone. As for his own tomb, Shepseskaf chose to forsake Giza and have his burial at South Saqqara. Not only was the tomb location changed, but also the pyramidal design was forsaken in favor of a mastaba-like structure, known today as the Mastabat Faroun.

Shepseskaf

The Mastabat Faroun is a large stone mastaba with sides measuring 99.6 x 74.4 m. and a height of 18 m. Unlike the traditional mastaba, the narrow ends were raised, thus making the structure look a great deal like the hieroglyphic determinative for a shrine, 🏛.

We do not know the reason for the move to South Saqqara. Verner has suggested it might have been that the site wasn't far from Seneferu's two pyramids at Dahshur and could have represented "an expression of Shepseskaf's sense of belonging to this dynastic line." We do not know why Shepseskaf built a mastaba instead of the traditional pyramid. Verner posits that the mastaba might have been a temporary solution, since the major thrust of a vast amount of the economic structure of the government was geared to finishing the Menkaure complex. Stadelmann sees the reversion to a mastaba as an attempt to return to the tomb style of the first kings of Egypt. Some scholars have seen Shepseskaf's rejection of the pyramid as an attempt on his part to break away from the sun worship the pyramids represented and bolster their theories by pointing out that he does not have a name compounded with that of the god Re. Quirke mentions the possibility that the mastaba was only the first level of a step pyramid, left incomplete by the pharaoh's death. Perhaps in support of Quirke's consideration is the fact that the main fragment of the Palermo Stone mentions a "Selection of the Place for the pyramid [called] 'Shepseskaf is Pure'."

The Turin Canon gives Shepseskaf's reign as four years, although it should be noted that the king's name is not preserved, only the regnal years. The Palermo Stone preserves a record of the first year of his rule. The phrase "Year of the 2nd occurrence, 2nd. Month of prt, Day 10(?)" was discovered on a fragment of limestone found in a shaft of the Giza mastaba of Seshemnefer II (G5080), but there is absolutely no evidence that the years mentioned refer to Shepseskaf.

References:

Clagett 1989 pp. 53, 86-87
Dodson 2003 p. 64
Dodson and Hilton 2004 pp. 50, 52-53, 55-56, 59, 61
Gardiner 1961 p. 83, 434
Jánosi 1992 p. 53
Jéquier 1928a
Kanawati 2003 p. 2
Lehner 1997 p. 139
O'Connor 1995 p. 5 boats at Umm el Qa'ab
Quirke 2001b p. 126
Spalinger 1994 pp. 291-292
Stadelmann 2001a p. 597
Verbrugghe and Wickersham 1996 pp. 135, 190
Verner 1997 pp. 157-158, 245, 254-259, 463
Verner 2001b pp. 378, 588, 597
Verner and Callender 1997 pp. 32-33
von Beckerath 1999 pp. 54 #7, 55 #7
Waddell 1940 p. 47
T. Wilkinson 2000 pp. 149-151

Shepseskare — Dynasty V

Horus Name: sḫm-ḫꜥw

Nomen: nṯr(?)-wsr / Netjer(?)-user

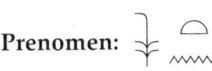

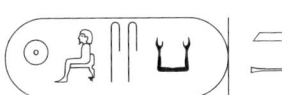

Prenomen: špss-kꜣ-rꜥ / Shepseskare

Two Ladies: Unknown

Golden Falcon: Unknown

Length of Reign:	1 year(?)
Tomb:	Unknown; probably at Abusir
Mummy:	Unknown

Consorts:	Unknown	**Variant Names:**	Neter(?)-user
Manetho:	Sisires (A)		
King Lists:	S: (28); T: (G [3.20])		

Although the Saqqara king-list records Shepseskare as the successor to Neferirkare (I) and the predecessor of Neferefre, archaeological evidence points to this king actually succeeding Neferefre. The Turin Canon is of little help in this case, as the names of both Shepseskare and Neferefre are missing, although traces of the years reigned are visible. While it has been common practice to follow the Saqqara list and place Shepseskare before Neferefre, there is, in fact, not one whit of evidence for such a placement. Seal impressions giving Shepseskare's Horus name have been found in the temple complex of Neferefre's pyramid and he is very possibly responsible for part of the structure's completion. Thus, he is regarded herein as the fifth king of Dynasty V.

Shepseskare's parentage is unknown. It has been suggested that a dynastic rivalry may have existed between the families of Sahure and Neferirkare (I) and that the Sahure faction managed to elevate Shepseskare (possibly Sahure's son?) to the throne upon the premature death of Neferirkare's son Neferefre.

Sheshi

No monuments attest to Shepseskare's reign. He is known from two cylinder-seals, four seal-impressions of unclear provenance and half a dozen impressions found in Neferefre's mortuary temple. A scarab bearing Shepseskare's name dating from the Saite Period may commemorate a petty king of Dynasty XXV.

At Abusir, mid-way between Userkaf's sun temple and the pyramid of Sahure, lies an unfinished platform, without question the beginning of a foundation for a pyramid. Also present are the rough-cuts for the building's substructure. By process of elimination, Shepseskare would seem to be the most likely candidate for interment therein, had it been completed.

Manetho gives his Sisires a reign of seven years, as does the Turin Canon, although the king's name is missing from the papyrus and the position may have been occupied by Neferefre. Considering the dearth of material attesting to Shepseskare's reign, it is probably safe to estimate a period of only months or perhaps a year in which this king held the throne.

References:

Dodson 2003 p. 69
Kaplony 1981 vol. IIA pp. 289-294, vol. IIB pl. 81-82
Krejcí 2000 p. 479
Gardiner 1959 pl. II, Col. III #20
Gardiner 1961 p. 435
Lehner 1997 pp. 142, 147, 148
Petrie 1902a p. 74, fig. 44
Petrie 1924 vol. I p. 85, fig. 56
Verbrugghe and Wickersham 1996 pp. 136, 191
Verner 2000b pp. 581-602
Verner 2002 pp. 54, 58, 111
von Beckerath 1999 pp. 56 #4, 57 #4
Waddell 1940 p. 51

Sheshi   Dynasty XIV

Horus Name: Unknown

Nomen: š-š-i
Sheshi

Prenomen: m3ˁ-ib-rˁ
Maaibre

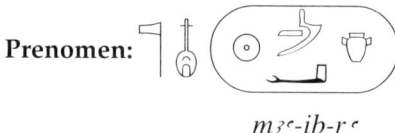

Two Ladies: Unknown

Golden Falcon: Unknown

Sheshi

Length of Reign:	Unknown		
Tomb:	Unknown		
Mummy:	Unknown		
Consorts:	Tati	**Variant Names:**	Mayibre
Manetho:	Not given		Scheschi
King Lists:	None		Shesha

Possibly the fifth king of Dynasty XIV, Sheshi is not listed in the Turin Canon, but is known from over 390 scarab-seals and seal impressions. While Sheshi's sphere of influence was in the eastern Delta, his scarab-seals and seal-impressions have been found at various sites in Canaan (e.g., Gezer, Jericho and Tell el-Ajjul), throughout Egypt (as far south as Elephantine) and in Nubia, from at least eleven sites including the fortresses of Mirgissa and Uronarti. The Uronarti seal-impression was found in context with several seal-impressions of kings of Dynasty XIII (Khabau and Djedkheperu). Since the two dynasties were contemporaneous, this seal-impression gives us a clear picture of Sheshi's dynastic position. The massive amount of scarab-seals strongly suggests that Sheshi's reign was a long one.

Sheshi's ties with Nubia seem to have been such that he appears to have married a Nubian woman, perhaps a princess. This woman, Tati, is the only known queen of Dynasty XIV. It is interesting to note that her name is found surrounded by a cartouche; in this period, this was strictly the prerogative of the king, the heir apparent and the Royal Treasurer. Tati was almost certainly the mother of Sheshi's successor, Nehsy.

It would seem that, sometime prior to Sheshi's death, prince Neshy was made coregent.

It should noted be that in the past some Egyptologists considered Sheshi a king of Dynasty XV.

References:

Petrie 1952 p. 7 #'s 4-5, pl. IX #'s 5 7
Rowe 1936 p. 53-54 #'s 204-207
Ryholt 1997a pp. 42-44 and table 11
    and note 119, 53, 55 fig. 7, 98 table 19 #5, 198-199 and table 38, 252-253, 299, 322 and table 93, 366 376
File 14/5, 409 table 95 #5
von Beckerath 1999 pp. 116 #f, 117 #f

Sihathor — Dynasty XIII

Horus Name: Unknown

Nomen: *mn-w3d-r'*
Menwadjre

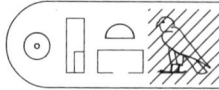

Prenomen: {r'-}s3-hwt-hr
Sihathor{re}

Two Ladies: Unknown
Golden Falcon: Unknown

Length of Reign:	T: "0 years, 1 + x months, 3 days"
Tomb:	Unknown
Mummy:	Unknown

Consorts:	Unknown	**Variant Names:**	Menuazra Sahathor
Manetho:	Not given		
King Lists:	T: (G 6.26: R 7.26; vB 6.26)		

The brother of Neferhotep I, Sihathor may never have had an independent reign, perhaps only serving as his older brother's coregent; if that is so, the Turin Canon's listing of a reign of 1 + x months and 3 days would record his coregency.

Attestations for Sihathor are very few. As a prince, he is known from two inscribed statues found on the island of Elephantine (one is Aswan Museum 1347, the other's location is unknown) and rock inscriptions from Sehel and Philae, where he is listed as a member of the family of Neferhotep I. As a king, Sihathor is known only from a cylinder-seal (Petrie Museum 11571) and a single bead (Brooklyn 44.123.163), neither of whose provenance is known.

Sihathor was probably born at Thebes, and it is interesting to note that all of his confirmed attestations come from the areas south of that city.

References:

Dewachter 1976 pp. 66-73
Dewachter 1984 pp. 195-199
Dodson and Hilton 2004 pp. 100, 105, 106-107, 108-109
Gardiner 1959 pl. III, Col. VI #26
Gardiner 1961 p. 440 #6.26
Habachi 1981 pp. 79-80, fig.s 8 and 9
Petrie 1925a pp. 30, pl. XXIV #13.24
Ryholt 1997a pp. 71 fig. 10, Col. 7

#26, 73, table 17 # 28, 192 table 33 and note 7/6, 225-230 and notes, 345 File 13/28, 408 table 94 #28
Seidlmayer 1988 pp. 173, 181-182 and fig. 15, pl. 58a
Simpson 1969 pp. 154-158 and pl. VIIa
von Beckerath 1999 pp. 96 #23, 97 #23

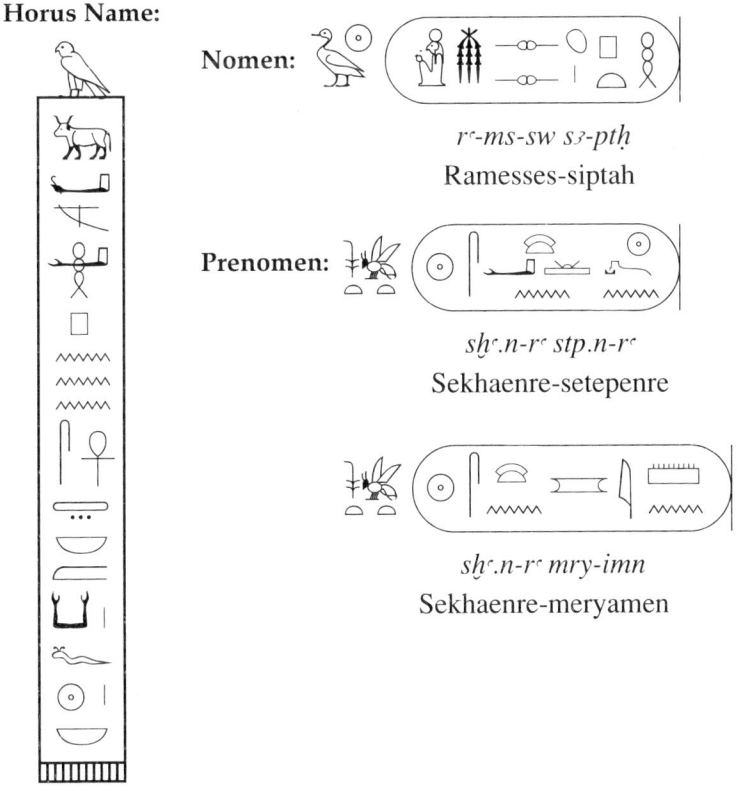

Siptah   Dynasty XIX

Horus Name:

Nomen:

r^c-ms-sw $s3$-pth

Ramesses-siptah

Prenomen:

$sh^c.n$-r^c $stp.n$-r^c

Sekhaenre-setepenre

$sh^c.n$-r^c mry-imn

Sekhaenre-meryamen

$k3nht$ mri-h^cpis\`nh-$t3$-nb-m-$k3.f$-r^c=nb

Siptah

Horus Name:

kꜣnḫt wr-pḥti

Nomen: *sꜣ-ptḥ mry-n-ptḥ*
Merenptah-siptah

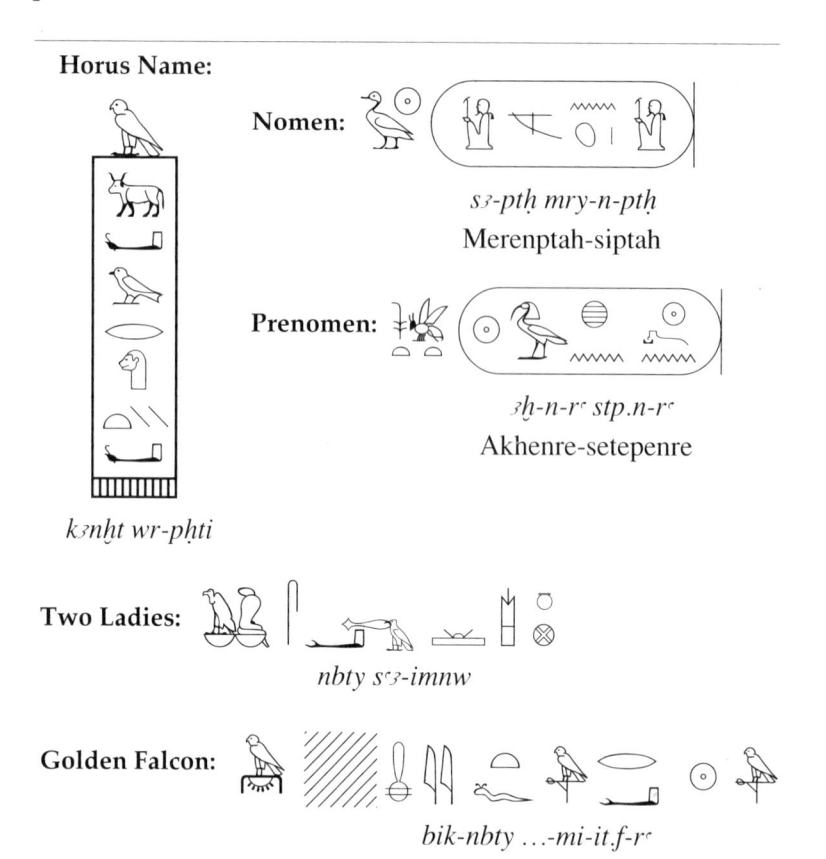

Prenomen: *ꜣḫ-n-rꜥ stp.n-rꜥ*
Akhenre-setepenre

Two Ladies: *nbty sꜣ-imnw*

Golden Falcon: *bik-nbty ...-mi-it.f-rꜥ*

Length of Reign:	6 years
Tomb:	Valley of the Kings: KV47
Mummy:	Tomb of Amenhotep II: Now at Cairo Museum: JE34563; CG61080

Consorts:	Unknown	**Variant Names:**	None
Manetho:	Not given		
King Lists:	None		

The seventh pharaoh of Dynasty XIX, Siptah succeeded Sety II, who may or may not have been his father; Egyptologists are divided as to whether that distinction should go to Sety II or his predecessor, Amenmesse. The name of Siptah's mother has also been in question, however recent research has turned up a relief which gives her name as Sutailja; it has been suggested that her name may be of Canaanite origin, and that she was most likely a concubine.

Siptah was not Sety II's original heir-apparent; this honor went to Sety-Merenptah, son of Sety II and his chief wife, Tawosret. However, Sety-Merenptah predeceased his father. When Siptah was chosen as the next king, he may have been next in line based on his lineage, but this cannot be said with certainty. He was only 10 or 11 years old at the time of his accession, and some scholars have suggested that Siptah was maneuvered onto the throne by Queen Tawosret and her confidante, a Syrian courtier named Bay. Because of his youth and poor health, Siptah required a regent (a role filled by Queen Tawosret) and would have been easily manipulated.

What is known is that early in Siptah's reign, Bay, a commoner and a foreigner, became unusually powerful and rose to the position of "Great Chancellor of the Entire Land." Bay's influence over the young king is shown in many ways. He claimed to have been responsible for placing Siptah on the throne, had himself portrayed on the same scale as the pharaoh on reliefs, was granted a large tomb in the Valley of the Kings (KV13), and even got himself included in the cult of Siptah's mortuary temple. As quickly as he rose, he also fell. In year five of Siptah's reign, the workmen preparing Bay's tomb were informed in no uncertain terms that Siptah "killed the great enemy, Bay." Work upon the tomb was abandoned.

Outside of Egypt, attestations for Siptah are few. From Palestine we have scarabs found at Beth Shemesh and Gezer. He is the first king of the dynasty *not* to leave attestations at the mines in Sinai. In Nubia, Siptah had texts and reliefs added to temples at Amada (which also show Bay), Abu Simbel (dated to regnal year one), in the south temple at Buhen, and also in Buhen town, where various inscriptions give dates of regnal years three and six.

Attestations for Siptah in Egypt are equally scarce. A graffito near Aswan, left by Serty, the Viceroy of Kush, pictures Siptah followed by Bay. At Gebel Silsila, in the Great Speos of the Dynasty XVIII pharaoh Horemheb, Siptah is shown making an offering to the gods Amen-Re and Ptah. At Thebes, Siptah appears to have started two mortuary temples, both of which were excavated by Petrie in 1896. One, between the temples of Thutmose III and Ramesses II (the Ramesseum), yielded more than half a dozen foundation deposits, the contents of which included copper tools, gold and faience plaques, and glazed pottery, some of which bore the name of Bay. The second temple, almost completely gone, was built between the temples of Merenptah and Thutmose IV and was usurped by Tawosret. Siptah's tomb in the Valley of the Kings, which seems to have held the burials of Siptah and his mother, was evidently entered not long after the interments and the cartouches of the king were chipped out, only to be replaced by painted ones at a later date.

In the long run, it seems as though Siptah merely exchanged one master for another. Almost certainly, Queen Tawosret, who had perhaps been forced to take a back seat to Bay (and may have plotted and engineered his downfall), seized upon the opportunity to strengthen her position as regent, a position she held until the young king's death only one year later. She immediately took on the trappings of a pharaoh and became the next king of Egypt, backdating her regnal years to the death of Sety II, and ignoring Siptah's reign completely. This led to Siptah's exclusion in all king lists, including Manetho.

Siptah's mummy was found in the tomb of Amenhotep II (KV35), in the Valley of the Kings. When unwrapped the pharaoh was found to have been in his late teens or early twenties at the time of death. Siptah's left foot was deformed; the original diagnosis had been a club foot, but this conclusion has been challenged and x-rays taken in the late 1960's seem to point to the king having had poliomyelitis. Cerebral palsy has also been suggested. The king's mummy was 1.638 m. in height.

References:

Brier 1994 pp. 115, 173, 272, 273-275, 276
Bucaille 1990 p. 55, fig. 15
Callender 2006 pp. 52-55
T. Davis 1908
Dodson and Hilton 2004 pp. 140, 176-177, 178, 181, 183, 285 notes 122 and 127
El Madhy 1989 pp. 90, 91
Forbes 1993 pp. 56-58
Forbes 1998a pp. 684-685
Harris and Weeks 1973 pp. 112, 159-160, 166
Ikram and Dodson 1998 pp. 84, 121, 264, 288, 315, 318, 326, ills. 98-99, 101, 385
G. Johnson 1998 pp. 47-64

Partridge 1994 pp. 168-170
Peden 2001 pp. 115-116 and note 361, 165-166
Petrie 1897 pp. 13-16, 16-20, pl. XVI-XIX, XXII, XXVI
Reeves 1990b pp. 105-108
Reeves and Wilkinson 1996 pp. 24, 37, 45, 77, 80, 84, 147, 150, 151, 154-158, 165, 183, 187, 191, 199, 200, 203, 207
G. Smith 1912 pp. 70-73, pl. LX-LXIII
H.S. Smith 1976 pp. 149-150, pl. XL #4, LXXVIII #2
von Beckerath 1962 pp. 70-74R
von Beckerath 1999 pp. 160-163 #7
R. Wilkinson 2000 pp. 182, 187

Sma   Dynasty 0

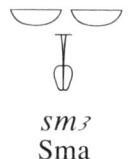

sm3
Sma

Length of Reign:	Unknown
Tomb:	Abydos, B 15(?)
Mummy:	Unknown

Consorts:	Unknown	**Variant Names:**	None
Manetho:	Not given		
King Lists:	None		

This king's existence is extremely doubtful. Like other possible rulers of Dynasty 0, "Sma" was discovered by Petrie at Abydos. Several broken stone bowls and ivory pieces bearing what appears to be the hieroglyph for Sma, surmounted by what may be abbreviated symbols for the epithet Two Ladies (nebty) or Two Lords (nebwy), led Petrie to believe that he had found a new ruler. The artifacts were excavated near tomb B 15, which Petrie believed to be Sma's tomb. Today it is believed that B 15 is a part of the tomb of king Aha of Dynasty I.

An ivory box from the tomb of Queen Neithhotep at Naqada may bear the name Sma, but more likely the hieroglyphs are part of the queen's title *ywts* (*smɜ.w nbty*), "She who is united to the king."

References:

Kaiser 1982 pp. 212-213
Kemp 1966 p. 22
Legge 1904 pp. 130-131
Petrie 1901a pp. 4-5, 9, 19-20 and pl. II .11, LVI . 2
Petrie 1902a pp. 3, 9, 14
Petrie 1902b pp. 5, 7
Petrie 1905 pp. 284-285

Smenkhkare   Dynasty XVIII

Horus Name: Unknown

Nomen: *smnḫ-kɜ-rʿ ḏsr-ḫprw*
Smenkhkare (djoserkheperre)

Prenomen: *ʿnḫ-ḫprw-rʿ*
Ankhkheperure

Two Ladies: Unknown

Golden Falcon: Unknown

Length of Reign:	3 years
Tomb:	Valley of the Kings, KV55
Mummy:	Cairo Museum: CG61075

Consorts:	Meryetaten	**King Lists:**	None
Manetho:	Rathotis (J) Rhathos (A)	**Variant Names:**	Sakara

Smenkhkare

The eleventh king of Dynasty XVIII, an exceptionally shadowy figure living in confused times, even Smenkhkare's parentage is unsure. He may have been a son of Akhenaten by Queen Nefertiti, the minor queen Kiya, or possibly (though not likely) a son of Amenhotep III by Tiye, Princess Sitamen, or a minor queen or concubine whose name is lost. At present, Kiya seems the most likely choice. Serological tests performed on Smenkhkare's skeletal remains show he was closely related to Tutankhamen. The two were probably brothers.

Smenkhkare was married to Meryetaten, eldest daughter of Akhenaten and Nefertiti. Whatever his parentage, this marriage cemented the succession for the young heir apparent. At the time of the wedding, Akhenaten evidently elevated young Smenkhkare to the position of coregent. It seems likely that Smenkhkare reigned for only a few years and predeceased Akhenaten; if so, then he was never sole king of Upper and Lower Egypt. His age at death is much debated; estimates range from the early 20's to the mid-30's.

Both Smenkhkhare and Nefertiti adopted the prenomen Ankhkheperure, and this contributed to confusion among Egyptologists about which of them was actually Neferneferuaten Ankhkheperure, now generally believed to be the twelfth pharaoh of Dynasty XVIII. Current scholarship supports the theory that Nefertiti, rather than Smenkhkare, filled this role.

The location of the tomb Smenkhkare originally occupied is unknown, but he was probably buried at Amarna. His mummy was found in the Valley of the Kings, in a cache given the designation KV55. The "mummy" was, in fact, reduced to a skeleton. The body had rested in a coffin originally belonging to Queen Kiya. Part of the tomb ceiling had fallen and damaged the coffin and the mummy, and water damage had done the rest. Some of Smenkhkare's funerary equipment, including four gold canopic containers and a gold-plated coffin, were reused in the burial of Tutankhamen.

Several Egyptologists believe the "body" found in KV55 to be that of Akhenaten and not Smenkhkare. To date, this theory has not found much acceptance.

References:

Allen 1991 pp. 74-85
Bell 1990 pp. 97-137
T. Davis 1907/90
Dodson 1994a pp. 92-103
Forbes 1998a pp. 249-317
Grajetzki 2005 p. 62
Ikram and Dodson 1998 pp. 324-325
Kadry 1982 pp. 191-194
Murnane 1977 pp. 169-179, 234
Partridge 1994 pp. 122-128, 135
Perepelkin 1978
Samson 1978 pp. 112-115
Samson 1982 pp. 61-67
G. Smith 1912 pp. 51-56
Tyldesley 2006 pp. 136-137
Verbrugghe and Wickersham 1996 pp. 141, 149
von Beckerath 1999 pp. 144 #11, 145 #11
Waddell 1940 pp. 103 ff.

Sobek SIP

Horus Name: Unknown **Nomen:**

sbk
Sobek

Prenomen: Unknown

Two Ladies: Unknown

Golden Falcon: Unknown

Length of Reign:	Unknown		
Tomb:	Unknown		
Mummy:	Unknown		

Consorts:	Unknown	**Variant Names:**	Sebek
Manetho:	Not given		Sebk
King Lists:	T: (?)		Sobk

This nomen is found on three scarab-seals of unknown provenance and is otherwise not attested. Tufnell gives the name as Sobekhotep, but this is incorrect. According to Ryholt, the cutting of the seals and their border design would seem to date them before the reign of Sobekhotep III (see Dynasty XIII in Dynastic King List). Ryholt further suggests that Sobek may be the nomen of king Nerikare of Dynasty XIII or, more likely, king Khabau, also of Dynasty XIII.

References:

Newberry 1906 p. 123 #27, pl. X #27
Tufnell 1984 p. 368 #3531, pl. LXIV #3531

Ryholt 1997a pp. 34 note 89, 401 File N/4

Sobekemsaf SIP

Horus Name: Unknown **Nomen:**

sbk-m-s3.f
Sobekemsaf

Sobekemsaf I

Prenomen: Unknown

Two Ladies: Unknown

Golden Falcon: Unknown

Length of Reign:	Unknown
Tomb:	Unknown
Mummy:	Unknown

Consorts:	Unknown	**Variant Names:**	Sebekemsaf Sobkemsaf
Manetho:	Not given		
King Lists:	T: (?)		

The nomen Sobekemsaf is known from a stele found at Thebes, several statues discovered at Karnak, a statuette from Tod, a graffito from Shatt el-Rigal, and a scarab-seal in a gold mount and a statuette, both of unknown provenance. All of these finds undoubtedly belong to either one or both of the reigns of Dynasty XVII kings Sobekemsaf I or Sobekemsaf II. It is highly unlikely that there was a third king with this name.

References:

Helck 1983 p. 61 #91, 64 #95, 64 #96, 71 #s 101 and 102
Newberry 1906 p. 123 #24, pl. X #24
Ryholt 1997a p. 401 File N/5
Winlock 1924 p. 243
Winlock 1947 p. 134, pl. 148

Sobekemsaf I   Dynasty XVII

Horus Name: Unknown

Nomen:

sbk-m-$s3.f$

Sobekemsaf

Prenomen:

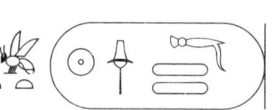

shm-r^c-$šd$-$t3wy$

Skehemre-shedtowy

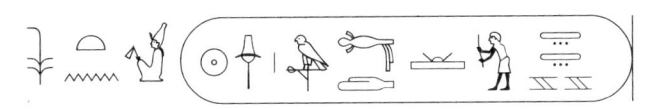

Sobekemsaf I

sḫm-rʿ šd-tȝwy
Sekhemre-shedtowy

Two Ladies: Unknown

Golden Falcon: Unknown

Length of Reign:	Unknown
Tomb:	Pyramid at Dra Abu el-Naga
Mummy:	Destroyed
Consorts:	Nubkhaes
Manetho:	Not given
King Lists:	K: (58)
Variant Names:	Ra-sekhem-shedti-taui

Sebekemsaf
Sobkemsaf

The second pharaoh of Dynasty XVII, Sobekemsaf's parentage is unknown. It has been posited that this king was the son of his predecessor, Rehotep, but there is no evidence to support such a theory.

Aside from a broken stone block bearing parts of his nomen and prenomen and a "finger ring" of unknown provenance, all attestations for Sobekemsaf I come from the Theban area. From Dra Abu el-Naga come a fragment of a shrine giving the king's cartouches and showing the king making offerings to Amen-Re and other deities, and a private stele bearing his nomen. From Qurna comes a four-sided stele belonging to the temple scribe Sobekhotep, inscribed with texts listing offerings granted by the pharaoh to Ptah-Sokar and Anubis. From Thebes proper come a lintel and a doorjamb. The doorjamb, recovered from a Dynasty XVII temple, is of special interest as it points to a father-son relationship between Sobekemsaf I and Intef VI, and therefore a similar relationship with Intef VI's older brother, Intef V.

Late in Dynasty XX, officials in Thebes apprehended, tried and convicted a number of people involved in tomb robbery. During the investigation it was discovered that the pyramid tomb of Sobekemsaf I and his queen Nubkhaes had been invaded, the burial chambers looted of all valuables and the mummies stripped of all valuables and burned.

Sobekemsaf II

References:

Budge 1913 p. 8, pl. 17-21
Dodson 2000 pp. 20-21, 134-135
Dodson 2003 p. 106
Dodson and Hilton 2004 pp. 116, 117, 118, 120
Helck 1983 pp. 70 #99, 71 #s 100 and 101
Peet 1930 pp. 38, 181
Petrie 1903 p. 35 #s 4 and 5, pl. XXXII #s 4 and 5
D. Redford 1997 p. 9 #51 (as Sobekemsaf II)
Ryholt 1997a pp. 167 and notes 599 and 602, 169-170, 171, table 28, 266, 270, 271, table 79, 309, 393 File 17/2, 410, table 98
von Beckerath 1999 pp. 128 #10, 129 #10 (as Sobekemsaf II)
Winlock 1924 pp. 237-243
Winlock 1947 p. 134, pl. 48

Sobekemsaf II   Dynasty XVII

Horus Name:

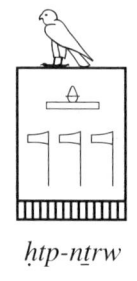

ḥtp-nṯrw

Nomen:

sbk-m-s3.f
Sobekemsaf

Prenomen:

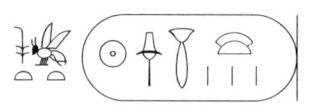

sḫm-rʿ w3ḏ-ḫʿw
Sekhemre-wadjkhau

Two Ladies:

nbty ʿš-ḫprw

Golden Falcon:

bik-nbw inḵ-t3wy

Length of Reign:	7 + ? years
Tomb:	Dra Abu el-Naga
Mummy:	Unknown

Consorts:	Nubemhat	**Variant Names:**	Sebekemsaf
Manetho:	Not given		
King Lists:	K: (48)		

Sobekemsaf II

The sixth pharaoh of Dynasty XVII, Sobekemsaf II's parentage is unknown, as is his relationship to his predecessor, Intef VII.

Attestations for Sobekemsaf II range from a statue found at Abydos to the Dyad statue in Elephantine; the latter is the first known reference to a Theban king that far south. A series of inscriptions at Wadi Hammamat, the first to be carved there in many reigns, attest to trading expeditions to the Red Sea.

Sobekemsaf did restoration work at Abydos, Coptos and Medamud and certainly built at Abydos and Medamud. From Abydos comes a red granite standing statue inscribed with a dedication by the king to Osiris; it also bears a figure of the King's Son, also named Sobekemsaf (who did not succeed him). From Medamud come a great many "architectural elements," including decoration added to a gateway built by the Dynasty XII pharaoh Senwosret III. Also from Medamud we have an inscription giving the details of endowments given to the temple of the god Montu. This text is carved on the base of a statue usurped from the Dynasty XIII pharaoh Sobekhotep III, who in turn had usurped it from his immediate predecessor, Seth.

Although Sobekemsaf's tomb has not been discovered, it is safe to say that he was almost certainly entombed beneath a small, steep-sided pyramid at Dra Abu el-Naga, near the pyramids of his predecessors. Evidently, Sobekemsaf's burial survived the tomb robbers of ancient times only to be looted in the early nineteenth century: A heart scarab and a canopic chest, both part of his funeral equipment, became "available" in 1827. The scarab is interesting because of its human face. The chest is of note because, being too small to actually hold real canopic jars, it has the jars and their spells painted and inked on the underside of the chest's lid.

An obelisk bearing Sobekemsaf's full fivefold titulary, along with a lintel, a statue and a statuette have been discovered at Karnak. Farther south have been found a pedestal and part of an inscribed block from Tod, remains of a shrine from Gebelein, and a Dyad statue from Elephantine.

A regnal year seven is given in one of the Wadi Hammamat inscriptions.

References:

Andrews 1990 pp. 12, 89, Illustration 65
Couyat and Montet 1912 p. 78 #111
W. Davies 1981b pp. 29 #45, 30 #s 46-48
Dodson 1994b pp. 37-47, 118 #26, 152-153, pl. XIV-XVI
Dodson 1994c p. 35, color photograph
Dodson 2000 pp. 119-120 and fig. 15, 21
Dodson and Hilton 2004 pp. 116, 117, 118-119, 120, 122, 124
Gasse 1987 pp. 207-218
Hall 1913 pp. 22-23 #211
Hein 1994 pp. 146 #116, unnumbered color plate
Helck 1983 pp. 61 #91, 62 #92, 63 #93, 64 #94
Ikram and Dodson 1998 pp. 141, 281-282, Illustrations 150, 410 and 413a

Sobekhotep

D. Redford 1997 p. 8 #s 47-49
Ryholt 1997a pp. 146, 168, 169-170, 171, table 28, 174, 176, note 628, 181, note 650, 272 and table 80, 395-396, File 17/6, 410, table 98

von Beckerath 1999 pp. 124 #3, 125 #3 (as Sobekemsaf I)
Winlock 1924 pp. 231-233, 268-269, pl. XV

Sobekhotep   SIP

Horus Name: Unknown

Nomen: sbk-ḥtp
Sobekhotep

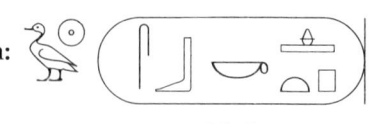

Prenomen: Unknown

Two Ladies: Unknown

Golden Falcon: Unknown

Length of Reign:	Unknown
Tomb:	Unknown
Mummy:	Unknown

Consorts:	Unknown		Sebkhotp
Manetho:	Not given		Sobekhotpe
			Sobkhotep
King Lists:	T: (?)		Sobkhotpe
Variant Names:	Sebekhotep		
	Sebekhotpe		

This nomen is found on a dozen items including a statuette from Heliopolis, a stele from Abydos and another from Armant, two statues from Karnak, a sphinx from Atfih, a cylinder-seal from Kom Ombo and another from el-Mahamid Qibli, a doorjamb from Elephantine and another jamb whose provenance is unknown. The name Sobekhotep stands alone on all of the above mentioned artifacts with the exception of one of the statues from Karnak, which shows a partially preserved prenomen that reads $ḫ^c$-...-r^c and could therefore belong to Sobekhotep II (Khaankhre), Sobekhotep IV (Khaneferre), or Sobekhotep VI (Khahotepre).

References:

Englebach 1942 p. 222
Hall 1913 p. 270 #2640
Helck 1983 p. 36 #40
Legrain 1903a p. 7 #4

Ryholt 1997a pp. 401-402 File N/6
Stewart 1979 p. 17 #77
Stewart 1983 pp. 28-29, pl. 38

Sobekhotep I   Dynasty XIII

Horus Name:

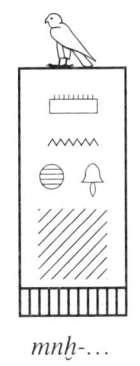

mnḫ-...

Nomen:

imn-m-ḥꜣt (sꜣ)sbk-ḥtp
(Amenemhet's Son) Sobekhotep

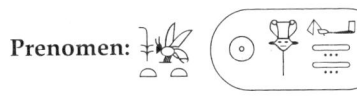

Prenomen:

سḫm-rꜥ-ḫw-tꜣwy
Sekhemrekhutowy

Two Ladies:

nbty ꜥnḫ-n ṯrw

Golden Falcon: Unknown

Length of Reign:	4 +? years
Tomb:	Unknown
Mummy:	Unknown

Consorts:	Unknown	Sebekhotpe
Manetho:	Not given	Sebkhotp
		Sobekhotpe
King Lists:	T: (G 6.19; R 7.19; vB 6.19)	Sobkhotep
		Sobkhotpe
Variant Names:	Sebekhotep	

Sobekhotep is the first Pharaoh of Dynasty XIII, although due to a scribal error, he is listed as the twelfth ruler of this dynasty in the Turin Canon. Ryholt gives a strong argument in favor of Sobekhotep having been the son of Amenemhet IV of Dynasty XII. Certainly Sobekhotep's full nomen may be given as either "Amenemhet-Sobekhotep" or "Amenemhet's (son) Sobekhotep"; Ryholt's interpretation for the two names being an example of filial nomina is quite convincing. The strongest evidence in favor of this pharaoh having been the first ruler of Dynasty XIII comes from Nile height records found at the Second Cataract near Semna and Kumma. These records list a series of kings' names which begins with Amenemhet

Sobekhotep II

III of Dynasty XII and runs in what is undoubtedly chronological order, through the reign of Nerikare of Dynasty XIII. Sobekhotep is listed under his prenomen, Sekhemrekhutowy. It gives a year four date for this king, which is, at present, the highest regnal date known for him.

While early Dynasty XIII is basically a continuation of Dynasty XII, and Sobekhotep ruled Egypt from Dynasty XII capital of Itjtowy in the Faiyum, there is evidence that a part of the eastern Delta was under the control of a Caanite overlord, probably Yakbim, one of the first rulers of what would become Dynasty XIV. As Ryholt points out, it is undoubtedly true that Sobekhotep was wary of this situation and that his prenomen, Sekhemrekhutowy, "The Might of Re which protects the Two Lands," reflects this concern.

Attestations for Sobekhotep I include remains from Medamud, just north of Thebes, e.g., the lintels and doorjamb of a heb-sed chapel (copied from a similar temple built by Senwosret III). Also from the Theban area comes a lintel found at Deir el-Bahri and architraves from Luxor. From Gebelein, just south of Thebes, comes a cylinder-seal. Besides the Nile-markers mentioned above, there is the bottom half of a statuette, discovered at Kerma. To date, there have been no attestations for this king discovered in Lower Egypt

References:

W. Davies 1981b p. 23 #9 (as Sobekhotep II)
Dunham and Janssen 1960 p. 131 RIS #'s 2 and 3, pl. 93 #B
Gardiner 1959 pl. III, Col. VI #19
Gardiner 1961 p. 440 #6.19
Helck 1983 p. 13 #20
Naville 1910 pp. 11-12, 21 pl. X, Pl. X -B
Newberry 1906 p. 195 #3, pl. XLIII #3

Ryholt 1997a pp. 12-13, 71 fig. 10 Col. 7 #19, 73 table 17 #1, 208 and table 46, 209, 296-297 and table 88, 315-316 and table 91, 318, 319-320 and table 92, 336 File 13/1, 408 table 94 #1
von Beckerath 1999 pp. 92 #16, 93 #16 (As Sobekhotep II)
Willems 1984 pp. 103-104

Sobekhotep II   Dynasty XIII

Horus Name:

Nomen:

sbk-ḥtp
Sobekhotep

Prenomen:

ḫʿ-ʿnḫ-rʿ
Khaankhre

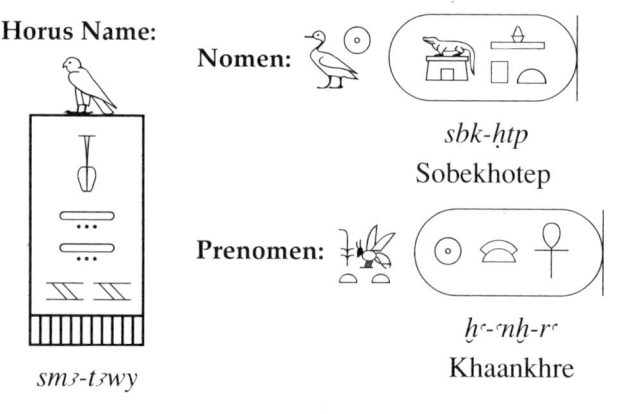

smꜣ-tꜣwy

Sobekhotep II

Two Ladies: nbty dd-ḥʿw

Golden Falcon: bik nbw kȝw-nṯrw

Length of Reign:	Unknown	
Tomb:	Unknown	
Mummy:	Unknown	
Consorts:	Unknown	Sebekhotep
Manetho:	Not given	Sebek[hot]pe
		Sebkhotpe
King Lists:	T: (G 6.15; R 7/15; vB 6.19)	Sobekhotpe
		Sobkhotpe
		Sobkrehotep
Variant Names:	Re'?-	

Sobekhotep II would seem to be the thirteenth pharaoh of Dynasty XIII, although von Beckerath places him as the sixteenth. Sobekhotep II may have been a usurper; the Turin Canon at one time gave the name of his father, but the papyrus is very much damaged and that name is lost. We can, however, be fairly certain that Sobekhotep's father was a commoner: there isn't enough room in the lacuna for a cartouche.

Another interesting feature of Sobekhotep's cartouche on the Turin Canon is that, through what is probably a scribal error, a ☉ has been added to the nomen, making the name read Sobekhotep*re*. There are several such errors in the Canon, however, Kitchen has called the "Re" "an integral part of the name" and gives the name as Sobekrehotep. Ryholt has shown that this reading is highly unlikely.

A further problem with Sobekhotep II is that his titulary had, until recently, been confused with the titulary of Sobekhotep I.

Attestations for Sobekhotep are few—some inscribed blocks and an altar from a chapel at Abydos, the pedestal from a statue found at Karnak, and a column whose provenance is unknown.

References:

Bourriau 1984 p. 131 #268
W. Davies 1981b p. 22 #5 (as Sobekhotep I)
Gardiner 1959 pl. III, Col. VI #15
Gardiner 1961 p. 440 #6.15
Helck 1983 p. 5 #10 (as Sobekhotep I)
Kitchen 1967 p. 46 note 2
Reeves 1986 p. 165-167, pl. 19
Ryholt 1997a pp. 71 Col. 7.15, 73 #13, 209, 215 and note 741, 284 table

Sobekhotep III

83, 339 File 13/13, 408 table 94 #13
Stewart 1979 p. 17 #76

von Beckerath 1999 pp. 90-92 #12, 91-93 #12 (as Sobekhotep I)

Sobekhotep III Dynasty XIII

Horus Name:

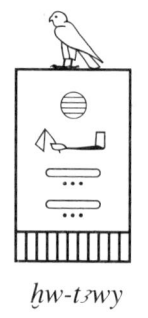

ḥw-tꜣwy

Nomen: *sbk-ḥtp*
Sobekhotep

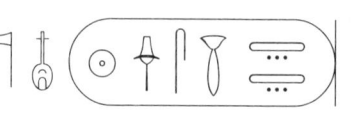

Prenomen: *sḫm-rꜥ swḏ-tꜣwy*
Sekhemre-sewadjtowy

Two Ladies: *nbty ḫꜥ-m-sḫm.f*

Golden Falcon: *bik-nbw ḥtp-ḥr-mꜣꜥt*

Length of Reign:	T: "4 years, 2 months, ..."
Tomb:	Unknown
Mummy:	Unknown

Consorts:	Neni Sonbhenas II	**Variant Names:**	Sebekhotep Sebekhotpe Sebkhotp Sobekhotpe Sobkhotpe
Manetho:	Not given		
King Lists:	K: (36); T: (G 6.24; R 7.24; vB 6.24)		

Sobekhotep III was probably the twenty-fifth pharaoh of Dynasty XIII, although Ryholt places him as the twenty-sixth and von Beckerath places him as the twenty-first. Sobekhotep III was no relation to his predecessor, Meribre Seth, nor to any of the previous

Sobekhotep III

rulers of Dynasty XIII. Making no secret of his non-royal birth, he issued a series of "genealogical seals" which gave the names and titles of his parents as "God's Father Montuhotep" and "King's Mother Iuhetibu." It is also possible that the "Elite Officer Sobekhotep, son of the Elite Officer Montuhotep" mentioned on more than a dozen scarab-seals is the future Sobekhotep III: A position of high rank and connections in the military would have made usurping the throne a great deal easier. Other attestations of Sobekhotep and his family come from a stele found at Coptos and now in the Louvre (C8), an altar from the island of Sehel, just south of Elephantine, and a monumental rock inscription from Wadi el-Hol (recently destroyed by vandals).

Although Sobekhotep reigned no more than five years, he is one of the best-documented pharaohs of the Second Intermediate Period. Attestations for this reign have been found as far north as Saqqara(?) (a scarab-seal) to as far south as the fortress of Mirgissa (a seal-impression) at the Second Cataract in Lower Nubia. Seal-impressions and scarab-seals are known from Lisht and Abydos and there are more than a dozen scarab-seals of unknown provenance.

The Theban area has yielded a fair amount of material attributable to Sobekhotep III. From Karnak come an altar (now lost), a sphinx (Cairo JE52810) and the statue of the vizier Ayameru, which gives the king's nomen. A papyrus found at Thebes gives dates of regnal years one and two. Medamud has yielded a series of architectural structures, including a lintel, stone blocks and the base of a statue which had once belonged to Sobekhotep's direct predecessor, Seth. In almost every case, the nomen and prenomen of Seth had been chipped away and replaced by those of his successor, certainly strong evidence for a coup placing Sobekhotep III on the throne.

Attestations for Sobekhotep III south of Thebes include inscribed blocks from a Sed chapel at El Kab, a doorjamb from Edfu, an offering table and altar from Sehel, a pedestal and feet of a statue whose provenance was most likely Elephantine and finally the seal impression from Mirgissa mentioned above.

Ryholt posits a serious political change during the reign of Sobekhotep III, and this may well have been the case: Sobekhotep very likely claimed the throne after some sort of military action, and his "genealogical seals," which made it clear that the new pharaoh had no blood ties to his predecessors, certainly suggests a desire to break completely with the old regime.

References:

W. Davies 1981b pp. 24-25 #s 17 and 18
Dodson 2003 p. 104
Dodson and Hilton 2004 pp. 25, 100, 101, 104-105, 106-107, 108-109, 111-113
Dunham 1967

Eder 2002
Gardiner 1959 pl. III Col. VI.24
Gardiner 1961 p. 440 6.24
Hayes 1955 pp. 15, 16, 73, 99, 111-114, 124, 125, 128, 145-148
Helck 1983 pp. 13-17 #s 21-25, 62 #92
Macadam 1946 p. 60, pl. VIII

Sobekhotep IV

Peden 2001 p. 47 and note 153
Ryholt 1997a pp. 17, 33-37 and fig. 1a and b and table 9, 38, 39-40 and table 10, 71 Col. 7.24, 73 #26, 74 note 7/24, 80 and Note 244, 192 table 33, 195 and note 691, 222-223, 224, 225 table 55, 284-286 and table 83 and note 1031, 296 table 88, 297-298, 343-344 File 13/26, 408 table 94 #26
Tufnell 1984 p. 366 #s 3099-3108, pl. LIV #s 3100-3108
von Beckerath 1999 pp. 94 #21, 95 #21
Wild 1951 pl. IV.2

Sobekhotep IV   Dynasty XIII

Horus Name:

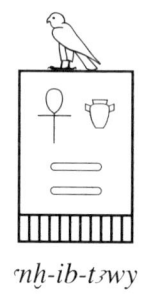

ʿnḫ-ib-tꜣwy

Nomen: sbk-ḥtp
Sobekhotep

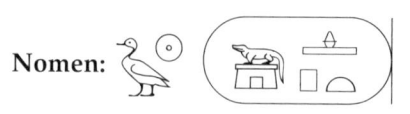

Prenomen: ḫʿ-nfr-rʿ
Khaneferre

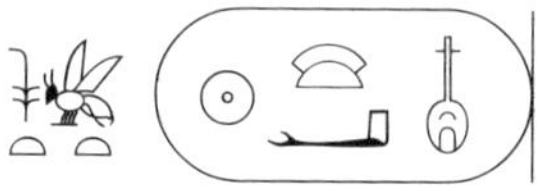

Two Ladies: nbty wꜣḏ-ḫʿw

Golden Falcon: bik-nbw wsr-bꜣw

Length of Reign:	Unknown
Tomb:	Unknown
Mummy:	Unknown

Consorts:	Tjin	Ra-Kho-Nefer
Manetho:	Not given	Sebekhotep
		Sebekhotpe
King Lists:	T: (G 6.27; R 7.27; vB 6.27)	Sebkhotp
		Sobekhotpe
Variant Names:	Chenephrês	Sobkhotep
		Sobkhotpe

448

Sobekhotep IV

The younger brother to pharaohs Neferhotep I and Sihathor, Sobekhotep IV was probably the twenty-eighth ruler of Dynasty XIII, although von Beckerath places him as twenty-fourth and Ryholt sees him as twenty-ninth. Like his brothers, he was evidently born at Thebes, although he undoubtedly resided at Itjtowy. After the death of his brother Sihathor (who seems to have died while still a coregent to Neferhotep I), Sobekhotep IV became coregent, and upon Neferhotep's death, succeeded to the throne. He is the best attested ruler of the entire Second Intermediate Period.

Although no item bearing Sobekhotep IV's name has been found outside of Egypt, the names of officials known to date to his reign have turned up in the Levant, in particular at Tell el-Ajjul. Tufnell suggests that a scarab-seal found at Jericho may bear Sobekhotep's prenomen, Khaneferre, but the seal is very stylized and the "Re" hieroglyph is not present, making the reading doubtful. A private stele discovered at Karnak informs us that Sobekhotep had two sets of doors for the temple of Amen fashioned from cedars from Lebanon. This is the final known example we have of timber from that region being imported into Egypt during Dynasty XIII.

For all his many attestations, no record of Sobekhotep IV appears north of the Memphite area, save for a single scarab-seal found at Tell el-Maskhuta (Pithom) in the southeastern Delta. This may mean that Egyptologists simply haven't found anything, or it may mean that the Delta area was no longer under complete control of this pharaoh. (Sobekhotep's immediate predecessor, Sihathor, shows no attestations north of the Theban area; neither do his two successors, Sobekhotep V and Sobekhotep VI.) However, Ryholt has documented some 68 scarab-seals whose provenance is unknown, any number of which may have been found north of Memphis.

Items bearing Sobekhotep's name from the Memphite area include a statuette from Heliopolis; from Memphis itself come a pair of colossal statues of the king and a statue (now lost) dedicated to Ptah; from Saqqara(?) two scarab-seals are known.

Attestations for Sobekhotep are known from the Faiyum region, Abydos, Dendera and, most importantly, a stele (now lost) dated to regnal year nine in the Wadi Hammamat. A little farther south, the Karnak area has given us doorjambs, a stele, the lower half of a statue of the king, and statues of the vizier Ayemeru and Army Commander Amenemhet. From Mo'alla comes a beautiful inscribed statue of Sobekhotep. Two stelae found at Edfu (now lost) were dated to regnal year eight.

Five stelae, two royal and three private, at the amethyst quarries at Wadi el-Hudi attest to Sobekhotep's interest in that stone as well as to mining for garnet, quartz, green feldspar and other semi-precious gems. At least one expedition to the mine occurred in regnal year six, as evidenced by the dating of four of the five stelae.

Evidently, at least some of the fortresses in Nubia (i.e. Semna and Kumma, at the second cataract) continued to function during the reign of Sobekhotep IV. It has been suggested that a war with Wawat, in Nubia, had occurred during this reign. However, the single limestone block upon which this theory is based is badly damaged and, as Ryholt has pointed out, the inscription does not mention Wawat, nor a war. It more probably refers to the establishing of offerings for a god whose name is now lost.

For some unknown reason, Sobekhotep IV was remembered long after his death. New Kingdom scarab-seals and other amulets were inscribed with both his nomen and prenomen. Even later, during the early Ptolemaic period, the Jewish historian Artapanus of Alexandria, in his history of the Jews, writes that Moses lived during the reign of Sobekhotep IV (equating the prenomen Khaneferre with the grecianized Chenephrês). It is interesting that Chenephrês is described as "king over the regions beyond Memphis, for at this time there were many kings of Egypt." Artapanus also tells us that Chenephrês was "the first of all men to contract elephantiasis and he died." While Artapanus never names his pharaoh of the Exodus, it seems certain he was referring to Chenephrês. Clement of Alexandria also equates Chenephrês with the pharaoh of the Exodus.

References:

Budge 1913 p. 9, pl. 23 # 278 [1060]
Collins 1985 pp. 891, 898-903
W. Davies 1981b pp. 25-27 #s 22-30
Debono 1951 pp. 81-82, pl. XV
Dodson and Hilton 2004 pp. 100, 105, 106-107, 108-109, 112-113, 284 note 84
P.M. Fraser 1972 pp. 704-706
Gardiner 1959 pl. III, Col. VI #27
Gardiner 1961 p. 440 #6.27
Habachi 1981 pp. 78 figs. 4-6, 79-81
Hein 1994 pp. 85-86 #2, pl. 2
Helck 1969 pp. 194-200, pl. XVII
Helck 1983 pp. 30-39 #s 36-49
Holladay 1982 pp. 45,50, pl. 45
Martin 1971 p. 120 #1554, pl. 22 #8
Peden 2001 pp. 45, 48-50
Petrie 1902b pp. 29, 42, pl. LIX
Petrie 1903 pp. 34, 43, pl. XXVIII
Petrie 1978 p. 23 (as Sobekhotep III), pl. XVIII 13.23.1-9, pl. XIX 13.23-10-16

Ryholt 1997a pp. 34, 35 fig. 1 e and f/fig. 2 a, 37, 38, 71 fig. 10, Col. 7 #27, 73 table 17 #27, 75, 77, 78, 84-86, 89-90 notes 287 and 291, 225-226, 227-231 and table 56, 284 table 83, 348-352, 408 table 94 #29
Sadek 1980 pp. 46-52
Sadek 1985 pp. 5-7, pl. XI, XII
Simpson 1969 pp. 154-158, pl. VIIa
Tufnell 1984 pp. 69, 158-160, 178, 180, 184-187, 200, 365-366 #s 3131-3161 and pl. LIV and LV 3131-3161
von Beckerath 1999 pp. 96 #24, 97 #24
Weigall 1908 p. 107

Sobekhotep V   Dynasty XIII

Horus Name: **Nomen:**
Unknown

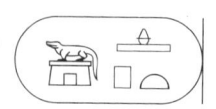

sbk-ḥtp
Sobekhotep

Sobekhotep V

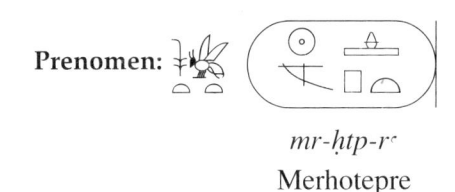

Prenomen: *mr-ḥtp-rˁ*
Merhotepre

Two Ladies: Unknown

Golden Falcon: Unknown

Length of Reign:	Unknown
Tomb:	Unknown
Mummy:	Unknown

Consorts:	Nubkhaes(?)	Sebekhotep
Manetho:	Not given	Sebekhotpe
		Sebkhotp
King Lists:	T: (R 7.28 lost)	Sobekhotpe
Variant Names:	Merhetepre	Sobkhotep
		Sobkhotpe

Most likely the twenty-ninth pharaoh of Dynasty XIII, Sobekhotep V was unrelated to his predecessors and would seem to have usurped the throne. Two scarab-seals name a lady Nubhotepti as "King's Mother", but she does not bear the title "King's Wife" and in fact, Sobekhotep's father, as attested by a broken scarab-seal found by Petrie at Tukh (ancient Nubt), held the title of God's Father, but his name has been lost.

Although von Beckerath would identify this king's prenomen as belonging to Sobekhotep VI, Ryholt has built a strong case for Sobekhotep V.

With the exception of the seal mentioned above, and two scarab-seals of unknown provenance, no attestation for Sobekhotep V has been found outside the Karnak area. The Karnak finds are two black granite seated statues (one being only the bottom half) and a standing statuette whose head is missing.

References:

W. Davies 1981b p. 27 #s 31-33 (as Sobekhotep VI)
Dodson and Hilton 2004 pp. 100, 105-106, 106, 106-107, 111, 113
Helck 1983 p. 40 #s 51-52
Petrie 1896a p. pl. LXXX #5
Ryholt 1997a pp. 22, 34, 35 fig. 1g and h, 36 fig. 4a, 73 table 17 #30, 79, 154-155, 231-232 and table 57, 240-241, 284 table 83, 352-353 File 13/30, 408 table 94 #30
von Beckerath 1999 pp. 98 #28, 99 #28 (as Sobekhotep VI)

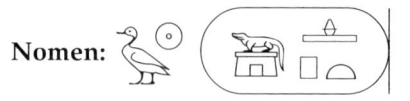

Sobekhotep VI — Dynasty XIII

Horus Name: Unknown

Nomen: *sbk-ḥtp* — Sobekhotep

Prenomen: *ḫʿ-ḥtp-rʿ* — Khahotepre

Two Ladies: Unknown

Golden Falcon: Unknown

Length of Reign:	T: "4 years, 8 months, 29 days"
Tomb:	Unknown
Mummy:	Unknown

Consorts:	Nubhotepti(?)	Sebekhotpe
Manetho:	Not given	Sebkhotp
King Lists:	T: (G 8.1; R 8.1; vB 7.1)	Sobekhotpe Sobkhotep Sobkhotpe
Variant Names:	Sebekhotep	

Probably the thirtieth pharaoh of Dynasty XIII, although von Beckerath places him twenty-fifth and Ryholt as thirty-first. For many years, the prenomen for this king was thought to be Merhotepre (which is in fact the prenomen of Sobekhotep V) and because of this the dynastic positions of the two rulers were reversed. Ryholt has recently corrected this error. Sobekhotep VI bore no known relationship to his predecessor and was probably a usurper.

Objects bearing Sobekhotep VI's name are few in spite of the fact that the Turin Canon gives the pharaoh a reign of over four years. Known are a scarab-seal found at Abydos and a kneeling statuette of the pharaoh found at Kerma(?). Items of unknown provenance include a cylinder seal, a seal impression, and half a dozen scarab-seals. A scarab bearing his prenomen, Khahotepre, was found in a tomb at Jericho, but it may have been a trade object and does not necessarily imply more than that.

References:

Dodson and Hilton 2004 pp. 100, 106, 106-107, 108
Gardiner 1959 pl. III, Col. VII.1
Gardiner 1961 p. 440 #7.1
Hein 1994 p. 115 #53, pl.: Kat. Nr. 53
Petrie 1925b p. 18, pl. XXVI #13.26.5
Petrie 1978 pl. XIX #s 13.24.1-2
Ryholt 1997a pp. 34, 36 fig. 3 a, 63, 71 fig. 10 Col. 8 #1, 73 table 17
#31, 192 table 195, 233, 240-241, 353 File 13/31, 408 table 94 #31
Tufnell 1984 pp. 5, 70, 180, 368 #3162-3167, pl. LV #3162-3167 (as Sobekhotep V)
von Beckerath 1999 pp. 96 #25, 97 #25 (as Sobekhotep V)

Sobekhotep VII   Dynasty XIII

Horus Name: Unknown

Nomen:

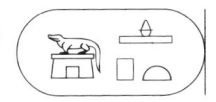

sbk-ḥtp
Sobekhotep

Prenomen:

mr-k3w-rʿ
Merkaure

Two Ladies: Unknown

Golden Falcon: Unknown

Length of Reign:	T: "2 years, ...months, 3 days"
Tomb:	Unknown
Mummy:	Unknown

Consorts:	Unknown	Sebekhotpe
Manetho:	Not given	Sebkhotp
		Sobekhotpe
King Lists:	T: (G 7.8; R 8.8; vB 7.8)	Sobkhotep
		Sobkhotpe
Variant Names:	Merkawre Sebekhotep	

Sobekhotep VII was probably the thirty-seventh king of Dynasty XIII, though Ryholt sees him as the thirty-eighth and von

453

Sobekhotep VIII

Beckerath places him as number thirty-two. Aside from a scarab-seal of unknown provenance, attestations for Sobekhotep VII are limited to two seated statues found at Karnak, both of which were dedicated to the Theban deity Amen.

References:

W. Davies 1981b p. 28 #s36 and 37
Dodson and Hilton 2004 pp. 100, 106-107, 108, 112
Gardiner 1959 pl. III, Col. VII #8
Gardiner 1961 p. 441 #7.8
Ryholt 1997a pp. 71 fig. 10, Col. 8 #8, 73 table 17 #38, 357-358 File 13/38, 408 table 94 #38

Sobekhotep VIII		Dynasty XVI

Horus Name: Unknown

Nomen:

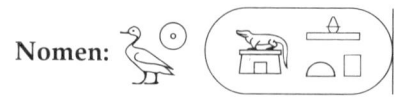

sbk-ḥtp
Sobekhotep

Prenomen:

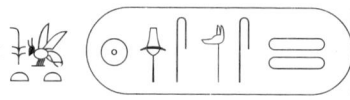

sḫm-rˁ s.wsr-tʒwy
Sekhemre-sewosertowy

Two Ladies: Unknown

Golden Falcon: Unknown

Length of Reign:	16 years
Tomb:	Unknown; probably at Dra Abu el-Naga
Mummy:	Unknown

Consorts:	Unknown	**Variant Names:**	Sebekhotep
Manetho:	Not given		
King Lists:	T: (G 11.2; R 11.2)		

The third king of Dynasty XVI, Sobekhotep VIII's parentage is unknown, as is his relationship to his predecessor, Djehuty. It should be noted that some scholars believe this king to have belonged to Dynasties XIII or XVII, although recent scholarship places him in Dynasty XVI.

The only contemporary attestation for Sobekhotep VIII is a stele from the Temple of Amen-Re at Karnak. Used as filler for the Third Pylon, built by Amenhotep III, the stele is dated to Sobekhotep's fourth regnal year and records a flooding of the temple during a particularly high inundation. The stele would have us believe that "His majesty was wading in it [the water] together with the workmen."

The Turin Canon records a sixteen-year reign for this pharaoh.

References:

Dodson and Hilton 2004 p. 116
Gardiner 1959 pl. IV, Col. XI #2
Gardiner 1961 p. 442
Habachi 1974 pp. 207-214 and pl. 1 and 2
Helck 1983 pp. 46-47 #63
D. Redford 1984 p. 100
D. Redford 1997 p. 3 #5
Ryholt 1997a pp. 152, 153 fig. 14 #2, 158, table 24, 305 table 97, 388 File 16/3, 410 table 97 #3
von Beckerath 1999 pp. 104 #g, 105 #g

Sobekneferu   Dynasty XII

Horus Name: mr(y)t-rˁ

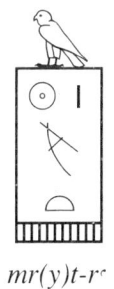

Nomen: sbk-nfrw
Sobekneferu

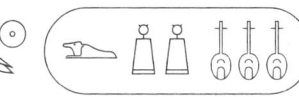

Prenomen: sbk-kȝ-rˁ
Sobekkare

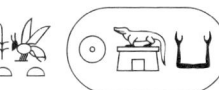

Two Ladies: nbty sȝt-shm nbt-tȝwy

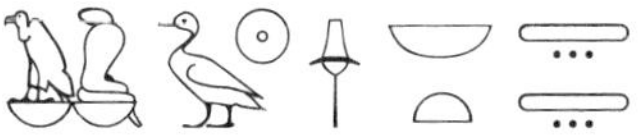

Golden Falcon: hik-nbw ddt-hˁw

Length of Reign:	T: "3 years, 10 months, 24 days"
Tomb:	Pyramid at Mazghuna(?)
Mummy:	Unknown

Sobekneferu

Consorts:	Amenemhet IV	**Variant Names:**	Kasobkre
Manetho:	Skemiophris (A)		Neferusebek
King Lists:	S: (46); T: (G 6.2)		Sebekneferu

Probably the daughter of Amenemhet III and therefore the sister or half-sister of Amenemhet IV, Sobekneferu was the eighth and last ruler of Dynasty XII. While she was not the first woman to rule Egypt (see MERNEITH), she was the first to actually refer to herself as the female Horus and to possess the full pharaonic fivefold titulary.

It is very likely that Sobekneferu was married to her brother Amenemhet IV and, upon his death, became his successor as Pharaoh of Upper and Lower Egypt. It is possible that Amenemhet IV never ruled independently (see Amenemhet IV) and that his queen (regent?) simply fell into the position of Ruler of Upper and Lower Egypt. There are no signs or records of a dynastic struggle, so it is probable that she was the only surviving potential successor.

Not a great deal has survived from Sobekneferu's time; however, enough has been discovered to make it fairly certain that she continued the dynastic tradition of residing in the city of Itjtowy, in the Faiyum. She was also extremely fond of another town in that same area, Shedet, the site of a shrine to the god Sobek, and she incorporated its name into some of her cartouches.

Sobekneferu's name has been discovered on several blocks and columns from the ruins of a building near the pyramid of Amenemhet III at Hawara. From the same location comes a plaque which bears the names of Amenemhet III and Sobekneferu. The juxtaposition of the names on the plaque has led a few Egyptologists to believe there may have been a coregency between Amenemhet III and Sobekneferu; however, this theory was never widely accepted and has no support from evidence beyond the plaque.

Tell el Dab'a, in the Delta, has yielded the greater portions of three near-life-sized granite statues of the female pharaoh. A basalt sphinx, bearing the ruler's prenomen, was found not far from the area where the statues were discovered.

At Ihnasiya (Herakleopolis), just to the south of the Faiyum, several architraves dating to Dynasty XII were unearthed, including a cartouche reading "Sobekneferu-Shedyt," a variant of Sobekhneferu's prenomen that incorporates the name of the town Shedyt. This same cartouche is preceded by the title "King."

A graffito found at the Second Cataract records the Nile's height during the inundation of the third regnal year of King Sobekneferu. This is the highest year we have for this pharaoh from a primary source.

The location of Sobekneferu's tomb, presumably a pyramid, has never been ascertained. To date the likeliest is at Mazghuna, where there are two pyramids very similar in their internal construction to the pyramid of Amenemhet III. Another possibility is that Sobekneferu was buried in her father's pyramid at Hawara.

References:

Callender 1998 pp. 45-46
Gardiner 1959 pl. III, Col. VI #2
Gardiner 1961 p. 439
Habachi 1954 pp. 458-470
Lehner 1997 pp. 181-184
Mackay 1912 pp. 36, 38
Mokhtar 1978 pp. 86, 90
Murnane 1977 pp. 20-23, 229

Peden 2001 p. 42
Ryholt 1997a p. 214 table 47
Verbrugghe and Wickersham 1996 pp. 138, 196
Verner 1997 pp. 388, 433
von Beckerath 1999 pp. 86 #8, 87 #8
Waddell 1940 p. 69

Sonbef   Dynasty XIII

Nomen:

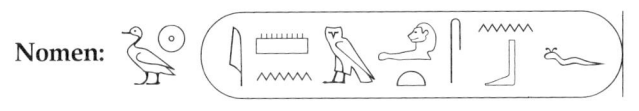

imn-m-ḥȝt (sȝ)snb.f
(Amenemhet's Son) Sonbef

Horus Name:

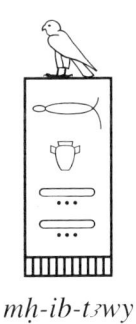

mḥ-ib-tȝwy

Prenomen:

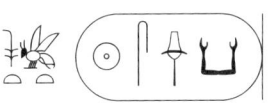

sḥm-kȝ-rʿ
Sekhemkare

Two Ladies:

nbty iṯ-sḥm.f

Golden Falcon: Unknown

Length of Reign:	4 + ?
Tomb:	Unknown
Mummy:	Unknown

Consorts:	Unknown	**Variant Names:**	None
Manetho:	Not given		
King Lists:	T: (G 6.6; R 7.6; vB 6.6)		

The second king of Dynasty XIII, Sonbef was, according to the use of filial nomina in his cartouche, probably the brother of his predecessor, Sobekhotep I, and the son of the Dynasty XII pharaoh Amenemhet IV. Although Sonbef most likely ruled from the Dynasty XII capital Itjtowy, in the Faiyum, no attestations for him have been found farther north than Tod, about fifteen miles south of Thebes. Very few items bearing Sonbef's name have been discovered. From Tod came two inscribed blocks; from Moalla came a very nicely made cylinder-seal. There is a scarab-seal of unknown provenance.

There are also Nile-records, at Askut and Semna in Nubia, that give regnal years three and four, respectively, and a much-damaged one at Semna that may record a year five. The Nile-records for this king bear his prenomen, Sekhemkare, and Smith initially identified this name as belonging to Sonbef (Smith 1991), but then decided the records refer to Amenemhet V, who bore the same prenomen . However, other scholars continue to identify the ruler in question as being Sonbef.

A papyrus found at el-Lahun, at the entrance to the Faiyum in Central Egypt, mentions a year three and some months and days of a pharaoh whose prenomen is given as Sekhemkare. As with the Nile records, this papyrus may refer to Sonbef or Amenemhet V (see also SEKHEMKARE).

References:

Beste 1979 pp. 150-160
Dunham and Janssen 1960 p. 132 RIS 8
Gardiner 1959 pl. III, Col. VI #6
Gardiner 1961 p. 440 #6.6
Newberry 1906 p. 114 #3, pl. VII #3
Parkinson 1991 p. 112 no. 38c
Ryholt 1997a pp. 71 Col. 7.6, 73 #2, 193, 208 and table 46, 209, 214 table 47, 297, 320 and table 92, 321, 336 File 13/2, 408 table 94 #2
S. Smith 1991 p. 118 and Note 56
S. Smith 1995 p. 27
von Beckerath 1999 pp. 88 #2, 89 #2

Tawosret   Dynasty XIX

Horus Name:

Nomen: tꜣ-wsrt
Tawosret

Prenomen: sꜣt-rꜥ mry-imn
Sitre-meryamen

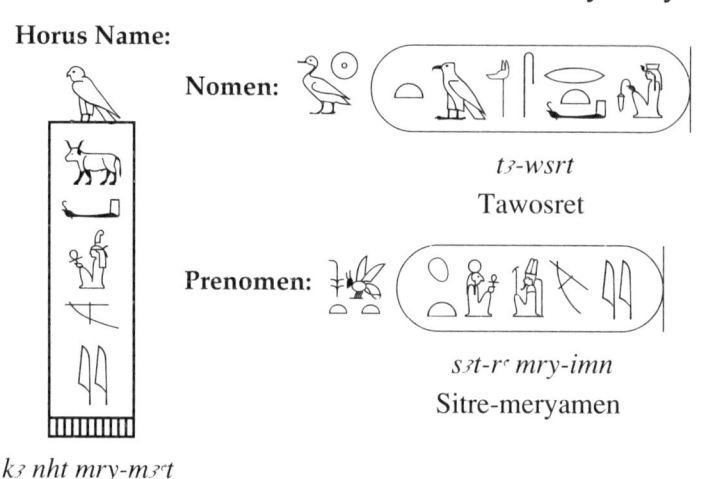

kꜣ nḫt mry-mꜣꜥt

Two Ladies: 𓎟𓏏𓀗𓐟𓍿𓅓𓏏 𓅱𓆑𓉐𓄡𓋴𓅓𓏏

nbty grg-kmt wf-ḫꜣswt

Golden Falcon: Unknown

Length of Reign:	2 years
Tomb:	Valley of the Kings: KV14
Mummy:	Tomb of Amenhotep II: Now at Cairo Museum: CG61082

Consorts:	None	**Variant Names:**	Tauosrit Twosre Twosret
Manetho:	Thouoris (A, E) Polybus (A, E)		
King Lists:	None		

The eighth and final pharaoh of Dynasty XIX was a woman named Tawosret, the former principal queen of the sixth pharaoh of the dynasty, Sety II. Nothing is known of Tawosret's background prior to assuming her role as queen. She only came to the fore upon Sety's death, when she became regent for the ten-to-twelve year old boy pharaoh Siptah. Sety II's chosen successor was his son, Sety-Merenptah, who appears to have predeceased his father. The throne, perhaps by default, passed to Siptah, a crippled young boy of (now) disputed paternity. His disability and youth meant that he required a regent, and Tawosret filled that role for the young king's six-year reign. Tawosret apparently had a close relationship with a Syrian courtier named Bay, who rose to the position of Great Chancellor of the Entire Land early in Siptah's reign. Bay undoubtedly exerted great power during Tawosret's regency, until he was executed during year five of Siptah's reign.

When Siptah died in his regnal year six, Tawosret immediately took on the trappings of a pharaoh and became the next ruler of Egypt, backdating her regnal years to the death of Sety II, and ignoring Siptah's reign completely. This led to Siptah's exclusion from all king lists.

Tawosret's two year independent reign has left few attestations, aside from scarabs, which are numerous. A seated statue found in Cairo is inscribed with her cartouches. Petrie excavated her mortuary temple in 1896. What was left of the temple (almost certainly never finished), which she shared with or usurped from Siptah, were a few decorated stone blocks. Foundation deposits (Petrie found nine) included hundreds of scarabs and glazed plaques, as well as hundreds of amulets and rings. In 1908, Davis found a cache of jewelry and other precious objects, much of which bore her name, in what he called the "Gold Tomb" (KV56) in the Valley of the Kings.

Tawosret's tomb is also in the Valley of the Kings (KV14). It was incomplete at the time of her death, but she was evidently interred there, as was her husband Sety II. Her tomb was later opened by her successor Setnakht, first king of Dynasty XX, who usurped it and completed the decorations for himself. It is assumed that Sety's mummy was moved to his original unfinished and abandoned tomb (KV15).

The highest known regnal year for Tawosret is year eight. Manetho, who gives his "Thouoris" a reign of seven years, also equates "him" with Homer's King Polybus (an Egyptian "king" who supposedly ruled at the time of the Trojan War).

A female mummy found in the tomb of Amenhotep II (KV35), in the Valley of the Kings and referred to as "Unknown Woman D," has been tentatively identified by some scholars as the remains of Tawosret. The mummification method certainly dates to the end of Dynasty XIX, and the mummy was found in company with that of Sety II. The body was resting beneath a coffin lid belonging to the pharaoh Setnakht, the king who usurped her tomb, although this may be accidental. The body measures 1.589 m. in length.

References:

Altenmüller 1992 pp. 141-164
Bakry 1971 pp. 17-26, pl. I-VI
Brier 1994 pp. 274-275
Bucaille 1990 p. 10, fig. 9
Callender 2006 pp. 48-63
T. Davis 1908 pp. 30-46 and plates
Dodson and Hilton 2004 pp. 18, 176-181, 183
Forbes 1993 pp. 57-59, 74
Forbes 1998a pp. 686-687
Forbes 1998c pp. 65-69
Gardiner 1956 pp. 40-44
Grajetzki 2005 p. 71
Harris and Weeks 1973 pp. 159, 160
Ikram and Dodson 1998 pp. 119, 264, 265, 315, 326-327
Partridge 1994 pp. 164-167
Petrie 1897 pp. 13-15, pl. XVI-XVII, XXII, XXVI
Petrie 1978 pl. XLIV #s 19.7.1-6
Reeves 1990b pp. 109-111
Reeves and Wilkinson 1996 pp. 32, 36, 37, 47, 53-54, 64, 77, 150, 152-154, 157-158, 199, 209, 211
G. Smith 1912 pp. 81-84, pl. LXVI-LXVII
Tyldesley 2006 pp. 163-166
Verbrugghe and Wickersham 1996 pp. 108, 112-113, 117 note 57, 143 and note 13
von Beckerath 1962 pp. 70-74
von Beckerath 1999 pp. 162 #8, 163 #8
Waddell 1940 pp. 149, 151, 153
R. Wilkinson 2000 p. 187

Teti — Dynasty VI

Horus Name: shtp-t3wy

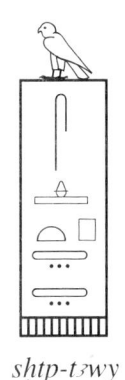

Nomen: tty / Teti

Prenomen: Unknown

Two Ladies: nbty shtp

Golden Falcon: bik-nbw sm3

Length of Reign:	11(?) years
Tomb:	Pyramid at Saqqara: "The Places of Teti Endure"
Mummy:	Portion in Cairo Museum

Consorts:	Iput I Khent[kaues III?] Khuit A	**King Lists:**	Ab: (34); S: (33); T: (G [4.1])
		Variant Names:	None
Manetho:	Othios (E) Othius (E) Othoes (A, E)		

The first king of Dynasty VI, Teti seems to have attained the throne by marrying Iput, a daughter of his immediate predecessor, Unas, the last ruler of Dynasty V. Although Teti's father's name is unknown, his mother was the King's Mother, Sesheshet, whose name and title are found in the tomb of the early Dynasty VI Vizier Mehu, as well on the South Saqqara Stone Annals. Interestingly, the Ebers Medical Papyrus mentions a lady named Shesh(et) as Teti's mother; more than one scholar has posited that the two women are one and the same. However, as Dodson and Hilton point out, final proof is lacking.

The transition from Dynasties V to VI appears to have had little if any effect in Egypt itself, and foreign relations continued undisrupted, as evidenced by fragments of an inscribed stone vessel found at Byblos. An alabaster vessel, found at Naga ed-Deir in Upper Egypt, is inscribed with what has been called "a female personification of Punt," and has been used as evidence by a few scholars to show that trading with that land occurred during Teti's reign—perhaps reading more into it than the evidence warrants. As far as Nubia is concerned, Teti is named in graffiti at Tumas, where his cartouche joins those of other kings Dynasties, V and VI, including Pepi I, Isesi (Djedkare) and Sahure. There are no other known examples of his name beyond Egypt's borders.

In Egypt, attestations for Teti beyond his pyramid and its funerary complex are not plentiful. His nomen and Horus name are found on graffiti at the Hatnub quarries in Middle Egypt. A beautiful alabaster model of a sistrum complete with Teti's Horus name and nomen, crowned with a hawk and cobra, and bearing an inscription calling Teti "beloved of Hathor," probably comes from Hathor's temple at Dendera. The oldest known true obelisk, found at Heliopolis, is inscribed with Teti's name. A stone lintel from Memphis bears Teti's Horus name. Teti also built a ka temple at Bubastis. A large block of red granite, inscribed with Teti's nomen, Two Ladies and Golden Falcon names was found at Qantir, although it was brought from another location. Teti is also responsible for the completion of Unas' mortuary temple.

Teti's pyramid is at Saqqara, just to the north of Djoser's step pyramid. Originally standing about 52 m. high and with a base of 79 x 79 m., the pyramid today is a hill of rubble. The inner chambers, beneath the pyramid, were damaged by stone robbers, but the texts inscribed on the walls of the burial chamber, the antechamber, and a small portion of the passage are still legible. The inside of his sarcophagus is inscribed with spells recited by the goddess Nut.

When Teti's pyramid was first opened in May of 1881, the excavator, Gaston Maspero, found a shoulder and arm, all that remained of the pharaoh; these were on display at Cairo Museum for many years. Interestingly, the Egyptologist J.E. Quibell, while excavating the king's mortuary temple during the 1907-08 dig, turned up a death mask which might very well be the face of Teti.

Teti's mortuary temple has all but disappeared due to the activities of stone robbers, but the plan is very similar to the temple of Unas, having an open court, magazines and statue niches. Architects seem to hearken back to Dynasty IV by their use of square columns.

A small subsidiary pyramid lay near the south-east corner of the king's tomb, and about 100 m. to the north-east are found the pyramids of two of Teti's wives, Iput and Khuit.

The highest regnal date we have for Teti comes from one of the graffiti at Hatnub and is dated to the "Year after the 6th. occurrence...," of the cattle count, which would be either year seven or 11/12, depending on whether the count was conducted biennially or yearly. The Turin Canon is much damaged at this point, and so we have only "...6 months and 21 days," the years being unknown. The South Saqqara Stone Annals give us only Teti's first year. Manetho gives a reign of 30 years and also informs us that the pharaoh was murdered by his own bodyguard. Egyptologist Naguib Kanawati has done an in-depth study and concludes that Teti was most likely assassinated, though, as Kanawati himself points out, the evidence is open to many interpretations.

Certainly Teti's memory remained alive. His funerary cult was maintained until at least the time of Amenemhet I of Dynasty XII. In a graffito found at Saqqara and dated to year 34 of Ramesses II, a scribe named Nashuy enlists the aid of Teti-beloved-of-Ptah (as well as Djoser-Discoverer-of-Stonecutting). Teti also has this title on a late XVIII/early XIX Dynasty stele, which would seem to bear evidence to a cult of the king at Saqqara.

References:

Altenmülier 2001 p. 602
Anthes 1928 p. 18, pl. 9a, gr. 1 and 2, pl. 9, gr. 1 and gr. 2
Daressy 1902 p. 29
N. Davies 1920 pp. 69-72, pl. VIII
Dodson 2003 pp. 71, 74-75, 126
Dodson and Hilton 2004 pp. 64, 67, 68, 70, 72-73, 76-78
Firth and Gunn 1926 vol. I pp. 2, 7-10, 11-14
Gardiner 1961 p. 436
Hamza 1930 p. 34
Hayes 1953 p. 125
Ikram and Dodson 1998 pp. 9, 82, 250, 314, 317
Jéquier 1933a
Kanawati 2003

Lehner 1997 pp. 31, 33, 63, 83, 156-157, 158, 172
Magee 2001 pp. 379-381
Peden 2001 pp. 7, 12, 99
Petrie 1924 vol. I pp. 100-101
Quibell 1909 pp. 19-20, 112-113, 113-114, 115, pl. LV, LVII, LXI
Ryholt 2000 p. 91
W. Smith 1971 pp. 189-191
Spalinger 1994 p. 303
Verbrugghe and Wickersham 1996 pp. 135, 136, 193
Verner 1997 pp. 141, 322, 335, 342-351, 370
Waddell 1940 pp. 51, 53
Weigall 1907 p. 108, pl. LVI-LVIII
R. Wilkinson 2000 p. 110, 124-125

Thutmose I   Dynasty XVIII

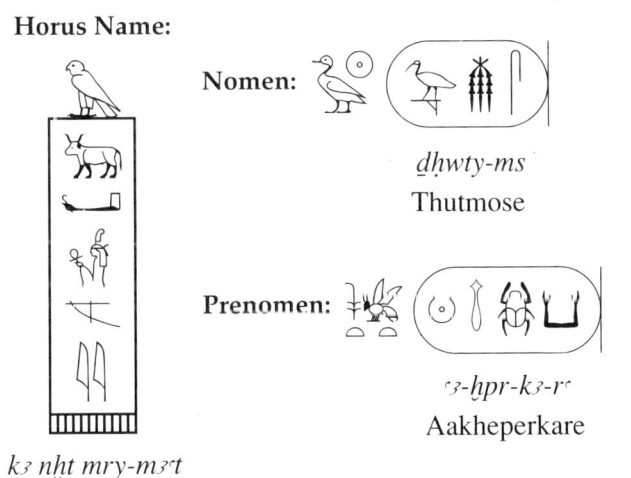

Horus Name:

Nomen:

dḥwty-ms
Thutmose

Prenomen:

ꜥꜣ-ḫpr-kꜣ-rꜥ
Aakheperkare

kꜣ nḫt mry-mꜣꜥt

Thutmose I

Two Ladies: nbty ḥʿ-m-nsrt ʿ3-pḥti

Golden Falcon: bik-nbw nfr-rnpwt sʿnḫ-ibw

Length of Reign:	9-13 years
Tombs:	Valley of the Kings, KV20 Valley of the Kings, KV38
Mummy:	Royal cache at Deir el-Bahri: Now at Cairo Museum: JE26217; CG61065(?)

Consorts:	Ahmose Mutneferet	Okheperkere Tahutimes
Manetho:	Memphres (E) Mephres (J) Miphres (E) Misaphris (A)	Tehutimes Thothmes Thotmes Thoutmosis Thuthmosis
King Lists:	Ab: (68); S: (49 lost)	Tuthmosis
Variant Names:	Djehutymes	

    The third pharaoh of Dynasty XVIII, Thutmose I had no known familial relationship with his predecessor, Amenhotep I, although it is possible that he may have been distantly related to him. While we know the name of Thutmose's mother, Senisonbe, we have no idea who his father might have been. Senisonbe's only title, King's Mother, makes it clear that she was not the child of, or married to, a pharaoh. It appears as though Thutmose I was an army commander under Amenhotep I and was named as successor to the throne by the childless king. A coregency between the two kings has been suggested, but the only "evidence" is a set of inscriptions on a shrine at Karnak begun by Amenhotep I and completed by Thutmose I. It is possible that Ahmose, Thutmose's principal queen, was a sister of Amenhotep I, since she is called King's Sister. However, she is never called King's Daughter; as a sister to Amenhotep, her father would have been the pharaoh Ahmose. It has also been proposed that she was actually the sister of Thutmose I. On the other hand, Thutmose's second queen (and the mother of his son and successor, Thutmose II) was most likely a daughter of Ahmose.

Early in the reign Thutmose I moved his court from Thebes to Memphis, where it would be centrally located within Egypt, and much closer to western Asia with its myriad city-states and the emerging superpowers of Hatti and Mitanni. However, Thebes was not forgotten. The temple of Amen at Karnak received two pylons, numbers IV and V, and the space between them was converted into a columned hall. (Two 20 m. tall obelisks honoring Thutmose's Sed Festival were probably completed during the joint reigns of Hatshepsut and Thutmose III.). Thutmose I also added a sandstone wall that enclosed the Middle Kingdom shrine and a goodly portion of the western area of the temple grounds, and completed the alabaster chapel begun by Amenhotep I. He finished another of Amenhotep I's structures, a building to house the vast amount of treasure which was beginning to accrue to the Temple of Amen. Across the Nile, Thutmose constructed his mortuary temple, and some distance further from the river, in the desolate series of wadis known as the Valley of the Kings, Thutmose I constructed his tomb. Other building activities were undertaken throughout Egypt from el-Hiba, 50 km. south of the Faiyum region, to Elephantine. Unfortunately they are mostly represented by a few decorated blocks of stone. A stele at Abydos records the offerings and works presented by Thutmose I and tells us that he was recognized and greatly honored as the son of Osiris.

A campaign in Nubia occurred in years two and three. Although it seems as though the actual boundary between Egypt and Nubia remained firmly at the island of Sai, 100 km. south of the Second Cataract, Thutmose's troops went overland, southeast across the desert, until they reached the Nile where it bends north, between the Fourth and Fifth Cataracts. At this point, he left a stele at Kurgus. At Tombos, just above the Third Cataract, a fort was erected. Some time later a large stele was carved near the fort to commemorate the king's victories in Nubia and western Asia. Two veterans, Ahmose Pennekhbet and Ahmose, son of Ebana, each record the expedition. The latter tells us that the king had come to suppress raiders from the desert highlands and that Thutmose wrought havoc among the Nubians, finally returning to Egypt with an unfortunate Kushite chieftain hanging head downward from the bow of his ship. Pennekhbet only tells us that he personally captured five prisoners. Inscriptions left by the Viceroy of Kush, Turi, at Aswan and on the island of Sehel, describe Thutmose I's victorious return in regnal year three.

After dispensing with Nubia, Thutmose I turned his eyes, and the Egyptian army, toward western Asia, and he conducted two campaigns in the region. Syria-Palestine had probably been of interest to Egypt since the expulsion of the Hyksos under the pharaoh Ahmose. Ahmose pursued his enemies into the area, where he laid siege and eventually conquered the city of Sharuhen, evidently the last Hyksos stronghold. The riches of the land would have been noted and coveted by the Egyptians, and the weakness of

Thutmose I

the individual little kingdoms certainly borne in mind. Thutmose was in command of a well-trained and victorious army. The veterans, Ahmose Pennekhbet and Ahmose Ebana, both describe triumphant battles against the kingdom of Naharain (Mitanni) when horses and chariots and a great many men were captured. Ahmose Pennekhbet presented the king with the severed hands of 21 enemies.

The Egyptian army could remain at such a distance from home for only a short while as supply bases would of necessity have been great distances apart, and reinforcements almost impossible to depend upon. However, Thutmose stayed in the region long enough to have an inscribed stele placed on the distant side of the river Euphrates and to conduct an elephant hunt at Niy. The Egyptian army returned in triumph.

Thutmose was the possessor of two tombs in the area now known as the Valley of the Kings. The first, constructed during the pharaoh's lifetime and now numbered KV20, was enlarged after his death by his daughter Hatshepsut so that she might be buried with her father. This is the tomb mentioned in the autobiography of the architect Ineni. Thutmose was later moved to the second tomb, KV38, which was built by order of Thutmose I's grandson, Thutmose III. Hatshepsut was left alone in KV20.

A mummy from the Royal Cache at Deir el-Bahri was found in a set of sarcophagi identified as belonging to Thutmose I, but the outer coffin had been reused by Dynasty XXI pharaoh Pinudjem I. It was unclear to whom the body belonged, especially since the mummy of Pinudjem was also found in the cache. The mummy was eventually identified as Thutmose I simply because it bore a resemblance to the mummies identified as Thutmose II and Thutmose III, the son and grandson of Thutmose I. The mummy's age at death was originally estimated to be about 50. More recent X-ray examinations suggest that age at time of death was 18-22 years. This is much too young to be Thutmose I. Another factor that mitigates against the mummy having been any pharaoh is the position of the hands and arms. Beginning with Amenhotep I, all pharaohs were buried with arms crossed and hands positioned to hold scepters, or the crook and flail. The mummy found in Thutmose I's coffins had arms extended downward, with the palms of the hands also down.

Thutmose I was succeeded by his son, Thutmose II, who was a child by Queen Mutneferet and was married to Hatshepsut, his half-sister and the daughter of Queen Ahmose. Hatshepsut would one day rule Egypt as pharaoh in her own right.

Manetho gives his Mephres a reign of 12 years, 9 months. The highest known date from a source contemporary with Thutmose I is a regnal year nine, found on an inscribed block at Karnak.

References:

Bradbury 1992 pp. 51-77
Breasted 1906 vol. II pp. 24-46 §54-§61, §65, §67-§108, §109-§114
Brier 1994 pp. 107, 262, 264, 265, 266-267, 278
Bryan 2000 pp. 230-235
Dodson and Hilton 2004 pp. 15, 22, 25, 31, 122, 123, 126-127, 126, 128-131, 132-133, 137-140, 284 note 53
El Madhy 1989 pp. 26, 36, 37, 88, 131
Forbes 1998a pp. 620-625
Gabolde 1987 pp. 61-87
Gardiner 1961 pp. 443, 444
Grajetzki 2005 p. 51
Harris and Weeks 1973 pp. 102, 130-132, 137
Ikram and Dodson 1998 pp. 37, 122, 170, 230, 255, 315, 318, 322, 329, ills. 301, 354, 356, 356, 360, 413c, 415
Jacquet 1983
Manuelian 2006 pp. 413-429
Murnane 1977 p. 115, 230
D. Redford 1967 pp. 28, 51
Reeves 1990b pp. 13-18
Reeves and Wilkinson 1996 pp. 15, 22, 29, 37, 53-54, 69, 75, 80, 84, 89, 91-96, 172-173, 195, 196, 200, 204, 206-207
Partridge 1994 pp. 69-73
Peden 2001 pp. 84, 86, 88-89, 135
D. Redford 1992 p. 153
Reeves and Wilkinson 1996 pp. 91-94
G. Smith 1912 pp. 25-28, pl. XX-XXII
Spalinger 2005 pp. 49-51, 58-59, 70-71, 76, 137
Strudwick 1999 pp. 33, 51, 80, 97, 174
Tyldesley 2006 pp. 91, 92
Verbrugghe and Wickersham 1996 pp. 140, 141, 159, 198
von Beckerath 1999 pp. 132-135 #3
Waddell 1940 pp. 101, 109, 113, 115, 117

Thutmose II   Dynasty XVIII

Horus Name:

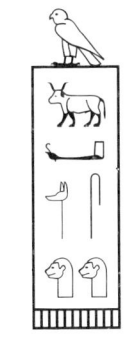

$k\!\!\;^\prime$ nḫt wsr-pḥti

Nomen:

ḏḥwty-ms
Thutmose

Prenomen:

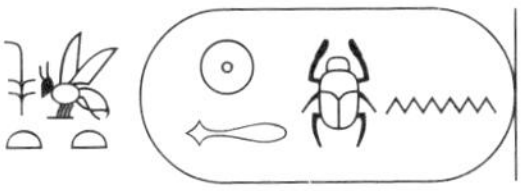

$\!\!\;^\prime$-ḫpr-n-r$\!\!\;^\prime$
Aakheperenre

Two Ladies:

nbty nṯr-nsyt

Golden Falcon:

bik-nbw sḫm-ḫprw

Thutmose II

Length of Reign:	3-18 years(?)
Tomb:	Unknown
Mummy:	Royal cache at Deir el-Bahri, DB 358(?) Now at Cairo Museum: JE26212; CG61066

Consorts:	Hatshepsut	Okheperenre
	Iset	Tahutimes
Manetho:	Chebron (E) (J)	Tehutimes
	Chebros (A)	Thothmes
	Khebron (E) (J)	Thotmes
	Khebros (A)	Thoutmosis
		Thuthmosis
King Lists:	Ab: (69); S: (50 lost)	Tuthmosis
Variant Names:	Djehutymes	

    The son of Thutmose I and his queen Mutneferet, Thutmose II was the fourth pharaoh of Dynasty XVIII. He had been third in line for the succession, but his older brothers Amenmose and Wadjmose seem to have predeceased him. It is likely that Thutmose was a teenager when he ascended the throne, perhaps as young as 12 or 13, and that his father's principal wife, Ahmose, served as regent for a time. It was probably at this point that the young king was married to his half-sister, Hatshepsut, thus further stabilizing his right to the throne.

    Attestations for Thutmose II are comparatively rare. At Karnak are two large statues of the king, and two empty pedestals mark where obelisks of his once stood. There are also a dismantled limestone gateway and a jumble of inscribed blocks from some unidentified structure belonging to his reign that were used as filler in the Third Pylon, built by Amenhotep III. Across the Nile, a little north of the temple/palace of Ramesses III at Medinet Habu, a small temple dedicated to Thutmose II was completed, or perhaps built entirely, by the king's son, successor and namesake, Thutmose III. Thutmose II is also known from a fragment of inscription, the construction of a doorway, and an ebony shrine (the latter probably finished by Hatshepsut) from Deir el-Bahri.

    An inscription found on the island of Sehel, just south of Aswan, relates information concerning a rebellion in Nubia (Kush). In year one (actually, on the day of his accession to the throne) Thutmose II was brought the news that a group of Kushites had stolen cattle near one of the forts at the Third Cataract, whereupon an army was dispatched at once. Naturally, the Egyptians were victorious: "...they did [not] let live anyone among their males, according to all the command of his majesty...," except for the son of a chief who was taken back to Egypt.

Thutmose II seems to have fought at least one campaign in Asia, as evidenced by the veteran Ahmose Pennekhbet, who tells us that the number of prisoners taken was too many to count. Fragments of relief from Karnak and Thutmose's small temple near Medinet Habu show scenes of battles with Asiatics, and some fragments show the Egyptians using chariots.

The tomb of Thutmose II has never been identified. Several tombs and locations have been suggested, but none of them bear so much as a trace of evidence that the pharaoh was ever buried there. Perhaps the tomb has yet to be discovered. We do have the king's mummy. It was found in the Royal Cache at Deir el-Bahri. The body when unwrapped was found to have been hacked to pieces, probably by an axe, and had to be reconstructed. The king seems to have stood about 1.68 m. tall and is estimated to have been around thirty years old at time of death. Scabrous growths were found on his body; their cause is unknown, but they are also present on the mummies of Thutmose III and Amenhotep II, his son and grandson.

Although a great many Egyptologists have followed Manetho in giving Thutmose II a reign of 12-13 years, a few others have opted for 18 years, based on a doubtful reading of an inscription on a statue that is now lost. The highest regnal date we possess for Thutmose II is the year one mentioned in the inscription from Aswan. His reign was probably longer than that by some years, especially since Queen Mutneferet is known to have acted as regent for some time.

A red granite statue of Thutmose II dressed in the Heb Sed costume found at Elephantine was dedicated by his widow, Hatshepsut. It is very unlikely that such a celebration took place.

References:

Breasted vol. II 1906 pp. 48-50 §119-§122, 50-51 §123
Brier 1994 pp. 107, 111, 263, 264, 267
Bryan 2000 pp. 235-237
Bucaille 1990 pp. 10, 27, 56-57, 84, 85, 97, 102, 103, 112, 129, 141-142, 167, fig. 18
Dodson and Hilton 2004 pp. 16, 31, 130-131, 132-133, 138-140
Dorman 2006 pp. 46-47
El Madhy 1989 pp. 35, 37, 87, 88
Forbes 1998a pp. 626-629
Forbes 2005a pp. 68-81
Gabolde 1987 pp. 61-87
Gabolde 1993 pp. 1-82
Grajetzki 2005 p. 52
Harris and Weeks 1973 pp. 101, 133
Ikram and Dodson 1998 pp. 28, 88, 255, 258, 315, 318, 322, 323, ill. 355
Partridge 1994 pp. 73-76
Peden 2001 p. 89
Reeves 1990b pp. 18-19
Reeves and Wilkinson 1996 pp. 44, 71, 88-89, 91, 96, 195, 196, 201, 203, 207
G. Smith 1912 pp. 28-31, pl. XXIII-XXIV
Spalinger 2005 pp. 10, 13, 50, 59, 62, 76, 107, 121, 123, 170
Tyldesley 2006 pp. 89, 94-95
Verbrugghe and Wickersham 1996 113, 114, 140, 159, 179, 198
von Beckerath 1999 pp. 134 #4, 135 #4
Waddell 1940 pp. 101, 109, 111, 115, 117, 241

Thutmose III　　　　　　　　　　　　　　　　Dynasty XVIII

Horus Name:

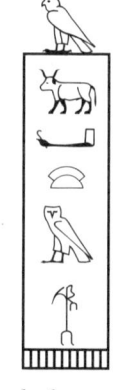

Nomen: *ḏḥwty-ms*
Thutmose

Prenomen: *mn-ḫpr-rʿ*
Menkheperre

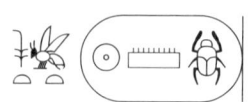

kȝ nḫt ḫʿ-m-wȝst

as Coregent:

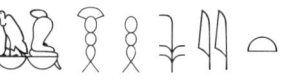

Two Ladies: *nbty wȝḥ-nsyt*

Golden Falcon: *bik-nbw ḏsr-ḫʿw*

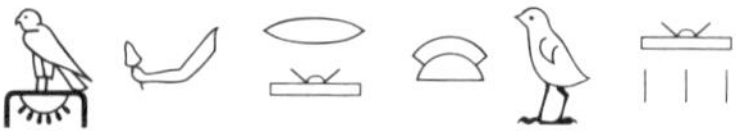

as Sole Ruler:

Two Ladies: *nbty wȝḥ-nsyt-mi-rʿ-m-pt*

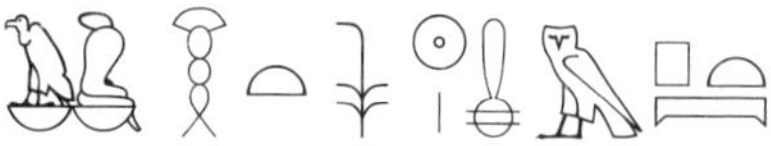

Golden Falcon: *bik-nbw ḏsr-ḫʿw sḫm-pḥti*

Length of Reign:	T: "53 years, 10 months, 26 days"
Tomb:	Valley of the Kings, KV34
Mummy:	Royal Cache at Deir el-Bahri Now at Cairo Museum: JE26213; CG61068

Consorts:	Menhet Menwi Merti Merytre-Hatshepsut Nebtu Neferure Sitiah		Myspharmou-thosis (E)
		King Lists:	Ab: (70); K
		Variant Names:	Djehutymes Tahutimes Tehutimes Thothmes Thotmes Thoutmosis Thuthmosis Tuthmosis
Manetho:	Mephramu-thosis (J) Mispharmuthosis (A, E) Misphragmou-thosis (A, E) Misphragmu-thosis (A, E)		

The sixth king of Dynasty XVIII, Thutmose III was the son of Thutmose II and of a minor wife or concubine named Iset (Isis). Hatshepsut, the King's Great Wife of Thutmose II, was Thutmose III's aunt as well as his stepmother. Thutmose was very young when he succeeded to the throne upon his father's death, perhaps not more than three or four years old, and a regent was required to rule in his name until he came of age (18 years old); Hatshepsut assumed the role. Also about this time, Thutmose III may have been married to his half-sister Neferure, the daughter of Thutmose II and Hatshepsut, although proof of this marriage is based on one possible reading of a cartouche which had been partially erased and recarved with the name of another Thutmose III's wives.x

Writers of history and fiction have speculated for more than a century upon the exact relationship between the young king and his aunt/stepmother/mother-in-law(?), but we will never truly know what that relationship was. We do know that, for a time, Hatshepsut remained the dutiful regent until, sometime between years two and seven of Thutmose's reign, she usurped the throne and the boy found himself the junior partner in an enforced coregency. The dual monarchs appeared on inscriptions and monuments which were dated from Thutmose's ascension, giving the illusion that Hatshepsut had been coregent since the beginning of Thutmose's reign. The young king was most definitely the lesser power and there is little doubt that Egypt was governed by Hatshepsut. Thutmose, it would appear, spent a good deal of time with the military, eventually commanding the entire Egyptian army.

Once thought to have been a time of peace, it is now known that several military actions, perhaps as many as six, were fought during the joint rule. While we do not know if Thutmose III was involved with the first of two campaigns in Syria-Palestine, it seems certain that he commanded the second, and was responsible for the capture of the important city of Gaza. Of the four campaigns sent to Nubia during this period, Thutmose III is known to have led the last three, between regnal years 12 and 20. The Gaza campaign appears to have occurred immediately after the final Nubian venture.

Hatshepsut's length of rule is given as "22 years, 6 months and 10 days" on a stele from Armant in Nubia. While theories abound regarding her fate, it is probably safe to assume that she simply died a natural death.

Soon after Hatshepsut's death, when Thutmose became sole ruler, he began the first of 17 campaigns in Asia. During the joint rule, Egyptian garrisons in Syria-Palestine were not well supported, yearly tribute from the region had likely begun to slow, and the chiefs and princes were beginning to show signs of rebellion. By late in Thutmose's twenty-third regnal year (his first year of sole rule), the princes in Syria-Palestine were in open revolt. Led by the prince of Kadesh, the rebellious armies were gathered at the city of Megiddo.

In the first Asian campaign, Thutmose III proved himself to be a superb strategist and commander. Marching from the fortress of Tjel in the eastern Delta, he was able to reach Gaza, in Palestine, in a mere ten days. Having taken Gaza on the twenty-third anniversary of his accession to the throne, an undoubtedly jubilant pharaoh rapidly moved his army north toward Megiddo. Halting only long enough to gather his straggling troops, Thutmose succeeded in routing the enemy forces camped outside the city's walls. It is likely Megiddo would have fallen at this time had the Egyptian soldiers not paused to plunder the deserted enemy camp; instead, a seven-month siege ensued before Megiddo was taken. By the time the city fell, the prince had escaped back to Kadesh. It required five campaigns and seven years before Thutmose was able to take Kadesh.

By the end of the seventeenth and final campaign in Syria-Palestine in year 42, Thutmose had expanded and solidified Egyptian control in that area to an extent unequaled by any other pharaoh either before or after him. Tribute and gifts flowed into the Egyptian coffers from Babylon, the Hittites, Kadesh, Mitanni, Megiddo and literally hundreds of other cities and city-states. There is evidence for tribute being received from as far away as the land of Punt, though scholars are unsure whether an actual expedition was mounted to this region. Expeditions to the turquoise mines at Serabit el-Khadim, well attested for the coregency period, continued during the sole rule.

There is a possibility that Thutmose led a small punitive force to Nubia in year 50. However, for the greater part of his reign, tribute and gifts from the south arrived regularly.

Despite the long years of campaigning, Thutmose III did not neglect Egypt. The riches pouring in from foreign conquest funded building and renovation of parts of the temple of Amen at Karnak as well as a temple at Deir el-Bahri. Other projects included a temple of

Ptah at Memphis and a temple at Gurob. In Nubia, the king built extensively, including shrines constructed at Qasr Ibrim, temples at Wadi Halfa, Semna, Kumma and Sai, and a temple begun at Soleb.

The wholesale removal of the names and titles of Queen Hatshepsut, ordered by Thutmose and once thought to have begun immediately following her death, now appears to have occurred much later in Thutmose's reign. The reason for this is unclear, though it is probably because the king had been too busy to attend to it earlier.

About two years prior to his death, Thutmose appointed his son Amenhotep II as coregent. It was a clever move: there would be no doubt who would rule the Egyptian Empire once Thutmose died.

Thutmose III was buried with all the trappings in the Valley of the Kings in a most interesting tomb, now numbered KV34. This tomb has been called one of the most sophisticated architectural achievements in the Valley. In a blend of art, architecture literature, and theology, its antechamber and cartouche-shaped burial chamber were plastered and then painted with a list of divinities and the earliest known complete version of the *Amduat*, "The Book of What is in the Otherworld." Indeed, the walls of the burial chamber are made to represent a gigantic illustrated magical papyrus.

Thutmose III's mummy was discovered in the Royal Cache at Deir el-Bahri in 1881 and was unwrapped shortly afterward. The body had suffered badly at the hands of tomb robbers. The head, arms and legs were broken from the torso, and the feet were broken off at the ankles. The mummy, which had been rewrapped during Dynasty XX, was held in place by four oars, three of which were placed inside the bandages, one being held on the outside by strips of linen. Like that of his father, Thutmose III's mummy shows scabrous growths; the cause is unknown. When the mummy was first measured, the disarticulated feet were not included and so the height was erroneously given as 1.615 m. This supposed short height, coupled with his many campaigns and conquests, led many Egyptologists to refer to him as "the Napoleon of Egypt." It has been estimated that, with the feet added, the king would have stood about 1.638 m.; a recent, unofficial measurement of the mummy (with the feet in place) gives the height as 1.75 m.

References:

Aldred 1998 p. 152
Breasted 1906 vol. II pp. 53-75
Brier 1994 pp. 109, 111 fig. 37, 171, 172 fig. 60, 263, 267
Bryan 2006
Bucaille 1990 pp. 56-57, 82, 135, 142
Della Monica 1991
Dodson and Hilton 2004 pp. 16, 31, 86, 130, 131-133, 137-141
Dorman 1988 pp. 78-79
El Madhy 1989 pp. 17, 36, 37, 57, 87
Faulkner 1946 pp. 39-42
Forbes 1998a pp. 630-631
Forbes 2005a pp. 88, 108, 131, 133, 140-173, 175, 176, 178
Forbes 2005/2006 pp. 18-31
Gardiner and Peet 1952 pls. XIV, LVI-LXV
Gardiner and Peet 1955 pp. 10, 13, 24, 36, 37, 38, 39, 74 #44, 122, 124, 150-151 #s 174A-176, 151-153 #s 179-181, 154-155 #s 184-186, 155-163 #s 188-204, 198 #320
Gibson 2000 pp. 60-65
Grajetzki 2005 pp. 53-55
Grimal 1992 pp. 207-209, 213-217

Thutmose IV

Ikram and Dodson 1997 p. 30
Ikram and Dodson 1998 pp. 81 fig. 79, 91, 122, 128, 160, 209, 210, 226, 256-257 figs. 358-359, 315, 316, 318, 322, 323, 371 fig. 386
Murnane 1977 pp. 32-57
Partridge 1994 pp. 77-81
Peden 2001 pp. 58-60, 62, 89-90, 106-108, 120-121, 145, 207, 272
Petty 1997 pp. 45-53
Petty 2000 pp. 50-59
D. Redford 1965 pp. 107-122
D. Redford 1967 pp. 60-63
D. Redford 2003
Reeves 1990a pp. 8, 20, 26, 29, 35, 37-38, 43, 47, 69, 71, 84, 91, 93-99, 101-103, 105, 118, 150, 172-173,183, 187, 194, 195, 196
Reeves 1990b pp. 19-24
Reeves and Wilkinson 1996 pp. 8, 9, 26, 29, 35, 37, 38, 47, 69, 71, 84, 91, 93-99, 101, 102-103, 105, 118, 172-173, 183, 187, 194, 195, 196, 206-207
Romer 1981 pp. 158-160, 163-165
G. Smith 1912 pp. 32-36, pl. XXVIII
Tulhoff 1984
Tyldesley 2006 110-112
Verbrugghe and Wickersham 1996 pp. 141, 198
von Beckerath 1999 pp. 136-139 #6
Waddell 1940 pp. 109, 113, 115, 117

Thutmose IV   Dynasty XVIII

Horus Name:

k₃ nḫt twt-ḫʿw

Nomen: dḥwty-ms
Thutmose

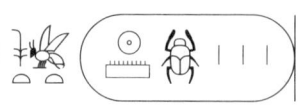

Prenomen: mn-ḫprw-rʿ
Menkheperure

Two Ladies: nbty ḏd-nsyt-mi-itm

Golden Falcon: bik-nbw wsr-ḫpš dr-pḏt-9

Length of Reign:	8-12 years
Tomb:	Valley of the Kings: KV43
Mummy:	Tomb of Amenhotep II Now at Cairo Museum JE34559; CG61073

Consorts:	Iaret Mutemwia Nefertari Tenettepihu(?)	**Variant Names:**	Djehutymes Tahutimes Tehutimes Thothmes
Manetho:	Thmosis (J) Thummosis (J) Touthmosis (A, E, J) Tuthmosis (A, E, J)		Thotmes Thoutmosis Thuthmosis Tuthmosis
King Lists:	Ab: (72); S: (53-missing)		

The son of Amenhotep II and Queen Tiaa, Thutmose IV was the eighth king of Dynasty XVIII. Amenhotep had ten children, one daughter, Iaret, and nine sons including Thutmose. It is not certain that Thutmose was the chosen heir to the throne, as any or all of his brothers might have been older than Thutmose. At least one of the brothers, Webensenu, evidently predeceased his father and was buried in Amenhotep II's tomb, where his mummy was discovered in 1898. It has been suggested that Thutmose IV may have usurped the throne, but there is little evidence of this beyond the defacement or erasure of several stelae at the temple of Amenhotep II at Giza. Sometimes also cited in support of the theory that Thutmose was a usurper is a story on the stele erected between the paws of the Sphinx at Giza. The inscription tells a tale of Prince Thutmose coming across the Sphinx buried in the desert sands; the Sphinx later speaks to Thutmose in a dream and promises him the throne. One interpretation of this tale is that Thutmose was not, at that time, the designated heir. The possibility of a coregency with Amenhotep II has also been suggested, but evidence is slight and inconclusive.

As with his father, Thutmose IV's "consort" for much of his reign was his mother. Queen Tiaa did not step down from her position as first lady of Egypt until well into the reign. Eventually, the role of queen was assumed by Nefertari, Thutmose's principal wife.

While some sort of military action in Syria-Palestine took place during Thutmose's reign, records are few and fragmentary and do not tell us the number, length, or extent of any such forays. However, a list of offerings to Amen at Karnak lists items "which his majesty captured in Naharin (Mitanni)...on his first victorious campaign." The stele of an official named Amenhotep makes mention of action against Mitanni and a scene in the tomb of the treasurer Khaemhet shows Thutmose receiving tribute from a group of bowing and scraping Asiatic princes; such a scene is also found in the tomb of the courtier Tjaneni. A treaty between Egypt and Mitanni was eventually concluded and a Mitannian princess was sent as a wife for the pharaoh.

An uprising by a group of Nubian tribes threatened the gold mines in the desert east of Edfu and necessitated military action in regnal year 7/8. No actual attestations for any sort of conflict in Nubia are known, although the stele of the official Amenhotep referenced above mentions Thutmose IV's presence on the battlefield not only in Syria, but also in Nubia.

In addition to military actions of one sort or another, Thutmose also built in Nubia. Decorated blocks, a statue base and a foundation deposit were found at the Amen temple at Gebel Barkal, and a re-used lintel, a stele, and jar-sealings come from Buhen. At Amada, Thutmose IV's additions to the temple of Amen-Re and Re-Horakhty, originally built during the coregency of Thutmose III and Amenhotep II, included converting the courtyard into a pillared hall, and decorating the columns with inscriptions bearing wishes for a first and subsequent occurrences of the Sed Festival. A large number of sandstone blocks bearing Thutmose's name have been found on Argo Island.

At the turquoise mine at Serabit el-Khadim in Sinai, Thutmose added to the temple of Hathor. There are also rock inscriptions dating to regnal years four and seven.

The reign of Thutmose IV was a time of great prosperity. Foreign trade thrived, as did the tribute and booty from Egypt's neighbors. The riches, coupled with the relative peace of the period, allowed Thutmose to devote a great deal of attention to art and architecture throughout Egypt. Attestations include more than two dozen monuments from Giza, including a relief added to the temple built by Amenhotep II, and 18 stele, the Sphinx stele mentioned above among them. Red granite columns found at Alexandria were probably brought there from Heliopolis, where they were most likely from the temple of Re or Atum. A statue of King's Mother Tiaa comes from Crocodilopolis in the Faiyum. A mud brick chapel was built at Abydos; inscribed fragments of walls, a lintel, and a red granite statue also come from there. Inscribed blocks, architraves, columns, and the like come from Armant, Tod, Edfu, El Kab and Elephantine.

The Theban area saw most of Thutmose's building activity. At Karnak, construction included the addition of a decorated portico to the Fourth Pylon (demolished by his son Amenhotep III and used as filling for the Third Pylon), and the building of a barque shrine. A single obelisk, 32 m. tall, was erected in the eastern precinct; also built were a new porch and doorways for the temple of Montu. Two large stelae were erected at Luxor.

Across the Nile from Luxor and Karnak, Thutmose built his mortuary temple slightly southwest of the future mortuary temple of Ramesses II. A tomb was also built in the Valley of the Kings.

The mummy of Thutmose IV was found in the tomb of Amenhotep II, having been moved there during Dynasty XXI. Unwrapped, the mummy proved to be that of "an extremely emaciated man, 1.646 m. in height." The hair was of a reddish-brown color, possibly tinted with henna. Age at death has been estimated at 25 to 40 years old.

The highest regnal date known for Thutmose IV, year eight from a stele at Konosso, jibes well with Manetho's nine years, eight months, as given by Josephus.

References:
Brier 1994 pp. 115, 173, 187, 267
Bryan 1991
Bryan 1998 pp. 27-62
Dodson and Hilton 2004 pp. 18, 132-133, 134-135, 137-140, 140, 181, 283 note 31
El Madhy 1989 pp. 39, 76, 87, 88, 131, 157
Forbes 1998a pp. 674-675
Forbes 2002 pp. 40-56
Forbes 2005a pp. 199-223
Murnane 1977 pp. 117-123
Partridge 1994 pp. 94-95
Peden 2001 pp. 90, 91, 95, 142-143
Reeves 1990b pp. 34-38
Reeves and Wilkinson 1996 pp. 28-29, 33, 37-38, 42-43, 47, 70, 74-75, 77, 80-81, 105, 106, 107-108, 111, 112, 113-115, 126, 132, 142, 178, 180, 182-184, 187, 191-193, 199, 203, 207
Gardiner and Peet 1952 pl. XIX-XX, LVIII, LXII
Gardiner and Peet 1955 pp. 38, 39, 81 #58, 82 #60, 164 #s 207-208, 165 #209
Grajetzki 2005 pp. 56-57
Harris and Weeks 1973 pp. 60, 112, 136, 138, 139, 140
Ikram and Dodson 1998 pp. 62, 74, 84, 96-97, 210, 258, 315, 324, Ills. 69-70, 360, pl. XXXVII
G. Smith 1912 pp. 42-46, pl. XXIX-XXX
Soliman and Johnson 1994 pp. 40-49
Tyldesley 2006 pp. 89, 113-114
Verbrugghe and Wickersham 1996 pp. 159, 199
von Beckerath 1999 pp. 138-141 #8
Waddell 1940 pp. 87, 109, 113, 115, 117

Tiu   Predynastic

tiw
Tiu

Length of Reign:	Unknown
Tomb:	Unknown
Mummy:	Unknown

Consorts:	Unknown	**Variant Names:**	Tau
Manetho:	Not given		Teyew
King Lists:	P		

Tiu is one of a group of nine kings known only from the Palermo Stone. Each name is followed by a representation of a squatting king wearing the crown of Lower Egypt. Whether these names are to be taken as historic personages or mythic "ancestors" is not known.

References:
Clagett 1989 pp. 66, 97-98
Edwards 1971 pp. 3-4
T. Wilkinson 2000 pp. 62, 85-86, 87
Gardiner 1961 pl. III
O'Mara 1979 p. 5

Tjesh   Predynastic

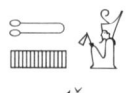

tš
Tjesh

Length of Reign:	Unknown
Tomb:	Unknown
Mummy:	Unknown

Consorts:	Unknown	**Variant Names:**	Itjiesch Thesh
Manetho:	Not given		
King Lists:	P		

Tjesh is one of a group of nine kings known only from the Palermo Stone. Each name is followed by a representation of a squatting king wearing the crown of Lower Egypt. Whether these names are to be taken as historic personages or mythic "ancestors" is not known.

References:
Clagett 1989 pp. 66, 97-98
Edwards 1971 pp. 3-4
Gardiner 1961 pl. III
O'Mara 1979 p. 5
T. Wilkinson 2000 pp. 62, 85-86, 87

Tutankhamen — Dynasty XVIII

Horus Name:

kꜣ nḫt-twt-mswt

Nomen:

twt-ꜥnḫ-itn
Tutankhaten

twt-ꜥnḫ-imn
Tutankhamen

Prenomen:

nb-ḫprw-rꜥ
Nebkheperure

Two Ladies:

nbty nfr-hpw sgrḥ-tꜣwy

Golden Falcon:

bik-nbw wṯs-ḫꜥw sḥtp-nṯrw

Length of Reign:	9 years
Tomb:	Valley of the Kings: KV62
Mummy:	Valley of the Kings: KV62

Consorts:	Ankhsenamen	**Variant Names:**	Toutankh-amanou
Manetho:	Chebres (A) Khebres (A)		Tutankhamon
King Lists:	None		Tutankhamun

Tutankamen

Tutankhamen is the thirteenth king of Dynasty XVIII. Originally named Tutankhaten, Tutankhamen ascended the throne as a child, presumably upon the death of the pharaoh Akhenaten. He evidently shared the throne with Neferneferuaten (Nefertiti), who was most likely coregent throughout the early years of his reign. His parentage is unknown, though he may have been the son of Akhenaten and Queen Nefertiti or of a secondary queen named Kiya. Serological tests on his mummy show him to have been closely related to the remains found in the Royal Cache in Valley of the Kings tomb KV55, usually identified as Smenkhkare. Whatever his parentage, his claim to the throne was strengthened by marriage to Ankhsenpaaten (later called Ankhsenamen), third and oldest surviving daughter of Akhenaten and Nefertiti.

In about year two of the new king's reign, his name was changed from Tutankh*aten* to Tutankh*amen* and the seat of government was moved from Akhenaten's capital, Akhetaten, to the city of Memphis. What is now known as the "Restoration Stele" was erected near the Third Pylon of the temple of Amen-Re at Karnak. The stele was engraved with an edict restoring and reopening temples throughout Egypt. The period of Akhenaten's religious "heresy" was, for all practical purposes, at an end (see AKHENATEN).

There is very little doubt that circumstances beyond the control of the boy king caused these events. It seems almost certain that, although Tutankhamen was pharaoh, Egypt was actually controlled by the vizier and regent, Ay (who had served under Akhenaten in various positions of influence), perhaps in collusion with the priesthood of Amen, and possibly with assistance from the Great Commander of the Army, Horemheb.

Building activities during Tutankhamen's reign included not only the restoration of temples but also additions to them, examples being the Processional Colonnade at Luxor and the continued construction of the temple of Amen at Karnak. A tomb in the Valley of the Kings was begun, as well as a mortuary temple near Medinet Habu. Neither of these was completed.

An Apis bull was buried during Tutankhamen's reign.

Decorations in the tomb of Huy, Viceroy of Kush under Tutankhamen, show the young king receiving tribute from Nubia. It is unclear whether there was an actual military campaign in this area; the tribute was probably a mere continuation of a long established practice. Tutankhamen did build a temple to himself at Faras, where he was worshipped as a living god.

There is evidence from the Hittite archives that attests to an attack upon the Hittite-held city of Kadesh by a combined Egyptian and Hurrian army. Reliefs from the Saqqara tomb of Horemheb would seem to record this war. In any case, the Egyptians seem to have been defeated. These events evidently occurred just prior to the king's death. Van Dijk suggests that the titles granted to Horemheb, in particular "Eldest Son of Horus," indicate that Tutankhamen had selected Horemheb as his successor. However, Ay, rather than Horemheb, became the next pharaoh. Quite possibly, Horemheb was leading the army in northern Syria at the time of the young king's death; if so, this might explain why Ay took over the throne.

Tutankhamen's tomb was discovered in the Valley of the Kings by British archaeologist Howard Carter in November, 1922. The tomb, numbered KV62, was found to have been entered in antiquity by robbers on two separate occasions; in both cases it was resealed by officials of the royal necropolis. The amount of loot the robbers carried away could not have been substantial, as the tomb was found virtually intact and proved to be a treasure trove.

Nestled within a series of gilt and/or golden shrines and coffins lay the mummy of the king. Tutankhamen was about eighteen or nineteen years old at his death. Although fairly extensive testing has been done on the remains, no cause of death has been determined.

References:

Carter 1923-33
Deroches-Noblecourt 1963
Forbes 2005b pp. 38-50
Grajetzki 2005 p. 64
Ikram and Dodson 1997 p. 38
Ikram and Dodson 1998 p. 325
Murnane 1995 pp. 211-223
Partridge 1994 pp. 128-140, 141-144
D. Redford 1984 pp. 204-217
Reeves 1990a
Reeves 1990b pp. 61-69
Tyldesley 2006 pp. 137-139
van Dijk 1996 pp. 29-42
Verbrugghe and Wickersham 1996 pp. 142, 199
von Beckerath 1999 pp. 144 #12, 145 #12
Waddell 1940 p. 113
Welsh 1993

Tutimaios   Fictitious

A Manetho listing is found in Josephus that has been interpreted as being one King Tutimaios. However, there is general agreement among Egyptologists that this is a mistranslation and that no such king ever existed.

References:

Bülow-Jacobsen 1997 pp. 327-329

Unas — Dynasty V

Horus Name: wȝḏ-tȝwy

Nomen: wnis / Unas

Prenomen: wnis / Unas

Two Ladies: nbty wȝḏ-m

Golden Falcon: bik-nbw wȝḏ

Length of Reign:	30-33 years
Tomb:	Pyramid at Saqqara: "Perfect are the Places of Unas"
Mummy:	Cairo: TR2.12.25.1
Consorts:	Nebet I / Khenut I
Manetho:	Onnos (A) / Onnus (A)
King Lists:	Ab: (33); S: (32); T: (G 3.25)
Variant Names:	Unis / Wenis

The ninth and final king of Dynasty V, Unas might have been the son of his predecessor, Djedkare, although there is no direct evidence to confirm this theory. Indeed, aside from his pyramid and its complex, we know very little about Unas' reign.

An alabaster vase, inscribed with the king's name, was found at Byblos, on the Lebanese coast. A relief from the causeway of his pyramid complex shows Egyptian troops battling an "Asiatic" enemy; on another block Asiatic prisoners are shown being brought to Egypt in ships. However, it should be borne in mind that the latter relief is an exact duplicate of a scene from the temple complex of Sahure at Abusir and may not represent an actual occurrence. Similarly, a representation of Unas bashing in the head of a Libyan might very well be spurious, such a scene having become a convention of pharaonic iconography long before.

A large carving at Elephantine may represent a visit by Unas to the southern border of his kingdom, perhaps to receive homage from Nubian chieftains, as did one of his successors, Merenre of Dynasty VI. At any rate, reliefs from Unas' causeway show ships loaded with columns and blocks of Aswan granite.

Unas chose to have his pyramid built near the southwest corner of Djoser's step pyramid at Saqqara. Measuring some 57.75 m. to the side and reaching a height of 43 m., it is the smallest of all of the Old Kingdom pharaohs' pyramids. Despite the size, Unas' monument is one of the most important pyramids, for it is the first one to be inscribed with the series of spells, prayers, incantations, etc., that have come to be known as the "Pyramid Texts." Walls of the burial and antechamber as well as part of the corridor were incised with row upon row of these texts. In the burial chamber itself, the ceiling was painted a dark blue with golden stars.

A 750 m. long causeway runs between Unas' valley and mortuary temples. The inner walls of the causeway were decorated with painted reliefs that included such varied scenes as ships loaded with granite columns and blocks sailing down the Nile from Aswan toward Saqqara, battle scenes, ships carrying prisoners from the Levant, scenes of starving desert-dwellers, laborers of various professions, gathering of honey, wild animals and much more. To the south of the causeway were discovered two boat pits, each 45 m. long.

Instead of pyramids, Unas' two consorts, Khenut and Nebet, were buried in a fine double mastaba to the northeast of his mortuary temple.

When opened in 1881, the burial chamber of Unas' pyramid was found to contain not only a beautifully preserved black basalt sarcophagus, but also fragments of the king's mummy. The remains consisted of a left arm and hand and several pieces of the royal skull, some of the latter still retaining skin and hair.

The Turin Canon gives Unas a reign of 30 years, which fits well with the 33 given by Manetho. Scenes of a Sed Festival have survived in the king's mortuary temple, which implies he likely saw his thirtieth regnal year.

References:
Altenmüller 2001 pp. 600-601
Dodson 1994b pp. 12, 13 note 46, 109 #3
Dodson 2003 pp. 23, 25, 37, 38, 72-73, 125
Dodson and Hilton 2004 pp. 62, 64-65, 67-70, 77, 78
Gardiner 1959 pl. II, Col. III #25
Gardiner 1961 p. 435
Hassan 1955 pp. 136-139

Userkaf

Ikram and Dodson 1998 pp. 82, 113, 249, 315, 317, 321
Jidejian 1968 p. 17
Lehner 1997 pp. 20, 31, 32, 33, 38, 62, 82, 83, 149, 202
Malek 2000 pp. 250-251, 256
Petrie 1924 vol. I p. 93 fig. 62.
Verbrugghe and Wickersham 1996 pp. 112, 192
Verner 1997 pp. 141, 273-274, 332-340, 464
Verner 2002 pp. 37
von Beckerath 1999 pp. 60 #9, 61 #9
Waddell 1940 p. 51
R. Wilkinson 2000 p. 128

Userkaf   Dynasty V

Horus Name:

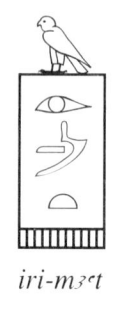

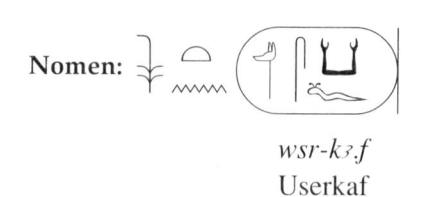

iri-m3't

Nomen:

wsr-k3.f
Userkaf

wsr-k3.f
Userkaf

Two Ladies:

nbty iri-m3't

Golden Falcon:

(bik) nbw ntr-nfr

Length of Reign:	T: "7 years"
Tomb:	Pyramid at Saqqara: "Pure are the Places of Userkaf"
Mummy:	Unknown

Consorts:	Khentkaues I(?)	**Variant Names:**	Weserkaf Woserkaf
Manetho:	Ouserkheres (A) Usercheres (A)		
King Lists:	Ab: (26); P; S: (25); T: (G 3.17)		

The first pharaoh of Dynasty V, Userkaf may have been a son of the Dynasty IV king Menkaure or perhaps the brother of that ruler's son, Shepseskaf, Userkaf's immediate predecessor. It has also been suggested that he was the grandson of Dynasty IV's Djedefre by way of that king's daughter, Neferhetepes, and an unknown, possibly non-royal, father. To further complicate the issue, some scholars believe Neferhetepes to be the consort, rather than the mother, of Userkaf.

Userkaf returned to Saqqara for the building of his pyramid, forsaking the Giza Plateau and its environs, which the Dynasty IV kings had favored. It has been suggested that this was a political move: possibly on shaky ground succession-wise, Userkaf perhaps wanted to be associated with the great Dynasty III pharaoh Djoser. After all, Userkaf went so far as to return to using what Lehner describes as "'Djoser-type' elements," i.e., the north-south orientation of a rectangular funerary enclosure and its internal structures.

Userkaf's pyramid is now known as "El Haram el-Mekharbesh" (the Scratched Pyramid). It originally measured 73.3 m. square, rose to a height of 49 m. and was encased in white limestone. It was so poorly constructed internally that when the casing fell away and/or was pilfered, a large part of the structure collapsed; it is now a great pile of blocks and rubble. The same fate came to the mortuary temple, and the injury there was compounded by three Late Period (Dynasty XXVI) tombs that had been cut into the floor. Excavations in the temple courtyard yielded the remains of a granite statue that originally stood 5 m. tall, the oldest known colossal statue of a pharaoh, discounting the Sphinx at Giza. The temple also revealed fragments of beautifully executed raised relief.

In addition to a small satellite pyramid built inside the wall of the funerary complex, Userkaf also ordered constructed a third pyramid that has, very tentatively, been ascribed to Queen Neferhetepes; as mentioned above, she is either this pharaoh's mother or wife.

The worship of the sun god Re, first gaining ascendance during Dynasty IV, continued unabated during Dynasty V, as evidenced by the building of a "sun temple" by Userkaf, the first royal structure to be built at Abu Gurob, some 3 km. north of Saqqara. Called Nekhen-Re (Stronghold of Re), the valley temple was connected by a causeway to an upper cultic site that held an immense, blunted obelisk. The upper temple area may not have been finished during Userkaf's reign. In any case, the structure was completed or added to by two of the pharaoh's successors, Neferirkare (I) and Niuserre. Recent work at the site by a Czech archaeological team has shown that the obelisk was not initially part of the temple, but was added by Userkaf's son, the future pharaoh Neferirkare (I).

The Turin Canon gives Userkaf a reign of seven years. The Palermo Stone and its Cairo fragments record some of the events for years five through seven of the reign; they include endowments to various deities including Re, Horus, Wadjet and Nekhbet, the building of a shrine for the goddess Hathor at the king's pyramid complex, and inventories and cattle counts. The entry for regnal year three mentions 70 "women of foreign countries" (or hill-country?) and 303 prisoners(?) who were also given to the king's mortuary cult, probably as servants.

Userkaf is mentioned in a tomb of Nykaankh, a priest of Hathor at Tehna, in Middle Egypt. Excavations at Tod, near Luxor have shown the king to have been responsible for additions to the temple of the god Montju. He may have ordered a campaign into Nubia.

A marble cup bearing the name of Userkaf's mortuary temple was discovered on the Aegean island of Kythera, just off the shore of the Peloponesian Peninsula, which may or may bear witness to Dynasty V's trade with that region.

Manetho gives Userkaf a reign of 28 years, but the highest date known comes from a mason's graffito in the king's sun temple and is for the "Year of the 3rd. occurrence, 3rd. Month of prt...," which would be in the regnal year seven and thus in accordance with the Turin Canon.

References:

Altenmüller 2001 p. 598
Clagett 1989 pp. 87-89
Dodson 2003 pp. 65-66, 124
Dodson and Hilton 2004 pp. 62, 63, 64-65
Fakhry 1961b pp. 167-171
Gardiner 1959 pl. II, Col. III #17
Gardiner 1961 p. 84, 85, 435
Lehner 1997 pp. 140-141, 149, 150-151
Ricke 1965
Ricke 1969
W. Smith 1971 pp. 180-182
Spalinger 1994 pp. 294-296
Stadelmann 2000 pp. 530-542
Verbrugghe and Wickersham 1996 pp. 135, 191
Verner 1997 pp. 111, 141, 265-267, 274-280, 463
Verner 2000a pp. 561-562, 563
Verner 2001b p. 588
Verner 2002 pp. 71-77
von Beckerath 1999 pp. 56 #1, 57 #1
Waddell 1940 p. 51
R. Wilkinson 2000 pp. 121, 126
T. Wilkinson 2000 pp. 152-159, 217-219

Userkare   Dynasty VI

Horus Name: Unknown   **Nomen:**

wsr-k3-rˁ
Userkare

Prenomen: Unknown

Two Ladies: Unknown

Golden Falcon: Unknown

Length of Reign:	1 to 5 years		
Tomb:	Unknown		
Mummy:	Unknown		
Consorts:	Unknown	**Variant Names:**	Woser-ku-re
Manetho:	Not given		
King Lists:	Ab: (35); SSA		

The second king of the Dynasty VI, Userkare is an ephemeral ruler who may or may not have been related to his predecessor, Teti. It has been suggested that Userkare might have been Teti's son by Queen Khuit II, but there is no actual evidence to support this proposition. It is also possible that Userkare was a descendant of the pharaoh Unas, last king of Dynasty V. Whatever his familial position, it is possible that Userkare was a usurper, although it is unknown whether he was involved in the possible assassination of king Teti that Manetho mentions (see TETI). Another school of thought sees Userkare as an older brother of Pepi I who held the throne, perhaps as a regent, until Pepi was old enough to rule in his own right.

Userkare is listed in the Abydos King List of Sety I and may have been listed in the Turin Canon, where he would seem to represent the ruler whose name, now lost, occupied a space between kings Teti and Pepi I. Userkare is also given the same position on the Dynasty VI annals from Saqqara. Physical attestations of this king amount to nothing more than two cylinder seals and an inscribed knife blade made of copper.

The Dynasty VI king Userkare has been confused with the Dynasty XIII ruler, Khendjer, whose prenomen was Userkare.

References:

Altenmüller 2001 vol. 2 p. 602
Kanawati 1984 pp. 34, 35
Kanawati 1990 pp. 60-63
Ryholt 2000 p. 91
Spalinger 1994 pp. 305-306, 309

Verbrugghe and Wickersham 1996 pp. 192
Verner 1997 pp. 340, 349, 352, 355, 370
von Beckerath 1999 pp. 62 #2, 63 #2

Wadjin   Predynastic

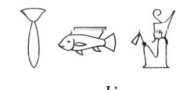

w3djn
Wadjin

Wadjkare

Length of Reign:	Unknown
Tomb:	Unknown
Mummy:	Unknown

Consorts:	Unknown	**Variant Names:**	Uatch-Nar Wadjenedj Wazenez
Manetho:	Not given		
King Lists:	P		

Wadjin is one of a group of nine kings known only from the Palermo Stone. Each name is followed by a representation of a squatting king wearing the crown of Lower Egypt. Whether these names are to be taken as historic personages or mythic "ancestors" is not known.

References:
Clagett 1989 pp. 66, 97-98
Edwards 1971 pp. 3-4
Gardiner 1961 pl. III
O'Mara 1979 p. 5
T. Wilkinson 2000 pp. 62, 85-86, 87

Wadjkare   Dynasty VII/VIII

Horus Name: Unknown

Nomen: Unknown

Prenomen:

w₃ḏ-k₃-rʿ
Wadjkare

Two Ladies: Unknown

Golden Falcon: Unknown

Length of Reign:	Unknown
Tomb:	Unknown
Mummy:	Unknown

Consorts:	Unknown	**Variant Names:**	Uadjkare
Manetho:	Not given		
King Lists:	Not given		

This prenomen is known only from a decree issued by the king Horus Demedjibtowy to the temple of Min at Coptos. It is fairly certain that Demedjibtowy was, in fact, the Horus name of the seventeenth ruler of Dynasty VII/VIII, Neferirkare (II). However, von Beckerath believes that Wadjkare was a different king altogether and lists him as "unplaced" in Dynasty VII/VIII. Hayes sees Wadjkare as being a scribal error for Neferkare and equates him with Neferkaure, the fifteenth pharaoh of this dynasty. Hayes also makes the point that the prenomen in the inscription does not belong to Demedjibtowy but to the king "in whose reign the official charged with the delivery of the decree was born…," i.e., Neferkaure.

References:
Gardiner 1961 p. 437
Hayes 1946 pp. 20, 21, 23
Sethe 1933 pp. 304-308
von Beckerath 1999 pp. 70 #b, 71 #b

Wazad   Dynasty XIV

Horus Name: Unknown   **Nomen:** Unknown

Prenomen:

wꜣḏ-d
Wazad

Two Ladies: Unknown

Golden Falcon: Unknown

Length of Reign:	Unknown
Tomb:	Unknown
Mummy:	Unknown

Consorts: Unknown
Manetho: Not given
King Lists: None
Variant Names: Uatched
Uazed
Wadjed
Wasa

Wazad is known only from five scarab-seals, all of unknown provenance. His position within Dynasty XIV is uncertain; scarab seriation places him after Nehsy. He is probably represented in the Turin Canon by his prenomen, the name Wazad having been lost due to the deterioration of the papyrus. Ryholt suggests the

489

...webenre (a)

possibility that he may be identified with either Sehebre or Merdjefare. None of Wazad's scarab-seals gives a prenomen. As with all kings of Dynasty XIV, Wazad's rule would have been confined to the eastern Delta.

It should be noted that in the past many Egyptologists have placed Wazad in Dynasty XVI, which until recently was considered to be made up of a series of Hyksos vassals, or "little Hyksos," as they were sometimes called.

References:
Newberry 1906 p. 152 #'s 7-9, pl. XXIII #'s 7-9
Ryholt 1997a pp. 52 table 13, 96-97, 99 table 20, 102, 323-325, 381 File 14/d
von Beckerath 1999 pp. 120 #y, 121 #y

...webenre (a)   Dynasty XIV

Horus Name: Unknown   **Nomen:** Unknown

Prenomen:

...wbn-rˁ
...webenre

Two Ladies: Unknown

Golden Falcon: Unknown

Length of Reign:	Unknown
Tomb:	Unknown
Mummy:	Unknown

Consorts:	Unknown	**Variant Names:**	...ubenre ...[we]ben[re]
Manetho:	Not given		
King Lists:	T: (G 8.11; R 9.11; vB 8.11)		

Possibly the sixteenth king of Dynasty XIV, ...webenre is one of a group of kings known only from the Turin Canon. The papyrus' fragile state allows for varying interpretations as to the positioning of some of the kings of this dynasty. However, ...webenre's place seems secure.

References:

Gardiner 1959 pl. III, Col. VIII #11
Gardiner 1961 p. 441 #8.11
Ryholt 1997a pp. 95 Col. 9.11, 98 #16, 198 table 37 and note 9/11, 379
File 14/16, 409 table 95 #16
von Beckerath 1999 pp. 108 #12, 109 #12

...webenre (b)   Late SIP

Horus Name: Unknown

Nomen: Unknown

Prenomen:

...[wb]n-rʿ
...webenre

Two Ladies: Unknown

Golden Falcon: Unknown

Length of Reign:	3-4 years
Tomb:	Unknown
Mummy:	Unknown

Consorts:	Unknown	**Variant Names:**	[...]-uben-[re]
Manetho:	Not given		
King Lists:	T: (G fr. 163 #5; R 11.30)		

Due to the fragile condition of the Turin Canon, nothing beyond a partial name survives for this king. No other attestations to his reign are known. Ryholt gives this king as [...]hebre, but what signs are visible do not warrant that reading. Ryholt would also place this ruler in his "Abydos Dynasty," but there is no evidence to support such a dynasty.

References:

Gardiner 1959 pl. IV, Col. XI, Fragment 163 #5
Ryholt 1997a pp. 153, fig. 14 #30, 203, table 43, 392, File Abydos/15

...webenre (c) — Late SIP

Horus Name: Unknown

Nomen: Unknown

Prenomen: ...*wbn-rˁ* / ...webenre

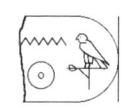

Two Ladies: Unknown

Golden Falcon: Unknown

Length of Reign:	3-4 years
Tomb:	Unknown
Mummy:	Unknown

Consorts:	Unknown	**Variant Names:**	[...]-uben-[re]
Manetho:	Not given		
King Lists:	T: (G frag. 163 #6; R 11.31)		

Due to the fragile and worn condition of the Turin Canon, nothing beyond a partial name survives for this king. No other attestations to his reign are known. Ryholt suggests that ...webenre belonged to what he calls the "Abydos Dynasty," but there is no evidence to support such a dynasty.

References:

Gardiner 1959 pl. IV, Col. XI, Fragment 163 #6

Ryholt 1997a pp. 153, fig. 14 #31, 203, table 43, 392, File Abydos/16

Webenre — Dynasty XIV

Horus Name: Unknown

Nomen: Unknown

Prenomen:

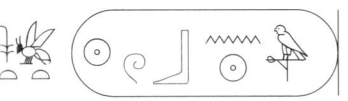

wbn-rʿ
Webenre

Two Ladies: Unknown

Golden Falcon: Unknown

Length of Reign:	Unknown
Tomb:	Unknown
Mummy:	Unknown

Consorts:	Unknown	**Variant Names:**	Ubenre
Manetho:	Not given		
King Lists:	T: (G 8.8; R 9.8; vB 8.8)		

Perhaps the thirteenth king of Dynasty XIV, Webenre is one of a group of kings known only from the Turin Canon. The papyrus' fragile state allows for varying interpretations as to the positioning of some of the kings of this dynasty. However, Webenre's place seems secure.

References:

Gardiner 1959 pl. III, Col. III #8
Gardiner 1961 p. 441 #8.8
Ryholt 1997a pp. 95 Col. 9 #8, 98 #, 198 table 37, 198 table 37, 379 File 14/13, 409 #13

von Beckerath 1999 pp. 108 #9, 109 #9

Wegaf   Dynasty XIII

Horus Name: *sḫm-nṯrw*

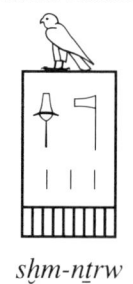

Nomen: *wgȝ.f*
Wegaf

Prenomen: *ḫw-tȝwy-rʿ*
Khutowyre

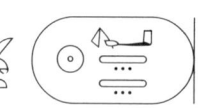

Two Ladies: *nbty ḥʿ-bȝw*

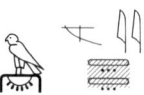

Golden Falcon: *bik-nbw mry-[tȝwy]*

Length of Reign:	T: "2 years, 3 months, 24 days"
Tomb:	Unknown
Mummy:	Unknown

Consorts:	Unknown	**Variant Names:**	Ougaf Ugaf
Manetho:	Not given		
King Lists:	K: (56); T: (G 6.19[?]; R 7.5)		

Wegaf is the twentieth pharaoh of Dynasty XIII, although von Beckerath, following an earlier interpretation of the Turin Canon, lists him as the first ruler of this dynasty. (A scribal error confused Wegaf's prenomen, Khutowyre, with Sobekhotep I's prenomen, Sekhemrekhutowy, resulting in Wegaf's position in the dynasty being exchanged with that of Sobekhotep I.)

Wegaf would seem to have no familial connection with his predecessor, Amenemhet VII, and, like him, was almost certainly a usurper to the throne. Wegaf may have been a senior commander in the army prior to seizing the kingship.

Attestations for Wegaf are few, and none has been found north of Abydos, where a stele dedicated to the Abydene deity Wepwawat was usurped by Neferhotep I. A regnal year four given on the stele may belong to Wegaf, as suggested by Leahy; if so, it would contradict the two-plus years given by the Turin Canon. A statue and a stele from Karnak have survived; Wegaf's name is carved into a banque-stand at Medamud, near Thebes; a stele from Mirgissa and a statuette from Semna are also known and would seem to indicate that Egypt still controlled Nubia at least as far as the Second Cataract. Known, too, are an ostracon from Elephantine and a scarab-seal of unknown provenance.

References:

W. Davies 1981b p. 22 #s 1 and 2
Franke 1988 pp. 249 and note 5
Gardiner 1959 pl. III, Col. VI #19 [?]
Gardiner 1961 p. 440 #6.19 [?]
Helck 1983 pp. 1 #s 1 and 2, 2 #3
Legrain 1905 pp. 130, 133
Legrain 1907 pp. 248-252
Leahy 1989 pp. 46, 47-49
Martin 1971 no. 439

Ryholt 1997a pp. 13, 71 fig. 10 Col. 7 #5, 73 table 17 #20, 192 table 33, 195, 219-220 and note 759, 284 table 83, 315-317, 341 File 13/21, 408 table 94 #
Vercoutter 1975 pp. 222, 227-228 and fig., pl. 22a and b
von Beckerath 1999 pp. 88 #1, 89 #1

Weneg   Dynasty II

Horus Name:
Unknown   **Nomen:**

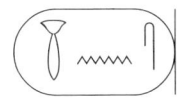

w3ḏ-ns
Wadjnes

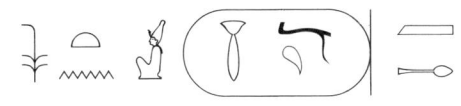

w3ḏ-ns
Wadjnes

Nomen and Two Ladies:

wng
Weneg

Golden Falcon: Unknown

Wepwawetemsaf

Length of Reign:	Unknown
Tomb:	Unknown
Mummy:	Unknown

Consorts:	Unknown	**Variant Names:**	Uneg Wenig
Manetho:	Tlas (A)		
King Lists:	Ab: (12); S: (60); T: (G 2.23 lost)		

Outside of the Saqqara and Abydos King Lists (where he is referred to as Wadjnes), Weneg is known only from a dozen stone bowls discovered at Djoser's Step Pyramid complex at Saqqara and two inscriptions found in Mastaba S3014 at North Saqqara. To date, these inscriptions are the sole attestations for this ruler; no other trace of him has been found. However, later generations certainly considered him as a legitimate king, as is evidenced by his inclusion on king lists. According to these later king lists, Weneg (as Wadjnes) was the immediate successor to King Ninetjer. In any case, Weneg was without a doubt an ephemeral ruler whose reign was very short. His tomb has not yet been discovered, if there ever was one. It may lie beneath a section of the Step Pyramid complex, or it may lie beneath an area of Saqqara, south of the Step Pyramid, that was leveled to accommodate the pyramid and causeway of the Dynasty V king Unas.

References:

Edwards 1971 p. 31
Gardiner 1959 p. 15 note II.23, pl. I Col. II #23
Gardiner 1961 pp. 415, 431, 432
Grdseloff 1944 pp. 288-292
Lacau and Lauer 1959 pp. 6, 16-17, 50-53, pl. V #6, 19 #105 and 20 #101-107
Lauer 1936-39 p. 20, 16-17, 74, pl. XIX #s 3 and 4
Verbrugghe and Wickersham 1996 pp. 133: 188
von Beckerath 1999 pp. 42 #4, 43 #4
Waddell 1940 p. 37
T. Wilkinson 1999 pp. 87-88
T. Wilkinson 2000 pp. 59, 73, 74, 135

Wepwawetemsaf Dynasty XIII/?

Horus Name: Unknown **Nomen:**

wp-w3wt-m-s3.f
Wepwawetemsaf

Wepwawetemsaf

Prenomen: (cartouche)

sḫm-rʿ nfr-ḥʿw
Sekhemre-neferkhau

Two Ladies: Unknown

Golden Falcon: Unknown

Length of Reign:	Unknown
Tomb:	Unknown
Mummy:	Unknown

Consorts:	Unknown	Oupouaout
Manetho:	Not given	Upwautemsaf
King Lists:	None	Wepwawemsaf
Variant Names:	Apuatemsaf	

This king is known from a single, poorly made stele, discovered at Abydos and now in the British Museum (EA969). Because the stele was found at Abydos, and this king's nomen honors the Abydene deity Wepwawet, Ryholt sees this ruler as having belonged to what he calls the "Abydos Dynasty." Von Beckerath would place this king at the end of Dynasty XIII.

A hieratic graffito in a tomb (no. 2) at Beni Hasan in central Egypt, (glyphs), has been posited as giving Wepwawetemsaf's prenomen, Sekhemreneferkhau, but the reading is far from sure.

References:

Bourriau 1988 pp. 72, 73 fig. 58
Budge 1913 p. 9 pl. 25
W. Davies 1982 p. 72 fig. 1
Ryholt 1997a pp. 163 and note 593,
    165 table 27, 392 File Abyd/a
von Beckerath 1964 p. 69
von Beckerath 1999 pp. 104 #1, 105 #1

Woserkhau SIP

Horus Name: Unknown
Nomen: Unknown
Prenomen: Unknown

Two Ladies:

nbty wsr-ḫꜥ(w)
Woserkhau

Golden Falcon: Unknown

Length of Reign:	Unknown
Tomb:	Unknown
Mummy:	Unknown

Consorts:	Unknown	**Variant Names:**	None
Manetho:	Not given		
King Lists:	None		

This Two Ladies (*nbty*) name was found on a stone block at the site of an unfinished pyramid at South Saqqara. The pyramid is dated by its architectural features to the middle of Dynasty XIII. It is often described as being built for an anonymous ruler, but this inference is belied to a certain extent by Jéquier's discovery of the above mentioned inscribed block. An interesting feature of the pyramid is that it contains two burial chambers. It would appear that neither chamber was ever occupied, as the lid of the sarcophagus found in the main chamber was never lowered and the portcullis had never been closed.

References:
Dodson 1987 p. 41
Jéquier 1933b p. 55-67, 63 fig. 47
Lehner 1997 p. 187

Ryholt 1997a pp. 80-81 especially note 245, 404 File D/1

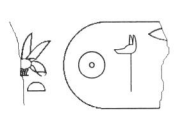

Woser...re (I) — Late SIP

Horus Name: Unknown

Nomen: Unknown

Prenomen: *wsr...-rꜥ*
Woser...re

Two Ladies: Unknown

Golden Falcon: Unknown

Length of Reign:	Unknown
Tomb:	Unknown
Mummy:	Unknown

Consorts:	Unknown	**Variant Names:**	User...re
Manetho:	Not given		
King Lists:	T: (G 11.16; R 11.16)		

Due to the fragile condition of the Turin Canon, nothing beyond a partial name survives for this king. No attestations have been found. Ryholt suggests that Woser...re belonged to what Ryholt calls the "Abydos Dynasty," but there is little evidence to support such a dynasty.

References:

Gardiner 1959 pl. IV, Col. XI #16
Gardiner 1961 p. 442

Ryholt 1997a p. 153, fig. 14 #16, 165, table 26, 392 File Abyd/1

Woser...re (II) — Late SIP

Horus Name: Unknown

Nomen: Unknown

Prenomen: *wsr...-rꜥ*
Woser...re

Two Ladies: Unknown

Golden Falcon: Unknown

Ya-k-'-r-b(?)

Length of Reign:	Unknown
Tomb:	Unknown
Mummy:	Unknown

Consorts:	Unknown	**Variant Names:**	User…re
Manetho:	Not given		
King Lists:	T: (G 11.17; R 11.17)		

Due to the fragile condition of the Turin Canon, nothing beyond a partial name survives for this king. No attestations have been found. Ryholt suggests that Woser…re belonged to what Ryholt calls the "Abydos Dynasty," but there is little evidence to support such a dynasty.

References:
Gardiner 1959 pl. IV, Col. XI #17
Gardiner 1961 p. 442
Ryholt 1997a p. 153, fig. 14 #17, 165, table 26, 392 File Abyd/1

Ya-k-'-r-b(?) Dynasty XIV

Horus Name: Unknown

Nomen: *ya-k-ʿ-r-b (?)*
ya-k-'-r-b (?)

Prenomen: Unknown

Two Ladies: Unknown

Golden Falcon: Unknown

Length of Reign:	Unknown
Tomb:	Unknown
Mummy:	Unknown

Consorts:	Unknown	**Variant Names:**	Jakba'al(?) Yekeb-Bor Ykb-l
Manetho:	Not given		
King Lists:	None		

Ya-k-'-r-b is known from only two scarab-seals, both of unknown provenance. His position in Dynasty XIV is unknown. It is possible that his prenomen is given in the Turin Canon, the nomen being lost due to the Canon's poor preservation. As with all kings of Dynasty XIV, Ya-k-'-r-b's rule would have been confined to the eastern Delta.

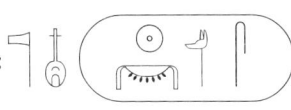

References:
Newberry 1906 pl. XXII #8
Petrie 1978 pl. XXII H1, p. xxii 16. H. 1
Ryholt 1997a pp. 52 table 13, 99 table 20, 102 note 340, 323-325, 383 File 14/g
Tufnell 1984 p. 384 #3493, 385 pl. LXIII #3493

Ya'ammu — Dynasty XIV

Horus Name: Unknown

Nomen: *ya-'-mw*
Ya'ammu

Prenomen: *nbw-wsr-r'*
Nubwoserre

Two Ladies: Unknown

Golden Falcon: Unknown

Length of Reign:	Unknown
Tomb:	Unknown
Mummy:	Unknown

Consorts:	Unknown	**Variant Names:**	Ja'mmu Ya'mu Yamu'
Manetho:	Not given		
King Lists:	None		

Perhaps the second king of Dynasty XIV, Ya'ammu is known from 26 scarab-seals, only one of whose provenance (Pella in Canaan) is known. Although nothing else is known about this ruler, it seems likely that his reign was relatively long. As with all kings of this dynasty, Ya'ammu's sphere of control did not exceed the eastern Delta. Von Beckerath places Ya'mmu (as Ja'mu) in his XV./XVI. Dynasties.

Yakbim

References:

Newberry 1906 p. 151 #s 4-6, pl. XXII #s 4-6

Ryholt 1997a pp. 41, 44 table 11, 47 fig. 6/a, 49, 101 and note 328, 199 table 38, 299, 323-325 and note 1115, 363 File 14/2, p. 409 table 95 #2

Tufnell 1984 p. 384 #s 3487-3492, pl. LXIII 3s 3487-3492

von Beckerath 1999 pp. 118 #h, 119 #h

Yakbim   Dynasty XIV

Horus Name: Unknown

Nomen:

ya-k-b-mw
Yakbim

Prenomen:

s.ḫꜥ-n-rꜥ
Sekhaenre

Two Ladies: Unknown

Golden Falcon: Unknown

Length of Reign:	Unknown
Tomb:	Unknown
Mummy:	Unknown

Consorts:	Unknown	**Variant Names:**	Jakebmu Yakbemu
Manetho:	Not given		
King Lists:	None		

Perhaps the first king of Dynasty XIV, Yakbim was undoubtedly of Canaanite origin, but whether he actually came to Egypt as an invader or was one of the thousands of Asiatics to have lived in the Delta area for many generations is unknown. He is not found in the Turin Canon but is represented by some 126 scarab-seals. Seven of these seals come from Canaan (e.g., Tell el-Fara and Tell el-Ajjul), four from Egypt (as far south as Abydos) and three from Nubia (Aniba, Buhen and Kerma); the rest are of unknown provenance.

Like all of his successors of Dynasty XIV, Yakbim's sphere of influence was the eastern Delta. Von Beckerath places Yakbim (as Jakebmu) in his XV./XVI. Dynasties.

References:

Clayton 1994 p. 94
Ryholt 1997a pp. 40-41, 44 and table 11 and note 119, 47 fig. 6a, 49, 100 and note 326, 112 and note 372, 199 table 38, 251, 299, 323-325, 359-363 File 14/1, 409 table 95 #1

Tufnell 1984 p. 378 #s 3380-3392, pl. LX #s 3380-3392
von Beckerath 1999 pp. 118 #i, 119 #i

Ya'qub-Har   Dynasty XIV

Horus Name: Unknown

Nomen: ya-ʿ-ḳ-b-h-r
Ya'qub-Har

Prenomen: mr-wsr-rʿ
Merwoserre

Two Ladies: Unknown

Golden Falcon: Unknown

Length of Reign:	Unknown
Tomb:	Unknown
Mummy:	Unknown

Consorts:	Unknown	Jakoblier
Manetho:	Not given	Ja'qobher
King Lists:	None	Yakubher
Variant Names:	Iquebher	

Although his position is uncertain, it would appear that Ya'qub-Har's reign came near the end of Dynasty XIV. His nomen and prenomen, Merwosserre, are found on various scarab-seals and the latter is very likely to be the ...woser found on a misplaced fragment in the Turin Canon.

Ya'qub-Har is represented by 27 scarab-seals. Three of these are from Canaan (Pella, Shikmona and one of unknown origin, but bought in Jerusalem and therefore probably from Canaan), four from Egypt (two from Tell el-Yahudiya, one from Hu and one probably from Saqqara) and one from Kerma in Nubia; the remaining 19 are of unknown provenance. The distribution of the scarabs of known provenance make it safe to assume that trade relations with Canaan and Nubia still continued in the latter portion of Dynasty XIV.

Prior to the discovery of the Shikmona scarab-seal, it was customary to place Ya'qub-Har among the Hyksos rulers of Dynasty XV. However, the archaeological context of the Shikmona find places this king as contemporary with the mid-to-latter part of Dynasty XIII—exactly where a king of the contemporaneous Dynasty XIV should be.

References:

Hein 1994 p. 143 Catalogue # 106
Kempiinski 1985 pp. 132-134
Newberry 1906 p. 151 #29, pl. XXII 329
Ryholt 1997a pp. 26 and note 65, 41, 42-43, 44 table 11 and note 119, 45, 49 and notes 133-135, 99 table 20,
102 and note 324, 254, 256, 382-383 File 14/f
Tufnell 1984 pl. LVII #3230
von Beckerath 1999 pp. 116 #g, 117 #g
Yeivin 1959 pp. 16-18

Zeser   Dynasty 0

ḏsr
Zeser

Length of Reign:	Unknown
Tomb:	Unknown
Mummy:	Unknown

Consorts:	Unknown	**Variant Names:**	Djoser
Manetho:	Not given		
King Lists:	None		

Zeser is one of the "kings" Petrie proposed to have ruled prior to Dynasty I. As with some other supposed rulers, Zeser's existence is based on a single find, in this case a broken piece of stone fragment inscribed with the "name" Zeser, beneath what Petrie saw as the Two Ladies or Two Lords name of the royal titulary. (The hieroglyph (*ḏsr*) is given here as Zeser to lessen confusion with the Dynasty III king Djoser.)

Although the inscribed stone was discovered in the tomb of the Dynasty I king Den, (Abydos Tomb T), Petrie assigned Tomb B9 to Zeser. (Tomb B9, along with B7, is now considered to be the tomb of the late Dynasty 0 ruler Ka.)

References:

Petrie 1900 pl. IV. 3, pp. 19, 38
Petrie 1901a pp. 4-5, 6, 14, 19, 48

Petrie 1902a p. 6

Appendix: Apocryphal Kings of the Fourteenth Dynasty

The Turin Canon shows a group of cartouches in Gardiner's columns IX and X. Von Beckerath is the only modern authority to consider the possibility that these cartouches actually represent kings of Dynasty XIV. Gardiner shows the names in his transcription of the papyrus, but considers them to be "obviously fantastic" and not representing real kings; he therefore does not include them in his king list. Ryholt has demonstrated that Gardiner's basic premise is correct, and that these names represent a series of gods and demigods. The following names are included in this group:

Name [Variant Spellings]	Cartouche	Transliteration	References
Aped(?) [Sa]		ꜣpd(?)	Gardiner 1959 pl. III, Col. IX #18 von Beckerath 1984 pp. 76 #50, 160 XIV Dynasty #50, 214 #50
Hapu (I) [Hape, Hapi]		ḥpw	Gardiner 1959 pl. III, Col. IX #19 von Beckerath 1984 pp. 76 #51, 160 XIV Dynasty #51, 214 #51. Author gives name as both "Hape" and "Hapi."
Hibe		hꜣb	Gardiner 1959 pl. III, Col. IX #17 von Beckerath 1984 pp. 76 #49, 160 XIV Dynasty #49, 214 #49
Hor… (II)		ḥrw…	Gardiner 1959 pl. III, Col. X #4 von Beckerath 1984 pp. 76 #67, 161 XIV Dynasty #67, 215 #67

APPENDIX

Name [Variant Spellings]	Cartouche	Transliteration	References
Inib[ef] [Enibef(?)]		*n-ib[f]*	Gardiner 1959 pl. III, Col. X #7 von Beckerath 1984 pp. 77 #70, 161 #70, 215 #70
Iwf... [Ef...]		*iwf*	Gardiner 1959 pl. III, Col. X #1 von Beckerath 1984 pp. 76 #64, 161 XIV Dynasty #64, 215 #64
Kherhimwet-shepsut [Cherhimweschepse]		*ḫr-ḥmwt-špswt*	Gardiner 1959 pl. III, Col. X #10 von Beckerath 1984 pp. 77 #73 as "Cherhimweschepse", 161 XIV Dynasty #73, 215 #73
Khuhimwet... [Chuhimwe...]		*ḫw-ḥmwt...*	Gardiner 1959 pl. III, Col. X #11 von Beckerath 1984 pp. 77 #74 as "Chuhimwe", 161 XIV Dynasty #74, 215 #74
Meni...		*mni*	Gardiner 1959 pl. III, Col. IX #21 von Beckerath 1984 pp. 76 #53, 160 XIV Dynasty #53, 214 #53

APPENDIX

Name [Variant Spellings]	Cartouche	Transliteration	References
Peneset-en-sepet		pnst-n-spt	Gardiner 1959 pl. III, Col. 10 #9 von Beckerath 1984 pp. 77 #72, 161 XIV Dynasty #72, 215 #72
Seth (II) [Set (II)]		stḫ	Gardiner 1959 pl. III, Col. X #32 von Beckerath pp. 76 #65, 161 XIV #65, 215 #65
Shemsu [Schamse]		šmsw	Gardiner 1959 pl. III, Col. IX #20 von Beckerath 1984 pp. 76 #52, 160 XIV Dynasty #52, 214 #52
Sunu [Saine]		swnw	Gardiner 1959 pl. III, Col. X #3 von Beckerath 1984 pp. 76 #66, 161 #66, 215 #66
Werka [Werqa]		wr-kꜣ…	Gardiner 1959 pl. III, Col. IX #22 von Beckerath 1984 pp. 76 #54, 161 XIV Dynasty #54, 214 #54

References:
The following references are applicable to all kings listed above:
Gardiner 1961 p. 441
Ryholt 1997a pp. 24-25, including notes 59 and 60

The Royal Titulary

The Royal Titulary, a series of five names or titles for the pharaoh, was developed over a period of several hundred years, and was not really codified until some 1,100 years after the first pharaoh sat on the throne of the two lands.

The pharaoh was considered a god on Earth and an intermediary between the gods and the people of Egypt. The powers he was believed to possess, in his manifestations as various deities, are expressed in the royal appellations listed below.

The Horus Name: From the late Predynastic Period (Naqada III, often referred to as Dynasty 0) until the end of Dynasty III, the Horus name was the king's primary name. It was written within a vertical rectangular frame called a "serekh," which was surmounted by the falcon god, Horus. The serekh (srh), with its recessed paneling at the bottom, probably represented the facade of the royal palace, which was in turn imitated on the facades of the royal mastaba tombs at Abydos, Naqada and Saqqara. The Horus falcon perched atop the serekh represented not only the god's protection of the palace, and therefore Egypt, but also the king in his earthly manifestation of the god.

While the serekh described above is considered the standard type, there were exceptions. It is not uncommon to find variations in the falcon's headgear, or to find the bird crownless, as was common in earlier Horus names. During the Dynasty II reign of King Peribsen, for reasons that are disputed, Horus was displaced by the unknown animal that represented the god Set, while the serekh of King Khasekhemwy was surmounted by both the falcon and the Set animal:

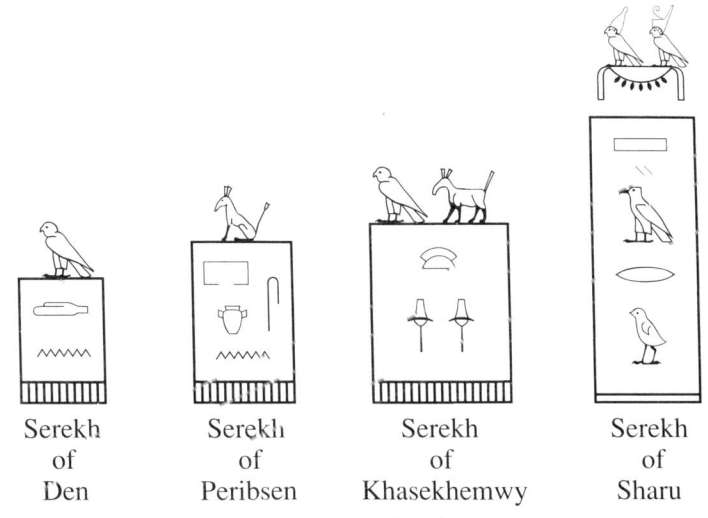

| Serekh of Den | Serekh of Peribsen | Serekh of Khasekhemwy | Serekh of Sharu |

This name was given upon accession to the throne.

The Royal Titulary

The Two Ladies Name: So called because the probable reading of the group is *nbty*, i.e., "the two ladies," this name shows the king as being protected by the goddess (*nḫbt*), or Nekhbet, the Vulture Goddess of Upper Egypt, and (*wȝdt*), or Uadjet, the Cobra Goddess of Lower Egypt. The earliest example of this name, although not connected with the royal titulary, comes from an ivory label dated to king Aha of Dynasty I. By the reign of Semerkhet of Dynasty II, the two ladies name was an established part of the royal titulary. The title was given upon accession to the throne.

The Golden Falcon Name: The significance of this title is much disputed. It may represent the king as Horus, victorious over (*nbt*[*y*]), "the Ombite," that is, the god Set who was worshipped at the city of Ombos. On the other hand, it may represent the king in his incarnation as Horus the Sun God. The hieroglyph shows Horus standing above the hieroglyph for "gold." Gold was considered a divine metal; the flesh of the gods was golden. The king, as the Horus name signifies, is equated with the god and therefore is himself golden.

This name dates at least from the time of the Dynasty I ruler Den. Eventually the title came to be given upon accession to the throne.

The Prenomen: The prenomen is the name that follows the hieroglyphs (*nswt-bity*) for "he who belongs to the sedge and the bee," the plant (*swt*) symbolizing Upper Egypt and the bee (*bit*) representing Lower Egypt. This title is usually translated as "King of Upper and Lower Egypt." The name, written within a cartouche, is almost always compounded with the name of the sun god Re in the earlier dynasties, and always included Re's name from Dynasty XI onward.

The Nomen: The nomen, written in a cartouche, is usually preceded by (*sȝ rꜥ*), "Son of Re." This name is the personal or birth name of the king. The first kings to distinguish between the nomen and prenomen were those of Dynasty V.

Note: "Cartouche" is a French word meaning an ornamental tablet of stone, wood or metal designed to receive an inscription. The Egyptian word for cartouche, (*šnw*), comes from the verb *šni*, to encircle, and probably represents the king as the ruler of all that was encircled by the sun.

Glossary

Abydos King List: Inscribed on the walls of Sety I's temple at Abydos, this list gives the cartouches of 76 kings beginning with Meni and ending with Sety. The list is still in place.

Abydos King List 2: A much-damaged king list from the temple of Ramesses II at Abydos. The list originally gave the cartouches of 78 kings. Now in the British Museum.

Africanus: Sextus Julius Africanus (ca. 220 AD). Christian chronographer. He wrote a history of the world which included passages from Manetho's "History of Egypt."

Amarna Letters: Also known as the Amarna Tablets. A series of 382 clay tablets, inscribed in cuneiform and discovered in the "records office" at El Amarna in the late nineteenth century. The letters, written in Akkadian, the lingua franca of the day, date to the reigns of Amenhotep III, Akhenaten, and Tutankhamen. The letters come from the kings of Hatti, Mitanni, Babylon, Assyria, Alashiya (Cyprus?), Arzawa (in Anatolia), and from the "kings" of various petty city-states in Palestine-Syria. There are also a few copies of letters sent by a pharaoh.

Apis bull: A sacred bull, identified with the god Ptah. A ceremony known as the "Running of the Apis" was an important event which may have been associated with the Sed Festival and, in any case, was a ceremony of renewal during which the bull was seen as a manifestation of the pharaoh as Ptah.

Artapanus: A Jewish historian who lived in Alexandria some time during the middle Ptolemaic Period (ca. 250-100 BC), writer of a history of the Jews. His actual book has not come down to us, but is paraphrased by Eusebius.

Canopic jars: A set of four vessels used to hold the viscera (lungs, stomach, intestines and liver) of a mummy. By the New Kingdom, these jars had evolved from the linen-wrapped organs of the Old Kingdom to animal and human headed containers bearing the likenesses of the four "Sons of Horus." Royal canopic jars often bore the heads of goddesses or queens.

Cartouche: An ovoid representing a length of rope, knotted at one end. The prenomen and nomen of pharaohs, and the names of queens, were enclosed in cartouches.

Cataracts: A series of six rapids found in the Nile between Egypt's border at Aswan and Khartoum in the Sudan. In some

GLOSSARY

	areas the ancient Egyptians cut canals to bypass the rushing and unnavigable waters. During the Middle Kingdom, a series of fortresses were built above and below the Second Cataract.
Coregency:	The practice in which an established ruler takes on a junior partner, usually a son. There is no proof to support the implementation of this practice prior to Dynasty XII.
Demotic:	Used on documents, the demotic script replaced the hieratic script in the seventh century BC. It, too, was a form of cursive writing.
Electrum:	An alloy of silver and gold which occurs naturally in Egypt and Nubia. It was used during all periods of Egyptian civilization, most commonly for making jewelry, although it has been suggested that some pyramid capstones were made of the substance.
Ennead:	A group of nine gods. The group can be of any nine deities, or can be a designated set of nine deities, such as the Great Ennead of Heliopolis, which consists of the creator gods and the most ancient of the gods of Egypt.
Eusebius:	Bishop Eusebius of Caesarea (ca. 260 AD). He wrote an epitome of world history which included passages from Manetho's "History of Egypt." His other writings include a paraphrasing of the "History of the Jews" by Artapanus.
Faience:	A glazed ceramic made from a mixture of sand, lime and natron used from predynastic times onward for the making of jewelry, small vessels, statuettes (including ushabti figures) and the like. The color was almost always turquoise or blue-green, but was sometimes varying shades of brown.
Filiative Nomina:	The practice of adding the name of the royal father and predecessor to a king's name in order to show legitimacy of succession.
Funerary Enclosures:	Large rectangular structures, usually of mud brick construction, which seem to have come into use during Aha's reign, in Dynasty I. The actual purpose of these structures is not known, but probably had to do with the mortuary cults of the kings for whom they were built. These structures were often surrounded with subsidiary burials of servants, especially concubines. They are sometimes referred to as "funerary palaces"; Petrie called them "forts." They were discontinued by the middle of Dynasty III.

GLOSSARY

God's Father: A priestly title dating back to the Old Kingdom. The God's Father was originally responsible for seeing to the chanting of prayers, leading processions and similar duties. In the Middle Kingdom, the title was evidently given to a non-royal father of a king. During the New Kingdom, God's Father may have signified the father-in-law of a king.

Golden Falcon: The meaning of this name has been long debated. One explanation sees the gold in this title as representing the divinity of the pharaoh. Gold never decays; the flesh of the gods is made of gold. The name is seen as a falcon perched atop the hieroglyph for gold. Given upon ascension to the throne.

Heb-sed: See Sed Festival.

Herakleopolitans: A group of "pharaohs" who hailed from the nome and like-named city of *Nn(w)-nswt* (Greek Herakleopolis), located just south of the entrance to the Faiyum in Middle Egypt. Originally nomarchs, they took on the trappings of pharaohs and claimed to be rulers of all Egypt. Just how much of Egypt the Herakleopolitan pharaohs actually controlled at the height of their power is unknown, although to the south they might never have held sway much beyond Abydos. They came to power at the close of Dynasty VII/VIII, which is considered the end of the Old Kingdom, and are classified as belonging to the First Intermediate Period. The Herakleopolitan rulers are for the most part contemporaneous with the rulers of the early half of the Theban Dynasty XI. While the much-damaged Turin Canon originally listed 18 kings for Herakleopolis, only a few of the names survive, and these are much damaged.

Hieratic: A cursive form of the hieroglyph script, for writing on papyrus and ostraca. Used for literature, business documents and similar writings, it was employed from the Early Dynastic Period until demotic replaced it in the seventh century BC.

Horus Name: The earliest of the five titular names of the pharaoh, this name represented the ruler's affiliation with the deity Horus. The name was enclosed in a rectangle, called a "serekh," which represented a palace façade, and was surmounted by a hawk. Given upon ascension to the throne.

Hyksos: A group of foreign rulers who claimed kingship of Egypt during a portion of the Second Intermediate Period (see Chronology of Ancient Egypt). Although the origins of these usurpers are contested, they were most likely from Syria-Palestine. They were a Semitic-speaking people.

Glossary

Josephus: Flavius Josephus (ca. 70 AD). A Jewish historian whose writings are a main source for excerpts from Manetho.

Karnak List: Originally in the temple of Amen-Re at Karnak and now in the Louvre, this list was inscribed for Thutmose III. It originally gave the cartouches of 61 kings from Meni to Thutmose III.

Lacuna: A missing section; a gap.

Manetho: An Egyptian priest from Sebennytos in the Delta. He lived during the time of Hellenistic control of Egypt (ca. 300 BC) and wrote a history of his country in Greek. No intact version of this book has survived and we know of its contents only through mostly garbled extracts from later writers.

Menat: A beaded necklace or collar that was an emblem of the goddess Hathor and symbolized the life force. The necklace was traditionally worn by pharaohs, queens, and the priests and priestesses of Hathor. Menat amulets were thought to bring good luck.

Mnevis bull: The sacred bull at the temple of Re at Heliopolis. Mnevis (Mer-Wer in Egyptian) was believed to be an earthly manifestation of the sun god. Mnevis was considered an intermediary between Re-Atum and the priests at Heliopolis. The Mnevis bull, like the better-known Apis bull, was buried in state.

Naos: The inner part of a temple, the shrine. The dwelling place of a god.

Nomarch: Governor of a nome.

Nome: An ancient Egyptian administrative province ruled over by a nomarch. There were a total of 42 nomes in Upper and Lower Egypt.

Nomen: The personal name of the king, given at birth or shortly thereafter. This name is encircled by a cartouche and is almost always preceded by the hieroglyphs spelling out "Son of Re."

Palermo Stone: Fragments of a basalt stele which dates to Dynasty V. Originally over 2 m. long and 0.6 m. high, the stone was inscribed on both sides with annals of Egyptian rulers from mythological times to the middle of Dynasty V. Named for the location of its principal fragment, there are smaller sections in the Cairo Museum and the Petrie Museum (at University College, London).

Glossary

Prenomen: The name taken by a pharaoh at his ascension to the throne. It is preceded by the hieroglyph symbols of a reed and a bee, representing the title "King of Upper and Lower Egypt." It is encircled in a cartouche.

Protodynastic Period: Same as the Archaic Period.

Punt: A land somewhere on the African side of the Red Sea coast, perhaps part of modern Sudan or Eritrea. Often referred to as "God's Land." Egyptians had begun to send expeditions there as early as the reign of Sahure of Dynasty V. The country was famous for its myrrh and incense as well as exotic animals (and their pelts), rare timbers, gold and electrum. Much of the carved relief in the temple of Hatshepsut at Deir el-Bahri deals with an expedition to Punt.

Pyramid Texts: A series of more than eight hundred spells, incantations, prayers and utterances found inscribed in nine pyramids of the Old Kingdom and First Intermediate Period. No one pyramid had all of the texts inscribed within it. Large parts of the texts deal with the king's celestial journey in the boat of Re and with the cult of Osiris.

Qasr el-Aini Hospital: A hospital in Cairo whose Anatomy Department houses a great many mummies, including many of royal personages.

Royal Cache: A group of mummies, mostly royalty, including about a dozen pharaohs, gathered from various tombs during Dynasty XXI and deposited in a tomb, DB320, in the cliffs not far from Hatshepsut's temple at Deir el-Bahri, where they were discovered in 1881.

Saff-tomb: Named for the Arabic word for "row," the saff-tomb consisted of a wide open court that fronted a row of pillars cut into the rock. The room behind the colonnade was long and narrow; in its rear wall were cut a number of entrances leading into a chapel, burial and storage chambers. In the case of royal tombs, a shaft is sunk that leads to the tomb chamber. Examples of this tomb type come from Thebes, Dendera and Gebelein.

Saqqara List: Now in the Cairo Museum, this list, discovered in the tomb of a royal scribe, originally held the cartouches of 58 kings from Anedjib of Dynasty I to Ramesses II of Dynasty XIX. Today the list shows only 47 names.

Scarab: An amulet made in the shape of the sacred scarab beetle. This form of amulet was extremely popular in Egypt, Syria-Palestine and Nubia. The earliest scarabs date to the late Old Kingdom and carry no inscriptions. During the

GLOSSARY

	Middle Kingdom, these amulets began to be inscribed on the flat underside and were used as seals. Scarabs were also carved or molded (in faience) with good luck symbols or the names of kings. While the use of scarabs bearing royal names is not always an accurate way to date archaeological material found with them, it is often possible to use scarab design for this purpose. In different periods, scarabs underwent design changes which can be traced from reign to reign and/or period to period.
Second Intermediate Period:	1795-1550 BC. The second period of political unrest in ancient Egypt, comprised of Dynasties XIII through XVII.
Sed Festival:	A festival of renewal for the kings of Egypt. The Sed, or Heb-sed, dated back to at least late predynastic times. It was ideally celebrated after 30 years of rule and thereafter, usually in three-year increments. However it might be celebrated at any year of rule at the king's discretion. It has been suggested that the Sed Festival was a replacement for the ritual murder of a king who had lost the ability to rule properly because of age.
Serekh:	See Horus Name
South Saqqara Stone Annals:	The lid of the sarcophagus of the queen Ankhsenpepi, a wife of Pepi II of Dynasty VI. It was discovered by Jéquier in his 1932-33 excavation of Pepi's pyramid complex at Saqqara. Both sides of the lid are inscribed with records of events occurring during the reigns of the Dynasty VI pharaohs Teti, Userkare, Pepi I and Merenre.
Stele:	A tablet, usually rounded at the top, carved or painted with inscriptions usually of a funerary or commemorative type, although other uses are known; for instance, the pharaoh Akhenaten set up a series of stelae to mark the boundaries of the city of Akhetaten.
Subsidiary Burials:	Burials of servants, the majority being women, who were killed in order to accompany a king into the afterlife. This custom was prevalent in Dynasty I and in several cases in Dynasty II, but did not survive these two dynasties.
Titulary:	The various forms of titles given to a pharaoh at birth and/or coronation. See Horus Name, Golden Falcon, Nomen, Prenomen, Two Ladies and Two Lords.
Turin Canon:	A papyrus dating from the time of Ramesses II and inscribed in hieratic with a list of the names of about three hunddred kings. This list, when complete, gave not only

the names in chronological order but also an account of the years, months and days each ruler reigned. It is in a much-damaged state and subject to a great amount of controversy. The standard reconstruction of the papyrus has been that of Sir Alan Gardiner (see Gardiner 1959). A new study of the papyrus by K.S.B. Ryholt has resulted in major changes in the placement of papyrus fragments, primarily in the renumbering of columns and reconstruction of some of the kings' names based on the matching of the fragments' fibers (see Ryholt 1997, pp. 9-33). We follow Ryholt's example by using Roman numerals for the columns of the Gardiner reconstruction and Arabic numerals for the columns of the Ryholt reconstruction.

Two Ladies: Taken upon ascension, this name is preceded by the vulture and cobra goddesses who signified that the king was protected by Upper and Lower Egypt. Also known as the "Nebty" name.

Two Lords: This title referred to the king as the embodiment of the gods Horus and Set. Not a part of the conventional titulary. Also known as the "Nebwy" name.

Ushabti: A small mummiform statuette frequently found in burials. The ushabti figure, often called a "servant figure," was intended to perform any physical labor in the afterlife, thus relieving the tomb owner of that responsibility. Figures may be made of clay, wood or stone, but most frequently are faience. Ushabti figures appear to have originated early in the Middle Kingdom. Variant spellings include "shawabti."

Wadi: A valley created by a river or flood; a dry river bed.

Wadi Hammamat: A Wadi that begins on the east side of the Nile, at Qift (ancient Coptos) in Upper Egypt, and leads to the Red Sea. Stone quarries and gold mines made this area very important. Certain parts of the Wadi are inscribed with graffiti, including over four hundred carvings from the Dynastic Period.

Wadi Hammamat List: A graffito which gives five names of Dynasty IV: three kings, Khufu, Djedefre and Khafre, and two princes, Baufre and Djedefhor.

Abbreviations

A = Sextus Julius Africanus (see Glossary)

Ab = Abydos King List of Sety I (see Glossary)

Ab2 = Abydos King List of Ramesses II (see Glossary)

AJA = American Journal of Archaeology

AJSL = American Journal of Semitic Literature, Chicago, 1884-1941

ARCE = American Research Center in Egypt

ASAE = Annales du Service des Antiquities de l' Égypte, Le Caire, 1900–

BACE = The Bulletin of the Australian Centre for Egyptology, North Ryde, Australia 1990–

BASOR = Bulletin of the American School of Oriental Research, Ann Arbor, 1919–

BES = Bulletin of the Egyptological Seminar, New York, 1979–

BIFAO = Bulletin de l'Institut Français d'Archéologie Orientale, Cairo, 1901–

BSAE = British School of Archaeology in Egypt

BSFE = Bulletin de la Société Française d'Égyptologie, Paris, 1949–

CAH = The Cambridge Ancient History, Cambridge, 3rd ed., 1970-73

CRIPEL = Cahier de recherches de l'Institut de papyrologie et égyptologie de Lille

DAWW = Dinkschriften der Akademie der Wissenschaften in Wien, Wien.

DE = Discussions in Egyptology, 1983–

E = Eusebius (see Glossary)

EA = Egyptian Archaeology: The Bulletin of the Egypt Exploration Society, London, 1991–

EEF = Egypt Exploration Fund. Later known as EES

EES = Egyptian Exploration Society

FIFAO = Fouilles de l'Institut Français d'Archéologie Orientale, Le Caire.

G = Gardiner.

GM = Göttinger Miszellen, Göttingen, 1972–

IE J = Israel Exploration Journal, Jerusalem, 1950–

IFAO = Publications de l'Institut Français d'Archéologie Orientale, Le Caire

J = Josephus (see Glossary)

JARCE = Journal of the American Research Center in Egypt, N.Y., 1962–

JEA = Journal of Egyptian Archaeology, London, 1914–

JNES = Journal of Near Eastern Studies, Chicago, 1942–

JSSEA = Journal of the Society for the Study of Egyptian Antiquities, Toronto, 1970–

K = Karnak King List of Thutmose III (see Glossary)

KMT = KMT, A Modern Journal of Ancient Egypt, Sebastopol, Ca., 1989–. In 2004, "KMT" was changed to "Kmt."

KV = Kings Valley, i.e., Valley of the Kings

MDAIK = Mitteilungen des Deutschen Archäologischen Instituts Abtteilung Kairo, Weisbaden, 1930–

MIFAO = Mémoirs publiés par les Membres de l'Institut Francais d'Archéologie Orientale (IFAO) du Caire, Berlin and Cairo.

MMA = Metropolitan Museum Of Art

OMRO = Oudheidkundige Mededelingen uit het Rijksmuseum van Oudheden te Leiden (Nuntic ex Museo antiquarioLiedensi), Leiden.

OR = Orientalia commentarii trimestres a facultae studorium orientis antiqui pontificci Instituti biblici in lucem editi in urbe, Rome, 1932–

P = Palermo Stone (see Glossary)

PSBA = Proceedings of the Society of Biblical Archaeology, London, 1879-1918.

QV = Queens Valley, i.e., Valley of the Queens

Rd'E = Revue d'Egyptologie, La Société Française d'Égyptologie, Paris, 1933–

RDSO = Rivista Degli Studi Orientali, Rome

RecTrav = Receuil des Travaux Relatifs à la philologie et à l'archéologie égyptiennes et assyriennes, Paris.

S = Saqqara King List (see Glossary)

SAK = Studien zur Altägyptischen Sprache Kultur, 1972–

SAOC = Studies in Ancient Oriental Civilization. University of Chicago Press.

SIP = Second Intermediate Period (see Glossary)

SSA = South Saqqara Stone Annals

T = Turin Canon (see Glossary)

WH = Wadi Hammamat King List (see Glossary)

WV = West Valley, i.e., the West Valley in the Valley of the Kings

ZÄS = Zeitschrift für ägyptische Sprache und Altertumskunde, Akademie-Verlag, Berlin, 1863–

Bibliography

Abd el-Raziq, M, G. Castel, P. Tallet, V. Ghica 2002
"Les inscriptions d'Ayn Soukhna," in *MIFAO* Vol 122.

Abitz, Friedrich 1992
"The Structure of the Decoration in the Tomb of Ramesses IX," in Reeves, C.N., ed., *After Tutankhamun. Research and Excavation in the Royal Necropolis at Thebes*.

Adams, Barbara and Cialowicz, Krzysztof M. 1997
Protodynastic Egypt. Shire Egyptology Series. Buckinghamshire, UK.

Adams, William Y. 1985
"Doubts about the Lost Pharaohs," in *JNES* vol. 44.

Aldred, Cyril 1955
"A Statue of King Neferkare Ramesses IX," in *JEA* vol. 41.
— 1965
Egypt to the End of the Old Kingdom. McGraw-Hill, N.Y.
— 1988
Akhenaten, King of Egypt. Thames and Hudson, New York and London.
— 1998
The Egyptians. 3rd edition, revised and updated by Aidan Dodson. Thames and Hudson Ltd, London.

Allen, James P. 1976
"The Funerary Texts of King Wahkare Akhtoy on a Middle Kingdom Coffin," in Johnson, Janet H., and Wente, Edward F., eds., *Studies in Honor of George R. Hughes*. University of Chicago Press, Chicago.
— 1991
"Akhenaten's 'Mystery' Coregent and Successor," in *Amarna Letters* vol. 1.

Altenmüller, Hartwig 1992
"Bemerkungen zu den neu gefundenen Daten im Grab der Königin Twosre (KV 14) im Tal der Könige von Theben," in C.N. Reeves, ed., *After Tut'ankhamun; Research and Excavation in the Royal Necropolis at Thebes*. Kegan Paul Int. London and New York.
— 2001
"Old Kingdom: Sixth Dynasty," in Donald B. Redford, ed., *The Oxford Encyclopedia of Ancient Egypt*, vol. 2, Oxford University Press, Oxford and New York.

Amélineau, E. 1899
Le tombeau d'Osiris. Paris.

BIBLIOGRAPHY

Amer, Amin A.M.A. 1981
"A Unique Theban Tomb Inscriptionn under Ramesses VIII," in *GM* vol. 49.
— 1982
"Notes on Ramesses IX in Memphis and Karnak," in *GM* vol. 57.
— 1985
"Reflections on the Reign of Ramesses VI," in *JEA* vol. 71.

Andrews, Carol 1990
Ancient Egyptian Jewelry. London.

Anthes, Rudolf 1928
Die Felseninschriften von Hatnub. Leipzig.

Arkell, A. J. 1956
"Stone bowls of Khaba (Third Dynasty)," in *JEA* vol. 42.
— 1958
"Stone bowls of Khaba (Third Dynasty)," in *JEA* vol. 44.
— 1963
"Was King Scorpion Menes?" in *Antiquity* vol. XXXVII.

Arnold, Dieter 1974
Der Tempel des Königs Mentuhotep von Deir el-Bahari. vols. I and II. Von Zabern, Mainz.
— 1976
Gräber des Alten und Mittleren Reiches in El-Tarif. Von Zabern, Mainz.
— 1979
The Temple of Mentuhotep at Deir el-Bahari. MMA. New York.
— 1981
Der Tempel des Königs Mentuhotep von Deir el-Bahari. vol. III. Von Zabern, Mainz.
— 1987
Der pyramidenbezirk des Königs Amenemhet III. In Dahshur. Von Zabern Mainz am Rhein.
— 1988
The Pyramid of Senwosret I (The South Cemeteries of Lisht, vol. I). MMA.
— 1992
The Pyramid Complex of Senwosret I (The South Cemetery of Lisht, vol. II). MMA.
— 1998
"Royal Cult Complexes," in *Temples of Ancient Egypt*, I.B. Tauris, London (ed. Byron E. Shafer).
— 2002
The Pyramid Complex of Senwosret III at Dahshur. Architectural Studies. MMA.

Arnold, Dieter and A. Oppenheim 1995
"Reexcavating the Senwosret III Pyramid Complex at Dahshur," in *KMT* vol. 6, #2.

Arnold, Dorothea 1996
   The Royal Women of Amarna: Images of Beauty from Ancient Egypt. Metropolitan Museum of Art. New York.

Arnold, Felix 1990
   Control Notes (The South Cemeteries of Lisht, vol. II), Metropolitan Museum of Art, New York.

Ayrton, E.R. 1908
   "The Tomb of Rameses Mentuherkhepshef: (No. 19)," in Theodore M. Davis, ed., *The Tomb of Siptah; The Monkey Tomb and the Gold Tomb.* Archibald Constable & Co. Ltd. London.

Ayrton, E.R.; Currelly, C.T. and Weigall, A.E.P. 1904.
   Abydos Part III. EEF.

Baines, John and Málek, Jaromír 1980
   The Atlas of Ancient Egypt. Facts on File. New York and Oxford.

Bakry, H. 1971
   "The Discovery of a Statue of Queen Twosre (1202-1194? B.C.) at Madinet Nasr, Cairo," in *RDSO* vol. 46.

Bares, Ladislav 2000
   "The destruction of the monuments at the necropolis of Abusir," in Miroslav Bárta and Jaromír Krejcí, eds, *Abusir and Saqqara in the Year 2000.* Prague.

Barsanti, Alexandre 1902
   "Fouilles autour de la pyramide d'Ounas (1901-1902)" in *ASAE* vol. III.
— 1908
   "Stèle inédite au nom du roi Radadouhotep Doudoumes," im ASAE vol. IX.
— 1912
   "Fouilles de Zaouiét el-Aryân 1911-1912," in *ASAE* vol. XII.

Barsanti, Alexandre and Maspero, Gaston 1906
   "Fouilles de Zaouiét el-Aryân" in *ASAE* vol. VII.

Barta, Winfried 1981
   "Die Chronologie der 1. bis 5. Dynastie nach den Angaben des rekonstruierten Annalensteins," in *ZÄS* vol. 108.

Batrawi, A. 1947
   "The Pyramid Studies: Anatomical Reports," in *ASAE* vol. XLVIII.
— 1951
   "The Skeletal Remains from the Northern Pyramid of Sneferu," in *ASAE* vol. LI.

Bibliography

Baud, Michel and Dobrev, Vassil 1995
"De nouvelles annales de l'Ancien Empire égyptien: Une Pierre de Palerme pour la VI dynastie," in *BIFAO* vol. 95

Baumgartel, Elise J. 1966
"Scorpion and Rosette and the Fragment of the Large Hierakonpolis Mace Head," in *ZÄS* vol. 93.

Bell, Martha R. 1975
"Climate and the History of Egypt: The Middle Kingdom," in *AJA* Vol 79.
— 1990
"An Armchair Excavation of KV55," in *JARCE* vol. XXVII.

Bennett, John 1966
"Pyramid Names," in *JEA* vol. 52.

Ben-Tor, Daphna 1989
The Scarab, A Reflection of Ancient Egypt. The Israel Museum, Jerusalem.

Berg, D.A. 1987
"Early Eighteenth Dynasty Expansion into Nubia," in *JSSEA* vol. 17, #1/2.

Berlandini, Jocelyne 1979
"La pyramid 'ruinée' de Sakkara-Nord et le roi Ikaouhor-Menkaouhor," in *Rd'E* vol. 31.

Berlev, Oleg 1974
"A Contemporary of King Sewaḥ-en-re," in *JEA* vol. 60.

Berman, Lawrence M. 1986
Amenemhet I. Unpublished dissertation. Yale University.
— 1998
"Overview of Amenhotep III and His Reign," in David O'Connor and Eric H. Cline, eds., *Amenhotep III: Perspectives on His Reign*. University of Michigan Press, Ann Arbor.

Beste, Irmtraut 1979
Skarabäen vol. III Von Zabern, Mainz am Rhine.

Bierbrier, M.L. 1975
"The Length of Reign of Ramesses X," in *JEA* vol. 61.

Bietak, Manfred 1970
"Vorläufiger Bericht über die dritte Kampagne der österreichischen Ausgrabungen auf Tell ed Dab'a im Ostdelta Ägyptens (1968)," in *MDAIK* vol. 26.
— 1981
"Eine Stele des ältesten Königssohnes des Hyksos Chajan," in *MDAIK* vol. 37.

— 1986
"Avaris and Piramesse: Archaeological Exploration in the Eastern Nile Delta," in *Proceedings of the British Academy, London, vol. LXV*, Oxford University Press.
— 1991
"Egypt and Canaan During the Middle Bronze Age" in *BASOR* vol. 281.
— 2001
"Hyksos," in Donald B. Redford, ed., *The Oxford Encyclopedia of Ancient Egypt*, vol. 2. Oxford.

Bietak, M. and Strouhal, Eugene 1974
"Die Todesumstände des Pharaos Seqenenre (17. Dynastie)," in *Annalen des Naturhistorischen Museums in Wein*.

Birrell, Michael 1997
"Was Ay the Father of Kiya?" in *BACE* #8.

Bisson de la Roque, F. 1937
Fouilles de Tôd (1934 Ab936) FIFAO 17, Cairo.

Björkman, Gun 1971
Kings at Karnak. A Study of the Treatment of the Monuments of Royal Predecessors in the Early New Kingdom. Uppsala.

Blankenberg-van Delden, C. 1969
The Large Commemorative Scarabs of Amenhotep III. E.J. Brill. Leiden.

Bleiberg, Edward 2001
"Amenhotpe I," in Donald B. Redford, ed., *The Oxford Encyclopedia of Ancient Egypt*, vol. 1. Oxford.

Borchardt, Ludwig 1907
Das Grabdenkmal des Königs Ne-user-Re. Leipzig.
— 1909
Das Grabdenkmal des Königs Nefer-ir-ke-re. Leipzig.
— 1910
Das Grabdenkmal des Königs Sa-hu-re. vol. I. Leipzig.
— 1913
Das Grabdenkmal des Königs Sa-hu-re. vol. II. Leipzig.
— 1935
Die Mittel zur Zeitlichen Festlegung von Punkten der ägyptischen Geschichte und ihre Anwendung. Cairo.

Bothmer, Bernard V. 1971
"A bust of Ny-User-Ra from Byblos, in Beirut, Lebanon." in *Kemi* Vol 21.

Bourriau, Janine 1976
"Egyptian antiquities acquired in 1974 by museums in the United Kingdom,"in *JEA* vol. 62.

Bibliography

— 1984
(ed.) "Egyptian antiquities acquired in 1982 by museums in the United Kingdom." *JEA* vol. 70.

— 1988
Pharaohs and Mortals: Egyptian Art in the Middle Kingdom. Cambridge.

— 2000
"The Second Intermediate Period (c. 1650-1550 B.C.)", in Shaw, Ian (ed.) *The Oxford History of Ancient Egypt.* Oxford.

Bradbury, Louise 1992
"Following Thutmose I on His Campaign to Kush," in *KMT* Vol 3, #3.

Brand, Peter 1998a
"Seti the First, His Reign & Monuments," in *KMT* vol. 9, #3.

— 1998b
" The Seti Reliefs Inside the Hypostyle Hall of the Amen Temple at Karnak," in *KMT* vol. 9, #3.

Breasted, James Henry 1906
Ancient Records of Egypt. 5 vols. Russell and Russell, N.Y.

Brier, Bob 1994
Egyptian Mummies. Quill, William Morrow and Company, Inc., New York.

Brock, Edwin C. 1992
"The Tomb of Merenptah and its Sarcophagi," in Reeves, C.N., ed., *After Tutankhamun. Research and excavation in the Royal Necropolis at Thebes.* Kegan Paul International, London and New York.

— 1995
"The Clearance of the Tomb of Ramesses VII," In Wilkinson, Richard H., ed., *Valley of the Sun Kings, New Explorations in the Tombs of the Pharaohs.* University of Arizona Egyptian Expedition, Tucson.

Brunton, Guy 1937
Mostagedda and the Tasian Culture. British Museum Expedition to Egypt, London.

Bryan, Betsy M. 1991
Reign of Thutmose IV. Johns Hopkins University Press, Baltimore.

— 1998
"Antecedents to Amenhotep III," in David O'Connor and Eric H. Cline, eds., *AmenhotepIII: Perspectives on His Reign.* Ann Arbor.

— 2000
"The Eighteenth Dynasty Before the Amarna Period (c. 1550-1352 BC)," in Ian Shaw, ed., *The Oxford History of Ancient Egypt.* Oxford.

— 2006
    "Administration in the Reign of Thutmose III," in Eric H. Cline and David O'Connor, eds., *Thutmose III, A New Biography*. Ann Arbor.

Bucaille, Maurice 1990
    Mummies of the Pharaohs: Modern Medical Investigations. St. Martin's Press, New York.

Budge, E.A. Wallis 1908
    The Book of the Kings of Egypt. Vols. I and II. London.
— 1913
    Hieroglyphic Texts from Egyptian Stelae, &c., in the British Museum. Part IV, British Museum, London.
— 1914
    Hieroglyphic Texts from Egyptian Stelae, &c., in the British Museum. Part V, British Museum, London.
— 1922
    Hieroglyphic Texts from Egyptian Stelae, &c., in the British Museum. Part VI, British Museum, London.
— 1968
    A History of Egypt, vol. I. Anthropological Publications, Oosterhout N.B., Netherlands (Reprint of the 1902 edition originally published by Routledge & Kegan Paul Ltd., London).
— 1976
    The Book of the Kings of Egypt, vol. I AMS Press, New York (A reprint of the 1908 edition originally published by Kegan Paul, Trench, Trübner & Co. London).

Bülow-Jacobsen 1997
    "The Abdication of Tutimaios?" in Ryholt, K.S.B., ed, *The Political Situation in Egypt during the Second Intermediate Period c. 1800 – 1550 B.C.* University of Copenhagen.

Callender, Gae 1995/1996
    "Problems in the Reign of Hatshepsut," in *KMT* vol. 65, #4.
— 1998
    "What Sex was King Sobekneferu, and What is Known About Her Reign?" in *KMT* vol. 9, #1.
— 2000
    "The Middle Kingdom Renaissance," in Ian Shaw (ed.) *The Oxford History of Ancient Egypt*. Oxford.
— 2006
    "The Cripple, the Queen & the Man from the North," in *KMT* vol. 17, #1.

Calverly, A. M. et al. 1933-38
    The Temple of King Sethos I at Abydos, Vols I-IV. London and Chicago.

Caminos, Ricardo A. 1974
    The New-Kingdom Temples of Buhen. Vols. I & II. EES.

Bibliography

Capart, Jean 1938
"Deuxième rapport sommaire sur les Fouilles de la Fondation Égyptologique, Reine Élisabeth à El-Kab (janvier à mars 1938)," in *ASAE* Vol XXXVIII.

Carnarvon, Earl of, and Carter, Howard 1912
Five Years Exploration at Thebes. Oxford.

Carter, Howard 1916
"Report on the Tomb of Zeser-Ka-Ra Amen-Hetep I, Discovered by the Earl of Carnarvon in 1914," in *JEA* vol. 3.
— 1917
"A Tomb Prepared for Queen Hatshepsut and Other Recent Discoveries at Thebes," in *JEA* vol. 4.
— 1923-33
The Tomb of Tut-Ankh-Amen. 3 vols. Cassel, London.

Castel, Georges and Soukiassian, Georges 1985
"Dépôt de stèles dans le sanctuaire du Novel Empire au Gebel Zeit," in *BIFOA* vol. 85.

Caulfield, A. St. G. 1902
The Temple of the Kings at Abydos. BSAE 8. London.

Clagett, Marshall 1989
Ancient Egyptian Science. vol. One, Tome One. American Philosophical Society, Philadelphia.

Clayton, Peter A. 1994
Chronicle of the Pharaohs. Thames and Hudson, N.Y.

Cledat, J. 1914
"Les vases de El-Béda" in *ASAE* vol. XIII.

Clère, J.J. 1982
"La stèle de Sânkhptah, Chambellan du Roi Râhotep," in *JEA* vol. 68.

Clère, J.J. and Vandier, J. 1948
Textes de la Première Période Intermédiare et de la Xième Dynastie. Brussels.

Cline, Eric 1987
"Amenhotep III and the Aegean: A Reassessment of Egypto-Aegean Relations in the 14th. Century B.C.," in *Orientalia* vol. 56.

Collins, J.J. 1985
"Artapanus (Third to Second Century B.C.)" in James H. Charlesworth, ed., *The Old Testament Pseudepigrapha*, vol. 2. Doubleday & Co., Inc., Garden City, N.Y.

Couyat, J. and Montet, P. 1912
   Les inscriptions hiéroglyphiques du Ouâdi Hammâmât. IFAO.

Cron, Rodney L. and Johnson, George B. 1995a
   "De Morgan at Dahshur: Excavations in the 12th. Dynasty Pyramids, 1894 – '95, Part One," in *KMT* vol. 6, #2.
— 1995b
   "De Morgan at Dahshur: Excavations in the 12th. Dynasty Pyramids, 1894 – '95, Part Two," in *KMT* vol. 6, #4.

Daoud, Khaled 2000
   "Abusir during the Herakleopolitan Period," in Miroslav Bárta and Jaromír Krejcí (eds.) *Abusir in the Year 2000*. Prague.

Daressy, Georges 1902
   "Le temple de Mit Rahineh," in *ASAE*, Vol III.

Darnell, J.C. 2002
   Theban Desert Road Survey in the Egyptian Western Desert," vol. I, Chicago.

Darnell, J.C. and D . 1997a
   "The Theban Desert Road Survey," in *The Oriental Institute 1996-1997 Annual Report*, Chicago 1997.
— 1997b
   "Exploring the 'Narrow Doors' of the Theban Desert," in *EA* vol. 10.

Davies, Benedict G. 1995
   Egyptian Historical Records of the Later Eighteenth Dynasty. Fascicle VI. Aris & Phillips Ltd., Warminster.
— 1997
   Egyptian Historical Inscriptions of the Nineteenth Dynasty. Paul Aströms förlag. Jonserad.

Davies, N. de Garis 1902
   The Rock Tombs of Deir el-Gebrawi. EEF, London.
— 1903-08
   The Rock Tombs of El-Amarna. 6 Vols. EEF, London.
— 1920
   "An Alabaster Sistrum Dedicated by King Teti," in *JEA* vol. 6.

Davies, W. Vivian 1981a
   "Two Inscribed Objects from the Petrie Museum," in *JEA* vol. 67.
— 1981b
   A Royal Statue Reattributed. British Museum Occasional Paper #28, London.
— 1982
   "The Origin of the Blue Crown," in *JEA* vol. 68.

— 1987
   Catalogue of Egyptian Antiquities in the British Museum. vol. VII, London.

Bibliography

Davis, Theodore M. 1906
The Tomb of Hâtshopsîtû. Archibald Constable & Co., London.
— 1907
The Tomb of Iouiya and Touiyou. Archibald Constable & Co., London.
— 1907/90
The Tomb of Queen Tiyi. A 2nd and updated edition of the original 1907 publication. KMT Communications, San Francisco.
— 1908
The Tomb of Siptah; the Monkey and the Gold Tomb. Archibald Constable & Co. London.
— 1912
The Tombs of Harmhabi and Touatânkhamanou. Archibald Constable & Co. London.

Davis, Whitney 1992
Masking the Blow. University of California Press, Berkeley.

Dawson, W.R. 1925
"A Bronze Dagger of the Hyksos Period," in *JEA* Vol 11.

Debono, F. 1951
"Expédition archéologique royale au désert 0riental (Keft-Kosseir)," in *ASAE* vol. 51.

de Buck, A. 1937
"The Judicial Papyrus at Turin," in *JEA* vol. 23.

Delia, Robert D. 1991/1992
"New Rock Inscriptions of Senwosret III, Neferhotep I. Penpata, and Others at the First Cataract," in *BES* vol. 11.
— 1993
"First Cataract Rock Inscriptions: Some Comments, Maps, and a New Group," in *JARCE* vol. 30.
— 1995
"Khakaure Senwosret III: King & Man," in *KMT* vol. 6, #2.

Della Monica, M. 1991
Thoutmosis III: Le Plus Grand Des Pharaohs. Le Leopard d'Or, Paris.

de Morgan, Jacques. 1895
Fouilles à Dahchour, mars-juin, 1894. Vienna.

de Rougé, Emmanuel 1866
Recherches sur les Monuments Qu'on Peut Attributer aux Six Premieres Dynasties de Manéthon. Paris.

Deroches-Noblecourt, Christiane 1963
Tutankhamen: Life and Death of a Pharaoh. New York Graphic Society, N.Y.

Derry, Douglas E. 1934
"An X-Ray Examination of the Mummy of King Amenophis I," in *ASAE* vol. XXXIV.

Dewachter, M. 1976
"Le roi Sahathor et la famille de Neferhotep I," in *RdÉ* vol. 28.
— 1984
"Le roi Sahathor," in *RdÉ* vol. 35.
— 1985
"Nouvelles informations relatives à l'exploitation de la nécropole royale de Drah Aboul Neggah," in *RdÉ* vol. 36.

Dobrev, Vassil 2003
"Builders' Inscriptions from the Pyramid of King Pepi I (Sixth Dynasty)," in Zahi Hawass and L.P. Brock, ed., *Egyptology at the Dawn of the Twenty-First Century*. American University in Cairo Press. Cairo and New York.

Dodson, Aidan 1985
"The Tomb of Amenmesse: Some Observations," in *DE* vol. 2.
— 1987
"The Tombs of the Kings of the Thirteenth Dynasty in the Memphite Necropolis," in *ZÄS* 114.
— 1994a
"Kings' Valley Tomb 55 and the Fates of the Amarna Kings," in *Amarna Letters* vol. 3. KMT Communications, San Francisco, Calif.
— 1994b
The Canopic Equipment of the Kings of Egypt. Keegan Paul International, London
— 1994c
"From Dahshur to Dra Abu el Naga: The Decline & Fall of the Royal Pyramid," in *KMT* vol. 5, #3.
— 1995
Monarchs of the Nile. Rubicon Press, London.
— 1996
"The Mysterious 2nd Dynasty," in *KMT* vol. 7, #2.
— 1997
"The Sons of Rameses III," in *KMT* vol. 8, #1.
— 1997-98
"The So-called Tomb of Osiris," in *KMT* vol. 8, #4.
— 1998
"On the Threshold of Glory: the Third Dynasty," in *KMT* vol. 9, #2.
— 1999
"The Decorative Phases of the Tomb of Sethos II and Their Historical Implications," in *JEA* vol. 85.
— 2000
After the Pyramids: The Valley of the Kings and Beyond. Rubicon Press, London.
— 2000/2001
"The Intact Pyramid Burial at Hawara of 12th. Dynasty Princess Neferuptah," in *KMT* vol. 11, #4.

BIBLIOGRAPHY

— 2003
The Pyramids of Ancient Egypt. New Holland Press, London.
— Forthcoming
"Amarna Sunset: the late-Amarna succession revisited."

Dodson, Aidan and Hilton, Dyan 2004
Complete Royal Families of Ancient Egypt. Thames and Hudson, London.

Dodson, Aidan and Reeves, C. Nicholas 1988
"A Casket Fragment of Ramesses IX in the Museum of Archaeology and Anthropology, Cambridge," in *JEA* vol. 74.

Doret, Eric 2001
"Ankhtifi of Mo'alla," in Redford, Donald B., ed., *The Oxford Encyclopedia of Ancient Egypt.* Oxford.

Dorman, Peter F. 1988
The Monuments of Senenmut. Kegan Paul. London & New York.
— 2006
"The Early Reign of Thutmose III: An Unorthodox Mantel of Coregency," in Eric H. Klein and David O'Connor, eds., *Thutmose III. A New Biography.* Ann Arbor.

Drews, Robert 1993
The End of the Bronze Age; Changes in Warfare and the Catastrophe Ca. 1200 B.C. Princeton.

Dreyer, Gunther 1990
"Umm el-Qaab: Nachuntersuchungen im frühzeitlichen Königsfriedhof. 3./4. Vorbericht," *MDAIK* vol. 46.
— 1992a
"Recent Discoveries at Abydos Cemetery U" in Edwin C.M. van den Brink, ed., *The Nile Delta in Transition: 4th. - 3rd. Millenium B.C.* Tel Aviv.
— 1992b
"Horus Krokodal, ein Gegenkönig der Dynastie 0" in Renée Friedman and Barbara Adams, eds., *The Followers of Horus: Studies Dedicated to Michael Allen Hoffman.* Egyptian Studies Associate Publication #2. Oxbow Publications, Oxford.
— 1993a
"Umm el-Qaab: Nachuntersuchungen im früzeitlichen Königsfriedhof. 5./6. Vorbericht" in *MDAIK* vol. 49.
— 1993b
"A Hundred Years at Abydos" in *EA* #3.
— 1998
Umm El-Qaab I: Das prädynastische Königsgrab U-j und seine frühen Schriftzeugnisse. Philipp von Zabern, Mainz.

Dreyer, G.; Engel, E.-M.; Hartung, U.; Hikade, T.; Köhler, E.C. and Pumpenmeier, F. 1996
"Umm el-Qaab. Nachuntersuchungen im Frühzeitlichen Königsfriedhof. 7./8 .Vorbericht" in *MDAIK* vol. 52.

Drioton, E. 1954
"Une liste de rois de la IV Dynastie dans l'Ouâdi Hammâmât" in *BSFE* vol. 16.

Dunham, Dows 1967
Second Cataract Forts, vol. II: *Uronarti Shalfak Mirgissa*, Boston.
— 1978
Zawiyet el-Aryan: The Cemetries Adjacent to the Layer Pyramid. Musum of Fine Arts, Boston.

Dunham, Dows and Janssen, J.M.A. 1960
Second Cataract Forts, vol. I: *Semna-Kumma*, Boston

Eaton-Krauss, Marianne 2001
"Akhenaten," in Redford, Donald B., ed., *The Oxford Encyclopedia of Ancient Egypt*. vol. 1. Oxford.

Edel, Elmar and Wenig, Steffen 1974
Die Jahreszeitenreliefs aus dem Sonnenheiligtum des Königs Ne-User-Re. Berlin.

Eder, Christian 2002
El KAB VII: Die Barkenkapelle des Königs Sobekhotep III in El Kab. Brepols.

Edgerton, Wm. F. and Wilson, John A. 1936
Historical Records of Ramses III, The Texts in Medinet Habu. SAOC, 12. Chicago.

Edwards, I.E.S. 1965
"Lord Dufferin's Excavations at Deir el-Bahri and the Clandeboye Collection," in *JEA* vol. 51.
— 1971
"The Early Dynastic Period in Egypt," in *CAH* vol. I, Part 2, Chapter XI.
— 1993
The Pyramids of Egypt. 3rd edition. Penguin Books, London.
— 1994
"Chephren's Place Among the Kings of the Fourth Dynasty," in Eyre, C, Leahy, A and Montagno, L (eds.) *The Unbroken Reed: Studies in the Culture and History of Ancient Egypt in Honour of A.F. Shore.* EES, Occasional Publications 11.

El-Alfi, Mostafa 1991
"La Liste de Rois de Karnak," in *DE* vol. 19.

El Madhy, Christine 1989
Mummies, Myth and Magic in Ancient Egypt. Thames and Hudson. NY.

El Maksoud, Mohamed Abd 1983
"Un monument du roi 'Aa-sh-r' Nhsy à Tell Heboua (Sinaï Nord)" in *ASAE* vol. LXIX.

Bibliography

— 1989
"Excavations on "The Ways of Horus" in A. Nibbi (ed.) *The Archaeology, Geography and History of the Egyptian Delta in Pharaonic Times*. Discussions in Egyptology Special Number 1.

Emery, Walter B. 1938
Excavations at Saqqara: The Tomb of Hemaka, Cairo.
— 1939
Hor-Aha. Excavations at Saqqara,1937-8. Government Press, Cairo.
— 1949-58
Great Tombs of the First Dynasty. 3 vols. Cairo and London.
— 1961
Archaic Egypt. Penguin Books, N.Y.
— 1963
"Egypt Exploration Society: Preliminary Report on the Excavations at Buhen, 1962," in *Kush* vol. 11.

Englebach, Rex 1921
"Notes of Inspection, April 1921", in *ASAE* vol. XXI
— 1942
"A List of the Royal Names on the Objects in the 'King Fouad I Gift' Collection with Some Remarks on its Arrangement", in *ASAE* vol. XLI.

Erman, A. (Ed.) 1911
Hieratische Papyrus aus den königliche Museen zu Berlin. vol. III, Leipzig.

Ertman, Earl L. 1992
"Is there visual evidence for a "King" Nefertiti?" in *Amarna Letters* vol. 2.
— 1993
"A First Report on the Preliminary Survey of Unexcavated KV10 (The Tomb of Amenmesse)," in *KMT* vol. 4, #2.
— 2001/2002
"An Electrum Ring of Nefertiti: Evidence of Her Co-Kingship?" in *KMT* vol. 12, #4.

Eyre, C.J. 1980
"The reign-length of Ramesses VII, in *JEA* vol. 66.

Fairservis, Jr., W.A. 1991
"A Revised View of the Na'rmr Palette" in *JARCE* vol. XXVIII.

Fakhry, Ahmed 1952
The Inscriptions of theAmethyst Quarries at Wadi El Hudi. Cairo.
— 1959
The Monuments of Sneferu at Dahshur. vol. I. Cairo.
— 1961a
The Monuments of Sneferu at Dahshur. vol. II. Cairo.
— 1961b
The Pyramids. University of Chicago Press, Chicago.

Farag, Nagiv and Iskander, Zaki 1971
The Discovery of Neferwptah. Cairo.

Farag, Rifaat Abdallah 1980
"A Stele of Khasekhemui from Abydos" in *MDAIK* vol. 36.

Faulkner, Raymond O. 1946
"The Euphrates Campaign of Tuthmosis III" in *JEA* vol. 32.

Fay, Biri 1988
"Amenemhat V – Vienna/Assuan" in *SAK* vol. 44.
— 1996
The Louvre Sphinx and Royal Sculpture from the Reign of Amenemhat II. Von Zabern, Vienna.

Firth, Cecil M. 1924
"Two Mastaba Chapels of the IIIrd. Dynasty at Saqqara" in *ASAE* vol. XXIV.

Firth, Cecil M. and Gunn, Battiscombe 1926
Teti Pyramid Cemeteries. 2 Vols. IFAO.

Firth, Cecil M. and Quibell, James E. 1935
The Step Pyramid. 2 Vols. IFAO.

Fischer, Henry G. 1963a
"Varia Aegyptiaca" in *JARCE* vol. 2.
— 1963b
"A Stela of the Heracleopolitan Period at Saqqara: the Osiris 'Iti," in *ZäS* vol. 90.
— 1987
"Archaeological Aspects of Epigraphy and Palaeography" in Ricardo Caminos and Henry G. Fisher (eds.) *Ancient Egypt Epigraphy and Palaeography*, 3rd edition, New York, 1987.

Forbes, Dennis C. 1990
"Pharaoh was a Fat Man," in *KMT* vol. 1, #2.
— 1991/1992
"Senusert I," in *KMT* vol. 2, #4.
— 1992
"Nebmaatre Amenhotep III," in *KMT* vol. 3, #2.
— 1992/1993a
"Cache KV35, Amenhotep II's tomb yields more kings," in *KMT* vol. 3, #4.
— 1992/1993b
"End Paper: The MMA Displays Rameses I Again," in *KMT* vol. 3, #4.
— 1993
"The Rameses II Legacy," in *KMT* vol. 4, #1.
— 1994
"Amenhotep I, Last King of the 17$^{th.}$ Dynasty? Or Fifth of the 18th?," in *KMT* vol. 5, #2.
— 1997
"The Oldest Royal Mummy in Cairo" in *KMT* vol. 8, #4.

BIBLIOGRAPHY

— 1998a
Tombs, Treasures and Mummies: Seven Great Discoveries of Egyptian Archaeology. KMT Communications, Inc. Sebastopol and Sante Fe.

— 1998b
"Horemheb, the New Kingdom's In-Between Pharaoh," in *KMT* vol. 9, #1.

— 1998c
"Another Ayrton/Davis King's Valley Discovery: the Gold Hoard of Queen Tausert & King Seti II," in *KMT* vol. 9, #4.

— 2002
"Menkheperure Djehutymes IV: The Fourth & final Thutmose" in *KMT* vol. 13, #2.

— 2004
"Egypt Update: What was new in 2003," in *KMT* vol. 15, #1.

— 2005a
Imperial Lives, Illustrated Biographies of Significant New Kingdom Egyptians. vol. One. KMT Communications Inc.

— 2005b
"Beyond the Tomb: The Historical Tutankhamen from His Monuments," in *KMT* vol. 16, #2.

— 2005/2006
"Thutmose III: Warrior-Pharaoh & Master Builder," in *KMT* vol. 16, #4.

Franke, D. 1984
Personendaten aus dem Mittleren Reiches, Ägyptologische Abhandlungen 41, Weisbaden.

— 1988
"Zur Chronologie des Mittleren Reiches Teil II: Die sogenannte 'Zweite Zwischenzeit' Altägyptens." in *Orientalia* vol. 57.

— 2001
"First Intermediate Period," in Donald B. Redford (ed.) *The Oxford Encyclopedia of Ancient Egypt*, vol. 1. Oxford University Press, Oxford and New York.

Frankfort, Henri 1926
"Egypt and Syria in the First Intermediate Period" in *JEA* vol. 12.

Fraser, George 1900
A Catalogue of Scarabs Belonging to George Fraser. Bernard Quaritch, London.

Fraser, P.M. 1972
Ptolemaic Alexandria, Oxford.

Freed, Rita E.; Markowitz, Y.J. and D'Auria, S.H. 1999
Pharaohs of the Sun: Akhenaten+Nefertiti+Tutankhamen. Museum of Fine Arts, Boston.

Friedman, Renée and Stan Hendrickx 2002
"Gebel Tjauti Rock Inscription 1" in John C. Darnell (ed.) *Theban Desert Road Survey in the Western Egyptian Western Desert* vol. 1.

Gabolde, Luc 1987
"La Chronologie du règne de Thoutmosis II, ses conséquences sur la datation des momies royales et leurs répercutions sur l'histoire du développement de la Vallée des Rois," in *SAK* 14.
— 1990
"Nerkarê, a-t-il existé?" *BIFAO* vol. 90.
— 1993
"La "Cour des fêtes" de Thoutmosis II à Karnak," in *Karnak* #9.

Gabra, Gawdat 1976
"Preliminary Report on the Stela of *Ḥtpi* from El-Kab from the Time of Wahankh Inyôtef II," in *MDAIK* vol. 32.

Gardiner, Alan 1916
"The Defeat of the Hyksos by Kamose: The Carnarvon Tablet, No. I," in *JEA*, vol. 3.
— 1941-48
The Wilbour Papyrus. Vols. I-III. Oxford.
— 1956
"The Tomb of Queen Twosre," in *JEA* vol. 40.
— 1957
Egyptian Grammar, Third Edition, Revised Oxford.
— 1958
"The Personal Name of King Serpent," in *JEA* vol. 44.
— 1959
The Royal Canon of Turin Griffith Institute, Oxford.
— 1960
The Kadesh Inscriptions of Ramesses II. Oxford.
— 1961
Egypt of the Pharaohs. Oxford University Press, Oxford.

Gardiner, Alan and Peet, T. Eric 1952
The Inscriptions of Sinai, vol. 1 EES, London.
— 1955
The Inscriptions of Sinai, vol. II EES, London.

Garstang, John 1903
Mahasna and Bet Khallaf. London.

Gasse, Annie 1987
"Un expédition au Ouadi Hammamat sous le regne de Sebekemsaf Ier," in *BIFAO* Vol 87.

Gauthier, Henri 1907-17
Le Livre des rois d'Égypte, vol. 1-5, *MIFAO* 17-21.

Bibliography

— 1923
"Quelques additions au Livre des rois d'Égypte." in *RecTrav* vol. 40.
— 1931
"Deux sphinx du Moyen Empire originaires d'Edfou (avec 1 planche)," in *ASAE* vol. XXXI.

Gibson, Gayle 2000
"How Tall Was Thutmose III" in *KMT* vol. 11 #1.
— 2000/2001
"Names Matter: The Unfinished History of the Niagara Falls Mummies," in *KMT* vol. 11, #4.

Gibson-Kirwin, Gayle 1992/1993
"Excellent Mummies, Dated Labels," in *KMT* vol. 3, #4.

Giddy, Lisa 1996
"Digging Diary 1995-1996," in *EA* Vol 9.
— 1997
"Digging Diary 1996," in *EA* vol. 10.

Giles, Fredrick J. 1997
The Amarna Age: Western Asia. Aris and Phillips Ltd., Warminster, UK.

Giveon, Raphael 1965
"A Sealing of Khyan from the Shephela of Southern Palestine," in *JEA* vol. 51.
— 1974a
"A Second Relief of Sekhemkhet in Sinai," in *BASOR* vol. 216.
— 1974b
"The XIIIth Dynasty in Asia," in *Rd'E* vol. 30.
— 1985
Egyptian Scarabs from Western Asia from the Collections of the British Museum. Orbis Biblicus et Orientalis 3, Freiburg.

Godron, Gerard 1990
Études sur L'Horus Den, Geneva.

Goedicke, Hans 1956
"The Pharaoh Ny-Swth," in *ZÄS* vol. 81.
— 1971
Re-used Blocks from the Pyramid of Amenemhet I at Lisht. Metropolitan Museum of Art, N.Y.
— 1986
The Quarrel of Apophis and Seqenenre. Van Siclen Books, San Antonio.
— 1988
"The Death of Pepi II – Neferkare" in *SAK* vol. 15.
— 1990
"Two Mining Records from the Wadi Hammamat" in *Rd'E* vol. 57.

— 2000
"Abusir – Saqqara – Giza," in Miroslav Bárta and Jaromír
Krejcí (eds.) *Abusir and Saqqara in the Year 2000*. Prague.
— 2004
The Speos Artemidos Inscription of Hatshepsut and Related Discussions. Halgo. Connecticut.

Gohary, Jocelyn 1992
Akhenaten's Sed-festival at Karnak. Keegan Paul International. London and New York.

Gomaa, Farouk 2001
"Upper Egypt," in Donald B. Redford, ed., *The Oxford Encyclopedia of Ancient Egypt* vol. 3. Oxford.

Goneim, M. Zakaria 1956
The Lost Pyramid. Rinehart & Company, Inc. New York.
— 1957
Horus Sekhem-khet- The Unfinished Step Pyramid at Saqqara. IFAO.

Gophna, Ram 1987
"Egyptian Trading Posts in Southern Canaan at the Dawn of the Archaic Period" in Anson F. Rainey, ed., *Egypt, Israel, Sinai: Archaeological and Historical Relationships in the Biblical Period*. Tel Aviv University.

Görg, Manfred 1981
"Zur Erklärung des Namens des Hyksosprinzen," in *MDAIK* vol. 37.

Goyon, Georges 1957
Nouvelles inscriptions rupestres du Wadi Hammamat. Paris.

Grajetzki, Wolfram 2005
Ancient Egyptian Queens, a Hieroglyphic Dictionary. Golden House Publications. London.
— 2006
The Middle Kingdom of Ancient Egypt. Duckworth, London.

Grandet, Pierre 1993
Ramsès III, Histoire d'un règne. Pygmalion. Paris.

Grdseloff, Bernard 1939
"Le roi Iti divinisé" in *ASAE* vol. XXXIX.
— 1944
"Notes d'épigraphie archaïque" in *ASAE* vol. XLIV.

Green, F.W. 1903
"Notes on an Inscription at El Kab" in *PSBA* vol. XXV.

Grimal, Nicolas 1992
A History of Ancient Egypt. Basil Blackwell, Cambridge, USA.

Bibliography

Gunn, Battiscombe 1928
"Inscriptions from the Step Pyramid Site III. Fragments of Inscribed Vases" in *ASAE* vol. MCMXXIII.

Habachi, L. 1950
"Was Anukis Considered as the Wife of Khnum or as His Daughter?" in *ASAE* vol. L.
— 1954
"Khata'na-Qantir: Importance" in *ASAE* vol. LII.
— 1957
"Two Graffiti at Sehel from the Reign of Queen Hatshepsut," in *JNES* vol. XVI, #2.
— 1958
"God's fathers and the role they played in the history of the first intermediate period," in *ASAE* vol. LV.
— 1963
"King Nebhepetre Menthuhotp: His Monuments, Place in History, Deification and Unusual Representations in the Form of Gods," in *MDAIK* vol. 19.
— 1972
The Second Second Stele of Kamose. Glückstadt.
— 1974
"A High Innundation in the Temple of Amenre at Karnak in the Thirteenth Dynasty," in *SAK* vol. 1.
— 1975
"Building Activities of Sesostris I in the Area South of Thebes," in *MDAIK* vol. 33.
— 1981
"New Light on the Neferhotep I Family, as Revealed by their Inscriptions in the Cataract Area," in *Studies in Ancient Egypt, the Aegean, and Sudan*," eds. W.K. Simpson and W. M. Davis, Boston.
— 1985
Elephantine IV, The Sanctuary of Heqaib. Mainz am Rhein.

Hall, H.R. 1913
Catalogue of Egyptian Scarabs, etc, in the British Museum vol. I, British Museum.

Hamza, Mahmud 1930
"Excavations of the Department of Antiquities at Qantir (Faqus District) (Season, May 21st.-July 7th., 1928)," in *ASAE*, vol. XXX.

Hardwick, Thomas 2006
"The Golden Horus name of Amenmesse?" in *JEA* vol. 92.

Haring, Ben 2001
"Deir el-Medina," in Donald B. Redford, ed., *The Oxford Encyclopedia of Ancient Egypt* vol. 1. Oxford.

Harris, James E. and Weeks, Kent R. 1973
X-Raying the Pharaohs. Chas. Scribner's Sons. NY.

Harris, James E. and Wente, Edward F. 1980
   An X-Ray Atlas of the Royal Mummies. University of Chicago Press.

Hart, George 1991
   Pharaohs and Pyramids. The Herbert Press Ltd., London.

Harvey, Stephen 1994
   "Monuments of Ahmose at Abydos," in *EA* vol. 4, #4.

Hassan, Selim 1937
   "The Great Limestone Stela of Amenhotep II," in *ASAE* vol. XXXVII.
— 1938
   "Excavations at Saqqara (1937-1938), in *ASAE* vol. XXXVIII.
— 1955
   "The causeway of *Wnis* at Sakkara," in *ZÄS* vol. 80.

Hawass, Zahi 1995
   "The Programs of the Royal Funerary Complexes of the Fourth Dynasty," in David O'Connor and David P. Silverman (eds.) *Ancient Egyptian Kingship*, E.J. Brill, New York.
— 2000
   The Mysteries of Abu Simbel. The American University in Cairo Press. Cairo and New York.
— 2001
   "Menkaure," in Donald B. Redford, ed., *The Oxford Encyclopedia of Ancient Egypt*. vol. 2, Oxford.
— 2006
   "Quest for the Mummy of Queen Hatshepsut," in *KMT* vol. 17, #2.

Hawass, Zahi and Brock, Lyla Pinch 2003
   Egyptology at the Dawn of the Twenty-first Century. Three Vols. American University in Cairo Press.

Hayes, Wm. C. 1939
   The Burial Chamber of the Treasurer Sobk-mose from Er Rizeikat. Papers #9. Metropolitan Museum of Art. New York.
— 1946
   "Royal Decrees from the Temple of Min at Coptus," in *JEA* vol. 32.
— 1953
   The Scepter of Egypt. vol. I. Harper & Brothers, New York.
— 1955
   A Papyrus of the Late New Kingdom in the Brooklyn Museum [Papyrus Brooklyn 35.1446]. The Brooklyn Museum.
— 1959
   The Scepter of Egypt. vol. II. HarvardUniversity Press, Cambridge, Massachussets.
— 1973
   "Egypt: From the Death of Ammenemes III to Seqenenre II," in *CAH* vol. II, part 1, chapter II.

BIBLIOGRAPHY

Hein, I. (editor) 1994
    Pharaonen und Fremde-Dynastein im Dunkel, Vienna.

Helck, Wolfgang 1969
    "Ein Stele Sebekhoteps IV. aus Karnak," in *MDAIK* vol. 24.
— 1983
    Historisch-biographische Texte der 2 . Zwischenzeit und neue Texte 18. Dynastie 2nd edition. Wiesbaden.

Hendrickx, Stan 1999
    Review of *State Formation in Egypt. Chronology and Society* by Toby A.H. Wilkinson, in *JEA* vol. 85.

Herodotus 1954
    The Histories. Translation by A. deSélincourt. Penguin Books Ltd., Harmondsworth.

Hintze, F. and Reineke, W.F. 1989
    Felsinschriften aus dem sudanesischen Nubien, vol. I. Berlin.

Hoffman, Michael A. 1982
    The Predynastic of Hierakonpolis — An Interim Report. Cairo and Illinois.
— 1991
    Egypt Before the Pharaohs. University of Texas Press, Austin.

Holladay Jr., John S. 1982
    Cities of the Delta, Part 3, *Tell el-Maskhuta* Malibu, Calif.

Hölscher, Uvo 1912
    Das Grabdenkmal des Königs Chephren. J.C. Hinrichs, Leipzig.

Hornung, Erik 1999
    Akhenaten and the Religion of Light. Cornell University Press.
— 2006
    "The New Kingdom," in Hornung, Erik, Krauss, Rolf, and Warburton, David A., eds., *Ancient Egyptian Chronology.* Brill, Leiden and Boston.

Hornung, Erik and Staehelin, Elisabeth 1976
    Skarabäen und andere Siegelamulette aus Basler Sammlungen, Philipp von Zabern, Mainz.

Huyge, Dirk 1984
    "Horus Qa-a in the El Kab area, Upper Egypt," in *Orientalia Lovaniensia Periodica* vol. 15.

Ikram, Salima 2004
    Personal communication. April, 2004.

Ikram, Salima and Dodson, Aidan 1997
    Royal Mummies in the Egyptian Museum. The American University in Cairo Press.

— 1998
   The Mummy in Ancient Egypt. Thames and Hudson. New York.

Ikram, Salima and Rossi, Corinna 2004
   "An Early Dynastic serekh from the Kharga Oasis," in *JEA*, vol. 90.

Jacquet, Jean 1983
   Le Trésor de Thoutmosis Ier: Étude Architecturale. Vols. 1 and 2. IFAO.

James, Susan E. 2001/2002
   "Mutnodjmet, Sister-in-Waiting & Great Royal Wife," in *KMT* vol. 12, #4.

James, T.G.H. 1961
   "A Group of Inscribed Egyptian Tools," in *The British Museum Quarterly*, vol. XXIV, London.
— 1965
   "Egypt: From the Expulsion of the Hyksos to Amenophis I," in *CAH* vol. II, Part 1, Chapter VIIII.
— 1974
   Corpus of Hieroglyphic Inscriptions in the Brooklyn Museum I. The Brooklyn Museum, Brooklyn, NY.

Jánosi, Peter 1992
   "The Queens of the Old Kingdom and Their Tombs," in *BACE* vol. 3.

Janssen, Jac. J. 1978
   "Year 8 of Ramesses VI Attested," in *GM* vol. 29.

Jeffreys, Alan L. 1993
   "Mysterious Middle Kingdom Monument on Thoth Hill, Luxor." In *KMT* vol. 4, #1.

Jenkins, Nancy 1980
   The Boat Beneath the Pyramid. Holt, Rinehart and Winston, N.Y.

Jéquier, Gustave 1928a
   Le Mastabat Faraoun. Fouilles à Saqqarah. IFAO.
— 1928b
   La pyramide d'Oudjebten. IFAO, Cairo.
— 1931
   Rapport préliminaire sur les fouilles éxecutées en 1930-1931 dans la partie méridionale de la nécropole memphite. ASAE vol. XXXI.
— 1933a
   Les pyramides des reines Neit and Apouit. Fouilles à Saqqarah IFAO.
— 1933b
   Deux pyramides du Moyen Empire. Fouilles à Saqqarah. IFAO.
— 1935
   La pyramide d'Aba. Fouilles à Saqqarah. IFAO.

Bibliography

— 1936-40
Le monument funéraire de Pépi II. Vols. I-III IFAO, Cairo.

Jidejian, Nina 1968
Byblos Through the Ages. Dar el-Machreq Publishers. Argonaut, Inc.

Johnson, George B. 1998
"KV47, the Theban Royal Tomb of Siptah," in *KMT* vol. 9, #2.
— 2000
"The Royal Tomb of Horemheb in the Valley of the Kings: Its Discovery, Design & Decoration," in *Amarna Letters* vol. 4.
— 2000/2001
"KV16: The Tomb of Rameses I in the Valley of the Kings," in *KMT* vol. 11, #4.
— 2002
"Senwosret One, Building for Eternity," in *KMT* vol. 13, #3.
— 2003/2004
"Where was Amenhotep I Buried? A Look at Three Candidates for His Tomb," in *KMT* vol. 14, #4.

Johnson, Sally 1990
The Cobra Goddess of Ancient Egypt. Kegan Paul International, London.

Johnson, W. Raymond 1991
"The Dazzling Sun Disk," in *KMT* vol. 2, #2.
— 1996
"Amenhotep III and Amarna: Some New Considerations," in *JEA* vol. 82.

Jordan, Paul 1998
Riddles of the Sphinx. New York University Press, New York.

Junker, Hermann 1912
Bericht über die Grabungen der Kaiserlichen Akadamie der Wissenschaften in Wien, auf dem Friedhof in Turah. Winter 1909-1910, in *DAWW* 56, Wien.

Kadry, Ahmed 1982
"Semenkhkare, the Ephemeral King," in *ASAE* vol. LXVIII.

Kahl, Jochem; Kloth, Nicole and Zimmermann, Ursula 1995
Die Inscriften der 3. Dynastie. Harrassowitz. Wiesbaden.

Kaiser, Werner 1964
"Einige Bemerkungen zur ägyptischen Früzeit," in *ZÄS* vol. 91.
— 1982 (with Gunter Dreyer)
"Umm el-Qaab. Nachuntersuchungen im frühzeitlichen Königsfriedhof 2. Vorbericht," in *MDAIK* vol. 38.

Kamal, Ahmed Bey 1912
"Fouilles à Dara et à Qoçéîr el-Amarna," in *ASAE* vol. XII.

Kanawati, Naguib 1984
    "New Evidence on the Reign of Userkare?" in *GM* vol. 83.
— 1990
    "Saqqara Excavations Shed New Light on Old Kingdom History," in *BACE* vol. 1.
— 2003
    Conspiracies in the Egyptian Palace: Unis to Pepi I, London.

Kaplony, Peter 1958
    "Sechs Königsnamen der I. Dynastie in neuer Deutung," in *Orientalia Suecana*, vol. 7.
— 1963
    Die Inschriften der Ägyptischen Frühzeit, vol. I-III. Wiesbaden.
— 1965
    "Eine Schminkpalette von König Skorpion aus Abu Umuri," in *Orientalia* vol. 34.
— 1968
    Steingefässe mit Inschriften der Frühzeit un des Alten Reichs. Fondation Égyptologique Reine Élisabeth. Brussels.
— 1973
    Beschriftete Kleinfunde in der Sammlung Georges Michailiidis, Istanbul.
— 1981
    Die Rollsiegel des Alten Reichs Vol IIA and IIB. Fondation Egyptologique Reine Elisabeth, Brussels.

Karkowski, Janusz 1981
    Faras V: The Pharaonic Inscriptions from Faras. Warsaw.

Kees, Hermann 1928
    Das Re-Heiligtum des Königs Ne-woser-re (Rathures). vol. III. Berlin.

Kemp, Barry J. 1966
    "Abydos and the Royal Tombs of the First Dynasty," in *JEA* vol. 52.
— 1967
    "The Egyptian 1st Dynasty Royal Cemetery," in *Antiquity*, vol. XLI.
— 1989
    Ancient Egypt: Anatomy of a Civilization. Routledge. London.

Kempiinski, Aaron 1985
    "Some Observations on the Hyksos (XV) Dynasty and its Canaaite Origins" in Sarah Israelit-Ghroll (ed.) *Pharaonic Egypt: The Bible and Christianity*, The Hebrew University, Jerusalem

Kitchen, Kenneth A. 1967
    "Byblos, Egypt, and Mari in the second millenium B.C.," in *Orentalia* vol. 36.
— 1972
    "Ramesses VII and the Twentieth Dynasty," in *JEA* vol. 58.

Bibliography

— 1982
Pharaoh Triumphant; The Life and Times of Ramesses II. Aris & Phillips Ltd. Wiltshire.
— 1984
"Family Relationships of Ramesses IX and the Late Twentieth Dynasty," in *SAK* vol. 11.
— 1987
"Amenmesses in Northern Egypt," in *GM* vol. 99.

Kozloff, Arielle P.; Bryan, Betsy M. and Berman, Lawrence M. 1992
Egypt's Dazzling Sun: Amenhotep III and His World. Cleveland Museum of Art.

Krauss, Rolf and Ullrich, Detlaf 1982
"Ein gläserner Dopplering aus Ägypten," in *Jahrbuch Preussischer Kulturbesitzungs* 19.

Krejcí, Jaromír 2000
"The origins and development of the royal necropolis at Abusir during the Old Kingdom," in Miroslav Barta and Jaromír Krejcí (eds) *Abusir and Saqqara in the Year 2000*. Prague.

Kuper, Rudolph and Förster, Frank 2003
"Khufu's 'mefat' Expeditions into the Libyan Desert" in *EA* #23.

Lacau, P. and Lauer, J.-PH. 1959
La Pyramide à Degrés, vol. IV, 1st Fascicule, IFAO.
— 1961
La Pyramide à Degrés, vol. IV, 2nd Fascicule, IFAO
— 1965
La Pyramide à Degrés, vol. V, IFAO.

Lacovara, Peter 1994
"In the Realm of the Sun King: Malkata, Palace City of Amenhotep III," in *Amarna Letters: Essays on Ancient Egypt* vol. Three. KMT Communications, San Francisco.

Lange, H.O. and Schäfer, H. 1908
Grab- und Denksteine Vols. I and II. Catalogue Général des Antiquités Égyptiennes du Musée du Caire; Cairo 1904/Berlin 1908.

Lauer, Jean-Philippe 1936-39
La Pyramide à Degrés, Vols. I-III, IFAO.
— 1976
Saqqara- The Royal Cemetery of Memphis: Excavation and Discoveries since 1850. Chas. Scribner's Sons. New York.

Leahy, Anthony 1989
"A Protective Measure at Abydos in the Thirteenth Dynasty" in *JEA* vol. 75.

Legge, F. 1904
"The Kings of Abydos," in *PSBA* vol. XXVI.
— 1906
"The Early Monarchy of Egypt," in *PSBA* vol. XXVIII.

Legrain, Georges 1903a
"Second rapport sur les travaux exécutés à Karnak," in *ASAE* vol. IV.
— 1903b
"Notes d'inspection," in *ASAE* vol. IV.
— 1905
"Notes d'inspection," in *ASAE* vol. VI.
— 1907
"Notes d'inspection," in *ASAE* vol. VIII.

Lehner, Mark 1985
The Pyramid Tomb of Hetep-heres and the Satellite Pyramid of Khufu. Von Zabern, Mainz.
— 1997
The Complete Pyramids. Thames and Hudson, N.Y.

Leprohon, Ronald J. 1980
The Reign of Amenemhet III. Unpublished thesis. University of Toronto.

Lesko, Leonard H. 1980
"The Wars of Rameses III," in *Serapis* #6.

Lichtheim, Miriam 1975
Ancient Egyptian Literature, vol. I. University of California Press, Los Angeles.
— 1976
Ancient Egyptian Literature, vol. II. University of California Press, Los Angeles.
— 1988
Ancient Egyptian Autobiographies, Chiefly of the Middle Kingdom. Göttingen.

Lilyquist, Christine 1995
Egyptian Stone Vessels, Khian through Tuthmosis IV. The Metropolitan Museum of Art. New York.

Loeben, Christian E. 1994
"No Evidence of Coregency: Two Erased Figures from Tutankhamen's Tomb," in *Amarna Letters* vol. Three. KMT Communications. San Francisco.

Lorton, David 1987
"The Internal History of the Herakleopolitan Period," in *DE* vol. 8.

Macadam, M.F. Laming 1946
"Gleanings from the Mankes Mss.," in *JEA* vol. 32.

Bibliography

— 1951
"A Royal Family of the Thirteenth Dynasty" in *JEA* vol. 37.

Mace, Arthur 1922
"A Group of Scarabs Found at Lisht," in *JEA* vol. 8.

Mackay, Ernest 1912
"The Cemeteries of Mazghuna," in W. M. F. Petrie, ed., *The Labyrinth, Gerzeh and Mazghuna*. London.

Magee, Diana 2001
"Teti," in` Donald B. Refford, ed., *The Oxford Encyclopedia of Ancient Egypt*. vol. 2. Oxford University Press. Oxford and New York.

Malaise, Michel 1981
"Inventaire des stèlés égyptiennes du Moyen Empire porteuse de representations divines," in *SAK* vol. 9.

Malek, Jaromír 1992
"The Annals of Amenemhet II," in *EA* #2.
— 2000
"Old-Kingdom rulers as 'local Saints' in the Memphite area during the Middle Kingdom," in Barta, Miroslav and Krejcí, Jaromír, eds., *Abusir and Saqqara in the Year 2000*. Prague.

Manassa, Colleen 2003
The Great Karnak Inscription of Merneptah: Grand Strategy in the 13Th Century BC. Yale Egyptological Studies 5. Yale.

Manuelian, Peter der 1987
Studies in the Reign of Amenophis II. Hildesheim.
— 1990/1991
"Boston at Giza. The Museum of Fine Arts Race Against Time in the Shadow of the Pyramids," in *KMT* vol. 1, #4.
— 2006
"The End of the Reign and the Accession of Amenhotep II," in Eric H. Cline & David O'Connor, eds., *Thutmose III, A New Biography*. Ann Arbor.

Maragioglio, Vito and Rinardi, Celeste 1967
L'Architettura delle Piramidi Menfite. Part VI. Rapallo, Italy.
— 1968
"Note sulla piramide di Ameny 'Aamu" in *Orientalia* vol. 38.

Marcus, Ezra 2002
"Early Seafaring and Maritime Activity in the Southern Levant from Prehistory through the Third Millennium BCE," in van den Brink, Edwin C.M. and Levy, Thomas E. (eds) *Egypt and the Levant: Interrelations from the 4th. through the Early 3rd. Millennium BCE*. Leicester University Press, London.

Mark, Samuel 1997
 From Egypt to Mesopotamia. Texas A&M University Press.

Martin, G.T. 1971
 Egyptian Administrative and Private Name Seals. Griffith Institute, Ashmolean Museum, Oxford.
— 1974
 The Royal Tomb at El-Amarna. vol. 1: *The Objects*. EES.
— 1989a
 The Royal Tomb at El-Amarna. vol. 2: *The Reliefs, Inscriptions and Architecture*. EES.
— 1989b
 The Memphite Tomb of Horemheb Commander-In-Chief of Tutankhamun. vol. I: *The Reliefs, Inscriptions, and Commentary*. EES.
— 1991
 The Hidden Tombs of Memphis, New Discoveries from the Time of Tutankhamun and Ramesses the Great. Thames and Hudson Ltd., London.

Maspero, Gaston 1902
 "Notes sur les objets recueilles sous la pyramide d'Ounas" in *ASAE* vol. III.

Matouk, Fouad S. 1972
 Corpus du Scarabée egyptien. vol. I l'Académie Libanaise, Beirut.

McIntyre, Glen V. 1990
 "Rameses III & the End of the Empire," in *KMT* vol. 1, #3.

Mellink, Mechthild J 1995
 "New Perspectives and Initiatives in the Hyksos Period," in *Ägypten und Levant* 5.

Meltzer, Edmund S. 1971
 "A Reconsideration of ⟨𓏏𓈖𓊃⟩," in *JEA* vol. 57.

Mey, P.; Castel, G. and Goyon, J.-P. 1980
 "Installations rupestres du Moyen et du Nouvel Empire au Gebel Zeit (près de Râs Dib) sur la Mer Rouge," *MDAIK* 36.

Meyer, Marvin W. 1983
 "Archaeological Survey of the Wadi Sheikh Ali December 1980," in *GM* 64.

Millet, N B. 1990
 "The Narmer Macehead and Related Objects" in *JARCE* vol. XXVII.

Mokhtar, Mohamed G. 1978
 Ihnasya El-Medina. IFAO.

BIBLIOGRAPHY

Montet, Pierre 1981
    Everyday Life in Egypt in the Days of Rameses the Great.
       Philadelphia.

Montserrat, Dominic 2000
    Akhenaten: History, Fantasy and Ancient Egypt. Rutledge.
       London.

Moran, William L. 1992
    The Amarna Letters. Johns Hopkins University Press. Baltimore
       and London.

Morkot, Robert G. 1990
    "NB-M3'T-'R'—United-with-Ptah," in *JNES* vol. 49, #4.

Murnane, William J. 1977
    Ancient Egyptian Coregencies. University of Chicago.
— 1981
    "The Sed Festival: A Problem in Historical Method," in *MDAIK*
       vol. 37.
— 1983
    The Guide to Ancient Egypt. Penguin Books Limited,
       Harmondsworth, England.
— 1995
    Texts from the Amarna Period in Egypt. Scholars Press, Atlanta.
— 2001
    "Coregency," in D.B. Redford, ed., *The Oxford Encyclopedia of*
       Ancient Egypt. vol. 1. Oxford University Press, New York
       and London.

Murray, Margaret 1903
    The Osireion at Abydos. BSAE 9. London.

Naville, Edouard H. 1891
    Bubastis (1887-1889). EEF.
— 1895-1908
    Temple of Deir el Bahari, The Vols. 1-7. EEF.
— 1907
    The XI Dynasty Temple at Deir El-Bahari. Part I. EEF.
— 1910
    The XI Dynasty Temple at Deir El-Bahari. Part II. EEF.

Newberry, Percy E. 1905
    "Extracts from My Notebooks VIII" in *PSBA*, vol. 27.
— 1906
    Scarabs. Archibald Constable and Co. LTD, London.
— 1907
    The Timmins Collection, London.
— 1909
    "Impressions on seals from Abydos," in *Annals of Archaeology*
       and Anthropology #2.
— 1912
    "King [hieroglyphs] of the Story of the Eloquent Peasant," in
       ZÄS Vol 50.

— 1913
"Notes on the Carnarvon Tablet No. I," in *PSBA* vol. 35.
— 1932
"King Ay, Successor of Tutankhamun," in *JEA* vol. 32.
— 1943
"Queen Nitocris of the Sixth Dynasty," in *JEA* vol. 29.

Newberry, Percy E. and Wainwright, George A. 1914
"King Udy-Mu (Den) and the Palermo Stone," in *Ancient Egypt*, Part IV.

O'Brien, Alexandra A. 1996
"The Serekh as an aspect of Iconography of Early Kingship," in *JARCE* vol. XXXIII.

Obsomer, Claude 1995
Sésostris Ier, Etude chronologique et historique du regne. Brussels.

Ockinga, Boyo 2000
"The Saqqara Tomb of the Overseer of Craftsmen and Chief Goldworker, Amenemone," in Miroslav Bárta and Jaromír Krejcí, eds., *Abusir and Saqqara in the Year 2000*. Prague.

O'Connor, David 1989
"New Funerary Enclosures (*Talbezirke*) of the Early Dynastic Period at Abydos," in *JARCE* vol. XXVI.
— 1991
"Boat Graves and Pyramid Origins,"in Expedition vol. 33 #3.
— 1995
"The Earliest Royal Boat Graves," in *EA* #6.

O'Connor, David and Cline, Eric H.,eds. 1998
Amenhotep III, Perspectives on His Reign. University of Michigan. AnnArbor.

O'Mara, Patrick F. 1979
The Palermo Stone and the Archaic Kings of Egypt. Paulette Publishing, La Canada.

Oppenheim, Adela 1995
"A First Look at Recently Discovered 12th. Dynasty Royal Jewelry from Dahshur," in *KMT* vol. 6, #1.

Pankhurst, Richard 1984
"Early Pharaonic Contacts with the Land of Punt," in *Quaderni Di Studi Etiopici*, #5.

Parkinson, R.B. 1991
Voices from Ancient Egypt: An Anthology of Middle Kingdom Writings. University of Oklahoma Press, Norman, Oklahoma.

Partridge, Robert B. 1994
Faces of Pharaohs. The Rubicon Press, London.

BIBLIOGRAPHY

— 2002
Fighting Pharaohs: Weapons and Warefare in Ancient Egypt. Peartree Publications. London.

Peden, A.J. 1989
"The Usurped Karnak Stela of Ramesses V," in *GM* vol. 110.
— 1994a
Egyptian Historical Inscriptions of the Twentieth Dynasty. Paul Aströms förlag. Jonsered, Sweden.
— 1994b
The Reign of Ramesses IV. Aris & Phillips Ltd. Warminster.
— 2001
The Graffiti of Pharaonic Egypt: Scope and Roles of Informal Writings (c. 3100 – 332 B.C.). Brill, Leiden.

Peet, T. Eric 1925
"A Possible Year Date of King Ramesses VII," in *JEA* vol. 11.
— 1930
The Great Tomb-Robberies of the Twentieth Egyptian Dynasty. vol. I. Oxford.

Peet, T.E.; Woolley, C.L.; Frankfort, H.; Pendlebury, J.D.S. 1961
The City of Akhenaten. Parts I-III. EES. London.

Perepelkin, G. 1978
The Secret of the Gold Coffin. "Nauka" Publishing House, Moscow.

Petrie, W. M. F. 1885
Tanis I, EEF, London.
— 1888
Tanis II, EEF, London.
— 1889
Historical Scarabs.
— 1890
Kahun, Gurob, and Hawara, London.
— 1891
Illahun, Kahun and Gurob, EEF, London.
— 1894
Tell El Amarna. Methuen & Co. London.
— 1896a
Naqada and Ballas, EEF, London.
— 1896b
Koptos, Bernard Quaritch, London.
— 1897
Six Temples at Thebes 1896, Bernard Quaritch, London.
— 1900
The Royal Tombs of the First Dynasty, Part I. EEF, London.
— 1901a
The Royal Tombs of the Earliest Dynasties, Part II. EEF, London.
— 1901b
Diospolis Parva: The Cemeteries of Abadiyeh and Hu 1898-9. EEF, London.

— 1902a
>   *A History of Egypt.* vol. I. Reprint of the fifth edition. Ayer Co., 1989.
— 1902b
>   *Abydos I*. EES, London.
— 1903
>   *Abydos II*. EES, London.
— 1905
>   "The Early Monarchy of Egypt," in *PSBA* vol. XXVII.
— 1906a
>   *Hyksos and Israelite Cities*. BSAE 12, London.
— 1906b
>   *Researches in Sinai*. John Murray, London.
— 1907
>   *Gizeh and Rifeh*, BSAE, London.
— 1909
>   *Qurneh*. BSAE, London.
— 1912
>   *The Labyrinth, Gerzeh and Mazgumeh*. BSAE, London.
— 1913
>   *Tarkhan I and Memphis V*. Bernard Quaritch, London.
— 1914
>   *Tarkhan II*. Bernard Quaritch, London.
— 1924
>   *A History of Egypt.* 3 volumes. Methuen and Co. Ltd., London.
— 1925a
>   *Tombs of the Courtiers and Oxyrhynkhos*. Quaritch, London.
— 1925b
>   *Buttons and Design Scarabs*. BSAE 38, London.
— 1933
>   "Rare Scarabs" in *Ancient Egypt*, Part 1.
— 1952
>   *City of the Shepherd Kings and Ancient Gaza V*. Bernard Quaritch, London.
— 1978
>   *Scarabs and Cylinders with Names*, Aris & Phillips, Ltd. (Reprint of the 1917 edition originally published by BSAE).

Petty, William 1997
>   "Hatshepsut & Thutmose II Reconsidered: Some Thoughts on the Nature of Their Relationship," in *KMT* vol. 8, #1.
— 2000
>   "Some Problems with the Reign of Thutmose III," in *KMT* vol 11, #1.
— 2002/2003
>   "Redating the Reign of Hatshepsut," in *KMT* Vol 13, #4.

Pinches, Theophilus G. and Newberry. Percy E. 1921
>   "A Cylinder-Seal Inscribed in Hieroglyphic and Cuneiform in the Collection of the Earl of Carnarvon," in *JEA* 7.

Polz, Daniel 1995
>   "The Location of the Tomb of Amenhotep I: A Reconsideration," in Richard H. Wilkinson, ed., *Valley of*

the Sun Kings. New Explorations in the Valley of the Kings. University of Arizona Egyptian Expedition.
— 2001
"Thebes," in Donald B. Redford, ed., *The Oxford Encyclopedia of Ancient Egypt*, vol. 3. Oxford.
— 2003
"The pyramid complex of Nubkheperre Intef," in *EA* #22.

Polz, Daniel and Seiler, Anne 2003
Die Pyramidenanlage des Königs Nub-Cheper-Re Intef in Dra' el-Naga. Philipp von Zabern, Mainz.

Posener-Kriéger, Paule 1991
"Quelques pièces du matériel cultuel du temple funéraire de Rêneferef," in *MDAIK* vol. 47.

Quibell, James 1898
El Kab. EES.
— 1908
The Tomb of Yuaa and Thuiu. IFAO.
— 1909
Excavations at Saqqara (1907-1908). IFAO.
— 1923
Excavations at Saqqara (1912-1914): Archaic Mastabas. IFAO.
— 1934
"Stone Vessels from the Step Pyramid," in *ASAE* vol. XXXIV.

Quibell, James E. and Green, F.W. 1902
Hierakonpolis II. Egyptian Research Account, Fifth Memoir, London.

Quibell, James E. and Petrie, W.M.F. 1900
Hierakonpolis I. Egyptian Research Account, Fourth Memoir, London.

Quirke, Stephen 1986
An Investigation into Problems of Thirteenth Dynasty Kingship with Special Reference to Papyrus Boulaq 18. Unpublished dissertation, Cambridge University.
— 1990
Who were the Pharaohs? Dover Publications, Inc., N.Y.
— 1991
"Royal Power in the 13th Dynasty," in Stephen Quirke (ed.) *Middle Kingdom Studies*. Sia Publishing, Surrey.
— 1992
Ancient Egyptian Religion, Dover Publications, N.Y.
— 2001a
"Second Intermediate Period," in Donald B. Redford (ed.) *The Oxford Encyclodedia of Ancient Egypt*, vol. 3. Oxford University Press, Oxford and New York.
— 2001b
The Cult of Ra. Sun-Worship in Ancient Egypt. Thames and Hudson, New York.

Randall-MacIver, D. 1902
   El Amrah and Abydos. EEF, London.

Randall-MacIver, D. and Woolley, C. Leonard 1911
   Buhen. Philadelphia.

Ratié, Suzanne 1979
   La Reine Hatchepsout; sources et problèmes. Leyden.

Redford, Donald B. 1965
   "The Coregency of Tuthmosis III and Amenophis II," in *JEA* vol. 51.
— 1967
   History and Chronology of the Eighteenth Dynasty of Egypt: Seven Studies. Toronto.
— 1974
   "A New Dated Inscription from the Reign of Horemheb," in *JSSEA* vol. 4.
— 1984
   Akhenaten: The Heretic Pharaoh. Princeton University Press, Princeton.
— 1986
   Pharaonic King-Lists, Annals and Day-Books. Benben Publications, Mississauga.
— 1992
   Egypt, Canaan, and Israel in Ancient Times. Princeton University Press, Princeton.
— 1997
   "Textual Sources for the Hyksos Period," in Oren, Eliezer D. (ed.) *The Hyksos: New Historical and Archaeological Perspectives*. University of Pennsylvania.
— 2003
   The Wars in Syria and Palestine of Thutmose III, Brill, Leiden and Boston.

Redford, Donald B. (Ed.) 2001
   The Oxford Encyclopedia of Ancient Egypt, Oxford University Press, Oxford.

Redford, Susan 2002
   The Harem Conspiracy: The Murder of Ramesses III, Northern Illinois University Press, Dekalb.

Reeves, N. 1986
   "Miscellanea Epigraphica," in *SAK* vol. 13.
   1988
   "New Light on Kiya from Texts in the British Museum," in *JEA* vol. 74.
— 1990a
   The Complete Tutankhamun. Thames and Hudson, London.
— 1990b
   Valley of the Kings, The Decline of a Royal Necropolis. Kegan Paul International.

BIBLIOGRAPHY

— 2000
>*Ancient Egypt: The Great Discoveries.* Thames and Hudson, London.

— 2001
>*Akhenaten, Egypt's False Prophet.* Thames & Hudson, London and New York.

Reeves, N. and Wilkinson, Richard 1996
>*The Complete Valley of the Kings.* Thames and Hudson, London.

Reisner, George A. 1931
>*Mycerinus.* Harvard University Press, Cambridge, Massachusetts.

— 1942
>*A History of the Giza Necropolis vol. I.* Harvard University Press, Cambridge, Massachusetts.

— 1955
>*A History of the Giza Necropolis vol. II.* Harvard University Press, Cambridge, Massachusetts.

Rice, Michael 1990
>*Egypt's Making.* Routledge, N.Y.

— 1999
>*Who's Who in Ancient Egypt.* Routledge, London.

Ricke, Herbert 1965
>*Das Sonnenheiligtum des Königs Userkaf.* vol. I, Cairo.

— 1969
>*Das Sonnenheiligtum des Königs Userkaf.* vol. II, Wiesbaden.

Ridley, R.T. 1973
>*The Unification of Egypt.* Shield Press, Deception Bay, Australia.

Robbins, Gay 1999
>"The Names of Hatshepsut," in *JEA* vol. 85.

Romer, John 1981
>*Valley of the Kings.* Henry Holt and Company, N.Y.

Rose, John 1985
>*The Sons of Re: Cartouches of the Kings of Egypt,* JR-T, Cheshire, England.

Rose, Mark 2002
>"King Scorpion: A Pretty Bad Dude" in *Archaeology*, May/June 2002.

— 2003
>"*Mystery Mummy*," in *Archaeology*, March/April 2003.

Rothe, Russel D.; Rapp Jr., George; and Miller, William K. 1996
>"New Hieroglyphic Evidence for Pharaonic Activity in the Eastern Desert of Egypt," in *JARCE* vol. XXXIII.

Rothenberg, Beno 1979
    Sinai: Pharaonen, Bergleute, Pilger und Soldaten. Kümmerly + Frey, Bern.

Rowe, Alan 1936
    A Catalogue of Egyptian Scarabs. IFAO, Cairo.

Ryan, Donald P. 1990
    "Who is Buried in KV60?." In *KMT* vol. 1, #1.

Ryholt, K.S.B. 1997a
    The Political Situation in Egypt during the Second Intermediate Period, Carsten Niebuhr Publications, vol. 20. Museum Tusculanum Press, University of Copenhagen.
— 1997b
    "A Bead of King Ranisonb and a Note on King Qemaw," in *GM* vol. 156.
— 1998a
    "King Qareh, A Canaanite King of Egypt during the Second Intermediate Period" in *IEJ* vol. 48.
— 1998b
    "Hotepibre, a Supposed Asiatic King in Egypt with Relations to Ebla," in *BASOR* vol. 311.
— 2000
    "The Late Kingdom in the Turin King-list and the Identity of Nitocris," in Zäs vol. 127.

Rzepka, Slawomir 2000
    "A recarved Old Kingdom statue. Some observations on the statue of *ꜣhj-Jp* (CG44)," in Miroslav Bárta and Jaromír Krejcí, eds., *Abusir and Saqqara in the Year 2000*. Prague.

Saad, Zaki Y. 1951
    Royal Excavations at Helwan, IFAO.
— 1969
    The Excavations at Helwan. University of Oklahoma Press, Norman, Oklahoma.

Sadek, Ashraf I. 1980
    The Amethyst Mining Inscriptions of Wadi el-Hudi Part I, Aris & Phillips, Warminster.
— 1985
    The Amethyst Mining Inscriptions of Wadi el-Hudi Part II, Aris & Phillips, Warminster.

Samson, Julia 1978
    Amarna, City of Akhenaten and Nefertiti. Aris & Phillips Ltd., Warminster.

— 1982
    "Neferneferuaten-Nefertiti "Beloved of Akhenaten," Ankhkheperure Neferneferuaten "Beloved of Akhenaten," Ankhkheperure Smenkhkare "Beloved of Aten," in *GM* vol. 57.

Bibliography

Sanchez, Gonzalo M. 2003
"Injuries in the Battle of Kadesh," in *KMT* vol. 14, #1.

Sayce, A.H. 1899a
"A New Egyptian King; The Predecessor of Kheops," in *PSBA* vol. XXI.
— 1899b
"Some Old Empire Inscriptions from El-Kab," in *PSBA* vol. XXI.
— 1904
"The Egyptian King Sharu, or Soris," in *PSBA* vol. XXVI.

Schaden, Otto J. 1992
"The God's Father Ay," in *Amarna Letters* vol. 2. KMT Communications, San Francisco.
— 1994
"Some Observations on the Tomb of Amenmesse (KV-10)," in Bryan, Betsy, and Lorton, David, eds., Essays in Egyptology in Honor of Hans Goedicke. Van Siclen, San Antonio.
— 2000
"Paintings in the Tomb of King Ay (WV23)," in *Amarna Letters* vol. 4. KMT Communications, Sebastopol, California.

Schäfer, Heinrich 1902
Ein Bruchstück altägyptischer Annalen. Berlin.

Schmidt, John D. 1973
Ramesses II. A Chronological Structure for His Reign. Johns Hopkins. Baltimore and London.

Schmitz, B. 1977
"Bemerkungen zu einigen Königlichen Geschenken," in *SAK* vol. 5.

Schmitz, Franz-Jürgen 1978
Amenophis I. Versuch einer Darstellung der Regierungszeit eines ägyptischen Herrschers der frühen 18. Dynastie. Hildesheim.

Schulman, A.R. 1983
"On the Dating of Egyptian Seal Impressions from 'En Besor," in *JSSEA* 13.

Schulz, Regine and Seidel, Matthias, editors. (date not given)
Egypt: The World of the Pharaohs. Könemann.

Seidlmayer, Stephan J. 1988
"Stadt und Tempel von Elephantine. 15./16. Grabungsbericht," IX Ausgewählte Einzelfunde, in *MDAIK* vol. 44.
— 2000
"The First Intermediate Period in Egypt (c. 2160-2055 B.C.)," in Ian Shaw (ed.), *The Oxford History of Ancient Egypt*. Oxford.

Sethe, Kurt 1897
>   "Die ältesten geschichtlichen Denkmäler der Agypter" in *ZÄS* vol. XXXV.
— 1933
>   *Urkunden Des Alten Reichs* vol. II. Leipzig.

Seyfried, K-J. 1984
>   *Beiträge zu den Expeditionen des Mittleren Reichs in die Ost-Wüste.* HAB 15. Hildersheim.

Sharp, David 2001
>   "Funerary Enclosures: Early Dynastic 'Forts' Re-Examined," in *KMT* vol.12, #1.

Shaw, Ian and Nicholson, Paul 1995
>   *The Dictionary of Ancient Egypt.* British Museum Press, London.

Siliotti, Alberto 1996
>   *Guide to the Valley of the Kings.* Barnes and Noble, New York.
— 1997
>   *Guide to the Pyramids of Egypt.* Barnes and Noble, New York.

Simpson, William Kelly 1956
>   "A Statuette of King Nyneter," in *JEA* vol. 42.
— 1969
>   "The Dynasty XIII Stela from the Wadi Hammamat," *MDAIK* vol. 25.
— 1974
>   *The Terrace of the Great God at Abydos: The Offering Chapels of Dynasties 12 and 13.* Yale University and University of Pennsylvania. Newhaven and Philadelphia.

Smith, G. Elliot 1912
>   *The Royal Mummies.* IFAO.

Smith, H.S. 1976
>   *The Fortress of Buhen. The Inscriptions.* EES Memoir, 48. London.

Smith, M. 1980
>   "A Second Dynasty King in a Demotic Papyrus of the Roman Period," in *JEA* vol. 66.

Smith, Stuart Tyson 1991
>   "*Askut and the Role of the Second Cataract Forts,*" in *JARCE*, vol. XXVII.

— 1995
>   *Askut in Nubia: The Economic and Ideology of Egyptian Imperialism in the Second Millenium B.C.,* Kegan Paul International, London and New York.

Smith, W. Stevenson 1971
>   "The Old Kingdom in Egypt and the Beginning of the First Intermediate Period" in *CAH* vol. I, Part 2, Chapter XIV.

Bibliography

— 1981
The Art and Architecture of Ancient Egypt. 2nd. Revised edition with additions by W.K. Simpson. Yale University Press.

Smolarikova, Kveta 2000
"The Greek Cemetery at Abusir," in Miroslav Bárta and Jaromír Krejcí, (eds.) *Abusir in the Year 2000.* Prague.

Soliman, Isabella and Johnson, George B. 1994
"KV43: The Tomb of Thutmose IV," in *KMT* vol. 5, #1.

Sotheby's (Auctioneers) 1988
Darius. 12th December, 1988. London.

Sourouzian, Hourig 1989
Les Monuments du roi Merenptah. Philipp von Zabern, Mainz am Rhein.

Spalinger, Anthony J. 1994
"Dated Texts of the Old Kingdom," in *SAK* vol. 21.
— 2005
War in Ancient Egypt. Blackwell Publishing, Oxford.

Spencer, A.J. 1993
Early Egypt: The Rise of Civilisation in the Nile Valley. British Museum Press, London.

Stadelmann, Rainer 1985
"Die Oberbauten der Königsgräber der 2. Dynastie in Saqqara," in *Melanges Gamal Eddin Mokhtar* vol. II, IFAO.
— 2000
"Userkaf in Saqqara und Abusir. Untersuchungen zur Thronfolge in der 4. Und frühen 5. Dynastie," in Miroslav Bárta and Jaromír Krejcí, eds, *Abusir and Saqqara in the Year 2000.* Prague.
— 2001a
"Old Kingdom: Fourth Dynasty," in Donald B. Redford, ed., *The Oxford Encyclopedia of Ancient Egypt.*, vol. 3, Oxford.

— 2001b
"Sphinx," in Donald B. Redford, ed., *The Oxford Encyclopedia of Ancient Egypt.*, vol. 3. Oxford.

Stewart, H.M. 1979
Egyptian Stelae, Reliefs and Paintings from the Petrie Collection. vol. II. Warminster.
— 1983
Egyptian Stelae, Reliefs and Paintings from the Petrie Collection. vol. III. Warminster.

Stone, Mark C. 1997
"Reading the Highest Attested Regnal Year Date for Senwosret II: Stela Cairo JE59485," in *GM* vol. 159.

Strouhal, Eugen and Callender, Gae 1992
"A Profile of Queen Mutnodjmet," in *BACE* vol. 3.

Strouhal, Eugen; Fawzi Baballah, M.; Bonani, G.; Woelfli, W.; Nemeckova, A. and Saunders, S. 1998
"Re-investigation of the Remains Thought to be of King Djoser and those of an Unidentified Female from the Step Pyramid at Saqqara," in C.J. Eyre (ed.), *Proceedings of the Seventh International Congress of Egyptologists*. Uitgeverij Peeters, Leuven.

— 2003
"Three Mummies from the Royal Cemetery at Abusir," in Zahi Hawass and Lyla Pinch Brock (eds) *Egyptology at the Dawn of the Twenty-first Dynasty*. American University in Cairo Press.

Strouhal, Eugen and Gaballah, Mohammad Fawzi 1993
"King Djedkare Isesi and His Daughters," in W. Vivian Davies and Roxie Walker (eds) *Biological Anthropology and the Study of Ancient Egypt*. British Museum Press, London.

Strouhal, Eugen and Vyhnánek, Lubos 2000
"The identification of the remains of King Neferefra found in his pyramid at Abusir," in Miroslav Bárta and Jaromeír Krejcí (eds) *Abusir and Saqqara in the Year 2000*. Prague.

Strudwick, Nigel and Helen 1999
Thebes in Egypt. A Guide to the Tombs and Temples of Ancient Luxor. Cornell University Press, Ithaca, N.Y.

Swelim, Nabil M.A. 1974
Horus Seneferka, an essay on the fall of the First Dynasty. Archaeological & Historical Studes 5, The Archaeological Society of Alexandria, Alexandria.

— 1983
Some Problems on the History of the Third Dynasty. The Archaeological Society of Alexandria, Alexandria.

— 1987
The Brick Pyramid at Abu Rowash, Number '1' by Lepsius: A Preliminary Study. The Archaeological Society of Alexandria, Alexandria.

Swelim, Nabil M.A. and Dodson, Aidan 1998
"On the Pyramid of Ameny-Qemau and its Canopic Equipment," in *ZÄS* vol. 54.

Taylor, John H. 1991
Egypt and Nubia. Harvard University Press, Cambridge, Mass.

Teeter, Emily 1990
"Hatshepsut," in *KMT* vol. 1, #1.

Tefnin, Roland 1979
> *La statuaire d'Hatshepsout, Portrait royal et politique sous la 18e Dynastie*. Momumenta Aegyptiaca, Vol 4. Brussels.

Thomas, Angela 1994
> "The Other Woman at Akhetaten, Royal Wife Kiya," in *Amarna Letters* vol. 3. KMT Communications, San Francisco.

Tidyman, Richard A.J. 1995
> "Further Evidence of a Coup d'Etat at the End of Dynasty 11?," in *BACE* vol. 6.

Trad, May and Mahmoud, Adel 1995
> "Amenhotep III in the Egyptian Museum, Cairo," in *KMT* vol. 6, #3.

Trigger, Bruce G. 1976
> *Nubia Under the Pharaohs*. Boulder, Colarado.

Trope, Betsy Teasley and Lacovara, Peter 2003
> "A Pharaoh in Atlanta? The Michael C. Carlos Museum Royal Mummy is Probably Rameses I," in *KMT* vol. 14, #2.

Troy, Lana 1986
> *Patterns of Queenship in Ancient Egyptian Myth and History*. Acta Universitatis Upsaliensis. Boreas. Uppsala Studies in Ancient Mediterranean and Near Eastern Civilization 14, Uppsala.

Tufnell, Olga 1984
> *Studies on Scarab Seals*, vol. II, Aris & Phillips, Warminster.

Tulhoff, Angelika 1984
> *Thutmosis III*. Callwey, Munich.

Tyldesley, Joyce 1996
> *Hatchepsut, The Female Pharaoh*. Viking. London.

— 1998
> *Nefertiti, Egypt's Sun Queen*. Viking. New York.

— 2000
> *Ramesses, Egypt's Greatest Pharaoh*. Penguin. New York and London.

— 2006
> *Chronicle of the Queens of Egypt*. Thames & Hudson. London.

Uphill, Eric P. 1984
> "The Sequence of Kings for the First Dynasty" in *Studien zu Sprache und Religion*. Festschrift W. Westendorf, Gottingen.

— 2000
> *Pharaoh's Gateway to Eternity. The Hawara Labrynth of King Amenemhet III*. Kegan Paul International. NY.

Valbelle, Dominique and Bonnet, Chas. 1996
Le sanctuaire d'Hathor, maîtresse de la turquoise Sérabit el-Khadim au Moyen Empire. Picard Editeur, Paris.

Valloggia, Michael 2003
"Radjedef's pyramid complex at Abu Rawash." in *EA* vol. 23.

van den Brink, Edwin C. M. 1992
"Preliminary Report on the Excavations at Tell Ibrahim Awad, Seasons 1988-1990" in Edwin C.M. van den Brink, ed., *The Nile Delta in Transition 4TH. -3RD. Millennium B.C.*, Tel Aviv.

— 1996
"The incised serekh-signs of Dynasties 0-1, Part One: Complete Vessels," in Jeffery Spencer, ed., *Aspects of Early Egypt*, London.

van den Brink, Edwin C. M. and Braun, Eliot 2002
"Wine Jars with Serekhs from Early Bronze Lod: Appelation Vallée du Nil Contrôlée, but for Whom?" in C.M. van den Brink and Eli Yannai, eds., *In Quest of Ancient Settlements and Landscapes*, Tel Aviv.

Vandersleyen, C. 1971
Les guerres d'Amosis. Brussels.
— 1993
"Rahotep, Sébekemsaf Ier et Djéhouti, rois de la 13e Dynastie," in *RdÉ*, vol. 44.

Vandier, Jacques 1968
"Une stèle égyptienne portant un nouveau nom royal de la troisième dynastie" in *CRAIBL* 1968.

van Dijk, Jacobus 1996
"Horemheb and the Struggle for the Throne of Tutankhamun," in *BACE* vol. 7.
— 2000
"The Amarna Period and the Later New Kingdom," in Ian Shaw, ed., *The Oxford History of Ancient Egypt*. Oxford.

van Siclen III, Charles C. 1989
"New Data on the Date of the Defacement of Hatshepsut's Name and Image on the Chapelle Rouge," in *GM* vol. 107.

Vassilika, Eleni 1995
"Museum Acquisitions, 1993" in *JEA* vol. 81.

Velikovsky, Immanuel 1960
Oedipus and Akhnaton. Doubleday, New York.

Ventura, Raphael 1983
"More Chronological Evidence from Turin Papyrus Cat. 1907 + 1908," in *JNES* vol. 42, #4.

Bibliography

— 1985
"Snefru in Sinai and Amenophis I at Deir el-Medina," in Israel-Groll, Sarah, ed., *Pharaonic Egypt, the Bible and Christianity*. Jerusalem.

Verbrugghe, Gerald P. and Wickersham, John M. 1996
Berossos and Manetho, Introduced and Translated. University of Michigan Press, Ann Arbor.

Vercoutter, J. 1975
"Le roi Ougaf et la XIIIe Dynastie sur la Iime Cataracte" in *Rd'E* vol. 27.

Verner, Miroslav 1991
"Remarks on the Pyramid of Neferirkare," in *MDAIK* vol. 47.
— 1994
Forgotten Pharaohs, Lost Pyramids. Abusir. Academia Skodaexport, Prague.
— 1995
Abusir III. The Pyramid Complex of Khentkaus. Universitas Carolina Academia, Prague.
— 1997
The Pyramids. Grove Press, N.Y.
— 2000a
"Newly discovered royal sarcophagi from Abusir," in Miroslav Bárta and Jaromír Krejčí (eds), *Abusir and Saqqara in the Year 2000*. Prague.
— 2000b
"Who was Shepseskara and when did he reign?" in Miroslav Bárta and Jaromír Krejčí (eds), *Abusir and Saqqara in the Year 2000*. Prague.
— 2001a
"Pyramid," in Donald B. Redford, ed., *The Oxford Encyclopedia of Ancient Egypt*, vol. 3, Oxford.
— 2001b
"Old Kingdom: An Overview," in Donald B. Redford, ed., *The Oxford Encyclopedia of Ancient Egypt*, vol.2, Oxford.
— 2002
Abusir. Realm of Osiris. The American University in Cairo Press. Cairo.

Verner, Miroslav and Callender, Gae 1997
"Image and Reflection: Two Old Kingdom Queens Named Khentkaus," in *KMT* vol. 8, #3.

Vernus, Pascal 1989a
"La Stèle du roi Sekhemsankhtaouyrê Neferhotep Iykhernofert et la domination Hyksôs (Stèle Cairo JE59635) (avec une planche)," in *ASAE* vol. MCMLXXXIX.

— 1989b
"La stèle du pharaon *Mntw-ḥtpi* à Karnak," in *Rd'E* vol. 40.
— 1990
"À propos de la stèle du pharaon *Mntw-ḥtpi*," in *Rd'E* vol. 41.

Vittmann, Günther 1974
"Was there a coregency of Ahmose with Amenophis I?," in *JEA* vol. 60.

von Beckerath, Jürgen 1962
"Queen Twosre as Guardian of Siptah," in *JEA* vol. 48.
— 1963
"Ein neuer König des späten Mittleren Reiches" in *ZÄS* vol. 88.
— 1964
Untersuchungen zur politischen Geschicte der Zweiten Zwischenzeit in Ägypten. Glückstadt.
— 1984
Handbuch der ägyptische Königsnamen. Müncher Ägyptologische Studien 20, Mainz.
— 1997
Chronologie des pharaonischen Ägypten. Die Zeithestimmung der ägyptischen Geschicte von der Vorzeit bis 333 v. Chr. Mainz.
— 1999
Handbuch der ägyptische Königsnamen Müncher. Ägyptologische Studien 49, Mainz.

von Bissing, Fredrick W. 1905
Das Re-Heiligtum des Königs Ne-woser-re (Rathures). vol. I. Berlin.

von Bissing, Fr. W. and Kees, Herman 1913
"Vom Wadi Es S'aba Rigale bei Beiträgen Gebel Silsile," in *Sitzungsberichte der Königlich Bayerischen Akademie der Wissenschaftenn*, #10.
— 1923
Das Re-Heiligtum des Königs Ne-Woser-Re (Rathures). vol. II. Berlin.

von der Way, Thomas 1993
Untersuchungen zur Spätvor- und Frügeschichte Unterägyptens. Studien zur Archäologie und Geschichte Altägyptens: Bd. 8. Heidelberg.

von Falck, Martin et al. 1985
"Neufunde ergäzen Königsnamen eines Herrschers der 2. Zwischenzeit," in *GM* Vol 87.

Vörös, Győző 1998
Temple on the Pyramid of Thebes. Hungarian Excavations on Thoth Hill at the Temple of Pharaoh Montuhotep Sankhkara 1995-1998. Százszorszép Kiadó és Nyomda Ltd., Budapest.
— 2003
"The Ancient Nest of Horus above Thebes: Hungarian Excavations on Thoth Hill at the Temple of King Sankhkare Montuhotep III (1995 – 1998)," in Hawass, Zahi and Brock, Lyla Pinch, eds., *Egyptology at the Dawn of the 21st. Century*, vol. 1. American University in Cairo Press, Cairo.

Waddell, W.G. 1940
   Manetho. Loeb Classical Library. Harvard University Press, Cambridge, Mass.

Ward, William A. 1970
   "The Origin of Egyptian Design-Amulets," in *JEA* vol. 56.
— 1978
   Studies on Scarab Seals. vol. I. Warminster.

Watterson, Barbara 1999
   Amarna: Ancient Egypt's Age of Revolution. Tempus, Gloucestershire.

Weeks, Kent R. 1992
   "The Theban Mapping Project and Work in KV 5," in Reeves, C.N., ed., *After Tutankhamun. Research and excavation in the Royal Necropolis at Thebes.* Kegan Paul International, London and New York.
— 1998
   The Lost Tomb. The Greatest Discovery in the Valley of the Kings Since Tutankhamun. Weidenfeld & Nicolson, London.
— 2001
   "Tombs," in Donald B. Redford, ed., *Oxford Encyclopedia of Ancient Egypt.* vol. 3. Oxford.

Wegner, Josef W. 1995
   "Old & New Excavations at the Abydene Complex of Senwosret III," in *KMT* vol. 6, #2.
— 1996
   "The Nature and Chronology of the Senwosret III-Amenemhat III Regnal Succession: Some Considerations Based on New Evidence from the Mortuary Temple of Senwosret III at Abydos," in *JNES* vol. 55, #4.

Weigall, Arthur E.P. 1907
   A Report on the Antiquities of Lower Nubia (The First Cataract to the Sudan Frontier) and Their Condition in 1906-7. Oxford.
— 1908
   "Upper Egyptian Notes," in *ASAE* vol. IX.
— 1925
   A History of the Pharaohs. vol. I. Thornton Butterworth, Ltd. London.
— 1927
   A History of the Pharaohs. vol. II. Thornton Butterworth, Ltd. London.

Weill, Raymond 1908
   Les origines de l'Égypte pharaonique, I, la IIe et la IIIe Dynasties. Paris.
— 1961
   Recherches sur la Ier Dynastie et les Temps Prépharaoniques. IFAO, Cairo.

Welsh, Frances 1993
Tutankhamun's Egypt. Shire Egyptology Series. Buchinghamshire, UK.

Wente, Edward F. 1963
"Two Ramesside Stelas Pertaining to the Cult of Amenophis I," in *JNES* vol. 22.
— 1980
"Age at Death of Pharaohs of the New Kingdom, Determined from Historical Sources," in Jas. E. Harris and Edward F. Wente, eds., *An X-Ray Atlas of the Royal Mummies.* Chicago.

Wild, Henri 1951
"A Bas-Relief of SekhemRe'-Sewadjtowe Sebkhotpe from Sehel," in *JEA* vol. 37.

Wilkinson, Richard H. 2000
The Complete Temples of Ancient Egypt. Thames & Hudson, New York.
— 2003
The Complete Gods and Goddesses of Ancient Egypt. Thames & Hudson. New York.

Wilkinson, Toby A.H. 1993
"The identification of Tomb B1 at Abydos: refuting the existence of a king Ro/Iry-Hor," in *JEA* vol. 79.
— 1995
"A New King in the Western Desert" in *JEA* vol. 81.
— 1999
Early Dynastic Egypt. Routledge, London and New York.
— 2000
Royal Annals of Ancient Egypt. The Palermo Stone and its associated fragments. Kegan Paul International, London and New York.

Willems, H.O. 1984
"A Second Look at the Reconstruction of Two Festival Gates from the Middle Kingdom," in *JSSEA* vol. XIV.

Williams, Bruce Beyer 1980
"The Lost Pharaohs of Nubia," in *Archaeology* vol. 33.
— 1986
Excavations between Abu Simbel and the Sudan Frontier, Keith C. Seele, Director. Part 1: The A-Group Royal Cemetery at Qustul: Cemetery L. Oriental Institute Nubian Expedition, vol. III. Chicago.
— 1987
"Forebearers of Menes in Nubia," in *JNES* vol. 46.

Willoughby, Karin L. 1988 (with Elizabeth B. Stanton)
The First Egyptians. The McKissick Museum, University of South Carolina.

Bibliography

Wilson, J.A. 1941
"The Egyptian Middle Kingdom at Megiddo," in *AJSL* vol. 58.

Winkler, Hans A. 1938
Rock Drawings of Southern Upper Egypt. EES, London.

Winlock, Herbert E. 1924
"The Tombs of the Kings of the Seventeenth Dynasty at Thebes," in *JEA* vol. 10.
— 1937
The Temple of Rameses I at Abydos. MMA.NY
— 1942
Excavations at Deir el Bahri 1911-1931. New York.
— 1947
The Rise and Fall of the Middle Kingdom in Thebes. Macmillan, New York.

Yeivin, S. 1959
"Ya'qob'el" in *JEA* vol. 45.

Yoyotte, Jean 1957
"Le Soukhos de la Maréotide," in *BIFAO* vol. 56
— 1989
"Le Roi Mer-djefa-Rê et le Dieu Sopdou," in *BSFE* vol. 114.

Yurco, Frank J. 1998
"Narmer: First King of Upper and Lower Egypt. A Reconsideration of his Palette and Macehead," in *JSSEA* vol. XXV.

Zaba, Zbynek 1974
Rock Inscriptions of Lower Nubia (Czechoslovak Concession). Czechoslovak Institute of Egyptology, Prague.

Ziegler, Christiane 1990
Catalogue des stèles, peintures et reliefs égyptiens de l'Ancien Empire et de la Première Période Intermédiaire. Paris.

Zuhdi, Omar 1997/1998
"Reassessing Rameses II at Kadesh," in *KMT* vol. 8, #4.
— 2000/2001
"A Tale of Two Ahmoses, or How to Begin an Empire," in *KMT* vol. 11, #4.
— 2001/2002
"Imperial Twilight: End of the Egyptian New Kingdom in Syria-Palestine," in *KMT* vol. 12, #4.

Index: Alphabetical King List

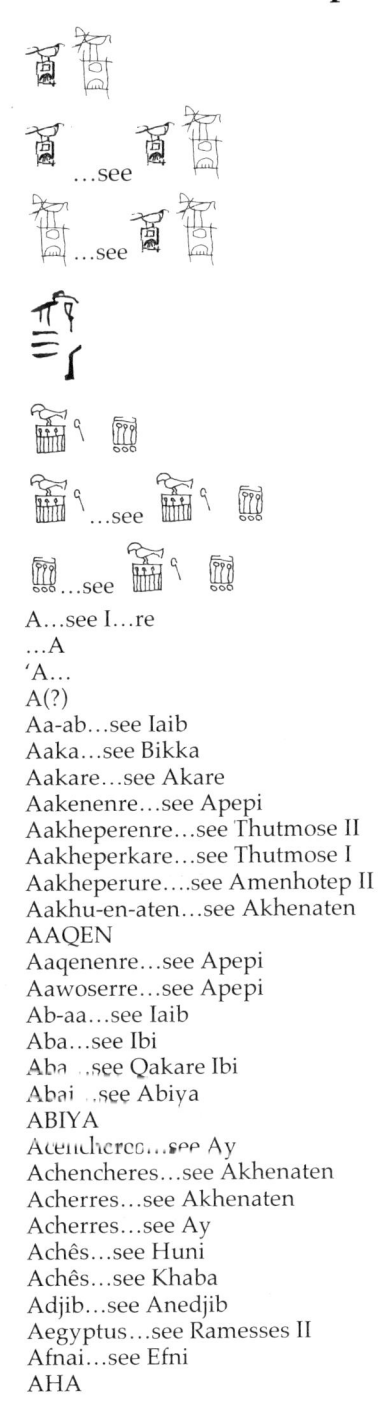

[hieroglyphs] ...see [hieroglyphs]

[hieroglyphs] ...see [hieroglyphs]

[hieroglyphs]

[hieroglyphs]

[hieroglyphs] ...see [hieroglyphs]

[hieroglyphs] ...see [hieroglyphs]

A...see I...re
...A
'A...
A(?)
Aa-ab...see Iaib
Aaka...see Bikka
Aakare...see Akare
Aakenenre...see Apepi
Aakheperenre...see Thutmose II
Aakheperkare...see Thutmose I
Aakheperure....see Amenhotep II
Aakhu-en-aten...see Akhenaten
AAQEN
Aaqenenre...see Apepi
Aawoserre...see Apepi
Ab-aa...see Iaib
Aba...see Ibi
Aba...see Qakare Ibi
Abai...see Abiya
ABIYA
Acencheres...see Ay
Achencheres...see Akhenaten
Acherres...see Akhenaten
Acherres...see Ay
Achês...see Huni
Achês...see Khaba
Adjib...see Anedjib
Aegyptus...see Ramesses II
Afnai...see Efni
AHA
Ahmes...see Ahmose
AHMOSE
Ahmosi...see Ahmose
Ahotepre...see 'Ammu
Ai...see Ay
Aigyptos...see Sety I
Aïtnou...see Iytjenu
Aka...see Neferkare
AKARE
Akauhor...see Menkauhor
Akenkheres...see Ay
AKHENATEN
Akhenkheres...see Akhenaten
Akhenkherses...see Akhenaten
Akhenre-setepenre...see Siptah
Akherres...see Akhenaten
Akherres...see Ay
Akhes...see Huni
Akhes...see Khaba
Akhthoes...see Khety I
Akhtoy...see Khety
AMENEMHET I
AMENEMHET II
AMENEMHET III
AMENEMHET IV
AMENEMHET V
AMENEMHET VI
AMENEMHET VII
Amenhirkopshef I...see Ramesses V
Amenhirkopshef II...see Ramesses VI
Amenhirkopshef III...see Ramesses X
AMENHOTEP I
AMENHOTEP II
AMENHOTEP III
Amenhotep IV...see Akhenaten
AMENMESSE
Amenmesses-heqawaset...see Amenmesse
Amenmessu...see Amenmesse
Amenophath...see Merenptah
Amenophis...see Amenhotep
Amenophthis...see Amenhotep I
Amenses...see Hatshepsut
Amensis...see Hatshepsut
Ameny-Amu...see Qemau
Ameny Kemau...see Qemau
Ameny Qemau...see Qemau
Amersis...see Hatshepsut
Amesse...see Hatshepsut

573

INDEX

Amessis...see Hatshepsut
Aminikimau...see Qemau
Ammanemes...see Amenemhet
Ammenemes...see Amenemhet
Ammenemes...see Amenmesse
Ammenemnes...see Amenmesse
Ammenephthes...see Merenptah
Ammenephthis...see Merenptah
Ammenophis...see Amenhotep I
'AMMU
Amnophis...see Amenhotep II
Amonhotep...see Amenhotep
Amophis...see Amenhotep I
Amos...see Ahmose
Amoses...see Ahmose
Amosis...see Ahmose
'Amu...see 'Ammu
Amunemhat...see Amenemhet
Amunemhet...see Amenemhet III
Amunhotpe...see Amenhotep
Ana...see Ini
'ANATI
Andjyeb...see Anedjib
ANEDJIB
Ani...see Ini
An(jotef)...see In(tef)
Anjotef...see Intef
Ankhetkheperure-mer(y)etwaenre...see Neferneferuaten
Ankhkheperure-merywaenre...see Neferneferuaten
Ankhkare...see Akare
Ankhkare...see Sekhem(?)kare
Ankh(?)kare...see Sekhem(?)kare
Ankhkeperure...see Smenkhkare
An(tef)...see In(tef)
Antef...see Intef
Antefaa...see Intef V
Antiemdjaf...see Merenre
Antyemsaf...see Merenre
Any...see Niuserre
An(yotef)...see In(tef)
Anyotef...see Intef
'AP...
Ap...see Ka
APED(?)...see Appendix
Apep...see Apepi
APEPI
Apepi...see Ap...
'APER-'ANATI
Aphobis...see Apepi
Aphôphis...see Apepi

Apophis...see Apepi
Apopi...see Apepi
Apuatemsaf...see Wepwawetemsaf
Aqen...see Aaqen
A...re...see I...re
Asehre...see Nehsy
Armais...see Horemheb
Armeis...see Horemheb
Asosi...see Djedkare
Asu...see Isu
Asychis...see Huni
Aten-khu-en...see Akhenaten
Athothis...see Aha
Auibre...see Awibre (II)
Auibre...see Hor (I)
Auserre...see Apepi
Auyibre...see Hor (I)
Awibre (I)...see Hor(I)
AWIBRE (II)
AY
Ay...see Aya
AYA
Aye...see Ay
Aye...see Aya
Azab...see Anedjib
BA
Babnem...see Bebnum
Baenre-meryamen...see Merenptah
Baka...see Bikka
Bakare...see Baufre
Bakare...see Bikka
Baneteren...see Ninetjer
Baneteru...see Ninetjer
Banetjeren...see Ninetjer
Banetjeru...see Ninetjer
Bauefre...see Baufre
BAUFRE
Bauneter...see Hotepsekhemwy
Baunetjer...see Hotepsekhemwy
Beb'anch...see Bebiankh
BEBIANKH
Bebnem...see Bebnum
BEBNUM
Bebty...see Khasekhemwy
Beby...see Khasekhemwy
Bedjau...see Hotepsekhemwy
Bicheris...see Bikka
Bienekhes...see Qa'a
Bikheris...see Bikka
BIKKA
Binothris...see Ninetjer
Biophis...see Ninetjer

INDEX

Boethos...see Hotepsekhemwy
Bokchos...see Hotepsekhemwy
Bokhos...see Hotepsekhemwy
Chaba...see Khaba
Chaires...see Sekhemib/Peribsen
Chamudi...see Khamudi
Chebres...see Tutankhamen
Chebron...see Thutmose II
Chebros...see Thutmose II
Chefren...see Khafre
Chendjer...see Khendjer
Chenephrês...see Sobekhotep IV
Cheneres...see Khasekhemwy
Cheops...see Khufu
Chephren...see Khafre
Cheres...see Neferefre
Cherhimweschepse...see
  Kherhimwet-shepsut
Choös...see Nebre
Chuhimwe...see Khuhimwet...
Chui...(?)...see Neferkauhor
Chui-oqre...see Khuiqer
Chuiqer...see Khuiqer
Chuwihapi...see Neferkauhor
CROCODILE
Dad-nefer-ra...see Dedumose II
Daduihetepre...see Dedumose I
Danaos...see Horemheb
Danaus...see Horemheb
DE
Dedui-ankh-ra...see Montuemsaf
Dedumes...see Dedumose
DEDUMOSE
DEDUMOSE I
DEDUMOSE II
Demedjibtowy...see Neferirkare
  (II)
DEN
Dewen...see Den
Dhout...see Djehuty
Dhuti...see Djehuty
Djadjay...see Khasekhemwy
Djadkere...see Djedkare
Djait...see Djet
Djaiti...see Djet
Djed...see Djedkare
DJEDEFHOR
Djedefra...see Djedefre
DJEDEFRE
Djedhotepre...see Dedumose I
DJEDKARE
Djedkare Schemai...see Djedkare
  Shemai
DJEDKARE SHEMAI

Djedkare...see Anati
Djedkheperew...see Djedkheperu
DJEDKHEPERU
DJEDKHERURE
Djedneferre...see Dedumose II
DJED...RE
Djed...re...see Anati
Djedankhre...see Montuemsaf
Djefakare...see Nerikare
...DJEFARE
DJEHUTY
Djehutymes...see Thutmose
DJER
Djeserkare...see Amenhotep I
DJET
DJOSER
Djoser...see Zeser
Djoserit(?)...see Djoser
Djoserkare...see Amenhotep I
Djoserkheperre...see Horemheb
Djosersa...see Djoser
Djoser-teti...see Sekhemkhet
Djoserty...see Sekhemkhet
Doser...see Djoser
DOUBLE FALCON
Dudumes...see Dedumose
Dudumesu...see Dedumose I
Edjo...see Djet
Ef...see ...Iwf
EFNI
Emramescha'...see Imyremeshau
Enezib...see Anedjib
Enibef(?)...see Inib[ef]
En(yotef)...see In(tef)
Enyotef...see Intef
Eye...see Aya
Eye...see Ay
H...
Haa-ka...see In(tef)
Hakara...see In(tef)
Hamudi...see Khamudi
Hape...see Hapu (I)
Hapi...see Hapu (I)
HAPU (I)...see Appendix
HAPU... (II)
Har...see Hor (I)
Harmais...see Horemheb
Harmesses Miamun...see
  Ramesses II
Harmhab...see Horemheb
Harnedjheritef...see
  Hornedjheritef
Hashepsowe...see Hatshepsut
HAT-HOR

575

INDEX

Hatasu...see Hatshepsut
Hatchepsut...see Hatshepsut
Hati...see Hat-Hor
HATSHEPSUT
...HEBRE
Hen-Nekht...see Sanakht
Hepu...see Hapu... (II)
Heqamaatre-setepenre...see
   Ramesses IV
Her-Kai...see Bikka
HERIBRE
Heruemheb...see Horemheb
Heru-ta-ta-f...see Djedefhor
Hetep...see Hotep
Hetepibre...see Hornedjheritef
Hetepkare...see Hotepkare
Hetepsekhemui...see
   Hotepsekhemwy
HIBE ...see Appendix
Ho-ka-ra...see In(tef)
HOR (I)
HOR... (II)...see Appendix
...HOR
Hor-A-Kau...see Menkauhor
Hor-Aha...see Aha
Hordedef...see Djedefhor
Hordjedef...see Djedefhor
Hordjedef[re]...see Djedefhor
HOREMHEB
...HORI
Horka...see Bikka
HORNEDJHERITEF
Hor-nefer-hen...see Pepi I
HOTEP
Hotep...see Hotepsekhemwy
Hotep Ahaui...see
   Hotepsekhemwy
Hotepibre...see Hornedjheritef
Hotepibre...see Khamudi
HOTEPKARE
...HOTEP[RE?]
HOTEPSEKHEMWY
Hotpe...see Hotep
Hu...see Huni
HUDJEFA (I)
HUDJEFA (II)
HUNI
I...see 'A...
IAIB
Iamu-Sahornedjheriotef...see
   Hornedjheritef
Iannas...see Khyan
Ia'yeb...see Iaib
...ib-[re?]Seth...see Seth (I)

IBI
Ibi...see Qakare Ibi
Ibi I...see Qakare Ibi
Ibiaw...see Iaib
Iby...see Ibi
Iby...see Qakare Ibi
Ijchernofre...see Neferhotep III
Ijibchentre...see Iyibkhentre
Ikaouhor...see Menkauhor
I-khent-yeb-Re'...see Iyibkhentre
Ikhernofret...see Neferhotep III
Ikhnaton...see Akhenaten
IMHOTEP
Imichet...see Mekh
Immureya...see Amenhotep III
IMYREMESHAU
In...see In(tef)
In...see Intef
Inai...see Ini
Ind...see INED
INED
Ineb...see Inek(?)
Ineb(?)...see 'A...
INEK(?)
Ini...see Niuserre
INI I
INI II
INIB[EF]...see Appendix
In(j)...see Ini
Ink...see Inek(?)
IN(TEF)
INTEF
INTEF I
INTEF II
INTEF III
INTEF IV
INTEF V
INTEF VI
INTEF VII
In(yotef)...see In(tef)
Inyotef...see Intef
Ip...see 'Ap...
Iquebher...see Ya'qub-Har
I...RE
Iri (-Hor)...see Iry-Hor
Iri-neter...see Semerkhet
Irj-Hor...see Iry-Hor
IRY-HOR
Isesi...see Djedkare
Isi...see Neferefre
ISU
Ita...see Djet
Itamen...see Ramesses VII
Iteti...see Djer

Iti...see Djer
Itjiesch...see Tjesh
ITY
Iucha...see Khayu
IWF......see Appendix
Iy...see Aya
IYIBKHENTRE
Iykhernofret...see Neferhotep III
Iytenu...see Iytjenu
IYTJENU
Izezi...see Djedkare
Izozi...see Djedkare
Ja'ib...see Iaib
Jakba'al...see Ya-k-'-r-b
Jakebmu...see Yakbim
Jakobher...see Ya'qub-Har
Ja'mmu...see Ya'ammu
Ja'qobher...see Ya'qub-Har
Jer...see Djer
Jewefni...see Efni
KA
Ka'a...see Qa'a
Kahedjet...see Qahedjet
Kaiechos...see Nebre
Kaiekhos...see Nebre
Kakai...see Neferirkare (I)
Kakare...see In(tef)
Kakare...see Qakare Ibi
Kakau...see Nebre
Kakaure...see Qakare Ibi
Ka?kaure...see Qakare Ibi
KAKEMETRE
Kakemure...see Kakemetre
Ka-ku-Re...see In(tef)
Kames...see Kamose
KAMOSE
Kanefertemre...see Nefertum...re
Ka(?)-pu-ib(I)(?)...see Neferkauhor
...ka[re?]...see Akare
...ka[re?]...see 'Anati
...ka[re?]...see Khakare
...kare...see Behnem
[...]kare...see Djedkheperu
Kasobkre...see Sobekneferu
Kay...see Sebkay
Kay-Amenhemhet...see Amenemhet VII
Kebh...see Qa'a
Kebhu...see Qa'a
Kechoos...see Nebre
Kemau...see Qemau
Kenkenes...see Djer

Ker(?)-taui-f...see Iyibkhentre
Kerpheres...see Huni
Khaankhre...see Sobekhotep II
Khaau...see Khayu
Kha'-[bau(?)]...see Neferkaure
KHABA
KHABAU
Khabaw...see Khabau
Khaemwaset I...see Ramesses IX
Khaemwaset II...see Ramesses XI
KHAENPTAH
Khafkhufu...see Khafre
KHAFRE
Khahotepre...see Sobekhotep VI
Khaires...see Sekhemib/Peribsen
KHAKARE
Khakaure...see Senwosret III
Khakheperre...see Senwosret II
Khakherewre...see Khakherure
KHAKHERURE
KHAMUDI
KHAMURE
Khaneferre...see Neferefre
Khaneferre...see Sobekhotep IV
KHA...RE
Kha...re...see Khakare
Khasekhem...see Khasekhemwy
Khasekhemre...see Neferhotep I
Khasekhemui...see Khasekhemwy
KHASEKHEMWY
Khasty...see Den
Khatire...see Khakherure
Khatyre...see Khakherure
Khawoserre...see Qareh
Khayan...see Khyan
KHAYU
Khebres...see Tutankhamen
Khebron...see Thutmose II
Khebros...see Thutmose II
Khekure...see Senwosret III
KHENDJER
Khendu...see Neferkare Khendu
Kheneres...see Khasekhemwy
Khent...see Djer
KHENTKAUES (I)
Khenzer...see Khendjer
Kheperkare...see Senwosret I
[Kheper?]kare...see Nerikare
Kheperkheperure...see Ay
Khepermaatre-setepenre...see Ramesses X
Khephren...see Khafre

577

Index

Kheres...see Neferefre
KHERHIMWET-SHEPSUT...see Appendix
KHETY I
KHETY II
KHETY III
KHETY IV
KHETY V
Khety Neferkare...see Khety III
Khian...see Khyan
Khnemka...see Bikka
Khnum-khufu...see Khufu
Khnumkhufwey...see Khufu
Kho-kau-ra...see Senwosret III
Kho-kheper-ra...see Senwosret II
Kho-Ra...see Khamure
Khoba...see Khaba
Khondy...see Khamudi
Khoös...see Nebre
Khu-en-aten...see Akhenaten
KHUFU
Khufukhaf...see Khafre
Khufwey...see Khufu
KHUHIMWET...see Appendix
KHUI
Khuihapy...see Neferkauhor
KHUIQER
Khutowyre...see Wegaf
Khuwi...see Khui
Khuwihapi...see Neferkauhor
Khuy...see Khui
KHYAN
Krokodil...see Crocodile
Lachares...see Amenemhet III
Lamares...see Amenemhet III
Lamaris...see Amenemhet III
Lampares...see Amenemhet III
Maaibre...see Sheshi
Maakherure...see Amenemhet IV
Maat-Ra-neb...see Amenhotep III
Maatkare...see Djedkare
Maatkare...see Hatshepsut
...maatre...see Ibi
Maka...see Bikka
Makare...see Hatshepsut
Makere...see Hatshepsut
Maot-en-Re...see Amenemhet III
Mayibre...see Sheshi
Mehti-em-saf...see Merenre II
MEKH
Mekha...see Mekh
Memphres...see Thutmose I
Memphses...see Semerkhet
Merbiape...see Anedjib

Men......see Narmer
Men-ma-re...see Sety I
Menchaoure...see Snaiib
Mencheres...see Menkauhor
Mencheres...see Menkaure
Menes...see Narmer
MENI...see Appendix
Meni...see Narmer
Men[ib]re...see Men...re
Menibre...see Men...re
Menkaouhor...see Menkauhor
MENKARE
MENKAUHOR
MENKAURE
Menkhaure...see Senaaib
Menkhe...see Mekh
Menkheperre...see Thutmose III
Menkheperure...see Thutmose IV
Menkheres...see Menkauhor
Menkheres...see Menkaure
Menkhkare...see Segerseni
Menmaatre...see Sety I
Menmaatre-setepenptah...see Ramesses XI
Menmire-setepenre...see Amenmesse
Menpehtire...see Ramesses I
MEN...RE
Mentehotep...see Montuhotep
Mentehotpe...see Montuhotep
Mentemsaf...see Montuemsaf
Menthesouphis...see Merenre II
Menthotep...see Montuhotep
Menthotep...see Montuhotepi
Menthotpe...see Montuhotep
Menthotpe...see Montuhotepi
Menthuhotep...see Montuhotep
Menthuhotepo...see Montuhotep I
Mentu-user...see Montuwoser
Mentuemsaf...see Montuemsaf
Mentuhotep...see Montuhotep
Mentuhotep-aa...see Montuhotep I
Mentuhotepi...see Montuhotepi
Mentuwoser...see Montuwoser
Menuazra...see Sihathor
Menwadjre...see Sihathor
Mephramuthosis...see Thutmose III
Mephres...see Thutmose I
Mer-Nar...see Narmer
Merankhre...see Montuhotep VI
Merbiapen...see Anedjib

INDEX

Mercheperre...see Merkheperre
MERDJEFARE
MERENHOR
MERENPTAH
Merenptah-siptah...see Siptah
MERENRE I
MERENRE II
Merhetepre...see Ini I
Merhetepre...see Sobekhotep V
Merhotepre...see Ini I
Merhotepre...see Sobekhotep V
MERHOTEPRE
Meribre...see Seth (I)
Merikara...see Merykare
Merire...see Pepi I
Meritneith...see Merneith
MERKARE
Merkaure...see Sobekhotep VII
Merkawre...see Sobekhotep VII
MERKHEPERRE
Mermeshau...see Imyremeshau
Merneferre...see Aya
Merneit...see Merneith
MERNEITH
Merneptah...see Merenptah
Mernere...see Merenre
Mernoferre...see Aya
Merpibia...see Anedjib
MER...RE
Mersekha...see Semerkhet
MERSEKHEMRE
Mersekhemre...see Ined
Mersekhemre...see Neferhotep II
Mershepsesre...see Ini II
Merunar...see Narmer
Meruserre...see Ya'qub-Har
Merwoserre...see Ya'qub-Har
Mery...(?)...see Mery...[hathor?]
Meryet-nit...see Merneith
MERY...[HATHOR?]
Meryibre...see Khety I
MERYKARE
Meryre...see Pepi I
Mery...(re) Khety...see Khety IV
Meryt-neith...see Merneith
MERYTOWY
Merytowy...see Pepi I
Mesôchris...see Khaba
Mesôchris...see Sedjes
Mesokhris...see Khaba
Mesokhris...see Sedjes
Methousouphis...see Merenre I
Methusuphis...see Merenre I
Nebkaure...see Khety V

Miebidos...see Anedjib
Mimmareya...see Amenhotep III
Miphres...see Thutmose I
Mirnire-Mihtimsaf...see Merenre
Misaphris...see Thutmose I
Mispharmuthosis...see Thutmose III
Misphragmouthosis...see Thutmose III
Misphragmuthosis...see Thutmose III
Monthhotep...see Montuhotep
Monthhotepi...see Montuhotepi
Monthwoser...see Montuwoser
Montjuhotep...see Montuhotep
MONTUEMSAF
MONTUHOTEP I
MONTUHOTEP II
MONTUHOTEP III
MONTUHOTEP IV
MONTUHOTEP V
MONTUHOTEP VI
MONTUHOTEPI
MONTUWOSER
...mose...see ...Mosre
...MOSRE
Mycerinus...see Menkaure
Mykerinos...see Menkaure
Myspharmouthosis...see Thutmose III
Nakhtnebtepnefer...see Intef III
Nar...see Narmer
NARMER
Narmeru...see Narmer
Neb-towi-re...see Montuhotep IV
NEBDJEFARE
Nebennati...see Anati
Nebennu...see Nebnennu
Neberaw...see Nebiryraw
Nebfaure...see Nebfawre
NEBFAWRE
Nebhepetre...see Montuhotep
Nebhepetre...see Montuhotep II
Nebi...see Neferkare Neby
Neb(i)-Ka(i)...see Bikka
Nebiriau...see Nebiryraw
Nebirieraw...see Nebiryraw
NEBIRYRAW I
NEBIRYRAW II
Nebitau...see Nebiryraw II
Nebka...see Bikka
Nebka...see Sanakht
Nebkare...see Bikka
Nebkaure Khety...see Khety V

579

INDEX

Nebkheperure...see Tutankhamen
Nebkhepeshre...see Apepi
NEBMAATRE
Nebmaatre...see Amenhotep III
Nebmaatre-meryamen...see Ramesses VI
Nebmare...see Amenhotep III
NEBNENNU
Nebnun...see Nebnennu
Nebpehtire...see Ahmose
NEBRE
NEBSENRE
Nebtowyre...see Montuhotep IV
Nebuahab...see Qareh
Necherôchis...see Sanakht
Necherôphês...see Sanakht
NEDJEMIBRE
Nefer...see Neferkamin Anu
NEFEREFRE
NEFERHOTEP
NEFERHOTEP I
NEFERHOTEP II
NEFERHOTEP III
Neferhotpe...see Neferhotep
NEFERIBRE
NEFERIRKARE (I)
NEFERIRKARE (II)
Neferka...see Bikka
Neferka...see Neferkare
Neferka...see Neferkare Pepi-Sonb
NEFERKAHOR
Neferka Khered-Sonb...see Neferkare Pepi-Sonb
Nefer<kamin>...see Neferkamin Anu
NEFERKAMIN
NEFERKAMIN ANU
NEFERKARE (Dynasty II)
NEFERKARE (Dynasty VII/VIII)
NEFERKARE (Dynasty IX/X)
Neferkare...see Huni
Neferkare...see Nebiryraw II
Neferkare...see Neferkare Nebi
Neferkare...see Pepi II
Neferkare...see Sanakht
Neferka<re>...see Neferkare Pepi-Sonb
Neferkare Chendu...see Neferkare Khendu
NEFERKARE KHENDU
Neferkare Khered...see Neferkare Pepi-Sonb
Neferkare Nebi...see Nefer Neby
NEFERKARE NEBY
NEFERKARE PEPI-SONB
Neferkare-setepenre...see Ramesses IX
NEFERKARE TERERU
NEFERKASEKER
Neferkasokar...see Neferkaseker
NEFERKAUHOR
NEFERKAURE
Neferkawhor...see Neferkauhor
Neferkawre...see Neferkaure
Neferkheperure-waenre...see Akhenaten
NEFERNEFERUATEN
Neferneferuaten-merywaenre...see Neferneferuaten
Neferre...see Neferefre
Nefersahor...see Pepi I
Neferseka...see Seneferka
Nefertemre...see Nefertum...re
Nefertiti...see Neferneferuaten
NEFERTUM...RE
Neferusebek...see Sobekneferu
Nehasi...see Nehsy
NEHEB
Nehesi...see Nehsy
NEHSY
Neitiqerty...see Netjerkare Siptah
Nekherokhis...see Sanakht
Nekherophes...see Sanakht
Nemtyemsaf...see Merenre
Nephercheres...see Neferkare
Nephercheres...see Neferirkare (I)
Nepherkheres...see Neferkare
Nepherkheres...see Neferirkare (I)
NERIKARE
Ner(?)kare...see Nerikare
Nerkare...see Nerikare
Netcherikhe...see Djoser
Neteren...see Ninetjer
Neterikhet...see Djoser
Neterkare...see Netjerkare Siptah
Neter(?)-user...see Shepseskare
Neterymu...see Ninetjer
Nether-er-Inhet...see Djoser
Nether-er-Khet...see Djoser

INDEX

Netjer(?)-user...see Shepseskare
NETJERKARE SIPTAH
Netjeren...see Ninetjer
Netjerikhet...see Djoser
Neuserre...see Niuserre
Newoserre...see Niuserre
Ni-heb...see Neheb
Nibmuareya...see Amenhotep III
Niebais...see Anedjib
NIKARE
Nimaatre...see Amenemhet III
Nimmureya...see Amenhotep III
NINETJER
Ninutjer...see Ninetjer
Nitacrit...see Netjerkare Siptah
Nitocris...see Netjerkare Siptah
Nitokerty...see Netjerkare Siptah
Nitokris...see Netjerkare Siptah
NIUSERRE
...nnat...see 'Anati
Nofrehotpe...see Neferhotep III
Noutirkere-Hotep...see Hotep
Nubkaure...see Amenemhet II
Nubkheperre...see Intef VI
NUBNEFER
Nubwoserre...see Ya'ammu
Nufe...see Neferkamin Anu
Nutjeren...see Ninetjer
Nu-Hor...see Ny-Hor
NUYA
NY-HOR
Nykare...see Nikare
Nymaatra...see Amenemhet III
Nyneter...see Ninetjer
Nyswth...see Huni
Nyuserra...see Niuserre
Oa-qenen-ra...see Apepi
Ochthois...see Khety I
Okheperenre...see Thutmose II
Okheperkere...see Thutmose I
Okheperure...see Amenhotep II
Onnos...see Unas
Onnus...see Unas
Onta...see 'Apor-'Anati
Ontha...see 'Aper-'Anati
Oros...see Amenhotep III
Orus...see Amenhotep III
Osymandias...see Ramesses II
Othios...see Teti
Othius...see Teti
Othoes...see Teti
Oubienthis...see Qa'a
Ouenephis...see Djet

Ougaf...see Wegaf
Oupouaout...see Wepwawetemsaf
Ousaphaidos...see Den
Ousaphais...see Den
Ouserkara...see Khendjer
Ouserkheres...see Userkaf
PALMANTHOES
Pantini...see Pantjeny
PANTJENY
Paramesses...see Ramesses I
PE-HOR
PENESET-EN-SEPET...see Appendix
Penthen...see Pantjeny
Pentini...see Pantjeny
Pentjeny...see Pantjeny
PEPI
PEPI I
PEPI II
Peribsen...see Sekhemib/Peribsen
Pepy...see Pepi
Peryebsen...see Sekhemib/Peribsen
PHARETHOTHES
Phiops...see Pepi
Phiops...see Pepi II
Phios...see Pepi I
Phius...see Pepi I
Piopi...see Pepi
Pipi...see Pepi
Piramesses...see Ramesses I
Polybus...see Tawosret
Pramesses...see Ramesses I
"Priestly Figure"...see Semerkhet
...PU
Pu(?)...hapi...see Neferkauhor
Qa...see Qa'a
QA'A
Qaa...see Qa'a
QAHEDJET
Qaikare...see Qakare Ibi
Qakare...see Intef
Qakare...see Qakare Ibi
QAKARE IBI
Qakaure...see Qakare Ibi
Qar...see Qareh
QAREH
Qay-a...see Qa'a
QEMAU
Ra...see Iry-Hor
Ra-aa-qenen...see Apepi

581

INDEX

Ra-ab-khent...see Iyibkhentre
Ra-...-ab-khent...see Iyibkhentre
Ra-Kho-Nefer...see Sobekhotep IV
Ra-Kho-Seshes...see ...sekhem[re?]
Ra-Maat-neb...see Amenhotep III
Ra-mer-kheper...see Merkheperre
Ra-nub-kheper...see Intef VI
Ra-oa-user...see Apepi
Ra-qa-ka...see In(tef)
Ra Sa?...see Hotep
Ra-se-beq-ka...see Amenenhet VII
Ra-se-beq-ka...see Sebkay
Ra-sekhem-shedti-taui...see Sobekemsaf I
Ra-Senefer-Ab...see Senwosret IV
Ra-seshes-her-maat...see Intef VII
Ra-seshes-up-maat...see Intef V
Ra-uah-ab...see Iaib
Ra-u-aqer...see Khuiqer
Ra-Zed-Nefer...see Dedumose II
Ra-Zedui-Hetep...see Dedumose I
Rabauwf...see Baufre
Radjedef...see Djedefre
Rahotep...see Rehotep
Rahotpe...see Rehotep
Rakhaef...see Khafre
Rameses...see Ramesses
RAMESSES I
RAMESSES II
RAMESSES III
RAMESSES IV
RAMESSES V
RAMESSES VI
RAMESSES VII
RAMESSES VIII
RAMESSES IX
RAMESSES X
RAMESSES XI
Ramesses-meryamen...see Ramesses II
Ramesses-siptah...see Siptah
Ramessu...see Ramesses
Rampses...see Ramesses II
Raneb...see Nebre
Ranebsen...see Nebsenre
Ranefer...see Neferefre
Raneferef...see Neferefre
RANISONB
Ranisonbe...see Ranisonb

Ra-Kha-Seshes...see Neferhotep I
Ra-kho-kheper...see Senwosret II
Rapses...see Ramesses II
Rathotis...see Smenkhkare
Rathures...see Niuserre
...RE (one in Dynasty XIII)
...RE (two in Dynasty XIV)
...[RE] (two in Dynasty XIV)
Re'?-...see Sobekhotep II
Re-Amenemhe...see Amenemhet V
Rebaef...see Baufre
Rebauf...see Baufre
Redjedef...see Djedefre
REHOTEP
Rehotpe...see Rehotep
Re...ka...see Se...kare
Rekhaef...see Khafre
Reneb...see Nebre
Reneferef...see Neferefre
Rensonb...see Ranisonb
Rhamesses...see Ramesses I
Rhamessês Miamoun...see Ramesses II
Rhampses...see Ramesses II
Rhapsakes...see Ramesses II
Rhathos...see Smenkhkare
Rhathoures...see Niuserre
Ro...see Iry-Hor
Sa...see Aped(?)
Sa-Nekht...see Sanakht
Sahathor...see Sihathor
SAHURE
Saine...see Sunu
Saites...see Sharek
Sakara...see Smenkhkare
Sakarher...see Sakir-Har
SAKIR-HAR
Salitis...see Sharek
Šamuqēnu...see Semqen
SANAKHT
S'ankhibre...see Seankhibre
SANKHPTAHI
S'ankhre'enswadjtu...see Sewadjtu
Saqnounri...see Seqenenre
Scemiophris...see Sobekneferu
Schamse...see Shemsu
Scheschi...see Sheshi
Schesti...see Djer
SCORPION
SCORPION I
SCORPION II
Se'anchptah...see Sankhptahi

INDEX

Seankhenre…see Montuhotepi
Seankhenre…see Sewadjtu
SEANKHIBRE
Seankhibtowy…see Montuhotep II
Seankhkare…see Montuhotep III
Seankhptah…see Sankhptahi
Seankhtowy…see Montuhotep III
Seanra…see In(tef)
Seb…see Sebkay
Sebek…see Sobek
Sebekai…see Sebkay
Sebeka-ka-ra…see Amenemhet VII
Sebekemsaf…see Sobekemsaf
Sebekhotep…see Sobekhotep
Sebekhotpe…see Sobekhotep
Sebek-ka-ra…see Sebkay
Sebekneferu…see Sobekneferu
Sebercheres…see Shepseskaf
Seberkheres…see Shepseskaf
Sebk…see Sobek
Sebka-re(?)…see Amenemhet VII
Sebka-re(?)…see Sebkay
Sebkai…see Sebkay
SEBKAY
Sebkhotp…see Sobekhotep
Sechen…see Ka
Sedjefakare…see Amenemhet VII
SEDJES
SE…ENRE
SEGERSENI
Sehabre…see Sehebre
SEHEBRE
Seheqenre…see Sankhptahi
Sehertowy…see Intef I
SEHOTEPIBRE
Sehotepibre…see Amenemhet I
Sehotepibre…see Hornedjheritef
Sehotepkare…see Intef IV
SEKA
Sekanefer…see Seneferka
SE…KARE
Sekenenre…see Seqenenre
Sekhaenptah…see Khaenptah
SEKHAENRE
Sekhaenre…see Yakbim
Sekhaenre-meryamen…see Siptah
Sekhaenre-setepenre…see Siptah
Sekhem…see Ka
Sekhem-uah-kha-ra…see Rehotep
Sekhemib…see Sekhemib/Peribsen

Sekhemib-perenmaat…see Sekhemib/Peribsen
SEKHEMIB/PERIBSEN
Sekhemkare…see Amenemhet V
Sekhemkare…see Sonbef
SEKHEM(?)KARE
SEKHEMKARE
SEKHEMKHET
SEKHEMRE…
SEKHEM…RE
…SEKHEM[RE?]
Sekhemre-herhermaat…see Intef VII
Sekhemre-neferkhau…see Wepwawetemsaf
Sekhemre-seankhtowy…see Neferhotep III
Sekhemre-sementowy…see Djehuty
Sekhemre Se'onkhtowy…see Neferhotep III
Sekhemre-sewadjtowy…see Sobekhotep III
Sekhemre-sewosertowy…see Sobekhotep VIII
Sekhemre-shedtowy…see Sobekemsaf I
SEKHEMRE-SHEDWASET
Sekhemre-wadjkhau…see Sobekemsaf II
Sekhemre-wahkau…see Rehotep
Sekhemre-wahkau…see Wa-ka'-u
Sekhemre-wepmaat…see Intef V
SEKHEMREKHUTOWY
Sekhemrekhutowy…see Khabau
Sekhemrekhutowy…see Pantjeny
Sekhemrekhutowy…see Sobekhotep I
Sekhen…see Ka
Sekhenptah…see Khaenptah
Sekhentenre…see Senakhtenre
SEKHEPERENRE
Sekheperenre…see Ramesses V
Sekherseny…see Segerseni
Sekhty…see Djer
Selk…see Scorpion
Selkh…see Scorpion
Sem-ken…see Semqen
Semempses…see Semerkhet
Semenenre…see Hapu… (II)
Semenenre…see Semenre
Semenkare…see Nebnennu
Semenkhkare…see Imyremeshau
Semenmedjat(?)re…see Semenre

583

INDEX

Semenptah...see Semerkhet
SEMERKHET
SEMQEN
Semsem...see Semerkhet
Semty...see Den
Sena'aib...see Senaaib
SENAAIB
SENAKHTENRE
Sendi...see Sened
Senebmaui...see Senebmiu
SENEBMIU
SENED
Senedi...see Sened
Senedji...see Sened
Seneferibre...see Senwosret IV
SENEFERKA
Seneferka...see Neferkamin
Senefer{ka?]re...see Senefer...re
Seneferka-Anu...see Neferkamin Anu
SENEFER...RE
SENEFERU
Senefru...see Seneferu
SENEN...
Sennaib...see Senaaib
Senne...see SENEN...
Senofru...see Seneferu
Senusert...see Senwosret
Senusret...see Senwosret
SENWOSRET I
SENWOSRET II
SENWOSRET III
SENWOSRET IV
Seonkhare...see Montuhotep III
Seonkhibtaui...see Montuhotep II
Sephouris...see Sedjes
Sephres...see Sahure
Sêphuris...see Sedjes
SEQENENRE
Sequenenre...see Seqenenre
Se...re Akhtoy...see Se...re Khety
SE...RE KHETY
Seshes-Ra-up-maat...see Intef V
Sesochris...see Neferkaseker
Sesokhris...see Neferkaseker
Sesonchosis...see Senwosret I
Sesonkhosis...see Senwosret I
Sesorthos...see Djoser
Sesostris...see Senwosret
Set...see Seth
Setepenre...see Ramesses IV
SETH (I)
SETH (II)...see Appendix
Sethenes...see Sened

SEMENRE
Sethirkopshef...see Ramesses VIII
Seth?ka...see Bikka
Sethnakhte...see Setnakht
Sethos...see Sety II
Seti...see Sety
Setka...see Bikka
SETNAKHT
Setui...see Sety
SETY I
SETY II
Seusekhtowy...see Sehotepibre
Seuserenre...see Bebiankh
Seuserenre...see Khyan
Sewadjare...see Montuhotep V
Sewadjenre...see Montuhotepi
Sewadjenre...see Nebiryraw I
Sewadjenre...see Sewadjtu
Sewadjkare...see ...hori
SEWADJKARE I
SEWADJKARE II
SEWADJ...RE
Sewadjre...see Montuhotep V
Sewadjtew...see Sewadjtu
SEWADJTU
Sewahenre...see Montuhotepi
Sewahenre...see Senebmiu
Sewesekhtowy...see Sehotepibre
Sewoserenre...see Bebiankh
Sewoserenre...see Khyan
Sezes...see Sedjes
Shaaru...see Sharu
Shairu...see Sharu
Shalek...see Sharek
SHAREK
SHARU
SHED...Y
Shemay...see Djedkare Shemay
SHEMSU...see Appendix
SHENEH
Shenes...see Sheneh
Shens...see Sheneh
SHENSHEK
SHEPSESKAF
SHEPSESKARE
Shesha...see Sheshi
SHESHI
Shub...see Qareh
Siharnedjheritef...see Hornedjheritef
SIHATHOR
[Si?]kare...see Nerikare
SIPTAH
Sisires...see Shepseskare

INDEX

Sitre-meryamen...see Tawosret
Skehemre-shedtowy...see Sobekhemsaf I
Skemiophris...see Sobekneferu
Skheperenre...see Sekheperenre
Skorpion...see Scorpion
SMA
SMENKHKARE
Snaaib...see Senaaib
Snaiib...see Senaaib
"Snake"...see Djet
Sneferka...see Neferkamin
Sneferka...see Seneferka
Sneferka-Anu...see Neferkamin Anu
Sneferu...see Seneferu
Snefru...see Seneferu
Snofru...see Seneferu
SOBEK
Sobekai...see Sebkay
SOBEKEMSAF
SOBEKEMSAF I
SOBEKEMSAF II
SOBEKHOTEP
SOBEKHOTEP I
SOBEKHOTEP II
SOBEKHOTEP III
SOBEKHOTEP IV
SOBEKHOTEP V
SOBEKHOTEP VI
SOBEKHOTEP VII
SOBEKHOTEP VIII
Sobekhotpe...see Sobekhotep
Sobekkare...see Sobekneferu
SOBEKNEFERU
Sobk...see Sobek
Sobkemsaf...see Sobekemsaf
Sobkhotep...see Sobekhotep
Sobkhotpe...see Sobekhotep
Sobkrehotep...see Sobekhotep II
SONBEF
Sonbmijew...see Senebmiu
Soris...see Seneferu
Sosorthus...see Djoser
Souphis I...see Khufu
Souphis II...see Djedefre
Souphis II...see Khafre
S...re Akhtoy...see Se...re Khety
Staan...see Khyan
Suah-n-ra...see Nebiryraw I
Suat'en-ra...see Nebiryraw I
Suazenra...see Nebiryraw I
SUNU...see Appendix

Suphis I...see Khufu
Suphis II...see Djedefre
Suphis II...see Khafre
Swadj[en?]re...see Montuhotepi
Swadjkare...see Sewadjkare
Swaz-en-re...see Nebiryraw I
Taa...see Senakhtenre
Taa...see Seqenenre
Taa-a...see Senakhtenre
Tahuti...see Djehuty
Tahutimes...see Thutmose
Tancheres...see Djedkare
Tankheres...see Djedkare
Ta'o...see Senakhtenre
Ta'o...see Seqenenre
Tau...see Tiu
Tauosrit...see Tawosret
TAWOSRET
Tcheser-kheperu-ra...see Horemheb
Tehuti...see Djehuty
Tehutimes...see Thutmose
Telulu...see Neferkare Tereru
Te'o...see Senakhtenre
Te'o...see Seqenenre
Tepya...see Montuhotep I
Tereru...see Neferkare Tereru
Tesau...see Khayu
TETI
Teti...see Aha
Teti...see Sekhemkhet
Tewosre...see Tawosret
Teyew...see Tiu
Thamphthis...see Djedefhor
Ther...see Djer
Thesh...see Tjesh
Thmosis...see Thutmose IV
Thothmes...see Thutmose
Thotmes...see Thutmose
Thouoris...see Tawosret
Thoutmosis...see Thutmose
Thummosis...see Thutmose IV
Thuoris...see Tawosret
Thuthmosis...see Thutmose
THUTMOSE I
THUTMOSE II
THUTMOSE III
THUTMOSE IV
Thuty...see Djehuty
TIU
TJESH
Tlas...see Weneg
Tosertasis...see Sekhemkhet

585

INDEX

Tosorthros...see Djoser
Toutankhamanou...see Tutankhamen
Touthmosis...see Thutmose IV
TUTANKHAMEN
Tutankhamon...see Tutankhamen
Tutankhamun...see Tutankhamen
Tutankhaten...see Tutankhamen
Tuthmosis...see Thutmose
TUTIMAIOS
Twosre...see Tawosret
Twosret...see Tawosret
Ua-qer-ra...see Khuiqer
Uadji...see Djet
Uadjkare...see Wadjkare
Uah-onkh...see Intef II
Uatched...see Wazad
Uatch-Kheper-Re...see Kamose
Uatch-Nar...see Wadjin
Uaz-ka-ra...see Segerseni
Uaz-Kho...see Dedumose I
Uazed...see Wazad
Ubenre...see Webenre
...ubenre...see ...webenre
[...]-uben-[re]...see ...webenre
Udimu...see Den
Ugaf...see Wegaf
UNAS
Uneg...see Weneg
Unis...see Unas
Upwautemsaf...see Wepwawetemsaf
Usaphais...see Den
Usefemsaf(?)...see Merenre II
Useranat...see 'Aper-'Anati
Usercheres...see Userkaf
USERKAF
USERKARE
Userkare...see Khendjer
Userkhau...see Neferirkare (I)
Userkhau-setepenre...see Setnakht
Usermaatre-akhenamen...see Ramesses VIII
Usermaatre-meryamen...see Ramesses III
Usermaatre-sekheperenre...see Ramesses V
Usermaatre-setepenamen...see Ramesses IV
Usermaatre-setepenre...see Ramesses II
Usermaatre-setepenremeryamen...see Ramesses VII
User...re...see Woser...re
Usertsen...see Senwosret
Usimare...see Ramesses III
Usimare-akhenamen...see Ramesses VIII
Usimare-sekheperenre...see Ramesses V
Usimare-setepenre...see Ramesses IV
Usimare-setepenremeryamen...see Ramesses VII
Uthkere...see Segerseni
Vavenephis...see Djet
Vibenthis...see Qa'a
Vogel...see Ba
Wadj-ku-Re...see Segerseni
Wadjed...see Wazad
Wadjenedj...see Wadjin
Wadji...see Djet
WADJIN
WADJKARE
Wadjkare...see Segerseni
Wadjkheperre...see Kamose
Wadjnes...see Weneg
Wahibre...see Iaib
Wahkare...see Khety II
Wahonkh...see Intef II
Wasa...see Wazad
WAZAD
Wazenez...see Wadjin
Wazkara...see In(tef)
WEBENRE
...[we]ben[re]...see ...webenre
...webenre...see ...hor
...WEBENRE (a)
...WEBENRE (b)
...WEBENRE (c)
Wedymuw...see Den
WEGAF
Wehemka...see Bikka
WENEG
Wenig...see Weneg
Wenis...see Unas
Wepwawemsaf...see Wepwawetemsaf
WEPWAWETEMSAF

INDEX

WERKA...see Appendix
Werqa...see Werka
Weserkaf...see Userkaf
Woser-ku-re...see Userkare
Woserkaf...see Userkaf
Woserkare...see Khendjer
WOSERKHAU
Woserkhaure-sepepenre...see
  Setnakht
Woserkheperuremeryamen...see
  Sety II
WOSER...RE (I)
WOSER...RE (II)
Ya...see I...re
YA'AMMU
YA-K-'-R-B(?)
Yakbemu...see Yakbim
YAKBIM
Yakubher...see Ya'qub-Har
Yamu'...see Ya'ammu
Ya'mu...see Ya'ammu
YA'QUB-HAR
Yayebi...see Iaib
Yekeb-Bor...see Ya-k-'-r-b(?)
Ykb-l...see Ya-k-'-r-b(?)
Zadneferre...see Dedumose II
Zanakht...see Snakht
Zegerzenti...see Segerseni
Zer...see Djer
ZESER
Zeser...see Djoser
Zeser-kheperu-ra...see
  Horemheb
Zeserkara...see Amenhotep I
Zet...see Djet
Zoser...see Djoser